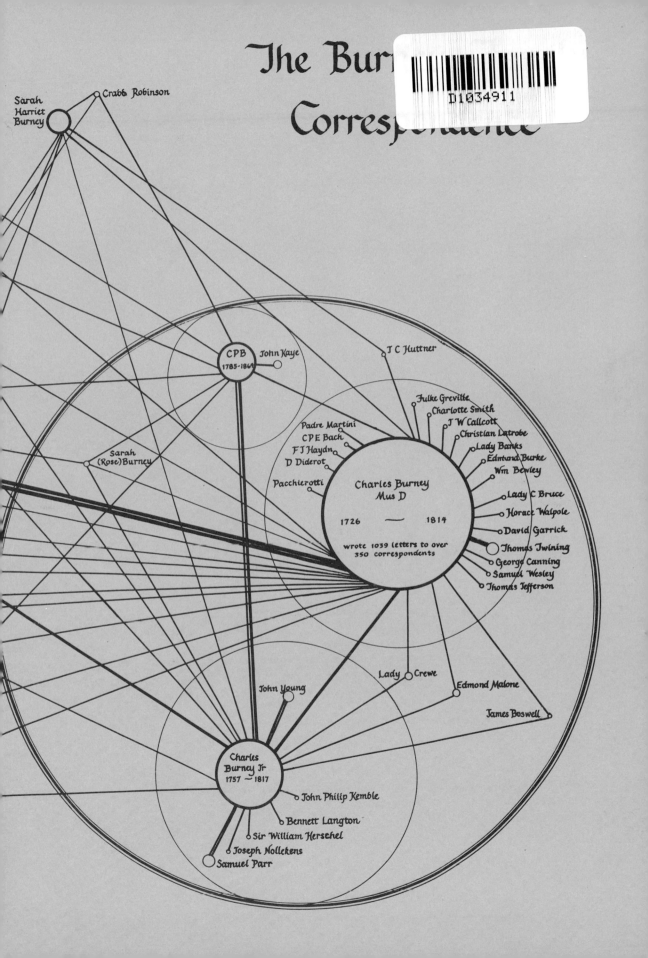

A CATALOGUE OF THE
BURNEY FAMILY CORRESPONDENCE
1749–1878

A CATALOGUE

OF

THE BURNEY FAMILY

CORRESPONDENCE
1749–1878

By

JOYCE HEMLOW

with

JEANNE M. BURGESS *and* ALTHEA DOUGLAS

NEW YORK
The New York Public Library
MONTREAL *and* LONDON
McGill–Queen's University Press

THIS WORK HAS BEEN PUBLISHED WITH THE HELP OF A GRANT FROM THE HUMANITIES RESEARCH COUNCIL OF CANADA, USING FUNDS PROVIDED BY THE CANADA COUNCIL; AND A GRANT FROM THE JOHN SIMON GUGGENHEIM MEMORIAL FOUNDATION

Library of Congress Catalog Card Number: 67–31117

NYPL   ISBN 0–87104–037–9

McGill–Queen's ISBN 0–7735–0055–3

Printed at The New York Public Library

form p737 [vii-12-71 750]

To

JOHN D. GORDAN

in ever grateful memory

Table of Contents

*   *   *

Illustrations

end papers: The Extent of the Burney Family Correspondence, multi-cycle design by Althea Douglas, calligraphy by Marilyn Henrion

following page xvi: The Burney Family Tree, prepared by Althea Douglas, calligraphy by Marilyn Henrion

INTRODUCTION

THIS CATALOGUE AND INDEX of the Burney Family correspondence locates and arranges in chronological groupings a family correspondence of some ten thousand extant letters written by over a thousand persons between the middle of the eighteenth century and the last quarter of the nineteenth.

As catalogued here, the Burney Correspondence may be defined as the letters written or received by the following persons:

CHARLES BURNEY [CB] [1] (1726–1814), Mus Doc (1769) and historian of music;

his first wife née Esther Sleepe (1723–1762); and the children of this marriage,

> Esther (Burney) Burney [EBB] (1749–1832), harpsichordist and music teacher,
>
> James Burney [JB] (1750–1821), Rear-Admiral (1821),
>
> Frances (Burney) d'Arblay [FBA] (1752–1840), journalist and novelist,
>
> Susannah Elizabeth (Burney) Phillips [SBP] (1755–1800),
>
> Charles Burney [CB Jr] (1757–1817), DD (1812), schoolmaster and Greek scholar, and
>
> Charlotte Ann (Burney) Francis Broome [CBFB] (1761–1838);

his second wife Elizabeth (Allen) Allen (1725–1796); and the children of this second marriage,

> Richard Thomas Burney (1768–1808), schoolmaster at Kiddepore, India; and
>
> Sarah Harriet Burney [SHB] (1772–1844), novelist;

his stepchildren,

> the Rev Stephen Allen (1755–1847) and
>
> Maria (Allen) Rishton (1751–1820); and

his numerous sons-in-law, daughters-in-law, and grandchildren.

---

[1] Abbreviations are used in referring to the chief correspondents; see page xxi.

With social and literary gifts and a wide range of interests and associations, the Burney family seem to have met most of the writers and musicians in the London of their day, and as well artists, politicians, and divines, actors and actresses, "foreigners," eccentrics, "royals," and common folk. The correspondence is similarly varied, ranging from the illiterate pennings of such obscure personages as James Sleepe to the elegant effusions of Princess Elizabeth; from the brisk, witty letters of Mrs Thrale or the sly and humorous comment of Mrs Locke to the concise diplomacies of a Lord of the Admiralty or a Chancellor of the Exchequer. A stream of letters from Alexandre d'Arblay [M d'A] and from the d'Arblay acquaintance in France (from, for instance, Lafayette or Madame de Maisonneuve, sister of the general and diplomat Victor de Latour-Maubourg) make their characteristic effects; while the letters exchanged between members of the Burney family oscillate from heart-rending recountals of domestic woe to the jubilant triumphs of their professional and social careers.

This catalogue will provide outlines for an edition of the letters of Dr Burney himself, with his wit, humour, learning, and close observation of the political as well as musical and social scenes of his day. Guide lines are similarly supplied for printings in whole or in part of the journal-letters of his daughter Susannah Elizabeth Burney with their first-hand accounts of theatrical and musical events in London, of village life in Mickleham, and of the rebellion of '98 in County Louth. The letters of his grand-daughter Marianne Francis reflect an active participation in the evangelical reforms of the nineteenth century. It is also hoped that the catalogue, by occasionally indicating letters hitherto unknown, may be of use to such biographers as may be concerned with some one or other of the 1,100 persons who corresponded with the Burney family.

The Provenance of the Burney-d'Arblay Manuscripts

Though Madame d'Arblay has been roundly blamed for destroying family papers and given little thanks for the accumulations she did preserve, the history of both the burnings and the preservations, and the policy governing both, can be dated from November 1797, when in Dr Burney's study and under his direct supervision and example all the letters of his second wife lately deceased were consigned to the flames, together with the hundreds he had written to her, all of which *she* had preserved. As Madame d'Arblay was living in the years 1797–1801 in West Humble, Surrey, the joint work of destroying or preserving Dr Burney's letters could be continued only at rare intervals, she reading, he listening and deciding the issue. During her exile in France (1801–1812) the effort ceased.

Meanwhile in 1800, with the death of Susannah Elizabeth (Burney) Phillips and the return of the sacks of journal-letters that since their young girlhood Fanny had composed for her, Madame d'Arblay's "hoards" of journal-letters, as distinct from Dr Burney's packets of letters, became so augmented as to need a trunk for their containing. On her return from France (1812–1814) the editorial work on the Doctor's papers was resumed at Chelsea, and sacrificed to a second holocaust were the letters of Fulke Greville along with other records and reminders of former painful episodes.[2] Dr Burney (d 12 April 1814) had expressed a desire that Fanny should continue to edit his papers, and on her departure for France in November 1814 she had apparently carried them with her, as may be seen from the anguish attendant on the supposed confiscation of royalist property that she feared and believed must have taken place in Paris with the return of Napoleon in March 1815:

> . . . we have lost all we possessed in France — Even all my dear Fathers MSS & all my own, & unprinted works, from *my youth upwards*, with all *my* Letters, & *my* Susan's. — & our Journals! ——[3]

Having survived, however, the vicissitudes of war, the trunks, retrieved at Calais, were brought safely in 1816 to Bath, where the d'Arblays lived until the General's death in May 1818, at which time his writings and those of his French associates were painfully added to the store. With the death of the d'Arblay's only son the Reverend Alexander (January 1837) the accumulation of letters as well as sermons and poems was so augmented as to become oppressive. In 1838 Madame d'Arblay, by then eighty-two years of age, wrote with mounting anxiety to her sister Mrs Broome and her niece Charlotte (Francis) Barrett [CFBt]:

[2] ALS (Barrett Collection, British Museum, Eg 3690 ff 128–35b) FBA to EBB, 28 Nov [1820].
[3] AL (Berg Collection, The New York Public Library) FBA to CB Jr, 7 Apr 1815. Also AL (Berg) FBA to M d'A, 30 Mar 1815; and AL (Pierpont Morgan Library) FBA to JB, 27 Mar 1815.

My dear Charlottes both — think for me . . . what I had best do with this killing mass of constant recurrence to my calamity. — Shall I burn them? — at once — or shall I, & can I . . . spare for future times various collections that may be amusing, & even instructive? [4]

Alexander saw how "the myriads and Hoards of MSS." were beginning to weigh on his mother's mind and health, and his counsel while he lived had been "Burn them, mama." Madame d'Arblay's will, made on 6 March 1839 and probated on 17 February 1840 (P.C.C. Arden 88), settled the question. In her will she divided the manuscript accumulations into two parts which may be called, though each contained sections or runs of letters properly belonging to the other, the Burney Papers and the d'Arblay Papers.

> . . . to my Nephew Doctor Charles Parr Burney I leave the entire arrangement of the correspondence of my dear Father excepting my own Letters which I give to my Niece Charlotte Barrett   I had already in the last year made it over to my beloved son who was preparing it for the press   I now commit it to Doctor Charles Parr Burney either for a small select publication or for the flames   I leave to him likewise indiscriminately and without reserve or direction whatever composition may remain in the handwriting of my dear Father whether in prose or in verse well assured that I cannot do more honor to his memory

> but the whole of my own immense Mass of Manuscripts collected from my fifteenth year whether personal or collateral consisting of Letters Diaries Journals Dramas Compositions in prose and in rhyme I bequeath to the care and sole and immediate possession of my Niece Charlotte Barrett with full and free permission according to her unbiased taste and judgment to keep or destroy them simply but strictly stipulating that she faithfully bequeath at her death whatsoever she has not disposed of or annihilated to her son the said Richard Barrett. . . .

The Burney Papers and the d'Arblay Papers continued in separate courses, the first being handed down in a direct line to the descendants of Charles Parr Burney (1785–1864), the second (the d'Arblay Papers), in a collateral line beginning with Charlotte (Francis) Barrett (1786–1870). And the two divisions are separate to this day, even though, more or less intact, they lie only as far apart as New York is distant from New Haven.

The d'Arblay Papers that Madame d'Arblay had bequeathed to her niece Charlotte (Francis) Barrett would have been augmented immediately in Charlotte's home by the lively journals and the neatly docketed correspondence of her mother, Madame d'Arblay's sister, Charlotte Ann (Burney) Francis Broome, who had died in 1838. Annexed to them also at the time would

---

[4] ALS (Berg) FBA to CBFB and CFBt, [20 Apr 1838].

have been the papers of the Francis family: the correspondence of Charlotte Barrett's brother Clement Robert Francis (who had died in 1829) and that of her sister Marianne Francis (1790–1832). The collection was in future to be augmented by the papers of Charlotte's daughter Julia Charlotte (Barrett) Thomas Maitland (1808–1864), a selection of whose letters, including those from Madras, has been printed. Subsidiary therefore to the d'Arblay Papers, but still contained within them as they descended in the Barrett family, was a considerable body of material which may be called for the moment a Barrett accretion, though in time it came to be separated out and called the Barrett Collection. (For in the course of time this d'Arblay-Burney-Barrett-Francis material was in turn to be divided, one part to be housed in The New York Public Library, the other in the British Museum.)

To trace the course as initiated in Madame d'Arblay's will, the d'Arblay material would have come, with the death of Charlotte (Francis) Barrett in 1870, to her son the Reverend Richard Arthur Francis Barrett (1812–1881), rector of Stower Provost, Dorset (1858–1881), and from him to his niece, Charlotte Barrett's grand-daughter Julia Maitland (1843–1890), who in 1861 had married the Reverend David Wauchope (1825–1911), rector of Church Lawford near Rugby, Warwichshire, with an address of Banister Gate, Southampton.

The Reverend David Wauchope had hoped that the manuscripts could be deposited in the British Museum, but nevertheless in the year 1924 a huge part of the d'Arblay accumulations was sold by the Wauchope family to a London bookseller in Oxford Street who presently sold them to the lawyer-industrialist Mr Owen D. Young of Van Hornesville, New York, and of New York City. Mr Young had his Librarian Miss Sarah Dickson, later Curator of the Arents Collections, The New York Public Library, sort the acquisition into its several parts, after which it was encased in beautiful boxes of blue morocco, made in sizes to fit the manuscripts and fireproofed, and though scholars sometimes puzzled their heads about Fanny Burney's manuscripts, for their known Johnsonian content, there were few people in the scholarly world who knew where they were.[5]

---

[5] Many indeed were led by R. Brimley Johnson's Preface to *Fanny Burney and the Burneys* (1926) to believe that the d'Arblay manuscripts had been burned in April 1919 with Camilla Lacey, the house in West Humble that the d'Arblays had built and occupied in the years 1797–1801, whereas in that fire there was lost the d'Arblay archive perhaps only a Paris Letter Book containing copies in M. d'Arblay's hand of some of the letters and journals that Madame d'Arblay wrote in Paris in the years 1801–1812, this being an autograph loaned among a few other items by Miss Ann Julia Wauchope to Leverton Harris, the owner of Camilla Lacey at the time. See the letters of acknowledgement (Barrett, Eg 3707 ff 280–86) Leverton Harris to Miss Ann Julia Wauchope, 12, 16, 18, and 19 May 1911.

In the year 1941, however, Mr Young's manuscripts were transferred, partly by gift and partly by sale, into the care and keeping of the Henry W. and Albert A. Berg Collection of The New York Public Library.[6] There, broken down into chronological runs of letters and sometimes catalogued item by item by the cataloguer at that time, Miss Adelaide Smith, they have been made available to qualified scholars since the year 1945. The manuscripts include, besides correspondence in French and English, a manuscript (though incomplete) of *Evelina*, manuscripts of unpublished plays, and the long-sought manuscripts of the *Diary and Letters*, these last being the letters and journals that Charlotte Barrett selected from the whole for possible printing in her edition *The Diary and Letters of Madame d'Arblay* (7 vols, 1842–1847). These selections, the considerable body of material sent as copy to the publisher Henry Colburn around 1841–47, were held by him and had to be brought back into the collection by purchase, that of Charlotte Barrett herself, a sum of £200 being mentioned in the surviving records of the transaction.[7]

Barrett Collection

The Barrett Collection may be defined as the residue of the d'Arblay-Burney-Barrett-Francis material that remained in the Wauchope family after the sale of 1924.

If scholars did not know what had become of the Burney-d'Arblay papers included in that sale, still less was its destination known to the Wauchope family at Bannister Gate, Southampton. A query, sent by the editor in 1951 to various descendants of the Burney and Barrett families, reached Miss Ann Julia Wauchope (d 1962), then at Howton, Bushey Heath, who thus learned for the first time that the papers sold at Southampton in 1925 had crossed the ocean and had come to rest and safe-keeping in The New York Public Library. Her kind response to the query included such startling manuscript enclosures, sent by post, that one needed no second invitation to come to tea and to enter thereupon into Eldorado.

---

[6] John D. Gordan, "A Doctor's Benefaction: The Berg Collection of the New York Public Library" *The Papers of the Bibliographical Society of America* xlviii (1954) 308–311.

[7] ALS (Barrett, Eg 3705 ff 101–02b) Henry Foss to CFBt, 30 Apr [1857] and a manuscript "Extract from Catalogue of Sale of Stock & Copyrights of late Mr. Colburn G^t. Marlborough Street May 21 &c 1857" (Barrett, Eg 3707 ff 271–72). Charlotte Barrett had also offered the publisher the manuscripts of the Juvenile Diaries, those later edited very ably by Annie Raine Ellis, *The Early Diary of Frances Burney* 1768–1778 (2 vols 1889) and these manuscripts she regained with the others in the purchase.

I shall never forget that tea party nor the room into which I was presently conducted. On the walls were the miniatures and portraits (see Sotheby's illustrated Catalogue for Monday 19 Dec 1960, Lots 294, 295, 296, 297) and in bookcases, first and now rare editions of d'Arblay and Burney publications. Old reliquaries still kept their old keepsakes — the gold watch, enamelled in translucent dark blue, with its matching chatelaine, one of Queen Charlotte's gifts to Fanny Burney (Sotheby, as above, Lot 291), a paperknife once the property of James the Admiral (Lot 293), and a sampler worked in 1732 by Fanny Burney's mother née Esther Sleepe (Lot 290). On a Library table covered over for the occasion with manuscript letters, were Fanny Burney's letters to her first publisher Thomas Lowndes, for instance, and his to her. On shelves were the marble-covered letter boxes, now empty, but once the receptacle of the larger part of the d'Arblay-Burney archive that had crossed the ocean. Other boxes, however, were still filled with eighteenth- and early nineteenth-century letters, some of them folded in the shapes in which a century before they had been posted. With successive visits, still more papers came to light, including an accumulation of the papers of the Broome, Francis, and Barrett families. I cannot tell what this archive, intact in spirit, meant to me or to *The History of Fanny Burney* (1958), but I should like to pay a tribute of respect and gratitude to the aged keeper of the archive (born in 1866, she was then well over eighty years old) with her high intelligence, integrity, and matchless knowledge of all things Burneyean. Unmoved by the fortune this residue of the collection could bring if, for instance, it could be united with the larger part that had gone to New York, she chose only to remember that her father had wished the manuscripts to go to the British Museum, and this *she* wished with a tenacity of purpose matched only by her diffidence in approaching the Keepers. She wished the manuscripts to go where every one might read them.

The mission so strongly suggested by the circumstances was soon accomplished and thus it was that this section of d'Arblay-Burney papers with its rich inheritance of Broome-Francis-Barrett-Maitland and Wauchope material passed into the care and keeping of the British Museum, an accession described by Dr C. E. Wright, "The Barrett Collection of Burney Papers" *The British Museum Quarterly* xviii 2 (June 1953) 41–43. Catalogued item by item and mounted, the series of over 2,000 items is described in a temporary typed Catalogue "The Barrett Collection of Burney Papers," Egerton 3690–3708, and made available in the Manuscript Room of the British Museum.

The Comyn and the Osborn Collections

Meanwhile the letters and papers of Charles Burney, Mus Doc (1726–1814) which in 1839 Madame d'Arblay had willed to his grandson, her nephew, Charles Parr Burney (1785–1865), proved, like the d'Arblay Papers, a nucleus of an expanding collection. Added to them at once no doubt were the juvenile pieces, the social and business letters, and some of the manuscript works of Charles Burney, DD, the Greek scholar and divine, who had died in December 1817. After 1865 this Collection was augmented by the hundreds of letters written to Dr Charles Parr Burney, Archdeacon of St Alban's, by divines, artists, and booksellers, friends of his father's and his own the kingdom over. And as, further, his wife née Frances Bentley Young (c1792–1878) and his daughters were industrious autograph collectors, the Burney Papers grew appreciably as they passed down the line, conjecturally, to Charles Parr's son, the Venerable Charles Edward Burney (1815–1907), Vicar of St Mark's, Surbiton, Archdeacon of Kingston-on-Thames, Hon Canon of Rochester, and thus on to the fifth Charles (1840–1912), Master in the Chancery Division, and his six daughters. One of these daughters, Fanny, later Mrs Atherton Cumming (1869–1954) of St Albans, inherited a very fine grangerized edition of *The Diary and Letters of Madame d'Arblay* lavishly illustrated with priceless manuscript letters, now, among other letters, portraits, and mementoes, the possession of her grandson Mr John Comyn of The Cross House, Turnestone, Herefordshire.

This is the only collection of any size known to be in the possession of the Burney family.

Whether or not the bulk of the Burney archive came to Miss Mabel Burney (1870–1953) of Wandsworth Common, it was not long after her death in 1953 when large packages containing hundreds, if not thousands, of Burney letters, suddenly released on the markets and acquired by the well-known collector and benefactor Mr James M. Osborn of Yale University, came permanently to rest there in the James Marshall and Marie-Louise Osborn Collection, Beinecke Library, New Haven, Connecticut. Containing, like all the other collections, a cross-section of family papers, the Osborn Collection of Burney Papers is distinguished by its high incidence of the papers of all five Charles Burneys, from which chronological increments it can be immediately recognized as the direct hereditament of Burney papers as they were passed down the Burney line. Enriched by successive purchases, as letters kept falling into the markets, and housed luxuriously in the Beinecke Library,

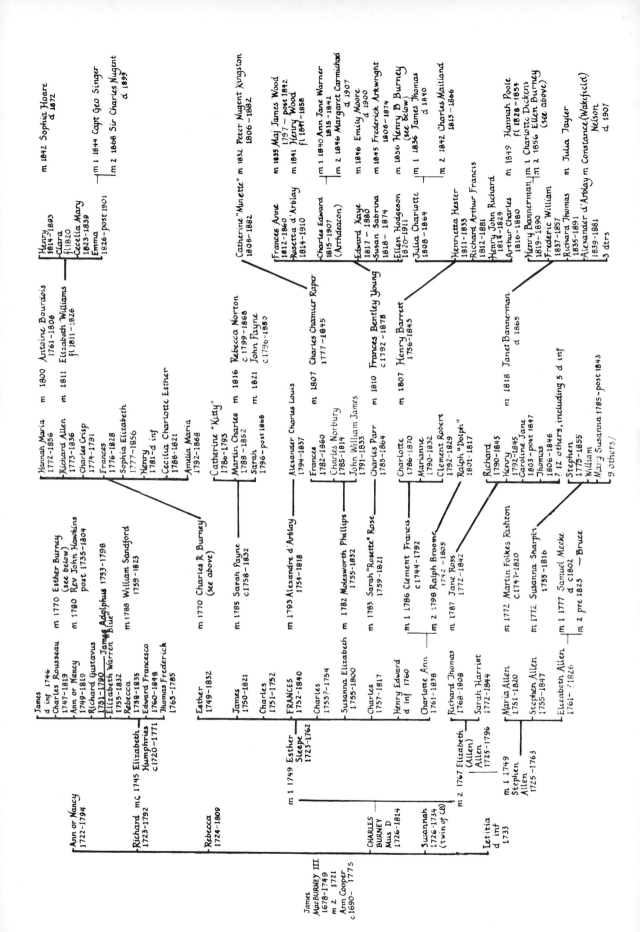

the Osborn Collection of Burney Papers, by the well-known liberality of its owner, has been made generously available to scholars, its material having already contributed significantly to Roger Lonsdale's brilliant investigations into the literary career of Dr Burney (*Dr. Charles Burney, A Literary Biography* 1965) while nuggets of its wealth are to be seen as well in *The History of Fanny Burney* (1958).

Such is the main outline of the provenance of the Burney, Barrett, and d'Arblay papers in the three largest Collections, the Henry W. and Albert A. Berg Collection of The New York Public Library, the James Marshall and Marie-Louise Osborn Collection in the Beinecke Library, Yale University, and the Barrett Collection of Burney Papers in the British Museum, with some indication of the origins of the Comyn Collection.

It is useful to remember, however, that while it was customary in the letter-writing ages to return at the deaths of recipients of letters complete packets of the same, neatly docketed and tied, to the senders or writers, this was not always done, and so it was that hundreds of fugitive Burney letters, kept by their recipients, were handed down in families other than the Burneys, and in the course of time sold to booksellers or deposited in libraries, museums, county record offices, or other repositories. In this way, for instance, Burney, Barrett, and Francis letters were deposited with Thrale-Piozzi material in the John Rylands Library, Manchester, and the correspondence of James the Admiral, in the Pierpont Morgan Library, New York City.

In an effort to locate stray letters, a query was mailed in 1964–65 to nearly 1,000 libraries and manuscript repositories in the United Kingdom and to some 1,500 in the United States of America. Though compunction must be felt at ever having troubled no less than 2,500 librarians or archivists to read such a letter and deal with such a request, the response was prompt, conscientious, and kind. Letters *to* and *from* members of the Burney family came to light in 100 or more libraries from Salt Lake City, Utah, to Newcastle-upon-Tyne, from Aberdeen and Armagh to McGill.

Unfortunately lacking in the Check List and to be added, it may be hoped, in future times if still extant is the correspondence of Susannah Elizabeth (Burney) Phillips and Madame d'Arblay with Frederica Augusta (Schaub) Locke (1750–1832) of Norbury Park and with her daughter Amelia (Locke) Angerstein (1777–1846), the existence of which is indicated not only by reference to it in known letters but also by copies of parts of it taken presumably c1840–1847 by Charlotte (Francis) Barrett. (See also the source material used by Vittoria Calonna Caetani, Duchess of Sermoneta, *The Locks of Norbury* (1940).)

The catalogue, however, lists only the letters that the compilers know to be presently extant in manuscript, most of which they have seen either in manuscript or in photographic reproduction. Though every effort has been made to trace letters known from their printings to have existed, such letters, unless to be seen, are not included in the catalogue. Omitted notably for example is that part of the correspondence between Fanny (Burney) d'Arblay and Hester Maria (Thrale) Elphinstone, Viscountess Keith, as seen printed by the Marquis of Lansdowne in *The Queeney Letters* (1934). And the catalogue may bring other letters to light.

The catalogue will nevertheless unite much of that which has been divided or dispersed. It locates replies to letters, completing correspondences. It restores letters, the sheets of which have become separated, one sheet in one library or continent, the other far away. It assembles the ribboned cuttings of mutilated letters; it completes sentences, part of the text of which may be on one side of the ocean, part on the other; and in words split by the scissors, it sometimes supplies the cross for the t's, the dots for the i's.

More significantly the catalogue will show the parts of a family saga more dramatic, more varied, interesting, and moving than fiction. Implicit in the series of 10,000 letters from the years 1749 to 1878 is a history of changing manners and customs, of changing social and religious life, and a comment on or a reflection of political and military events to rival that provided in the Paston Letters.

JOYCE HEMLOW

A Note on the Use of the Catalogue

Arrangement

The correspondence is arranged chronologically within family groupings under the names of the chief correspondents in the Burney family, Dr Burney, his children, and grandchildren. In the first Section, the *letters to* and *letters by* Charles Burney, Mus Doc (1726–1814) are arranged chronologically under his name, and following his letters, are those of his wives and their immediate connections. The correspondence of each of his children follows by a similar plan according to the order given in the Contents. Letters between members of the Burney family are listed once only. The Index gives the numbers of the pages on which the *letters to* and *letters by* all correspondents (both within and without the Burney family) are to be found.

To conserve space on the second lines of the entries, the names of most of the Burneys are represented by the symbols listed on p xxi. Other names appear in shortened form; the Index should be consulted for the full names.

Dating

Items are listed in each Section under the year of the correspondence. The year will be repeated in entries only when 1) in undated letters, the date is derived from internal evidence (in which case it is given in square brackets); and 2) when it is derived from postmarks (in which case the postmarks are given in abbreviated form). For example:

28 AU 94 pmk		a postmark supplying the full date, day, month, and year
18 pmk	Aug	partial use of a postmark to supply the day; the month is derived (or confirmed) from dating in the letter
18 Aug	pmk 1794	partial use of a postmark to give the year; the day and month are derived from the letter.

If the date could not be fixed exactly, but is narrowed down by internal evidence to a span of possible years, the letter is listed at the end of the entries for the first possible year. Journals and Journal-Letters covering a series of dates are listed under the first date of the series even though the journals may have been composed at a much later date.

Locations

The locations of the autograph letters are indicated at the ends of the first lines of the entries by symbols or abbreviations, the explanations of which (the name and address of owners, etc) will be found on p xxii–xxvii.

As a further means of identification, the first lines of the letters are printed (see the *third* lines of the entries) but without editorial emendations of any kind. Angle brackets indicate conjectural readings.

Copies or drafts of extant letters are noted in smaller type under the original entry. Letters which, torn in two, appear in their several pieces in different collections, are gathered together under the same entry, with a listing of the several locations and the first lines of the separated pieces.

For the most part, the Cataloguers undertook to list only the holograph letters they have seen (either in the original or in photo-copies). Added sparingly to the list, however, are manuscript letters they have seen described in bookseller's catalogues or those cited in such works on the Burneys as G. E. Manwaring's *My Friend the Admiral* (London 1931) or Dr Percy A. Scholes's *The Great Dr Burney* (2 vols, London 1948). It is hoped that the present location or ownership of these letters may again come to light.

Abbreviations

Postmarks appearing on both English and French letters have the month in an abbreviated form: e.g., MR = March; AP or AV = April; MA or MY = May; JU = June; JY = July.

[ ]	editorial insertion
< >	conjectural reading or illegible word
c	circa
AJ	autograph journal
AL(S)	autograph letter (signed)
inc	incomplete
JL(S)	journal letter (signed)
kt	knighted
LB	letter book
MB	manuscript book
pmk	postmark
post	after
PS	postscript

Major Correspondents

AA	Alexander Charles Louis d'Arblay
CAB,	Charlotte Ann Burney,
CBF,	after 11 Feb 1786 Mrs Francis,
CBFB	after 1 Mar 1798 Mrs Broome
CB	Charles Burney (1726–1814), Mus Doc
CB Jr	Charles Burney (1757–1817), DD
CB IV	Charles Edward Burney (1815–1907)
CFBt	Charlotte (Francis) Barrett
CPB	Charles Parr Burney (1785–1864), DD
EBB	Esther (Burney) Burney
FB,	Frances Burney,
FBA	after 20 July 1793 Madame d'Arblay
GMAPWaddington	Georgiana Mary Ann (Port) Waddington
HHBt	Henrietta Hester Barrett
HLTP	Hester Lynch Salusbury,
	after 11 Oct 1763 Mrs Thrale,
	after 23 July 1784 Mrs Piozzi
JB	James Burney
JCBTM	Julia Charlotte (Barrett) Thomas Maitland
M d'A	Alexandre Jean Baptiste Piochard d'Arblay
MF	Marianne Francis
SEB	Susanna Elizabeth Burney,
SBP	after 10 Jan 1782 Mrs Phillips
SHB	Sarah Harriet Burney

Note: AMR are the initials of an otherwise unidentified Edinburgh lady.

ABBREVIATIONS

Manuscript Collections

AECB	in the collection of the late Lt-Col A. E. C. Burney (31:1931)
All	Prof Marcia Allentuck English Department The City College The City University of New York New York, New York 10031
AN	Archives Nationales Palais Soubise Hôtel de Rohan 60 rue des Francs-Bourgeois Paris 3ᵉ, France
APS	American Philosophical Society Library 105 South Fifth Street Philadelphia, Pennsylvania 19106
Arm	The Public Library Armagh, Ireland
Bath	Municipal Libraries and Victoria Art Gallery Bath, Somerset, England
Belf	Public Record Office of Northern Ireland Law Courts Building May Street Belfast 1, Northern Ireland
BM	The British Museum London W.C. 1, England
BM(Bar)	The Barrett Collection of Burney Papers The British Museum London W.C. 1, England
BM(NH)	The British Museum (Natural History) Cromwell Road London S.W. 7, England
BN(M)	Département de la Musique Bibliothèque Nationale 58 rue de Richelieu Paris 2ᵉ, France
Bol	Civico Museo Bibliografico Musicale Piazza Rossini 2 Bologna, Italy
Bord	in the collection of the late Richard Border Lane End Pulborough, Sussex, England
BPL	Boston Public Library Copley Square Boston, Massachusetts 02117
Buff	Lockwood Memorial Library State University of New York at Buffalo Buffalo, New York 14214
BYU	Brigham Young University Library Provo, Utah 84601
Cal(B)	General Library University of California at Berkeley Berkeley, California 94720

Cal(SB)   The Library
        University of California at Santa Barbara
        Santa Barbara, California 93018

Camb   University Library
        University of Cambridge
        Cambridge, England

Camb(F)   Fitzwilliam Museum
        University of Cambridge
        Cambridge, England

Camb(T)   Trinity College Library
        University of Cambridge
        Cambridge, England

Car   Carnegie Book Shop
        [311(247): Catalogue 311 (1970), item no 247]
        140 East 59th Street
        New York, New York 10022

Coke   The Gerald Coke Collection
        Jenkyn Place
        Bentley, Hants, England

Colb   Colbeck Radford & Co
        (30: Oct 1930) — referred to in Scholes *The Great Dr.
        Burney* (London 1938)

Comyn   The John Comyn Collection of Burney Papers
        The Cross House
        Vowchurch, Turnastone, Hereford, England

Cox   Cox's and King's Branch
        Lloyds Bank Ltd
        6 Pall Mall, P.O. Box 220
        London S.W. 1, England

Essex   County of Essex Record Office
        County Hall
        Chelmsford, England

FLP   The Free Library of Philadelphia
        Logan Square
        Philadelphia, Pennsylvania 19103

Folger   The Folger Shakespeare Library
        201 East Capitol Street
        Washington, D.C. 20003

Glouc   County of Gloucester Records Office
        Shire Hall
        Gloucester, England

Good   Goodspeed's Book Shop
        (65:1965)
        18 Beacon Street
        Boston, Massachusetts 02108

Ham   Hammersmith Public Libraries
        Brook Green Road
        London W. 6, England

Harv(H)   Houghton Library
        Harvard University
        Cambridge, Massachusetts 02138

HEH   Henry E. Huntington Library & Art Gallery
        San Marino, California 91108

Manuscript Collections, continued

Hilles   Prof Frederick W. Hilles
Department of English
Yale University
New Haven, Connecticut 06520

HSP   The Historical Society of Pennsylvania
1300 Locust Street
Philadelphia, Pennsylvania 19107

Hyde   The Hyde Collection
Four Oaks Farm
Somerville, New Jersey 08876

Iowa   Iowa State Department of History & Archives
Historical Building
Des Moines, Iowa 50319

KL   The Borough Museum
King's Lynn, Norfolk, England

LC   Library of Congress
Washington, D.C. 20540

LC(J)   The Thomas Jefferson Papers
Library of Congress
Washington, D.C. 20540

Leeds   Brotherton Library
University of Leeds
Leeds 2, England

Leigh   R. A. Leigh, Esq
Trinity College
University of Cambridge
Cambridge, England

Lewis   Mr Wilmarth S. Lewis
Farmington, Connecticut 06032

Liv(P)   City of Liverpool Public Library
William Brown Street
Liverpool 3, England

Liv(U)   University Library
University of Liverpool
Liverpool 3, England

Mag   Maggs Brothers
[20: 1920; 230(96): Catalogue 230, item no 96; 349(1220):
Cat 349, no 1220; 352(1785?): Cat 352, no 1785?;
916(23): Cat 916, no 23]
50 Berkeley Square
London W. 1, England

McG   McGill University Library
Montreal 110, Quebec, Canada

MdHS   Maryland Historical Society
201 West Monument Street
Baltimore, Maryland 21201

Mich   William L. Clements Library
University of Michigan
Ann Arbor, Michigan 48104

Myers   Winifred A. Myers (Autographs) Ltd
                 80 New Bond Street
                 London W. 1, England

Newc   University Library
                 University of Newcastle upon Tyne
                 Queen Victoria Street
                 Newcastle upon Tyne 1, England

Nor   Norfolk & Norwich Record Office
                 Central Library
                 Norwich, Norfolk, England

NPG   National Portrait Gallery
                 Trafalgar Square
                 London W.C. 2, England

NSW   The Public Library of New South Wales
                 Macquarie Street
                 Sydney, Australia

NYPL(B)   The Henry W. & Albert A. Berg Collection of English and
                 American Literature
                 The New York Public Library
                 Fifth Avenue & 42nd Street
                 New York, New York 10018

NYPL(MS)   Manuscript Division
                 The New York Public Library
                 Fifth Avenue & 42nd Street
                 New York, New York 10018

NYPL(Mus)   Special Collections, Music Division
                 Research Library of the Performing Arts
                 The New York Public Library at Lincoln Center
                 111 Amsterdam Avenue
                 New York, New York 10023

NWUL   Northwestern University Library
                 Evanston, Illinois 60201

Osb   The James Marshall and Marie-Louise Osborn Collection
                 Yale University Library
                 New Haven, Connecticut 06520

Oxf(A)   Ashmolean Museum
                 The Department of Western Art
                 Oxford, England

Oxf(AS)   John Sparrow, Esq
                 Warden of All Souls College
                 University of Oxford
                 Oxford, England

Oxf(Bod)   The Bodleian Library
                 University of Oxford
                 Oxford, England

Penn   University of Pennsylvania Library
                 Philadelphia, Pennsylvania 19104

Pforz   The Carl H. Pforzheimer Library
                 41 East 42nd Street
                 New York, New York 10017

Plat   H. L. Platnauer, Esq
                 14 St George's Close
                 Westbourne Road
                 Edgbaston
                 Birmingham 15, England

ABBREVIATIONS

PML   The Pierpont Morgan Library
33 East 36th Street
New York, New York 10016

Prin   Princeton University Library
Princeton, New Jersey 08540

PRO   Public Record Office
Chancery Lane
London W.C. 2, England

RAA   Royal Academy of Arts
Piccadilly
London W. 1, England

Ray   Mr Gordon N. Ray, President
The John Simon Guggenheim Memorial Foundation
90 Park Avenue
New York, New York 10016

RF   The Philip H. & A. S. W. Rosenbach Foundation
2010 DeLancey Place
Philadelphia, Pennsylvania 19103

Roch   University of Rochester Library
Rochester, New York 14627

RS   The Royal Society
Burlington House
London W. 1, England

RSA   The Royal Society of Arts
Adelphi
John Adam Street
London W.C. 2, England

RWB   Mr Roger W. Barrett
231 South La Salle Street
Chicago, Illinois 60604

Ryl   The John Rylands Library
150 Deansgate
Manchester M3 3EH, England

Schol   in the collection of the late
Dr Percy A. Scholes

Scot   The National Library of Scotland
Edinburgh 1, Scotland

Shef   Sheffield City Libraries
Central Library
Sheffield 1, England

Shep   Mr Brooks Shepard
155 Linden Street
New Haven, Connecticut 06511

Shep(D)   Mr & Mrs David A. Shepard
Creamer Hill Road
Greenwich, Connecticut 06833

Soth   Sotheby & Co
(26: 1926; 30: 1930; 67: 1967)
34 & 35 New Bond Street
London W. 1, England

ABBREVIATIONS

StMar   St Margaret's Church
King's Lynn, Norfolk, England

StMi   St Michael's College Library
Tenbury Wells, Worcestershire, England

Taylor   Mr Robert H. Taylor
511 Lake Drive
Princeton, New Jersey 08540

TexCh   The Mary Couts Burnett Library
Texas Christian University
Fort Worth, Texas 76129

UAB   University Library
King's College
Aberdeen, Scotland

V&A   The Victoria & Albert Museum
South Kensington
London S.W. 7, England

Vas   The Library
Vassar College
Poughkeepsie, New York 12601

Vin   Service Historique de l'Armée
Vieux Fort
94 Vincennes, France

Wales   The National Library of Wales
Aberystwyth, Wales

WHM   The Wellcome Historical Medical Library
The Wellcome Building
Euston Road
London N.W. 1, England

Win   The Winchester College Library
Winchester, England

Wms   Dr Williams's Library
14 Gordon Square
London W.C. 1, England

Wy   Wellesley College Library
Wellesley, Massachusetts 02181

Yale(Be)   The Beinecke Rare Book and Manuscript Library
Yale University Library
New Haven, Connecticut 06520

Yale(Bo)   The Boswell Papers
Yale University Library
New Haven, Connecticut 06520

Yale(MS)   Historical Manuscripts Department
Yale University Library
New Haven, Connecticut 06520

Acknowledgements

FOR financial support contributing to the preparation and publication of the *Catalogue*, I wish to thank the Committee on Research at McGill University, the Humanities Research Council of Canada, and the John Simon Guggenheim Memorial Foundation. Grants given by the Canada Council for the editing of *The Journals and Letters of Fanny Burney (Madame d'Arblay), 1791–1840*, helped as well, when the work was one and indivisible, as did a grant donated (1964) by the American Council of Learned Societies. The support of Dr Stanley B. Frost, formerly the Dean of Graduate Studies and Research at McGill University and that of Mr Robin H. Strachan, Director of the McGill-Queen's University Press, is also gratefully acknowledged.

In recollecting early stages of the cataloguing when a large part of the Burney Correspondence was a jumbled mass, unsorted as yet, even with respect to writers and recipients, my thoughts go back to the late Ann Julia Wauchope, at Howton, Bushey Heath, Hertfordshire, and to Dr C. E. Wright, Deputy Keeper of Manuscripts at the British Museum, who took an interest in the Wauchope-Barrett archive as it entered the Museum; and, in The New York Public Library in those early days, to Miss Adelaide Smith, who once contributed a summer vacation to cataloguing Burney manuscripts. It was the late Dr John D. Gordan, Curator of the Berg Collection, who first suggested that the *Catalogue* be published, and to him in ever grateful memory the *Catalogue* is dedicated. It is also with great pleasure that one remembers the co-operation of his successor, Dr Lola L. Szladits, as well as that of the skilful librarians and archivists of the Local History and Genealogy Division of the Library, not to forget that of the genial editors of the *Bulletin*.

When in the 1950s and 60s Burney letters began to accrue in large packets, in the James Marshall and Marie-Louise Osborn Collection, at New Haven, Connecticut, Dr Osborn and the late Mrs Osborn repeatedly accorded a welcome to their home; and in later years when the Collection had been moved to the Beinecke Rare Book and Manuscript Library at Yale University, Mr Herman W. Liebert, the Librarian, kindly found a spare room in the library for work in progress. For pleasant associations, collaborations in cataloguing, and for prompt notices (often with Xeroxes) of new acquisitions, the compilers are indebted not only to Dr Osborn, but also to Dr Stephen Parks, Associate Curator of the Osborn Collection, and in former years, to Dr Roger H. Lonsdale and to Mr G. A. M. Woods.

ACKNOWLEDGEMENTS

That the priceless letters of the John Comyn Collection are included in the list is owing to the personal kindness and hospitality of Mrs Cecily Comyn of the Cross House, Vowchurch, Turnastone, Hertfordshire; and it is owing similarly to the personal kindness of the owners that the list includes the Burney letters in the Hyde Collection, Four Oaks Farm, Somerville, New Jersey, as well as a collection, the possession of Mr John Sparrow, Warden of All Souls College, Oxford. Mr Herbert T. F. Cahoon of the Pierpont Morgan Library helped to locate French correspondence that had strayed there from its d'Arblay base; and by the kindness of the late Carl H. Pforzheimer and of the former curator Dr Kenneth N. Cameron, Burney letters in the Pforzheimer Library reached the lists. Professor Frederick W. Hilles and Mr Brooks Shepard of Yale University, and Mr Wilmarth S. Lewis of Farmington, Connecticut, made their Burney letters available, both in the original and Xeroxes.

To all the owners, archivists, curators, and librarians listed on pages xxii–xvii, similar thanks are due. Doubtless others would have helped, had they known about the list, and doubtless by co-operative efforts of a similar kind, the list will be in time completed.

J. H.

A CATALOGUE OF THE
BURNEY FAMILY CORRESPONDENCE
1749–1878

I

CHARLES BURNEY, MUS DOC 1726–1814

(CB)

See also letters from FBA and CB Jr.

Holograph works and original documents of Dr Charles Burney are located chiefly in the Osborn, Berg, and British Museum collections, but some are in the following: Barrett, Bodleian, Folger, John Comyn, John Rylands, Hilles, Hyde, Pforzheimer, and the Royal Society.

1749

29 July   1 p fol   Harv(H)
from Christopher Smart
I have left your last unanswered so long that
also   copy   1 p 4to   Harv(H)

1752

[1752]   2 p 4to   Osb
to Esther (Sleepe) Burney
Now My Amiable Friend let me unbosom

1755

1 Feb   copy   ?   StMar
to Parish of St Margaret's, Lynn
The subscription being expired which first

7–16 Feb   draft   2 p 4to   TexCh
to Samuel Johnson
Though I have never had the happiness of a
also   typescript   Hyde

14 Apr   draft   2 p fol   Hyde
to Samuel Johnson
That you w^d. think my letter worthy of Notice,

14 Apr   draft   2 p 4to   Osb
to Samuel Johnson
Without exercising the greatest self-denial, I

1757

[14 Mar 1757]   1 p 4to   Osb
from William Bewley
I would have taken the present opportunity of

26 Mar   draft?   3 p 4to   NYPL(B)
to Samuel Johnson
Sir — Without exercising the greatest

1758

8 Mar   3 p 4to   NYPL(B)
from Samuel Johnson
Your kindness is so great, and my claim to any

1760

27 Feb   2 p fol   Osb
from Vicenzio Martinelli
La vostra umanissima de i 24 mi è stata di

1761

[1761]   ½ p fol   NYPL(B)
to William Bewley
Think not, my dearest Bewley, that you can

1762

4 Aug   4 p fol   Osb
from William Bewley
After a silence of 2 years, I sit down this

1 Dec   4 p 4to   NYPL(B)
to Elizabeth (Allen) Burney
Letters of Condolence are full as difficult to

16 Sept   1 p 4to   PML
from John Montagu, 4th Earl of Sand-
      wich
On my return from London I rec^d

1763

18–21 Mar   4 p fol   Osb
from William Bewley
In the note which I enclosed in Tartine I gave

5 Nov   3 p fol   Osb
from William Bewley
And so you think to *wash your hands of me*!

15 Oct   2 p 4to   Comyn
from [Jules, comte de] Polignac
C'est pour vous prouver Monsieur et tres Cher

26–28 Nov   3 p 4to   Osb
from William Bewley
Ecce iterum Crispinus! — but in 4to. only upon

1764

5 Feb   4 p 4to   Comyn
from David Garrick
I have defer'd keeping my promise to you

also   copy   4 p (in Memoirs)   NYPL(B)

[Apr? 1764]   3 p 4to   Osb
to Elizabeth (Allen) Burney
L^y. Susan Strangways marriage with M^r.

1 June   3 p fol   Osb
from William Bewley
I'll write no more Letters upon Franks — They

13 June   4 p 4to   NYPL(B)
to FB
I write to my dear Fanny again, to tell her, to

18–20 June   4 p 4to   NYPL(B)
with EBB to FB
I am sure it will please my dear Fanny

9–10 Sept   3 p fol   Osb
from William Bewley
With due gratitude I acknowledge the receipt

12 Sept   3 p fol   Osb
from William Bewley
D^r. Reid you must know endeavours to

10 Oct   3 p 4to   Osb
from William Bewley
Quousque tandem abutore, Burneie, patientia

14 Nov   3 p fol   Osb
from William Bewley
This is to inform you that I have taken this

[14] Nov   3 p 4to   Osb
from Fulke Greville
Tho I shall see you soon I sit down to write you

1765

14 Oct   draft   2 p fol   Hyde
to Samuel Johnson
The Translation I am going to mention to you

1766

27 June   2 p 4to   PML
from David Garrick
I have sent you a [f]ine copy of the prologue

27 Aug   3 p 4to   Osb
from   de Grange Blanche
Me permettrez vous de rapeller à votre

3 OC pmk [1766]   4 p 4to   Osb
from Fulke Greville
I am much obliged to you for your letter

29 Nov   1 p 4to   Comyn
from David Hume   to [CB?]
I have a Letter from Paris, by which I learn,

14 Dec   4 p fol   Osb
from Fulke Greville
I beg leave to prove to you that the old Proverb

1767

21 Mar   1 p 4to   Osb
from Thomas Hutcheson
I give you, my dear Sir, this immediate Answer,

9 May   1 p 4to   Osb
from Keane FitzGerald
[tear] [pre]sents his compliments to M^r

29 Oct   2 p 4to   Osb
from Frances (Macartney) Greville
I was favoured with yours this morning for

16 Nov   2 p 8vo   Osb
from Frances (Macartney) Greville
I do most heartily condole with you on the

1768

4 Jan   1 p 4to   Harv(H)
from Christopher Smart
Many thanks for your kind & generous

[pre 1769?]   2 p 4to   BM(Bar)
from William Bewley
This very instant, seated by my fireside with

Dec [pre 1769?]   ½ p 4to   Osb
from Fulke Greville
une bonne <poularde>, un bon feu, un

1769

6 Feb   2 p 4to   Comyn
from William Mason
As I was about to leave the Country for this

also   2 p 4to   copy   Lewis

2 Apr   1 p 4to   Comyn
from John Hawkesworth
M^r. Greville tells me that you have been so

20 Aug   2 p 4to   Osb
from William Bewley
As I did not tear myself away from you the

27 Sept   2 p fol   Osb
from [William Bewley]
I rec^d. your agreeable *Impromptu* from

[1769?]   2 p 4to   Osb
from William Bewley
Have not you a brother who lives at Salisbury?

1770

27 May   7 p 4to   Osb
to William Mason
Several Friends, who through partiality,

28 May   2 p 4to   Osb
from Samuel Crisp
I am so crippled with this sharp unseasonable

1770, continued

30 May   1 p 4to   Osb
from Vicenzio Martinelli
Il nome del renditone di questo

6 June   1 p 4to   BM(Bar)
to FB
I cannot set sail ere I have given you a word

18 June   3 p fol   Osb
from William Bewley
I snatch a moment amidst a thousand

17 Oct   4 p 4to   V&A
to David Garrick
"Thus far into the Bowels of the Land have we

20 Oct   2 p 4to   Bol
to Padre Martini
Altro non m'avrebbe impedito fin adesso

23 Oct [1770]   2 p 4to   Osb
from Sir William Hamilton
Having been prevented from coming to Naples

19–[20] Dec   draft   3 p 4to   Osb
to Samuel Crisp
But few things have lain heavier on my

1771

16 Jan   1 p 4to   Osb
from Padre Martini
Per mezzo del Sig: Perkins <spedisco> a VS.

6 Feb   3 p 4to   Osb
from William Bewley
At last I have it in my power to thank you for

[1 Mar 1771]   draft & copy   2 p 4to
to Pierre Gui   Leigh
Comme il m'est impossible d'oublier Jamais

7 Apr   1 p fol   Osb
from Padre Martini
Essendo <stato> favorito d'una visita a me

8 Apr   4 p 4to   Osb
from [Pierre?] Gui
J'ay bien recu la lettre que vous avez pris la

24 Apr   3 p fol   Osb
from William Bewley
I will for once condescend to overlook the high

8 May [1771]   2 p 4to   NYPL(B)
from Sir Alexander Macdonald
Sir Alex^r. Macdonald presents his Compliments

9 May [1771]   1 p 4to   Osb
from William Mason
I am going out of Town for a few days, &

15 May   2 p 4to   Osb
from Denis Diderot
Si vous n'avez point encore entendre parler de

18 May   3 p fol   Osb
from [William Bewley]
If my mind does not misgive me, the journal of

23 May   copy   3 p 4to   NYPL(B)
to Baron d'Holbach
The Happiness I enjoyed under your hospitable

24 May   copy   4 p 4to   NYPL(B)
to [Jean-Baptiste-Antoine] Suard
After so much politeness, so many friendly

27 May   copy   2 p 4to   NYPL(B)
to Denis Diderot
The National Music of your Country

[31] May [1771]   draft   3 p fol Osb
to Samuel Crisp
You w^d. have had my acknowledgm^t. sooner

31 May   3 p 4to   Osb
from Montagu North
I saw your late Book advertised in the Papers,

28 July   1 p 4to   Osb
from Jean Monnet
par une lettre que viens de ecrire a Mr Garrick

9 Aug [1771]   1 p fol   Harv(H)
from David Garrick
The enclos'd from my learned Friend D^r.

18 Aug   4 p 4to   Leigh
from Denis Diderot
Je ne perdrai Jamais une occasion monsieur, de

20 Aug   ?   Schol
from Christoph Daniel Ebeling
Though I have as yet not the honour to know

26 Sept   2 p 4to   Osb
from Denis Diderot
Je vous ai adressé, monsieur, Par monsieur

[Sept 1771?] 2 p 4to Osb
from William Bewley
I hazarded a letter to you this morning in the

10 Oct copy extract 3 p fol
to Denis Diderot Leigh
Le traité du *Melo Drame* is well written, full

23 Oct 3 p fol Osb
from William Bewley
It was an event of evil omen that Jemmy's

26 Oct 3 p 4to Osb
from William Bewley
It is scarce worth while to put you to the

[28 Oct 1771] 4 p 4to Leigh
from Denis Diderot
L'instrument que je veux, monsieur, et très

26 Nov 3 p 4to Osb
to John Alcock
There is a circumstance relative to the Birth &

Nov copy ? Schol
to Christoph Daniel Ebeling
I know so much already of the candour of your

15 Dec 3 p 4to Osb
from Baron d'Holbach
J'ai différé si longtems à répondre à votre lettre

[1771?] draft 3 p 4to Osb
to Denis Diderot
As I am convinced you Read English better

[1771?] 1 p 4to BPL
from David Garrick
I have got 3 places for you in a front Row —

[c 1771] 2 p 4to PML
from David Garrick
Ten thousand thanks for your Journals

[c 1771] fragment 1 p Osb
from Regina (Valentini) Mingotti
Ho pregato il Sig^{re}. Metastasio nella lettera di

1772

Mar ? Schol
to Christoph Daniel Ebeling
[no text available]

2 June copy 5 p fol Osb
to Baron d'Holbach
It is very painful to me to think how insensible

21 June copy 2 p fol Osb
to Felice de Giardini
I am again going to ramble over different parts

22 June copy 4 p fol Osb
to Count Firmian
An address from one who has the honour of

24 June 1 p 4to Osb
from Joseph Baretti
I have not the honour of being personally

25 June copy 4 p fol Osb
to Sir James Gray
When I had the honour of seeing you last, you

28 June 1 p 4to Osb
from Sir James Gray
It gives me great pleasure to hear you continue

30 June 1 p 4to Osb
from James Harris
Understanding from M^{rs}. Castle, that you

3 July draft 1 p 8vo NYPL(B)
to Charles Davy
Apology to Mr. Davy. after answering Mr.

20 Sept 4 p 4to Osb
from Louis DeVisme
Lord Stormont, who is equally kind, hospitable,

1[0] Oct 6 p 4to Osb
from J Mumssen
It might appear hazardous to attempt a

20–23 Nov 2 p 4to Osb
from William Bewley
Foreseeing a busy day tomorrow, I retire for

30 Nov 5 p 4to Osb
from Louis DeVisme
If my Letter was so long in reaching you how

[1772?] draft 2 p fol Osb
to [Joseph Warton]
Your voluntary offer of assistance to a person

[post 1772] 1 p 4to Osb
from William Bewley
What a Land tortoise must I appear in the eyes

1773

12 Jan   2 p 4to   Osb
from Henry Harington
You will Excuse this address from a Lover of

20 Jan   7 p 4to   Osb
from John Osborn
Quand il s'agit to make Enquiries of any sort

7 Apr   copy   3 p 4to   BM
from Thomas Twining
When I was in town in February last, I took

27 Apr   1 p 4to   Osb
from Johann Adolph Hasse [to CB?]
Comme en passant par ici Vous m'avez fait

28 Apr   6 p 4to   BM
to Thomas Twining
Few consequences of the Enterprise in wᶜʰ.

also   copy extracts   3 p LB   Osb

8 May   copy   1 p 4to   BM
from Thomas Twining
I beg your pardon for not returning your plan

15 May   2 p 4to   Osb
from William Bewley
Hurried & tossed about as I am, will you be

28 May   copy   6 p 4to   BM
from Thomas Twining
I seem to have many things to say to you, &

10 June   ?   Schol
from Christoph Daniel Ebeling
. . . This Declaration of war is not against your

[post 10 June 1773]   ?   Schol
from Christoph Daniel Ebeling
[no text available]

23 June   3 p 4to   Osb
from William Bewley
Your bribe — had you intended it as one —

2 July   2 p 4to   Osb
from James Hutton
Mr Hutton of Lindsey House Chelsea (whom

15 July   copy   4 p fol   Osb
to Christoph Daniel Ebeling
I never was more mortified at the receit [sic]

17 July   copy   4 p fol   Osb
to James Hutton
A few words may raise doubts & suspicions

22 July   copy   4 p 4to   BM
from Thomas Twining
As to Geminiani's *opinions* of Music &

27 July   ?   Schol
from Christoph Daniel Ebeling
. . . Mr. Klopstock was only on rancour with

30 July   copy   1 p 4to   NYPL(B)
from Chandler & Davidson (in ALS CB
    to S Crisp 21 Jan 1774)
we are directed by a friend of ours

8 Aug   draft 2 p 4to   NYPL(B)
to Mrs Crewe
As nothing has been a more constant source of

22 Aug   1 p 4to   Osb
from George, 1st Marquis Townshend
It was with much pleasure I heard you was

30 Aug   11 p 4to   BM
to Thomas Twining
My Friends often upbraid me for not more

also   draft   4 p 4to   NYPL(B)
It has often happened when my Friends

also   copy, extracts   1 p 4to   NYPL(B)
—— I have often seen with disgust the

[pre Oct 1773]   2 p 4to   NYPL(B)
to   ?
dear Madam, in the perusal of my Nonsense,

3 Oct   2 p 4to   Osb
from William Bewley
These are to notify you that your forte piano

11 Oct   3 p 4to   BM
to Arthur Young
You understand the *Arcana* of the Bibliopolean

16 Oct   copy   10 p 4to   BM
from Thomas Twining
Though you have not time to be happy why

3–[4] Nov   5 p 4to   NYPL(B)
to [William Bewley?]
When I sent you the German Books, I hardly

9 Dec   receipt   1 p 4to   Hyde
to George Robinson
Recᵈ. of Mʳ. George Robinson the sum of one

30 Dec   4 p 4to   Osb
from Garret Wesley, Earl of Mornington
Some time ago Mʳ Rigby wrote to me

[Dec 1773]   2 p 4to   Osb
from Thomas Pennant
Mʳ Pennant presents his compliments to Doctor

[1773?]   3 p 4to   Osb
from William Bewley
We have been all in the dumps since Sunday

[post 1773]   1 p 4to   Osb
from [Horace?] Twiss
In the year 1768 I visited the celebrated

1774

8 Jan & 5 Feb   3 p fol   Osb
from William Bewley
Where are you? & what are you doing? & what

11 Jan   2 p 4to   Osb
from Thomas Pennant
I cannot sufficiently acknowledge your polite

21 Jan   4 p 4to   NYPL(B)
to Samuel Crisp
I have long seen a Storm of Business brewing

21 Jan   copy extract?   3 p LB   Osb
to Thomas Twining
Ruckers makes the best Piano Fortes, but they

24 Jan   3 p 4to   Osb
from James Hutton
All that I have read of yours charmed & all

31 Jan   copy   3 p 4to   BM
from Thomas Twining
A thousand blessings upon you, for your

Jan   copy   3 p fol   Osb
to Thomas Pennant
If your kind offer of favouring me with a sight

7 Mar   copy   2 p 4to   BM
from Thomas Twining
You are certainly "ans coot a man ans efer

14 Mar   1 p 4to   Osb
from Horace Twiss
Mʳ. Twiss presents his Respects to Dʳ. Burney

2 Apr   3 p 4to   Osb
from James Hutton
In committing that Robbery on your time

[4 Apr 1774]   1 p fol   Comyn
from [Oliver Goldsmith]
Plain dress, for an ordinary man or woman

11 Apr   copy   7 p 4to   BM
from Thomas Twining
"Ay, marry, now my soul hath elbow room!"

3 May   draft   4 p 4to   Osb
to [Regina (Valentini) Mingotti]
It is now more than 12 months since I

23 May   1 p 4to   Comyn
from Leonard Smelt
Mʳ. Smelt's Compliments to Dʳ. Burney

27 May   2 p 4to   Osb
from Thomas Pennant
I thought myself very unfortunate in not seeing

30 May   3 p fol   Osb
from William Bewley
I would call you a Churl, & a Niggard of your

28 June   copy   3 p 4to   BM
from Thomas Twining
I know too well how you are hurried & plagued

3–6 July   copy   7 p 4to   BM
from Thomas Twining
—— I seize the first leisure hour to begin

4 July   1 p 4to   Comyn
from Felice Giardini
Oggi sono impegniato in fino le otto della sera.

13 July   copy extract?   4 p LB   Osb
to Thomas Twining
Shall I scribble a few words to you, en

26 July   copy   1 p 4to   BM
from Thomas Twining
You are afraid of Mrs T., & she is afraid of you.

25 JY pmk [1774]   1 p 4to   Osb
from Charles, 1st Earl Whitworth
I am allways [sic] happy to give you every

29 July [1774]   1 p 4to   Osb
to Dr William Hunter
Dr. Burney presents his Compᵗˢ. to

1 Aug [1774]   1 p 4to   Osb
from Charles, 1st Earl Whitworth
Lady Whitworth & Myself are this instant come

1774, continued

21 Aug   1 p 4to   PML
from John Montagu, 4th Earl of Sandwich
The Otaheita man is to be here on Saturday

29 Aug   1 p 4to   Osb
from Leonard Smelt
Altho I find that there hath been a

30 Aug   copy   1 p 4to   BM
from Thomas Twining
—— And so now we begin again with this

5 Sept   2 p 4to   Osb
from William Bewley
Fye upon you! — To be within a stone's throw

17 Sept   copy   3 p 4to   BM
from Thomas Twining
I must just scratch you a line or two, if it be

13 Oct   copy   2 p 4to   BM
from Thomas Twining
Now then for a little chat with you: I should

20 Oct   13 p fol   Osb
from [James Bruce]
I have employed the first Leisure that Bad

3 Nov   2 p 4to   Osb
to [Charles Davy]
I hasten to thank you for the Pleasure you have

11 Nov   8 p 4to   Osb
from Dr James Lind
I am sorry that I should have been so long of

14 Nov   copy   9 p 4to   BM
from Thomas Twining
I was heartily concerned, my dear Sir, to

26 Nov   4 p 4to   Osb
to Dr James Lind
The post that brought your kind & obliging

30 Nov   copy   7 p 4to   BM
from Thomas Twining
I was very glad to find you could make shift to

[1774]   1 p 4to   Osb
from Charles, 1st Earl Whitworth
Sir Charles Whitworth's Com^ts to Dr Burney &

[c 1774]   1 p 4to   Osb
from Felice de Giardini
Domani mi ritrovo impegniato d'andare

[post 1774]   1 p 4to   Comyn
from Venanzio Rauzzini
C'est avec regret, que je suis Constraint de

[1774–75]   draft   3 p 4to   Osb
to Dr James Lind
In the summer of 1772 I had the Honour of

27   [1774–76]   3 p 4to   Osb
from Jean-Baptiste-Antoine Suard
Je voudrois bien, mon cher Monsieur, meriter

1775

3 Jan 177[5?]   2 p 4to   Osb
from William Bewley
Your letter found me mourning the recent loss

28 Feb   copy extract?   2 p LB   Osb
to Thomas Twining
It is only in the broken-stick way that I can

10 Mar [1775]   copy extract?   3 p LB
to Thomas Twining   Osb
Here's another week gone & it is in vain I find

26 Mar   copy   2 p 4to   BM
from Thomas Twining
I have been good for nothing ever since I got

1–6 May   3 p fol   Osb
from William Bewley
—— What would you have a Man say who

9 May   1 p 4to   Comyn
from James Harris
D^r. Burney is desired to accept from M^r.

12 May   copy   3 p 4to   BM
from Thomas Twining
How is your patience? — you desired me not

9 June   copy   2 p 4to   BM
from Thomas Twining
I fear I must appear an ungrateful wretch, for

also   another copy extract?   1 p LB   Osb
Q. would Plut's dial. on Music translated into

22 June   copy   2 p 4to   BM
from Thomas Twining
First of all let us say all we have to say more

28 June   copy extract?   1 p LB   Osb
to Thomas Twining
You work & mortify me by saying that my being

29 June [1775?]   2 p 4to   Comyn
from Anthony Chamier
I most truly & sincerely my dear Doctor lament

22 July   copy extract   1 p LB   Osb
from Thomas Twining
My jokes taken seriously again. It was always

24 July   copy   2 p 4to   BM
from Thomas Twining
Will you excuse me, my good friend, for trying

2 Aug   2 p 4to   Camb
to [Charles Davy]
It has given me great Concern that I have been

19 Aug   1 p 4to   Osb
from Padre Martini
I favori che VS. si è degnata compartirmi, col

21 Aug   copy   2 p 4to   BM
from Thomas Twining
Any degree of hurry takes away the use of my

Sept   copy   4 p 4to   BM
from Thomas Twining
Ay — why now, when you talk of your work as

16 Oct   copy   4 p 4to   BM
from Thomas Twining
You will think me the most poking, dawdling,

also   copy extract   1 p LB   Osb

18 Oct   copy extracts   4 p LB   Osb
to Thomas Twining
I am quite ashamed to see how much there was

27 Oct [1775]   copy   4 p 4to   BM
from Thomas Twining
To talk of the antients *tempering*, without some

31 Oct [1775]   copy   10 p 4to   BM
from Thomas Twining
I'll be hanged if I think

Oct   copy extract?   1 p LB   Osb
to Thomas Twining
It grieves me sorely, my dear friend, to be

13 Nov   copy   4 p 4to   BM
from Thomas Twining
At last, I am able to sit down quietly, & write

15 Nov   copy extract   3 p LB   Osb
to Thomas Twining
I was carried out of a sick-bed to the Opera on

19 Nov   copy extract   1 p LB   Osb
to Thomas Twining
O! — the awkward scrawls you wish to have

Nov   copy extract   2 p LB   Osb
to Thomas Twining
The Gab[riella] comes on, I think, in favour.

1 Dec   2 p fol   Osb
from William Bewley
At this busy season — your hands full — both

3 Dec   copy extract   1 p LB   Osb
to Thomas Twining
The Gab[riella] sang divinely last night Sat^y.

3 Dec   copy   4 p 4to   BM
from Thomas Twining
The parcel arrived safe last night, — How good

18 Dec   3 p 4to   Osb
from Lucrezia Agujari
Spero che Ella <venia> gradire le mie nuove

24 Dec   copy extract   2 p LB   Osb
to Thomas Twining
If my book & self should live till a 2nd Edit. is

[post 24 Dec 1775]   2 p 8vo   Osb
from Thomas Twining
When I put my letter into the post, I received

Dec   copy extracts   2 p LB   Osb
to Thomas Twining
I remember 30 years ago in some ridiculous

[post Dec 1775]   draft   4 p fol   Osb
to Matthew Raper
Such active Zeal as you have kindly manifested

[1775?]   draft   2 p fol   Osb
to Garret Wesley, Earl of Mornington
Crosdill, whom your Lord^p. may have heard

[1775?]   1 p 4to   PML
from James Cook
Capt. Cook presents his Compliments to D^r.

[1775–78]   2 p 8vo   Osb
from David Garrick
Thank you for your Journals — I am much

[post 1775]   extract?   2 p 8vo   Osb
from   ?
I think the Letter which describes the meeting

1776

3 Jan   1 p 8vo   Osb
to Thomas Twining
My dear Friend — How fares it wth. your

7 Jan   1 p 4to   Osb
from Robert Darcy, 4th Earl of Holdernesse
Lord Holdernesse laments that he has not been

8 Jan   6 p 4to   BM
from Thomas Twining
—— You have flung me so behind-hand, & so

27 Jan   4 p 4to   BM
from Thomas Twining
There is something so solemn & frightful in this

30 Jan   copy of extract 2 p 4to Osb
to William Bewley
I cannot find in my Heart to let this Child of

30–31 Jan   3 p fol   Osb
from William Bewley
Though I am ill disposed at present to answer

3 Feb   copy extract? 6 p LB Osb
to Thomas Twining
That I should ever live to see the day when my

5 Feb   1 p 4to   Osb
from Anthony Chamier
I could not find time to call on you my dear

18 Feb   draft   2 p fol   Osb
to Garret Wesley, Earl of Mornington
and condescend to Interest yourself in my

19 Feb   6 p 4to   BM
from Thomas Twining
—— ah! me voici, moi! — I have just been

3 Mar   2 p fol   Osb
from William Bewley
You have been very good lately, & I seemingly

5 Mar   3 p 4to   Osb
from Lucrezia Agujari
Ricevo con infinito piacere la gentiliss^{ma}. sua

7 Mar   7 p 4to   BM
from Thomas Twining
—— A word with you, first, — about the

20 Mar   3 p 4to   BM
from Thomas Twining
This is only a little Letter of business, in which

28 Mar   4 p 4to   BM
from Thomas Twining
Well, I wow now you're a good creechure to

30 Mar   3 p 4to   Coke
from Garret Wesley, Earl of Mornington
I receiv'd your letter of the 20th. of last month

also   photostat   Osb

5 Apr   1 p 4to   Shep
to Brigg[s] Price [Fountaine]
I witheld [sic] my Thanks for the kind

9 Apr   15 p 4to   BM
from Thomas Twining
It is high time I shou'd say something to you;

12 Apr   2 p 4to   NYPL(B)
to Mrs Raper
It gave me great concern that I had not the

[14] Apr   3 p 4to   BM
from Thomas Twining
—— I long to know in what manner M^r. Bruce

27 Apr   1 p 4to   BM
from Thomas Twining
I have but just time, in the midst of the

16 May   1 p 4to   Osb
from Garret Wesley, Earl of Mornington
I ought before this to have acknowledg'd the

18–20 May   10 p 4to   BM
from Thomas Twining
Now you will think, I suppose, that I have

20 May [1776]   2 p 4to   Osb
from [Hugh] Kelly
a fair Musical Petitioner has applyed to me to

25 May   3 p 4to   BN(M)
to Jean-Baptiste-Antoine Suard
As you can read English with infinitely more

also   draft   2 p fol   Osb

18 June   2 p 8vo   Osb
from Giambatista Mancini
Il suo Servitore Giambatista *Mancini,* non

9 July   3 p 4to   Osb
from Andrew Lumisden
I received, by means of M. Payne, your

16 July   1 p 4to   Osb
from Anthony Chamier
I now return you the 2ᵈ. Vol. of M.

19 July [1776?]   3 p 8vo   Osb
from Daines Barrington
I shall spend the day tomorrow at E. Sheen

28 July   4 p 4to   BM
from Thomas Twining
I feel exceedingly shabby & ashamed, my good

22 Aug   4 p 4to   BM
from Thomas Twining
I write directly, that you may hear from me

5 Sept   3 p 4to   Osb
from C E P Bach
Je Vous rendre mes très humbles graces pour

17 Sept   6 p 4to   BM
from Thomas Twining
It always vexes me, when I can't do just as you

7 Oct   3 p 4to   BM
from Thomas Twining
This is the Lacedaemonian letter. It is only to

21 Oct   3 p 4to   BM
from Thomas Twining
Well — I have look'd over all your alterations

29 Nov   9 p 4to   BM
from Thomas Twining
'Twas a charming, communicative, comfortable

17 Dec   6 p 4to   Osb & NYPL(B)
from Samuel Crisp
[Osb] Your letter gave me great Content — I
[NYPL(B)] what a strange power of

[Dec 1776?]   2 p 4to   BM
from Thomas Twining
Ay — Ay, you may lock me up — but I detest

[1776?]   2 p 4to   Osb
from Denis Diderot
Voulez vous bien accepter mes tres sinceres

[1776?]   2 p 4to   Osb
from Anna (Dillingham) Ord
Mˢ. Ord presents her Compliments to Dʳ.

[1776?]   draft   1 p 4to   Osb
to Anna (Dillingham) Ord
Dʳ. B presents his Respects to Mʳˢ. Ord & has

[c 1776?]   3 copies   4 p 4to   Osb
to Jean-Jacques Rousseau
Je suis bien sensible de l'Honneur que

[1776–86]   3 p 4to   BM
to Thomas Twining
by Longman, to the 3 <pts> of his Lessons

[post 1776]   3 p 8vo   Hyde
with FB to Lady Banks
I was grieved to find, after my ride, the 1ˢᵗ. I

[1776–90]   1 p 4to   Osb
from Giusto Ferdinando Tenducci
Tenducci reverisce distintamente il Sigʳᵉ.

1777

24 Jan   8 p 4to   BM
from Thomas Twining
My hat, my shoe, ink, coal, soot, — no black

[Jan? 1777]   1 p 4to   BM
from Thomas Twining
Last night, in a chosen circle when your

22 Feb [1777]   1 p 4to   Ryl
to HLTP
To cut short all *Hes* & *shes,* & equivocal

5 Mar [1777]   2 p 4to   Osb
from HLTP
Lest you should hear of this hateful Accident

17 Mar [1777?]   1 p 8vo   Osb
to Mr Baker
Dr. Burney presents his Compᵗˢ. to Mr. Baker,

12 Apr   1 p 8vo   Osb
from Denis Diderot
Diderot Salue Monsieur Burney et le remercie

25 Apr   3 p fol   Osb
from William Bewley
I am quite *au desespoir* at not having a syllable

19 May   3 p fol   Osb
from William Bewley
You hint willingness to give me some *sense,*

9 June [1777?]   2 p 4to   Comyn
from Antonio Sacchini
Sacchini fà i suoi più distinti complimenti al

11 June   3 p 4to   Osb
from William Bewley
Necessity will have it so — the Knight's final

1777, continued

16 June   8 p 4to   BM
from Thomas Twining
You desired me to write "before *hot-weather*

18 [June 1777]   2 p 4to   Osb
from HLTP
I am so perpetually put out of my own Way

25 July   1 p 4to   BN(M)
to Signor   ?   Long
Il Dottore Burney a pregato il Signor Long de

26 July   4 p 4to   Osb
from Ralph Griffiths
I can only thank you for your late liberalities

5 Aug   2 p 4to   Cal(B)
to Gabriel Piozzi
Ho ricevuto le sue stimati<ssim> e Lettere

30 Aug   8 p 4to   BM
from Thomas Twining
Now this shews plainly, what a parcel of poor,

6 Oct   8 p 4to   BM
from Thomas Twining
I have no excuses to make now, or, if I have,

31 Oct   3 p 4to   BM
from Thomas Twining
Un mot seulement pour cette fois, pour

1 Nov   4 p 4to   Ryl
to HLTP
If my long Silence has <transt> into your

6 Nov [1777]   4 p 4to   Osb
from HLTP
What News shall I tell you of a Place that will

18 Nov   4 p 4to   BM
from Thomas Twining
—— Well? — has your great patience-peg

17 Dec   5 p 4to   BM
from Thomas Twining
How cou'd you, my dear friend, think that I

[1777]   draft   2 p 4to   Osb
to [Charles?] Grant
It is my fervent wish that the Letter wch. I have

[1777?]   2 p 4to   Osb
from HLTP
What a Heart must yours be for Friendship and

[1777]   2 p 4to   Osb
from HLTP
I have written out & enclosed the Invitation

[1777]   1 p 4to   Osb
from Garret Wesley, Earl of Mornington
A Friend of mine in Ireland whom I desir'd to

16 [1777–91]   1 p 4to   NYPL(B)
from Simon Nicolas Henri Linguet
M. Linguet est passé hier chez Monsieur

1778

11 Jan   3 p 4to   Yale(Be)
to HLTP
What a way you have to make obligations of

13 Jan   1 p 4to   Osb
from Padre Martini
Ricevei per mezzo del Sig. Long la bellissima

27 Feb [1778]   3 p 4to   Plat
from HLTP
I talked so to you yesterday about my Wood

8 Mar   3 p 4to   Ryl
to HLTP
Why, what a Lady Bountiful you are! most

[pre 15 Apr 1778]   copy   1 p 4to   BM
from Thomas Twining
Dr. Montgomeryman presents his respects to

[pre 15 Apr? 1778]   2 p 4to   BM
from Thomas Twining
The compliments of D^r. Montgomeryman

15 Apr   5 p 4to   BM
from Thomas Twining
"What have I been about? — Have I been

4 May   2 p 4to   Osb
from William Bewley
—— —— What a Chasm is here! — Let me

22 June   2 p 4to   Bol
to Padre Martini
Siccome niente me sià più prezioso della cara

29 June 1778   3 p 4to   Bol
to Padre Martini
Avendo Scritto una Lettera pochi giorni fà

also   draft   1 p 4to   Osb
Si il reverendo e molto Venerato padre Martini

29 June   1 p 4to   Bol
to HLTP
Since the departure of my Letter this morning,

22 [July 1778]   2 p 4to   Comyn
from HLTP
I forgot to give you the Novels home in your
also   facsimile   NPG
also   copy (in ALS SEB to FB 23 Jul 1778)
                                         NYPL(B)

28 July   8 p 4to   BM
from Thomas Twining
You have been gnawing & tearing the very

14 Aug [1778]   2 p 4to   Osb
from HLTP
Did not I tell you all would be well again? &

18 Aug [1778]   3 p 4to   Osb
from HLTP
When Scarson was dying his Friends lamenting

[23–29 Aug]   1 p 4to   Plat
from HLTP
Mrs. Thrale sends dear Dr. Burney his

29 Aug   2 p 4to   Osb
from Francesco Roncaglia
Arrivato che fui a bologna mi portai subito dal

25 [Sept 1778]   2 p 4to   Ryl
to HLTP
You are a good Creature for thinking of us

6 Oct   2 p 4to   Osb
to Francesco Roncaglio
La ricordanza su mi sta molto a Cuore, e le

14 [Oct 1778]   2 p 4to   Comyn
from HLTP
When every body goes to look for their Letters

19 Oct [1778?]   1 p 8vo   Lewis
from Arthur Murphy
I have long wished for the opportunity, which

23 Oct   2 p 4to   Osb
from Francesco Roncaglia
Con commo piacere ho ricevuto il di lei foglio

28 Oct   2 p 4to   Osb
from HLTP
Your sweet Letter followed me hither & gave

6 Nov   3 p 4to   Ryl
to HLTP
Having commissioned Secretary Fanny to

21 Nov [1778]   2 p 4to   Comyn
from HLTP
By the way of waking me agreably [sic]

1 Dec   copy extract   1 p LB   Osb
to Thomas Twining
Now for a little opera music. Come along as
also   another copy extract   1 p LB   Osb
If ever you are so idle & so silly as to read

7 Dec   3 p 4to   BM
from Thomas Twining
Your silence went on, my dear good friend, in

12 Dec   1 p 4to   Osb
from Anthony Chamier
Mr. Chamier's compliments to Mr Burney begs

16 Dec   1 p fol   Osb
from Gasparo Pacchierotti
The efficacy of your reasoning, ought to induce

19 Dec   8 p 4to   BM
from Thomas Twining
Well, then —— we have shaken hands, &
also   copy extract   3 p LB   Osb
I hope I shall never attain to that degree of

28 Dec   1 p 8vo   NYPL(B)
from ⟨Magellais⟩
Mr. ⟨Magellais's⟩ resps. to Dr. Burney and

[1778]   4 p fol   Osb
from William Bewley
A longer silence would render me criminal

[1778?]   1 p 4to   Osb
from HLTP
Queeney says Dear Sir that you talked of

[1778]   1 p 4to   Osb
from HLTP
How tender & kind is your good Advice! and

[1778]   2 p 4to   Osb
from HLTP
And so Baretti's Benefit went off charmingly,

30 [1778]   2 p 4to   Osb
from HLTP
No Letter, no note, no Satten Wig, from Dear

[1778–80?]   1 p 4to   Comyn
from Gasparo Pacchierotti
Pacchierotti's best Compts. wait on Dr Burney

1778, continued

[1778–84]   3 p 4to   Ryl
to HLTP
What a too good Creature you are to enquire

[1778–84?]   1 p 8vo   BPL
from Samuel Johnson
Mr Johnson received an invitation from Mrs

3 Jan [pre 1779]   1 p 8vo   PML
from David Garrick
Another much <fine> Letter from Gossip

[pre 1779]   1 p 8vo   RWB
from David Garrick
[first line not yet available]

1779

8 Jan   4 p 4to   BM
from Thomas Twining
I have hardly more than just time to tell you

also   copy extract   1 p LB   Osb
Well but — so ho! there — are not you a

1 Feb   4 p 4to   BM
from Thomas Twining
And so, as I was a saying of, — here is your

9 Feb   1 p 4to   RS
to William Hunter
As your curiosity seemed much excited by the

12 Feb   draft   2 p 4to   Osb
to [Jacob Schuback?]
Je ne veux pas perdre une occasion nouvelle

21 Feb   4 p 4to   Osb
to Benjamin Archer
If you imagine my silence has been voluntary,

also   copy [dated 1 Mar 1778]   5 p fol   Osb

[Feb 1779]   draft   2 p 4to   Osb
to [?James Harris]
As you seemed to interest yourself abt. little

12 Mar   7 p 4to   BM
from Thomas Twining
I shou'd not have been so terribly behind-hand

also   copy extract   2 p LB   Osb
I had procured Evelina upon your mention of

15–16 Mar   3 p 4to   Osb
from James Harris
I have perused yr. ingenious acct. of the little

29 Mar   2 p fol   Osb
from William Bewley
Without meaning to write you a *letter* — *That*

12 May   8 p 4to   BM
from Thomas Twining
No *parcellina* yet — I only mention that for

also   copy extract   2 p LB   Osb
I am glad we felt so much alike about Evelina.

1<5> May [1779]   ½ p 4to   Osb
from HLTP
Will you try to make Fryday suit you next

29 May   4 p 4to   Osb
from William Bewley
I learn just now, on my return home, that, in

3 June   6 p 4to   BM
from Thomas Twining
The Musicalisch parcel, my dear friend, with

7 June [1779]   1 p 4to   Osb
from HLTP
My dear Doctor Burney who never forgets a

14 June   2 p 4to   Osb
from William Bewley
I write — *stans pede in uno* — merely to

21 June   1 p 4to   Liv(P)
to Paul Panton
Doctor Burney presents his best Compts to Mr.

26–28 June   2 p fol   Osb
from William Bewley
Though you rightly suppose that Mr. Slater

7 July   2 p 4to   Osb
from Philip Hayes
In consequence of your favour, I did every

27 Aug [1779]   2 p 4to   Osb
from HLTP
I find Letters come *from* Chessington for your

29 Aug [1779?]   4 p 4to   Ryl
to HLTP
I thought, as how, we were to *throw notes* at

30 Aug [1779]   3 p 4to   Osb
from HLTP
And so I will to be sure, & so here is the

3 Scpt   3 p fol   Osb
from William Bewley
I received your letter just as I was stepping

15 Sept   1 p 4to   Osb
from Anthony Chamier
In consideration of Dr. Burney's active zeal

[16?] Sept   3 p 4to   Osb
from Jacob Schuback
Vous me faites trop d'honneur, en me

29 Sept   7 p 4to   BM
from Thomas Twining
It has vexed me that I have not been able to

13 [Oct? 1779]   2 p 4to   Osb
from HLTP
Are you come from Oxford, & have you been

14 Oct   2 p 4to   Osb
from James Harris
I have a thousand thanks to return you for

16 Oct   3 p 4to   Osb
to HLTP
Lord bless me! & so you waited for a Letter! &

20 Oct   4 p 4to   Bol
to Padre Martini
L'inestimabile Lettera, ed anche

[Oct 1779]   draft   2 p 4to   Osb
to Sir William Herschel
Memdums for Lettr. to Herschel — / "Authors

3–4 Nov   8 p 4to   BM
from Thomas Twining
If I had not been bother'd with preparations

also   copy extract   1 p LB   Osb

7 Nov   1 p 4to   Osb
from Padre Martini
In occasione che ritornono alla Patria due SSri.

9 Nov   2 p 4to   Hyde
from HLTP
Now my Dear Sir, Mr. Murphey will soon I

17 Nov   3 p 4to   BM
from Thomas Twining
I write this in the midst of the hurries &

[Dec? 1779]   1 p 4to   Osb
from HLTP
You are very kind Dear Sir, be still more so, &

[Dec 1779?]   1 p 4to   Osb
from HLTP
Your Cecchina has had a good Night, & will do

[1779]   3 p 4to   BM(Bar)
to FB
I love originals of good Things & good Folk

[1779]   1 p 4to   BM(Bar)
to FB
Dear Fanny, I have had a sad drabbled tailed

[c 1779]   2 p 4to   Hilles
from Lord Monboddo
Lord Monboddo returns Compliments to Dr

14   [1779?]   3 p 4to   Osb
from HLTP
My Dear Doctor Burney & his sweet Daughter

[1779?]   1 p 4to   Osb
from HLTP
Only six Words just to tell my Dear Dr Burney

[1779–80]   2 p 4to   Osb
from HLTP
No coming to Chessington my dear Sir — no

[1779–80]   1 p 4to   Osb
from HLTP
Well my dear Sir! when I returned home I

[1779–81]   1 p 4to   Osb
from HLTP
I must keep your sweet Daughter two days

[1779–84]   1 p 4to   Ryl
to HLTP
I hope you'll be soon well enough to get into

[1779–84]   2 p 4to   Ryl
to HLTP
I did not like the *Tone* of your Letter at all, it

1780

6 Jan   4 p 4to   BM
from Thomas Twining
—— Your letter found me *out* — that is, it

23 Mar   5 p 4to   BM
from Thomas Twining
It is high time, my good friend, to confess my

30 Mar   3 p 4to   BM
from Thomas Twining
I perceive, cher ami, that I am going to write

[Apr – June]   3 p 4to   Plat
from HLTP
A Thousand Thanks my Dear Sir — but don't

1780, continued

11 May   copy extract   12 p LB   Osb
to Thomas Twining
Ah my ever dear & worthy friend, into what a

18 May   8 p 4to   BM
from Thomas Twining
—— I skulk in to your presence with my tail

[21 May]   1 p 4to   Plat
from HLTP
When I am thanking Friends for Favours, let

24 May   3 p fol   Osb
from William Bewley
I know full well that I am in your debt, in the

1 June   3 p 4to   Bol
to Padre Martini
Son passati più di otto Mese ch'io avesse

16–17 June   4 p 4to   BM
from Thomas Twining
"Suave, mari magno turbantibus aequora ventis

also   copy   4 p LB   Osb

19 June [1780]   3 p 4to   Osb
from HLTP
Oh my Dear Doctor Burney what dreadful

24 June   1 p 4to   Osb
from Padre Martini
Sara presentata questa mia a VS. dal Sig.

[June? 1780]   3 p 4to   NYPL(B)
with CAB to FB
We are all safe & well, after our

10 July   3 p 4to   Osb
from Anthony Chamier
I'll take a new pen for You for you are by far

10 July   3 p 4to   Osb
from Andrew Lumisden
I return you a thousand thanks for your

14 July   6 p 4to   BM
from Thomas Twining
Your kind & communicative letter was most

31 July   1 p 4to   Oxf(Bod)
from Samuel Johnson
You did very kindly in

11 Aug   1 p 4to   NYPL(B)
from Ferdinando Bertoni
Eccomi arrivato in pochi giorni

11 Aug   3 p fol   Osb
from William Bewley
I need not say how pleased I was to see your

27 Aug [1780]   2 p 4to   Osb
from HLTP
What my dear Sir is become of our fair Fanny

18 Sept   1 p 4to   Osb
from Padre Martini
Per mezzo del Sig. Ferdinando Bertoni ho

12 Oct   8 p 4to   BM
from Thomas Twining
—— I am alive, well, & your's — il ne se peut

23 Oct   copy extract   1 p LB   Osb
to Thomas Twining
In the mean time comes home my eldest son

4 Nov   3 p 4to   BM
from Thomas Twining
Well, now then. The parcellina arrived safe: I

7 Nov   copy extract   3 p LB   Osb
to Thomas Twining
The passage from Euripides was first pointed

21 Nov   3 p 4to   BM
from Thomas Twining
Imprimis, — the parcellina arrived safe. — /

4 Dec   4 p 4to   BM
from Thomas Twining
—— Now then, for another little run, that I

[1780?]   1 p 4to   Ryl
to HLTP
"Still harping on my Daughter!" — Ah! my

[1780?]   copy extract   1 p LB   Osb
to Thomas Twining
Every one I talk to on the subject frights me

[1780]   1 p 4to   Osb
from HLTP
Accept five Words from me when there come

[1780]   3 p 4to   Osb
from HLTP
How I reproach myself for saying, though only

[1780?]   1 p 4to   Osb
from HLTP
My dear Dr. Burneys friendly Attention has

[1780 – May 1781]   1 p 4to   Osb
from HLTP
Oh my dear dear Sir how glad I am you called,

1781

9 Jan   7 p 4to   BM
from Thomas Twining
Well, *if* I *a'n't* ashamed of myself! — it often

12 Feb   4 p 4to   BM
from Thomas Twining
—— How long is it since you have given me

25 Feb   4 p 4to   Comyn
to CB Jr
Your present Situation is doubtless very critical,

4 May   8 p 4to   BM
from Thomas Twining
What *have* I been about? — / Why, truly, my

22 May   2 p fol   Osb
from Luigi Mattei Marchetti
Sappia che consegnai la lettera al Pe. Maestro

8 June   12 p 4to   BM
from Thomas Twining
Ah! — mon cher ami! — only think of it —

16 July   2 p fol   PML
from JB
I arrived here yesterday after a short cruize off

[Aug 1781]   3 p 4to   Ryl
to HLTP
I was, for once in my life, sorry to see your hand

6 Oct   1 p 4to   Osb
from Padre Martini
Se la pazienza del <lettore> di questa mia

10 Oct   10 p 4to   BM
from Thomas Twining
A trance indeed! — however, assure yourself

5 Nov   3 p fol   Osb
from William Bewley
As I can have no claim to a letter from you,

9 Nov   4 p 4to   BM
from Thomas Twining
I am sorry, my dear friend, to have kept your

19 Nov   2 p 4to   BM
from Thomas Twining
I must content myself, for once, with taking

8 Dec   7 p 4to   BM
from Thomas Twining
How are your patience-pegs? — Have they

14 Dec   copy extract   7 p LB   Osb
to Thomas Twining
—— You think of the old stuff just as I

28 Dec   4 p 4to   BM
from Thomas Twining
I am always sinning — I ought to have told

[1781]   3 p 4to   Osb
from HLTP
And so you *do* shirk us sure enough, but you

[1781]   2 p 4to (inc)   Oxf(A)
to   ?
. . . now Earl of Aylesbury, & Chamberlain

1782

27 Jan [1782?]   1 p 4to   Comyn
to Thomas Lowndes
Doctor Burney sends his Compts to Mr.

Jan   copy extract   1 p LB   Osb
to Thomas Twining
With respect to the application of *shouting* to

14 Feb   3 p 4to   BM
from Thomas Twining
—— I am so shamefully behind-hand with

24 Feb   copy extract   3 p LB   Osb
to Thomas Twining
But there is a fade & pumpkin-kind of

21 Apr   copy extract   2 p LB   Osb
to Thomas Twining
Mr Mason's work is well digested, & contains

5 May   4 p 4to   BM
from Thomas Twining
I am quite ashamed, my dear friend, of my

14 June   2 p 4to   Osb
from HLTP
You will think me mad about

26 June   3 p 4to   BM
from Thomas Twining
What will you have thought of me, my dear

1782, continued

8 July   2 p fol   Osb
from William Bewley
My Neighb^r, the Bearer, Mr Tite, my Taylor,

[July 1782]   not completed   3 p 4to
to FB & SEB   Hyde
I came from Ches. this morning where I left

Aug   2 p 4to   Plat
from HLTP
Through Featherbed Lane & over Crackskull

18 Sept   10 p 4to   BM
from Thomas Twining
—— Do you remember the man walking up
also   copy extract   4 p LB   Osb
I need not tell you that I gobbled up Cecilia

22 Sept [1782]   2 p 4to   NYPL(B)
to SBP
You must not think yourself forgotten, or less

21 Oct   4 p 4to   Osb
from William Bewley
I thank you most sincerely for your letter. I

Oct [1782]   2 p 4to   Comyn
from HLTP
Fanny says, My Dear Sir, that She cannot

2 Nov   2 p 4to   Osb
from HLTP
A Thousand Thanks my dear Doctor for your

6–[8] Nov   2 p 4to   BM(Bar)
to FB
It makes me feel uncomfortable to let your

[10 Nov 1782]   4 p 4to   BM(Bar)
from SBP
M^r. Fisher has brought us your letter,

15 [Nov]   2 p 4to   Osb
from HLTP
Why what a *Shoal* of kind Words &

19 NO pmk [1782]   2 p 4to   BM(Bar)
with CAB to FB
I wished you to see what Charlotte to save post,

28 Nov   4 p fol   BM
from Thomas Twining
—— again, I fear, I have sinned in not being
also   copy extract   6 p LB   Osb
Your account of the various opinions of Critics

27 Dec   2 p 4to   Osb
from Brownlow North
We have a very agreeable party of Burneys at

[1782]   2 p 4to   Osb
to FB
I have been trapsing & sweltering all over

[1782]   draft   2 p 4to   Osb
to William Mason
It w^d. subject me to great self-reproach if I did

[1782?]   1 p fragment   BM(Bar)
from William Bewley
I hope I was not misinformed the other day

[1782?]   1 p 4to   Comyn
from HLTP
Why this is delightful Dear Sir! ay and ten

[1782?]   2 p 4to   Osb
from HLTP
It is your Letters that are irresistible at last my

[pre 1783]   2 p 4to   Osb
from William Bewley
How you sport with my inquisitorial Character,

1783

27 Jan   4 p 4to   BM
from Thomas Twining
Am I never to come near you without throwing
also   copy extract   2 p LB   Osb
I was rejoiced to see so *handsome* a review of

3 Feb   10 p 4to   BM
from Thomas Twining
Alas alas! 'tis too true — I did promise to write

9 Feb   3 p 4to   BM(Bar)
from W Cutler
What shall I say to you? — Say? — say

19 Feb   4 p 4to   BM
from Thomas Twining
Your little letter, my dear friend, was a cordial

23 Feb   draft   1 p 4to   Osb
to Henry Blencowe
It is a little cruel to throw the sins of a man's

1 Mar   2 p 4to   Osb
from Jean-Pierre Brissot de Warville
Si vous vous rappelez le jeune françois qui eut

[Mar 1783?]   draft   2 p 4to   Osb
to Jean-Pierre Brissot de Warville
Le ressouvenir du plaisir que Je ressentis chez

[post 12 Apr 1783]   2 p 4to
to FB   NYPL(B)
Ah! my dear Fanny — your last Letter has

26 Apr   4 p 4to   BM
from Thomas Twining
Imprimus — I commit Monsieur votre MS to

⟨2⟩ May   3 p 4to   Osb
from Gasparo Pacchierotti
Hardly had I been here, that come your

4 May [1783]   1 p scrap   NYPL(B)
from Lady Banks
Lady Banks presents her Compᵗˢ. to Dʳ.

[post 4 May 1783]   1 p scrap
to FB   NYPL(B)
I am much more afflicted than Surprised at the

25 May   3 p 4to   Osb
to [Sir James Lake]
The perusal of your friend's humane & excellent

5 July   7 p 4to   BM
from Thomas Twining
—— Nay, — I am determined I *will* have a
also   copy, extract   1 p LB   Osb
"Your character of your poor friend, Mʳ Crisp,

29 July   2 p 4to   Osb
from Jean-Pierre Brissot de Warville
J'espere bien, Monsieur, avoir le plaisir de

6 Sept   1 p 4to   Osb
to CB Jr
I was sent for hither on Tuesday, in a great

6 Sept   copy extract   5 p LB   Osb
to Thomas Twining
I had some thoughts of going this summer &

9 Sept   1 p fol   Osb
from George Walpole, Earl of Orford
twas with ⟨deepest⟩ Concern I read

12 Sept [1783]   2 p 4to   NYPL(B)
to CB Jr
I thank you for your two Letters

20 Sept   2 p 8vo   Comyn
from Samuel Johnson
I came home on the 18th at noon to a very

22 Oct   7 p 4to   BM
from Thomas Twining
—— I have no comical apology *this* time, my
also   copy, extract   1 p LB   Osb
"Alas! your poor friend, Bewley! Your story

2 Nov   1 p fol   Osb
from Padre Martini
Sono infinite le obbligazioni, che io professo a

10 Nov   6 p fol   BM
to Thomas Twining
At length, dearest friend, I take my large sheet,
also   copy extract   4 p LB   Osb
There is a philosophical French Duke here at

12 Nov   4 p 4to   Osb
from Gertrude E (Schmeling) Mara
Monsieur; l'amitié que Vous m'avez

[14 Dec 1783]   4 p 4to   Osb
to SBP
How much pleasanter an employmᵗ. would it

[c 1783?]   1 p 4to   BM(Bar)
from W Cutler
Dr Burney will please, at his entire Leisure

[1783]   2 p 8vo   NYPL(B)
from Lady Mary Duncan
Lady Mary Duncan presents her Compᵗˢ. to

[c 1783]   1 p 8vo   NYPL(B)
from Lady Mary Duncan
Lady Mary Duncan was extreamly[sic]

[1783]   2 p 8vo   Comyn
from Eva Maria (Veigel) Garrick
Mʳˢ. Garrick presents her kind Compliments to

[1783]   copy extract   1 p LB   Osb
from Thomas Twining
"Do you know a certain Dʳ. *Loftus Wood?*

[1783]   draft   3 p 4to   Osb
to George Walpole, Earl of Orford
after so long an absence, & privation of the

15 Sept [pre 1784]   1 p 4to   Comyn
from Richard Owen Cambridge
We are all greatly obliged to you & Mʳˢ. Burney

[pre 1784]   1 p 4to   Osb
from Lady Mary Duncan
Lady Mary Duncan finding that wretched stuff

1783, *continued*

[pre 1784]   1 p 4to   Osb
from HLTP
As you want Comfort, and I have some to

[pre 1784]   3 p 4to   BM(Bar)
from William Seward
I dind yesterday with Mrs Bowcowens &

See also p 33 below

1784

7 Feb [1784?]   1 p 4to   Osb
to Christian Latrobe
Here is the *Histoirette* for poor Madlle.

30 July   2 p 4to   Ryl
to HLTP
If my wishes for your felicity shd. seem to

16 Feb   1 p 4to   Osb
from Padre Martini
Tempo <fa feci> acquisto di un esemplare

31 July   9 p 4to   NYPL(B)
to Thomas Twining
Ah my good & ever dear Friend, what a while

[7] Mar [1784]   1 p fol   Osb
from Ralph Griffiths
I am almost dead, my Dear Frd. with a

2 Aug   ?   Soth 30
from Samuel Johnson
The Post at this devious town goes out so soon

7 Apr   4 p 4to   BM
from Thomas Twining
—— A cart-load of thanks for your letter, &

2 Aug   2 p 4to   Osb
from HLTP & Gabriel Piozzi
The Compliments of Congratulations which we

21 Apr   2 p 4to   Coke
from John Stanley
Mr Stanley presents his Compts. to Dr Burney

6 Aug   3 p 4to   NYPL(B)
from Count Benincasa
Je suis de retour depuis huit jours

21 Apr   3 p 4to   NYPL(B)
from Arthur Young
The Duke de Liancourt at present on his

27 Aug   4 p 4to   BM
from Thomas Twining
It is more than time to thank you for your kind

26 Apr   3 p 4to   Osb
to SBP
What pity it is, my ever dear Susey! That such

28 Aug   1 p 4to   PML
from Samuel Johnson
You see that I am not a tardy correspondent,

26 May   2 p 4to   Hyde
to [Sir Joseph Banks]
I was not five minutes at home the whole day,

1 Sept   copy extract   5 p LB   Osb
to Thomas Twining
About the 13th. you say. Why I am obliged to

7 June   7 p 4to   Coke
from Count Benincasa
La Commémoration de Handel celebrée à

4 Sept   2 p 4to   Osb
to FB
I shall take your advice, & venture to take

26 June   8 p 4to   BM
from Thomas Twining
I am — "Tutto dispirito di rossore" my dear

4 Sept   2 p 4to   Coke
from Samuel Johnson
I have not the least objection to the little

6 July   3 p 4to   Coke
from Count Benincasa
Mi permetta e gradisca il mio Sigr. Dottore

18 Sept   3 p 4to   BM
from Thomas Twining
If I *cou'd* have told you, my dear friend, when

24 July   1 p fol   NYPL(B)
to FB & SBP
All my my [sic] fine Castle, built as I thought

20 Sept   3 p 4to   Osb
from Gasparo Pacchierotti
I have been many times in the point to send

27 July [1784]   4 p 4to   BM(Bar)
with CAB & EBB to FB
Sweet Pacchierotti called here this morning, to

24 Sept   3 p 4to   Osb
to CB Jr
I have never been in great intimacy with Dr.

1 Oct   3 p 4to   Coke
from Count Benincasa
N'auriez-vous pas par hazard reçu deux lettres,

14 Oct   draft   2 p 4to   Coke
to John Montagu, 4th Earl of Sandwich
The Letter with wch. your Lord^p. honoured me

26 Oct [1784]   4 p 4to   BM(Bar)
from CAB
I have received your kind favour, & am much

1 Nov   2 p 4to   Comyn
from Samuel Johnson
Our correspondence paused for want of topicks,

9 Nov   4 p 4to   BM
to [Sir Robert Murray Keith]
You formerly honoured me with such

12 Nov   4 p 4to   BM
from Thomas Twining
—— I'm afraid I am a naughty boy —— I

17 Nov [1784]   1 p 8vo   Comyn
from Samuel Johnson
Mr Johnson who came home last night, sends

22 Nov   3 p 4to   Osb
from Richard Bull
I have been inform'd, and I readily believe it,

27 Nov   draft   2 p 4to   Coke
to John Montagu, 4th Earl of Sandwich
The time being nearly elapsed, when my

[pre 13 Dec 1784]   copy extracts
from Samuel Johnson   2 p 4to   Osb
fall." / "I have left dear M^r. Allen, & wherever

14 Dec   2 p 4to   Comyn
from John Montagu, 4th Earl of Sand-
    wich [to CB]
Before I left London I got hold of Mr Wyatt,

[25 Dec]   copy extract   3 p LB   Osb
to Thomas Twining
Poor Johnson is gone! I truly reverenced his

29 Dec   1 p 4to   Osb
to Christian Latrobe
If you w^d. favour me with a literal prose

30 Dec [1784?]   1 p 4to   Osb
to Christian Latrobe
I have but time to give you, in the lump,

30 Dec   3 p 4to   BM
from Thomas Twining
When shall I cease pestering you, my dear

[Dec 1784]   2 p 4to   Comyn
to SBP
We have at length lost poor Johnson!

[1784]   1 p 4to   Osb
from George, Earl of Ashburnham
I yesterday spoke to the Prince of Wales, as

[1784?]   draft   4 p 8vo   Osb
to Richard Bull
Men may talk of *Free-will* as much as they

[c 1784?]   1 p 8vo   PML
to Edmond Malone
I am sorry that I cannot be as obedient to you,

also   copy   1 p   NYPL(B)

[1784]   6 p 4to   NYPL(B)
from SBP
She is growing very fond I will not get into

[1784?]   1 p 4to   Osb
from Sir John Bridger
Sir John Bridger presents his Comp^ts. to D^r.

[post 1784]   draft   2 p 8vo
to Mr Lee   NYPL(B)
D^r. B. is ashamed to own to M^r. Lee, that the

[post 1784]   1 p 4to   Comyn
from M[ary] Carter
haveing [sic] only occasion for Females

[1784–87]   2 p 4to   HSP
to Edmond Malone
It gave me much concern that it was utterly

[1784–92]   draft   1 p 4to   Comyn
to Elizabeth Ann (Linley) Sheridan
D^r. Burney presents his best compliments to

1785

2 Jan [1785?]   1 p 4to   Osb
to Christian Latrobe
As I have hopes of assembling together a *small*

14 Jan   1 p 4to   Cal(B)
from Jean Arthur
The bearer of this is a gentleman, I should be

1785, continued

1 Feb   4 p 4to   NYPL(B)
from SBP
It is so long since I have had an opportunity of

2 Feb   1 p 4to   NYPL(B)
from Christian Latrobe
Here I have the pleasure of sending You my

5 Feb [misdated 1784]   4 p 4to   BM
from Thomas Twining
What an ungrateful wretch you will think me:

9 Feb [1785?]   2 p 4to   Osb
to Christian Latrobe
I entirely agree with your Rev^d. & most worthy

11 Feb   1 p 4to   Osb
to Mary (Hamilton) Dickenson
D^r. Burney is too sensible of the value of Miss

11 Feb   1 p 4to   BM
from Thomas Twining
You wish, as I understand, to know, as soon as

15 Feb   4 p 4to   BM
from Thomas Twining
Here I am — & I hope in good time. But what

15 Feb   1 p 4to   BM
from Thomas Twining
Another dab! — It is best, I think, for fear of

16 Feb   4 p 4to   Osb
from Gasparo Pacchierotti
You will think me a forgetful Dog, having drop

18 Mar   1 p 4to   BM
from Thomas Twining
I have just been frighten'd out of my wits by

1 Apr   4 p 4to   BM
from Thomas Twining
—— Well — what *can* be said? — I can say

4 May [1785]   1 p 4to   Comyn
from George Colman to [CB?]
I have seen D^r. Arnold, & we have settled next

17 May   3 p 4to   Hilles
to Lady Herries & Mary (Hamilton)
      Dickenson (with FB to the latter)
I receive my dear Miss Hamilton's temptation

16 June   4 p 4to   BM
from Thomas Twining
What shall I do or say? — they tell me you are

17 June   1 p ½ 4to   Osb
to Mary (Hamilton) Dickenson
D^r. Burney presents his best respects to Miss

28 Aug   2 p 4to   Osb
from Henrietta Maria (Bannister)
      North
Do what you will Sir with your poetical Talents

6 Sept   1 p 4to   Comyn
from Horace Walpole
Mr. Walpole is very happy that Dr Burney can
also   copy typescript   Lewis

16 Sept   4 p 4to   BM
from Thomas Twining
—— Ay, Ay, we are a couple of dishclouts, as

[7 Oct 1785]   1 p scrap   BM
from Thomas Twining
parcel, w^h. I hope you'll receive safe. — Joy

17 Oct   3 p 4to   Comyn
from Edmond Malone
I should have thanked you this morning

31 Oct   2 p 4to   Osb
to FB
I shall not recover my fright for some time,

7 Nov [1785]   1 p 4to   Comyn
from Mary (Granville) Delany
Mrs. Delany presents Her Compliments to Dr

5 Dec [1785]   2 p 4to   Osb
from George Selwyn
I am very sorry that you had not that meeting

[1785]   2 p 4to   Osb
to FB
I must have seemed very glum of late — but I

[1785]   draft   2 p 4to   Coke
to François Hippolite Barthélémon
many apologies are due to you from me for the

24 [pre 1786]   card   BM(Bar)
from Hester (Mulso) Chapone
Mrs Chapone presents compliments to D^r. &

[pre 1786]   1 p 8vo   Osb
from Dr John Gillies [to CB?]
D^r. Gillies is informed that the Great

1786

31 Jan   1 p 4to   Hyde
to   ?
I am sorry that I was not at home when you

1 Feb [1786?]   3 p 4to   Osb
to Christian Latrobe
In order to save the trouble of transcription I

2 Feb   3 p fol   Osb
from Gasparo Pacchierotti
I have been excessively pleased with the favor

17 Feb [1786]   card   Osb
to Mrs & Misses Davies
Dr. & Mrs. Burney present their Compliments

25 Feb   3 p 4to   BM(Bar)
to CBF
You must not imagine, my ever dear Charlotte,

[19] June [1786]   3 p 4to   Osb
to FB
As there is no one who deserves better writing

19 June   2 p 8vo   LC(J)
to John Paradise
I beg you will acquaint Mr. Jefferson that he

6 July   copy typescript   1 p 4to
from Horace Walpole   Lewis
You cannot possibly imagine, dear Sr, how I

10 July   press copy   2 p 8vo   LC(J)
from Thomas Jefferson
I took the liberty, through mr Paradise, of

20 July   2 p 4to   Lewis
to Horace Walpole
Few consequences of the honour so graciously

21 July   draft   4 p 4to   Osb
to Leonard Smelt
If it be true that severe

31 July   2 p 4to   Osb
to FB
We returned here last Night, my dear Fanny,

[July 1786]   copy   1 p 4to   Osb
to FB
"Well, but I must tell my dear Fanny that I

1 Aug   3 p 4to   BM
to Arthur Young
What have I, without an inch of land, to do

5 Aug   3 p 4to   Osb
to FB
All that you have so feelingly described

4 Sept   2 p 4to   Osb
to FB
I never rec'd a Letter from you wch. gave me

20 Sept   1 p 4to   NYPL(B)
from Count Benincasa
J'avois écrit la lettre ci-jointe

2 Oct   3 p 4to   Osb
to FB
I was obliged to go to Town upon other

17 Oct   2 p 4to   Osb
to FB
I trembled all the time I read your letter at the

30 Oct   1 p 4to (inc)   Comyn
from Gasparo Pacchierotti
which I bought for you and of which

3 Nov   3 p 4to   Osb
to FB
Ah! my dear Fanny! How I wish to jump at

3 Nov   copy extract   2 p LB   Osb
to Thomas Twining
We came to Town for the winter about the

4 Dec   3 p 4to   Osb
to FB
I am at the moment working hard at one of the

26 Dec   1 p 4to   Osb
to Christian Latrobe
Your kind inquiries oblige & flatter us very

30 Dec   1 p 4to   Osb
to FB
Why now, Fanny! we have only made bad

[post 1786]   2 p 8vo   Comyn
from Lady Lucan
Ly Lucan begs Doct Burney will do her the

[pre 1787]   amanuensis?   1 p 4to
to [Thomas Percy?]   Osb
Dr. Burney presents his Respects to the Dean

1787

6 Jan   1 p 4to   Coke
from Count Benincasa
Je vous écrivez, mon ami, une longue lettre à

8 Jan   3 p 4to   Osb
to FB
My heart smote me, some how, this morning

20 Jan   4 p 8vo   LC(J)
to Thomas Jefferson
Few things have given me more concern than

7 pmk [Feb 1787]   4 p 4to   NYPL(B)
to FB
I yesterday called on Mrs. Boscawen, who is

12 Feb   press copy   1 p 8vo   LC(J)
from Thomas Jefferson
I have been honoured with your favor of the

13 Feb [1787?]   1 p 4to   Osb
to Christian Latrobe
My daughter Fanny (the mistress of the Robes)

3 Mar   3 p 4to   NYPL(B)
from Count Benincasa
Quoiqu'il me revienne quelque reponse

20 Mar   3 p fol   NYPL(B)
from Mr Cutler
[line of music] A Youth, in the Painter way —

1 May   1 p 4to   Osb
to FB
As you give me my choice, I'll send or call for

14 May [1787]   4 p 4to   NYPL(B)
from SBP
Your kind letter did not reach me till my return

14 June [1787]   2 p 4to   Osb
to Christian Latrobe
The *dumpty* book wch. accompanies this note

15 June   1 p 4to   HEH
to Robert Adam
D^r. Burney presents his Compliments to M^r.

18 July [1787]   3 p 4to   Osb
to Christian Latrobe
I am now obliged to hasten you in the

8 Oct   2 p 4to   Osb
to FB
When people are ill, & give no sign of life, the

15 Oct   1 p 4to   Comyn
from William Jackson
I have had for some Years past an Idea of a

22 Oct   3 p fol   Osb
from Gasparo Pacchierotti
Why should I complain with my friends, when

23 Nov   copy extract   1 p LB   Osb
from [or to?] Thomas Twining
Then <you> talk of Music so masterly, & so

15 Dec   1 p 4to   Osb
to Christian Latrobe
Will you gratify your own curiosity, and mine,

18 Dec [1787?]   1 p 4to   Osb
to Christian Latrobe
If it will afford you any amusement to go to

19 Dec   1 p 8vo   Lewis
from Horace Walpole
I have been very unlucky twice when you have

22 Dec [1787]   1 p 4to   Osb
to Christian Latrobe
I am sorry to teaze you ab^t. these Germ. books,

22 June [pre 1788]   1 p 4to   HEH
to Edward Jerningham
D^r. Burney presents his respects to M^r.

1788

2 Mar   1 p ½ 4to   Osb
to Maria Cecilia Louisa Cosway
Dr. Burney presents his best Compliments to

8 May   2 p 4to   Osb
from John Dixon
M^r. Dixon is sorry he is obliged to

27 May   3 p 4to   Osb
from William Mason
I am extreamly [sic] sorry that Mr Dixon, as

16 July   3 p fol   Comyn
from Dr H Quin
Some Paragraphs in your Letter to Mrs Crew

8 Aug   2 p 4to   Shef
to Edmund Burke
The manner in which you have kindly relieved

also   [dated 4 Aug] draft   1 p 4to   Osb

25 Aug   1 p fol   Osb
from Felice de Giardini
Il lattore della Presente, Sig^r Ascanio Bono,

28 Aug [1788?]   2 p 8vo   Osb
from Ralph Griffiths
Arrah, Dear Sir, if you are *not* returned from

4 Nov [1788]   4 p 4to   BM(Bar)
to CBF
Why! my dear Charlottenburg! Do you begin

[post 18] Nov   2 p 4to   Osb
to Humphry Repton
If, after calling you *whore*, I were now standing

13 pmk   Dec   3 p 4to   Osb
to FB
I am to dine here, wch. I did not expect, & get

[1788]   2 p 4to   Osb
to Christian Latrobe
You don't know, my dear & worthy friend, how

[1788?]   1 p 4to   Osb
to Christian Latrobe
I am now so surrounded & bewildered with

2 OC pmk [1788–91]   2 p 4to   Osb
to CB Jr
Thank you for your *no news*; w^{ch}., in the

12 Mar [1788–90]   1 p 4to   NYPL(B)
from Luigi Marchesi
Marchesi fa i suoi complimenti al Sig^r. D^r.

[1788–91]   2 p 4to   Osb
to Sarah "Rosette" (Rose) Burney *
I am sorry I was out when my dear Rosette's

———————

* Printed, hereafter: Rosette (Rose) Burney.

1789

8 Mar   1 p fol   Osb
to Christian Latrobe
I forgot to tell you when I had the Pleasure of

1 May   copy extract   2 p LB   Osb
from Thomas Twining
O it is a charming thing: I have read it 3 or 4

3 May   2 p 4to   Folger
from Edmond Malone
On opening one of your volumes yesterday,

10 May   1 p 4to   Osb
to [Sir Joseph Banks]
I wish much to mention your Lituus in the last

30 May   draft   2 p 4to   Osb
to [Joseph Cooper Walker]
As the time that I was honoured with your

[8] June   2 p 4to   Osb
to Joseph Cooper Walker
At the time when I was honoured with your

8 June   1 p 4to   PML
from William Mason
I beg leave to congratulate you upon your

31 JY pmk [1789?]   2 p 4to   NYPL(B)
to Rosette (Rose) Burney
Having, perhaps, nothing better to do,

2 Sept [1789]   2 p 4to   NYPL(B)
to CB Jr
Dear Charlotte, whose kindness & attention are

2 Sept   copy   3 p 4to   Osb
from Thomas Twining
Yes, yes, I have seen, & carefully examined the

2 Oct   4 p fol   Hilles
to FB
I have been under arms for several days in

9 Oct   2 p 4to   Comyn
from David, 7th Viscount Stormont
as I know how much disposed you are

29 Oct [1789]   4 p 4to   BM
with Elizabeth Young to Arthur Young
I am much obliged to you for a letter which

4 Nov   1 p 4to   Comyn
from David, 7th Viscount Stormont
Lord Stormont presents His best compts to

8 Nov   ½ p 4to   Hyde
to Thomas Cadell
D^r. Burney presents his Compliments to M^r.

5 Dec   4 p 4to   Osb
from Arthur Young
It gave me much concern that your favour

1789, continued

20 Dec   1 p 4to   Osb
from James Hutton
I shall have an opportunity to send this to

[Dec 1789]   ½ p 4to   Osb
from Ralph Griffiths to [CB?]
As the weather is, at present, so unfriendly, &

[1789–91]   1 p 4to   Osb
to CB Jr
Your Bill of health is a shabby one — I hope

24 Dec [1789–91]   1 p 4to   Osb
to CB Jr
There are very few things in the gift of *Time*

1790

15 Jan   1 p 4to   Osb
from Sir William Scott
I have been prevented by a great Pressure of

[Jan 1790?]   card   Osb
from Charles, 11th Duke of Norfolk
Duke of Norfolk / requests the honor of/ D^r

20 Apr   3 p 4to   Osb
from Ralph Griffiths
Bushels of thanks to you, my Dear Sir! for

24 Apr   pmk ⟨1790⟩   4 p fol   Comyn
from SBP
I was writing to you my dearest Sir yesterday

12 June [1790]   2 p 4to   Osb
to CB Jr
I was so hemmed in by important engagem^ts

21 July   3 p 4to   Osb
to CB Jr
You will not I hope, my dear Chas. ascribe the

29 Aug   2 p 4to   Osb
to FB
I will not say that I was not glad to see your

6 Sept   2 p 4to   Osb
to Rosette (Rose) Burney
I am really vexed that such a kind invitation &

25 Oct   1 p 4to   Osb
from William Crotch
Sensible as I am how great a friend you have

27 Oct [1790]   2 p 4to   BM(Bar)
to FB
I have sent to London to bespeak *3 copies* of

6 Nov   2 p 4to   Osb
from William Mason
I believe you know that I keep myself in a kind

8 Nov   1 p 4to   Folger
to George Steevens
I supposed, in a thorough rummage of my

[20 Nov 1790]   3 p 4to   Osb
to SBP
I have millions of things to talk to you about,

8 Dec [1790]   3 p 4to   BM(Bar)
with Elizabeth (Allen) Burney to CBF
Fan tells me that she has rec^d. so kind &

[13] Dec [1790]   6 p 4to   Hilles
to FB
I thought it possible for a letter to come from

[c 1790]   draft   4 p 4to   Osb
to   ?
It is a fortunate circumstance for writers when

[1790]   draft   2 p 4to   Osb
to William Mason
It has given me much concern to find that in

[1790–94]   4 p 4to   Osb
to the Association of the Crown &
    Anchor
Every Englishman not tainted with French

[1790–95?]   1 p 8vo   Comyn
from James Boswell to [CB?]
Did not you say you would come and take

[1790–1802]   4 p 4to   NYPL(B)
from George Symes Catcott
The Antiquity of the use of the Bow in the

1791

5 Jan   4 p 4to   Osb
from Christian Latrobe
Your very kind note of the 24 Dec 90 — I did

7 Jan   3 p 4to   Osb
to CB Jr
I lost your last scrap, & knew not where to

7 Jan   3 p 4to   BM
to Arthur Young
the precipice on wch. you have been so long

15 Jan   3 p 4to   Hyde
to Rosette (Rose) Burney
In the midst of your social enjoym^t.

31 Jan [1791?]   1 p 4to   Osb
to Christian Latrobe
If you sh^d. happen to be at leisure on Wed^y.

3 Feb   2 p 4to   Osb
from Christian Latrobe
I send you here a *literal* Translation of Y^r.

16 Feb   3 p fol   BM
to Arthur Young
I arranged your numbers, and gave them to

3 Mar   2 p 4to   Osb
to Christian Latrobe
It must appear very strange to you, that I have

8 Mar   2 p 4to   Osb
from William Crotch
The arrival of Haydn in this country has

23 Mar [1791]   2 p 4to   Osb
to CB Jr
It has appeared to *me* a long while since we

11 Apr   3 p 4to   Osb
from Arthur Young
It is rather late in the day to tell you that the

17 Apr   draft   2 p 4to   NYPL(B)
to Horace Walpole
It was upon a very melancholy occasion that

24 Apr   2 p 4to   Osb
to Christian Latrobe
We want much to see you at Chelsea, & think

30 Apr   2 p fol   NYPL(B)
from Horace Walpole
On my return to this Cottage from Houghton

[Apr 1791]   draft   2 p 4to   NYPL(B)
to Horace Walpole
I feel so much flattered by the honour

8 May   ½ p 4to   Osb
to Maria Hester (Hughes) Park
D^r. Burney presents his Compliments to M^rs.

14 June   2 p fol   Osb
to FB
Let me see — Where did we leave off? Oh, on

28 June   2 p fol   Osb
to FB
What times are these in France! & indeed

June   ½ p 4to   Osb
to FB
I am glad of anything that gives you spirits, &

[pre July 1791]   1 p 8vo   Lewis
from Lady Banks
Lady Banks will be very glad to have the

6 July   1 p 4to   Osb
to FB
Your last letter relieved my mind from great

6 July   copy   2 fol   BM(NH)
to Sir Joseph Banks
You have been such a constant Patron & Friend

16 July   4 p 4to   Yale(Bo)
to James Boswell
So much time has elapsed between the

also   draft   2 p 4to   Hyde

28 July   2 p 4to   Osb
from William Windham
I am shocked that circumstances of different

also   copy   2 p 4to   NYPL(B)

31 July [1791?]   4 p 4to   Osb
from Arthur Young
A thousand thanks for your very kind letter, in

[July 1791]   draft   1 p 8vo   Lewis
to Horace Walpole
You have done me the honour so long & so

also   photostat   Osb

3 Aug   draft   2 p 4to   NYPL(B)
to Edmund Burke
Not having been so fortunate as to find you at

10 Aug   2 p 4to   Osb
to FB
I cannot inclose your 2 Letters without "a few

also   copy extract   1 p 4to   NYPL(B)
I dined on Tuesday with a most pleasant party

10 Aug   1 p 4to   Osb
from Charles Clagget
I have the pleasure of informing you I am in

[post 10 Aug 1791]   draft   2 p 4to
to John Horne Tooke   Osb
The best articles of the Fr. Constitution are

1791, continued

17 Aug   3 p 4to   Osb
to FB
I have been so awkwardly circumstanced since

9 Sept   7 p 4to   Osb
to Mrs Crewe
I would not write in answer to your most kind

[13] Sept   3 p 4to   Osb
to Molesworth Phillips & FB
I never recᵈ. a more welcome letter in my life.

21 Sept   3 p 4to   Osb
to FB
I intended writing you a long letter; but I have

21 Sept   4 p 4to   BM
to Arthur Young
I am quite ashamed of not answering yʳ kind

29 Sept   4 p 4to   Liv(P)
to Joseph Cooper Walker
I fear my letter will scarce reach Dublin before

4 Oct   4 p 4to   Osb
to FB
I have written neither to you nor our beloved

8 Oct   3 p 4to   NYPL(B)
to FB
As I shall with great pleasure, send the Carr.

11 Oct   copy   2 p 4to   BM
from Thomas Twining
Why, my dear friend! — Where are you? —

8 Nov   2 p fol   NYPL(B)
from Horace Walpole
I am Favoured with your letter and am much

21 Nov   2 p 4to   Osb
from Richard Cox
I send you by the Andover Carrier which sets

[28 Nov 1791]   2 p 4to   Lewis
to SBP
I told our Capt. that poor Lᵈ. Orford is

[Dec? 1791]   draft 3 p 4to   Osb
to Richard Cox
Yesterday arrived safe (hormis 3 bonnes

[Dec 1791?]   3 p 4to   Osb
from Ralph Griffiths
I am afraid, my Dear Sir, that poor Becket's

[1791]   1 p 4to   Osb
to CB Jr
I dined after the *Abbey performance* with Sʳ.

22 Jan [1791–95] amanuensis 1 p 4to
from Franz Josef Haydn   Osb
La sua gentilissima lettera colla prontezza

[post 1791]   3 p 4to   Osb
from Elizabeth (Milbanke) Lamb, Viscountess Melbourne
Lᵈ. Melbournes Complᵗˢ to Docʳ Burney she

[pre 1792]   1 p 12mo   Comyn
from Sir Joshua Reynolds
Sir Joshua Reynolds presents his Compᵗˢ. to

[pre 1792]   2 p 4to   Osb
from Elizabeth Ann (Linley) Sheridan
Altho Mrs. Sheridan has not the pleasure of a

1792

17 Jan   2 p 4to   Osb
from William Mason
I never trouble you with my Letters, except

8 Feb   2 p 4to   Osb
from Gasparo Pacchierotti
Tho late, I trust you will not refuse reading

[Feb 1792]   1 p 4to   Comyn
to SBP
I am heartily grieved to tell you that poor Sʳ.

3 Mar [1792]   card   Comyn
from the Executors of Sir Josua Reynolds
The favour of your Company is requested to

Apr   1 p 4to   NYPL(B)
to FB
Adieu my ever dear & worthy Fanny!

Apr   1 p 4to   BM(Bar)
to CBF
Farewell! my dear & good Charlotte! It will

Apr   1 p 4to   NYPL(B)
to SBP
Adieu my dear, kind, & tender, Susan!

[c 17 May 1792]   copy 1 p 4to   Osb
to Charles Blagden
"Dʳ Burney has been at Broadwood's, . . ."

19 June   1 p 4to   Yale(Bo)
to James Boswell
I am truly concerned, that it will not be

17 July   3 p 4to   BM
to Arthur Young
Your very kind & hearty invitation to Bradfield

27 Aug   5 p 4to   Osb
to Mrs Crewe
How good & kind it was of you to write so soon

19 Sept   4 p 4to   Osb
to Mrs Crewe
How agreeably you flatter me, my dearest

19 SE 1792 pmk   4 p 4to   Osb
to SBP
I am always *mollen* choly as a *cot*, my dear

2 Oct [1792]   3 p 4to   NYPL(B)
to FB
Why you, Fanny. — Why won't you write

8 Oct   3 p 4to   NYPL(B)
to FB
I sh^d. have thanked you instantly for your most

8 Oct   4 p 4to   Osb
to Mrs Crewe
Though you have an infinitely better

18 Oct   2 p 4to   NYPL(B)
to CB Jr
Pauca verba, with you — for being more a man

22 Oct   2 p 4to   BM(Bar)
to CBF
I intended writing to my dear Charlotte on the

29 Oct   4 p 4to   NYPL(B)
to FB
The 1st. acc^t. I received of the very melancholy
also   copy   3 p 4to   NYPL(B)

31 Oct   7 p 4to   Osb
to Mrs Crewe
Two letters, unanswered, on my hands and

1 Nov   2 p 4to   Hyde
to Joseph Cooper Walker
I was driven to Bath the latter end of Sept^r.

2 Dec   5 p 4to   Osb
to Mrs Crewe
Politics are now got quite out of my reach —

25 Dec   2 p 4to   Osb
to Mrs Crewe
I am all astonishment & fear. — you wonder

31 Dec   2 p 4to   Harv(H)
to Edmond Malone
I w^d. not take my *corporal* of it, but as far as I

[c 1792?]   4 p 8vo   Comyn
from Mrs Crewe
Hope you go on well & will keep up your

[c 1792]   draft   1 p 4to   Osb
to Thomas Twining
Your gloomy silence alarms & terrifies me so

[1792–93]   2 p 4to   Osb
from William Seward to [CB?]
I could wish that you would be so good as to

[1792–98]   2 p 8vo   Osb
from Frederic, 5th Earl of Guilford
Your Reasons are unanswerable as to seeing the

1793

1 Jan   5 p 4to   Osb
to Mrs Crewe
I am glad that my *fat* letter came to hand;

10 Jan   2 p 4to   Osb
to Mrs Crewe
Supposing that you will hardly set out for

31 Jan   2 p 4to   NYPL(B)
to FB & SBP
I have little stomach to write. The horror of

13 Feb [1793]   4 p 4to   Osb
to Mrs Crewe
I have just been reading the debates of last

14 Feb   2 p 8vo   NYPL(B)
to CB Jr
Thanks for your Note & the *Notice* you took of

[19 Feb 1793]   3 p 4to   NYPL(B)
to FB
Why Fanny! What are you ab^t. & where are

19 Feb [1793]   2 p 4to   Osb
to Mrs Crewe
There is no picking up anything in the way of

21 Feb [1793]   1 p 4to   Osb
from James Hutton to CB & Elizabeth
      (Allen) Burney
I came to town the 18th and return the 22.

1793, continued

22 Feb   1 p 4to   NYPL(B)
from James Hutton
I wrote a L^r yesterday of great Consequence

12 Mar   copy   3 p 4to   BM
from Thomas Twining
Let us talk of other things. And alas!

3–[7] Apr   3 p 4to   Folger
to George Steevens
though confined to a sick room, of wch. I have

12 May   4 p 4to   BM
to Arthur Young
I cannot let M^rs. Young return without sending

[22?] May   3 p 4to   NYPL(B)
to FB
I have for some time seen very plainly that you

1 July   3 p 4to   Yale(Be)
to Joseph Cooper Walker
Want of health prevented me from

2 July   copy   1 p 4to   BM
from Thomas Twining
I was sorry I could not manage to reach

[3 July 1793]   3 p 8vo   NYPL(B)
from M d'A (with copy LS William
     Locke to CB)
Les expressions me manquent p^r rendre tout

[3 July 1793]   draft   1 p   NYPL(B)
from FB drafted by M d'A
C'est plus encore à mon ami qu'à mon Pere

3 July   copy   2 p 8vo   NYPL(B)
from William Locke Sr
finding you have been informed of Monsr.

10 July   3 p 4to   NYPL(B)
to William Locke Sr
I have been out of town for some days, or sh^d.

11 July [1793]   1 p 4to   NYPL(B)
to M d'A
Sir. If I have not been eager in manifesting a

11 July   2 p 4to   BM(Bar)
to Frederica Locke
I thought it utterly impossible that I could

16 July   3 p 4to   Plat
to CB Jr
I was very impatient to hear from you, and to

13 Aug   4 p 4to   Osb
from Charlotte Smith
An address, and of the nature that I am about

19 Aug   draft   2 p 4to   Comyn
to Charlotte Smith
Much flattered & gratified by the opportunity

⟨20⟩ Aug   4 p 4to   Osb
from Charlotte Smith
I am extremely honour'd & oblig'd by your

26 Aug   3 p 4to   Osb
to Mrs Crewe
I shall write to day to tell you what I *have*

7 Sept [1793]   3 p 4to   Osb
to Mrs Crewe
This is sad work, doing business by letter! I

10 Sept   3 p 4to   BM
to William Windham
You have escaped several letters from me

12 Sept   2 p 4to   BM(Bar)
to FBA
In this season of leisure, I am as fully

13–16 Sept   4 p 4to   NYPL(B)
from SBP
It is an age since I have given *signe de vie* to

15 Sept   4 p 4to   Comyn
from Edmund Burke
M^rs. Burke has just written a long Letter

25 Sept   4 p 4to   Osb
to FBA
My *secretaryship* occupies me more & more

4 Oct   4 p 4to   NYPL(B)
to FBA
This is a terrible Coup, so soon after your

15 Oct   3 p 4to   Osb
from Charlotte Smith
Your last most obliging & friendly Letter, as

23 Oct [1793]   2 p 4to   NYPL(B)
to FBA
In the utmost hurry & want of time, I cannot

[post 23 Oct 1793]   3 p 4to   NYPL(B)
to FBA
I have done nothing night & day since I wrote

24 Oct   3 p 4to   Osb
to Mrs Crewe
I am just returned from Mr. Wilmot's with

1–5 Nov [1793?]   4 p 4to   Osb
to [Mrs Crewe?]
M. Jamard dined with me on Sunday, and I

27 Dec   1 p 4to   Comyn
from the Bishop of St Pol de Léon
Mr. L'ar de Leon presente ses Respects à Mr

[1793]   5 p 4to   Osb
to Mrs Crewe
You will doubtless be furnished with more

20 ⟨Oct⟩ [pre 1794: 1783?]   1 p 4to
                                     Osb
from Louis-Marie-Joseph d'Albert d'-
    Ailly, duc de Chaulnes
Le Duc de ⟨Chaulnes⟩ est bien reconnaissant

[pre 1794: 1783?]   1 p 4to   Osb
from Louis-Marie-Joseph d'Albert d'-
    Ailly, duc de Chaulnes
The Duke of Chaulnes best compliments to

[pre 1794]   1 p fol   Osb
from George Colman [to CB?]
I really have scarce had a moment to read or

1794

[25 Jan 1794]   3 p 4to   NYPL(B)
to FBA
It is so long since I have been able to give you

29 Jan   1 p 4to   Yale(Bo)
to James Boswell
Dr. Burney presents his best compliments

[5 Feb 1794]   3 p 4to   NYPL(B)
to FBA
Capt. Phil. dines with us & allows me to run

19 Mar   4 p 4to   BM(Bar)
to FBA
I am so deeply in your debt, that I know not
also   copy   4 p 4to   NYPL(B)

14 Apr   4 p 4to   Osb
to FBA
After boasting so much of freedom from pain,

30 Apr   1 p 4to   Hyde
to [Thomas] Cadell
Dr. Burney presents his Compliments to Mr.

10 June   2 p 4to   BM(Bar)
to FBA
our dear Susan's acct. of your health at her

5 July   3 p 4to   Osb
to Mrs Crewe
Only think of your being at Wilbury the very

7 July   4 p 4to   BM(Bar)
to FBA
Why this seems to have been a very serious &
also composite copy? 6 p 4to NYPL(B)
Our Susanna's account of your health at her

7 July   2 p 4to   NYPL(B)
to CB Jr
You sneaked away in a *shabbyish*

20 July   3 p 4to   Osb
to Mrs Crewe
Your letter arrived just when I was winding up

5 Aug   4 p 4to   Osb
to Mrs Crewe
It was an observation of my old friend Mrs.

18 Aug   3 p 4to   Osb
from Richard Cox
I had a very sincere pleasure in the perusal of

28 AU 94 pmk   4 p 4to   BM(Bar)
to FBA
[page deleted] . . . At Mr. Carr's dinner I met
also   copy (inc)   3 p 4to   NYPL(B)

9 Sept   3 p 4to   Osb
from William Mason
Your valuable Present did not reach me till

23 Sept   3 p 4to   Osb
from Richard Cox
I will say that for my much beloved friend,

16 Oct   3 p fol   Osb
from William Keate
The perusal of Mattei's exposition of our

18 Oct   3 p 4to   NYPL(B)
to FBA
I waited for today's post bringing an acct. of

1794, continued

20 Oct   4 p 4to   Cox
to Richard Cox
Public affairs have gone so ill lately, &

2 Nov   3 p 4to   Osb
from William Keate
I fear you will have a right to say — In publica

3 Nov   3 p 4to   Osb
from William Keate
I thank you much for your kind & just

17 Nov   3 p 4to   NYPL(B)
to FBA
I have wanted to know how you do, & how the

20 Nov   2 p 4to   Osb
from Richard Cox
I cannot sufficiently thank you for your last

21 Nov   1 p 4to   APS
from Sir Joseph Banks
These are to give Notice that on the First Day

28 Nov   3 p 4to   Hilles
to Joseph Cooper Walker
In the last letter with wch. you favoured me

[1794–1811]   1 p 8vo   Osb
to CB Jr
I shall be very glad to see you at 4 o'clock

1795

1 Jan   1 p 4to   Osb
from William Keate
At length / The first of January I appear in

30 Jan   2 p 4to   NYPL(B)
from William Keate
I have been entertaining myself highly with

31 Jan   4 p 4to   Osb
from William Keate
Though I had made a hop step & jump from

1 Feb   3 p 8vo   Osb
from William Keate
Your servant went away too soon for me to

3 Feb   4 p 8vo   Osb
from William Keate
It would be the highest presumption in me to

18 Feb   1 p 4to   Osb
from Dorothy Young
I am extremely obliged for the valuable present

2 AP 1795 pmk   1 p 4to   NYPL(B)
to FBA
I honour your heroism. I always feared

[7] May   4 p 4to   NYPL(B)
to FBA
What a while has our correspondence slept! —

also   copy   8 p 4to   NYPL(B)

8 May   4 p 4to   Osb
to SBP
I never forgot my promise to write again, after

11 May   4 p 4to   Camb(F)
to William Mason
I have long wished to write to you; but

also   draft   3 p 4to   Osb

23 May   3 p 4to   Osb
from William Mason
About the time I rec^d your last obliging Letter

May   copy extract   2 p LB   Osb
from Thomas Twining
How superior her novels are to the sickening

8 June   6 p fol   NYPL(B)
to William Mason
I was very much flattered by your exclusive

9 June   4 p 4to   NYPL(B)
to FBA
I have been such an *évaporé* lately, that if I

also   copy   6 p 4to   NYPL(B)

9 June   1 p 4to   Comyn
from Franz Joseph Haydn
Mi rincresce infinamente, che non

28 June   4 p 4to   Osb
from William Mason
I am much oblged to you for pointing out such

15 Aug   1 p 4to   BM(Bar)
to CBF
"A few pleasing words" ere I depart hence.

19 Sept   3 p 4to   Osb
from Richard Cox
What a melancholy account do you give me of

19 Sept   3 p 4to   Osb
from Gasparo Pacchierotti
E per le mari di Morsellari ch'io ricevo un

5 Oct   ?   Soth26
from Edmund Burke
[first line not available]

23 Oct   2 p 4to   PML
from William Mason
Tho I have not answerd your instructiv[tear]

[1795–1800]   draft   2 p 4to   Osb
to [Jean-Pierre Brissot de Warville]
The analytical discourse of M. le Baron de W.

[1795–1800]   draft   1 p 4to   Osb
to [John] Gillies
For Dr. Gillies, only. *sub sigillo confessionis*

[post 1795]   3 p 4to   Osb
to Christian Latrobe
Your Packet was delivered to me at Breakfast

[post 1795]   1 p 4to   Osb
to Christian Latrobe
I have looked-over & played your VIth. sonatina

8 June [pre 1796]   1 p 4to   Osb
from Ralph Griffiths
As I know not Mr. Twining's address, I must

1796

5 Jan   1 p 4to   NYPL(B)
from Horace Walpole
Lord Orford is very sorry he was too ill to

also   copy   1 p 4to?   Lewis

7 [Jan]   3 p 4to   Cox
to Richard Cox
I was unwilling to break in upon the chearful

11 [Jan]   1 p 4to   NYPL(B)
to CB Jr
What *is* all this, my dear Carluch? What! no

6 Feb   2 p 4to   NYPL(B)
to FBA
I was in hopes to have scribbled a *few pleasing*

8 Feb   copy extract   1 p LB   Osb
to Thomas Twining
Fanny's novel is called CAMILLA, or a picture of

16 Feb   2 p 4to   Folger
to George Steevens
Your reverence & zeal for the "God of your

[18? Feb 1796]   draft   1 p 8vo   Lewis
to Horace Walpole
For the ease of your Lordship's conscience the

also   photostat   Osb

19 Feb   1 p 4to   Osb
from George Steevens
Accept my best thanks for your present,

20 Feb   1 p 4to   Lewis
from Horace Walpole
I thank you very much for your Books, which

22 FE 1796 pmk   4 p 4to   Osb
from Arthur Young
It gave me much pleasure to receive your very

21 Mar   2 p 4to   Osb
to Thomas Twining
It is not to fulfill the mechanical duties of

[Mar 1796]   copy   1 p 4to   NYPL(B)
from Edmund Burke
As to MISS BURNEY — the subscription ought

8 Apr [1796]   2 p 4to   Oxf(Bod)
to CB Jr
As I foresaw & dreaded, Robinson is piqued

11 Apr   1 p 12mo   NYPL(MS)
to [Thomas?] Cadell
Dr Burney presents his Compts to Mr Cadel —

18 Apr [1796]   1 p 4to   NYPL(B)
to CB Jr
I inclose you Robinson's list for Fanny

1 May   4 p 4to   Osb
from Joseph Cooper Walker
Presuming you would wish to be in possession

23 May [1796?]   3 p 8vo   Osb
to CB Jr
If you have not already seen the Pater-noster

30 June   1 p 4to   Camb(F)
to Rosette (Rose) Burney
It gives me great pleasure to find that you are

6 July   1 p 4to   Comyn
from Horace Walpole
You cannot imagine, dear Sr, how I rejoice for

1796, continued

12 July   2 p 4to   NYPL(B)
to FBA
You disappointed us sadly, by sneaking off,

12 July   2 p 4to   PML
to Joseph Cooper Walker
I last week consigned to the care of the Earl

[14 July 1796]   2 p 4to   NYPL(B)
to FBA
We go on rarely! I was in London all yesterday

[16 July 1796]   4 p 4to   NYPL(B)
with SHB to FBA
Well! Notwithstanding the number & size of

[16? July 1796]   copy extract   2 p 4to
                                        NYPL(B)
to CB Jr (in AL SBP to FBA 19 July
  1796)
"What think you all of your little Niece &

22 JY 1796 pmk   1 p 4to   Osb
to FBA
Though I have much to say, it must be

3 Aug   2 p 4to   Oxf(Bod)
to CB Jr
It was always my opinion that if Robinson had

6 Aug   2 p 4to   NYPL(B)
to FBA
More — More — More! — Thank you for your

8 Aug   1 p 4to   NYPL(B)
to SBP
Camilla — The governess, Miss Margland

12 Aug   1 p 4to   BM
to Samuel Rose
Supposing that abt. this time you may be

23 Aug   4 p 4to   NYPL(B)
with SBP to FBA
I have wanted for some days to thank you for

26 Aug   6 p 4to   Osb
from Joseph Cooper Walker
I have read, re-read your *Memoirs of*

31 Aug   1 p 4to   NYPL(B)
to CB Jr
I have seen Mr. Huttner since I was at

5 Sept   1 p 4to   NYPL(B)
to CB Jr
Dr. Chas. — As I am going a journey on Wedy.

20 Sept   2 p 4to   Osb
from Gasparo Pacchierotti
Only the other day I received from Mr

24 Sept   copy extract   3 p LB   Osb
to Thomas Twining
And — not a word yet of *Camilla*! ! I have

Sept   2 p 4to   NYPL(B)
to FBA
Your 2d. acct. of our poor dear Susan's health

13 Oct   3 p 4to   BPL
to Joseph Cooper Walker
I have been long waiting for an opportunity to

[20 Oct 1796]   copy   2 p 4to   Osb
from Dorothy Young
In my last I endeavored to convey something

20 Oct   3 p 4to   Osb
from Edward Miller
Our correspondence has certainly been

22 Oct [1796]   4 p 4to   NYPL(B)
from SBP
My dearest Father will I am sure wish to hear

29 Oct   3 p 4to   Osb
from Christian Latrobe
It was with the most heartfelt concern that I

31 Oct   4 p 4to   NYPL(B)
from SBP
I hasten, not to lose a mail, to tell my dearest

1 Nov [1796]   2 p 4to   BM(Bar)
from Maria (Allen) Rishton
I have been waiting a few days in hopes of

2 Nov   3 p 4to   Oxf(Bod)
to Ralph Griffiths
Your letter is so different from the generality
also   draft   3 p 8vo   Osb
also   copy (in ALS E. H. Barker to S. Allen
                2 AP 1836)   Osb

14 Nov   2 p 4to   Osb
to Christian Latrobe
Your kind condolance has administered all the

21 Nov   4 p 4to   BM(Bar)
from SBP
How long, how *very* long it is since I have

26 Nov   3 p 4to   Osb
from Joseph Cooper Walker
I am honored with your obliging & valuable

[Nov 1796]   3 p 4to   NYPL(B)
to FBA
I must thank you for your prompt letter and

[Nov 1796]   2 p 8vo   NYPL(B)
to CB Jr
Having had a pen in my hand, wth. wch. I was

2 Dec   4 p 4to   NYPL(B)
to FBA
I have been tolerably well, in body; but in

6 Dec   3 p 4to   NYPL(B)
to Thomas Twining
There is something so endearing in fellowship

[1796?]   copy extract   1 p 4to   Osb
to Dorothy Young
"We are thoroughly sensible of your humanity

[post 1796]   draft   1 p 8vo
to George Canning   NYPL(B)
I was unwilling to trouble you with the

[post 1796?]   draft   2 p 4to   Osb
to Sir William Herschel
When I last had the pleasure of seeing you at

[pre 1797]   1 p 4to   Osb
from William Seward
Your whole family accus'd me last night of

[pre 1797]   1 p 12mo   Lewis
from Lady Banks
Lady Banks will be very glad to have the

[pre 1797]   draft   1 p 4to   Osb
to Charles Davy
I have not Leisure to discuss from the use w^ch.

1797

16 Jan   pmk 1797   4 p 4to   BM(Bar)
from Maria (Allen) Rishton
Why don't I write to you? Why my dearest

24 Jan   1 p 8vo   Osb
to John Wall Callcott
D^r. Burney presents his best Compts to M^r.

6 Feb   3 p 4to   NYPL(B)
to FBA
I shall prepare a scrap for parcellina — w^ch.

7 Feb   2 p 4to (inc)   NYPL(B)
to [Arthur Young]
It seems, nay is, a great while since I have

25 Apr   1 p 4to   Osb
to John Wall Callcott
I hasten to thank you for the new present

20 May   2 p 4to   Osb
from Jamard
Permettez moi de vous témoigner

31 May   4 p fol   NYPL(B)
from Thomas Twining
"Commas & Points I set exactly right!

4 June   3 p 4to   KL
to FBA
Whence came it, my dear Fanny, that our

9 July   1 p 4to   NYPL(B)
from Edmund Nagle [to CB?]
I am grieved to tell you that your late friend

[c 10–12 July 1797]   1 p 4to   BM(Bar)
to William Windham
Mrs Crewe wishes me to attend poor dear M^r.

13 July [1797]   1 p 4to   BYU
to Edmond Malone
M^r. Windham has been so kind as to try to

20–[24] July [1797]   4 p 4to
to FBA (with PS by JB)   NYPL(B)
The close of the season is always hurry scurry

25 July   3 p 4to   Osb
from Arthur Young
Your feeling & consolatory letter was no slight

19 Aug   3 p 4to   Comyn
to CB Jr
I am sorry that your door still creaks on the

22 Aug   3 p 4to   Osb
from Richard Cox
It was but the day before I receiv'd your Letter

13 Sept   4 p 4to   NYPL(B)
to FBA
When did I leave off? — hang me if I know!

1797, continued

15 Sept   3 p 4to   Osb
to Mrs Crewe
I was all last week at Richmond where two of

[15 Sept 1797]   2 p 4to   NYPL(B)
to CBF
"A few pleasing words", you have a right to

28 SE 1797 pmk   1 p copy   4 p 4to
to FBA   NYPL(B)
I read your letter pen in hand, & shall try to

30 Sept [1797]   3 p 4to   Osb
to Mrs Crewe
Let me begin my letter, by asking whether

7 Oct   3 p 8vo   Shep
to [Samuel] Arnold
on my return to Chelsea, after scampering

24 Oct   draft?   2 p 4to   BM
to   ?
Your letter is too flattering to an author to

26 Oct   4 p 4to   BM(Bar)
to SBP
I have long felt uncomfortable at not writing

18 Nov   2 p 4to   Osb
from Richard Cox
I have deferred writing to you so long since I

28 Nov   2 p 4to   Osb
from Sir William Herschel
It seems to be an established custom with me

9 DE 1797 pmk   1 p 4to   Osb
from [Lady Lucan]
I am very much pleased with yᵉ alterations I

[1797]   12 p 4to   NYPL(B)
from Mrs Crewe
I will as you desire it endeavour to collect

[1797]   2 p fol   NYPL(B)
from Mrs Crewe
proper praises of many *good* improvements in

[1797]   4 p 8vo   NYPL(B)
from Mrs Crewe
I wᵈ. have every subject in the world treated

[1797]   4 p 4to   NYPL(B)
from Mrs Crewe
Oh I pity you indeed. I wish with all my

[post 1797]   1 p fol   Osb
from George Colman Jr
I really have scarce had a moment to read or

[1797–98]   1 p 4to   NYPL(B)
from Sir William Herschel
Unavoidable business has prevented my

Mar [1797–98?]   1 p 8vo   Osb
to John Wall Callcott
I never had a 2ᵈ. vol. of Forkel; nor am I

[1797–99?]   2 p 8vo   Osb
to John Wall Callcott
Nothwithstanding I am almost smothered with

[1797–1806]   1 p 8vo   Osb
to John Wall Callcott
My dear friend — if you think I have got my

1798

1 [Jan]   4 p fol   Folger
to Thomas Twining
Why, my dear friend! / What *is* become of

4 Jan   3 p 4to   Osb
from Joseph Cooper Walker
Your obliging favor of 13ᵗʰ. Oct. 1796,

17 Feb   1 p 4to   Osb
to John Wall Callcott
I see nothing to alter or correct in your *Revise*,

24 AP 1798 pmk   2 p 4to   NYPL(B)
to FBA
Mrs. Crewe has frequent singing parties with

2 June   1 p 4to   Comyn
from Jean-Baptiste Cléry
M. Cléry fait bien ses Complimens à Monsieur

4 June   4 p 4to   Osb
to FBA
I shall begin to write a few words, many I shall

16 June   1 p 4to   Comyn
from Jean-Baptiste Cléry
M. Cléry Presente ses complimens à Monsieur

26 June [1798]   2 p 4to   Osb
to Mrs Crewe
I fully intended getting to Hampstead for 2 or

5 July   4 p 4to   Comyn
from Warren Hastings [to CB]
I hope I shall not trespass too far

10 July   2 p 4to   Comyn
from Warren Hastings
I return you many thanks, most gratefully,

22 July   draft   1 p 4to   Osb
to Sir William Herschel
I yesterday began my Summer rambles, and

23 Aug   draft   1 p 4to   Osb
to Charles Butler
In the late general rummage of my library &

23 Aug   draft   1 p 4to   Osb
to Lord Charles Bruce
Having been out of Town when so substantial

26 Aug   [1798?]   1 p 4to   Osb
to Christian Latrobe
Let us have the pleasure of seeing you as soon

3 Sept   draft   1 p 4to   Osb
to Lord Charles Bruce
I may literally say that I have been *comblé de*

5 Oct   1 p 4to   Osb
to Christian Latrobe
I have been from home 8 or 10 days on a visit

9 Oct   3 p 4to   Osb
from Christian Latrobe
Your kind lines of Oct. 5th. I recd. on Saturday

10 Oct   1 p 4to   BM
to Edmond Malone
I have been such a vagabond of late, as not to

26 Oct   4 p 4to   NYPL(B)
with Maria (Allen) Rishton to FBA
Mrs. R. has told you of all that was done

2 Nov   2 p 4to   Osb
to FBA
Mrs. R. having told you my thoughts in a

2 Nov   copy   1 p 8vo   NYPL(B)
from Lavinia (Bingham), Countess
        Spencer
I should have returned you my best thanks

3 NO 1798 pmk   1 p 4to   Osb
to CB Jr
I have written & set a Song on our last naval

8 Nov   2 p 4to   Osb
from Brownlow North
Excuse my troubling you, as you are on the

18 Nov   2 p 8vo   NYPL(B)
to William Windham
I have been much flattered by learning from

Nov [1798]   3 p 4to   Osb
to Rosette (Rose) Burney
I have been truly grieved to hear of your

3 Dec   2 p 4to   Osb
from Richard Cox
It was my full intention to have thank'd you

10 Dec   4 p 4to   NYPL(B)
to FBA
You must not expect a spritely or a long letter

[18 Dec 1798]   1 p 8vo   Osb
to CB Jr
Though my cough is so bad that I go out as

18 Dec   2 p 4to   Osb
to Christian Latrobe
A Hymn, or supplicatory Song for the

[post 1798]   draft   1 p 4to   Osb
to Lord Charles [Bruce?]
The acct of your sufferings grieves me to the

[pre 1799]   2 p 4to   Osb
from William Seward to [CB?]
I am much obliged to you for the attention you

1799

3 Jan   4 p 4to   NYPL(B)
to FBA
My wish & intentions have been every day, for

14 [Jan]   2 p 4to   HSP
to Joseph Cooper Walker
I postponed answering your last obliging letter,

1799, continued

26 Jan   1 p 8vo   Shep
from Benjamin Moseley
Dr. Moseley requests Dr Burney will have the

also   copy   1 p 4to   Osb

26 Jan   draft   2 p 8vo   Shep
to Benjamin Moseley
D^r. Burney presents his Compliments to D^r.

30 Jan   [1799]   3 p 4to   Osb
from Warren Hastings
It grieves me much that after the great trouble

[post 5 Feb 1799]   draft   2 p 4to
to [Samuel Hoole]   NYPL(B)
The vortex in wch. professional men & even

6 FE 1799 pmk   2 p 8vo   NYPL(B)
to CB Jr
We thought you had been smothered in snow;

7 Feb   3 p 4to   Osb
from Christian Latrobe
Your kind note of — I received the day before

8 Feb   3 p 8vo   Coke
to CB Jr
Among a heap of small-trash articles, w^ch.

11 Feb [1799?]   2 p 4to   Osb
from Ralph Griffiths
"Unreasonable man" that I am, (for so you

2 Mar [1799]   2 p 4to   Osb
from Ralph Griffiths
It was very good of you to take care of Walker's

14 Mar   2 p 4to   Osb
to Sir William Parsons
It was the opinion of Prior, the favourite bard

8 Apr   3 p 4to   BM(Bar)
to FBA
d'ye think I dont want to know how you all do

18 Apr   1 p 4to   Osb
to Christian Latrobe
Thank you for sending my books. I hope, in

[pre 24 Apr 1799]   1 p 4to   NYPL(B)
from William Seward
We <missed Sadly of> each other

22 May   1 p 8vo   Comyn
to CB Jr
I have not yet returned S^r. Chas. Blagden's

[25 May 1799]   3 p 4to   BM(Bar)
to FBA
I have time only for a very few *pleasing* words

28 MY 1799 pmk   1 p 8vo   NYPL(B)
to CB Jr
I shall try to keep myself disengaged on

21 June   4 p 4to   BM(Bar)
to FBA
I have been thinking of writing to you for

30 June   2 p 4to   PML
to Joseph Cooper Walker
It was impossible for me to answer

2 July   2 p 4to   BM(Bar)
to FBA
A very few pleasing words, only; that the dear

6 July   1 p 8vo   Osb
to Rosette (Rose) Burney
I am glad to find that you seem better in health

18 July   4 p 4to   NYPL(B)
to FBA
Why Lord help your head! my dear Fanny —

22 July   4 p 4to   NYPL(B)
to FBA
I believe I told you, on friday, that I was

16 Aug   4 p 4to   Osb
to Rosette (Rose) Burney
I had a pen in my hand this morn^g. to thank

16 Aug   1 p 4to   Osb
to Mrs Crewe
How be you, Dear Madam? I arrived here

21 Aug   3 p 4to   Osb
from Edward Miller
After fruitless enquiries respecting you, your

1 Sept   3 p 4to   NYPL(B)
from Sir Uvedale Price
When I had the pleasure of seeing you at

9 Sept   4 p 4to   Osb
to FBA
Why *you* Fanny. — I did not intend to write

17 Sept   draft   3 p 4to   Comyn
to Edward Miller
I have been scampering ab^t. so much

18 Sept   3 p 4to   Osb
from Joseph Cooper Walker
Since I acknowledged your kind & valuable

19 Sept   3 p 4to   Osb
from Edward Miller
Your kind letter has had such a balmy effect

25 Sept   2 p 4to   Osb
to Mrs Crewe
I never read any thing wth. such trepidation as

30 Sept   2 p 4to   Coke
from Sir Uvedale Price
Many many thanks to you for the Lullis, & for

1 Oct   4 p 4to   Osb
to Thomas Twining
Why not deal with principals? I hear of you

[3 Oct 1799]   3 p 4to   Osb
from Sir William Herschel
I have the pleasure of your letter and judging

12 Oct   2 p 4to   Osb
from Joseph Cooper Walker
Since I took the liberty to request a loan of

16 Oct   ?   Mag230(96)
to HLTP
[mentions FB, Dr Johnson, Judge Fielding]

19 Oct   2 p 4to   Osb
to FBA
I shall ruin you in letters — but I *must* tell

21 Oct [1799]   3 p 4to   Osb
from Ralph Griffiths
I beseech you, Dear Sir, not to blame me

26 Oct   1 p 8vo   Osb
to John Wall Callcott
I did not know what arrangem^{ts}. were made

29 Oct   3 p 4to   Osb
to FBA
I w^{d}. not put you to the expense of another

1 Nov   3 p 4to   Osb
to FBA
I did not think of writing to you again, the

1 Nov   2 p 4to   NYPL(B)
to CB Jr
I meant to *borrow*, not beg, steal, or ravish

1 Nov   3 p 8vo   Osb
to John Wall Callcott
If you will take the trouble of acquainting our

4 Nov   4 p 4to   Osb
from Joseph Cooper Walker
I have derived so much pleasure & instruction

5 Nov [1799]   1 p 4to   Osb
from Samuel Wesley
I address you *at a venture* of speedy success

13 Nov   3 p 4to   Osb
to CB Jr
I read the letter wch. you inclosed to me this

19 Nov   3 p 4to   Osb
to FBA
I have wanted to write to you a good while,

26 Nov   1 p 4to   Hyde
to Edmond Malone
I have only been in London, merely to dine

[post Nov 1799]   1 p 4to   Osb
to [Samuel Wesley]
I was on the point of reminding you of your

1 Dec   2 p 4to   Osb
to FBA
I sh^{d}. not have let this <side> of paper be

14 DE 1799 pmk   1 p 4to   NYPL(B)
to CB Jr
I have got a miserable cold, & am not half well

16 Dec   1 p 8vo   Osb
to [Elizabeth Iremonger]
I have long known the difficulty of arranging

20 Dec [1799]   2 p 4to   NYPL(B)
to CB Jr
Why you Charles! Why will you not write me

22 Dec   3 p 4to   Osb
from Sir William Herschel
On looking over the memoranda that were

24 Dec   2 p 4to   Osb
to FBA
I have been X^{massing} wth. M^{rs}. Crewe from

24 Dec [1799]   2 p fol   Osb
to CB Jr
I rec^{d}. both your letters last night.

[25 Dec]   pmk 1799   2 p 4to   Osb
to CB Jr
I wrote to you yesterday morning from Hamp-

1799, continued

30 Dec   2 p 4to   Osb
to CB Jr
Though your tidings, wch. I had been anxiously

30 Dec [1799]   2 p 4to   Folger
from Edmond Malone
Can you give me any information concerning

30 Dec   1 p 4to   BM(Bar)
from SBP
Oh my beloved Father — once more I tread

31 Dec   2 p 4to   BN(M)
to [Edmond Malone]
Packington's pound is a Tune so frequently

[1799]   20 p 4to   NYPL(B)
from Mrs Crewe
I was mair glad to hear from you, thought it

[c 1799]   2 p 8vo   Osb
to Christian Latrobe
I have been a Scold — miserable ever since I

[1799?]   2 p 4to   Osb
from Benjamin Moseley
I have another complaint against your

[post 1799]   2 p 8vo   Comyn
from Ellis Cornelia Knight
Miss Knight's compliments to D^r. Burney

1800

6 Jan   2 p 4to   Osb
to CB Jr
I went to Slough on Thursday morning, & did

8 Jan   2 p 4to   Osb
to CB Jr and SBP
I can only write you & our dear Susey a bit

8 Jan [1800]   2 p 8vo   Folger
from Edmond Malone
Many thanks for your researches on the subject

9 [Jan]   2 p 4to   Osb
to CB Jr
What a journey had you had! & what a

28 Apr   1 p 4to   Folger
from Edmond Malone
A set of my Dryden, which is to issue forth on

27 May   4 p 4to   Osb
to FBA
You have imposed a melancholy task on me —

28 May   2 p 4to   Osb
to CB Jr
I suppose you had been told, that you were

10 June   2 p 4to   Osb
to FBA
I hope you do not imagine that anything but

26 June   1 p 8vo   BM
to John Wall Callcott
I think it has long been settled among

27 June   1 p fol   Osb
from Gasparo Pacchierotti
Fui deliziato nel leggere il vostro foglio de 17

16 July   1 p 4to   Osb
to John Wall Callcott
Time, like the Sibyl's leaves, becomes more

25 July   ?   BM
to [a publisher]
I am obliged to you for informing me that Dr.

13 Aug   draft   1 p 4to   Osb
to William Locke Jr
Congratulations for a Union where probability

23 Aug [1800]   3 p 4to   Osb
to Mrs Crewe
I fear you will Number me among such

8 Sept   4 p 4to   NYPL(B)
to Mrs Crewe
I am over head & ears in debt wth. you, &

23 Sept   4 p 4to   NYPL(B)
to Mrs Crewe
I have been grubbing at home, without stiring

27 Oct   5 p 4to   NYPL(B)
to Mrs Crewe
I never wished to answer a letter of yours

27 Oct   4 p 4to   NYPL(B)
to Mrs Crewe
A 1000 thanks, dear Madam, for your

13 Nov   4 p 4to   NYPL(B)
to Mrs Crewe
I put off writing till after Tuesday, when there

26 Nov   2 p 4to   NYPL(B)
to Mrs Crewe
I begin a short letter to night, as I am not

8 DE 1800 pmk   1 p 4to   Osb
from William Locke Jr
I am sorry it will not be in my power to attend

[post 1800]   2 p 4to   Osb
to Christian Latrobe
I was obliged to quit the good place in w^{ch}.

[July-Aug post 1800?]   3 p 8vo   Osb
from Lady Bruce
Though I am most exceedingly obliged to you,

[post 1800]   1 p 8vo   Osb
from William Malings
M^{r}. & M^{rs} & Miss Malings are very sorry that

[1800–06]   2 p 8vo   Osb
with Frances (Phillips) Raper to CB Jr
I was sorry not to find you at Salomon's Con-

[1800–06]   draft   2 p 8vo   Osb
to [Christian Latrobe?]
I am just now hurried to death with preparing

15 Oct [1800–07]   2 p 4to   Osb
from Brownlow North
An Expedition to Winchester to pass the Week

1801

13 Jan   copy   1 p 4to   BM
from Thomas Twining
The orato*rium* has amused me

2 Feb   6 p 4to   Osb
to Joseph Cooper Walker
I am involuntarily, & of necessity, a very

also   typescript copy   9 p   Folger

23 Apr   pmk 1801   1 p 8vo   Ryl
to CB Jr
I dined to day at Burlington house, where I

9 May   2 p 4to   Osb
from Ralph Griffiths
It is so long since you & I *shook pens,* that I

27 June   2 p 8vo   Comyn
to CB Jr
M^{rs}. Crewe has often talked in her Notes

[6 July 1801]   2 p 8vo   Osb
to CB Jr
Your note did not arrive here till past 6 on

7 Aug   3 p 8vo   Osb
from [Ellis Cornelia?] Knight
Miss Knight returns her most grateful thanks

31 Aug   2 p 4to   Osb
from Ralph Griffiths
The Book herewith sent tumbled out of the

26 Sept   2 p 4to   Osb
to Mrs Crewe
Now let us have a *chat* — taking it for granted

6 Oct pmk 1801 3 p 4to NYPL(B)
from Miss Dowdeswell
And will not even the joyous prospect of peace

[post 6 Oct 1801]   draft   1 p 4to
to Miss Dowdeswell   NYPL(B)
You are very good to write first, though I had

12 OC 1801 pmk   1 p 8vo   Osb
to CB Jr
You give me no *Streatham tidings* — & I

[13 Oct 1801]   2 p 8vo   Osb
to CB Jr
I am to be at Nolly's on Thursday at ½ past 11,

[31 Oct 1801]   2 p 8vo   Osb
to CB Jr
Come here tomorrow by all means if you can

7 Nov   3 p 4to   NYPL(B)
to Mrs Crewe
I have been ten times a day, for the Lord

10 NO 1801 pmk   3 p 8vo   NYPL(B)
to CB Jr
I was last night at S^{r}. Joseph's and took the

27 Nov [1801?]   1 p 8vo   Comyn
to CB Jr
I shall certainly dine at home on sunday next,

18 Dec   pmk 1801   3 p 4to   Comyn
to CB Jr
Your application to me to interest myself in

20 Dec   4 p 4to   BM
to William Windham
I did myself the honour of calling in Pall-Mall

24 Dec   3 p 4to   Osb
from Brownlow North
That your feelings are at all times alive is

1801, continued

[1801]   2 p 8vo   NYPL(B)
to CB Jr
"A few pleasing words" only for to morrow

[post 1801]   1 p 12mo   NYPL(B)
to [Samuel Wesley]
The weather for some days past has been

[post 1801?]   3 p 8vo   Osb
from Samuel Wesley
Your kind note I would sooner have

[1801–06]   3 p 8vo   Osb
to Mrs Crewe
In answer to your kind remembrance of

[pre 1802]   1 p 8vo   NYPL(B)
from S[amuel] Arnold
I sincerely thank you for the trouble you have

1802

27 Jan   copy   3 p fol   BM
from John Wall Callcott
I have long wished for an opportunity to shew

29 Jan   3 p 4to   Osb
to John Wall Callcott
Your offer of assisting me in my Lexicographic

3 Feb   copy   3 p fol   BM
from John Wall Callcott
I am entirely of your Opinion concerning the

13 Feb   1 p 4to   Osb
from Abraham Rees
You will do me the justice to believe,

17 Feb   2 p 4to   Comyn
to CB Jr
When your note arrived this morn   I was just

13 Mar   2 p 8vo   Osb
to Johann Christian Hüttner
D Burney presents his best Comptm to

[post 8 Apr 1802]   draft   2 p 8vo
to Shute Barrington   NYPL(B)
D B. presents his humble respects to the

9 May   receipt   ⅓ p 4to   Osb
from Anker Smith
Received of D Charles Burney Twenty six

10 May [1802]   1 p 4to   Osb
to CB Jr
Herschel came hither to day to ask me if I c .

20 May   2 p 4to   Osb
to FBA
I waited with impatience for your journal, and,

9 June   2 p 4to   Oxf(Bod)
to Ralph Griffiths
I hasten to acknowledge the Receipt of your

also   draft   2 p 8vo   Osb

12 June   1 p 4to   Shep
to Mr Jones
D Burney presents his Compliments to M .

7 July 18[02]   1 p 4to   StMi
to Mr Doane
I inclose a draught on Messrs Fuller & Co. for

28 July   4 p 4to   Osb
to FBA
I am ashamed of my long silence, but was

1 Aug   1 p 8vo   Oxf(Bod)
to John Wall Callcott
I have comp . and am called on to dinner — I

also   photostat   Osb

4 Aug [1802]   2 p 8vo   Shep
to [Samuel] Arnold
I am very sorry that you have

8 Sept   copy   4 p fol   BM
from John Wall Callcott
I attended the Royal Society of Musicians on

9 Sept   2 p 4to   Osb
to John Wall Callcott
I was ab . to thank you for the book of Laws

12 Sept   copy   2 p fol   BM
from John Wall Callcott
If You wish for a Copy of the Charter I will

24 Sept   2 p 4to   Osb
to John Wall Callcott
I have been very little at home for the last

25 Sept   copy   4 p fol   BM
from John Wall Callcott
I am much gratified by Your kind favour &

25 SP 1802 pmk   4 p 4to   NYPL(B)
from Mrs Crewe
It does not signify talking, but I must have a

27 Sept   4 p 4to   NYPL(B)
to Mrs Crewe
I have thought it very long since I heard

[c Sept 1802]   2 p 4to   Osb
to Catherine (Graham) Greville
I am extremely sorry to find that this

5 Oct   copy   2 p fol   BM
from John Wall Callcott
I made the following Extracts on Sunday

9 Oct [1802]   copy   2 p fol   BM
from John Wall Callcott
Do you mean to insert the word LEGER or

9 Oct   2 p 4to   Osb
to John Wall Callcott
I have no doubt that a *Leger-line* in Music is

12 Oct   2 p 4to   Oxf(Bod)
to Ralph Griffiths
The melancholy account wch. you gave of the

also   draft   3 p 8vo   Osb

16 Oct [1802?]   3 p 4to   Osb
to Mrs Crewe
I have thought it long since I wrote to you,

25 Oct   2 p 4to   Prin
to William Ayrton
The performance of the very melancholy duty

31 Oct   4 p 4to   NYPL(B)
to Mrs Crewe
I have for some days been creaking & croaking

19 NO 1802 pmk   3 p 4to   Osb
to Mrs Crewe
I know, you are now saying "inwardly" — *My*

24 Nov   1 p 4to   Osb
from Sir William Hamilton
Sir W^m. Hamilton presents his Comp^ts. to

[6] Dec [1802]   2 p 4to   Osb
to Mrs Crewe
It grieves me when I cannot answer your

[post 6 Dec 1802?]   2 p 4to   Osb
to Samuel Wesley
Those that seldom go to a concert or Theatre

23 Dec   2 p 4to   NYPL(B)
to Mrs Crewe
Your are so indulgent to my scraps, such as

28 Dec   2 p 8vo   Comyn
to CB Jr
I yesterday rec^d. a very long letter

23 [?]   1 p 4to   Oxf(Bod)
to Edmond Malone
I am always flattered by your

24 June [post 1802?]   1 p 4to   Osb
from Abbé Morellet
je prens la liberté de rappeler à votre souvenir

[1802]   draft   4 p 8vo   Osb
to Anne (Home) Hunter
When ever I am honoured wth the present of a

[1802–06]   draft   2 p 4to   Osb
to Anne (Home) Hunter
Though the Philosoph Godwyn tells us that

[1802–07?]   draft   2 p 8vo   Osb
to Mrs Fermor & Miss Willes
my time To save (of wch I have little left) &

[1802–12]   3 p 8vo   Osb
to CB Jr
Your doings & calculations are all clear &

13 Jan [pre 1803]   2 p 4to   Osb
from Ralph Griffiths [to CB?]
For these 6 or 7 weeks have I been scheming

21 Feb [pre 1803]   3 p 4to   Osb
from Ralph Griffiths
It is a sad acc^t. my Dear Sir, that I have heard,

31 Dec [pre 1803]   3 p fol   Osb
from Ralph Griffiths
A thousand thanks to my kind Friend, for the

[pre 1803]   2 p 4to   Osb
from Ralph Griffiths
Your Letter, written the day after your return

1803

13 Jan   copy   4 p fol   BM
from John Wall Callcott
Whenever I am silent for a considerable time

14 Jan   1 p 8vo   Osb
to Edmund Ayrton
Dr. Burney, on his return home yesterday, was

14 Jan   3 p 8vo   Osb
to John Wall Callcott
I have been sorry not to be able to appoint a

14 Jan   1 p 4to   Osb
to Christian Latrobe
I shall not set abt. telling you how anxiously &

24 Jan [1803?]   amanuensis   2 p 4to
from Christian Latrobe   Osb
For your very generous punctuality in sending

26 Jan   2 p 4to   Osb
from Jamard
Jaurois dù vous écrire aussitôt après mon

9 Feb   ½ p fol   Osb
from Joseph Plymley
Archdeacon Plymley found the enclosed paper

23 Feb   3 p 4to   Osb
from Gasparo Pacchierotti
Fui colpito da un colpo di fulmine all'esordio

25 MR 1803 pmk   1 p 8vo   Osb
to CB Jr
Its a word & a blow, wth. you — your note had

5 May   pmk 1803   2 p 8vo   NYPL(B)
to CB Jr
The powers, the *power of business* every one

12 MY 1803 pmk   1 p 4to   NYPL(B)
to CB Jr
I hasten to thank you for thinking of me

16 MY 1803 pmk   2 p 4to   Osb
to Rosette (Rose) Burney
I rejoice very much that you are sufficiently

27 JU 180[3] pmk   1 p 4to   NYPL(B)
to CB Jr
I was sorry not to meet you at Hampstead

15 July   3 p 4to   Osb
from Christian Latrobe
Your kind letter I duly recd. and wish I may

22 Aug [1803]   1 p 8vo   Osb
to CB Jr
I am on the wing — & intend setting off for

4 Sept [1803]   2 p 8vo   Osb
to CB Jr
Mrs. Crewe will have told you my opinion abt.

20 Sept [c 1803?]   1 p 4to   Comyn
from John Courtenay [to CB]
I enclose your two songs, as you were formerly

20 Sept [1803]   3 p 4to   Shep
to Joseph Cooper Walker
I am always to have apologies to make

26 Sept [1803 misdated 1801]   3 p 4to
to Mrs Crewe   Osb
Without stop or stay, except to change horses

6 Oct   3 p 4to   Oxf(Bod)
to Edmond Malone
I have not been returned from Cheltenham

19 OC 1803 pmk   4 p 4to   Osb
to Mrs Crewe
Thanks for your scrap. I am sorry you go on

3 Nov   pmk 1803   2 p 8vo   Comyn
to CB Jr
Will you, Rosette, & Carluch, dine here on

14 Nov   1 p 8vo   Osb
to John Wall Callcott
Though I have no doubt of the abilities

18 Nov   3 p 4to   NYPL(B)
to Mrs Crewe
I go out so little that I have no opportunity of

[post Nov 1803]   draft   2 p 4to   Osb
to Lady Mary Lowther
You never manifested a more gratifying agree-

[1803–05]   2 p 8vo   NYPL(B)
to CB Jr
I have this morning been honoured with a very

[post 1803]   draft   1 p 4to   Osb
to Lady Banks
I am eager to thank your Ladp. for so

[pre 1804]   draft   2 p 8vo   Osb
to [Thomas Twining]
Your worthy frd. and Dr. C provoke me to say

[pre 1804]　copy　1 p fol　BM
from Thomas Twining
with you both. The former part of this letter

[pre 1804?]　1 p 8vo　Osb
from Frederic, 5th Earl of Guilford
　[to CB?]
Will you do me the Favour of passing

1804

9 [Jan]　3 p 4to　NYPL(B)
to Mrs Crewe
Why what a dead silence! you promised to tell

24 JA 1804 pmk　1 p 4to　Osb
to Rosette (Rose) Burney
You have sent me a long letter of apologies for

25 Apr　3 p 4to　Osb
from Cecilia Maria Henslow
I have long had it in my mind to take the

[post 25 Apr 1804?]　draft　4 p 8vo
to Cecilia Maria Henslow　Osb
There is no one of Dr Arne's family, frds. or

26 Apr [1804]　½ p 4to　Osb
from [Cecilia Maria Henslow]
According to Promise, I take the earliest

30 Apr　1 p 8vo　Osb
to Cecilia Maria Henslow
God knows who will live to see! For the letter

10 May　copy extract　7 p LB　Osb
to Thomas Twining
I cannot like the Grassini, the new opera

19 May　amanuensis　1 p 4to　Osb
from Franz Josef Haydn
J'ai reçu hier une lettre de monsieur Salomon

28 May　2 p 4to　Osb
to Rosette (Rose) Burney
I am all hurry & perturbation at this time of

15 July　2 p 4to　Osb
from William Lowther, *later* Lord
　Lonsdale
Dont imagine I am laying a Trap to draw you

20 July　2 p 4to　Osb
to Christian Latrobe
A Lady of high rank, for whom I have a great

July　2 p 8vo　Osb
to William Lowther, *later* Lord Lonsdale
I never was more gratefully flattered than by

13 Aug [1804]　draft　2 p 8vo　Osb
to [Richard Twining]
Ah! my dear Sir! What an afflicting &

1 Sept　3 p 8vo　Osb
to CB Jr
Will you present my best Compts. to Mr. Foss

12 Sept　3 p 4to　Osb
to Mrs [Thomas] Blore
After so long lamenting the ideal loss of that

21 Sept　1 p 4to　Osb
to CB Jr
After remaining in Clover, at Bulstrode, from

28 Sept　3 p 8vo　Osb
to CB Jr
I have done every thing in my power to get my

2 Oct　pmk 1804　2 p 8vo　Osb
to CB Jr
I have not yet seen Mr. <Glandhill>, he did

2 Oct　4 p 4to　NYPL(B)
to Mrs Crewe
In the midst of all your sights, hospitalities, &

5 Oct　3 p 8vo　Osb
to CB Jr
Thank you for calling on the Robinsons & for

23 Oct　draft　3 p 8vo　Osb
to Samuel Hoole
Though there are no people whom the world

31 Oct　1 p 8vo　NYPL(B)
to CB Jr
I have just recd. a letter from the Robinsons

2 Nov　2 p 4to　Shep
to George & John Robinson
after being much alarmed for myself, I was

3 Nov [1804?]　1 p 8vo　Oxf(Bod)
to Edmond Malone
I want to know very much

1804, continued

5 Nov [1804]   2 p 4to   Osb
to Christian Latrobe
I believe I never before suffered a letter of

⟨27⟩ pmk   Nov   4 p 4to   Osb
to Mrs [Thomas?] Blore
Your very kind & flattering letter certainly

11 Dec   pmk 1804   1 p 4to   Belf
to George, 1st Earl Macartney
I was in Town on Saturday last, and in visiting

13 DE 1804 pmk   2 p 8vo   Osb
to CB Jr
You are but a shabby fellow, in the way of

25 Dec   2 p 4to   NYPL(B)
to Rosette (Rose) Burney
However prepared we may be for the loss of

26 Dec   1 p 4to   Osb
from Richard Wroughton
There is not either Score or Harpsichord Part

[post 1804?]   draft   1 p scrap   Osb
to [Richard Twining]
As I was extremely [tear] from the long

[1804–06]   1 p fragment   Osb
to ?
I was so unwilling to put a negative on your

[pre 1805?]   ½ p 4to   Osb
from [Arthur?] Murphy
Mr. Murphy to see Docr. Burney ⟨revived⟩,

1805

14 [Jan]   3 p 8vo   Coke
to CB Jr
I wish you wd. look at a newspaper for the

17 Feb   8 p 4to   Coke
to William Crotch
Much as I want leisure, I am glad that you

15 Mar   1 p 4to   Osb
to Rosette (Rose) Burney
It has vexed me that I have not been able to

16 Mar   1 p 4to   NYPL(B)
from Samuel Rogers [to CB?]
What can I say to You in return for so much

24 Mar   2 p 8vo   Osb
to Christian Latrobe
I am much obliged to you for furnishing me

31 May   1 p 4to   Osb
with Frances (Phillips) Raper to FBA
The notice I recd. of our good friend Miss

10 June   pmk 1805   3 p 8vo   Osb
to CB Jr
I must relate to you the adventures of last

10 June   1 p 4to   NYPL(B)
to GMAPWaddington
The enclosed letter is just arrived —

12 July   copy   2 p 4to   NYPL(B)
to FBA
Your Brother Dr. Charles, and I, have had the

12 July   2 p 4to   NYPL(B)
to GMAPWaddington
It grieved me extremely to lose you so

27 Aug [1805]   3 p 4to   Osb
to Mrs Crewe
Abt. 2 hours after my letter was sent to the

12 Sept   3 p 4to   NYPL(B)
to GMAPWaddington
Pour entrer en matiere, *sans phrase,*

19 Sept   2 p 4to   Osb
from James Bindley
I suppose you & I are the only two Men in

31 Oct   pmk 1805   2 p 8vo   Osb
to CB Jr
I came home last Friday, dog tired, &

31 Oct   2 p 8vo   Osb
to Christian Latrobe
I have been scampering almost all over the

4 Nov   1 p 4to   Osb
to William Crotch
I am not certain whether I had the face to

[1805]   3 p 8vo   Osb
to Mrs Crewe
I have not been in the city since X^mas. till

[c 1805?]   draft   1 p 4to   NYPL(B)
to Longman Rees & Co
D^r. Burney presents his Comp^ts. to Messrs.

[Jan pre 1806]   2 p 4to   Osb
to Mrs Crewe
the objections to the present plan of raising

[pre 1806?]   draft   1 p 4to   Osb
to ?
I am sorry to say that a week will not be suffi-

[pre 1806]   1 p 8vo   Osb
to Edmond Malone
My cough is but *baddish*, & the weather much

22 Feb [pre 1806]   1 p 8vo   NYPL(B)
from Caroline Calvert
If you can favour us by taking your dinner

[pre 1806]   1 p 8vo   Osb
from Margaret Bingham, Countess of
   Lucan
It is very long I think since I have seen you —

1806

16 Jan   2 p 4to   Osb
from James Wyatt
Your Letter of the 13th Ins^t. has given me real

21 Feb   1 p 4to   Osb
from Joseph Cooper Walker
These lines will be presented to you by Mr.

16 Apr   3 p 4to   Comyn
to CB Jr
I am glad you begin to feel

18 Apr   3 p 4to   BM
to Lady Crewe
I had been so long hopeless as to Place or

19 Apr   2 p 4to   Comyn
to CB Jr
Thanks for your congratulations — I hope for

23 Apr   2 p 8vo   Comyn
to CB Jr
Much obliged for your Garrickiana —

24 Apr   3 p 4to   Osb
to Lady Crewe
I had been so long hopeless as to place or

8 May   1 p 4to   Bord
to Lady Banks
Dr Burney presents his best respects to Lady

4 June   2 p 4to   Osb
from Henry Harington
I am sorry that Your good Daughter gave you

17 June   2 p 4to   Osb
to T J Mathias
You c^d not have gratified me more by the

14 July   copy   6 p 4to   Osb
from John Phillipps
D^r. Burney's Hypothesis concerning the

19 July   pmk 1806   2 p 8vo   Osb
to Rosette (Rose) Burney
You well know what a hurry I am always in,

29 July   draft   2 p 4to   Coke
to Sir Joseph Banks
previous to my plunging into a subject w^ch.

29 July   with draft   5 p 4to   BM
to [John Phillipps]
Previous to my plunging into a subjcct [sic]

30 July   2 p 4to   Osb
to FBA
I shall not fill my letter, after such a long

1 Aug   4 p 4to   Osb
from Lady Mary Lowther
You have ever showed so kind an interest in

4 Aug   2 p 4to   Osb
from Sir Joseph Banks
In Return for your very Obliging Communica-

19 AU 1806 pmk   2 p 8vo   NYPL(B)
to CB Jr
F.P. & I set out for Hetty's Cottage, at M^rs.

22 AU 1806 pmk   2 p 8vo   Osb
to CB Jr
I have been at Bulstrode, and came away a

30 Aug   2 p 4to   NYPL(B)
to CB Jr
I begin to be uneasy at not having heard

1806, continued

3 Sept   1 p 4to   Osb
from Princess Charlotte (per M Udney)
Her Royal Highness The Princess Charlotte

17 Sept   3 p 4to   Osb
to CPB
You have long been a Cathedral hunter, & I

28 Sept [1806]   2 p 4to   Osb
from Gasparo Pacchierotti
Nel leggere la grata vostra del primo andante

[post Sept 1806]   draft   2 p 8vo   Osb
to Mrs Fermor & Miss Willes
I returned to Chelsea from Bath on Michs. day

[post Sept 1806]   draft   2 p 8vo   Osb
to [John] Flaxman
I went to the Bristol hotwell the latter end of

9 Oct   4 p 4to   NYPL(B)
to FBA
Your sweet friend, & I now hope, mine, having

12 Oct   1 p 4to   Osb
to FBA
The dear Made. D<   > is to dine with

22 OC 1806 pmk   1 p 4to   Osb
to CB Jr
The day before yesterday a gentleman brought

31 Oct   pmk 1806   1 p 4to   Osb
to CB Jr
I had a proof last night from Strahans — &

7 Nov   1 p 4to   Osb
to CB Jr
I have 4 Vols. of your old News-papers in

8 Nov   1 p 4to   BM
from JB
One Map came to me with Dr. Vincent's

9 Nov   3 p 4to   Oxf(Bod)
to Edmond Malone
I understood you that the obliging Mr.

11 Nov   2 p 4to   Osb
from John Belfour
Mr. Belfour presents his Compts to Dr.

12 Nov   2 p 8vo   Osb
to John Belfour
It grieves me to acquaint you, that the task

[post 12 Nov 1806?]   2 p 8vo   Osb
to John Belfour
The rapidity & gratification wth. which I have

17 NO 1806 pmk   1 p 4to   Osb
to CB Jr
I see a new edition of a Latin book advertised

17 Nov   3 p 4to   NYPL(B)
to Lady Crewe
Your Jolities [sic] please me in the *Echo* very

27 Nov   2 p 4to   Oxf(Bod)
to Edmond Malone
I have longed to see you & to thank you

[9? Dec 1806]   4 p 8vo   Comyn
from Lady Crewe
This is merely to say that I find it will not be in

18 Dec [1806?]   1 p 4to   Oxf(Bod)
to Edmond Malone
I hope you had a good Club yesterday; it

23 Dec   1 p 4to   Folger
from Edmond Malone
I wrote a few lines by the two penny post on

[1806?]   1 p 4to   Osb
from Lady Bruce
Lord Bruce saw the Catalani last Night, and

[1806?]   2 p 8vo   Osb
from Mr Lee
Mr. Lee's compts to Dr. Burney informs him

[1806?]   draft   2 p 8vo   Osb
to ?
I never was much more angry wth. myself,

[post 1806]   draft   1 p scrap   Osb
to ?
Now obliged me to <   > [tear] with wch. I

[post 1806]   draft   2 p 4to   Osb
to Lady Crewe
Though I am partly "as well as can be

[post 1806]   draft   2 p 8vo   Osb
to Lady Crewe
I shall begin my answer & thanks for your

[post 1806?]   draft   2 p 8vo   Osb
to Lord Cardigan
My cough has been extremely troublesome to

[post 1806]   5 p 4to   Osb
to Lady Crewe
It appears, by the news-papers, that the D.

[post 1806]   draft   1 p scrap   Osb
to Sir David Dundas
Dr. Burney presents his Respects to the Rt.

[post 1806]   draft   2 p 4to   Osb
to Elizabeth Iremonger
Why, you naughty Donna della Casa bianca

[post 1806]   draft   1 p 8vo   NYPL(B)
to Elizabeth, Lady Templetown
Dr. B. presents his most humble respects to

[1806–07]   2 p 8vo   NYPL(B)
to CB Jr
I grieve much for your sufferings and sincerely

[1806–07]   1 p 12mo   Comyn
from Henry Harington
Dr Harington's Comps to Dr Burney and is

[1806–07]   2 p 4to   Osb
from Lady Manvers
No words can express the Concern I felt at

[1806–10]   draft   2 p 8vo   Osb
to Lady Crewe
as before; and expected a letter from

[post 1806?]   draft   1 p scrap   Osb
to Lady Bruce
O my ever dear and kind Lady Bruce, by what

[post 1806?]   draft   1 p 12mo   Osb
to Lady Bruce
when I finished the letter of [blank] I was in

21 Sept [post 1806]   3 p 8vo   Osb
from Lady Bruce
I have been perfectly unable to comprehend

[pre 1807]   1 p 4to   Osb
to Rosette (Rose) Burney
I am lame of my right hand, from gout,

1807

[post 1 Jan 1807]   draft   1 p 8vo   Osb
to Lord Cardigan
I can no longer postpone my thanks for your

3 Jan   3 p 4to   NYPL(B)
to Lady Crewe
I have not written to Cheshire for a long time

[c 3 Jan 1807]   draft   2 p 8vo   Osb
to Lady Bruce
Nothing is so consoling and chearing under my

16 Jan   1 p 8vo   Osb
to CB Jr
I caught cold, either on Wedy. in my Visit at

17 Jan ⟨1807⟩   1 p 4to   Osb
from Lord Cardigan
I am much obliged to you for the favor of your

18 Jan   1 p 8vo   Osb
to CB Jr
How are you this morning? I was better of my

21 Jan   2 p 4to   Ryl
to HLTP
I was so animated by the honour of your visit,
also   2 drafts   3 p 8vo & 4to   Osb

21 Jan   1 p 4to   Hyde
to HLTP
We are not come to a right understanding yet.

21 Jan   2 p 4to   Osb
from HLTP
Dear Doctor Burney has no Reason to

24 Jan   2 p 4to   Ryl
to HLTP
It is with deep regret, that I submit to the

29 Jan   copy   1 p 4 to   Osb
from Longman & Co (in AL CB & F
    Raper to CB Jr 4 Feb 1807)
"Dr. Rees is aground for want of more Articles

2 Feb [1807]   copy   1 p 4to   Osb
from Andrew Spottiswood (in ALS CB
    to CB Jr 4 Mar 1807)
"I write to inform you that the Copy wch. was

[post 2 Feb 1807]   draft   1 p 4to
to ?   Osb
I had had a very pleasing account of my dear

4 Feb   3 p 4to   Osb
with Frances (Phillips) Raper to CB Jr
I want very much to know how your cold and

14 Feb   3 p 4to   Folger
from Edmond Malone
My brother and his family arrived here from

1807, continued

4 Mar   2 p 4to   Osb
to CB Jr
Your long silence made me uneasy for you, &

6 Mar   2 p 4to   NYPL(B)
to Johann Christian Hüttner
The letter wᶜʰ. you did me the favour to

also   draft dated 6 Feb   2 p 4to   Osb

14 Mar   3 p 4to   Comyn
to Johann Christian Hüttner
I was sorry that in my hurry to answer your

also   draft   2 p 4to   Osb

[post Mar 1807]   draft   1 p 8vo   Osb
to John Courtenay
After a dreadful state of health ever since my

22 Apr – 2 May [1807]   amanuensis
to Dr Caleb Hillier Parry   3 p 4to   Osb
After receiving such benefit under your

12 MY 1807 pmk   1 p 8vo   Osb
to CB Jr
You and James will soon hear from Mʳ.

23 May [1807?]   2 p 4to   Osb
from Mary (Palmer), Marchioness of
     Thomond
I ought to make a thousand apologies for not

22 June   2 p 8vo   Osb
from T J Mathias to [CB?]
This morning I had done myself the pleasure

3 July   4 p 8vo   Osb
with Frances (Phillips) Raper to Rosette
     (Rose) Burney
I heard of your terrible sufferings at the time

4 July   2 p 8vo   NYPL(B)
to Lady Crewe
Though I very much long to see your new

15 July   2 p 4to   Oxf(Bod)
to Lord Charles Bruce
My ever dear & too kind Lord. 10,000 thanks

17 July   3 p 4to   NYPL(B)
to CBFB
After more than usual difficulties in leaving

23 July   2 p 4to   Oxf(Bod)
to Edmond Malone
I have recᵈ. a letter in the most illegible hand,

24 July [1807]   draft?   2 p 4to
                                    BM(Bar)
to Thomas, 1st Earl of Ailesbury
The flattering note with wᶜʰ your Lordᵖ

25 July   4 p 4to   Folger
from Edmond Malone
Our old friend Boswell's second Son, whose

27 July   3 p 4to   NYPL(B)
to Lady Crewe
I arrived here the day after I had the honour

[28 July 1807]   2 p 4to   NYPL(B)
to Johann Christian Hüttner
I shall be extremely mortified if you have not

2 Aug   2 p 4to   Oxf(Bod)
to Edmond Malone
Your account of Mʳˢ. Boswell frights me —

15 Aug   4 p 4to   Osb
to Johann Christian Hüttner
Your letter of the 28ᵗʰ. ult. afflicted and

31 Aug   draft   2 p 4to   Osb
to Thomas, 1st Earl of Ailesbury
I am totally unable to express my thanks &

7 Sept   2 p 4to   Osb
to Lady Crewe
I have been here a week in good quarters &

2 Oct   4 p 4to   Osb
to [Lady Crewe?]
A chasm in our habitual correspondence of so

13 Oct   4 p 4to   Osb
from Lord Lonsdale
If I could not suppose you could not give

16 Oct   1 p 4to   Cal(B)
to Johann Christian Hüttner
Though I did not answer your most reasonable,

[26 Oct 1807]   2 p 4to   Osb
to Johann Christian Hüttner
I fear you will think it long ere Lord Lonsdale

27 Oct   pmk 1807   2 p 8vo   Osb
to Johann Christian Hüttner
I hasten to assure you that the happiness which

1 Nov   3 p 8vo   Osb
from Lord Lonsdale
Fifty pounds are well bestow'd in producing

5 Nov   2 p 8vo   Osb
to Johann Christian Hüttner
Only a word or two to let you know that *our*

9 Nov   draft   2 p 4to   Osb
to Lady Mary Lowther
How perverse is the order of small human

[post 9 Nov 1807]   draft   1 p 4to   Osb
to Louisa M Harris
When Dr. Johnson lost his friend Mr. Thrale

10 Dec   6 p 4to   Osb
from Lady Mary Lowther
Do not imagine that you alone are

24 Dec   5 p 4to   Osb
to Lady Crewe
The Moment I had perused your Ladyship's

[post 25 Dec 1807]   draft   1 p scrap
to Lord _____?   Osb
Having always had the honour of being treated

26 Dec [1807]   draft   2 p 8vo   Osb
to Anna (Dillingham) Ord
though unable to venture of my lofty apartmt.

29 Dec   2 p 4to   Osb
from Anna (Dillingham) Ord
The kind Remembrance of an old Friend, my

[1807?]   draft   2 p 8vo   NYPL(B)
to ?
There is no cordial to age & infirmities so

[c 1807]   4 p 8vo   NYPL(B)
to CB Jr
You "hope that I have gotten my books"! upon

[1807?]   draft   2 p fol   NYPL(B)
to Sir Walter Farquhar
I am unwilling to leave "this Valley of Tears"

[1807?]   2 p 4to   Osb
to Mrs Fermor
I thought frequently of you & your worthy

[1807?]   draft   ½ p fol   Osb
to Elizabeth Iremonger
How kind are the intentions della Carissima

[c 1807?]   draft   2 lines   Osb
to Elizabeth Anne (Smart) LeNoir
Mrs Le Noir, with directions how & where to

[c 1807?]   draft   ½ p fol   Osb
to [Brownlow North?]
My dear friendly and most kind Lord Bishop,

[c 1807?]   draft   2 p 8vo   Osb
to Lord Charles Bruce
My ever most constant, kind & friendly Lord

[c 1807?]   draft   ½ p fol   Osb
to Lord Charles Bruce & Lady Bruce
Dr. B. in return for Ld. & Ly. Bruce's very kind

[c 1807?]   draft   2 p 8vo   Osb
to [Lady Mary? Lowther]
I began to think you a little undutiful in not

[post 1807]   1 p 8vo   Osb
to CB Jr
We had so many courtly things to discuss, that

[post 1807]   3 p 8vo   Hyde
to Lord Lonsdale
When Dr. Johnson, a firm believer in the

5 Dec [post 1807]   1 p 4to   Osb
from [Jean-Gabriel] Peltier
M. Peltier a l'honneur de présenter ses devoirs

[post 1807]   draft?   1 p 8vo
NYPL(B)
from Frances (Phillips) Raper
We shall be truely happy to accept your very

[1807–10?]   2 p 8vo   Osb
to Lady Mary Lowther
As almost every body in their younger days has

[1807–12?]   2 p 4to   Osb
to Lady Bruce
How much and how long have I languished

[1807–12]   draft   1 p 8vo   Osb
to President & Council of the Royal
    Academy
Dr. Burney presents his best compliments &

1808

9 Jan   2 p 8vo   Osb
to CPB
I have not been able to thank you for your

Jan   6 p 4to   Osb
to Lady Crewe
If I did know the old trick of persons of great

1 Feb   2 p 4to   Osb
to Lady Crewe
I fear my thanks for your funny & very

24 Feb   2 p 4to   Oxf(Bod)
to Edmond Malone
I hasten to thank you for your curious &

25 Feb   3 p 4to   Osb
to Lady Banks
I did not know that your Ladyship had a

25 Feb   1 p 4to   BM
to Arthur Young
Your letter has given me great pleasure, in

27 Feb [1808]   2 p 4to   Osb
to Lady Crewe
How good it is of Your Lad^p. to let a body

27 Feb   3 p 4to   Osb
from Lord Lonsdale
To say I have been as active as I ought to have

also   copy   2 p 4to   Osb

29 Feb   1 p 4to   Osb
to Johann Christian Hüttner
It grieved me that I c^d. not immediately on the

4 Mar   3 p 4to   Osb
to Johann Christian Hüttner
I am sorry you tormented yourself with

9 Mar   pmk 1808   1 p 4to   Osb
to Johann Christian Hüttner
I rather fear that my last letter will seem to

9 Mar   4 p 4to   Osb
from Sir Uvedale Price
I have lately been employed in defending, to

13 Mar   1 p 8vo   Osb
from David, 11th Earl of Buchan
Lord Buchan begs leave to recommend young

16 Mar   2 p 4to   Hyde
to David, 11th Earl of Buchan
I had the honour of your Lordship's note,

also   draft   1 p 8vo   Osb

22 Mar   1 p 4to   Osb
from David, 11th Earl of Buchan
I write, I say Dear, for Dear to me is every

22 Mar   2 p 4to   Osb
from Samuel Wesley
Although your many and important

[post 22 Mar 1808]   draft   2 p 8vo
to Samuel Wesley   Osb
Your remembrance after (I do believe)

4 Apr [1808?]   draft   1 p 8vo   Osb
to Mrs Fermor & Miss Willes
D^r. B was preparing to sally forth this morning

10 Apr   2 p 4to   Osb
to David, 11th Earl of Buchan
The gracious manner with wch. your Lordship

also   draft   1 p scrap   Osb

11 Apr   1 p 4to   Osb
to Lady Banks
After being 5 Weeks confined to my bed & my

12 Apr [1808]   3 p 4to   Osb
from Samuel Wesley
Your kind letter has reached me only 5 minutes

14 Apr [1808]   1 p 8vo   Osb
from Charles Wesley Jr
I have sent your letter to Linley, who will be

14 Apr [1808]   draft   2 p 4to   Osb
to Lady Crewe
D^r. B. is codling himself during this terrible

4 May   draft   4 p 8vo   Osb
to Lady Bruce
Most dear & honoured L^r. Bruce will I humbly

5 May   2 p 4to   PML
to [Edmond Malone?]
In pursuance of my promise, I enclose you a

7 May   draft   ¼ p 4to   Osb
to James Ord
After having been honoured with the steady,

8 May   1 p 8vo   Osb
to Lady Banks
Dr Burney presents his best respects to Lady

13 May   2 p 4to   Osb
to CB Jr
I have now an opportunity of appointing a

20 May [1808]   1 p 8vo   Osb
to CB Jr
If, as usually happens, you come to Town

20 May   3 p 4to   Osb
to Johann Christian Hüttner
I am again thrown back into my bed room —

22 May   2 p 4to   Osb
to Johann Christian Hüttner
I never was more shocked in my life than by

[23 May 1808]   3 p 4to   Osb
to Johann Christian Hüttner
Be assured that I feel for and participate in

[26 May 1808]   2 p 4to   Osb
to Johann Christian Hüttner
I have been out this morn^g. making a visit to

26 May   6 p 4to   Osb
from Johann Christian Hüttner
Having yesterday, by the interment of my

28 MY 1808 pmk   1 p 4to   Osb
to CB Jr
I am made very happy to night (Thursday)

[28–29 May 1808]   2 p 4to   Osb
to Johann Christian Hüttner
A letter to our dear & best of Lords, was

30 May   2 p 4to   Osb
to Johann Christian Hüttner
To simplify our business as much as possible,

31 May   2 p 4to   Osb
to CB Jr
I must own that there was nothing I so much

1 June   1 p 4to   Osb
to Johann Christian Hüttner
I am all hurry this morning, & preparing to go

1 June   2 p 4to   Osb
to Johann Christian Hüttner
I was sorry to send you such a scrap of an

4 June   2 p 4to   BM(Bar)
to Martha (Allen) Young
Your huge packet frightened me —

7 June [1808]   1 p 4to   Osb
to Johann Christian Hüttner
I hope you have not been surprised or uneasy

8 June [1808?]   2 p 8vo   Oxf(Bod)
to Edmond Malone
I cannot rest till I have explained to you

8 June   4 p 4to   Folger
from Edmond Malone
I was just going to answer your letter of

10 June   5 p 4to   Oxf(Bod)
to Edmond Malone
Your reply to my long, catechistical, &

12 June   copy   2 p 4to   NYPL(B)
to FBA
The complaint made in one of two short notes

17 June 18[08]   3 p 4to   NYPL(B)
to CB Jr
You are a good-natured fellow for taking my

23 June [1808?]   1 p fol   Oxf(Bod)
to Edmond Malone
I know not how to thank you to my mind

23 June [1808?]   2 p 4to   Osb
from Samuel Wesley
I cannot advance a Step without your Advice

24 June   1 p 4to   Comyn
to CB Jr
I was much grieved to receive so melancholy

26 June   2 p 4to   Osb
to Johann Christian Hüttner
Your last letter was so cordial, that I collected

[30 June 1808]   1 p 12mo   Osb
to Johann Christian Hüttner
I left off abruptly this morn^g. & said I w^d.

[30 June 1808]   1 p 4to   Osb
from Johann Christian Hüttner
The enclosed was just going to be sent to You

2 July   pmk 1808   2 p 8vo   NYPL(B)
to CB Jr
I have set poor Huttner's mind, & his affairs,

1808, continued

2 July   2 p 4to   Osb
to Johann Christian Hüttner
Fearful, on reflexion, that I had been a little

4 July [1808]   3 p 8vo   Comyn
to CB Jr
I was not without hopes of having a glimpse

4 July   2 p 4to   Osb
from Johann Christian Hüttner
The noble present which You have sent me

[post 5 July 1808]   photostat of draft
     6 p 8vo   Osb
to Lord Lonsdale
I have wanted extremely to give your Lord^p.

[6 July 1808]   2 p 4to   Osb
to Johann Christian Hüttner
I can only *acknowledge* the rec^t. of your two

also   draft   2 p 8vo   Osb

7 July   3 p 4to   Osb
from Charles Wesley Jr
I am just returned from the Cambridge

9 July   3 p 4to   Oxf(Bod)
to Edmond Malone
I procured the last G. Magazine

10 July   3 p 4to   Osb
to Johann Christian Hüttner
How I envy you your Office — Pens, Ink, &

23 July [1808]   2 p 4to   Osb
to Johann Christian Hüttner
How do you do? — I hope tranquil, &

26 July   3 p 4to   Osb
to Johann Christian Hüttner
I wrote you a longish letter ab^t. a fortnight

26 July   copy   2 p 4to   Osb
to George Canning (included in ALS
     CB to J C Hüttner same date)
"I am extremely flattered & gratified by your

[c 26] July [1808]   2 p 4to   Osb
from George Canning (included in ALS
     CB to J C Hüttner 26 July 1808)
You wrote to me last year on behalf of a

27 July   4 p 4to   Osb
from Lord Lonsdale
The ordinary Excuse of constant Occupation,

[July 1808]   draft   2 p 4to   Osb
to Johann Christian Hüttner
I am extremely shocked, after your boasting of

[c July 1808]   draft   2 p 8vo   Osb
to Charles Long, Baron Farnborough
The notice wth. wch. you have been pleased to

[July 1808]   2 p 4to   Osb
to Lord Lonsdale
As, contrary to my expectations, after such an

July   ?   Colb30
from Samuel Wesley
. . . this Journey has advanced Sebastian Bach's

12 Aug   2 p 4to   Osb
from Edward Bunting
Having devoted 14 or 15 Years of my Life in

14 Aug   3 p 8vo   Osb
from Lord Lonsdale
I take the opportunity of the <return> of the

16 Aug   2 p 4to   Osb
to CB Jr
You give us not an acct. of your coasting

18 Sept   pmk <1808>   1 p 4to   Osb
to CB Jr
I returned to Chelsea from Tunbridge last

24 Sept   draft   2 p fol   Osb
to Edward Bunting
I never c^d. subscribe to the wild assertion of

11 Oct [1808]   1 p 4to   NYPL(B)
to CB Jr
I have been very uneasy ab^t. you for some

17 Oct   3 p 8vo   Osb
to Samuel Wesley
I am glad you like M^r. <Horn>; I have never

23 Oct [1808]   1 p 4to   Osb
from Lord Cardigan
I have many thanks to return to you for a very

25 Oct   2 p 4to   Comyn
to CB Jr
I *must* thank you for your 2^d. kind Cargo of

27 Oct   draft   1 p 4to   Osb
to Lady Crewe
I take it for granted that your Lad^p. is, if not

29 Oct   draft   1 p fol   Osb
to Lord Cardigan
I wish I c^d. have the honour & happiness of

12 Nov   3 p 4to   NYPL(B)
to FBA
The complaints made in one of the two short

20 Nov   draft   3 p fol   BM
to Louisa Margaret Harris
I have in my life been hon^d. wth. some very

30 Nov   receipt   ½ p 4to   NYPL(B)
from R[ichar]d Fuller & Co
Messrs Rd. Fuller & Co presents compliments

Nov [c 1808?]   draft   2 p 8vo   Osb
to Lady Banks
As Sir Joseph was not very stout when he left

[Nov 1808]   draft   1 p 4to   Osb
to Lady Crewe
How pinching & petrifying has the weather

16 Dec   3 p 4to   Osb
from Lady Banks
I can easily find an Excuse for doing what I

20 Dec   2 p 8vo   Osb
from Samuel Wesley
I am eternally pestering you, but you bear my

20 Dec [1808?]   draft   1 p 8vo   Osb
to Samuel Wesley
I am over head & ears in bed wth. my former

28 Dec   3 p 4to   Osb
from Edward Bunting
I consider myself highly honored by the

[1808]   4 p 8vo   Osb
from Mary Carter [to CB]
I have Forty good Reasons for my Long

[1808?]   1 p 8vo   Osb
to CB Jr
Ecce iterum Crispinus — here we *be* —

[1808?]   2 drafts   1 p scrap   Osb
to Lord Cardigan
Dr Burney presents his most humble respects

[1808–12]   draft?   ½ p 8vo   Osb
to FBA
Ever since M. d'A has been indulged wth. a

1809

⟨1⟩3 Jan   draft   3 p 4to   BM
to Louisa Margaret Harris
Then what I very much feared, really *did*

[post 18] Jan   draft   2 p 4to   BM
to Louisa Margaret Harris
I must own that I have been upon the fidget

[Jan 1809]   draft   2 p 4to   Osb
to Lady Crewe
The year has begun very inauspiciously

[post 4 Feb 1809]   draft   1 p 4to
to Louisa M Harris   Osb
Your letter in reply to my Scratch was right

[post 15 Feb 1809]   draft   3 p 4to
to Louisa M Harris   Osb
What a whimsical & capricious ⟨   ⟩ world

[Feb 1809]   draft   1 p scrap   Osb
to Louisa M Harris & Miss Benson
If 2 such puissant Heroines approach my

Mar   1 p 4to   NYPL(B)
to ?
I believe I told you in my last short & croaking

26 Apr   1 p 4to   Osb
from [Jean-Gabriel?] Peltier
M. Peltier a l'honneur de présenter Ses devoirs

7 June   1 p 4to   Osb
to CB Jr
Thank you for your information concerning

28 JU 1809 pmk   3 p 8vo   Comyn
to CB Jr
I think you have acted very wisely

29 June   draft   1 p fol   Osb
to Lady Bruce
Ah my ever dear L^y. Bruce, how very good

1 July   pmk 1809   2 p 8vo   Comyn
to CB Jr
The *Examine dono didit* is come:

4 July   2 p 4to   Osb
to CPB
I have just seen your Father for a few minutes,

18 July   draft   2 p 4to   Osb
to [Lady Manvers]
There is nothing so consolatory to ages

1809, continued

2 Aug   4 p 4to   Osb
from Lord Lonsdale
Few Kings could have afforded me greater

14 Aug   2 p 8vo   Osb
from William, 3rd Duke of Portland
The Information I received from you yesterday

4 Sept   3 p 4to   Osb
from Samuel Wesley
I am glad to find that your welcome Letter

8 Sept   3 p 4to   Osb
from Lady Mary Lowther
I know that it is not so, My dear D^r. Burney,

18 Sept   pmk 1809   1 p 4to   Osb
to CB Jr
I did not answer the letter from you wch. I

[post 27 Sept 1809]   draft   1 p 4to
to Lord Cardigan   Osb
Though I am always pleased & flattered by

28 Sept   1 p 8vo   Osb
from William, 3rd Duke of Portland to
   [CB?]
I rejoice at learning Your determination of

16 Oct [1809?]   1 p 4to   Osb
from Charles Long, Baron Farnborough
In transmitting the enclosed to you which I

18 Oct [1809]   1 p 8vo   Osb
from Lord Cardigan
I am very much obliged to you for the favor of

20 Oct   3 p 4to   Osb
to CB Jr
You are very good for thinking of my crooked

23 Oct [1809]   2 p 4to   Osb
to CB Jr
Can M^r. Payne's eloquence reconcile you or

31 Oct [1809]   2 p 4to   Osb
to CB Jr
I have just rec^d. the inclosed Letter from a

6 Nov [1809]   2 p 4to   Osb
to CB Jr
I was too much afflicted & dispirited to write

22 Nov   pmk 1809   2 p 8vo
to CB Jr   NYPL(B)
I have had a tolerable night, & therefore shall

[Nov 1809]   draft   2 p 8vo   Osb
to Lady Crewe
I shall not attempt to describe my affliction at

17 Dec   draft   7 p 8vo   Osb
to Lady Mary Lowther
I was extremely sorry when the message &

[1809?]   4 p 8vo   Osb
from Lady Mary Lowther
I cannot any longer defer writing to you, My

[1809–10?]   draft   2 p 8vo   NYPL(B)
to Samuel Wesley
But this morning's business more complicated

1810

21 Feb   3 p 8vo   Folger
from Edmond Malone
My friend Mr Bindley wishes that I should ask

23 Feb   amanuensis   3 p 4to
to Edmond Malone   Oxf(Bod)
Your Friend's plain & seemingly

28 Feb   1 p 4to   Folger
from Edmond Malone
I have great pleasure in telling you that we

1 Mar   1 p 4to   Oxf(Bod)
to Edmond Malone
I thank you most heartily for the gratification

11 AP 1810 pmk   2 p 4to   NYPL(B)
to CB Jr
The last time you & our Carluch were here

5 May   4 p 4to   Osb
to FBA
I never was so surprised and delighted at the

[post 5 May 1810]   3 p 4to   Osb
to FBA
I am not certain that you have rec^d. a letter

7 May   pmk 1810   1 p 4to   NYPL(B)
to CB Jr
I wish you w^d. have the goodness to write or

9 MY 1810 pmk   1 p 4to   NYPL(B)
to CB Jr
Carluch, in his way to Leatherhead, had told

1 June   2 p 4to   NYPL(B)
to CB Jr
I most sincerely congratulate you on your

27 June   1 p 8vo   BM
to Samuel Wesley
Since we last met, I have been but 3 days

17 July   1 p fol   Osb
from Samuel Wesley
I am right glad to find that upon examination

19 July [1810]   1 p 4to   BM
to Samuel Wesley & Vincent Novello
With best Comp[s] al Virtuosiss.mo. Sigre.

27 July   2 p 8vo   Folger
from Edmond Malone
I beg your acceptance of a very imperfect &

3 Aug   4 p 4to   Folger
from Edmond Malone
My friend, Courtenay, anticipated me, and

13 Aug   4 p 4to   Folger
from Edmond Malone
I am extremely obliged to you for your three

17 Aug   draft   2 p 8vo   Osb
to Lady Bruce
Ah! my ever dear & kind benefactress, How

20 Aug   3 p 8vo   Folger
from Edmond Malone
Many thanks for your last packet. I think

28 Aug   3 p 4to   Osb
from John Dixon
I was sorry not to see you & have called at your

25 Sept   draft   2 p 4to   Osb
to Lady Manvers
I certainly shd. not have suffered a post to

2 Oct   4 p 8vo   Osb
from Lady Manvers
I have two of your delightful Letters now

13 Oct   1 p 8vo   Osb
from T J Mathias
I will pay Mrs. D'Arblay's pension to your Son

[c Oct 1810]   draft   2 p 8vo   Osb
to CB Jr
As I have no carriage, & never intend going out

11 Nov   pmk 1810   1 p 8vo   Comyn
from ?
I trust my dear Sir, to be with you

19 Nov   3 p 8vo   Camb(F)
from Edmond Malone
A gentleman has lately furnished me with the

21 Nov   2 p 4to   Yale
to Edmond Malone
The Song for Three voices by Thomas Weelkes

22 Nov   draft   2 p 4to   Osb
to Lord Cardigan
My very old acquaintance, the worthy excellent

3 DE 1810 pmk   1 p 4to   Osb
to CB Jr
James brought last Night a list from Mr. Payne

26 Dec   ½ p 4to   Ryl
to CB Jr
I was abt. to condole you for the loss of your

26 Dec   1 p 4to   Osb
to CPB
You were not only a *shy* but a *sly*-boots, about

[1810]   draft   1 p 4to   Osb
to Lady Banks
Having been confined at home a month by a

[1810?]   draft   4 p 8vo   Osb
to Thomas James Mathias
You cd. not have gratified me more by a work

[1810–12]   draft   2 p 4to   Osb
to Mary Ann (Greenwood) Solvyns
When I had the honour to address you last

[1810–12]   draft   2 p 8vo   Osb
to Mary Ann (Greenwood) Solvyns
It gave me great pleasure to hear from my

1811

1 Jan   1 p 8vo   Osb
to CB Jr
The new Era I was determined first to use in

12 Jan   3 p 8vo   Osb
to CB Jr
Your dictated letter is so melancholy & full of

15 Jan   2 p 8vo   Osb
to CB Jr
I am very anxious to be informed of the exact

22 Feb [1811]   3 p 8vo   Osb
to Lady Manvers
If you have heard or read of the Melancholy of

[post 22 Feb 1811]   draft   2 p 4to
to Lady Manvers   Osb
The venison with wch I have been honᵈ. from

[post 22 Feb 1811]   draft   2 p 4to
to Lady Manvers   Osb
The revᵈ. & worthy Mr. Dixon a Friend of long

24 Mar   copy   2 p   Osb
to August Kollman (included in holo-
    graph memoirs p 169)
I was very sorry, when you did me the favour

8 Apr   copy   1 p   Osb
to August Kollman (included in holo-
    graph memoirs p 171)
Though I have not yet been able to quit my

17 Apr   1 p 4to   Osb
from Brownlow North
The Hour is so late, & your note so full of your

18 Apr   draft   1 p 4to   . Osb
to Brownlow North
Your Lorship's letter wᶜʰ. accompanied the

Apr   2 p 4to   Osb
to ?
You have been so jocose in your lively letter of

9 May   copy   1 p   Osb
to William Shield (in holograph
    memoirs)
Nothing within my competence wᵈ. give me

16 May   1 p 4to   Comyn
to CB Jr
I have caught a fresh cold of the catarrh kind,

19 June [1811?]   1 p 4to   Osb
to CB Jr
I am sorry Mʳ. Professor Young was engaged

20 Sept   4 p 8vo   Osb
from Lady Manvers
In any language My dear Sir, it would give

[Sept 1811?]   1 p fragment   Osb
to Elizabeth, Lady Templetown
The preceding memoranda concerning the

11 Oct   1 p 4to   Osb
to CB Jr
You have very kindly done all the business for

20 Oct   4 p 8vo   Osb
from Lady Manvers
Truly as I am Concerned that You do Not give

10 Nov [1811]   draft   2 p 8vo   Osb
to Lady Manvers
It is a double affliction to me, that I am unable

29 Dec 1811 & 4 Jan 1812   draft
    3 p 8vo   Osb
to [Mary Carter?]
I have been extremely ill of many maladies

1812

6 JA pmk [1812]   1 p 4to   Comyn
to CB Jr
I have been dreadfully alarmed & terrified

10 Jan   1 p 4to   Comyn
to CB Jr
I hope to God you may have had the *sound*

6 Feb [1812?]   draft   2 p scrap
to Lady Bruce   Osb
All the partial & obliging things you are

13 Mar   2 p 4to   Osb
from David, 11th Earl of Buchan
When you consider my Nestorian existance &

2 May   1 p 8vo   Osb
to CPB
I congratulate you & my worthy

6 May   1 p 4to   Osb
to Johann Christian Hüttner
When you have an hour in broad daylight, to

8 May [1812]   1 p 8vo   Osb
to [Thomas?] Brand
Dᵣ. Burney is extremely flattered by the

14 May [1812]   1 p 4to   Osb
to Johann Christian Hüttner
Your worthy friend & countryman, Mʳ.

16 May   2 p 4to   Bath
to Lady Banks
I am unable to describe the mental sensation
also   draft dated 16 May   1 p 4to   Osb

[post May 1812]   draft   2 p 8vo
to Mary Ann (Greenwood) Solvyns
I am unable to express my thanks for the   Osb

29 June draft   1 p 4to   Osb
to John Broadwood
Dᵣ. Burney sends his best Compliments to

[29 June 1812?]   draft   1 p 4to
to Elizabeth Iremonger   Osb
That diluvian day (Friday) wᶜʰ. filled your

1 AU pmk   3 p 12mo   Osb
from Elizabeth Iremonger
Indeed Dear Doctor Burney — your feelings

[Aug 1812]   ⅓ p 4to   Comyn
to FBA
Dear F. d'Arblay — I have scratched a bit of

4 Sept   2 p 4to   Osb
from Lady Charlotte Greville
I have just heard that your Daughter Mᵈᵉ

6 Sept   3 p 4to   Osb
from Lord Lonsdale
Few opportunities are likely to offer of

16 Sept   1 p 8vo   Osb
to FBA
I was honᵈ. wᵗʰ. the inclosed letter yesterday

23 Sept 1812   1 p 8vo   Ray
to William Shield
Dᵣ. Burney presents his best compliments to

9 Oct   2 p 8vo   Osb
to CB Jr
My dear Rector of Deptford & Coʸ. in a hearty

12 OC 1812 pmk   2 p 8vo   Osb
to CPB
I am quite ashamed of the many mistakes I

16 Oct   1 p 8vo   Osb
to CB Jr
My dear divine Dᵣ. thanks for the leases — &

[Oct 1812]   ½ p fol   Osb
to FBA
Our active Deptford Doctor called on me

Nov   1 p 4to   Osb
to FBA
I hasten, most urgently, to warn you against

[c 1812]   amanuensis   9 p 4to   Osb
to Joachim LeBreton
Je suis extrémement reconnoissant de la

1813

[pre 11 Jan 1813]   ?   ΛECB31
to JB
I cannot defer thanking you for your good

12 Jan   ?   ΛECB31
to JB
My noble Captain yesterday was inauspicious

19 Jan   1 p 4to   Osb
to Edward Smith Foss
If you will have the goodness to permit one of

9 Mar   2 p 4to   Osb
to CB Jr
I have been thinking of nothing else since I

2 ΛP 1813 pmk   3 p 4to   Osb
to FBA
Why, my dear F Burney d'Arblay! what a

6 Apr   1 p 4to   Osb
to Maria Hester (Hughes) Park
You seem to be mistaken in imagining that you

21 May   1 p 4to   Osb
to CB Jr
Your Sunday's letter, at least the part of it

25 May   1 p 4to   Osb
to FBA
To say nothing of other complaints, I am so

1813, continued

14 June   1 p 4to   Osb
to CB Jr
My dear Carluch — I am informed by Becky,

[July 1813]   2 p 4to   Osb
to FBA
I fully intended writing a few "pleasing

19 Aug   1 p 4to   Comyn
to SHB
Many thanks for your long and very comic

29 Aug   1 p 4to   BM
to Samuel Wesley
Though the weather grows daily more cold to

28 SP 1813 pmk   4 p 4to   Yale(Bo)
from Euphemia Boswell   & Osb
Under very painful circumstances I venture to

[post 28 Sept 1813]   3 p 8vo   Yale(Bo)
from Euphemia Boswell   & Osb
Words are inadequate to express my feelings

[post 28 Sept 1813]   3 p 4to   Yale(Bo)
from Euphemia Boswell   & Osb
I beg leave to inform you that my Harmonious

[1813]   2 p 4to   Osb
to FBA
Ah, my dear F. B d'—y I am sorry to tell you

[1813]   ½ p 4to   Hyde
to Charles Hague
I much wish to discharge my debt of

[1813]   draft   2 p 4to   Osb
to Lady Manvers
The game (a Fine Hare & beautiful Pheasant)

1814

19 Jan   3 p 8vo   Osb
from Elizabeth Iremonger
Have you any kind amanuensis, who, if it be

[Mar 1814]   draft   1 p 8vo   Osb
to FBA
Mem. for Mrs. d'Arblay (at Mrs. Broome's for

[1814?]   draft   2 p 8vo   Osb
to Elizabeth Iremonger
Such letters as yours are sufficient to make the

undated

draft   1 p 8vo   Oxf(Bod)
to Henry Colburn
Dr. Burney informs Mr. Colburn, or whoever

copy   3 p 4to   NYPL(B)
to Fulke Greville
I snatch a Moment from my eternal hurries to

?   ½ p 4to   BM(Bar)
to Dorothy Young
a conversation suivie of 7 or 8 people

?   2 p 8vo   Osb
from Lady Lucan
I have sent my Sert to save yours the trouble

ESTHER (SLEEPE) BURNEY 1723–1762

[c 1752]   2 p 4to & scrap   Osb
from J Pitt
I was afraid that not only my politeness, but

also   copy   3 p 4to   Comyn

30 Jan 1759   3 p 4to   NYPL(B)
from Fulke Greville
Mr. Burney's letter gave me very great pleasure

2 Oct [1760]   4 p 4to   Osb
from Frances (Macartney) Greville
Various things have prevented my having

Elizabeth (Allen) Allen Burney 1725–1796
See also letters to and from FBA and from CB and SHB.

[1778]   2 p 4to   BM(Bar)
from HLTP
My Dear Mrs. Burney will excuse my writing

July 1792   4 p 4to   BM
to Arthur Young
Nay if you talk of yr Difficulties fabricating an

12 Mar 1793   1 p 4to   NYPL(B)
from James Hutton
I am prevented coming to Town the 13th, so

[1793–96]   4 p 4to   BM
to Arthur Young
You, "the willing advocate of every feeling I

[Apr-Oct 1796]   verses   3 p 4to   Osb
from M[ary?] Hales
[letter p 3] I obey yr. commands my dear

5 May 1796   1 p 4to   NYPL(B)
from HLTP
Mrs. Piozzi returns a thousand Compliments to

Maria (Allen) Rishton 1751–1820
See also letters to and from FBA, CB, and JB.

21 Oct 1783   4 p 4to   NYPL(B)
from Jane Coke
I was not at all surprised to find by a letter

[c 1783]   3 p 4to   NYPL(B)
from Jane Coke
The commotions in the political world, have

12 Aug [1793]   3 p 4to   NYPL(B)
to SBP
Tho' I believe twenty years have elapsed since

4 Sept [1798]   copy   2 p 4to
                         BM(Bar)
to SHB (included in M Rishton to FBA
     5 Sept [1798]
God Bless you! and receive my most grateful

II

FRANCES (BURNEY) D'ARBLAY 1752–1840
(FB, FBA)

See also letters from CB, CB Jr, CPB, and CFBt.

Holograph works, documents, and other original material of Madame d'Arblay are chiefly to be found in the Berg and Barrett collections with some items in the following: British Museum; Emmanuel College, Cambridge; Hilles; John Comyn; National Portrait Gallery; Osborn; Pierpont Morgan.

1768

23 June　　2 p fol　　　　　　Osb
to CB
O aid me, ye muses of ev'ry Degree, / O give

11 July [1768]　　4 p 4to　　NYPL(B)
from Elizabeth (Allen) Burney &
　　[SBP?]
I can tell you but this, Madam Fanny,

⟨27⟩ pmk　Aug　4 p fol　NYPL(B)
to Rebecca Burney, Ann Burney & Mrs
　　Gregg
Ah! where shall I expression find / To soften

13 Oct　　2 p fol　　　　　NYPL(B)
from Elizabeth (Allen) Burney
I've but a bad excuse to make for not

[20 Nov 1768]　　1 p 4to　　NYPL(B)
from Richard Thomas Burney per
　　[Maria Rishton?]

Master New-Com's affectionate Love to his

[1768]　　3 p 4to　　　　　NYPL(B)
from Maria (Allen) Rishton
Come Fan Psa'w your a good girl and Ill write

[1768–71]　　3 p fol　　　NYPL(B)
from Maria (Allen) Rishton
Prepare a good stomach and good pair of shoes

1769

[1769–1775]　　2 p 4to　　　　PML
to SEB
Jem — will be quite a Lyon on his return —

1770

[1770?]　　4 p fol　　　　　NYPL(B)
from Maria (Allen) Rishton
Well girls — Such a piece of news — if it

[1770–74]　　2 p 4to　　　BM(Bar)
to Lady Hales
I am so much astonished, & so much confused

1771

[7 Sept 1771]　　5 p fol　　NYPL(B)
from Maria (Allen) Rishton
Dont scold so violently about my not writing,

21 Nov　　4 p fol　　　　　NYPL(B)
from Maria (Allen) Rishton
I conjure by our long Friendship & the love

[1771?]　　2 p 4to　　　　　NYPL(B)
from Maria (Allen) Rishton
Here I am at Warham I could not resist the

26 Feb [1771–74]　　3 p 4to　　　Osb
from Dorothy Young
Your melancholy disaster, my dear Fanny,

15 Oct [pre 1772]   4 p fol   NYPL(B)
from Maria (Allen) Rishton
I am most exceedingly obliged to you for the

1772

[6 Apr 1772]   2 p 4to   NYPL(B)
from Maria (Allen) Rishton
My dear Fanny — Copying the letter I have

8 JU pmk [1772]   4 p fol   NYPL(B)
from Maria (Allen) Rishton
All's over — Crisp knows I am Maria Rishton

1 Aug [1772]   1 p fol   NYPL(B)
from Maria (Allen) Rishton
Mr Rishton begs his Compliments — Stephen

11 Aug   mutilated   7 p 4to   Essex
from Samuel Crisp
that / these men What does he do? —

2 Sept [1772]   2 p 4to   BM(Bar)
from Dorothy Young
You will believe without my telling you

[1772]   4 p fol   NYPL(B)
from Maria (Allen) Rishton
I never received greater pleasure in my life

[1772]   2 p fol   NYPL(B)
from Maria (Allen) Rishton
Upon my word you very little deserve I shoud

[1772]   2 p fol   NYPL(B)
from Maria (Allen) Rishton
As Rishton is very deeply engaged at present in

[post 1772]   1 p 4to   BM(Bar)
from Dorothy Young
I do remember you huffed me for a more

1773

25 Apr [1773]   7 p 4to   NYPL(B)
from Maria (Allen) Rishton
Here we are arrived at our little retirement

13 Apr [1773]   5 p 4to   NYPL(B)
from Maria (Allen) Rishton
I know not whether I owe you a letter or not

22 Feb   4 p 4to   NYPL(B)
from Maria (Allen) Rishton
You are my best and kindest Friend to write to

[28 May 1773]   5 p 4to   NYPL(B)
from Maria (Allen) Rishton
You are really a very good Girl to write me so

6 June [1773]   3 p fol   NYPL(B)
from Maria (Allen) Rishton
I can no longer delay writing to enquire the

13 June [1773]   8 p 4to   NYPL(B)
from Maria (Allen) Rishton
So far from giving up the hopes of seeing you

[June 1773]   1 p 4to   NYPL(B)
from Maria (Allen) Rishton
Mr. & Mrs. Rishton hope Miss Burney will

25 [Aug? 1773]   4 p 4to   NYPL(B)
from Maria (Allen) Rishton
the most money of his Children — Think only

2 Oct   4 p fol   NYPL(B)
from Maria (Allen) Rishton
Many thanks for your very kind letter I hope

13 Nov   2 p 4to   Harv(H)
to Stephen Allen
It makes me extremely happy to find it in my

⟨13⟩ NO pmk [1773]   1 p 4to
from Samuel Crisp   BM(Bar)
I'll tell you what Fanny — I yesterday receivd

[Nov 1773]   4 p 4to   NYPL(B)
from Samuel Crisp
In consequence of our Agreement

[1773?]   1 p ¾ 4to   BM(Bar)
from Samuel Crisp
Tho the weak knotty Joints of my knuckles are

[1773]   3 p fol   NYPL(B)
from Maria (Allen) Rishton
& so here we are once More arrived at the Seat

1773, continued

[1773]   4 p fol   NYPL(B)
from Maria (Allen) Rishton
And so by way of return to the very Curious

[1773?]   2 p 8vo   NYPL(B)
from Maria (Allen) Rishton
I delay'd writing till to day as M^r R expected

1774

1 Jan [1774]   2 p 4to   BM(Bar)
from Samuel Crisp
A happy new year to the Fannikin! & I think I

[7 Feb 1774]   2 p 4to   BM(Bar)
to Samuel Crisp
Did you draw me into a Correspondence, my

7 Feb [1774]   2 p fol   NYPL(B)
from Maria (Allen) Rishton
& so Mr Cartwright has made Miss Burney a

[9 Feb 1774]   2 p fragment of fol
to Samuel Crisp   BM(Bar)
The sight of your Hand, once again directed

17 Feb   2 p fol   NYPL(B)
from Maria (Allen) Rishton
& so Miss Fanny Burney has mounted her little

[Apr 1774]   2 p 4to   NYPL(B)
from Samuel Crisp
I tell you what — You are a Jew — an Ebrew

21 May [1774]   3 p fol   NYPL(B)
from Maria (Allen) Rishton
Lord bless me what Silly Things Excuses are

13 JU pmk [1774?]   2 p fol   NYPL(B)
from Maria (Allen) Rishton
two or 3 lines in a flying hurry to thank you for

22 Aug [1774]   2 p 4to   BM(Bar)
from Samuel Crisp
You are a good Sort of Girl enough, & I don't

24 [Aug]   4 p fol   NYPL(B)
from Maria (Allen) Rishton
What your opinion of me must be I don't know

1 Dec [1774]   8 p 4to   BM(Bar)
to Samuel Crisp
What you have thought of me & of my

[1774]   4 p fol   NYPL(B)
from Maria (Allen) Rishton
Upon my life Fanny I very often am to blame

[1774?]   1 p fol   NYPL(B)
from Maria (Allen) Rishton
I am shocked to find on collecting the scattered

[1774?]   3 p fol   NYPL(B)
from Maria (Allen) Rishton
I am so afraid of forgetting the real business of

1775

[1 Jan 1775]   4 p fol   NYPL(B)
from Maria (Allen) Rishton
I have got a Bad sore throat yet I sit down to

25 Jan   2 p ½ fol   BM(Bar)
from Samuel Crisp
Hark ye Fanny You must know I had a mind to

[2] Feb [1775]   4 p 4to   BM(Bar)
to Samuel Crisp
I have been so long & so much distressed

[17 Feb 1775]   4 p fol   NYPL(B)
from Maria (Allen) Rishton
I hope e'er this you have all of you banished

[2] Mar   8 p 4to   BM(Bar)
to Samuel Crisp
I hope, by your Letter to my Mother,

27 Mar [1775]   2 p 4to   BM(Bar)
from Samuel Crisp
With a right hand half lame, & a left

Mar-Apr [1775]   12 p 4to   BM(Bar)
CB & FB to Samuel Crisp
Here Fanny desires me to write the prologue

2 Apr [1775]   3 p 4to   BM(Bar)
from James Hutton
I have wrote here a longish kind of Letter to

[14 Apr]   8 p 4to   BM(Bar)
to Samuel Crisp
I have complied with your commands without

24 Apr [1775]   8 p 4to   BM(Bar)
to Samuel Crisp
[obliteration] So you prohibit speechifying?

24 Apr [1775]   3 p 4to   BM(Bar)
from James Hutton
My little visit at your House on Saturday

8 May [1775]   6 p 4to   NYPL(B)
from Samuel Crisp
Tho' Fingers are Crippley & left Arm lame

16 May [1775]   3 p 4to   NYPL(B)
from James Hutton
I left off, my dear friend, because I saw I had

[22 May 1775]   3 p 4to   BM(Bar)
to Samuel Crisp
My Father cannot see you before Sunday

30 May   8 p 4to   BM(Bar)
to Samuel Crisp
I was extremely happy at the Receipt

[May 1775]   2 p 4to   BM(Bar)
from Thomas Barlow
Uninterrupted happiness we are told is of short

[May 1775]   2 p 4to   BM(Bar)
from Thomas Barlow
I have somewhere seen that powerful Deity

10 June   8 p 4to   BM(Bar)
to Samuel Crisp
Thank you a thousand Times my dear Daddy

18 July [1775]   3 p 4to   BM(Bar)
from Samuel Crisp
In a great hurry I sent off a Line

13 SE pmk [1775]   4 p fol   NYPL(B)
from Maria (Allen) Rishton
As this promised letter has never arrived I will

[26 Oct 1775]   4 p fol   NYPL(B)
from Maria (Allen) Rishton
I am really ashamed of not being more exact in

[30 Oct 1775]   6 p 4to   BM(Bar)
to Samuel Crisp
It is so long since I wrote to you that I suppose

5 Nov [1775]   4 p fol   NYPL(B)
from Maria (Allen) Rishton
I'll e'en try what writing to the minute will

[9 Nov 1775]   12 p 4to   BM(Bar)
to Samuel Crisp
The best apology I can make for the indolence

19 Nov   2 p 4to   NYPL(B)
from Samuel Crisp
That I wish for the remnant of your Evening

[10 Dec 1775]   12 p 4to   BM(Bar)
to Samuel Crisp
I have this moment received your Letter

14 Dec   4 p 4to   BM(Bar)
from Samuel Crisp
Dont imagine, that, because my letters are

[30 Dec 1775]   mutilated   2 p 4to
from Samuel Crisp   BM(Bar)
"There's no more faith in thee than in a stew'd

[1775]   2 p 4to   NYPL(B)
from JB
I am under a necessity of trusting

[1775]   4 p fol   NYPL(B)
from Maria (Allen) Rishton
You would have heard from me so long since to

[1775]   2 p fol   NYPL(B)
from Maria (Allen) Rishton
Only two or three Lines because I think it

1776

2 Jan   2 p 4to   NYPL(B)
from James Hutton
I had but just time to hasten the L^rs. to the

29 Jan [1776?]   4 p 8vo   NYPL(B)
from James Hutton
I did not find your kind Note sent with the

[Jan-Feb 1776]   2 p scrap   NYPL(B)
to   ?
My Sister has been very ill

[5 Apr 1776]   4 p 4to   BM(Bar)
to Samuel Crisp
I long to hear if you have got, & how you like

27 July   4 p 4to   BM(Bar)
to Samuel Crisp
Now really my dear Daddy, this is prodigiously

7 Aug   3 p 4to   BM(Bar)
from Mary Bruce Strange
Will you my dear Miss Burney forgive

1776, continued

24 Sept [1776]   4 p 4to   NYPL(B)
from Maria (Allen) Rishton
I should be glad to know which of us is the

[Sept 1776]   2 p 4to   BM(Bar)
from Samuel Crisp
[p 1 obliterated] What? — Do you believe I

[Nov 1776]   3 scraps   BM(Bar)
from Samuel Crisp
really concern'd, when you

[2 Dec 1776]   4 p 4to   BM(Bar)
to Samuel Crisp
[p 1 obliterated] The party consisted of —

25 Dec   1 p 4to   BM(Bar)
from Thomas Lowndes
I've not the least objection to what

29 Dec   1 p 4to   BM(Bar)
from Thomas Lowndes
I've read & like the Manuscript & if

Dec   draft   1 p 4to   BM(Bar)
to Thomas Lowndes
As an author has a kind of natural claim to a

also   facsimile   1 p 8vo ?   NPG

[1776]   4 p 4to   NYPL(B)
from Maria (Allen) Rishton
You may think perhaps I write this out of

[1776–81]   2 p 4to   BM(Bar)
from Lady Hales
You are to know my Dear Miss Burney we have

[post 1776?]   2 p 4to   NYPL(B)
from Elizabeth (Allen) Meeke
Pardon me for not sooner acknowledging your

1777

17 Jan   1 p 8vo   BM(Bar)
from Thomas Lowndes
I have read your Novel and cant see any reason

[post 17] Jan   1 p 4to   BM(Bar)
to Thomas Lowndes
I am well contented with the openness of your

also   facsimile   NPG

[15 Mar 1777]   4 p 4to   NYPL(B)
to SEB
Your Letter, my dear Susy, was a most

22 Mar [1777]   1 p 4to   NYPL(B)
from William Cutler
Mr Cutler presents his Compliments to Miss

27 Mar   2 p 4to   BM(Bar)
from Samuel Crisp
You can't imagine how we miss'd you as soon

[28 Mar 1777]   7 p 4to   BM(Bar)
to Samuel Crisp
My dear Father, seemed well pleased at my

2 Apr   5 p 4to & fragment   BM(Bar)
from Samuel Crisp
Why Fanny you young Torment, dʸᵉ think to

[July 1777]   2 p scrap   BM(Bar)
to SEB
for our young gentlemen will have their own

11 Nov   1 p 4to   BM(Bar)
from Thomas Lowndes
I've read this 3ᵈ. Vol & think it better than

[1777?]   2 p 4to   NYPL(B)
from James Hutton
I know not whether any of the He Saints

[1777–1780]   2 p 4to   Comyn
to Thomas Lowndes
As Business, with those who understand

[1777–1780]   2 p 4to   Comyn
to Thomas Lowndes
The frankness with which you favoured

[1777–1780]   2 p 4to   Comyn
to Thomas Lowndes
I have been much mortified that a multiplicity

[1777–1780]   1 p 4to   Comyn
to Thomas Lowndes
I return you my thanks for your attention to my

[1777–1780]   1 p 4to   Comyn
to Thomas Lowndes
I am much ashamed, after having been myself

[1777–1780]   1 p fol   Comyn
to Thomas Lowndes
The M.S. concerning which I troubled you last

[1777–1780]   1 p 4to   Comyn
to Thomas Lowndes
I now send you all the sheets of Evelina

7 OC pmk [1777–1780]   1 p 4to
to Thomas Lowndes
A long & dangerous illness having, for some   Comyn

[1777–1780]   2 p 4to   Comyn
to Thomas Lowndes
I am much gratified by your good opinion of

[1777–1780]   1 p 4to   Comyn
to Thomas Lowndes
I am extremely sorry to have kept the press

1778

7 Jan   1 p 4to   BM(Bar)
from Thomas Lowndes
I take the Liberty to send you a Novel

25 Jan   3 p 4to   BM(Bar)
from Mary Bruce Strange
Don't, my dear Miss Burney, examine your

Mar [1778]   17 p 8vo   NYPL(B)
Journal
March is almost over — & not a word

9 MA pmk [1778]   2 p 4to   NYPL(B)
from SEB
I will transcribe for you Bessy's last letter *on*

May [1778]   2 p 4to & scrap
to SEB   NYPL(B)
I thank you a thousand times

4 JU pmk [1778]   2 p 4to   NYPL(B)
from SEB
But, my dear Fanny, my Father has

[11 June 1778]   4 p 4to   NYPL(B)
from SEB
Yesterday I spent in Brook Street —

[post 11 June 1778]   2 p 4to
from SEB   NYPL(B)
They were got on in reading it as far as

16 June [1778]   4 p 4to   NYPL(B)
from SEB
My Mother was gone to < > My dear

[post 16 June 1778]   2 p 4to
from SEB   NYPL(B)
"I have *such* a thing to tell you,

18 June [1778]   2 p 4to   NYPL(B)
to SEB
Here I am, & here I have been this age

29 June   4 p 4to   NYPL(B)
from SEB
I have just recᵈ. your parcel

[June? 1778]   4 p 4to   NYPL(B)
to SEB
took leave, & returned to town.

2 July   1 p 4to   BM(Bar)
from Thomas Lowndes
I bound up a Sett for you the first Day I had

4 JY pmk [1778]   4 p 4to   NYPL(B)
from SEB
When Charlotte returned home the Coach

5 July   4 p 4to   NYPL(B)
to SEB
Don't you think there must be some wager

[5]–6 July [1778]   4 p 4to   NYPL(B)
from SEB
This Mornᵍ. between 7 & 8 I was woke

6 July   2 p 4to   NYPL(B)
to SEB
Your Letter, my dearest Susan, & the

[post 6 July 1778]   1 p 4to   NYPL(B)
from SEB
To my great disappointment My Mother was

8 JY pmk [1778]   4 p 4to   NYPL(B)
with Samuel Crisp to SEB
Pray Suzettikin go to a Colour Shop

13 July [1778]   4 p 4to   Hyde
from Elizabeth (Allen) Burney
Allow me to Congratulate you on the Merit and

16 July [1778]   4 p 4to   NYPL(B)
from SEB
At night my Father read as usual — I found

16 July [1778]   4 p 4to   NYPL(B)
from SEB
Tuesday my Father & Mother came home

[20 July 1778]   4 p 4to   NYPL(B)
to CB
I have just received from Susan an account

1778, continued

20 July-Aug [1778]   14 p 4to
to SEB   NYPL(B)
sweet Girl, & I have a real regard

23 JY pmk [1778]   2 p 4to NYPL(B)
from SEB
At Dinner yesterday my Father had a Letter

25 July [1778]   4 p 4to   NYPL(B)
to CB
My dear & most kind Father. — the *request*

[25 July 1778]   2 p 4to   NYPL(B)
to SEB
but repetitions of what I have heard from

[July 1778]   14 p 4to   NYPL(B)
to SEB
always affected the utmost sourness

[July or Aug 1778] 2 p 4to NYPL(B)
from Samuel Crisp
If I wish to hear the sequel

10 Aug   2 p 4to   BM(Bar)
from Isabella Strange
Much do I miss the benefit of the Courier

23 Aug [1778]   32 p 4to   NYPL(B)
to SEB
I was obliged, my dear Susy, to send

Aug [1778]   8 p 4to   NYPL(B)
to SEB
Indeed, my dearest Susy, I know not how

Sept [1778]   39 p 4to   NYPL(B)
to SEB
I must now begin a Journal to you

Sept [1778?]   2 p 4to   NYPL(B)
to SEB
Yesterday Morning Mr. Lort called

[Oct-Nov 1778]   12 p 4to   NYPL(B)
to SEB
Saturday Evening, Mr. & Mrs. Thrale took me

6 NO pmk [1778]   5 p 4to   NYPL(B)
from Samuel Crisp
Since Peace is proclaimed, & I am got our

22 Nov   2 p 4to   BM(Bar)
from Samuel Crisp
I imagine I have found out the Cause of the

[post Nov 1778]   2 p 4to   NYPL(B)
to SEB
I have now an opportunity to write a Folio

1 Dec   3 p 4to   NYPL(B)
from Catherine Coussmaker
And could you imagine my Dear Miss Burney

8 DE pmk [1778]   1 p fol   BM(Bar)
to SEB
called here twice to Day, & as usual was

8 Dec   4 p 4to   NYPL(B)
from Samuel Crisp
Exclusive of the high entertainment

24 Dec   1 p 4to   BM(Bar)
from Samuel Crisp
I have just read Evelina over again

[Dec? 1778]   4 p 4to   NYPL(B)
to SEB
I was extremely glad, my dearest Susan,

[Dec 1778]   3 p 4to   NYPL(B)
from HLTP
Though your Papa kindly told me the time of

[Dec 1778]   4 p 4to   BM(Bar)
from SEB
Indeed my dear Girl if my Father's wishes &

[1778?]   2 p fol   NYPL(B)
to Catherine Coussmaker
Y^r. kind & most flattering Letter, my dear Miss

[1778]   1 p fragment   NYPL(B)
to SEB
Head that he painted, &c, &c, / You are *very*

[1778]   2 p scrap   BM(Bar)
from SEB
very capable of writing such a Work.

[1778–79]   1 p 4to   BM(Bar)
from Isabella Strange
I was sorry I miss'd my sweet Girl. I was

[1778–82]   1 p scrap   Comyn
from HLTP
only three Words, to say that Evelina with all

[1778–86]   1 p 4to   NYPL(B)
from Henrietta Maria (Bannister)
     North
Will you & D^r: Burney come & dine with a poor

[1778–86?]   1 p 8vo   NYPL(B)
from Henrietta Maria (Bannister)
     North
I have a Box for Monday & still hope

1779

16 Jan   1 p 4to   NYPL(B)
from Anthony Chamier
Mʳ Chamier presents his compliments to Miss

19 Jan   3 p 4to   NYPL(B)
from Samuel Crisp
Extract of a Letter from Gast, dated Burford

27 Jan   1 p 4to   BM(Bar)
from Thomas Lowndes
I'll soon get ready 500 of the 1500 for wᶜʰ. the

Jan [1779]   52 p 4to   NYPL(B)
to Samuel Crisp & SEB
Your patience, my dear Daddy, in being

[Jan 1779]   4 p 4to   NYPL(B)
from HLTP
Instead of writing monitory Letters to Dick

Feb [1779]   21 p 4to   NYPL(B)
to SEB
I have been here so long, my dearest Susan,

11 MA pmk [1779]   2 p 4to   NYPL(B)
to Samuel Crisp
The kindness & honours I meet with from

29 Mar [1779]   1 p 4to   Osb
from Gasparo Pacchierotti
Mʳ. Pacchierotti returns his best respects to

4 May   4 p 4to   NYPL(B)
to Samuel Crisp
Oh! my dear Daddy —

[pre 15 May 1779]   1 p ⅔ 4to
from Samuel Crisp   BM(Bar)
You are a Jew, Fannikin, an Ebrew Jew — so

[pre 15 May 1779]   2 p 4to   BM(Bar)
from Samuel Crisp
As I know the goodness of your heart, I am

15 May   3 p 4to   BM(Bar)
from Samuel Crisp
My weak state of health can never destroy

[20] May [1779]   1 p fol   BM(Bar)
to Samuel Crisp
Your last sweet Letter was the most acceptable

[28?] May [1779]   16 p 4to   NYPL(B)
to SEB
Once more, my dearest Susy, I will attempt

28 May   3 p 4to   BM(Bar)
from Samuel Crisp
Symptoms of my Illness, of which in degree

28–30 May [1779]   21 p 4to
to SEB   NYPL(B)
To my no small concern, I am obliged

[May 1779]   2 p scrap   BM(Bar)
to SEB
I did not, therefore, want a Friend at *Table*,

13–15 June   34 p 4to   NYPL(B)
to SEB
Now, my dear Susan, hard & fast let me

[June 1779]   2 p 4to   BM(Bar)
to SEB
Gormandized with equal avidity, we sent a

5–10 July [1779]   10 p 4to   NYPL(B)
to SEB
I have hardly had any power to write

21 July   3 p 4to   BM(Bar)
from Samuel Crisp
You have now put me upon my Mettle

30 July [1779]   5 p 4to   NYPL(B)
to Samuel Crisp
Now my dear Daddy, let me attempt

1 Aug [1779]   4 p 4to   BM(Bar)
from SEB
I need not tell you that I left Town

3–6 Aug [1779]   4 p 4to   BM(Bar)
from SEB
Tuesday August 3ᵈ. — Yesterday was

4 Aug [1779]   2 p 4to   BM(Bar)
to CB
Your sweet Letter, my dearest sir, has quite

4 AU pmk [1779]   4 p 4to   BM(Bar)
from SEB
My Father then played over some songs

25–26 Aug [1779]   8 p 4to   BM(Bar)
from SEB
Wednesday August 25ᵗʰ — Tho' I really think

[Aug 1779]   4 p fol   NYPL(B)
to CB
The fatal knell then, is knolled

1779, continued

[Aug? 1779]   3 p fol   NYPL(B)
to Samuel Crisp
Well! — "God's above all! —

[Aug? 1779]   4 p 4to   NYPL(B)
from Samuel Crisp
I have known half a letter filled up

[25 Sept 1779]   3 p 4to   NYPL(B)
to HLTP
Your Letters, my Dearest Madam, have

10 Oct   4 p 4to   NYPL(B)
to CB
Here we are, all safe & all well, — *Mrs.*

10 pmk   Oct [1779]   4 p fol
to Samuel Crisp   NYPL(B)
Our Jem is at last come, — & I have quitted

20 Oct [1779]   8 p 4to   BM(Bar)
from SEB
reminding her either of Captn. Mirven

1–[2] Nov [1779]   8 p 4to   BM(Bar)
from SEB
Monday Novr. 1st. Saturday Se'night my

3–[27] Nov [1779]   58 p 4to
from SEB   BM(Bar)
Wednesday Novr. 3^d. It shall not be said

16 Nov [1779]   3 p 4to   Wales
to Samuel Johnson
And so — while I am studying to avoid the

also   photostat   Hyde
17 Nov [1779]   6 p 4to   BM(Bar)
to SEB
I am a little vexed, my dear Susy, & so I will

30 Nov–9 Dec [1779]   22 p 4to
from SEB   BM(Bar)
Tuesday Morn^g. Novr. 30^tn. I must get a

[5? Dec 1779]   2 p 4to   BM(Bar)
from Samuel Crisp
The Contents of your letter from Brighton our

[Dec]   2 p 4to   BPL
with HLTP to CB
Your Daughter Dear Sir is no longer *better* but

[Dec 1779]   4 p 4to   NYPL(B)
to Samuel Crisp
I have deferred Writing from Day to Day

[1779]   facsimile of copy   1 p 4to?
to Samuel Crisp   NPG
I am extremely gratified by your approbation

[1779?]   2 p 4to   NYPL(B)
to SEB
When I went down stairs, I found them all

[1779]   4 p 4to   BM(Bar)
from SEB
I cannot thank you sufficiently my dearest

[1779]   1 p 4to   Osb
from William Seward
Mr Seward presents his compts to Miss

[1779–80]   1 p 8vo   Shep(D)
to HLTP
Thanks, ever dearest Madam, for your most

[1779–84]   1 p 4to   Ryl
to HLTP
How should I *help* being uneasy, Dearest

⌊1779–86]   1 p 4to   BM(Bar)
from Sophia Streatfield
When Doc^r: Burney did us the favor

[1779–86]   1 p 4to   BM(Bar)
from Sophia Streatfield
Then my Dearest Fanny was really angry with

1780

1 Jan–13 Feb   22 p 4 to   BM(Bar)
from SEB
Jan 1st. had a very good social party

7 Jan [1780]   6 p 4to   BM(Bar)
to Samuel Crisp
Ah my dear Daddy now you are angry indeed!

16 Jan [1780]   3 p 4to   NYPL(B)
to HLTP
There it goes! sweet Letter as it is, & beyond a

22 Jan [1780]   10 p 4to   NYPL(B)
to Samuel Crisp
As this sheet is but to contain a sequel

[c 12 Feb 1780] 2 p 4to Plat
from HLTP
I could not Yesterday write half my Mind; &

[23 Feb 1780] 2 p 4to NYPL(B)
from Samuel Crisp
Our letters crossed each other

23 Feb mutilated 3 p 4to NYPL(B)
from Samuel Crisp
If my letter was acceptable to you

Feb–[13 Apr 1780] 4 p 4to BM(Bar)
to Samuel Crisp
I have received your very kind Letter but

8–17 Mar [1780] 16 p 4to BM(Bar)
from SEB
him — "If I sh^d. be so happy to return here",

[23]-30 Mar [1780] 12 p 4to
from SEB BM(Bar)
return to this he sent him a Letter

7–9 Apr 37 p 4to NYPL(B)
to SEB
A thousand thanks, my dearest Susy, for

10 Apr [1780] 6 p 4to NYPL(B)
to CB
I trouble you, my dearest Sir, much seldomer

10 Apr [1780] 4 p fol BM(Bar)
from CAB
I hope my Dearest Fonny that you are not in

[11]–12 Apr [1780] 4 p 4to BM(Bar)
from SEB
mine, wch. is that when you hear it the

13 Apr [1780] 4 p 4to BM(Bar)
to Samuel Crisp
So very much, my Dearest Daddy, & so very

13–15 Apr [1780] 16 p 4to BM(Bar)
from SEB
Thursday Morn^g. 13th Apr — Upon my loved

20–22 Apr [1780] 10 p 4to BM(Bar)
from SEB
Saturday I sent off my last despatch to you

24 Apr–9 May 44 p 4to BM(Bar)
from SEB
Monday Morn^g. April 24th M^r. Burney

27 Apr 4 p 4to NYPL(B)
from Samuel Crisp
I was much pleased with the sight

29 Apr [1780] 12 p 4to NYPL(B)
to SEB
Is it such an age since I have written

30 Apr [1780] 24 p 4to NYPL(B)
to SEB
It is not a shocking thing, my dearest Susette

[Apr 1780] 2 p scrap NYPL(B)
to SEB
This Evening we have all been at

Apr [1780] 4 p 4to Yale(Bo)
to Samuel Johnson
So mix our Studies, & so join our names

2 May 2 p 4to Osb
from Gasparo Pacchierotti
I begin for asking your pardon having provoked
also copy 2 p 4to NYPL(B)

9–16 May [1780] 8 p 4to BM(Bar)
from SEB
Tuesday May 9th. I sent off my last packet

13 May 2 p 4to NYPL
from Sophia (Crisp) Gast
How grateful to my Heart, and how flattering

21–22 May [1780] 8 p 4to BM(Bar)
from SEB
Sunday Morn^g. — May 21st. Oh My dear

[post 22] May 2 p 4to NYPL(B)
to SEB
Now, my Susy, will I begin this Budget with

23 MA pmk [1780] 4 p fol BM(Bar)
to CB
I was so incessantly engaged yesterday

28 May 7 p 4to NYPL(B)
to SEB [& CAB]
I was very happy, my dearest Girls, with the

31 May ? ? Mag 349 (1220)
to HLTP
[Describes a party at Mrs Montagu's]

May 14 p 4to NYPL(B)
to SEB
So he was *satisfied enough* though he only saw

1780, *continued*

4 June   16 p 4to   NYPL(B)
to SEB
To go on with Saturday Evening.

8–12 June [1780]   30 p 4to   BM(Bar)
from SEB
Thursday Eve^g. June 8th. Ah my dear Fanny!

9–10 June   6 p 4to   NYPL(B)
to CB
How are you — where are you — &

11 June [1780]   3 p fol   NYPL(B)
to CB
Here we are, dearest Sir, & here we mean

[11]–13 June   6 p 4to   NYPL(B)
to SEB
It is a great while indeed since I have written

[12–20] June [1780]   30 p 4to
from SEB   BM(Bar)
Monday night. — We have despatched a

13 June [1780]   2 p 4to   NYPL(B)
to CB
We arrived here yesterday about 7 in the

14 June [1780]   1 p 4to   NYPL(B)
to CB
Here we now are, — & *I* thinking of nothing

[17 June 1780]   4 p 4to   NYPL(B)
to CB
O with what joy, most dear Sir! did I see your

19 June   2 p 4to   NYPL(B)
to SEB
All your Letters, my dearest love, are now

20 June [1780]   4 p 4to   NYPL(B)
to CB
I cannot help again writing to you, my dearest

20–21 June [1780]   16 p 4to
from SEB   BM(Bar)
Tuesday Eve^g. 20th June I have just sent off

29 June   3 p 4to   BM(Bar)
from HLTP
Streatham detained me so scandalously late

June   40 p 4to   NYPL(B)
to SEB
To go on with Mrs. Lambart

1 July   4 p 4to   NYPL(B)
to HLTP
Have you no *Quality* yet, my Dearest Madam

5 July [1780]   4 p 4to   NYPL(B)
from HLTP
My dearest Miss Burney is very kind to her

8 July [1780]   5 p 4to   NYPL(B)
to HLTP
See but, Dearest Madam! my prompt

11 [July 1780]   4 p 4to   NYPL(B)
from HLTP
Now when will the Post be pleased to bring

19 July [1780]   4 p 4to   BM(Bar)
from HLTP
And so my Letters please you, do they

[July 1780]   5 p 4to   Hyde
to HLTP
Well, dearest Madam! & thus perversely goes

[July? 1780]   2 p 4to   NYPL(B)
from HLTP
My Dear Miss Burney shall have her Letters

2 Aug   2 p 4to   Osb
from Gasparo Pacchierotti
I am extremely rejoiced, but not at all surprised

13 Aug   2 p 4to   BM(Bar)
from Samuel Crisp
I am quite glad to hear the Burnean System

16 Aug [1780]   4 p 4to   NYPL(B)
to HLTP
I return you my most hearty thanks,

18 [Aug 1780]   4 p 4to   NYPL(B)
from HLTP
This Letter goes by Signor Piozzi, who has

24 Aug [1780]   4 p 4to   NYPL(B)
to HLTP
Here at length we are, — arrived just in Time

[Aug 1780]   5 p 4to   NYPL(B)
to HLTP
Nobody does write such sweet Letters as my

[Aug 1780]   3 p 4to   NYPL(B)
from HLTP
I am not happy my sweet Burney! my Master is

[Aug-Oct 1780]   1 p 4to   NYPL(B)
from HLTP
Treachery & Presbyterianism! O what indeed

3 Sept [1780?]   4 p fol   NYPL(B)
from Maria (Allen) Rishton
I make no excuses for not sooner answering

6 SE pmk [1780]   2 p 4to   BM(Bar)
to HLTP
No news — no not a word of news yet! — but

[26 Sept 1780]   2 p 4to   BM(Bar)
from Samuel Crisp
Such a poor miserable Invalid as S.C. is

20 Oct - Nov [1780?]   94 p 4to
to SEB   NYPL(B)
As you say you will accept Memorandums

31 Oct [1780]   1 p 4to   NYPL(B)
from HLTP
No more Fun my dear Miss Burney! we have

[Oct 1780]   3 p 4to   NYPL(B)
to CB
We have this Moment finished the Critic

2 NO pmk [1780]   1 p 4to   NYPL(B)
to HLTP
I write in the greatest hurry imaginable, & only

4 Nov [1780]   4 p 4to   NYPL(B)
to HLTP
I never managed matters so adroitly before

7 Nov   1 p 4to   Osb
from HLTP
The Coach — the *old* Coach shall fetch my

13 Nov   4 p 4to   NYPL(B)
to Samuel Crisp
I know now less than ever when I shall be

15 Nov   2 p 4to   BM(Bar)
from Samuel Crisp
If I was disappointed by your putting

[18 Nov 1780]   4 p 4to   BM(Bar)
to Samuel Crisp
You must know *I* am at this Time at Home

26 Nov [1780]   2 p 8vo   Harv(H)
to HLTP
Ah Dearest Madam what a World indeed! —

[Nov? 1780]   1 p 4to   NYPL(B)
from HLTP
Your sweet Letter drew the first Tears from my

[Nov? 1780]   1 p scrap   NYPL(B)
from HLTP
All goes on just as it did — my Master neither

[Nov? 1780]   1 p scrap   NYPL(B)
from HLTP
I thank you a thousand Times for your kind

[Nov-Dec 1780]   2 p 4to   NYPL(B)
from HLTP
Oh my dear! what a World is this! M^r. Thrale

[Nov-Dec]   2 p scrap   NYPL(B)
from HLTP
I am flirting with your Captain, but must just

[Nov-Dec 1780]   1 p 4to   NYPL(B)
from HLTP
This don't come to ask how you do: Sophy

[Nov-Dec 1780]   1 p 4to   NYPL(B)
from HLTP
The Truth is my Dear Master has by a glorious

[Nov-Dec 1780]   1 p 4to   NYPL(B)
from HLTP
Jebb said he w^d. call — did he? he is not so

[Nov-Dec 1780]   4 p 4to   NYPL(B)
from HLTP
This is the first Letter or Note I have written

[Nov-Dec 1780]   1 p 4to   NYPL(B)
from HLTP
My Dearest Miss Burney will not be pleased to

6 Dec [1780]   11 p 4to   NYPL(B)
to SEB
As I am now well enough to employ myself

14 Dec [1780]   2 p 4to   NYPL(B)
to HLTP
Three Days only have I left dear Streatham —

20 Dec [1780]   4 p 4to   Ryl
to Henry Thrale
Were I to tell you, my Dear Master, but half

⟨20⟩ Dec   3 p 4to   Osb
from Gasparo Pacchierotti
From Lucque they sent me a letter of yours,

1780, continued

[22 Dec 1780]   2 p 4to   NYPL(B)
from HLTP
My lovely Burney will believe that I have

22 Dec [1780]   1 p 4to   NYPL(B)
from François Sastres
Mᵣ. Sastres presents his Compliments to Miss

24 Dec [1780]   3 p 4to   NYPL(B)
from HLTP
I do not I thank God forbear to write because

[Dec? 1780]   1 p scrap   NYPL(B)
from HLTP
There is a dreadful deal of Danger, indeed

[Dec 1780]   4 p 4to   NYPL(B)
from HLTP
I received the enclosed from Mʳˢ. Lambart

[Dec 1780]   1 p 4to   NYPL(B)
from HLTP
Make yourself happy, make yourself easy says

[Dec 1780?]   4 p 4to   NYPL(B)
from HLTP
And so here comes your sweet Letter

[1780]   2 p 4to   NYPL(B)
to SEB
expensive Entertainments she makes, &

[1780]   1 p 4to   Comyn
from Elizabeth Montagu
I am very anxious to hear how Mʳ Thrales

[1780?]   2 p 4to scrap   NYPL(B)
from HLTP
Now I have picked

[1780]   3 p 4to   Wms
from HLTP
As I went Yesterday I stop'd to read Hoyley's

[1780]   2 p 4to   BM(Bar)
from HLTP
Well! and what have I to say to my

[1780]   2 p 4to   BM(Bar)
from HLTP
I am come to town partly to do some little

[1780]   1 p 4to   BM(Bar)
from HLTP
My sweet little Friend! how your true

[1780]   3 p 4to   BM(Bar)
from HLTP
On this Day is our dear Master gone to see our

[1780]   6 p 4to   BM(Bar)
to HLTP
O dear! O dear — What can I say — write —

[1780]   1 p 4to   BM(Bar)
to HLTP
How much do I long for more good news of

[1780–81]   2 p 4to   NYPL(B)
from SEB
I am extremely concerned at the *reason* wᶜʰ.

[1780–82]   1 p 4to   Newc
from HLTP
My dear Creature's charming Letter almost

17 AP pmk [1780–84]   3 p 4to   Comyn
to HLTP
Thanks, Dearest Madam, for this cordial

[1780–84]   2 p 4to   Ryl
to HLTP
I am quite delighted at this sweet *hint*. — I

1781

4 Jan [1781]   4 p 4to   NYPL(B)
from HLTP
Don't I pick up Franks prettily? I sent

5 Jan [1781]   3 p 4to   BM(Bar)
from HLTP
Tis good Fun enough to read your Father's

8 Jan   4 p 4to   NYPL(B)
to EBB
Your Letter to Mr. Crisp, my sweet Hetty,

[10 Jan 1781]   1 p 4to   NYPL(B)
to SEB
I can't suffer the Baker to go away to Day

11 [Jan 1781]   3 p 4to   NYPL(B)
from HLTP
I never was so glad of a Letter from you before:

[15 Jan 1781]   2 p 4to   NYPL(B)
to SEB
Your Letter of this Morning, my dearest Girl,

19 Jan [1781]   2 p 4to   BM(Bar)
from SEB
Friday, Jany. 19th. Yesterday was the Queen's

19 [Jan 1781]   3 p 4to   BM(Bar)
from HLTP
So on Wednesday Evening did I go to Town

20 Jan   3 p 4to   BM(Bar)
from HLTP & Susanna Arabella Thrale
I received your kind Letter

22 Jan [1781]   4 p 4to   BM(Bar)
to HLTP
Yes indeed, Dearest Madam, I do begin to

[post 22 Jan 1781]   3 p 4to   BM(Bar)
from HLTP
If you had not written just as you did

[23 Jan 1781]   4 p fol   NYPL(B)
to SEB
I will write to Mrs. Thrale myself about your

[26] Jan [1781]   4 p fol   NYPL(B)
to SEB
I am very sorry, my dearest Susy, for the letter

30 Jan [1781]   3 p 4to   BM(Bar)
to HLTP
Ah, Dearest Madam, this is a disappointment

[Jan? 1781]   2 p 4to   BM(Bar)
to HLTP
I rejoice that the people know their *own good,*

[Jan-Apr 1781]   3 p 4to   Ryl
to HLTP
God bless you, my Dearest Madam! — I think

[3 Feb 1781]   4 p 4to   NYPL(B)
to SEB
You are very good & sweet for accepting my

3 Feb [1781]   4 p 4to   Osb
from HLTP
My dear my lovely Burney cannot be too much

7 Feb [1781]   4 p 4to   BM(Bar)
from HLTP
What is become of our dear little Burney

8 Feb [1781]   4 p 4to   NYPL(B)
to HLTP
This moment have two sweet & most

8 [Feb 1781]   1 p 4to   NYPL(B)
from HLTP
You fright me sadly my dear Girl with shewing

10 Feb [1781]   2 p 4to   BM(Bar)
from SEB
Saturday, Feby 10th. M^r & Mrs Hoole drink tea

13 [Feb 1781]   4 p 4to   NYPL(B)
from HLTP
This Moment Dick Burney tells me how

[13 Feb 1781]   1 p 4to   Wms
from HLTP
works at us pretty hard — it is a new

14 Feb [1781]   4 p 4to   Ryl
to HLTP
What shall I do for another Heart to give you,

[19 Feb 1781]   3 p 4to   NYPL(B)
to CB, SEB & CAB
I am now got wondrously better, & mean to be

20 Feb [1781]   3 p 4to   BM(Bar)
from HLTP
Scarce was I got over the Common before

[Feb 1781]   2 p 4to   NYPL(B)
to SEB
My dearest Susy's last Letter made me sad, for

[Feb 1781]   3 p 4to   NYPL(B)
to HLTP
I was just beginning to feel a little languid

20 [Mar 1781]   3 p 4to   BM(Bar)
from HLTP
I can perhaps, now I am at a Distance

27 MR pmk [1781]   9 p 4to   NYPL(B)
to Samuel Crisp
Kitty has given me the utmost satisfaction

29 Mar   2 p 4to   BM(Bar)
from Samuel Crisp (with PS by CB)
You are a good soul to trouble your head

[c Mar 1781]   4 p 4to   Hyde
to HLTP
Sweeter than ever is my Dearest Mrs. Thrale,

[c Mar 1781]   1 p 4to   Hyde
from HLTP
I enclose my Tyo her Ticket — Peggy Pitches

1781, continued

[c Mar 1781]   2 p 4to   BM(Bar)
from HLTP
My dearest Fanny must accept a Letter today

[pre Apr 1781]   1 p 4to   NYPL(B)
from HLTP
My lovely Tyo had better go to M^rs. Ord's, &

[3–4 Apr 1781]   1 p fol   BM(Bar)
from Sophia Streatfield
Oh! Dearest Fanny — our Dear Master is

[4 Apr 1781]   1 p 4to   NYPL(B)
from HLTP
I go to Brighton to M^r. Scrase write to me, &

[4 Apr 1781]   3 p 4to   NYPL(B)
to HLTP
You bid me Write to you, & so I will

[post 4 Apr 1781]   2 p scrap
to [SEB]   NYPL(B)
Mr. G. C. exclaimed "Why I never heard

5 Apr   2 p 4to   NYPL(B)
from James Hutton
Yesterday was my dear late Louisa's Birthday

[5 Apr 1781]   1 p 4to   NYPL(B)
from HLTP
I fly to hide myself; Brighthelmston is the

6 Apr [1781]   3 p 4to   NYPL(B)
to HLTP
I would I had some Commission, some Business

7 Apr   1 p 4to   NYPL(B)
from HLTP
My Dearest Burney's Letter was doubly

8 Apr   1 p 4to   NYPL(B)
from HLTP
I *can* give you no Commissions my Dear

9 Apr [1781]   4 p 4to   NYPL(B)
to HLTP
How sweetly & unexpectedly consoling to me

10 Apr [1781]   2 p 4to   NYPL(B)
from HLTP
My Dear my lovely Tyo has by now forgiven

18 Apr   3 p 4to   Osb
from Gasparo Pacchierotti
What melancholy an Effect has made on me

18 Apr   4 p 4to   NYPL(B)
from HLTP
On Tuesday next my little Dear Tyo returns

20 [Apr 1781]   4 p 4to   NYPL(B)
from HLTP
Well my sweet Tyo! & how go things at the

[21 Apr]   2 p 4to   NYPL(B)
from HLTP
I will send for my Tyo o' Tuesday 24: & pray

23 [Apr 1781]   3 p 4to   NYPL(B)
from HLTP
I believe you *did* misunderstand me my Love,

29 Apr [1781]   4 p 4to   NYPL(B)
to Samuel Crisp
Have you not, my dearest Daddy, thought

10 May [1781]   2 p 4to   NYPL(B)
from HLTP
What shall I tell my Tyo? what? but that

15 May   3 p 4to   NYPL(B)
from Samuel Crisp
I was neither cross nor surprised

[post 15] May   18 p 4to   NYPL(B)
to SEB
I am much obliged to you, my Dearest Susy

28 May [1781?]   4 p 4to   NYPL(B)
to SEB
We had hardly gone 10 yards, before it began

31 May-5 June [1781]   4 p 4to   RF
to HLTP
How precisely have you forestalled my answer

[May 1781]   12 p 4to   NYPL(B)
to SEB
This was the great & most important Day

[May 1781]   1 p 4to   NYPL(B)
to SEB
Thanks, my Dearest Susy, for your most kind

[May 1781]   1 p 4to   NYPL(B)
from HLTP
You are *a truly Dear:* poor M^rs. Byron is almost

[May? 1781]   1 p 4to   NYPL(B)
from HLTP
With infinite Difficulty and long Delay, the

[May-Aug 1781]   1 p 4to   NYPL(B)
from HLTP
Now Christ thee save thou little Footpage /

[May-Aug 1781]   2 p 4to   NYPL(B)
from HLTP
Now will my Dear little Tyo be delighted —

[May-Aug 1781]   1 p scrap   NYPL(B)
from HLTP
Your poor Tyo was forced to send for Sir

[May-Aug 1781]   2 p 4to   NYPL(B)
from HLTP
Sir Richard Jebb breakfasted here today, and

[May-Aug 1781]   1 p 4to   NYPL(B)
from HLTP
That Kam & Presto have had another Battle,

[May-Aug 1781]   1 p 4to   NYPL(B)
from HLTP
No News yet! I am sorry to be sure, but I am

[May-Aug 1781]   1 p 4to   NYPL(B)
from HLTP
Just six words to my Tyo by Crutchley's Man

9 June [1781]   4 p 4to   BM(Bar)
to HLTP
My sweetest Tyo how cruelly have you

10–20 June 1781   2 p 4to   Osb
from Gasparo Pacchierotti
Per mancanza d'esercizio vado dimenticando

[c 10 June 1781]   2 p 4to   BM(Bar)
to HLTP
I have already written you, my Dearest Tyo

[14]–26 June   20 p 4to   NYPL(B)
to SEB & CAB
I found Dr Johnson in admirable good

26 June [1781]   14 p 4to   NYPL(B)
to SEB
I sent you off a most sad morsel, my Dearest

26 June   4 p 4to   BM(Bar)
from Samuel Crisp
The waiting for your long expected letter

June – 4 July   16 p 4to   NYPL(B)
to SEB & CAB
I will now go on with the scrape into

[2 July 1781]   2 p 4to   NYPL(B)
to SEB
I assure you I am much better, though I must

9 July   1 p 8vo   NYPL(B)
from Samuel Johnson
Pray let these books be given after the

[12 July 1781]   2 p 4to   NYPL(B)
to HLTP
Why where is there such another Witch? —

14–16 July   4 p 4to   NYPL(B)
to SEB & CAB
I will give you now, my dear Girls,

15 Aug [1781]   3 p 4to   BM(Bar)
to Samuel Crisp
Now do pray believe me when I assure you

17 Aug [1781]   4 p 4to   NYPL(B)
to HLTP
Now I am going to write a very tyo Letter, —

19 [Aug 1781]   4 p 4to   NYPL(B)
from HLTP
"Wretched doings Ma'am!" as old Blakeney

20 Aug [1781]   3 p 4to   NYPL(B)
to HLTP
"Harshly said!" — no, Dearest Madam, never

[pre 21 Aug 1781]   1 p 4to   Iowa
to SEB
I can merely write to — say I love you dearly,

25 Aug-3 Sept   28 p 4to   NYPL(B)
to SEB & CAB
My poor Journal is now so in arrears

Aug   12 p 4to   NYPL(B)
to SEB
I fear you will think me a long Time, my

[Aug 1781]   2 p 4to   NYPL(B)
to SEB
I thank you heartily, my dearest Susy, for your

[Aug 1781]   2 p 4to   NYPL(B)
to SEB
Your Journal Letter was very entertaining, —

[Aug? 1781]   3 p 8vo   Hyde
to HLTP
Never was I so shocked as at the sight of Jacob,

[Aug-Nov 1781]   2 p 4to   NYPL(B)
from HLTP
You know my ridiculous Whim of fearing &

1781, continued

11 SE pmk [1781]   3 p 4to   BM(Bar)
to CAB
So you say I *"intend sending you a Letter on*

18 SE pmk [1781]   2 p 4to   NYPL(B)
to Samuel Crisp
At length, my dear Daddy, I hope to have

[21 Sept 1781]   4 p 4to   NYPL(B)
to SEB
Though I now hope so very soon to see you, I

[21 Sept 1781]   copy   2 p 4to
to SEB   NYPL(B)
conclusion of a Letter / To Miss Susan Burney

21 Sept   3 p 4to   BM(Bar)
from Samuel Crisp
Before I take any Notice either of your Journal

25 Sept [1781]   2 p 4to   BM(Bar)
to Samuel Crisp
How perverse & how cross, my dearest Daddy,

2 Oct [1781]   3 p 4to   BM(Bar)
to Samuel Crisp
I will not wait to be *told* you wish to hear how

3 Oct [1781]   4 p 4to   NYPL(B)
to SEB
As I have so often been behind hand with your

17 Oct   2 p 4to   BM(Bar)
from Samuel Crisp
If I wish it, you will send me a few more sheets

Oct   10 p 4to   NYPL(B)
to SEB & CAB
The next Morning, the Instant I entered

10 Nov [1781]   3 p 4to   BM(Bar)
to HLTP
What more bleeding! more <villanous> pill

11 Nov [1781]   2 p 4to   BM(Bar)
to SEB
You are a most sweet Susan,

11 [Nov 1781]   2 p 4to   NYPL(B)
from HLTP
Sweet Burney / Your little Scrap to my Fit was

19 Nov [1781]   4 p 4to   BM(Bar)
to HLTP
Why then all hail, most excellent Sedition

19 Nov   2 p 4to   Osb
from Gasparo Pacchierotti
I dare say that in some istance [sic] I know

22 Nov   4 p 4to   BM(Bar)
to SEB
I was never so pleased with a visit

25 Nov [1781]   4 p 4to   BM(Bar)
to HLTP
Just now have I read Letters from my best Mrs.

28 Nov   4 p 4to   NYPL(B)
from HLTP
You are a sweet Soul and always were so; I

[Nov 1781]   mutilated   3 p 4to
from HLTP   NYPL(B)
sent the [paste-over] Philip!

2 Dec [1781]   4 p 4to   NYPL(B)
to SEB
I have not often wished any thing more

2 Dec [1781]   3 p 4to   NYPL(B)
to HLTP
Write to you, dearest Madam? — How must

3–4 Dec [1781]   2 p 4to   BM(Bar)
from SEB
Monday night. Decr. 3. I have just finished

[7 Dec 1781]   2 p 4to   BM(Bar)
to SEB
I don't know what to say! — I don't know what

[8 Dec 1781]   3 p 4to   NYPL(B)
from HLTP
Thanks dearest Burney, I waited for your

10 Dec [1781]   3 p 4to   NYPL(B)
to HLTP
And so Mrs. Shirley, Captain Phillips' sister

[13 Dec 1781]   3 p 4to   NYPL(B)
from HLTP
I have got D^r. Johnson home at last, so the

[14 Dec 1781]   3 p 4to   NYPL(B)
to SEB
I am now waiting in the utmost impatience for

16 Dec [1781]   3 p 4to   BM(Bar)
to HLTP
And *continue* still will I say, — but not *then*

[17–18 Dec 1781]   4 p 4to   NYPL(B)
to SEB
What cross purposes are we all at! — my

[20 Dec 1781]   4 p 4to   NYPL(B)
from HLTP
I was bled again today by dear Sir Richard's

[22 Dec 1781]   2 p 4to   NYPL(B)
to SEB
I have never been *ill*, so it's nothing to say

[Dec 1781]   3 p 4to   NYPL(B)
to HLTP
How sweet & kind & good you are to write to

[1781]   2 p ¼ 4to   BM(Bar)
to CB
when he considered that your present work

[1781?]   3 p 8vo   Wms
to HLTP
Dearest Madam pardon me that I behave so

[1781?]   2 p 4to   Wms
to HLTP
Ah, Dearest Madam, *Alive* — & yet not with

[1781?]   2 p 4to   Wms
to HLTP
How vexed am I, dearest Madam, at this

[1781?]   3 p 4to   Ryl
to HLTP
This penny post is more tormenting than ever.

[1781]   1 p 4to   Hyde
to HLTP
I found all at Home well, & *4 to 1* in good

[1781?]   ½ p 4to   NYPL(B)
to HLTP
You *are* a clever Creature indeed, — & so kind

[1781]   3 p 4to   NYPL(B)
to HLTP
My dearest Tyo has had charming Weather &

[1781?]   2 p 8vo   NYPL(B)
to HLTP
I believe, dearest Madam, I shall surely see

[1781]   1 p 8vo   NYPL(B)
to HLTP
Yesterday by the Pennypost I answered your

[1781]   2 p 4to   BM(Bar)
to HLTP
Thanks for your charming Letter, — but

[1781]   4 p 4to   BM(Bar)
from CAB
Thanks for your comique Letter —

[c 1781]   1 p 8vo   NYPL(B)
from Lady Frances Burgoyne
I have by chance heard a most affecting

8 AU pmk [1781–82]   1 p 4to
to CAB   NYPL(B)
Three words I have promised my dear

[1781–86]   1 p 4to   NYPL(B)
from James Hutton
there is a poor German, in real distress who

[1781–93]   1 p 4to   Comyn
from Henrietta Maria North
I should have acknowledged the receipt of

[pre 1782]   1 p 8vo   NYPL(B)
from Dorothea (Gregory) Alison
I did not know that Mrs M. had asked you for

1782

[2] Jan   2 p 4to   NYPL(B)
from HLTP
Why must my lovely Burney be so unadorned?

[c 10 Jan 1782]   1 p 4to   BM(Bar)
from HLTP
Oh my dear, I had no Time to Write

22 Jan   4 p 4to   NYPL(B)
to SBP
I was very sorry I could not write to you last

[Jan 1782]   1 p 4to   NYPL(B)
to HLTP
Next Thursday will you, dearest Madam,

[Jan? 1782]   1 p scrap   NYPL(B)
from HLTP
M^rs: Byron is with me! for a Week! what a

[Jan-Apr 1782]   3 p 8vo   Ryl
to HLTP
A little *chear up* from you, my dearest madam,

1782, continued

[Jan-Apr 1782]   2 p 4to   Ryl
to HLTP
Sweetest & dearest Madam don't say *you'll do*

11 FE pmk [1782]   4 p 4to   NYPL(B)
to SBP
I should, indeed have been grieved my dearest

14 Feb [1782?]   3 p 4to   BM(Bar)
to CAB
I am immensely ashamed of the Paper & other

25 FE pmk [1782]   4 p 4to   NYPL(B)
to SBP
Are you qute enragée with me, my dearest

25 Feb [1782]   4 p 4to   NYPL(B)
from Samuel Crisp
I do acquiesce (tis true) but not

[Feb 1782]   2 p 8vo   Hyde
to HLTP
I send you here. Dearest Madam, my third

[Feb-Apr 1782]   3 p 4to   NYPL(B)
from HLTP
I really am excessively hurt to think that my

[Feb-Apr 1782]   1 p 4to   NYPL(B)
from HLTP
Don't hurry your tender Spirits so for God's

[Feb-Apr 1782]   1 p 4to   NYPL(B)
from HLTP
On Tuesday I will send for my sweet Burney,

[Feb-Apr 1782]   1 p ½ fol   NYPL(B)
from HLTP
We meet at Mrs. Ord's tomorrow night, but I

[15 Mar 1782]   6 p 4to   NYPL(B)
to Samuel Crisp
Your letter, my dear Daddy, which I

[19 Mar 1782]   4 p 4to   NYPL(B)
to SBP
But that I am myself in continual disgrace

[Mar-Apr 1782]   2 p 4to   NYPL(B)
from HLTP
My sweetest Burney! I have been a *poor*

[Mar-Apr 1782]   2 p 4to   NYPL(B)
from HLTP
Sick again sweet Burney is thy simple Friend,

[Mar-Apr 1782]   1 p 4to   NYPL(B)
from HLTP
I need not to have dreaded my Conference

[Mar-Apr 1782]   2 p 4to   NYPL(B)
from HLTP
No my sweetest Soul, I only came for Prattle;

[post 4 Apr 1782]   2 p 4to   NYPL(B)
from HLTP
My dearest Burney will see that I write on a

6 AP pmk [1782]   2 p fol   NYPL(B)
to Samuel Crisp
Heartily do I thank you, my ever dear Daddy,

6 AP pmk [1782]   1 p 4to   NYPL(B)
from Samuel Crisp
< > some one < > in works of Genius,

[11 Apr 1782]   3 p 4to   BM(Bar)
to HLTP
Scarce had I answered the first Letter

[24 Apr 1782]   3 p 4to   NYPL(B)
from HLTP
I thought to have seen my sweet Fanny

[25 Apr 1782]   3 p 4to   NYPL(B)
from HLTP
Upon my Honour then my Dear I have

[30 Apr 1782]   2 p 4to   NYPL(B)
from HLTP
My Eyes red with reading & crying

[Apr 1782]   1 p scrap   NYPL(B)
from HLTP
And so I sha'nt see my Love any more till we

[Apr? 1782]   3 p 4to   NYPL(B)
from HLTP
My precious Burney will not wonder that I

[Apr 1782]   3 p 4to   NYPL(B)
from HLTP
Well my dear Burney, here is your little Friend

[Apr-Aug 1782]   1 p ½ 4to   NYPL(B)
from HLTP
My sweet Burney must send *this* Book, & bring

[Apr-Aug 1782]   2 p ½ 4to   NYPL(B)
from HLTP
Povo' was a Puppy, & wanted to be talking of

[pre May 1782]   3 p 8vo   BM(Bar)
to HLTP
Ever since you left me, Dearest Madam,

[30 May 1782]   2 p 4to   BM(Bar)
from HLTP
Well! I won't croak; but you know I

[May 1782]   4 p 4to   NYPL(B)
to Samuel Crisp
Who in the world has a Daddy so kind

[May 1782]   8 p 4to   NYPL(B)
to SBP
That I could but come to you, Dearest &

[May 1782]   2 p 4to   NYPL(B)
from Samuel Crisp
I deferred a return of my most sincere thanks

[c 12 June 1782]   1 p 8vo   Osb
to HLTP
Dearest Madam I *have* written by the Post, to

[June? 1782]   1 p 4to   BM(Bar)
from HLTP
And so the Dr. left the Letters at Home,

June – [July?]   8 p 4to   NYPL(B)
to SBP
At length, my ever dearest Susan. my long

9 July [1782]   1 p 4to   Ryl
to HLTP
Thanks, dearest Madam, for the sweet *Words*

14 July [1782]   2 p 4to   NYPL(B)
to SBP
How does my Heart yearn to see you, my

21 July [1782]   4 p 4to   BM(Bar)
with SBP to CB
I found our sweet Susan better both in Health

21 July [1782]   3 p 4to   NYPL(B)
to HLTP
Here I am, dearest Madam, & I know not when

25 July [1782]   3 p 4to   BM(Bar)
to CB
How sweet of you, Dearest Sir, to speed

⟨28⟩ July   3 p 4to   Osb
from Gasparo Pacchierotti
Nothing can give me consolation in your

29 July   2 p fol   Comyn
from Edmund Burke
I should feel myself exceeding to Blame

also   draft   2 p 4to   PML
I should feel exceedingly to blame, if I could

also   copy   2 p 4to   NYPL(B)

[30? July 1782]   2 p 4to   NYPL(B)
from HLTP
Well sweet Burney, I wrote your Father every

31 [July 1782]   3 p 4to   NYPL(B)
from HLTP
I could not keep your Father from his Nursery.

July [1782]   4 p 4to   NYPL(B)
to CB
I congratulate you, dearest Sir, upon my

[July 1782]   4 p 4to   PM(Bar)
from CAB
You will be surprised to hear from me encore

[July? 1782]   1 p ½ 4to   NYPL(B)
from HLTP
I pity my dear's real Sufferings, but Cecilia's

[July 1782]   2 p 4to   NYPL(B)
from HLTP
My charming Burney! & how sweetly you bring

4 Aug [1782]   3 p 4to   BM(Bar)
to CB
But now, dearest Sir, let me call

5 Aug   4 p 4to   NYPL(B)
to Samuel Crisp
Thanks, my dearest Daddy, for your very kind

9 Aug   4 p 4to   NYPL(B)
to SBP
I long to hear from you, my dearest most

9 Aug   2 p 4to   NYPL(B)
from François Sastres
I have read Cecilia. It has pleased and

12 [Aug 1782]   3 p 4to   NYPL(B)
from HLTP
I felt my Heart so lightened by the

16 Aug [1782]   4 p 4to   NYPL(B)
to SBP
Here I am, my ever dearest Susy, & here as

1782, continued

[17 Aug 1782] 4 p 4to NYPL(B)
to HLTP
How welcome did your Letter make

24 Aug [1782] 6 p 4to NYPL(B)
to SBP
My Writing is very irregular, my dearest Susy,

[27 Aug 1782] 7 p 4to NYPL(B)
to SBP
engagements, write at his leisure, & make

31 Aug [1782] 4 p 4to BM(Bar)
to SBP
Your Letter. Errata, & account

Aug 2 p 4to NYPL(B)
to HLTP
I have been kept in hot water in defiance

10 [Aug-Sept 1782] 3 p 4to
from HLTP NYPL(B)
You are very charming my beloved Burney,

10 [Sept 1782] 3 p 4to NYPL(B)
from HLTP
Why here is a Letter that I suppose will be of

[14 Sept 1782] 2 p 4to NYPL(B)
to SBP
till about a Week before my departure

16 Sept 1 p 4to Comyn
to Thomas Lowndes
The Author of Evelina is much surprised that

[19] Sept [1782] 4 p 4to NYPL(B)
to SBP
Don't be angry, my dearest Susy, at this week's

[20 Sept 1782] 2 p 4to NYPL(B)
from HLTP
My dearest Burney will find me quite tranquille

21 [Sept 1782] 1 p 4to NYPL(B)
from HLTP
Dearest Burney do date your Letters. I never

[24 Sept? 1782] 1 p 4to NYPL(B)
from HLTP
On Saturday then I shall expect my Love, I

[Sept-Oct 1782] 1 p 4to NYPL(B)
from HLTP
Oh never let my dearest Creature put herself

[post 5 Oct 1782] 3 p 4to BM(Bar)
from HLTP
I rec^d. *two* Letters last night, very sweet ones

8 pmk Oct 3 p 4to NYPL(B)
to Rosette (Rose) Burney
That I have so long deferred answering the

15 Oct 4 p 4to NYPL(B)
to Samuel Crisp
Thanks, my dear Daddy, for your kind &

16 Oct [1782] 3 p 4to NYPL(B)
to HLTP
I do now indeed, Dearest Madam, begin to

18 [Oct 1782] 2 p 4to Harv(H)
from HLTP
I have received your charming Letter my Love

[19 Oct 1782] 2 p 4to NYPL(B)
to HLTP
Sweet & most kind are your Letters, dearest

24 Oct [1782] 1 p 4to NYPL(B)
to HLTP
Now are you indeed *my own* Mrs. Thrale,

24 [Oct 1782] 1 p 8vo NYPL(B)
from HLTP
M^rs. Phillips's three Weeks are out next

26 Oct-20 Nov 40 p 4to NYPL(B)
to SBP
In pursuance of my promise, I will now begin

28 Oct [1782] 3 p 4to NYPL(B)
to SBP
The excessive & ceaseless hurry I have been in

30 pmk Oct [1782] 4 p 4to
to HLTP BM(Bar)
Thanks, ever dearest madam, for both

OC pmk [1782] 3 p 4to NYPL(B)
from HLTP
Dear generous, prudent, faithful, friendly

3 Nov 3 p 4to NYPL(B)
to CB
I long most impatiently Dearest Sir, to know

8 Nov 4 p 4to NYPL(B)
to CB
How good, sweet & most kind is my beloved

9 Nov   2 p 4to   Osb
from Gasparo Pacchierotti
You have no idea with what pleasure I received

14 Nov [1782]   4 p 4to   Hilles
to CB
I have this moment been in search of a little

[21 Nov 1782]   4 p 4to   NYPL(B)
from HLTP
My dear Mrs. Ord & Piozzi, & Harry Cotton, &

24 Nov   2 p 4to   NYPL(B)
to SBP
The Day after my return home

29 Nov   2 p 4to   NYPL(B)
to HLTP
How sweet are the Letters you write, Dearest

Nov   4 p 4to   NYPL(B)
to SBP
it a fine lady's Door without being upon the

[Nov 1782]   1 p 8vo   NYPL(B)
from HLTP
My dearest shall have the Coach at 3. o'clock

[Nov-Dec 1782]   2 p 4to   NYPL(B)
from HLTP
I am just come home from that sweet *seducing*

[Nov-Dec 1782]   2 p 4to   NYPL(B)
from HLTP
The only Creature that I love in any degree of

[Nov-Dec 1782]   1 p 4to   NYPL(B)
from HLTP
Tell me dear Creature how you got home:

2 Dec 1782–3 Jan 1783   54 p 4to
to SBP   NYPL(B)
Decr. 2d. Mr. Swinerton took it

[13 Dec 1782]   2 p 4to   NYPL(B)
to SBP
<Midonte> *is* a pasticcio, — Margi does *not*

17 Dec receipt 2 p scrap NYPL(B)
to Payne & Cadell
Recd of Messrs Payne & Cadell Fifty Pounds

[25 Dec 1782]   4 p 4to   NYPL(B)
to SBP
A merry Christmas to you, my Susy, — my

25 Dec [1782]   1 p 4to   NYPL(B)
from HLTP
Tell me dearest Creature how you found

[26? Dec 1782]   1 p 4to   NYPL(B)
from HLTP
My dearest Creature will receive a long Letter

[Dec 1782]   2 p scrap   NYPL(B)
to SBP
full of sensibility, her voice is penetrating

[Dec 1782]   1 p 4to   NYPL(B)
from HLTP
All goes well my dearest Creature, I have had

[1782]   2 p 4to   BM(Bar)
to CAB
No room for a line but in the Frank to thank

[1782]   2 p 4to   BM(Bar)
from CAB
Rose's at Chiswick, & I have made him leave

[1782]   3 p 8vo   Comyn
from Hannah More
We came to Town late to night

[1782]   8 p fol   NYPL(B)
to SBP
I thank You most heartily for your two

[1782]   1 p 4to   NYPL(B)
to HLTP
I should have been quite as bad as Miss Thrale

[1782]   3 p 8vo   NYPL(B)
to HLTP
How sorry am I, Dearest Madam, to have you

[1782]   1 p 4to   NYPL(B)
from Elizabeth (Robinson) Montagu
Mrs Montagu is very sorry she cannot have the

[1782]   2 p 4to   Osb
from E[lizabeth] Montagu
I know the goodness & tenderness of your heart

[1782]   4 p 4to   NYPL(B)
from HLTP
How go the Harrels on?

[1782]   2 p 4to   NYPL(B)
from HLTP
Why what a foolish Fellow that Ostler Man of

1782, continued

[1782]   2 p ½ fol   BM(Bar)
from HLTP
Why we have had *such* an Evening at the

[1782]   2 p ½ 4to   BM(Bar)
from HLTP
Nobody less than Daniel is of Dignity

[1782]   1 p 4to   BM(Bar)
from HLTP
the Clock strikes *three* I have finished

[1782]   3 p 4to   NYPL(B)
from HLTP
I have this Moment received the enclosed

[1782]   1 p 4to   NYPL(B)
from Maria (Allen) Rishton
May I hope you will be at home to Morrow as

[post 1782]   2 p scrap   NYPL(B)
to SBP
The rest of the folks were Dr <Gathshore>

[1782–84]   3 p 4to   Ryl
to HLTP
Now indeed, Dear Madam, this is too cruel, —

[1782–84]   1 p 8vo   NYPL(B)
to HLTP
I have never been much more

[1782–84]   1 p fol   NYPL(B)
to HLTP
The Sight of your Hand *almost* makes me

[1782–86?]   2 p 4to   NYPL(B)
to SBP
I am sure, on my part,

[1782–86?]   2 p scrap   NYPL(B)
to SBP
I had turned off upon her beginning, that I

[1782–86?]   2 p 4to   NYPL(B)
to SBP
It was really a singular notion of Mrs. Ord's

[1782–86]   ¼ p 4to   BM(Bar)
from Hester (Mulso) Chapone
I find Mrs Pepys had engaged you my dear

[1782–86]   2 p 12mo   Wms
from Elizabeth (Robinson) Montagu
Mrs Montague presents her compts to Miss

[1782–86]   2 p 8vo   NYPL(B)
from Henrietta Maria (Bannister)
      North
It is so long since you have seen the inside of

[1782–86]   1 p 4to   NYPL(B)
to Charlotte Cambridge
I will own to you, my Dearest Miss Cambridge,

[1782–86]   3 p 8vo   NYPL(B)
to Charlotte Cambridge
I was most truly concerned at your

[pre 1783]   2 p 4to   Osb
to Rosette (Rose) Burney
I was truly concerned, my dear Miss Rose, at

1783

4-[post 20] Jan   mutilated   76 p 4to
to SBP   NYPL(B)
[We had <an> invited party at Home, both

6 Jan [1783]   3 p 4to   Osb
to Rosette (Rose) Burney
Will my dear Miss Rose think me a very

12 Jan [1783]   2 p 4to   NYPL(B)
to SBP
If he had *not* got the better,

16 Jan [1783]   2 p 4to   Comyn
from Hester (Mulso) Chapone
I have let Mrs. Delany know that you are very
also   copy   1 p   NYPL(B)

[16 Jan 1783]   2 p 4to   NYPL(B)
from HLTP
Well my dearest! the moment you were gone

[17 Jan 1783]   1 p 4to   NYPL(B)
from HLTP
Here is a Present such as I *know* my sweetest

[18 Jan 1783]   2 p 4to   NYPL(B)
from HLTP
Why my sweetest Burney! why what an

[21? Jan 1783]   1 p 4to   NYPL(B)
from HLTP
Nothing but Mistakes — but you won't wonder

[23? Jan 1783]   3 p 4to   NYPL(B)
from HLTP
I will begin a Letter to my sweetest Friend &

[23? Jan 1783]   3 p 4to   NYPL(B)
from HLTP
Dear little Selwin will bring me the Money on

[25? Jan 1783] 2 p 4to NYPL(B)
from HLTP
Now dearest, loveliest, kindest Burney! *now*

[29? Jan 1783] 4 p 4to NYPL(B)
from HLTP
Mr. Scrase has refused — I have tried little

[Jan? 1783] 2 p 4to NYPL(B)
from HLTP
My dearest Creature was particularly kind in

[Jan? 1783] 3 p 4to NYPL(B)
from HLTP
Not hear of me my Love! not hear of me! with

[Jan? 1783] 3 p 4to NYPL(B)
from HLTP
Is your Sister's Complaint easier? & is your

[Jan? 1783] 1 p 4to NYPL(B)
from HLTP
Dear precious Burney "come into the Wessel

[Jan? 1783] 2 p 4to NYPL(B)
from HLTP
I have a notion my sweetest loveliest Friend

[1 Feb 1783] 1 p fol NYPL(B)
from HLTP
When I got home from you I found a very

[2–3 Feb 1783] 2 p fol NYPL(B)
from HLTP
Nosooner [sic] had you left me than my

[4–5? Feb 1783] 1 p 4to NYPL(B)
from HLTP
The first I recd. before I rose — — as to waked

[6 Feb 1783] 2 p 4to NYPL(B)
from HLTP
You gave me leave to pester you with Letters,

[7 Feb 1783] 4 p 4to NYPL(B)
from HLTP
Why my dearest loveliest Burney, why what

[8–10 Feb 1783] 3 p 4to NYPL(B)
from HLTP
It is neither Laziness nor Forgetfulness that

[11 Feb 1783] 2 p 4to NYPL(B)
from HLTP
My dearest Burney wishes to hear how I do, &

12 Feb [1783] 3 p 4to NYPL(B)
from HLTP
I am better today though the night was terrible

[13 Feb? 1783] 3 p 4to NYPL(B)
from HLTP
It is scarcely fair to plague you so;

[14 Feb 1783] 3 p 4to NYPL(B)
from HLTP
My dearest Creature — not *quite* says she: —

[post 14 Feb 1783] 1 p 4to NYPL(B)
from HLTP
Come to me do this Morng loveliest Burney;

[19–23 Feb 1783] 8 p 4to NYPL(B)
to SBP
Wednesday, I spent the afternoon &

24 Feb [1783] 4 p 4to NYPL(B)
to SBP
How sorry I have been, my sweetest Susy

[Feb? 1783] 2 scraps NYPL(B)
to SBP
Wednesday, I have misplaced my Days:

[Feb? 1783] 1 p 4to NYPL(B)
from HLTP
Oh my sweetest Soul! what talkest thou of

[Feb? 1783] 2 p 4to NYPL(B)
from HLTP
I am but little easier my dearest, and poor

⟨6⟩ [Mar? 1783] 1 p 4to NYPL(B)
from HLTP
My sweet Burney will say the last *Words* of

25 Mar [1783] 4 p 4to BM(Bar)
to SBP
I thank you heartily, my dearest Girl, for your

[Mar? 1783] 1 p 4to NYPL(B)
from HLTP
All goes ill I think about what I care most

[Mar? 1783] 1 p 4to NYPL(B)
from HLTP
In despite of Maids & Moppets, in despite of

[Mar? 1783] 1 p 4to NYPL(B)
from HLTP
When I tell you that I was so mortified after

1783, continued

[Mar? 1783]   1 p ½ 4to   NYPL(B)
from HLTP
Oh my Dear! why Tuesday is Siddon's Benefit

[Mar? 1783]   2 p 4to   NYPL(B)
from HLTP
Mrs. Siddons is angelick and we had an

[pre Apr 1783]   2 p scrap   NYPL(B)
to Samuel Crisp & SBP
believe, before he could be found

[pre Apr 1783]   1 p 4to   NYPL(B)
from Samuel Crisp
Let then the satisfaction of this Treaty on your

5–11 Apr   8 p mutilated 4to & fol
to SBP   NYPL(B)
Your Letter of to Day, my beloved Susy, has

[pre 6] Apr [1783]   2 p 4to   NYPL(B)
to SBP
I have much, very much to write to you already

6 Apr [1783]   2 scraps   NYPL(B)
to SBP
than [obliteration] That makes the wonderful

[7? Apr 1783]   1 p 4to   NYPL(B)
from HLTP
If my dearest Burney retains even a little of

[8 Apr 1783]   3 p 4to   NYPL(B)
from HLTP
I write to the dearest of Creatures from

11 Apr [1783]   3 p 4to   NYPL(B)
from SBP
I sent my Father a frightful letter yesterday, &

[pre 12 Apr 1783]   3 scraps   NYPL(B)
to SBP
Mr. Pepys began an eloge of Mrs. Thrale

12 Apr   4 p 4to   NYPL(B)
with CB to Samuel Crisp
My dearest — dearest Daddy — I am more

[14 Apr 1783]   4 p 4to   NYPL(B)
from HLTP
You are very good to remember me my

15 AP pmk [1783]   4 p 4to   NYPL(B)
with SBP to CB
We are in hourly hope of seeing Capt. Phillips

[19 Apr 1783]   1 p fol   NYPL(B)
from HLTP
I write at Reading 11 o'clock Sat'. Night, &

20 Apr [1783]   2 p 4to   NYPL(B)
to CB & CAB
I intended returning to Town on Saturday

25 Apr   7 p 4to   NYPL(B)
from HLTP
And have I really been Wretch enough to add

29 Apr [1783]   1 p 8vo   NYPL(B)
from HLTP
I am very anxious to know how poor Mr. Crisp

30 Apr   4 p 4to   NYPL(B)
from HLTP
I enclose my dearest Friend a Letter which I

1 May   1 p 4to   NYPL(B)
from John Young
The Editor of the Criticism on the Elegy

3 May   2 p scrap   NYPL(B)
to SBP
Mr. Cambridge told me how

3 May–19 June [1783]   2 p 4to
to SBP   NYPL(B)
At Lady Mary Duncan's the Party was really

10 May [1783]   4 p 4to   NYPL(B)
from HLTP
Charming Creature as you are, & able to make

12 ⟨M⟩ A pmk [1783]   4 p 4to
from Maria (Allen) Rishton   NYPL(B)
Oh my dear Fanny, my heart is almost broken

14 May [1783]   2 p fol   NYPL(B)
from HLTP
Dear charming, cruel Burney write to me, if

14 [May 1783]   2 p 4to   NYPL(B)
from HLTP
The Bishop is gone so you may send *his* Franks,

17 May [1783]   2 p 4to   NYPL(B)
from HLTP
I have been thinking my loveliest Friend that

18 May [1783]   4 p 4to   NYPL(B)
from HLTP
Oh my Dear! Cator has taken my letter amiss

23 [May 1783]   2 p 4to   NYPL(B)
from HLTP
My sweetest Burney need not doubt my

23 May [1783]   4 p 4to   NYPL(B)
from Maria (Allen) Rishton
Many thanks for the very kind part you have

[24 May 1783]   2 p fragment
to SBP   NYPL(B)
Mrs. Ord sent an invitation to me for

28 May [1783]   2 p 4to   NYPL(B)
to SBP
& therefore I neither went down into the

28 [May 1783]   5 p 4to   NYPL(B)
from HLTP
How kind is my beloved Burney to love &

30 [May 1783]   5 p 4to   NYPL(B)
from HLTP
Well! now I *do* believe that my Dear Burney

5 June [1783]   3 p 4to   NYPL(B)
from HLTP
Well my dearest I am a little better I think

8 June   2 p 4to   NYPL(B)
from HLTP
I have written to Lady Frances Burgoyne &

[11 June 1783]   1 p 4to   NYPL(B)
from James Hutton
at my coming home last night I found a

14 June [1783]   4 p 4to   NYPL(B)
from HLTP
Rough edged Paper to thank my dearest

[17 or 18 June 1783]   2 p scrap
to SBP   NYPL(B)
I Dined at Sir Joshua Reynolds, —

20 June [1783]   2 p 4to   BM(Bar)
to SBP
dreadful shock to himself, & a most anxious

also   copy   3 p 4to   NYPL(B)

[23 June – 7 July 1783]   8 p 4to
to SBP   NYPL(B)
"Why once I saw you at Mrs. Vesey's, when

26 June   2 p 4to   NYPL(B)
from Mary (Hamilton) Dickenson
In proportion as I felt myself flatter'd by Your

[31 June] – 7 July   2 p 4to   NYPL(B)
to SBP
Friends be as faithful, as my *new* ones

[c June 1783]   ½ p 4to   BM(Bar)
from May (Wilson) Bogle
I am extremely obliged by your kind attentions,

2 July   1 p 4to   NYPL(B)
from Charlotte Boyle-Walsingham
Miss Hamilton has told me you are engag'd

2 July   2 p 4to   BM(Bar)
from Mary (Hamilton) Dickenson
Indeed my Dear Miss Burney I feel quite

[5 July 1783]   3 p 4to   NYPL(B)
from HLTP
[obliteration] I think I have done wonders

⟨7⟩ July   7 p 4to   NYPL(B)
from HLTP
Though I wrote yesterday yet I begin again

11–12 July [1783]   4 p 4to   NYPL(B)
to SBP
July 11th We had a party given at home

12 July   2 p 4to   BM(Bar)
from Mary (Hamilton) Dickenson
May I flatter myself my Dr Miss Burney

[15 July 1783]   2 p 4to   NYPL(B)
to SBP
Soon after Mr. Cambridge asked me

17–19 July [1783]   4 p 4to   NYPL(B)
to SBP
His spirits, too, once more restored, — his

20 July   3 p 4to   NYPL(B)
from HLTP
Why what an old Owl your foolish Friend

[July? 1783]   4 p 4to   NYPL(B)
to SBP
Afterwards, when we were speaking of illness

[July? 1783]   2 p 4to   NYPL(B)
to SBP
"But what shall we do, said Miss Baker

[July 1783]   2 p 4to   NYPL(B)
to SBP
River beyond the Duke of Montague,

1783, continued

[2 Aug 1783]   2 p fol   NYPL(B)
from HLTP
And who would *not* love, honour, and (to the

8 Aug   4 p 4to   NYPL(B)
from HLTP
I thank you most kindly my charming Creature

[11 Aug 1783]   6 p 4to   NYPL(B)
from HLTP
Tis odd enough but true here is no Paper *but*

14 Aug   3 p 4to   NYPL(B)
from HLTP
In an evil Hour did I tell my sweetest Burney

⟨20⟩ Aug   1 p 4to   Osb
from Gasparo Pacchierotti
May I still boast to call you with this name or

24 Aug [1783]   5 p 4to   NYPL(B)
from HLTP
How strangely I must have misled my dear

30 Aug [1783]   3 p 4to   NYPL(B)
from HLTP
I *am* better my sweetest Soul, but your Letter

[6 Sept 1783]   4 p 4to   NYPL(B)
from HLTP
I received your charming Letter yesterday but

[8 Sept 1783]   4 p 4to   NYPL(B)
from Maria (Allen) Rishton
You really have been a sad Correspondent for

12 Sept   4 p 4to   NYPL(B)
from HLTP
Poor dear D^r. Burney! why 'tis almost fatal

[post 12 Sept 1783]   4 p 4to
from HLTP   NYPL(B)
My charming Burney! my tender sympathizing

24 Sept [1783]   2 p 4to   NYPL(B)
from HLTP
My dear Creature was exquisitely kind in

[29 Sept 1783]   2 p 4to   NYPL(B)
from HLTP
I long to enclose both Billetdoux but dare not

29 Sept   1 p 4to   NYPL(B)
from HLTP
so am forced to manage this way, but *do* say

3 Oct [1783]   2 p 4to   NYPL(B)
to SBP
Ah my Susy how I miss you already! —

[pre 8 Oct 1783]   3 p 4to   NYPL(B)
from HLTP
I'll warrant I can tell you my *Case* fast enough

[8 Oct 1783]   1 p fol   NYPL(B)
from HLTP
You'll see by the enclosed that I have had a

[11 Oct 1783]   3 p 4to   NYPL(B)
from HLTP
All you say in your last Letter my dearest

25 Oct [1783]   4 p 4to   NYPL(B)
from HLTP
What would you have my sweetest Soul! when

29 Oct [1783]   2 p 4to   NYPL(B)
to SBP
I sent one Letter to you, my dearest Susy,

31 Oct [1783]   2 p 4to   NYPL(B)
from Frances Brooke
I shou'd sooner have answer'd your obliging

1 Nov [1783]   2 p 4to   NYPL(B)
from HLTP
If you knew the Agonies of my Soul you would

6 Nov   2 p fol   NYPL(B)
from HLTP
I dreamed last Night that you were come to

9 Nov   2 p 4to   Osb
from Gasparo Pacchierotti
Lest I should loose intirely [sic] the courage of

10 [Nov 1783]   3 p 4to   NYPL(B)
from HLTP
Have you *quite* done with me dearest Burney?

16 Nov   3 p 4to   NYPL(B)
from HLTP
Tis I dearest Burney who am the sinner, and *I*

19–22 Nov   mutilated   4 p 4to
to SBP   NYPL(B)
Wednesday, Nov 19 I received a Letter

19 Nov   1 p 4to   Harv(H)
from Samuel Johnson
You have been at home a long time and I have

also   copy (in FB to SBP 19–22 Nov 1783)
                          NYPL(B)

[20? Nov 1783]   1 p 4to   NYPL(B)
to Samuel Johnson (copy in FB to SBP
    19–22 Nov 1783)
May I not say *dear*? — for *quarrelled* I am sure

20 Nov [1783]   2 p 4to   NYPL(B)
from HLTP
I think nothing but of Sophy; my poor Sophy

21 Nov [1783]   2 p fol   NYPL(B)
to SBP
An engagement of long standing obliged me to

21 [Nov 1783]   4 p 4to   NYPL(B)
from HLTP
Oh my loveliest, dearest Burney! I thought I

22 [Nov 1783]   1 p 4to   NYPL(B)
from HLTP
My dearest Burney will be sorry for me; poor

24 Nov [1783]   2 p scrap   NYPL(B)
to SBP
Alas — my dearest Susy, it was

24 Nov   4 p 4to   NYPL(B)
from HLTP
What Steps would you take? we *do* take every

25 Nov [1783]   4 p 4to   Osb
to Rosette (Rose) Burney
I am glad nobody persuaded you to burn *this*

25 Nov [1783]   4 p 4to   NYPL(B)
from HLTP
I worry you with Letters my Love, but you

26 Nov   2 p 4to   NYPL(B)
from HLTP
All *is* safe at last my lovely Burney, She has

29 Nov   2 p 4to   NYPL(B)
from HLTP
I would be composed if I could my dearest,

30 Nov   3 p 4to   NYPL(B)
from HLTP
You are an Angelick Creature, and will excuse

[2–]3 Dec   7 p 4to   NYPL(B)
from HLTP
I received a sweet Letter from you today my

9 Dec [1783]   4 p 4to   NYPL(B)
from HLTP
My sweetest Burney is right in thinking my

11 Dec [1783?]   1 p scrap
                          NYPL(B)
from Hester (Mulso) Chapone
Now Miss, don't you offer <tr   > for to say

12 Dec [1783]   2 p scrap   NYPL(B)
to SBP
Friday Decr. 12 continued. I had the happiness

13 Dec [1783]   4 p 4to   NYPL(B)
to SBP
But in the midst of this, — how

17–19 Dec [1783] mutilated 2 p 4to
to SBP   NYPL(B)
with Dr. Johnson, who indeed is very ill

[20]–22 Dec [1783]   2 p 4to
to SBP   NYPL(B)
At night I went to the Opera. / Monday, Dec^r.

26–27 Dec [1783]   7 scraps   NYPL(B)
to SBP
Friday — Decr. 26th. I had a double

27–[30] Dec [1783]   10 p 4to
to SBP   NYPL(B)
contradict Yet I must think had he that very

30 Dec [1783]   2 scraps   NYPL(B)
to SBP
I went afterwards, by long appointment.

30 Dec   4 p 4to   NYPL(B)
from HLTP
I thank you for your Letter sweetest Burney,

[Dec 1783]   2 p scrap   NYPL(B)
to SBP
at him, I saw his own Face almost convulsed

[Dec 1783]   2 p 4to   NYPL(B)
to SBP
"And how did Mrs. Montagu herself behave?

[Dec 1783]   4 p 4to   NYPL(B)
to SBP
with the most chilling gravity

[Dec 1783]   mutilated   4 p 4to
to SBP   NYPL(B)
side of the defenders of Lord Lyttelton

[Dec 1783]   4 p 4to   NYPL(B)
from HLTP
Yes my Dearest, I *shall* love *you* to the last

1783, continued

[Dec 1783]   2 p 4to   NYPL(B)
from HLTP
I would be well if I could, & God knows I take

[Dec 1783]   1 p 4to   NYPL(B)
from HLTP
You are a dear delightful Creature, & always

[1783]   2 p scrap   NYPL(B)
to SBP
was going to congratulate him upon the *Ear* &

[1783]   draft 2 p 4to   NYPL(B)
to Frances Brooke
I should long since have waited upon you, but

[1783]   3 p 4to   NYPL(B)
to HLTP
What can I say to you, Dearest Madam, but

[1783]   1 p scrap   NYPL(B)
from Mary (Monckton) Boyle, Countess
   of Cork & Orrery
I wish you would give me your company all

[1783]   1 p 8vo   BM(Bar)
from Mary (Hamilton) Dickenson
Mrs. Carter goes with the Veseys &

[1783]   scrap   BM(Bar)
from Mary (Hamilton) Dickenson
I have only time to say I shall be

[c 1783?]   1 p 12mo   NYPL(B)
from Margaret, Duchess of Portland
If Dear Miss Burney will like to go to the

[1783?]   1 p 4to   NYPL(B)
from Maria (Allen) Rishton
only two lines to Congratulate you all on the

[1783]   1 p 4to   NYPL(B)
from Maria (Allen) Rishton
I will Just hasard two or three lines tho I am

[1783?]   6 p 4to   NYPL(B)
from Maria (Allen) Rishton
It seems to me an Age since I heard from you

[1783]   2 p 4to   NYPL(B)
from Maria (Allen) Rishton
Nothing but a bad head Ache shoud have

[1783?]   1 p scrap   NYPL(B)
from Elizabeth (Vesey) Handcock
   Vesey
My D Mad I did not hear till last Night that

9 Feb 178[3–5]   4 p 4to   Osb
to Rosette (Rose) Burney
The candour with which you have answered

[1783–86]   1 p 4to   NYPL(B)
to Rosette (Rose) Burney
Now don't be in a passion, my dear Rosette, for

[1783–86]   1 p 4to   Osb
to Rosette (Rose) Burney
I hope, my dear Mrs. Burney, you are

[1783–85?]   2 p scrap   NYPL(B)
to SBP
"How Miss Hetty, cried I, who has such

[1783–87]   1 p fragment   Osb
to Rosette (Rose) Burney
know well my dear Rosette, I have vowed

[1783–86]   2 p scrap   NYPL(B)
to SBP
Tete à Tete, he again talked to me of *George*

[1783–86?]   2 p scrap   NYPL(B)
to SBP
that Mr. G. C. was actually at Twickenham,

[1783–86?]   2 p scrap   NYPL(B)
to [SBP]
My Wife's odd jealousy, said he,

[1783–86]   2 p 4to   NYPL(B)
to SBP
As soon as she walked away, Mr. G. C.

[1783–86?]   scrap   NYPL(B)
to SBP
Mr. Cambridge, lowering his voice

[1783–86]   2 p scrap   NYPL(B)
to SBP
your visit. How did you find the Roads?

23 [pre 1784]   1 p card   NYPL(B)
from Frances & Harriet Bowdler to
   HLTP & FB
Mrs & Miss Harriet Bowdler present their

[pre 1784]   2 p 4to   NYPL(B)
from Sophia Byron
I shall be happy to see Dear Miss Burney at the

[pre 1784]   4 p 4to   Comyn
from Susannah Dobson
There are some things dear Madam

8 MR pmk [pre 1784]   3 p 4to   Comyn
from Susannah Dobson
As it was the furtherest thing in ye World

[pre 1784]   2 p scrap   NYPL(B)
to SBP
The Moment Mrs. Thrale came into the Coach,

[pre 1784]   1 p ½ 4to   BM(Bar)
from HLTP
If I could I should have come to Newton house

[pre 1784]   1 p scrap   NYPL(B)
from HLTP
By all means beauteous Burney! I shall be most

[pre 1784]   facsimile   1 p scrap?
from HLTP   NPG
Come o'Tuesday as well as o'Sunday do. / Dine

1784

[5 Jan 1784]   4 p 4to   NYPL(B)
from HLTP
Why you little Dear! I thought my last letter

6–8 Jan [1784]   2 p 4to   NYPL(B)
to SBP
Tuesday, Jan. 6th. I spent the afternoon with

[15 Jan 1784]   2 p 4to   NYPL(B)
to SBP
But before I go on with my Journal, let me

15 Jan   2 p 4to   NYPL(B)
from HLTP
Well my dearest Burney, now Mrs. Byron

[23 Jan 1784]   2 p 4to   NYPL(B)
to [SBP]
That means to be thought my particular

24 Jan [1784]   8 p 4to   NYPL(B)
to SBP
Thursday continued. I had a very long

5 Feb   1 p 4to   NYPL(B)
from HLTP
My dearest Miss Burney will be glad to see

[5 Feb 1784]   3 p 4to   NYPL(B)
from HLTP
My sweetest Burney will wonder to see

17 Feb   1 p 4to   NYPL(B)
from HLTP
Cruellest of all Creatures! and dearest of all

18 Feb   4 p 4to   NYPL(B)
from HLTP
Thanks, Thanks, a Thousand; my prettiest

[28 Feb 1784]   1 p 4to   NYPL(B)
from HLTP
Will you my dearest be so kind as to send the

14 Mar   4 p 4to   NYPL(B)
from HLTP
It is very wicked of you charming Burney to

22 Mar [1784?]   1 p fragment
                    NYPL(B)
from Hester (Mulso) Chapone
I hope you are long ago perfectly recover'd,

22 Mar [1784]   2 p 4to   Hilles
to Rosette (Rose) Burney
Mrs. Meek, Mrs. Phillips, & myself, will accept

23 Mar   3 p 4to   NYPL(B)
from HLTP
You was a dear Creature to write so soon

[15 Apr 1784]   3 p 4to   NYPL(B)
from HLTP
What a world this is dearest Burney. two

17 Apr [1784]   2 p 4to   NYPL(B)
to SBP
The sight of your paw, any way,

19 Apr [1784]   5 p 4to   NYPL(B)
from HLTP
Sweet Burney! so you will be glad to see me,

22 Apr [1784]   4 p 4to   NYPL(B)
to SBP
Sweet & delectable to me was my dearest

27 Apr   2 p 4to   BM(Bar)
from Sophia (Crisp) Gast
Your much valued Friend, and my beloved

1784, continued

[28 Apr 1784]   4 p 4to   NYPL(B)
to SBP
please ask Capt. P. if he can recollect

[4 May 1784]   4 p 4to   NYPL(B)
to SBP
And now, my dearest Susy, for yet a new scene

[15? May 1784]   3 p 4to   NYPL(B)
from HLTP
I wrote this Morning to tell my dearest Burney

[17 May 1784]   4 p 4to   NYPL(B)
to SBP
Let me now, my Susy, acquaint you a little

20 May   5 p 4to   NYPL(B)
from HLTP
When I came home I found a Letter from M^rs.

[22–23 May 1784]   8 p 4to   NYPL(B)
to SBP
Read this at any time — but read the Frank at

30 May   1 p 8vo   NYPL(B)
to Mary (Hamilton) Dickenson
The encreasing illness of a Friend who has long

[May 1784]   2 p 4to   NYPL(B)
from HLTP
I am come dearest Burney; It is

2 June [1784]   1 p 4to   NYPL(B)
from HLTP
I only write six Words lest you sh^d. think me

5–[6] June [1784]   4 p 4to   NYPL(B)
from SBP
Your silence my dearest Fanny

[12 June 1784]   2 p 4to   NYPL(B)
to SBP
My dearest, dearest Susy — I have read your

22 June   2 p 4to   BM(Bar)
from Sophia (Crisp) Gast
The sight of that dear Hand, which has so

23 June   1 p 4to   NYPL(B)
from Charlotte Boyle-Walsingham
I grow frighten'd least [sic] you have forgot y^r.

23 June amanuensis   2 p 4to   Comyn
from Mary (Granville) Delany
My dear Miss Burney I have but a Moments

27 June [1784]   3 p 4to   NYPL(B)
from HLTP
I am delighted my sweetest Soul to receive

[29 June 1784]   3 p 4to   NYPL(B)
from HLTP
high time for me to write to you would I yet

30 June   5 p 4to   NYPL(B)
from HLTP
I *did* detain then till the last Moment my ever

1 July   3 p 4to   NYPL(B)
from HLTP
I cannot sleep — how should I! my Piozzi is

12 July [1784]   3 p 4to   NYPL(B)
from HLTP
I received your Letter *here* my Love, it was

25 July   2 p 4to   NYPL(B)
from HLTP
Wish me joy my dearest Miss Burney, and let

[26 July 1784]   2 p 4to   BM(Bar)
with SBP to CB
As to poor Mrs. Thrale — she only keeps

26 July   2 p 4to   Osb
from Mary (Hamilton) Dickenson
I delay'd telling you how sensibly I felt your

6 Aug [1784]   1 p 4to   NYPL(B)
from HLTP
I not only thought you unkind, but I think so

10 Aug   draft   2 p 4to   NYPL(B)
to HLTP
When my wondering Eyes first < > looked

10–[16] Aug [1784]   2 p fol   NYPL(B)
to SBP
Let me begin, my dearest Susy, with business.

13 Aug [1784]   2 p 4to   BM(Bar)
from HLTP
Give yourself no serious Concern sweetest

26 Aug [1784]   4 p 4to   BM(Bar)
to CAB
The accounts Susan has received from our sister

12 Sept [1784]   4 p 4to   Osb
to Rosette (Rose) Burney
Shall I begin with making apologies? No, for

[17–22? Oct 1784]   4 p fol   NYPL(B)
to SBP
My dearest, dearest Susy — if you knew but
also   copy dated 8 Oct   2 p 4to   NYPL(B)

21–23 Oct [1784]   2 p scrap
to SBP   NYPL(B)
I purpose always Dating, in case of a Letter

23 Oct   4 p 4to   NYPL(B)
to CAB
My dearest Charlotte need never complain of

25 Oct-3 Nov [1784]   8 scraps
to SBP   NYPL(B)
3 Letters in her Hand

1 Nov   1 p 4to   PML
from Samuel Johnson
My heart has reproached me with my

6 Nov   4 p 4to   Comyn
to CB Jr
I thank you very much for your entertaining &

9 Nov   2 p 4to   NYPL(B)
to SBP
Tuesday Novr. 9th. 1784. This is Mr. W^m.

14 Nov   copy   7 p 4to   NYPL(B)
to Frederica Locke
"on gracious errand bent," indeed!

[post 21 Nov 1784]   2 scraps
to SBP   NYPL(B)
Charles told me afterwards that Mr. Badcock

22 Nov   2 p 4to   NYPL(B)
to CB Jr
Why your rioting Mr. Hamilton has done him

24 Nov   1 p 4to   NYPL(B)
from Mary (Hamilton) Dickenson
I will not delay shewing D^r. Burney how

25 Nov – 9 Dec [1784]   8 p fol & 4to
to SBP   NYPL(B)
I am extremely sorry, my dearest Susy,

28 Nov [1784]   2 p 4to   NYPL(B)
to SBP
Norbury Park, Saturday Nov. 28th. How will

29 Nov   4 p 4to   NYPL(B)
to CB
I don't write because I have got any

7 Dec   copy   4 p 4to   NYPL(B)
to Frederica Locke
Why poor Norbury and I are now in greater
also   copy extract   2 p 4to   NYPL(B)
Another of his confessions was this. — Luckily

7–18 Dec   4 p fol   NYPL(B)
to SBP
Thursday Decr. 7th. we had Mr. LaTrobe's two

[15] Dec   1 p 4to   NYPL(B)
to Frederica Locke
I wish my Dearest Mrs. Locke joy of the sweet

18–31 Dec   mutilated   4 p fol
to SBP   NYPL(B)
I am so behind hand in my Journal

Dec [1784]   amanuensis   3 p 4to
from Mary (Granville) Delany   Comyn
The affair of the Musical Catalogue

[Dec 1784]   copy   7 p 4to   NYPL(B)
to [Mary (Granville) Delany?]
A little more, however, I must talk of my much

[1784]   copy   2 p 4to   NYPL(B)
to Mary (Granville) Delany
Mrs. Lock, though almost adored by all who

[1784]   2 p scrap   NYPL(B)
to SBP
Tuesday — I spent the afternoon

[1784?]   2 p 12mo   Wms
from Hester (Mulso) Chapone
Will my dear Miss Burney drink tea with me

[1784–85]   2 p 4to   NYPL(B)
from SBP
A thousand thanks to you my Fanny

[1784–85]   2 p 4to   Osb
from Richard Owen Cambridge
I write in the greatest hurry to tell you that I

[1784–86]   2 p scrap   NYPL(B)
to SBP
At length, Mr. George Cambridge walked up

[1784–86]   1 p 4to   BM(Bar)
from Hester (Mulso) Chapone
Mrs Delany's servant is come for an answer

[c 1784]   2 p scrap   NYPL(B)
to [SBP]
when Mr. Cambridge came back, he said he

1785

1–2 Jan   2 p scrap   NYPL(B)
to SBP
upon her arrival: — I can less than

3 Jan   3 p 4to   NYPL(B)
to GMAPWaddington
I was very sorry my sweet Friend had so

8–10 Jan [1785]   2 p scrap   NYPL(B)
to SBP
Jany. 8th. I spent sweetly with my venerable

12 Jan [1785]   4 p fol   NYPL(B)
to SBP
Much Time — & much incident —

15–19 Jan   8 p fol   NYPL(B)
to SBP
How different this parting that meeting! —

18 Jan   1 p 12mo   NYPL(B)
from Margaret, Duchess of Portland
The Dss D. of Portland presents her Comp^ts

20–22 Jan   4 p fol   NYPL(B)
to SBP
January 20th. 1785. To Day about noon, I

24 Jan   4 p fol   NYPL(B)
to SBP
"She was going to write a note, &, in her

24 Jan – 17 Feb [1785]   4 p fol
to SBP   NYPL(B)
Monday, January 24th. 1785

[Jan 1785]   1 p 12mo   NYPL(B)
from Margaret, Duchess of Portland
The Dss D. of Portland presents her Comp^ts.

18 Feb – 1 Apr   4 p fol   NYPL(B)
to SBP
Twickenham, Feby. 1785. I closed my last

20–22 Feb   2 p fol   NYPL(B)
to SBP
Does my dearest Susan think such would have

22 Feb   2 p 4to   BM(Bar)
to CB
How good of you, most Dear Sir, to write to

10–17 Mar   4 p 4to   Hilles
to Mary (Hamilton) Dickenson
When my Dear Miss Hamilton so kindly called

[post 14 Mar 1785]   3 p 4to   BM(Bar)
from CAB
I sent you a Quire of paper, which I hope will

23 Mar   4 p fol   Comyn
from Mary (Hamilton) Dickenson
If you knew my Sweet friend how my heart

[3 Apr 1785]   2 p fragment   NYPL(B)
to GMAPWaddington
I have been very much vexed at not being able

6 Apr   4 p 4to   NYPL(B)
to CAB
Why you most notorious Charlotte! — do you

13 Apr   1 p 4to   NYPL(B)
from Mary (Granville) Delany &
       GMAPWaddington
It has not been in my power sooner to thank

[20]–22 Apr [1785]   4 p scraps
to SBP   BM(Bar)
Friday, April 22; Today I have had another

17 May   3 p 4to   Hilles
to Mary(Hamilton) Dickenson (with
      CB to Lady Herries & Mary (Ham-
      ilton) Dickenson)
I receive my dear Miss Hamilton's temptation
D^r. Burney, who is but just come home

20 May   7 p 4to   NYPL(B)
to Charlotte Cambridge
Now indeed I shall be glad to see my dearest

[25 May 1785]   3 p 4to   NYPL(B)
to GMAPWaddington
O how truly, how warmly I rejoice with my

[28 May 1785]   1 p 4to   NYPL(B)
to GMAPWaddington
Dear naughty Miss Port what have you been

28 May [1785]   ½ p 4to   BM(Bar)
from Hester (Mulso) Chapone
Will you, my dear Miss Burney, favour me with

21 June [1785]   2 p 4to   BM(Bar)
to CB
Mrs. Delany sees my necessity of hastening

[11 July 1785]   2 p scrap   NYPL(B)
to SBP
"I have been this whole morning with Mme.

15 July copy 2 p 4to NYPL(B)
from Stéphanie-Félicité, comtesse de
   Genlis
Combien j'ai été fachée ma chère amie

17 July 1 p 4to Osb
to Mary (Hamilton) Dickenson
I am very much vexed to have missed you this

20 July 4 p 4to Osb
to Rosette (Rose) Burney
If I had not the greatest objection in the world

20 July amanuensis 2 p 4to
from Mary (Granville) Delany Comyn
I am too sensible of my Dear Miss Burneys

25 July 3 p 4to NYPL(B)
from Court Dewes
I do not believe there is one among the

29 July 3 p 4to NYPL(B)
to GMAPWaddington
With what thankful surprise did

2 Aug 1 p 4to BM(Bar)
from Payne & Cadell
Messrs Payne and Cadell present their

9 Aug 4 p 4to NYPL(B)
to Rosette (Rose) Burney
Let me congratulate you, my Dear Rosette,

19 Aug 2 p 4to BM(Bar)
to CB
You will hear, most Dear Sir, of my summons

23 Aug [1785] 2 p 4to NYPL(B)
from SBP
In hope of having an opportunity

24 Aug 4 p 4to NYPL(B)
to CB
I have been very much alarmed, Dearest Sir,

25 Aug mutilated 4 p 4to
to SBP NYPL(B)
My most dear Susan's Letter is this moment

29 Aug copy 4 p 4to NYPL(B)
to Frederica Locke
How is my beloved Fredy? and can she

[post Aug 1785] 1 p 4to BM(Bar)
to CB & SBP
What a singular scene was this!

11 Sept 3 p 4to NYPL(B)
from GMAPWaddington
We are really quite uneasy at not havg. heard

17 Sept 3 p 4to NYPL(B)
from Charlotte Cuenod
C'est toujours pour obtenir des faveurs de votre

23 Sept 1 p 4to Hyde
from John Hoole
Mr. Hoole presents his best compliments to

24 Sept 3 scraps NYPL(B)
to CB
I hope, Dearest Sir, you are quite well

[25 Sept 1785] mutilated 4 p 4to
to CB NYPL(B)
Wives, Maidens, & — no, there is never a

25 Sept 4 p 4to NYPL(B)
with SBP to EBB
I was half inclined my dearest Esther to

8 Oct 2 p 4to PML
from Charlotte Boyle-Walsingham
You was so good as to say you would let me

[8 Oct 1785] 4 p 4to BM(Bar)
from CAB
[torn] ground.—I thank you my sweet adviser,

23 Oct [1785] 1 p 4to Osb
to Rosette (Rose) Burney
Accept, Dear Rosette, my kind congratulations

30 Oct 2 p 4to Osb
from Charlotte Boyle-Walsingham
What a sad Fright you have had, I pity you

31 Oct 2 p 4to Comyn
to CB Jr
Though I cannot imitate your kind attention in

2 Nov 3 p 4to NYPL(B)
to CAB
Tell my dearest Father that our Susan goes

4 Nov 4 p 4to NYPL(B)
to Rebecca Burney & Anne Burney
I have now another adventure to tell you that

10 Nov 3 p 4to NYPL(B)
to CAB
I was very much mortified to be unable to

1785, *continued*

11 Nov   2 p 4to   Wales
to [Margaret] Owen
Can you, Dear Madam, look at the signature

[pre 1786?]   1 p scrap   NYPL(B)
from Hannah More
M^rs. Pepys tells us you are to be there to

14 Nov   4 p 4to   NYPL(B)
to Sophia (Crisp) Gast
Can you, Dear Madam, after a silence so long

22 Nov   2 p 4to   BM(Bar)
from Charlotte Boyle-Walsingham
I have just rec'd the Faver [sic] of y^r. kind

24 Nov – 20 Dec   56 p 4to   NYPL(B)
to CB & SBP
As you don't quite hate one another, you will

also   copy extract   4 p 4to   NYPL(B)
"I wish the Translator knew that! —" / "O —

29 Nov [1785]   1 p 8vo   BM(Bar)
from Hester (Mulso) Chapone
Thursday next is the day fix'd with M^r. & M^rs.

1 Dec   4 p 4to   BM(Bar)
to Charlotte Cambridge
It is very long indeed since I have heard from

5 Dec   2 p 4to   NYPL(B)
to EBB
And now, my dear Hester, when you see the

6 Dec   2 p 4to   Osb
from William Locke, Sr
"She shall have Fairies enough to do all her

15 Dec [1785]   20? p 4to   NYPL(B)
to SBP & Frederica Locke
Not a word more passed about him

17 Dec   copy   4 p 4to   NYPL(B)
to EBB
I am sorry I could not more immediately write

19 Dec [1785]   4 p 4to   NYPL(B)
from Elizabeth Montagu
It is dangerous to indulge an opinion

20 Dec   ?   Mag 352(1785?)
to Elizabeth Montagu
[concerning Mrs Delany and FB's introduction]

[1785?]   mutilated   4 p 4to
to SBP   NYPL(B)
< >, on *perspective:* [cut] thing, however,

[1785?]   2 p scrap   NYPL(B)
to [SBP]
what Rooms there were, what *family*

[1785]   2 p 8vo   BM(Bar)
from Charlotte Boyle-Walsingham
I am extremely oblig'd to you for your kind

[1785]   1 p 4to   PML
from William Seward
Mr Seward presents his compts to Miss Burney,

[1785–July 1786]   2 p 8vo   NYPL(B)
to GMAPWaddington
You oblige me very much, my dear Miss Port,

[1785–86]   1 p 8vo   NYPL(B)
to GMAPWaddington
Many thanks to my Dear Miss Port for her

[1785–86]   2 p scrap   NYPL(B)
from Mary (Hamilton) Dickenson
As I imagined y^r. Dear little questioning Note

[1785–86?]   4 p 4to   NYPL(B)
to SBP
Monday continued. Mr. Cambridge has called

[pre 1786]   2 p scrap   NYPL(B)
to [CB]
But — my Dearest Padre, — *what shall I do*

[1785–90]   37 p & 19 scraps
to SBP & Frederica Locke   BM(Bar)
Friday 5th. This morning

[pre 1786]   2 p scrap   NYPL(B)
to SBP
"Did you see Mrs. Hamilton?"

[pre 1786]   2 p scrap   NYPL(B)
to [SBP]
shall —" / "Nay, nay, cried he, I have a *right*

[pre 1786]   2 p scrap   NYPL(B)
to SBP
she had seen me *at Mr. Pepys.*

[pre 1786]   1 p scrap   NYPL(B)
to SBP
[wh]ere you have still some in hand

[pre 1786?]   2 p scrap   NYPL(B)
to SBP
to prevent *all* evil

[pre 1786]   2 p scrap   NYPL(B)
to SBP
himself. Lady Rothes was very elegant

[pre 1786]   2 p scrap   NYPL(B)
to SBP
Some time after, but I know not

[pre 1786]   2 p scrap   NYPL(B)
to [SBP]
"Did you go in, then, the

[pre 1786?]   2 p 4to   NYPL(B)
to ?
we were all absolutely shaking between fright

5 Apr [1785–86?]   1 p 4to   Roch
to Charlotte Boyle-Walsingham
The hope of being able to partake of the

1786

3 Feb   2 p fol   NYPL(B)
from SBP
You were very good to give way, & trust to us

[14 Feb]   4 p 4to   BM(Bar)
from CBF
I now sit down to fulfill the promise

20 Feb – 21 Mar   12 p 4to   NYPL(B)
to SBP
Feby. 20th. — 86 I must now give my dearest

21 Feb   4 p 4to   Oxf(Bod)
with CB Jr to CBF
Has my Dearest Charlotte thought us lost?

21–22 Feb   6 p 4to   NYPL(B)
to SBP
My Dearest Susan will wonder but too *little*

26 Feb   4 p 4to   NYPL(B)
to SBP
I am inexpressibly happy, my dearest Susan, —

[post Feb 1786]   2 p 4to   NYPL(B)
to SBP
He repeated that the attempt would *terrify*

1 Mar [1786]   1 p fragment
                              NYPL(B)
from Mary (Granville) Delany
I long to see you tell me what Day & hour and

8   pmk MR [1786]   4 p 4to
from Maria (Allen) Rishton   NYPL(B)
I make no Apologies for not having sooner

9–10 Mar   4 p 4to   NYPL(B)
to Charlotte Cambridge
As nothing can well more vary than

17 Mar   4 p 4to   NYPL(B)
to Charlotte Cambridge
Has Mr. Cambridge told you how

[Mar 1786]   1 p 4to   NPG
from Mary (Granville) Delany &
     GMAPWaddington
We have been quite alarmed for we sent

13 Apr   2 p scrap   BM(Bar)
to CB
Why this is sweeter than any thing ever was

13 Apr   4 p 4to   Osb
to Rosette (Rose) Burney
I must quite, I fear, have exhausted your

2 May [1786]   card   BM(Bar)
from Hester (Mulso) Chapone
Mrs. Chapone presents compliments to Miss

6 May [1786]   2 p 8vo   BM(Bar)
from Hester (Mulso) Chapone
I was exceedingly obliged, my dear Miss

8–[11] May [1786]   2 p 4to   BM(Bar)
to SBP
For this long time past, my Dearest Susan

[20]–21 May [1786]   2 p 4to
to SBP   NYPL(B)
As soon [paste-over] pleasant an acquaintance

21–22 May [1786]   4 p 4to   NYPL(B)
to SBP
When we got to Windsor, my Father saw me

24 May [1786]   3 p 4to   NYPL(B)
to SBP
Now, my Dearest Susan, for the history of

1786, continued

19 June   2 p 4to   NYPL(B)
to CB
How great must have been your impatience,

20 June   4 p 4to   NYPL(B)
to CB
I am sure you will be glad to hear

22 June   copy   2 p 4to   NYPL(B)
to Frederica Locke
I know no more than I did yesterday, when I

22 June   3 p 4to   Comyn
from Mary (Hamilton) Dickenson
Though I have been for some time

27 June   4 p 4to   NYPL(B)
to CBF
My sweet Charlotte's kind indulgence to my

28 June   4 p 4to   NYPL(B)
to Rebecca Burney & Anne Burney
I have so very long been silent, — & you have

[June 1786]   4 p 4to   NYPL(B)
to EBB
I must be myself my own narrator to you of an

June   6 p 4to   NYPL(B)
to Charlotte Cambridge
I shall share, says my dearest Miss Cambridge

1 July   2 p fol   NYPL(B)
from Rebecca & Ann Burney
I have not words to express, nor power to

4 July   3 p 4to   BM(Bar)
from Jane (Campbell) Smelt
I hope My Dear Miss Burney has before this

5 July   4 p 4to   BM(Bar)
from Frances Bowdler
As Letters of congratulation are but little

7 July   1 p 4to   BM(Bar)
from Charlotte Boyle-Walsingham
I cannot hear of any Thing interesting to you

7 July   2 p 4to   Osb
to Rosette (Rose) Burney
I little thought when I received your last Letter

[10 July1786]   3 p 8vo   NYPL(B)
to GMAPWaddington
In order to give every body all the trouble I

10 July   amanuensis   2 p 4to   Comyn
from Mary (Granville) Delany
My Dear Fanny the Living is bespoke

10 July   3 p 4to   BM(Bar)
from Thomas Twining
— Pray, pardon the embarrassment & *gaucheté*

11 pmk   July   3 p 4to   Yale(Be)
to Mary (Hamilton) Dickenson
Your kind congratulations, my Dear Mrs.

15 July   3 p 4to   Osb
from Gasparo Pacchierotti
I own myself vastly obliged to you, for your

[17]–24 July   43 p 4to   NYPL(B)
to SBP
Once more I take up my Pen, to give

18 July   4 p 4to   NYPL(B)
to SBP
In re-reading my Susan's first Letters

19 July [1786]   2 p 4to   BM(Bar)
to SBP
I know my two most loved Friends will be

20 July   4 p 4to   NYPL(B)
to CB
Never were *Tears* so sweet as those

23 July   3 p 4to   Comyn
from Dorothy Young
You well know my "lack lustre eyes

25 July – 9 Aug   56 p 4to   NYPL(B)
to SBP
I now begin my second week — with a scene a

[July 1786]   2 p 4to   NYPL(B)
from SBP
Ah my beloved Fanny! — Our M^rs. Lock has

3 Aug   4 p 4to   BM(Bar)
to CB
I am truly concerned, most Dear Sir, not to

10 Aug–[Sept]   97 p 4to   NYPL(B)
to SBP
I shall now begin a new pacquet, from my

14 Aug   3 p 4to   BM(Bar)
from Jane (Campbell) Smelt
There is not an obligation upon Earth, which

29 Aug   4 p 4to   BM(Bar)
to CB
Your sweet Letter must have an immediate

12 ⟨Sept⟩   3 p 4to   Osb
from Gasparo Pacchierotti
It was very unlucky for me, before I left

18 Sept   2 p 4to   BM(Bar)
from Charlotte Boyle-Walsingham
I was very glad to receive a Letter from you

23 Sept   12 p 4to   NYPL(B)
from SBP
I was called to town upon the illness of my

29 Sept – 4 Oct   2 p 4to   BM(Bar)
to SBP
How good —how kind — how like yourself

Sept   1 p fragment   NYPL(B)
to GMAPWaddington
I am quite sorry you did not send for me down,

[post Sept 1786]   5 p 4to NYPL(B)
to SBP
& Mrs. Laurel, I have seen, formerly, at

[1–]2 Oct   20 p 4to   NYPL(B)
to SBP
The following Evening I first saw the newly

⟨10⟩ Oct   4 p fol   NYPL(B)
to CB
I have now, Dearest Sir, an adventure for you

27 Oct   2 p 4to   BM(Bar)
to CB
I have a world of things to say to you, — none

Oct   18 p 4to   NYPL(B)
to SBP
My Dearest Friends will easily conceive how

1–[30] Nov   50 p 4to   NYPL(B)
to SBP
November 1st. We began this Month by

10 Nov   2 p 4to   Osb
to CB
Kew has quite changed its aspect to your

[1]–31 Dec   50 p 4to   NYPL(B)
to SBP
The next Day my own poor Head — then

3 D[ec 1786]   2 p 4to & scrap
to CB   BM(Bar)
I was hoping for some account from yourself

16 Dec   3 p 4to   Osb
to Rosette (Rose) Burney
I do indeed congratulate you, my poor Rosette,

26 Dec [1786]   2 p 4to   BM(Bar)
to SBP
No, my dearest, best loved Susan

[30 Dec 1786]   6 p 4to   NYPL(B)
to SBP
Hour; — & a short one it seemed to us all — &

[Dec 1786]   2 p 4to   BM(Bar)
to SBP
this moment how do I feel the truth of my

[1786]   1 p 4to   BM(Bar)
from Jacob Bryant
Mr. Bryant presents his best respects

[1786?]   8 p 4to   NYPL(B)
to SBP & Frederica Locke
My beloved Sisters' separate answers have

[1786]   2 p 4to   NYPL(B)
from JB
Two Tickets for to nights concert

[1786]   1 p 4to   Comyn
from Edward Jerningham
Mr. Jerningham presents his Respectful

[1786]   1 p scrap   NYPL(B)
from Hannah More
Sunday is our constant day of retirement, and

[1786]   2 p 8vo   Comyn
from Hannah More
Mrs. Garrick desires me to tell you

[post 1786]   4 p 4to   NYPL(B)
to SBP
Let me now finish — if *ever* that may be —

[1786–87]   6 p 4to   NYPL(B)
to SBP
I now laughed more naturally

[1786–87]   2 p 4to   NYPL(B)
to SBP
one moment's Law, but even

23 Dec [1786–87]   2 p 4to BM(Bar)
from Charlotte Boyle-Walsingham
On the strength of your Postscript, I

[1786–87?]   1 p 4to   Osb
from Jacob Bryant
I return You with many thanks the observations

1786, continued

[1786–88]   4 p 4to   BM(Bar)
to Frederica Locke
What a terror indeed for my dearest dearest

[July 1786– Apr 1788]   2 p 4to
to SBP   NYPL(B)
a Message soon after cleared up that mistake:

[July 1786 – Apr 1788]   4 p 4to
to SBP   NYPL(B)
A degree even of terror seemed to affect all his

[1786–May 1788]   1 p fragment
to GMAPWaddington   NYPL(B)
the receipt of these sweet & precious things

[1786–May 1788]   1 p fragment
to GMAPWaddington   NYPL(B)
This way I must take, since I have no other, to

[1786–May 1788]   1 p fragment
to GMAPWaddington   NYPL(B)
Your uncle is very good, my dear Miss Port,

[1786–May 1788]   ½ p 4to
to GMAPWaddington   NYPL(B)
I thank my sweet Miss Port for her note, &

[1786–May 1788]   2 p 4to
to GMAPWaddington   NYPL(B)
The Rain prevents my walking out this

[1786–88]   1 p fragment NYPL(B)
to GMAPWaddington
I am quite sorry you are not well, my dearest

[1786–88?]   1 p fragment   NYPL(B)
to GMAPWaddington
O who can we couple with Mrs. Delany?/

[1786–88]   1 p scrap   Harv(H)
to GMAPWaddington
Can my Dear Marianne meet me this Evening

[1786–88]   ½ p 4to   NYPL(B)
to GMAPWaddington
I long to see my Dear Miss Port — but cannot

[1786–88]   1 p fragment   NYPL(B)
to GMAPWaddington
Many thanks for this little news — I cannot

[1786–88]   1 p fragment   NYPL(B)
to GMAPWaddington
Let me know how you are to Day, my dear

[1786–88]   1 p 8vo   BM(Bar)
from Elizabeth, Lady Templetown
I agree to your proposal with the

Jan [1786–89]   2 p 4to   NYPL(B)
to SBP
Young Brother was certainly to marry Miss

Nov [1786–89]   2 p 4to   NYPL(B)
to SBP
Miss Berrys, as I heard in a visit from Miss

2 [1786–89]   2 p 4to   NYPL(B)
to SBP
yet of a gravity kind & impressive — the

17 [1786–89]   2 p 4to   NYPL(B)
to SBP
concerning some answer to be sent to a

21 [1786–89]   2 p 4to   NYPL(B)
to SBP
Charles. I came Home too late for any thing

27 [1786–89]   2 p scrap   NYPL(B)
to SBP
<   >rtown prevented this design.

5 [1786–89]   2 p 4to   NYPL(B)
to SBP
When they all happened to be engaged

[1786–89]   mutilated   4 p 4to
to SBP   NYPL(B)
This swallowed up all my walking time:

[1786–89]   2 p 4to   NYPL(B)
to SBP
"I wish it too, then! cried he, laughing;

[1786–89]   2 p 4to   NYPL(B)
to SBP
of his professed plainness, — highly flattering.

[1786–89]   2 p 4to   NYPL(B)
to SBP
After they joined us, we were just as long in

[1786–89]   2 p 4to   NYPL(B)
to SBP
I rose, to ring the Bell — a second time, — to

[1786–89]   2 p 4to   NYPL(B)
to SBP
company for the rest of the Evening, in Town.

[1786–89] 2 p 4to NYPL(B)
to SBP
[pr]oduced a Letter from this same Man, in

[1786–89] 2 p 4to NYPL(B)
to SBP
This brought us again to the old favourite

[1786–89] 2 p 4to NYPL(B)
to SBP
You may easily suppose all this passed from

[1786–89] 2 p 4to NYPL(B)
to SBP
I grew now more serious, & *insisted* on being

[1786–89] 2 p 4to NYPL(B)
to SBP
[th]us far gives me not, therefore, uneasiness,

[1786–89] 2 p 4to NYPL(B)
to SBP
He began, very quietly, upon general matters;

[1786–89] 2 p 4to NYPL(B)
to SBP
"Certainly, cried he, pretty concisely, I shall

[1786–89] 2 p 4to NYPL(B)
to SBP
when it was over, for having got so well

[1786–89] 2 p 4to NYPL(B)
to SBP
of raillery, which so little waits for Probability,

[1786–89] 2 p 4to NYPL(B)
to SBP
effect, he stayed loitering at a Closet

[1786–89] 2 p 4to NYPL(B)
to SBP
her manner enforced its power, by expressing

[1786–89] 2 p 4to NYPL(B)
to SBP
[pro]mised my sister, he answered, to drink

[1786–89] 2 p 4to NYPL(B)
to SBP
For myself, my own conversation

[1786–89] 2 p 4to NYPL(B)
to SBP
up at him, to see if I had not

[1786–89] 2 p 4to NYPL(B)
to SBP
knowing her unhappy situation

[1786–89] 2 p 4to NYPL(B)
to SBP
so plain a speech in return,

[1786–89] 1 p 4to NYPL(B)
to SBP
hardly knew whether to be vexed at such

[1786–89] 2 p 4to NYPL(B)
to SBP
-tions, by sorrow & disappointment,

[1786–89] 2 p 4to NYPL(B)
to SBP
My Fredy may here wonder I

[1786–89] 2 p 4to NYPL(B)
to SBP
When he was gone, Mr. Digby desired

[1786–89] 2 p 4to NYPL(B)
to SBP
O Heaven! exclaimed I, Mr. Digby! —

[1786–89] 2 p scrap NYPL(B)
to SBP
of a Physician, no one else

[1786–89] 2 p scrap NYPL(B)
to SBP
my avowed regard. But it gave me

[1786–89] 2 p scrap NYPL(B)
to SBP
After a profound silence, he took

[1786–89] 2 p scrap NYPL(B)
to SBP
speech, would induce me to

[1786–89] 2 p scrap NYPL(B)
to SBP
me, is an idea — That something

[1786–89] 1 p scrap NYPL(B)
to SBP
We go on very well for what we ought to

[1786–89] 2 p scrap NYPL(B)
to SBP
at the attack, & your Eyes, & I don't

1786, continued

[July 1786–89]   4 p 4to   NYPL(B)
to SBP
I was a good deal surprised, however, to see

21 [1786–89]   copy   1 p 4to
                              NYPL(B)
to William Windham (included in FB
     to SBP 21 [1786–89])
If Mr. Windham is not apprized of the former

21 [1786–89]   copy 1 p 4to   NYPL(B)
from William Windham
I am fully apprized of the fact you allude to;

22 Sept [1786–90]   1 p 4to   Hyde
to James & Ann Elizabeth Lind
Miss Burney presents her Comp^ts. & many

[1786–90]   2 p 4to   Comyn
from Lady Mary Duncan
Poor Rubinelli has this moment acquainted me

10 Mar [1786–91]   3 p 4to   PML
to JB
The very Day on which I wrote to you I was

22 Mar [1786–91]   2 p 4to   Hilles
to Rosette (Rose) Burney
Continued avocations, & total want of leisure

31 Oct [1786–91]   1 p 4to   BM(Bar)
from Jacob Bryant
Mr Bryant presents his best respects to Miss

[1786–91]   1 p scrap   NYPL(B)
from Jacob Bryant
I am glad to find by your letter, that You are

[July 1786–91]   2 p 8vo   BM(Bar)
from Richard Owen Cambridge
As a short answer to your tripartite I say

[1786–91]   1 p fol   NYPL(B)
from SBP
My Captain bids me say with his kind love he

[1786–91]   2 p scrap   NYPL(B)
to [SBP]
I begged him to be less heroic,

[1786–91]   1 p 4to   NYPL(B)
from Elizabeth Juliana Schwellenberg
     (per Elizabeth Stainforth)
I am desired by Mrs Schwellenberg to acquaint

[1786–91]   2 fragments   BM(Bar)
from William Seward
Mr. Suard presents his compts to Miss Burney

[1786–91]   1 p 8vo   BM(Bar)
from Elizabeth, Lady Templetown
My Dear Madame I fear there

[1786–93?]   1 p fol   BM(Bar)
from Richard Owen Cambridge
Witwood says to Petulant / Thou art a Retailer

[pre 1787?]   1 p scrap   NYPL(B)
from Elizabeth (Vesey) Handcock
     Vesey
I am very sorry my Dr Mad^m that any affliction

[pre 1787?]   2 p 4to   NYPL(B)
from Lady Mary Duncan
Lady Mary Duncan presents her Comp^ts:

1787

1–16 Jan   24 p 4to   NYPL(B)
to SBP
Monday Jany. 1st. I opened the new year with

2–3 Jan [1787]   2 p 4to   NYPL(B)
to CB
The sweetest of Queens has said to me that

9 Jan   2 p 4to   BM(Bar)
from Jane (Campbell) Smelt
The gracious manner in which Her Majesty

10 Jan   4 p 4to   NYPL(B)
to CB
What a charming, comfortable, sociable,

[14 Jan 1787]   4 p 4to   Osb
from SBP
Our dearest M^rs. Lock has a cold in her eyes

also   copy   3 p LB   Arm

15 Jan–17 Feb   48 p 4to   Osb
from SBP
I must briefly give my Fanny a detail of what

also   copy   38 p LB   Arm

16–31 Jan   46 p 4to   NYPL(B)
to SBP
I go back to the 16th. when I went to Town,

[Jan 1787]   1 p 4to   Comyn
from Jacob Bryant
Mr Bryant presents his best respects to Miss

1–9 Feb   23 p 4to   NYPL(B)
to SBP
Thursday, Feby. 1st. During the Drawing

2 Feb   4 p fol   NYPL(B)
from CBF & Clement Francis Sr
I have just rec^d. y^r. Letter of affec^{te}. Enquiries

10–29 Feb   44 p 4to   NYPL(B)
to SBP
Saturday, Feby. 10th. This little *partie* will not

11 Feb   1 p 4to   NYPL(B)
to SBP
How content will a few words have power to

16 Feb   4 p 4to   Osb
from SBP
How can I thank my beloved Fanny for her
also   copy   3 p LB   Arm

23 Feb–5 Mar   16 p 4to   Osb
from SBP
I have just heard I shall shortly have an
also   copy   9 p LB   Arm

1 Mar   2 p 4to   NYPL(B)
to SBP
March 1st. My beloved Susan will long since

1 Mar   4 p 4to   Osb
from SBP
I will now endeavour to tell my Fanny the
also   copy   6 p LB   Arm

6 Mar Apr   38 p 4to   NYPL(B)
to SBP
"Pray Mr. Griffardiere, cried she, hastily, What

25–31 Mar   13 p 4to   Osb
from SBP
Notwithstanding a most abominable propensity
also   copy   10 p LB   Arm

[3]–18 Apr   24 p 4to   Osb
from SBP
I finished my little Paquet of Journal to my
also   copy   14 p LB   Arm

9 Apr [1787]   amanuensis? 4 p 4to
from Mary (Granville) Delany   Comyn
I will not say a word of my disappointment last

22 May [1787]   4 p 4to   NYPL(B)
to CB
This Date alone will tell my dearest Father all

May   13 p 4to   NYPL(B)
to SBP
A fresh beginning now of Journal to the kind

1–10 June   20 p 4to   Osb
from SBP
Once more I resume my annals my dearest
also   copy   11 p LB   Arm

4–[30] June   41 p 4to   NYPL(B)
to SBP
I am now writing to the present moment, —

7 June   2 p 4to   Osb
from SBP
What a most sweet letter was my Fanny! &
also   copy   2 p 4to   Arm

14 June   2 p 4to   NYPL(B)
to CB
I could write no sooner, from the

17 June   3 p 4to   NYPL(B)
to SBP
Quite alive, my Dearest Susan, — & going

18 June   23 p 4to   Osb
from SBP
My dearest Fanny knows by my little letter of
also   copy   16 p LB   Arm

[20 June 1787]   2 p 4to   NYPL(B)
to SBP
Quite alive & quite well, my Dearest Dear

1–19 July   23 p 4to   Osb
from SBP
My last Journal brought me up, I think, to last
also   copy   12 p LB   Arm

1–31 July   44 p 4to   NYPL(B)
to SBP
July 1st. Sunday, Alarming to my Heart was

7 July   2 p 4to   NYPL(B)
from Lady Rothes
I am extremely obliged to you for your kind

8 July   2 p 4to   NYPL(B)
to CB
M. de la Blancherie has expressed an

1787, continued

8 July   1 p 4to   NYPL(B)
from M de la Blancherie (included in
    FB to SBP 1–31 July 1787)
M. De la Blancherie présente respect à Miss

16 July   3 p 4to   BM(Bar)
from Jane (Campbell) Smelt
My Dear Miss Burneys Letter which I received

20 July   4 p 4to   NYPL(B)
to SBP
How sweet & kind of my most dear person's

28 July   1 p 4to   PML
to JB
What have you to say for yourself now, Mr.

29 July   2 p 4to   NYPL(B)
to SBP
Are you safe Home, my beloved Susan? Have

[post 30 July 1787]   draft 1 p 4to
                              PML
from JB (on p 2 of FB to JB 28 July
    1787)
To be sure I did put on my red coat and I will

31 July   4 p 4to   BM(Bar)
to CBF
My sweet Charlotte's kind letter was most

2–[31] Aug   40 p 4to   NYPL(B)
to SBP
I had the happiness to begin this Month with

3 Aug 178[7]   2 p 4to   NYPL(B)
from Ann (Cholmley) Phipps, Lady
    Mulgrave
I was made very happy by the kind Letter I

6 Aug–9 Sept   78 p 4to   Osb
from SBP
Since the late sweet interruption my Journal
also   copy   44 p LB   Arm

19 Aug   2 p 4to   Osb
from SBP
I received my dearest Fanny's *Sonnet* with
also   copy   1 p LB   Arm

29 Aug   2 p 4to   Osb
from SBP
Our dearest Mrs Lock has sent me the largest
also   copy   1 p LB   Arm

31 Aug [1787]   4 p 4to   Osb
to Rosette (Rose) Burney
At length, my dear Rosette, — *at length*

[17 Sept 1787]   3 p 4to   NYPL(B)
to SBP
Dear best loved Friends — take warm from a

19 Sept   2 p 4to   Osb
from SBP
I felt that my best loved kindest Fanny would
also   copy   2 p LB   Arm

22 Sept [1787]   1 p 8vo   BM(Bar)
from Elizabeth, Lady Templetown
I cannot my dear Madam be in Windsor

23–27 Sept   36 p 4to   Osb
from SBP
Once more I resume my pen & ink conversation
also   copy   22 p LB   Arm

Sept   12 p 4to   NYPL(B)
to SBP
My memorandums of this Month are so scanty,

1 Oct   2 p 4to   Osb
from SBP
We could not look at our dearest Fanny long
also   copy   2 p LB   Arm

9–14 Oct [1787]   4 p 4to   NYPL(B)
to SBP
How kind was my Susan's dear note with the

11 Oct   18 p 4to   Osb
from SBP
I began Journalizing when I had yet scarce
also   copy   13 p LB   Arm

11–31 Oct   42 p 4to   Osb
from SBP
I think the Giornale I sent by M^rs: Delany left
also   copy   28 p LB   Arm

15 OC 1787 pmk   4 p 4to NYPL(B)
to CB
This narration was kind indeed, most Dear Sir,

21 Oct   2 p 4to   Osb
from SBP
I know not whether my dearest Fanny will
also   copy   2 p LB   Arm

23 Oct [1787]   2 p 4to   NYPL(B)
to SBP
It was with such difficulty I scrambled time for

Oct 8 p 4to NYPL(B)
to SBP
My brief memorials of this Month

Oct 1787–Jan 1788 7 p 4to NYPL(B)
to SBP & Frederica Locke
I send my beloveds the Three last months of

1–[30] Nov 14 p 4to NYPL(B)
to SBP
Thursday, 1st. I called upon Lady Louisa

[4 Nov 1787] 2 p 4to NYPL(B)
to SBP
I do not wonder my dearest Susan was in such

4 Nov 4 p 4to Osb
from SBP
I had written myself almost blind Wednesday

also copy 2 p LB Arm

6 Nov [1787] 4 p 4to BM(Bar)
to CB
I am quite disappointed to write word to my

11 Nov–22 Dec 40 p 4to Osb
from SBP
My folio sheet letter I think brought me up to

also copy 51 p LB Arm

13 Nov [1787] 4 p 4to NYPL(B)
to SBP
Certainly, my beloved Susan, what I put into

23 Nov 4 p 4to NYPL(B)
to SBP
Mr. William is perfectly right with regard to

1–[31] Dec 13 p 4to NYPL(B)
to SBP
Saturday 1st. 'Tis strange <that> two feelings

3 Dec [1787] 4 p 4to BM(Bar)
from SBP
wth Papa, who was giving Nordia plumbs

6 Dec 3 p 4to Hilles
to Mary (Hamilton) Dickenson
Is there such a thing as pardon in the Land? —

10 DE 1787 pmk 3 p 4to NYPL(B)
to SBP
I am most happy to hear my dearest Susanna

21 Dec 1787–22 Jan 1788 42 p 4to
from SBP Osb
that they will as it is very little out of their

23 Dec 4 p 4to NYPL(B)
to SBP
My dearest Susan will have heard by this time

24 Dec 4 p 4to BM(Bar)
to CBF
Ah, my Dearest Charlotte, how do I regret I

[1787] 2 p 4to NYPL(B)
from James Hutton
I must thank you for Evelyna which I have

[1787] 4 p 4to Osb
from SBP
but what a scene again awaited her wth. the

[May? 1787–88] 8 p 4to NYPL(B)
to SBP
curiosity, I will Copy the Card.

[1787–89] 2 p 4to NYPL(B)
to SBP
I saw, too, that he disliked this same

[1787–89] 2 p 4to NYPL(B)
to SBP
of extremest earnestness "*Do* come back one

[1787–89] 2 p 4to NYPL(B)
to SBP
I resolved, therefore, however disagreeable,

[1787–91] 1 p 4to NYPL(B)
from Jacob Bryant
It affords me always great happiness to obey

18 [1787–91] 1 p 8vo Wms
from Jacob Bryant
Though I have a bad cold, yet in confidence of

[1787–91] 2 p 8vo NYPL(B)
from Jane Gomm
How is it my dear Miss Burney that you & I

11 May [1787–91] 1 p scrap
to SBP? NYPL(B)
< > you, my dearest Nurse, — Companion,

[1787–91] 1 p 4to NYPL(B)
from Lady Rothes
I should not have been so long without paying

[pre 1788] 1 p 4to NYPL(B)
from Sophy Streatfield
I must intrude on your time Just to thank you

1788

1–7 Jan   18 p 4to   NYPL(B)
to SBP
Happy prove this year to my most beloved

1 Jan   2 p 4to   Osb
from SBP
I must send a mite to my Fanny — I shall not

also   copy   1 p LB   Arm

1 Jan–1 Apr   81 p 4to   NYPL(B)
from SBP
Once more I am enabled to Journalize my

8–[12] Jan   28 p 4to   NYPL(B)
to SBP
Tuesday, Jany. 8th. This Evening, according to

12–31 Jan   41 p 4to   NYPL(B)
to SBP
Accordingly, at half past 7 o'clock, I ordered

20 Jan [1788]   2 p 4to   NYPL(B)
from SBP
The account you wrote me of yourself last

20 Jan   4 p 4to   NYPL(B)
from Thomas Twining
I have no right, poor Sinner as I am, to come

31 Jan–20 Mar   4 p 4to   BM(Bar)
to CBF
This ancient beginning shall now have a more

1–13 Feb   71 p 4to   NYPL(B)
to SBP
Friday, 1st. Feb^y. — To Day I had a summons

[post 13] Feb   28 p 4to   NYPL(B)
to SBP
In coming down stairs, I met Lord

[post 13 Feb 1788]   ½ p fol
to GMAPWaddington   NYPL(B)
I am come home much tired from the Trial —

[Feb 1788?]   2 p 8vo   NYPL(B)
to GMAPWaddington
I have been truly mortified in missing you, my

30 Mar   4 p 4to   NYPL(B)
to CB
We go on prodigiously well here. Mr. Locke

Mar   6 p 4to   NYPL(B)
to SBP
I have only memorandums of this Month, as

[14 Apr 1788]   1 p 4to   NYPL(B)
to GMAPWaddington
A thousand thanks for this Morning's

[pre 15 Apr 1788]   1 p 4to   BM(Bar)
from Jane (Campbell) Smelt
My Dear Miss Burney will I hope accept

[pre 15 Apr 1788]   2 p 4to   BM(Bar)
from Jane (Campbell) Smelt
I cannot think of leting [sic] the opportunity

[pre 15 Apr 1788]   1 p 8vo   BM(Bar)
from Jane (Campbell) Smelt
My dear Miss Burneys kind *permission* must

17–20 Apr [1788]   4 p 4to   NYPL(B)
from SBP & Frederica Locke
Here am I my sweet Fanny, returned to my

18 Apr   1 p 4to   NYPL(B)
from Bernard Dewes
M^r. Dewes is much obliged to Miss Burney for

19 Apr–May   41 p 4to   NYPL(B)
from SBP
After the exquisite lecture I have just made,

[22 Apr 1788]   2 p 4to   NYPL(B)
from SBP
I rejoice at the idea of the Messenger from

Apr   24 p 4to   NYPL(B)
to SBP
I have scarce a memorandum of this fatal

[Apr 1788]   1 p 4to   NYPL(B)
from SBP
Heaven bless my beloved Fanny! — She will

[Apr 1788]   1 p fragment   NYPL(B)
from SBP
I can scarce ask my beloved Fanny how she

Apr [1788?]   1 p 4to   NYPL(B)
from Jacob Bryant
Mr Bryant presents his best respects to Miss

7 May [1788]   2 p 4to   NYPL(B)
from SBP
My dearest Fanny's letter was sweet &

14 May [1788] 2 p 4to NYPL(B)
from SBP
My dearest Fanny's sweet letter to our dear

[May 1788] 1 p 4to BM(Bar)
to CBF
I beg you to be ready here a few minutes

May–June 14 p 4to NYPL(B)
to SBP
Neither have I kept any Diary this Month: I

[13 June]–9 Sept 88 p 4to NYPL(B)
from SBP
My dearest Fanny must ere have rec'd

14 June 4 p fol NYPL(B)
from SBP
My dearest Fanny's commission shall be as

15 June [1788] 4 p fol NYPL(B)
from SBP
I will now proceed in my narrative — upon

16 June [1788] 4 p fol NYPL(B)
from SBP
I was sorry it was out of my power to conclude

23 June 4 p 4to NYPL(B)
to CB
How expeditious & kind you have been,

25 June [1788] 4 p 4to NYPL(B)
from SBP
I am vexed my dearest Girl that the haste in

[1–12] July 2 p 4to NYPL(B)
to SBP
I shall now briefly collect a few scattered

2 July 3 p 4to NYPL(B)
from Anne (Smelt) Cholmley
That I have not sooner acknowledg'd what I

[9 July 1788] 2 p 4to NYPL(B)
from SBP
I must write a few hurried lines to my sweet

13–22 July 48 p 4to NYPL(B)
to SBP
Sunday, July 13th. Now, my dearest Friends,

14 July–10 Aug [1788] 2 p ½ fol
from CBF BM(Bar)
the foot of M^rs. Adey's Box & took

17–21 July 4 p fol NYPL(B)
to CB
In all this length of time, Dearest Sir, I have

18 July [1788] 3 p 4to BM(Bar)
from Richard Owen Cambridge
Charlotte not being able to write to you

22–29 July 48 p 4to NYPL(B)
to SBP
How disappointed was I this Morning to see

30 July 2 p 4to NYPL(B)
from SBP
My dearest Fanny will have been surprised at

30 July–4 Aug 46 p 4to NYPL(B)
to SBP
In the Afternoon, I went again to the play,

[July 1788] 2 p 4to NYPL(B)
from William Seward
Mr Seward presents his Compts to Miss

5–16 Aug 40 p 4to NYPL(B)
to SBP
I was much better This morning,

[9 Aug 1788] ½ p 4to NYPL(B)
to GMAPWaddington
How most provokingly unfortunate, my dear

10 [Aug] 1 p 4to NYPL(B)
from Stephen Digby
Her Majesty may possibly not have heard that

also copy (included in FB to SBP 5–16
Aug 1788) 1 p 4to NYPL(B)

12 Aug [1788] 4 p 4to NYPL(B)
from SBP & Frederica Locke
I am *very* sorry, tho' not much surprised that

[13 Aug 1788] 2 p fragment
to GMAPWaddington
My dear Marianne will have heard of the

[16 Aug 1788] 2 p 12mo BM(Bar)
to GMAPWaddington
I find I cannot possibly manage the play to

17–30 Aug 14 p 4to NYPL(B)
to SBP
Aug^st. 17. Sunday. This Day after our arrival

[22 Aug 1788] 1 p fragment
to GMAPWaddington NYPL(B)
Can I see my Dear Marianne to Tea this

26 Aug–2 Oct   40 p 4to   NYPL(B)
from SBP
I left off at the 26th: of Augt. when the stage

1–30 Sept   16 p 4to   NYPL(B)
to SBP
Septr. 1st. Peace to the <Manes> of the poor

5 Sept [1788]   4 p 4to   NYPL(B)
from SBP & Frederica Locke
Looking over my dearest Fanny's sweet letter

[7 Sept 1788]   2 p 4to   NYPL(B)
to CB
This is an humble supplication, Dearest Padre,

7 Sept   4 p 4to   NYPL(B)
from SBP & Frederica Locke
<well> my dearest dear Fanny you will see

17 Sept   4 p 4to   NYPL(B)
from SBP & Frederica Locke
I think that my beloved Fanny will like to hear

21 Sept–22 Dec   48 p 4to   NYPL(B)
from SBP
In my last Partie I forgot to mention

22 SE pmk [1788]   3 p 4to   NYPL(B)
from SBP
My dearest Fanny has, I am grieved to find,

26 pmk [Sept 1788]   3 p 4to
from SBP   NYPL(B)
I promised to write to my Fanny to day, & will

29 Sept–9 Oct   4 p 4to   NYPL(B)
to GMAPWaddington
This Day twelvemonth you were with me, my

30 Sept [1788]   2 p 4to   NYPL(B)
from SBP
My dearest Fanny Shd: not have been

[Sept 1788]   2 p 4to   NYPL(B)
from SBP
It had seemed long to me indeed since we had

1–31 Oct   30 p 4to   NYPL(B)
to SBP
Octr. 2d. What a sweet nooning had I this

5 Oct [1788]   4 p 4to   NYPL(B)
from SBP & Frederica Locke
Must we not now reccommence our *Alives* my

8 Oct   4 p 4to   NYPL(B)
to EBB
I would write to Mr. B. but I foresee you

22 Oct   2 p 4to   BM(Bar)
from Jane (Campbell) Smelt
My Dear Miss Burney will I trust have the

[23 Oct 1788]   2 p 4to   NYPL(B)
to CB
I have intended every Day to write, since

28 Oct [1788]   2 p fol   NYPL(B)
from SBP & Frederica Locke
This time three years does my Fanny

1–30 Nov   134 p 4to   NYPL(B)
to SBP
Saturday 1st. Our King does not advance in

3 Nov [1788]   1 p 4to   Osb
from Lady Carmarthen
I feel extremely obliged indeed

10 NO 1788 pmk   2 p 4to   NYPL(B)
to CB
Could I give you comfort, Dearest sir, with

15 NO 1788 pmk   2 p 4to   NYPL(B)
to CB
My Heart almost *aches* with fullness —

16 Nov   2 p 4to   NYPL(B)
from SBP
I cannot sufficiently thank my beloved Fanny

[18] NO pmk [1788]   2 p 4to
to CB   NYPL(B)
I have the Heart delight to tell you

18 Nov [1788]   2 p scrap   NYPL(B)
to SBP
they would only mortify me."

[21] Nov [1788]   2 p 4to   NYPL(B)
from SBP
Your dear lines my *most* dear Fanny have

23 [Nov 1788]   2 p 4to   NYPL(B)
to SBP
To see *Mr. Digby* waiting alone next to a

29 Nov [1788]   2 p 4to   NYPL(B)
from SBP
I had intended writing to my beloved Fanny

⟨NO⟩ 1788 pmk   2 p 4to   NYPL(B)
to CB
The anxious hope of being able day after Day

[Nov? 1788]   1 p 4to   NYPL(B)
to SBP
I have one partie of November ready written:

1–[12] Dec   41 p 4to   NYPL(B)
to SBP
Monday, 1st. Mournful was the opening of the

8 Dec [1788]   2 p 4to   NYPL(B)
to CB
once again, my ever dearest Father, we are

13–15 Dec   14 p 4to   NYPL(B)
to SBP
Saturday, Decr. 13th. Accounts are now very

[15]–18 Dec   20 p 4to   NYPL(B)
to SBP
I went *forthwith* to Mrs. Schwellenberg,

[18–19] Dec   4 p 4to   NYPL(B)
to SBP
Hope that strikes where Hope should strike!

20–[31] Dec   19 p 4to   NYPL(B)
to SBP
Saturday, 20th. Accounts were much the same

·25 Dec   2 p 4to   NYPL(B)
from SBP
It is like my sweet Fanny to choose those days

28 Dec [1788]   3 p 4to   NYPL(B)
to CB
our sensations to Day are of such

[Dec 1788]   1 p 4to   NYPL(B)
to SBP
Notwithstanding I find it, as a *Composition*,

[Dec 1788]   2 p 4to   NYPL(B)
from SBP
My sweetest Fanny's consolatory tho' affecting

[1788]   1 p 4to   BM(Bar)
to Frederica Locke
[copy of] Impromptu by Mr Hastings during

[1788?]   2 p 4to   BM(Bar)
from Richard Owen Cambridge
I am told by those who read the Newspapers

[1788?]   1 p 8vo   NYPL(B)
from Stephen Digby
His Majesty came suddenly upon the Friday &

[c 1788]   2 p scrap   NYPL(B)
[from SBP?]
Do you recollect the K: having seen the

[1788–89]   ½ p 4to   BM(Bar)
from Jane (Campbell) Smelt
a thousand thanks to my Dear Miss Burney

[1788–89]   2 p 4to   NYPL(B)
to SBP
And now — my dearest Friends, — I must own

[1788–89]   1 p scrap   Osb
to GMAPWaddington
A *Walking ½ Hour* this morning is all I have

1789

1–18 Jan   44 p 4to   NYPL(B)
to SBP
Thursday, 1st. The year opened with an

4 Jan   4 p 4to   NYPL(B)
to GMAPWaddington
Nothing shall longer prevent my writing to my

4 Jan–11 Apr   123 p 4to   NYPL(B)
from SBP
I gave my Fanny an acc^t. of Sunday eve^g.

5 Jan   copy   1 p 4to   NYPL(B)
to Frederica Locke
Yesterday we were almost in agonies of

6 pmk   Jan [1789]   4 p 4to
to CBF   NYPL(B)
Nothing but the extreme disturbance of my

11 Jan [1789]   3 p 4to   NYPL(B)
to CB
Every thing here, most dear Sir, goes on as

13 Jan   copy   1 p 4to   NYPL(B)
to SBP
We go on very well for what we ought to

19–27 Jan   55 p 4to   NYPL(B)
to SBP
Monday 19th. This Morning the news was very

1789, continued

2⟨1⟩ Jan   2 p 4to   NYPL(B)
to CB
I think it, Dearest Sir, a very great while not

[21] Jan   11 p 4to   NYPL(B)
from SBP
My dearest Fanny's explanatory sheet affected

26 Jan   3 p 4to   Hyde
to Rosette (Rose) Burney
I have long been hoping, my dear Rosette, to

26 Jan   2 p 4to   NYPL(B)
to SBP & Frederica Locke
We go on here so much the same, at present,

[28]–31 Jan   14 p 4to   NYPL(B)
to SBP
The excellent Dr. Willis gave me a most

30 Jan [1789]   4 p 4to   NYPL(B)
to CB
How great is your kindness, Dearest sir, — &

[Jan 1789]   1 p 4to   Comyn
from Jane (Campbell) Smelt
What words, what Language can I use My

1–9 Feb   24 p 4to   NYPL(B)
to SBP
Sunday, Feb.ʸ 1ˢᵗ. The good King, thank

3 Feb   4 p 4to   NYPL(B)
to GMAPWaddington
Heaven send you happy, my Dear Marianne!

10–17 Feb   24 p 4to   NYPL(B)
to SBP
Tuesday, 10ᵗʰ. The amendment of the King is

13 FE 1789 pmk   4 p 4to   NYPL(B)
to CB
We are now in the sweetest of prospects,

13 Feb [1789]   4 p 4to   NYPL(B)
from SBP
It would be very difficult to say how delighted

14 Feb   2 p 4to   NYPL(B)
to SBP
The joint Letters are just arrived — & mine

[16 Feb 1789]   2 p 4to   NYPL(B)
from SBP
It wᵈ be impossible to tell my Fanny how

18–[28] Feb   31 p 4to   NYPL(B)
to SBP
Wednesday, 18ᵗʰ. I had this morning the

18 Feb   2 p 4to   NYPL(B)
from Elizabeth, Lady Templetown
When I address a few lines under the direction

[post 21 Feb 1789]   3 p 4to
to SBP   NYPL(B)
How reviving to innumerable tender &

[24 Feb 1789]   4 p 4to   NYPL(B)
to CB
I suppose you will hardly thank *me* for good

1–15 Mar   41 p 4to   NYPL(B)
to SBP
What a pleasure was mine this morning! how

1–29 Mar   copy   1 p 4to   NYPL(B)
to SBP
Yes my beloved Friend, all indeed is now safe

2 Mar   4 p 4to   PML
to JB
Many thanks, my dear Brother, for your kind

6 Mar [1789]   3 p 4to   NYPL(B)
from JB
We are but newly arrived from Town

15 Mar   4 p 4to   NYPL(B)
from SBP
I have heard, not without deep concern, of the

16 Mar   4 p 4to   NYPL(B)
to CB
I could no way procure Time for writing

16–17 Mar   14 p 4to   NYPL(B)
to SBP
Mʳ Falkland called just before he went out on

16 Mar   copy   2 p 4to   NYPL(B)
to GMAPWaddington
— I thought with greatly added satisfaction

also copy extract   1 p   scrap NYPL(B)

[17 Mar 1789]   4 p 4to   NYPL(B)
to GMAPWaddington
How tranquilizing a letter my sweet Friend

18–19 Mar   18 p 4to   NYPL(B)
to SBP
Wednesday, March 18ᵗʰ. ToDay, — suddenly

20 Mar   1 p 4to   NYPL(B)
to SBP
What a Susan is my Susanna! how dear —

[20–31] Mar   11 p 4to   NYPL(B)
to SBP
The rest of this month I shall not give by

23 Mar   4 p 8vo   NYPL(B)
from Mary (Hamilton) Dickenson
I will write you a Note my dear instead of a

26 Mar   4 p 4to   NYPL(B)
from SBP
What balm was my beloved Fanny's letter to

7 Apr   4 p 4to   NYPL(B)
to SBP
My most sweet Susanna, your last Letter is

8 Apr 4 p fol mutilated NYPL(B)
to GMAPWaddington
Your last Letter, my sweet Marianne, has

[Apr 1789] copy 2 p 4to NYPL(B)
to Frederica Locke & William Locke
I have her Majesty's commands to enquire

Apr   10 p 4to   NYPL(B)
to SBP
I shall abbreviate this month, also, of its

1 May   2 p 4to   NYPL(B)
to GMAPWaddington
Indeed, my sweet Marianne, I feel myself very

6–[7] May [1789] 4 p 4to NYPL(B)
from SBP
I am quite broken hearted my Fanny for this

[12] May–10 Oct 65 p 4to BM(Bar)
from Frederica Locke
My Aug^as birthday / My good dear Augusta

14 May [1789] 2 p fol NYPL(B)
from SBP
I have never forgotten my Fanny's wish to

17 May [1789] 2 p 4to NYPL(B)
from SBP
I will now make use of the Alive w^ch: our

17 May–15 June 65 p 4to BM(Bar)
from SBP
Sunday May 17 — My dearest Fanny has

21 May 3 p 4to   Taylor
to Mary (Hamilton) Dickenson
I could not but smile — though perhaps I

[pre 28 May 1789?] 1 p card Osb
from Bernardo, marquis del Campo
L'Ambassadeur d'Espagne prie Miss Burney

May   2 p 4to   NYPL(B)
to SBP
I must give the few incidents of this month in

May   7 p 4to   NYPL(B)
to SBP
Now, then, my beloved Friends, for the history

6 June–19 July [1789] 36 p 4to
from SBP   BM(Bar)
Our Fanny promises us a new treat

21 June [1789] 2 p 4to NYPL(B)
from SBP
My kind Fanny regretted that she could not

26 June   4 p fol   NYPL(B)
to CB
Anything *worse behaved* than I have seemed

June   26 p 4to   NYPL(B)
to SBP
June 1st. From my window, this morning I

2 July   4 p 4to   NYPL(B)
from SBP
With most unusual delight, was my beloved

12 July [1789] 4 p 4to NYPL(B)
from SBP & Frederica Locke
What a sweet treat was my beloved Fanny's

13 July   4 p 4to   NYPL(B)
to CB
My Dearest Padre's kind Letter was most truly

13 July   4 p 4to   NYPL(B)
to GMAPWaddington
Rejoiced was I with great joy at sight once

16 July   3 p 4to   NYPL(B)
from Sarah (Kirby) Trimmer
Though you were so kind as to encourage me

19 July   2 p 4to   NYPL(B)
to CB
Your kind Letter, & its accompaniment, most

1789, continued

20 July–5 Oct   72 p 4to   BM(Bar)
from SBP
Near a fortnight has elapsed

28 July   4 p 4to   NYPL(B)
from SBP, Norbury & Frances Phillips
A thousand thanks to my beloved Fanny for

29 July   3 p 4to   Comyn
from Jane (Campbell) Smelt
A thousand & a thousand thanks, to my Dear

July   20 p 4to   NYPL(B)
to SBP
Wednesday, 8th. We are settled here

July   2 p 4to   NYPL(B)
to SBP
for opening upon his new plan

[July-Aug 1789]   2 p scraps
to SBP   NYPL(B)
Mr. Digby looked much surprised

2 Aug   2 p 4to   NYPL(B)
from SBP
I must thank my beloved Fanny for her

16 Aug   2 p 4to   NYPL(B)
from SBP
What a delicious comfortable alive is my

18 Aug   4 p 4to   NYPL(B)
to CB
Your pacquet, Dearest sir, for which I return

21 Aug [1789]   10 p 4to   NYPL(B)
to SBP
written with the same frank openness

23 Aug   2 p 4to   NYPL(B)
from SBP & Frederica Locke
Another week has elapsed my dearest Fanny

Aug   54 p 4to   NYPL(B)
to SBP
Saty. 1st. I received to Day this Note. / An

[Aug 1789]   1 p 4to   NYPL(B)
to SBP
<a>n air of *most* devoted regard, &

[Aug? 1789]   3 p 4to   NYPL(B)
from James Hutton
As I made you acquainted with my Illness its

1 Sept 1789–Jan 1790   34 p 4to
to SBP & Frederica Locke   NYPL(B)
NB. So wearied am I now of copying, my

also   copy extracts   37 p 4 to   NYPL(B)

9 Sept   4 p 4to   BM(Bar)
to EBB
I promised my Esther, I know

20 Sept   copy   1 p 4to   BM(Bar)
to Frederica Locke
I am indeed very much pleased that my Fredy

22 Sept   2 p 4to   NYPL(B)
to CB
We returned to Windsor on Friday, to dinner

26 Sept [1789]   2 p 4to   NYPL(B)
from SBP
What a delightful letter is my Fanny's! —

[Sept 1789]   2 p 4to   NYPL(B)
to SBP
Waiting for an always promising, but never

Sept   16 p 4to   BM(Bar)
from SBP
I am never so much out of humour

3 pmk [Oct 1789]   2 p 4to   NYPL(B)
from SBP
It seems to me an age since I have written a

4 Oct [1789]   1 p 4to   Osb
to Rosette (Rose) Burney
At length I think I may appoint a meeting

5 Oct–23 Nov   52 p 4to   BM(Bar)
from SBP
Mes annales my beloved Fanny have been

7 pmk   Oct   4 p 4to   BM(Bar)
to CBF
What may my Dearest Charlotte have thought

13–29 Oct   16 p 4to   BM(Bar)
from SBP
I have this morning

21 Oct–28 Dec   68 p 4to   BM(Bar)
from Frederica Locke
I am just returned from a little walking

26 OC 1789 pmk   4 p 4to   Ray
to Rosette (Rose) Burney
Do you yet, my Dear Rosette, know me so

27 Oct   4 p 4to   NYPL(B)
to CB
We go on here amazingly well, though every

also   copy   5 p 4to   NYPL(B)

30 Oct   1 p 4to   NYPL(B)
to GMAPWaddington
Neither to see nor hear from you, my Dear

Oct   1 p 4to   NYPL(B)
to SBP & Frederica Locke
My dearest Friends must pardon me that I sit

Oct–15 Nov   16 p 4to   BM(Bar)
from SBP
I must now regale myself w^{th}

1 Nov   2 p 4to   Osb
to Rosette (Rose) Burney
I write to thank my Dear Rosette for her last

8 Nov   1 p 4to   NYPL(B)
to SBP & Frederica Locke
Is my most loved Susanna safe returned? —

10 Nov [1789]   1 p 4to   Osb
from Jacob Bryant
Mr Bryant presents his best compliments to

10 Nov [1789]   4 p 4to   BM(Bar)
from SBP & Frederica Locke
Yes my beloved Fanny — I *am* safely returned

26 Nov   4 p 4to   NYPL(B)
to SBP & Frederica Locke
So punctual are my dearest Friends that

29 Nov   2 p 4to   BM(Bar)
from SBP
Your letter my best loved Fanny has excited in

30 Nov   8 p 4to   BM(Bar)
from SBP
With Feelings how altered do I prepare

Nov   36 p 4to   NYPL(B)
to SBP
My memorandums of this month are very

[Nov or Dec 1789]   4 p 4to
from SBP   NYPL(B)
I have read with a Surprise almost

2–4 Dec [1789]   4 p 4to   NYPL(B)
to SBP & Frederica Locke
I am sorry to perplex my sweet Fredy about

2–28 Dec   24 p 4to   BM(Bar)
from SBP
Can these Journals give a temporary relief

6 Dec [1789]   2 p 4to   NYPL(B)
from Richard Owen Cambridge
After all I wrote to you I hear there is a

6 Dec   2 p 4to   Osb
from SBP
My sweet Fanny's affecting letter leaves me

also   copy   2 p LB   Arm

16 Dec [1789]   2 p 4to   BM(Bar)
from SBP
Have you concluded us *lost* my beloved

16 Dec   copy   7 p LB   Arm
from SBP
I sent off my answer to F. first, yesterday, &

22–24 Dec   21 p 4to   BM(Bar)
from SBP
My dearest Fanny's prudent caution

24 Dec   2 p 4to   Osb
to CB Jr
I think I have never in my life read a Letter

26 Dec [1789]   2 p 4to   BM(Bar)
from SBP
What a delightful long alive we have this week

Dec   22 p 4to   NYPL(B)
to SBP
Fair, brightly genial & smiling is this < >

[1789?]   2 p 4to   NYPL(B)
to SBP
"And *you*, he then added, *you* I should not

[c 1789?]   copy extract   1 p 4to
to GMAPWaddington   NYPL(B)
Only guard yourself *all you can* from

[1789?]   4 p 8vo   Osb
from SBP
How have I wished I could leave an eye

also   copy   1 p LB   Arm

[1789–90]   1 p 4to   NYPL(B)
from Margaret (Cooper) DeLuc
Ten thousand thousand thanks for the kind

1790

2–4 Jan   16 p 4to   NYPL(B)
from SBP
What an interesting lecture my Fanny was

4–6 Jan   14 p 4to   NYPL(B)
from SBP
May it prove more propitious

6–21 Jan   24 p 4to   NYPL(B)
from SBP
I sent my Fanny my last Paquet on Wednesday

7 Jan   4 p 4to   NYPL(B)
from Dorothea (Gregory) Alison
I seize with very great pleasure the

13–16 Jan   16 p 4to   NYPL(B)
from SBP
I have just finished Violetta's most agitating

17–23 Jan   12 p 4to   NYPL(B)
from SBP
What an exquisite Partie have I not

20 Jan   3 p 4to   Osb
to Dorothea (Gregory) Alison
I should instantly have told my dear Miss

26–27 Jan   15 p 4to   NYPL(B)
from SBP
What an unexpected delight was to receive

28 Jan–19 Feb   44 p 4to   NYPL(B)
from SBP
My memorandums for the last week

Jan   10 p 4to   NYPL(B)
to SBP & Frederica Locke
The briary, crowded, & thorny path being now

10 Feb [1790]   13 p 4to   NYPL(B)
from SBP
A thousand thanks to my Fanny for the Hymn

17 Feb [1790]   8 p 4to   NYPL(B)
from SBP
How affecting how penetrating is

19 Feb   10 p 4to   NYPL(B)
from SBP
I have this minute sent

[22 Feb 1790]   2 p 4to   BM(Bar)
to CB
I never did read so sweet a letter, Dearest,

24–25 Feb   12 p 4to   NYPL(B)
from SBP
I am really a virtuous person my Fanny

Feb   12 p 4to   NYPL(B)
to SBP & Frederica Locke
I shall take the liberty to give this month in

[pre Mar 1790]   1 p 4to   NYPL(B)
to Benjamin Waddington
What a solace to me is this account of my most

7–8 Mar   8 p 4to   NYPL(B)
from SBP
This time I hope to embrace my beloved

8 Mar–24 May   72 p 4to   NYPL(B)
from SBP
At length a moment I may call my own

9 Mar   4 p 4to   NYPL(B)
to GMAPWaddington
I have been quite touched, my sweet Friend,

Mar   16 p 4to   NYPL(B)
to SBP & Frederica Locke
Monday, 1st. I am now once more resolved

8 Apr   pmk 1790   4 p 4to   NYPL(B)
from SBP
I must, however hastily, write a few lines to

9–14 Apr   4 p fol   BM(Bar)
from CBF
Since I have been home I have found

11 Apr   2 p 4to   NYPL(B)
from SBP
My sweet Fanny received a letter from me, I

15 Apr   4 p 4to   NYPL(B)
from SBP
I must endeavour to send a short *response*

18 Apr   1 p 4to   Osb
from Jacob Bryant
I fully purposed to have had the honour of

Apr   18 p 4to   NYPL(B)
to SBP & Frederica Locke
I have involuntarily let this month creep along

[Apr 1790]   2 p 4to   NYPL(B)
from SBP
Our dearest Mrs. Lock tempts me to write a

1 May [1790]   4 p 4to   NYPL(B)
from SBP
I have just received my beloved Fanny's long

2 May   1 p 4to   Comyn
from Jacob Bryant
Accept of my best acknowledgements for the

21 May [1790]   2 p 4to   Osb
to CB Jr
Encouraged by his great general kindness, I

26 May–18 July   27 p 4to   NYPL(B)
from SBP
I have been very idle since

May   57 p 4to   NYPL(B)
to SBP & Frederica Locke
Saturday, 1st. My dear Susanna will remember

May   8 p 4to   NYPL(B)
to SBP & Frederica Locke
And now, my dear Sisters! — to a subject &

[May 1790]   1 p fragment
to GMAPWaddington   NYPL(B)
I have had nothing but mortification in missing

[May 1790]   1 p fragment   NYPL(B)
to GMAPWaddington
My Cold is so rough to my breast & my voice,

[May 1790?]   1 p 4to   NYPL(B)
from William Windham
I am fully apprized of the fact, you allude to,

1 June   3 p 4to   NYPL(B)
to GMAPWaddington
O what an unexpected grief! — my dear dear

9 June   1 p 4to   KL
to Jeremy Bentham
I am extremely concerned at the suspense in

10 June   3 p 4to   Osb
to CB Jr
I got home very well, my dear Carlos, though

11 June   3 p 4to   NYPL(B)
to GMAPWaddington
You were most kind to write again so soon, my

12 June   2 p 4to   NYPL(B)
from Jacob Bryant
Permit me through your hands most gratefully

12 JU pmk [1790]   2 p 4to   NYPL(B)
from SBP
I cannot *rest* without giving my Fanny *three*

21 June   4 p 4to   Osb
to Rosette (Rose) Burney
I know, my dear Rosette, you will be sorry as

[24 June 1790]   1 p 4to   BM(Bar)
from Jacob Bryant
When I had last the pleasure of seeing you

[post 24 June 1790]   1 p 4to
from Jacob Bryant   BM(Bar)
When your letter arrived, it was accompanied

26 pmk   June   2 p 8vo   Osb
to CB Jr
If you had *good* news, my Dear Carlos, I am

June   19 p 4to   NYPL(B)
to SBP & Frederica Locke
This month opened with the truly afflicting

June   1 p 8vo   NYPL(B)
from Hester (Mulso) Chapone
Tho' I was much mortified at my

9 JY 1790 pmk   2 p 8vo   Osb
to CB Jr
I am so impatient to hear from you again, that

14 July–7 Aug   36 p 4to   NYPL(B)
from SBP
I sent you my Fanny

15–25 July   23 p 4to   NYPL(B)
from SBP
Had the Cahiers reached us whilst the contents

17 JY 1790 pmk   3 p 4to   Osb
to CB Jr
My dearest Carlos, I was quite uneasy at your

25 July   pmk 1790   1 p 8vo   Osb
to CB Jr
If you come on Wednesday, a little after

29 July [1790]   4 p 4to   NYPL(B)
from SBP & Elizabeth, Lady Temple-
      town
Two opportunities have vainly

July   7 p 4to   NYPL(B)
to SBP & Frederica Locke
At the Chapel, about this time, while I was

1790, continued

2 Aug   2 p 4to   HSP
to Jeremy Bentham
I feel almost ashamed to thank you for the

2 Aug   pmk 17⟨90⟩   4 p 4to
to CB Jr   NYPL(B)
You will have been much disappointed

5–25 Aug   14 p 4to   NYPL(B)
from SBP
Having concluded a response

6 Aug   4 p 4to   NYPL(B)
to GMAPWaddington
I know your indulgence, my sweet Friend, to

17 Aug   4 p 4to   NYPL(B)
from SBP
I shall now proceed as fast as I am able with

23 Aug   4 p 4to   NYPL(B)
from SBP
I yesterday read & acknowledged & to day

24 Aug   2 p 8vo   PML
to JB
Lest you should take a waste walk, I hate the

25 Aug–7 Sept 19 p 4to   NYPL(B)
from SBP
I concluded Wedʸ. eveᵍ. Augt. 25ᵗʰ. in great

26 Aug   1 p 4to   Osb
to Jeremy Bentham
Your Letters cannot but encrease my desire to

31 Aug   3 p 8vo   PML
to JB
I am quite pleased to find myself in your

Aug   8 p 4to   NYPL(B)
to SBP & Frederica Locke
As I have only my Almanac memorandums for

2 Sept   2 p 4to   BM(Bar)
to CB
The sight how much your wrist was

2 Sept   4 p 4to   Osb
to Rosette (Rose) Burney
See how good I am *for once*! Your last Letter

7–17 Sept   10 p 4to   NYPL(B)
from SBP
I must now in a *summary way* resume

8 Sept   3 p 4to   NYPL(B)
from Clement Francis Sr
I should be very happy If I could contribute

13 Sept   4 p 4to   NYPL(B)
from SBP
As speedily as shall be in my power

16 Sept–15 Oct 29 p 4to NYPL(B)
from SBP
I shall immediately resume where I left off in

26 Sept–5 Oct   7 p 4to   NYPL(B)
from SBP
With what a feeling of anxious concern

30 Sept [1790]   2 p 8vo NYPL(B)
from Marie-Elisabeth (Bouée) de La
    Fîte
Oserois-je vous prier, ma tres chère

Sept   8 p 4to   NYPL(B)
to SBP
I must immediately proceed to the melancholy

10 Oct   3 p 8vo   PML
to JB
Before this can arrive, my dear Brother, you

15 Oct   8 p 4to   NYPL(B)
from SBP
The Fair intervening has stop'd our course

16–24 Oct   8 p 4to   NYPL(B)
from SBP
In my Pacquet by Mr. George I gave my

17 Oct [1790]   4 p 4to   BM(Bar)
to CB
I thank you for your kind concern: I must own

24–25 Oct   16 p 4to   NYPL(B)
from SBP
What a full, what an interesting & sweet Partie

24 Oct–9 Nov   11 p 4to NYPL(B)
from SBP
Our visit to Mr. Rogers on Sunday 24ᵗʰ. was

27 Oct   1 p 4to   BM(Bar)
from Francis Matthews
As I shoᵈ. be extremely sorry to take any legal
also   copy (included in ALS FB to CB
    20 Oct 1790)   2 p 4to   Lewis

29 Oct   3 p 4to   Lewis
to CB
Most unwilling as I am, my dearest Padre, to

[Oct? 1790]   draft   4 p 4to
to Queen Charlotte   BM(Bar)
With the deepest sense of your Majesty's

also   copy (in AJ FB to SBP 1790)   3 p
                                          NYPL(B)

Oct   22 p 4to   NYPL(B)
to SBP & Frederica Locke
I open again with my poor Collomb. How

3 Nov   1 p 4to   Comyn
from Horace Walpole
I am exceedingly vexed for you, and sorry to

also   copy   1 p 8vo   Lewis

3 Nov   3 p 4to   Comyn
from Horace Walpole
Mr Cambridge called on me this morning and

also   copy   6 p 8vo   Lewis

4–5 Nov   8 p 4to   NYPL(B)
from SBP
You will perhaps smile my dearest Fanny to

9–15 Nov   13 p 4to   NYPL(B)
from SBP
On Tuesday last, Nov^r: 9th: having hastily

15 Nov–4 Dec   8 p 4to   NYPL(B)
from SBP
My last Diary was concluded Monday night

16 Nov   4 p fol   BM(Bar)
from CBF
Before I rec^d: your last kind letter, & affecting

19 Nov   4 p 4to   Osb
to Rosette (Rose) Burney
Could you then, my dear Rosette, be uneasy at

19 Nov   2 p 4to   NYPL(B)
from SBP
The patterns are arrived safely my beloved

22–[23] Nov [1790]   4 p 4to
from SBP   NYPL(B)
Your letter was indeed a great Surprise to us

23 Nov   4 p 4to   NYPL(B)
to GMAPWaddington
Now, at last, I must have required your

[23 Nov]–3 Dec   10 p 4to   NYPL(B)
from SBP
The month of Octr. diverted me by its brevity

29 Nov   2 p 4to   NYPL(B)
from SBP
V. says that difficulties seem multiplying

Nov   2 p 4to   NYPL(B)
to SBP
This month will be very brief of annals: I was

[Nov 1790]   1 p 8vo   NYPL(B)
from Jacob Bryant
You are abundantly good in casting away a

[Nov 1790]   4 p 4to   NYPL(B)
from SBP
Your communication my dearest Fanny has

⟨3⟩ pmk   Dec   4 p 4to   BM(Bar)
to CBF
It seems almost *frigid* to be so long in

6–12 Dec   11 p 4to   NYPL(B)
from SBP
Enfin an evening is arrived

7 Dec [1790]   1 p 8vo   NYPL(B)
to CB
M. Hummel, who will take to you this note is

14–15 Dec   8 p 4to   NYPL(B)
from SBP
What a development indeed awaited Violetta!

⟨15⟩ DE 1790 pmk   1 p 4to   NYPL(B)
from SBP
Full of the tenderest gratitude & most extreme

18 DE 1790 pmk   4 p 4to   BM(Bar)
to CB
I will now try to be a little more circumstantial

20 DE 1790 pmk   3 p 4to   NYPL(B)
to CB
I am extremely obliged by my Mother's

20–31 Dec   10 p 4to   NYPL(B)
from SBP
Having finished the last most

27 DE 1790 pmk   3 p 4to   NYPL(B)
to CB
How much should I have to relate of matters I

[Dec 1790]   copy   1 p   NYPL(B)
to Queen Charlotte (included in AJ
     FB to SBP Dec 1790)
May I yet humbly presume to entreat your

1790, continued

Dec   20 p 4to   NYPL(B)
to SBP
Leaving a little longer in the lurch the late

[Dec 1790]   2 p 4to   NYPL(B)
from SBP
What an agitating period my beloved Fanny!

[1790?]   1 p scrap   NYPL(B)
from C (de Montmollin) d'Espere-en-
        Dieu
On ne peut être plus sensible que je ne la suis

[1790]   1 p 4to   BM(Bar)
from Elizabeth (Robinson) Montagu
Your kind & obliging note yesterday

[1790]   2 p 4to   NYPL(B)
from SBP
I wonder not that my Fanny is grieved at

[1790?]   2 p 4to   NYPL(B)
from William Seward
I took the Liberty to make use of your name

[1790–91]   1 p 4to   Osb
to CB Jr
I think it of importance sufficient to stop the

[1790–91]   1 p 4to   NYPL(B)
from SBP
my putting him off, he at last said very

1791

1–31 Jan   21 p 4to   NYPL(B)
from SBP
I have got out of all regularity in *the Journal*

2 Jan   4 p 4to   NYPL(B)
to CB
I had no opportunity to put in practice my

also   copy   4 p 4to   NYPL(B)

[3 Jan 1791]   2 p 4to   NYPL(B)
from SBP
How have I regretted my beloved Fanny the

4–5 Jan   8 p 4to   NYPL(B)
from SBP
Jany. 4th. 91 — oh may it prove prosperous to

7 Jan   2 p 4to   BM(Bar)
to CB
Smooth all goes on, most dear Sir — but *silent*

10 Jan   1 p 8vo   BM(Bar)
to CB
I have just heard we go to town on Friday

Jan   5 p 4to   NYPL(B)
to SBP & Frederica Locke
Adventures being now but few, Life more

Jan   2 p 4to & scrap   NYPL(B)
to SBP
All my reading moments are engrossed by Mr.

11 Feb–24 Mar   20 p 4to   NYPL(B)
from SBP
As I do not love long arrears, I shall briefly

13 Feb [1791]   4 p 4to   BM(Bar)
from Maria (Allen) Rishton
I was very sincerely grieved to find

[Feb 1791]   2 p fol   NYPL(B)
from SBP
With what sorrow did I lose sight of you on

[Feb 1791]   2 p fol   NYPL(B)
from SBP
Dat book what you call — dat *first* what they

Feb-Apr   6 p 4to   NYPL(B)
to SBP & Frederica Locke
This month, my dearest Susanna, has no

6 Mar   pmk 1791   4 p fol   NYPL(B)
from SBP
I can no longer remain without saying a word

8–11 Mar   8 p 4to   NYPL(B)
from SBP
How surprised was I to find *quattro mese* in

15 Mar [1791]   4 p 4to   NYPL(B)
from SBP
I had not half thanked you my Fanny for the

17 Mar   2 p fol   NYPL(B)
from SBP
Your letter of to day my beloved Fanny is I

19–[21] Mar [1791]   3 p 4to
from SBP   NYPL(B)
It is vain to tell you my Fanny how much I am

25 Mar–17 May   40 p 4to   NYPL(B)
from SBP
My last Diary was concluded my beloved

27 Mar   4 p 4to   NYPL(B)
from SBP
We agree then but too well my beloved

29–31 Mar   8 p 4to   NYPL(B)
from SBP
Let me now, having concluded our immediate

4 Apr [1791]   4 p 4to   NYPL(B)
from SBP
Ah my dearest Fanny! — Where is this

12 Apr   1 p 4to   BM(Bar)
from Jacob Bryant
I heard, that you was robbed, and I

[16 Apr 1791]   3 p 4to   NYPL(B)
from Mary (Palmer) O'Brien, March-
    ioness of Thomond
You are too well acquainted with sentiments

[post 16 Apr 1791]   2 p 4to   NYPL(B)
from Mary (Palmer) O'Brien, March-
    ioness of Thomond
The Mystery is explaind [sic] my dear Miss

Apr   2 p 4to   BM(Bar)
to CB
I think neither the sight of my hand nor my

Apr   2 p 4to   BM(Bar)
from Maria (Allen) Rishton
Your letter must have been written by

1 May   3 p 4to   NYPL(B)
from SBP
I have just with astonishment recollected how

15 May   1 p 4to   BM(Bar)
from Jacob Bryant
Your letter surprises and alarms me greatly:

17 May   1 p 4to   Osb
to Eva Maria (Veigel) Garrick
Mrs. Lock has been so kind as to indulge me

[post 27 May 1791]   1 p 4to   BM(Bar)
from Anne (Leigh) Frodsham
As I could not prevail upon myself

30 May   4 p 4to   NYPL(B)
from SBP
How affecting is all this period preceding the

May   23 p 4to   NYPL(B)
to SBP & Frederica Locke
Let me have the pleasure, for once, to begin

5 June [1791]   3 p 4to   NYPL(B)
from SBP & Frederica Locke
Your letter was *exquisitely chearing* this

June   33 p 4to   NYPL(B)
to SBP & Frederica Locke
Am I not the very mirror of scribble Errantry

[post June 1791]   2 p 4to   NYPL(B)
from SBP
I have so blotted my direction in my haste that

3 July   4 p 4to   NYPL(B)
to CB
Mademoiselle Jacobi, my destined successor is

5 July [1791?]   2 p 4to   BM(Bar)
from Ann (Astley) Agnew
It was my intention to have left this

5 July [1791]   4 p 4to   BM(Bar)
from CBF & James Sleepe
I am out of breath at yr. Letter my dearest

[pre 7 July 1791]   23 p 4to   NYPL(B)
to SBP & the Lockes
I come now to write the last week of my royal

[post 7]–31 July   8 p 4to   NYPL(B)
to SBP & Frederica Locke
Once more I have the blessing to address my

[c 7 July 1791]   2 p 4to   NYPL(B)
from SBP
How happy this news has made me, & the

8 July [1791]   4 p 4to   NYPL(B)
from Frances Bowdler
The Papers mention your resignation; & it has

9–[10] July   4 p 4to   BM(Bar)
from CBF
Huzza — Huzza — Huzza! — / I received

10 July [1791]   2 p 4to   NYPL(B)
from SBP
Oh my beloved Fanny! — Well might your

13 July   1 p 4to   NYPL(B)
from Elizabeth Juliana Schwellenberg
    (per E Lutterloh)
I am requested by Mrs. Schwellenberg to

1791, continued

19 July   1 p 4to   NYPL(B)
from Lady Charlotte Finch
Lady Charlotte Finch presents her best

23 July   2 p 4to   NYPL(B)
from Lady Rothes
I shall go to Windsor tomorrow as usual, &

29 July   2 p 4to   NYPL(B)
from Dr Francis Willis
I hope I have not deferr'd this so long that

[post July 1791]   1 p scrap   NYPL(B)
from Dr Francis Willis
[let] me know how You go on when in Surry.

13 Aug   6 p 4to   NYPL(B)
to CB
The *"few pleasing words"* were most

14–16 Aug   4 p 4to   NYPL(B)
from SBP
Did I my dearest Fanny understand right that

16 Aug   2 p 4to   NYPL(B)
from SBP
My beloved Fanny's letter of to day gave me

21–28 Aug   10 p 4to   NYPL(B)
from SBP
In utter despair of bringing up my long

28 Aug   2 p 4to   NYPL(B)
from SBP
I rec^d. the first acc^t. of the Madre's interview

Aug   60 p 4to   NYPL(B)
to SBP & the Lockes
I have now been a Week out *upon my Travels*

[post Aug 1791]   1 p 4to   NYPL(B)
from Dr Francis Willis
I am very happy to find the Bath waters agree

⟨6⟩ Sept   3 p 4to   NYPL(B)
from Leonard Smelt
You had every reason my dear Madam for

8–[10] Sept [1791]   4 p 4to   NYPL(B)
to EBB
My dearest Esther will I know rejoice to hear

12 Sept [1791]   3 p 4to   NPG
with Frederica Locke to EBB
I will not attempt to tell you, my dear M^rs.

Sept   12 p 4to   NYPL(B)
to SBP & the Lockes
With what pleased — & full sensations do I

7 Oct   4 p 4to   NYPL(B)
to GMAPWaddington
Were this the time of Fairies & Witches, the

14 Oct   4 p 4to   NYPL(B)
from SBP
I hope my beloved Fanny has not too much

18–21 Oct   4 p fol   NYPL(Bar)
from CBF
I have been incessantly taken up for there

19 Oct   4 p 4to   BM(Bar)
with CB to CBF
How do? / I have left Susanna delightfully

20 Oct   2 p 4to   NYPL(B)
from SBP
To send an alive to my Fanny is an irresistible

Oct   4 p 4to   NYPL(B)
to SBP & Frederica Locke
Though another month has begun since I left

[Oct 1791]   7 p 4to   NYPL(B)
from SBP
I am now arrived at the month of October, in

4 Nov [1791]   2 p 4to   PML
from Dr Francis Willis
Yours of the 18th. of Nov. did not come to

6 Nov   4 p 4to   NYPL(B)
from SBP
What a delightful alive was my Fanny's last!

12 Nov   4 p 4to   NYPL(B)
from SBP
I must not lose my Sunday's conveyance this

20 Nov   4 p 4to   NYPL(B)
from SBP
My beloved Fanny's last letter to our dearest

27 Nov   4 p 4to   NYPL(B)
to CBF
N^o. *19*, my dearest Charlotte, is the best Letter

Nov   mutilated   8 p 4to   NYPL(B)
to SBP & Frederica Locke
Too little has occurred for chronological order

3–10 Dec   4 p fol   BM(Bar)
from CBF
Y^r: last, dated Nov^r: 27th: my dearest Fanny,

6–7 Dec   8 p 4to   NYPL(B)
from SBP
I shall seize the first leisure moments I have

[post 19 Dec 1791]   4 p 4to
to CBF   NYPL(B)
Thanks imprimis for all your Letters

27 Dec [1791]   1 p 8vo   BM(Bar)
from Hester (Mulso) Chapone
Are you in Town my dear Miss Burney?

also   copy   1 p 4to   NYPL(B)

31 Dec   7 p 4to   NYPL(B)
from SBP
I was very much pleased with Lysias's letter

Dec   mutilated   14 p 4to   NYPL(B)
to SBP
I now omit mere family meetings, as I

[pre 1792]   1 p 8vo   Comyn
from Mary (Palmer) O'Brien, March-
      ioness of Thomond
If you have a mind to be goodnaturd

1792

3 Jan   8 p 4to   NYPL(B)
from SBP
I now proceed from Sidmouth, where I wonder

15 Jan [1792]   1 p 4to   NYPL(B)
to Benjamin Waddington
I am quite concerned to have yet no news to

28 pmk   Jan   4 p 4to   NYPL(B)
to CBF
I will sooner send a short Letter at once than

Jan   11 p 4to   NYPL(B)
to SBP & Frederica Locke
The year opened with a family party — James

13 Feb [1792]   2 p 4to   NYPL(B)
to SBP & Frederica Locke
It is a consolation my beloved Fanny having

Feb   19 p 4to & scraps   NYPL(B)
to SBP & the Lockes
I shall begin this month at the *13th*. The Day

[post 10 Mar 1792]   2 p 4to
from SBP   NYPL(B)
I must write 3 lines to my Fanny to thank her

[12–15 misdated 11] Mar   4 p 4to
to GMAPWaddington   NYPL(B)
I begin to grow very & very impatient for a

16 Mar   4 p 4to   NYPL(B)
from SBP
I will not lose the first moment I am able

21 Mar [1792?]   1 p 4to   NYPL(B)
from Mary (Palmer) O'Brien, March-
      ioness of Thomond
I am very sensible of yours & my dear good

29 Mar [1792]   4 p 4to   NYPL(B)
from SBP
My dearest Fanny is well I hope — & our

Mar   2 p 4to   NYPL(B)
to SBP & Frederica Locke
Sad for the loss of Sir Joshua, & all of us ill

[Mar 1792]   4 p 4to   NYPL(B)
from SBP
My heart smites me when I think I have not

[15 Apr 1792]   3 p 4to   Newc
to CB
How very kind, Dearest Sir, to let us see your

Apr   11 p 4to   NYPL(B)
to SBP & Frederica Locke
This wayward Month opened upon me with

12–13 May   4 p 4to   BM(Bar)
with Elizabeth (Allen) Burney to CBF
I[t] was quite a joy to me to see your hand

25 May   2 p 4to   NYPL(B)
from SBP
You must tell me if you have all had *enoff* of

30 May [1792]   2 p 4to   NYPL(B)
from SBP
a thousand thanks my beloved Fanny

1792, continued

May   48 p 4to   NYPL(B)
to SBP & Frederica Locke
The first of this Month I went again to

[May 1792]   17 p 4to   NYPL(B)
from SBP
Lady Mapomprey is a great favourite, &

[May or June 1792]   3 p 4to
from SBP   NYPL(B)
kind, & probably regreted & repented of by

2 June   4 p 4to   NYPL(B)
from SBP
A thousand thanks to you my beloved Fanny

[10? June 1792]   2 p 4to   NYPL(B)
from SBP
Take a thousand tenderest good wishes from

11 June [1792]   1 p 4to   NYPL(B)
from SBP
My dearest Fanny, I hasten to keep my word

12 JU 1792 pmk   2 p 4to   NYPL(B)
from SBP
Let me now thank my beloved Fanny for the

18 JU 1792 pmk   4 p 4to   PML
from Arthur Young
What a plaguy [sic] business tis to take up

also   copy   2 p 4to   NYPL(B)

28 June   3 p 4to   Osb
from Jacob Bryant
Any intimation from you will have a great

also   copy   3 p 4to   NYPL(B)

June mutilated 52 p 4to NYPL(B)
to SBP
told me, with much pleasure that he had that

2 July   pmk 1792   1 p 4to   Osb
to CB Jr
I have written a very full & ample letter to the

5 July   copy 3 p 4to   NYPL(B)
to GMAPWaddington
I must rejoice to see such long letters from my

[6 July 1792]   4 p 4to   NYPL(B)
from SBP
All *is* right my dear, & only too anxious Fanny

[15 July 1792]   2 p 4to   NYPL(B)
from SBP
My beloved Fanny — I am just now charged

[16 July 1792]   1 p 4to   NYPL(B)
from SBP
received — soit entendu if my dear Father

July   2 p 4to   NYPL(B)
to SBP & Frederica Locke
I have kept no memorandums of this Month,

1 Aug [1792]   2 p 4to   NYPL(B)
from Mary (Palmer) O'Brien, March-
      ioness of Thomond
I need not assure you how sensible I am of

5 Aug   2 p 4to   NYPL(B)
from Dorothy Young
An endeavour to relieve a mind under deep

[6 Aug 1792]   3 p 4to   NYPL(B)
to CBF
With what joy do I tell my dearest Charlotte

7 Aug   copy 3 p 4to   NYPL(B)
from Jacob Bryant
When I come to Town which will be probably

[23 Aug 1792]   3 p 4to   NYPL(B)
with Elizabeth (Allen) Burney to CBF
I was very happy to hear by M^rs <Pamieter>

[24 Aug 1792]   4 p 4to mutilated
to SBP   NYPL(B)
Esther's going so well on, my dearest Susan,

26 Aug [1792]   4 p 4to   NYPL(B)
from SBP
Give my most affectionate & loving duty to my

Aug   3 p 4to   NYPL(B)
to SBP & Frederica Locke
August is just in the same immemorial state.

17 SE 1792 pmk 3 p 4to   BM(Bar)
from Anne (Leigh) Frodsham
I ought to have made at least much earlier

18 Sept   1 p 4to   NYPL(B)
from Elizabeth Juliana Schwellenberg
M^rs: Schwellenberg's Compliments to Miss

[pre 23 Sept 1792]   3 p 4to   NYPL(B)
from SBP
I enclose a letter from our Esther my most

23 [Sept 1792]   3 p 4to   BM(Bar)
from Anne (Leigh) Frodsham
I am equally at a loss to express my gratitude

23 Sept [1792]   4 p 4to   NYPL(B)
from SBP & Frederica Locke
You see my beloved Fanny that I am not

Sept   4 p 4to   NYPL(B)
to SBP & Frederica Locke
The first, best half of this month my beloved

Sept   copy, extract   2 p 4to
                              NYPL(B)
from SBP (included in FB to SBP
    Sept 1792)
— We shall shortly, I believe, have a little

2 Oct   4 p 4to   NYPL(B)
to CB
I have just got your direction, in a Letter from

4 Oct 4 p 4to   NYPL(B)
from SBP
I have beg'd our dearest Mrs: Lock to grant

5–8 Oct   mutilated   28 p 4to
to SBP & the Lockes   NYPL(B)
I come now to a month I cannot pass over

10 Oct [1792]   4 p 4to   NYPL(B)
to CB
How cordially welcome to me, Dearest Sir,

12 Oct [1792]   4 p 4to   NYPL(B)
to GMAPWaddington
I trust my ever-dear Marianne is now too

20 Oct [1792]   1 p 4to   Comyn
to CB Jr
'Tis cruel, my dear Charles, to write so

20 Oct [1792]   4 p 4to   NYPL(B)
to EBB
If I were sure of your seeing our Brother

23 Oct   2 p 4to   NYPL(B)
from SBP
Yr. letter to my sister B- was forwarded to me

28 Oct   4 p 4to   NYPL(B)
from SBP & Frederica Locke
Your letter has been a very considerable

29 Oct   1 p 4to   BM(Bar)
from Jacob Bryant
My Treatise is at last finished in a more

[2] Nov–11 Dec   mutilated 60 p 4to
from SBP   NYPL(B) & BM(Bar)
I find it always impossible in a letter my Fanny
[BM(Bar) 2 p 4to] M: d'Arblay had agreed,

6 NO pmk   4 p 4to   NYPL(B)
from SBP
Let me not longer defer thanking my Fanny

11 Nov [1792]   4 p 4to   NYPL(B)
from SBP & Frederica Locke
How long has your silence appeared my

15 Nov   4 p 4to   NYPL(B)
from Jacob Bryant
Your very kind Letter afforded me uncommon

27 Nov [1792]   copy   3 p 4to
to SBP   NYPL(B)
My dearest Susannas details of the French

[Nov-Dec 1792]   2 p scrap   NYPL(B)
to SBP
Miss Howarth came & carried off Charlotte &

[Nov-Dec 1792]   2 p 4to   NYPL(B)
from SBP
I take the first moment in my power to thank

11 Dec [1792]   4 p 4to   NYPL(B)
to GMAPWaddington
Your intelligence was true, my dear Friend —

16 Dec   mutilated 9 p 4to   NYPL(B)
from SBP
It gratifies me very much to find I have been

17–22 Dec   mutilated   10 p 4to
from SBP   NYPL(B)
Saturday Decr. 22d. 92 [It] has seemed a long

20 Dec   copy   3 p 4to   NYPL(B)
to Frederica Locke
I rejoice Mr Lock will be able to attend the

[1792]   2 p 4to   BM(Bar)
from Dorothy (Smelt) Goulton
My Father — wishs [sic] to thank you — my

[1792?]   4 p 4to   NYPL(B)
from Maria (Allen) Rishton
I have so little to entertain you with in the dull

[1792]   2 p 4to   NYPL(B)
from SBP
I cannot send this off dryly without a word

1792, *continued*

[1792?]   2 p 4to   NYPL(B)
from SBP
I had hoped to have sent you as usual a paquet

[1792–93]   1 p 4to   NYPL(B)
from François de la Rochefoucauld, duc
   de Liancourt
<Le D> de Liancoeur [sic] a l'honneur

[pre 1793]   ½ p 4to   BM(Bar)
from Charlotte Boyle-Walsingham
I cannot tell you how pleased I am with

[pre 1793]   2 p 8vo   BM(Bar)
from Charlotte Boyle-Walsingham
I was quite grieved to find you gone

[pre 1793]   2 p 4to   BM(Bar)
from Dorothy Young
I requested Mrs Burney to present you with

1793

6 Jan   6 p 4to   NYPL(B)
from SBP
Sunday Jany. 6th: our most dear Mr: Lock's

6 [Jan 1793?]   1 p 4to   NYPL(B)
from SBP
I can now only beg my Fanny to apologize if

8 Jan   copy   2 p 4to   NYPL(B)
to Frederica Locke
It is quite out of my power my dearest Friend

9 Jan   pmk 1793   4 p 4to
from SBP   NYPL(B)
Lest my dearest Girl shd: suffer useless anxiety

[22 Jan 1793]   2 p 4to   mutilated
to SBP   NYPL(B)
You are very naughty, I fear, my own dearest

28 Jan   4 p 4to   NYPL(B)
to CB
I have been wholly without spirit for writing,

Jan   1 p 8vo   PML
from Anne-Louise-Germaine (Necker)
   de Staël-Holstein
tell me, my dear, if this day is a charming one,

also   copy   1 p 4to   NYPL(B)

[Jan? 1793]   1 p 8vo   PML
from Anne-Louise-Germaine (Necker)
   de Staël-Holstein
when I learn'd to read english I begun by

also   copy   1 p 4to   NYPL(B)

[Jan? 1793]   copy   1 p 4to   NYPL(B)
from Anne-Louise-Germaine (Necker)
   de Staël-Holstein
Your card in french, my dear, has already

4 Feb   4 p 4to   NYPL(B)
to CB
How exactly do I sympathise in all you say &

[7–8 Feb 1793]   thème   1 p 4to
to M d'A   NYPL(B)
Je n'ai jamais eu une envie veritable

[7–14 Feb 1793]   thème   2 p 4to
from M d'A   NYPL(B)
how have you / how Me S — has she

[7–14 Feb 1793]   thème   ½ p 4to
to M d'A   NYPL(B)
Cet orgueil, dont M. D'Arblay m'accuse

[7–14 Feb 1793]   thème   ½ p 4to
to M d'A   NYPL(B)
Combien nous esperons — Les Lockes —

[9 Feb 1793]   copy   3 p 4to
to Frederica Locke   NYPL(B)
Your kind letter, my beloved Fredy was most

[c 12 Feb 1793]   thème   1 p 4to
from M d'A   NYPL(B)
Mr Narbonnes abilities ought to discourage

[14 Feb 1793]   copy   2 p 4to
to Frederica Locke   NYPL(B)
I have no heart *not* to write and no time to

[16? Feb 1793]   imperfect copy
         2 p 4to   NYPL(B)
to Frederica Locke
My most dear Friends How do? — We go on

19 Feb   6 p 4to   NYPL(B)
to CB
Have you not begun, Dearest sir, to give me

[post 19 Feb 1793]   thème   1 p 4to
from M d'A   NYPL(B)
I'm in the utmost anxiety on account of

[19–22 Feb 1793]   thème   1 p 8vo
from M d'A   NYPL(B)
Mʳˢ. Phillips is a very good friend. Miss

[20–22 Feb 1793]   thème   4 p 4to
to M d'A   NYPL(B)
Par rapport de la lecture qu'on veut

22 Feb [1793]   4 p 4to   NYPL(B)
to CB
What a kind Letter is my dearest Father's! —

[c 22 Feb 1793] 1 p 8vo NYPL(B)
from Anne-Louise-Germaine (Necker)
    de Staël-Holstein
tell me, my dear, how you have past the night?

[23–24 Feb 1793]   thème   3 p 8vo
from M d'A   NYPL(B)
I have seen little miss Cecilia to day and I hope

24 Feb [1793]   3 p 4to   NYPL(B)
to CB
Good God, my dearest Father, what a dreadful

[c 24 Feb 1793]   thème   2 p 8vo
to M d'A   NYPL(B)
Mon dernier theme m'a presque effrayée

25 Feb [1793]   copy   2 p 4to
with SBP to Frederica Locke NYPL(B)
I need not tell you if I *could*, how unspeakably

[25–26? Feb 1793]   thème   1 p 8vo
from M d'A   NYPL(B)
I can't answer to your endearing letter.

[25–26 Feb 1793]   thème   2 p 4to
to M d'A   NYPL(B)
Me demander encore des thèmes est pour moi

27 Feb   1 p 4to   Osb
from James Hutton
Your dear Lʳ came to me this morning here

[28 Feb 1793]   thème   3 p 8vo
from M d'A   NYPL(B)
Tomorrow we shall have been deprived of

[Feb-Mar 1793] 4 p 8vo NYPL(B)
from M d'A
Je confie ce que je vais écrire à l'honneur de la

[28 Feb 1793]   thème   2 p scrap
from M d'A   NYPL(B)
a thousand thanks to my dear master I. G.

3 Mar   1 p 4to   Comyn
from James Hutton
Your Charming account of your visit —

[pre 6 Mar 1793]   thème   2 p 4to
to M d'A   NYPL(B)
J'ai bien peur que mon dernier theme m'a

[12] Mar [1793] 1 p 8vo BM(Bar)
to SBP
pray make known in Portland Place that I dine

[13 Mar 1793]   8 scraps   NYPL(B)
to SBP
& little Fanny is quite bemoaned. Pray let me

18 Mar   2 p 4to   BM(Bar)
to GMAPWaddington
How truly I shall rejoice to see my ever dear

21 Mar   8 p 4to   NYPL(B)
from Lady Keith
It would be strange indeed after what has

[c 23 Mar 1793]   thème   3 p 8vo
from M d'A   NYPL(B)
Pray you, my dear Master in all, to be

30 Mar   4 p 4to   NYPL(B)
to M d'A
Le peu de Mots, tout tristes qu'ils étoient, que

31 Mar   3 p 4to   NYPL(B)
from M d'A
Pardon si je ne vous renvoye pas aujourdhui

[Mar 1793]   4 p 4to   NYPL(B)
from SBP & M d'A
The dear *Postman* is just arrived my Fanny,

1 Apr   2 p 4to   BM(Bar)
from SBP
This is the first moment I have been able to

[2–3] Apr [1793] 3 p 4to NYPL(B)
to SBP
O my dearest Susan! what would I not give to

[3 Apr 1793]   1 p 8vo   NYPL(B)
to M d'A
Vous avez bien juger qu'il ne me seroit pas

1793, continued

[3 Apr 1793]   mutilated   4 p 4to
from SBP   NYPL(B)
I must begin with begging my dearest Girl to

[4 Apr 1793]   4 p 4to   NYPL(B)
from SBP
Thursday Morn^g. Your letter my beloved

5 Apr   3 p 8vo   NYPL(B)
from M d'A
Je suis monté ce matin à cheval — j'étois sur

5–6 Apr [1793]   4 p 4to   NYPL(B)
to SBP
I am quite in an agony, my dearest Susan, that

5–[7] Apr [1793]   4 p 4to   NYPL(B)
from SBP
Saturday morn^g: April 5. I cannot tell you

5–8 Apr [1793]   4 p 4to   NYPL(B)
to SBP
I am sure I need not tell my dearest Susan how

[6 Apr]   2 p 8vo   NYPL(B)
to M d'A
Non — elle ne vous savoir pas mauvais gré, —

8 Apr–9 May [1793]   53 p 4to
to SBP   NYPL(B)
I must begin by giving my own comfort to my

10 Apr [1793]   4 p 4to   BM(Bar)
from SBP
Ah my Fanny! were ever times so interesting

[11, misdated] 12 Apr [1793]   6 p 4to
from SBP   NYPL(B)
Thursday Morn^g. April 12th: I am more sorry

13 Apr [1793]   4 p 4to   NYPL(B)
to SBP
Is it possible my dearest Susan can talk of

15 Apr [1793]   2 p 8vo   BM(Bar)
from Hester (Mulso) Chapone
I don't know whether you remember any thing

18 Apr [1793]   2 p 4to   NYPL(B)
from SBP
Your letter my dearest Fanny has given me

19 Apr   2 p 4to   NYPL(B)
from M d'A
Je n'ai pu, mon aimable amie, vous remettre

[pre 20 Apr 1793]   1 p 8vo   NYPL(B)
to M d'A
J'ai lu ce que vous avez écrit — Je vous prie

20 [Apr 1793]   3 p 8vo   NYPL(B)
from M d'A
Je remercie mon amie de ce qu'elle veut bien

21 Apr [1793]   4 p 8vo   NYPL(B)
from M d'A
J'ai tout dit à notre amie et du moins j'aurai

[21 Apr 1793]   4 p 4to   BM(Bar)
from SBP
I promised to write to you to day my Fanny

22 Apr [1793]   3 p 8vo   NYPL(B)
to M d'A
Une personne qui se dise de vôtre connoissance

22 AP 1793 pmk   3 p 4to   NYPL(B)
to SBP
I think certainly nothing in the world shall

[23 Apr 1793]   2 p 8vo   NYPL(B)
from M d'A
Voilà encore une lettre de quelqu'etranger

[Apr? 1793]   3 p 4to   NYPL(B)
from SBP
at the moment of departure I write my beloved

3 May   3 p 4to   NYPL(B)
to GMAPWaddington
What my disappointment was in not meeting

[5 or 12 May 1793]   2 p scrap
from SBP   BM(Bar)
Sunday Morn^g — a thousand thanks for y^r:

[6–7 May 1793]   1 p 8vo   NYPL(B)
from M d'A
Je n'ai que le tems de vous dire que Mad^e de

[7–8 May 1793]   2 p 12mo   NYPL(B)
to M d'A
You were very good to spare me so great a

8 May [1793?]   4 p 4to   PML
from Anne-Louise-Germaine (Necker)
    de Staël-Holstein
pour cette fois vous me permettez

also   copy (misdated? 8 Mar)   4 p 4to
                                    NYPL(B)

[post 8 May 1793]   2 p 12mo
to M d'A   NYPL(B)
I cannot even a moment defer answering so

[pre 11 May 1793]   3 p 8vo   NYPL(B)
from M d'A
I hope my dear friend is no more angry against

[11–12 May 1793]   3 p 12mo
to M d'A   NYPL(B)
Yes, — your friend is quite appeased; she

11 May [1793]   copy   2 p 4to
                                  NYPL(B)
from Anne-Louise-Germaine (Necker)
    de Staël-Holstein
Je vois bien, my dear miss que vous voulez

14 May   pmk 1793   4 p 4to
from SBP   NYPL(B)
Tuesday May 14th. Trusting to the kindness

[14 May 1793]   4 p 4to
from SBP   BM(Bar) & NYPL(B)
Tuesday night — I have scarcely sent off one

[NYPL(B)] moreover my Fanny on the most

[15] May [1793]   1 p 8vo   BM(Bar)
from M d'A
I pray you, my dearest friend, to make your

[16 May 1793]   3 p 12mo   BM(Bar)
to M d'A
Come, little Pen! & tell me what you have been

[17] May [1793]   2 p 4to   NYPL(B)
to CB
The Common was miserably bad,

17 May [1793]   4 p 4to   BM(Bar)
from SBP
Friday eveg. May 17th. vexed as I am at the

[20 May 1793]   1 p 4to   BM(Bar)
from SBP
Monday — Juniper — I am here waiting

[20–30 May 1793]   3 p 4to   BM(Bar)
from SBP
My dearest dear I shall be able but to say

[pre 21 May 1793]   3 p 12mo
from M d'A   NYPL(B)
My little pen is very happy indeed! I never

[21 May 1793]   2 p 8vo   NYPL(B)
from M d'A (PS by SBP)
She is gone at ten this morning — and if She

[21–22 May 1793]   2 p 4to   NYPL(B)
from SBP
I owe my Fanny a world of details — but how

also   imperfect copy   4 p 4to   NYPL(B)

[24] May [1793]   2 p 8vo   NYPL(B)
to M d'A
I am quite grieved by both your Letters,

[24–26 May]   copy   3 p 4to
to Frederica Locke   NYPL(B)
I have been quite enchanted to day by my

27 May   4 p 4to   NYPL(B)
from M d'A & SBP
Je vous ecrirai aujourdhui dans la langue qui

[28 May 1793]   4 p 4to   NYPL(B)
from SBP
Let me now my Fanny however short may be

30 May [1793]   1 p 8vo   BM(Bar)
from Hester (Mulso) Chapone
I hope this will find Dear Miss Burney

30 May [1793]   2 p 4to   BM(Bar)
from SBP
Ah mechante mechante! Et vous laissez

[30–31 May]   copy   2 p 4to
to Frederica Locke   NYPL(B)
I have heard today all I can most wish of all

31 May [1793]   1 p 8vo   NYPL(B)
to M d'A
Though I cannot just now enter into the

31 May [1793]   4 p 4to   NYPL(B)
to SBP & Frederica Locke
My Heart finally so smites me this Morning

also   copy   4 p 4to   NYPL(B)

[31 May 1793]   4 p 8vo   NYPL(B)
from M d'A
Je suis enchanté de ce que vous avez la bonté

[May 1793]   4 p 4to   NYPL(B)
from SBP
I was most excessively vexed last night my

[May 1793]   2 p 4to   NYPL(B)
from SBP
I sent you per post a short letter

1793, continued

[May? 1793]   1 p 8vo   NYPL(B)
from SBP
I had this Morn^g. just sealed a paquet

3 June [1793]   3 p 4to   NYPL(B)
to M d'A
Ah, comme vous êtes fin! You answer every

3 June [1793]   4 p 4to   NYPL(B)
to GMAPWaddington
Your sweet Letter ought to have been

[3 June 1793]   3 p 4to   NYPL(B)
from SBP
& am almost afraid of being unintelligible —

5 June [1793]   1 p 4to   NYPL(B)
from SBP
Your letter was most welcome this morning —

[8 June 1793]   2 p 8vo   NYPL(B)
to M d'A
Vous avez bien raison; il ne faut point "eluder

[8 June 1793]   3 p 4to   NYPL(B)
from M d'A
Aprés avoir lu votre charmante lettre, mon

[8–10 June 1793]   2 p 4to   NYPL(B)
to CB
Do not be frightened, Dearest Sir, at the Sight

9 June [1793]   4 p 4to   BM(Bar)
from SBP & M d'A
I begin to feel anxious & uneasy my Fanny

9–10 June [1793]   4 p 8vo   NYPL(B)
from M d'A & SBP & Louis, comte de
     Narbonne-Lara
Des amours, des respects, et du desire de vous

[10–11 June 1793]   3 p 8vo   NYPL(B)
from M d'A (PS by SBP)
Vos amis, aimable Fanny, accompagnant leur

11 June [1793]   4 p 4to   NYPL(B)
to SBP & Frederica Locke
I had not intended writing again till my last

[12 June 1793]   1 p 8vo   NYPL(B)
from M d'A
On me permet d'écrire un mot à l'aimable

12 June   3 p 4to   BM(Bar)
from SBP & M d'A
May we be united & happy the anniversary of

[13 June 1793]   2 p 8vo   NYPL B)
to M d'A
Fachée? — O mon Dieu Non! — fachée d'une

[13 June 1793]   4 p 8vo   NYPL(B)
from M d'A
notre Soeur a reçu aujourdhui une boette [sic]

14 June [1793]   4 p 8vo   NYPL(B)
from M d'A
ah dites moi dites moi bien qu'en s'occupant

[14 June 1793]   3 p 4to   BM(Bar)
from SBP
Ah my Fanny! — how interesting is this crisis

[15 June 1793]   2 p 8vo   NYPL(B)
to M d'A
"Mais mon Dieu comme vous êtes bête!" vous

[15–16 June 1793]   8 p 4to   NYPL(B)
from SBP
How often have I lately wished my dearest

[16 June 1793]   2 p 8vo   NYPL(B)
from M d'A
Je vous ecris, mon aimable amie, avec une de

[18 June 1793]   4 p 8vo   NYPL(B)
from M d'A & SBP
à merveille, Mademoiselle l'Athanase à

7 July [1793 misdated 1791]   4 p 4to
                              BM(Bar)
from Marianne (Burney) Bourdois
My dear Aunt Fanny has indeed reason to

[20 July 1793]   1 p 8vo   NYPL(B)
from M d'A
fy for shame, my dearest friend! — Je suis

[20 July 1793]   2 p 4to   NYPL(B)
from M d'A
Par quelle fatalité une reponse qui d abord

23 July   3 p 4to   Comyn
to CB Jr
I am anxious for intelligence of your safe

27 July   4 p 4to   BM(Bar)
from CBF
Your letter has indeed astonished me! — I

[post 28 July 1793]   2 p 4to   NYPL(B)
from SBP
My dearest Fanny has not I hope suffered by

2 Aug   4 p 4to   NYPL(B)
to GMAPWaddington
How in the World shall I begin this letter to

3 Aug   amanuensis?   1 p 4to   NPG
from Elizabeth Juliana Schwellenberg
I received your Letter at the time the Royal

8 AU 1793 pmk   3 p 4to   Osb
to CB Jr
How happy was I to see again the Hand of my

9 Aug 179[3]   2 p 8vo   PML
from Anne-Louise-Germaine (Necker)
    de Staël-Holstein
on me dit une nouvelle qui me fait un extrême

also   copy   2 p 4to   NYPL(B)

12 Aug   3 p 4to   NYPL(B)
from Lady Keith
I have so long accustomed myself to think

12 [Aug 1793]   8 p 4to   BM(Bar)
from Maria (Allen) Rishton
had not this last week been so productive of

19 Aug [1793]   4 p 4to   BM(Bar)
from Marianne (Burney) Bourdois
Will you not look upon your *Immense* Niece

30 Aug [1793]   4 p 4to   BM(Bar)
to CB
I have been longing to write to my dearest

16 Sept [1793]   4 p 4to   NYPL(B)
to CB & Elizabeth (Allen) Burney
With what true happiness did I receive your

24 Sept   4 p 4to   NYPL(B)
from Marie-Elisabeth (Bouée) de La
    Fîte
Combien vous êtes aimable, ma chère Madame

[c 26 Sept 1793]   2 p 4to   NYPL(B)
to M d'A
Do not be astonished at my consternation —

[pre 29 Sept 1793]   2 p 4to   BM(Bar)
from CBF
I have enclosed you Ham's Bill, & when you

5 Oct   3 p 4to   PML
from Thomas Twining
— I find, I shall never be easy in my mind

18 Oct   3 p 4to   BM(Bar)
from Anne (Leigh) Frodsham
Tho discretion obliged me to omit answering

[20 Oct 1793]   2 p 4to   NYPL(B)
to CB
My dearest Father will think I have been very

27 Oct [1793]   2 p 4to   NYPL(B)
to CB
The terrible confirmation of this last act of

3–11 Nov [1793]   10 p 4to   BM(Bar)
from Maria (Allen) Rishton
Shall I interrupt your happiness

28 Nov   4 p 4to   NYPL(B)
to GMAPWaddington
Ah, my sweet unfortunate Friend! how have I

19 DE 1793 pmk   4 p 4to   NYPL(B)
to GMAPWaddington
The account of your surprise, my sweet

[1793]   copy extract   1 p scrap
to GMAPWaddington   NYPL(B)
M: Talleyrand highly deserves the character

[1793]   1 p 4to   BM(Bar)
from Frederica Locke
How *very* long it is since I have had the

30 July [post 1793]   3 p 8vo NYPL(B)
from Susanna Arabella Thrale
Your kind Heart will I am sure excuse our

15 Sept [post 1793]   1 p 4to   Comyn
from Elizabeth Juliana Schwellenberg
Mrs: Schwellenberg's Complts to Mrs:

[post 1793]   3 p 8vo   NYPL(B)
from Charlotte FitzGerald, Baroness
    Ros
& yet totally unspoiled. There are very few

[1793–1802]   3 p 12mo   NYPL(B)
from Harriet (Collins) de Boinville
After talking over the business with Mr.

1794

8 Jan   12 p 4to   BM(Bar)
to CB
I had invented, as our Charlotte was wont to

also   copy   14 p 4to   NYPL(B)

8 Jan   4 p 4to   Osb
to CB Jr
So how do do this new year, my dearest

[8 Jan 1794]   1 p 4to   NYPL(B)
from SBP
Here is sad news my dearest Fanny — the

9 Jan   4 p 4to   NYPL(B)
to EBB
Our Susanna encourages me, my dear Esther,

27 JA 1794 pmk   4 p 4to   BM(Bar)
to CB (with PS from M d'A)
My dear dear dear Father what very great

3 Feb [1794]   4 p 4to   BM(Bar)
from Maria (Allen) Rishton
Shall I call you unkind? surely I may without

[8 Feb 1794]   2 p 4to   BM(Bar)
to CB
The Times are indeed, as my dearest Father

also   copy   2 p 4to   NYPL(B)

14 [Feb 1794]   4 p 4to   NYPL(B)
from SBP
I must now write a little more satisfactorily

[15 Feb 1794]   1 p 4to   NYPL(B)
from SBP
I am vexed & embarrassed about yʳ. parcels

2 Mar   2 p 4to   BM(Bar)
to CB
How kind, my dearly beloved Father, how

2 Mar   copy   2 p 4to   NYPL(B)
from Charles-Maurice de Talleyrand-
     Périgord to M d'A & FBA
Adieu, mon cher d'arblay: je quitte votre pays

22 Mar   8 p 4to   BM(Bar)
to CB
I am this moment returned from reading your

also   copy   6 p 4to   NYPL(B)

[pre Apr 1794]   ½ p 4to   NYPL(B)
from SBP
I have just recᵈ the enclosed from the Captain

2 Apr [1794]   3 p fol   NYPL(B)
from Elizabeth (Allen) Burney
I have to thank you, repeatedly to thank you,

[5–27 Apr 1794]   2 p 4to   Newc
to CB
for any such deed against what they call that

25–27 Apr   4 p 4to   PML
to JB
A thousand thanks, my ever kind Brother, for

27 Apr   4 p 4to   BM(Bar)
to CB
M. d'Arblay, my dearest Father, is vext you do

[post 27] Apr   2 p 4to   BM(Bar)
to CB
Why what an exquisite Letter, my dearest

also   imperfect copy (composite of extracts
     from this AL and AL FBA to CB 17 Jan
     1794)   NYPL(B)
What a charming Letter was your

2 May   4 p 4to   NYPL(B)
to EBB
A little word I must send to my dearest Etty,

6 [May 1794]   3 p 4to   BM(Bar)
from Maria (Allen) Rishton
We will say nothing about punctuality

9 May [1794]   4 p 4to   BM(Bar)
to CB
How kind is my dearest Father, & how strait

also   imperfect copy   4 p 4to   NYPL(B)

6 June [1794]   1 p 4to   NYPL(B)
to GMAPWaddington
What is become of my dear Marianne? & her

16 June   3 p 12mo   NYPL(B)
to M d'A
I have just received a Letter too dear to let me

[16 June 1794]   2 p 4to   NYPL(B)
from M d'A
Ce matin, ma bonne amie, je suis moins

22 June [1794]   4 p 4to   BM(Bar)
from Maria (Allen) Rishton
I could not trust myself to write

5 July   1 p 4to   NYPL(B)
to GMAPWaddington
Ever since my last Letter to my dearest *Mary*

16–21 July   4 p 4to   BM(Bar)
to CBF
How long it is since I have written to my

28 July   2 p 4to   NYPL(B)
from SBP
It is hard not to be able to embrace you my

[10] Aug [1794]   4 p 4to   BM(Bar)
to CB
It is just a week since I had the greatest

also   copy   4 p 4to   NYPL(B)

2 Sept [1794]   4 p 4to   BM(Bar)
to CB
What very sweet Letters does my dearest dear

also   copy extract   2 p 4to   NYPL(B)
The meeting with Mr Erskine amused me

6 Sept [1794?]   1 p 4to   PML
with M d'A to JB
I feel so sincerely anxious for some intelligence

[14 Sept 1794]   4 p 4to   BM(Bar)
from Maria (Allen) Rishton
Where was that spirit of candour?

[post 15 Sept 1794]   2 p 4to   BM(Bar)
from Maria (Allen) Rishton
While you remained at Chelsea I heard

24 Sept   4 p 4to   NYPL(B)
from CBF to M d'A & FBA
Je ne peux allez vous remercier mon bien aimé

[Sept 1794]   1 p 8vo   NYPL(B)
from CB Jr
Write in my Father's name at once; He will

12 Oct [1794]   4 p 4to   BM(Bar)
to CB
I had purposed in quitting my dearest Father,

13 Oct [1794]   1 p 8vo   HEH
to Edward Jerningham
Mr. Jerningham would have received long ere

16 Oct   1 p 4to   NYPL(B)
to GMAPWaddington
How long it is since I have heard from my dear

21 Oct   2 p 4to   BM(Bar)
to CB
How infinitely sweet & soothing is my dearest

[Oct 1794]   1 p 4to   Comyn
from Edward Jerningham
At the suggestion of Miss Cambridge

[post 17 Nov]   2 p 4to   BM(Bar)
to CB
What a beautiful little poem! — 'tis almost a

8 DE 1794 pmk   4 p 4to   NYPL(B)
with M d'A to CBF
I love you with all my heart, i.e. as well as

[16 Dec 1794]   4 p 8vo   NYPL(B)
to M d'A
The Moment of danger now fast approaching

[Dec? 1794]   1 p 4to   NYPL(B)
from Cassandra (Leigh) Cooke
Will you dear Mad^m allow me to prescribe,

[1794]   2 p 4to   NYPL(B)
with M d'A to SBP
Unluckily, my Susan, we were out upon

[1794]   2 p 4to   NYPL(B)
from SBP
I send my Fanny a dear letter from our Esther

[1794]   2 p 4to   NYPL(B)
from SBP
I return my Brother his charming letter, & am

[1794]   2 p 4to   NYPL(B)
from SBP
The morning my Fanny has been filled w^th:

[1794]   2 p 4to   NYPL(B)
from SBP
How deliciously affected & delighted I have

1795

[9 Jan 1795]   1 p 4to   BM(Bar)
to CB
Could I tell my beloved Father half — half —

20 Jan   1 p 4to   NYPL(B)
from Elizabeth Juliana Schwellenberg
With Pleasure I Rec^d. your <   >

1795, continued

[Jan? 1795]   1 p 4to   NYPL(B)
from SBP
My own Fanny will I know be glad to see this

2 Feb   1 p 4to   NYPL(B)
from Cassandra (Leigh) Cooke
I am sincerely anxious, my dear Madam, to

17–21 Feb   8 p fol   NYPL(B)
from SBP
I sent away a long letter to our darling Friend

7 MR 1795 pmk   1 p 4to   NYPL(B)
to GMAPWaddington
ah my Marianne! — What an age since I have

[pre 21] Mar   2 p 4to   NYPL(B)
from SBP
I have had a much better night than I expected
also   copy   2 p LB   Arm

[c 21 Mar 1795]   2 p 4to   NYPL(B)
from M d'A
En y reflechissant davantage, je me confirme

15 Apr   4 p 4to   NYPL(B)
to GMAPWaddington
So dry a reproof from so dear a Friend? — —
also   copy   4 p 4to   NYPL(B)

17 AP 1795 pmk   2 p 4to   NYPL(B)
from SBP
I can find no way of giving my Fanny a journal

[Apr or May 1795]   1 p 4to   NYPL(B)
from SBP
The die is cast my Fanny, & the flattering hope

1 May   4 p 4to   BM(Bar)
to CBF
How many thanks I owe my kind Charlotte for

13 May   ½ p 4to   NYPL(B)
to M d'A
I have nothing appropriate for my beloved

13 May [1795]   4 p 4to   NYPL(B)
to CB
You have not one Letter to translate, my most
also   copy   4 p 4to   NYPL(B)

15 May   1 p 8vo   PML
to JB
It has just been whispered in my Ear that there

27 May [1795]   4 p 4to   BM(Bar)
from Maria (Allen) Rishton
My dear Friend will not wonder she has not

10 June   3 p 4to   Osb
to CB Jr
How are you? How are yours? I am well. So

13 June   4 p 4to   NYPL(B)
to CB
How I rejoice my business Letter did not arrive
also   composite copy of extracts 13 June,
18 June & 6 July (dated 18 June)   6 p
4to   NYPL(B)

[pre 15 June 1795]   2 p scrap
from SBP   NYPL(B)
I have been sadly disappointed in my hopes of
also   copy (dated 15 June)   2 p LB   Arm

15 June   1 p 4to fragment   NYPL(B)
from SBP
Ah my Fanny — I can but write one sad word

17 June   2 p fol   NYPL(B)
from SBP
I am sorry I cannot fill this enormous sheet my
also   copy   2 p LB   Arm

18 June   4 p 4to   NYPL(B)
to CB
I am quite penetrated by such a quick Letter.

18 June   2 p 4to   Osb
to CB Jr
I know you to be now so busy, that I shall

[18 June 1795]   2 p 8vo   PML
to JB
Thanks, my ever zealously kind Brother [tear]

19 June   4 p 4to   NYPL(B)
to GMAPWaddington
No, my dear Marianne, No — this "poor
also   copy dated 15 June   3 p 4to   NYPL(B)

24 June [1795]   4 p 4to   NYPL(B)
from SBP
I could not have been easy without sooner
also   copy   5 p LB   Arm

1 July   3 p 4to   Osb
to CB Jr
I entreat you, my dear Carlos, not to enrage,

3 July [1795]   4 p 4to   NYPL(B)
from SBP and CBF
I must hastily thank my Fanny for her kind
also   copy   5 p LB   Arm

[5 July 1795] 4 p 4to NYPL(B)
from SBP
I was not disappointed in my hopes of finding
also copy 4 p LB Arm

[6 July 1795] 2 p 4to NYPL(B)
to CB
I cannot refrain sending my dearest Father

7 July 4 p 4to Osb
with M d'A to CB Jr
How completely unfortunate, my dearest

8 July 1 p 4to NYPL(B)
to GMAPWaddington
I earnestly hope to hear speedily that my dear

10–11 July 4 p 4to NYPL(B)
from SBP
I wrote to you in a sad hurry the last time my
also copy 4 p LB Arm

15 July 4 p 4to NYPL(B)
to CB
Charles absolutely refuses to refund his powers,

15 July 4 p 4to Osb
with M d'A to CB Jr
Carte blanche, to our dear Don Quichote

21 July 4 p 4to NYPL(B)
to CB
I am in the uttermost amazement at no news of

[24 July 1795] 4 p 4to NYPL(B)
from SBP
If you & my Brother conceive me to be only
also copy 3 p LB Arm

24–25 July 3 p 4to NYPL(B)
with Frederica Locke to GMAPWaddington
I was extremely gratified, my dear Madame by

4 Aug 4 p 4to NYPL(B)
with SBP to EBB
The account of your "imbecillity," my dearest

25 Sept 1 p 4to Osb
from GMAPWaddington
I really am quite shocked my Dear M^{rs}.

12–13 Oct [1795] 4 p 4to NYPL(B)
from SBP
I promised my Fanny a shabby letter — & in
also copy 4 p LB Arm

17 Oct 4 p 4to NYPL(B)
from SBP
My Fanny — I must begin with saying this
also copy 6 p LB Arm

20–21 Oct 8 p 4to NYPL(B)
from SBP
I can find but this half sheet of paper that must
also copy 6 p LB Arm

3–5 Nov 4 p fol NYPL(B)
from SBP
I was beginning to be seriously uneasy my
also copy 8 p 4to Arm

13 Nov [1795] 2 p 4to NYPL(B)
from SBP
My Fanny entreats to know the subject of my

15 Nov [1795] 8 p 4to NYPL(B)
from SBP
Your letter not only gave me most touching
also copy 7 p 4to Arm

[19] Nov 4 p 4to NYPL(B)
to GMAPWaddington
How touched have I just felt myself with a

26 Nov [1795] copy 8 p LB Arm
from SBP
Ten days are past & over my Fanny since I last

26–27 Nov 4 p fol NYPL(B)
from SBP
M^{rs}. Boscawen's list rec^d. after the 6th: August
also copy 2 p LB Arm

27 Nov–4 Dec [1795] 6 p 4to
from SBP BM(Bar)
took his leave — I had then a tête à tête with

4 Dec 4 p 4to NYPL(B)
from SBP
Here w^d. be an excellent opportunity for
also copy 3 p LB Arm

[4]–8 Dec [1795] 4 p fol NYPL(B)
from SBP
I had given up the hopes of a long *causene*

26 Dec copy 2 p 4to NYPL(B)
to Louis, comte de Narbonne-Lara
What a Letter, to terminate so long and painful

26 Dec 2 p 4to NYPL(B)
from M d'A
True Angel! / On disait dernierement à

1795, continued

[1795?]   2 p 4to   NYPL(B)
from SBP
I send my dearest Fanny a letter w^ch: came to

[1795–96]   1 p 12mo   NYPL(B)
from Louis, comte de Narbonne-Lara
je rends a ma soeur l'ami qu'elle rend si

1796

[c 20 Jan 1796]   1 p fol   NYPL(B)
from SBP
Since my letter was written my dear Father has

22 JA 1796 pmk   2 p 4to   Osb
to Elizabeth (Allen) Burney
I must scribble a line or two without delay to

31 Jan – 1 Feb   4 p 4to   NYPL(B)
from SBP to Frederica Locke & FBA
Here then am I — returned to the dark City —
also   copy   5 p LB   Arm

3 Feb   4 p 4to   NYPL(B)
to M d'A
We are as well as we know how to be, without

7–[8] Feb   2 p 4to   NYPL(B)
from SBP to M d'A & FBA
Je me suis sentie tout à fait bouleversée mon
also   copy   2 p LB   Arm

26 Feb   1 p 4to   NYPL(B)
from Elizabeth Juliana Schwellenberg
Mad^m. I hope youre goodness will Excuse me

29 Feb – 1 Mar   2 p fol   NYPL(B)
from SBP
I have this moment dispatched Susan with a
also   copy   4 p LB   Arm

4 Mar [1796]   4 p 4to   NYPL(B)
to CB
I know my beloved Father will exactly feel

4 Mar [1796?]   4 p 4to   NYPL(B)
from Charlotte Cambridge
I went yesterday to dear M^rs <Rs> at <   >

7 Mar   1 p 4to   NYPL(B)
from Frances (Glanville) Boscawen
Indeed, Dear Madam your obliging, & most

9 Mar   4 p fol   NYPL(B)
from SBP to FBA & Frederica Locke
It is a very unusual thing to me to hesitate
also   copy   4 p LB   Arm

11 MR 1796 pmk   4 p fol   NYPL(B)
with M d'A to CB
Though I am very much affraid to make you

14 MR 1796 pmk   3 p 4to   Osb
with M d'A to CB Jr
Neither Cicero, Longinus, nor Dr. Johnson ever

15–16 Mar   4 p fol   NYPL(B)
from SBP
It is impossible to resist sending you a few
also   copy   5 p LB   Arm

19 Mar [1796]   4 p fol   NYPL(B)
from SBP
I feel that it is useless to tell you, my dearest
also   copy   4 p LB   Arm

[21 Mar 1796]   1 p 4to   NYPL(B)
to CB
The shabbyest little bit will be better than total

5 Apr   1 p 4to   NYPL(B)
from Elizabeth Juliana Schwellenberg
I feel myself ashamed at not writing sooner

[pre 12 June 1796]   4 p 4to
from SBP   NYPL(B)
My dearest Fanny & dear Brother received
also   copy   3 p LB   Arm

17 June   4 p fol   Comyn
with M d'A to CB Jr
The whole Copy we have sent to the two

[c 17 June 1796]   4 p 4to   NYPL(B)
with M d'A to SBP
Un mot seulement à notre bonne et indulgente

20 JU 1796 pmk   1 p 4to   Osb
to Rosette (Rose) Burney
I <grieve> at the impossibility of meeting this

23–24 June   1 p 4to   NYPL(B)
from SBP
To save my Fanny double postage, as I was
also   copy   2 p LB   Arm

[25 June]   4 p 4to   NYPL(B)
from SBP
Your dear letter gave me *very* great pleasure
also   copy   4 p LB   Arm
Sunday Morn. — our baby in a sweet sleep.

J⟨U⟩ pmk [1796]   4 p 4to   NYPL(B)
from SBP to M d'A & FBA
Je repondrai bien vite à votre lettre mon cher

also   copy   3 p LB   Arm

2 July   4 p 4to   NYPL(B)
from SBP (part as from AA) to FBA &
    M d'A
Aujourdhui je vous ecris en francais, ce que me

also   copy   2 p LB   Arm

10 July [1796]   4 p 4to   NYPL(B)
to CB
If I had as much of Time as of Matter, my

[post 16 July 1796]   3 p 8vo   NYPL(B)
to SBP
M. d'A. will write about the Money — but join

also   partial copy   2 p 4to   NYPL(B)
I grieve to return Mons.r de Lally's

17 July [1796]   1 p fol   NYPL(B)
from Elizabeth (Allen) Burney
how many long Letters of thanks I've written

18 JY 1796 pmk   4 p 4to   NYPL(B)
to CB
Almost immediately upon my return to the

18 July   1 p 4to   NYPL(B)
to GMAPWaddington
once again I have the pleasure of writing to

18 July [1796]   1 p 4to   NYPL(B)
from Frances (Glanville) Boscawen
I have receiv'd the Favour of a second Visit

19 July   4 p 4to   NYPL(B)
from SBP
Your young namesake & I were near an hour

also   copy   4 p LB   Arm

21 July   3 p fol   NYPL(B)
from Elizabeth (Allen) Burney (with
    SBP to M d'A)
I want to write a 1000 & ten thousand thanks

also   copy of SBP to M d'A   3 p LB   Arm
I wish to tell my dear Brother d'Arblay that I

[24–25] July   4 p 4to   NYPL(B)
from SBP
I am sorry my own dearest Fanny it was

also   copy   2 p LB   Arm

27 JY 1796 pmk   4 p 4to   NYPL(B)
to CB
Miss Planta arrived at 10. with Her Majesty's

[28] July   2 p 4to   NYPL(B)
from SBP
A little parcel from my Mother sent by the

also   copy   2 p 4to   Arm

29 July [1796]   4 p fol   BM(Bar)
from CBF
Tho' I have not yet quite finish'd my dear

30 July   4 p 4to   BM(Bar)
from EBB
I must say that in not having written

[July 1796]   4 p 4to   NYPL(B)
to CB
Just before we assembled to Dinner, M.lle

7 Aug [1796]   4 p 4to   BM(Bar)
from CBF
With great pleasure I seize the opportunity of

13 AU 1796 pmk   8 p 4to   NYPL(B)
to CB
We spent the remnant of Wednesday Evening

17 Aug [1796]   4 p fol   BM(Bar)
from CBF (with PS from Charlotte
    Cambridge)
At last I have it in my power to begin a letter

[22 Aug 1796]   4 p fol   NYPL(B)
from SBP to M d'A & FBA
Je ne sçais pas precisement ce que vous

also   copy   5 p LB   Arm

31 Aug   2 p fol   NYPL(B)
from SBP
I cannot help feeling very anxious my dearest

also   copy   3 p LB   Arm

[Aug – Sept 1796]   1 p 8vo   NYPL(B)
to M d'A
My most beloved ami will find he had more

[11]–15 Sept   2 p fol   NYPL(B)
from SBP
My heart yearns to converse again with my

also   copy   3 p LB   Arm

[28 Sept 1796]   1 p 4to   NYPL(B)
from Etiennette, Princesse d'Hénin
chere madame, vous ecrivez aisément

1796, continued

[pre Oct 1796]   1 p 4to   NYPL(B)
from [SBP?]
having My <drst> Sally. *She is a comfort to*

2 Oct – 11 Nov   4 p 4to   NYPL(B)
to GMAPWaddington
You allow so little, my dear Marianne, to even

[10–11 Oct 1796]   4 p 4to   NYPL(B)
to SBP
How touching is every line of my beloved

[11 Oct 1796]   2 p 4to   NYPL(B)
from SBP
I cannot resist an opportunity of sending a line

13–14 Oct   4 p 4to   NYPL(B)
from SBP
I have had — for these times — a fair day my
also   copy   4 p LB   Arm

[14] Oct   4 p 4to   NYPL(B)
to CB
How well I know — & feel the pang of this

21–24 Oct [1796]   3 p 4to   NYPL(B)
from SBP
Not till this morning have I been able to
also   copy   3 p LB   Arm

22 Oct   3 p 4to   NYPL(B)
to M d'A
How sweet a surprise was this Morning's post!

23 Oct   2 p 4to   NYPL(B)
from M d'A
Quelle bonne, aimable, charmante, et delicieuse

24 Oct   2 p 4to   NYPL(B)
to M d'A
What sweetly touching traits of my little

25–29 Oct   2 p 4to   NYPL(B)
from M d'A
Pourquoi mon amie, en achevant ta lettre ne

31 Oct   4 p 4to   NYPL(B)
from SBP
Safe landed at Dublin will I know suffice to my
also   copy   3 p 4to   Arm

[Oct 1796?]   3 p 8vo   NYPL(B)
from Frederica Locke
I hope my dearest Fanny & her lovely Bambino

[2 Nov 1796]   4 p 4to   NYPL(B)
to CB
I can make no delay in writing to my most dear

7 Nov   mutilated   4 p 4to   NYPL(B)
with CB to SBP   & BM(Bar)
[NYPL(B) begins] Yes, my most beloved
[BM(Bar) begins] I am delighted to see our

7 Nov   4 p 4to   NYPL(B)
from SBP
I can scarce persuade myself it is but a week
also   copy   4 p LB   Arm

8 Nov   4 p 4to   NYPL(B)
to CB
I had intended writing to my dearest Father by

9 Nov   4 p 4to   BM(Bar)
to CBF
On *Sunday* I received news that our beloved

11 Nov   1 p 4to   NYPL(B)
from Dorothy Young
I wish I had addressed you before I finished a

14 Nov   4 p 4to   NYPL(B)
to CB
I covet much to hear that the melancholy task

14 Nov   4 p fol   NYPL(B)
from SBP
Time passes heavily with me my beloved
also   copy   6 p LB   Arm

15 Nov   2 p 4to   NYPL(B)
with Frederica Locke to SBP
How sweetly does my Susan spread a Sun beam

22 Nov   1 p 4to   BM(Bar)
from Cassandra (Leigh) Cooke
I had an opportunity, yesterday, of inquiring

25–27 Nov   4 p 4to   NYPL(B)
with Frederica Locke to SBP
Never was a sweeter Letter written, my dearest

28 Nov [1796]   4 p fol   NYPL(B)
from SBP
At length I find a moment to begin a letter

28 Nov   copy   6 p LB   Arm
from SBP
I am truly rejoiced in what you say of Sarah, &

29 Nov   4 p 4to   NYPL(B)
to CB
This uncommon & so total silence begins to give

[1 Dec 1796]   2 p 4to   NYPL(B)
from JB
I will not lose another moment in acquainting

9 pmk   Dec   4 p 4to   NYPL(B)
to CB
What cruel & most unnecessary disturbance

24 Dec   16 p 4to   BM(Bar)
from Maria (Allen) Rishton
A thousand thanks for your kind interesting

30 Dec   2 p 4to   NYPL(B)
to SBP
I know how my beloved Susan will rejoice to

30 Dec   4 p fol   NYPL(B)
from SBP
What a time has passed since I last wrote to my

also   copy   8 p LB   Arm

[c 1796]   ½ p 4to   BM(Bar)
from JB
last month or six weeks [torn] that Lord

[post 1796]   copy   2 fragments
from SBP?   NYPL(B)
"Give yourself up to sweet Ariella (Camilla)

[June–July 1796–98?]   1 p scrap
                            NYPL(B)
from Marianne (Burney) Bourdois
We shall be very glad my dear Aunt if you can

[1796–98]   1 p scrap   NYPL(B)
from JB
Full three months, after your last visit here,

1797

7 pmk   Jan   4 p 4to   BM(Bar)
from Maria (Allen) Rishton
Your letter was brought me to day from

8 Jan [1797]   4 p 4to   NYPL(B)
to CB
I was extremely vexed at missing our uncertain

9 Jan   8 p 4to   BM(Bar)
from Maria (Allen) Rishton
The night I wrote to you from Holkham

15 Jan [1797]   2 p fol   NYPL(B)
from SBP
Once more let me begin a letter to my Sisters

also   copy   4 p LB   Arm

26 Jan [1797]   4 p 4to   NYPL(B)
to CB
How is it, my dearest kindest Father! — you

29 Jan   4 p fol   NYPL(B)
from FBA & M d'A to SBP (with Amelia
   (Locke) Angerstein to Norbury
   Phillips)
And can you, my beloved Susan, reproach

30 Jan   4 p 4to   NYPL(B)
to CBF
What a grievous & most unexpected

Jan   2 p 8vo   BM(Bar)
from Hester (Mulso) Chapone
You can hardly imagine the vexation I felt

also   copy   1 p   NYPL(B)

10 Feb [1797]   2 p 4to   NYPL(B)
with Amelia (Locke) Angerstein to SBP
My most beloved Susan will, I trust, be relieved

13 Feb   2 p 4to   NYPL(B)
to GMAPWaddington
What is become of my dear Marianne? I know

24 Feb [1797]   2 p 4to   BM(Bar)
from Maria (Allen) Rishton
I have been absent from home

27 FE 1797 pmk   4 p 4to   NYPL(B)
to CB
I hardly know whether I am most struck with

27 Feb–14 Mar   4 p fol   BM(Bar)
with M d'A & Frederica Locke to SBP
I rejoice that at least this our only converse may

3 MR 1797 pmk   1 p 4to   NYPL(B)
to GMAPWaddington
I am too desirous to hear you are well, & free

16 Mar   4 p fol   NYPL(B)
to CB
Relieved at length from a terror that almost

18 Mar   1 p 4to   NYPL(B)
to GMAPWaddington
I have been too much engrossed, mind & hands,

24 Mar [1797]   2 p fol   NYPL(B)
from SBP
I have scarce recovered sight my Fanny, for

also   copy   3 p LB   Arm

1797, continued

[1] Apr [1797]   4 p 4to   NYPL(B)
to CB & SHB
My dearest Father will have wondered I have

1 AP 1797 pmk   3 p 4to   NYPL(B)
to Rosette (Rose) Burney
I ought to have given a more immediate answer

3 Apr   4 p 4to   NYPL(B)
to EBB
Launcelot Gobbo — or Gobbo Launcelot was

3 Apr–17 May   1 p fol mutilated
to SBP   NYPL(B) & BM(Bar)
[BM(Bar)] Yesterday I joined to our beloved
[NYPL(B), 2 pieces] -ble impatience & anxiety

11 May   3 p 4to   BM(Bar)
to CBF
I am a good deal disappointed, my dearest

11 May   4 p 8vo   PML
to JB
I hate to torment you — but what can poor

[17 May 1797]   2 p 4to   PML
to JB
I have the joy to tell you a Letter is arrived

[pre 18 May 1797] copy   2 p 4to
to Frederica Locke   NYPL(B)
You are too good my dearest Friend almost

2 JU 1797 pmk   4 p 4to   NYPL(B)
to GMAPWaddington
It was a very sweet thought to make my little

24 JU 1797 pmk   1 p scrap   NYPL(B)
from SHB
just now for a few days — Papa has been out

29 JU 1797 pmk   4 p 4to   NYPL(B)
to EBB
I agree to your Quarterly payments, my

20–24 July   4 p fol   NYPL(B)
with Frederica Locke & Amelia (Locke)
     Angerstein to SBP
Your dear Letters, my most beloved Susan, are

[24 July 1797]   7 p fol   BM(Bar)
from Maria (Allen) Rishton
how is your little Darling? much better I hope

27 July   4 p 4to   NYPL(B)
to CB
a Letter of so many dates is quite delicious to

1 Aug   4 p 4to   NYPL(B)
to M d'A
I find I can have no joy that is not yours — I

10 Aug   6 p 4to   NYPL(B)
to CB
My dearest Father, will, I know, be grieved at

17–29 Aug   mutilated   8 p 4to
     BM(Bar) & NYPL(B)
with M d'A to SBP
I must not — dare not tell my own beloved
[2 scraps in NYPL(B)] one I mention, from his

20 Aug   4 p 4to   BM(Bar)
to SBP
Our best-loved & most precious Friend

29 Aug   4 p 4to   BM(Bar)
to CB
As I called upon my dearest Father to take part

Aug [1797]   2 p 4to   McG
to CB Jr
In the absence of my Lord & Master

15 Sept   1 p 4to   Comyn
from Lady Rothes
The two first Volumes I think

25 Sept   2 p 4to   NYPL(B)
to CB
How very kind is this, most dear — dear sir!

25 Sept   4 p 4to   NYPL(B)
to CB
I must vex my dearest Padre with my vexation

[18 Oct 1797]   1 p fragment
     NYPL(B)
from Cassandra (Leigh) Cooke
I am afraid I am selfish enough to look for an

[30 Oct 1797]   2 p 4to   NYPL(B)
to M d'A
I have waited to the last Minute in hopes of

1 Nov   2 p 4to   Osb
to CB Jr
In the midst of packing — alas, not of paying!

[1 Nov 1797]   3 p 4to   NYPL(B)
from M d'A
Merci cent et cent fois, ma tres chère amie

[pre 3 Nov 1797]   2 p 4to   NYPL(B)
to M d'A
J'étois toute agitée ce matin jusqu'à l'heure de

[10 Nov 1797]   copy   2 p 8vo
[to CBF or JB]   BM(Bar)
I come on an Embassy to demand one of yr.

10 Nov   4 p 4to   PML
to JB
I went to Town this morning Express upon

also   draft   2 p fol   BM(Bar)

14 Nov [1797]   3 p 4to   NYPL(B)
to SBP
The immense pacquet I enclose from our

16 Nov   4 p 4to   NYPL(B)
to CBF
Your Letter was most welcome to me, my

28 Nov   copy, extract   1 p fol
from SBP   NYPL(B)
You judged rightly of our poor Father, that the

10 Dec   4 p 4to   NYPL(B)
to CB
I am shocked inexpressibly — nay, alarmed, at

17 Dec   2 p 4to   NYPL(B)
to SBP
seems a most good & gentle creature, &

[26 Dec 1797]   1 p 4to   NYPL(B)
from Cassandra (Leigh) Cooke
I hope to hear, *quite* well of dear little Boy

Dec   8 p 4to   NYPL(B)
to SBP
This moment I receive, through our dearest

1798

4 Jan   4 p 4to   NYPL(B)
to EBB
I feel inclined to write you a very long Letter,

5–19 Jan   4 p fol   NYPL(B)
from SBP to FBA & M d'A
I feel as if I shd. like to fill half a quire of paper

also   copy (misdated 5 Jan)   10 p LB
                                    Arm

11 Jan   3 p 4to   NYPL(B)
to M d'A
Tell me if ever anything was half so vexatious?

15 Jan   4 p 4to   BM(Bar)
to CB
Your most kind invitation to my dear Partner

[18 Jan 1798]   4 p 4to   NYPL(B)
to SBP
I had meant to hear again from my beloved

[c 18 Jan 1798]   copy   2 p LB   Osb
to Ralph Broome
The alacrity with which I undertook to prepare

10 Feb [1798]   2 p 4to   NYPL(B)
from Ralph Broome
When I took the Liberty of addressing You on

[26? Feb–8 Mar 1798]   20 p 4to
to SBP   NYPL(B)
I will not give the real date when I resume my

also   copy   24 p LB   Osb

[26? Feb–10 Mar 1798]   18 p 4to &
        scrap   NYPL(B) & BM(Bar)
to SBP
But I have not told you of my renewed
[BM(Bar) scrap] Room. — But before that

[Feb 1798]   3 p 4to   BM(Bar)
from Maria (Allen) Rishton
I hardly know where to begin

[Feb 1798]   14 p 4to   NYPL(B)
to SBP
And now I have to prepare another Court

also   copy   15 p LB   Osb

[Feb–Mar 1798]   copy   1 p
                        NYPL(B)
from ? (included in FBA to SBP) [26?
        Feb–10 Mar 1798]
Madme d'Arblay need not have any scruple in

[Feb–Mar 1798]   copy   1 p
                        NYPL(B)
from Margaret Bremyere (included in
        FBA to SBP [26? Feb–8 Mar 1798])
Mrs. Bremyere has received the Queen's

[Feb–Mar 1798]   2 p 8vo   BM(Bar)
from Hester (Mulso) Chapone
You are very good, my dear Madam, to afford

also   copy (included in FBA to SBP [26?
        Feb–10 Mar 1798]   2 p 4to   NYPL(B)

1798, continued

1 Mar   3 p 4to   BM(Bar)
from CBFB & Ralph Broome
Many thanks for y^r. last kind Letter my dearest

2 Mar   2 p 4to   NYPL(B)
to CBFB
To feel, as well as say that I wish to both all

8 Mar   copy   1 p   NYPL(B)
from Margaret Planta (included in FBA
    to SBP [26? Feb–8 Mar 1798])
The Queen has commanded me to acquaint

12 Mar   4 p 4to   NYPL(B)
to SBP
What a world of materials have I for my

18 Mar   4 p 4to   Comyn
to CB Jr
How very provoking, my dearest Carlos, to be

18 Mar [1798]   4 p 4to   BM(Bar)
from Maria (Allen) Rishton
I think I may not with certainty demand your

20 Mar   24 p 4to   NYPL(B)
to SBP (first 4 p copied from Journal for
    3 Nov 1797)
Though I have so lately sent off a close

also   copy   33 p LB   Osb

3 Apr   3 p 4to mutilated   NYPL(B)
to CBFB   & BM(Bar)
[NYPL(B) fragment] Now that I see my
[BM(Bar)] Comfort to my Father, whom she

20 Apr   3 p 4to   Camb(F)
to Rosette (Rose) Burney
I most truly rejoiced at sight of your hand, my

25 Apr   4 p 4to   NYPL(B)
to CB
Bouder, my dearest Father? — But I am sure

2 May   copy   1 p 4to   Osb
to JB
I sh'd have been very glad to have had y^r letter

13 May   4 p 4to   NYPL(B)
to SBP (with PS by M d'A)
I begin to feel so compleatly uneasy at this

May [1798]   12 p 4to   BM(Bar)
from Maria (Allen) Rishton
How kindly do I feel the Interest

4 JU 1798 pmk   2 fragments of 4to
to CB   NYPL(B) & BM(Bar)
[BM(Bar) fragment] & much pitied &
[NYPL(B) fragment] March to the <Bank>:

5 June   4 p 4to   NYPL(B)
to EBB
How delighted am I to have a Commission

7 June   2 p 4to   NYPL(B)
to CB
Indeed, my dearest Father, Mr. Clery's

20 June   3 p 4to   NYPL(B)
from FBA & Md'A to SBP
O my beloved Susan how cruelly

20 June   3 p 4to   NYPL(B)
from FBA & M d'A to SBP
What I suffer from finding you receive none of

21 June   4 p 4to   NYPL(B)
to EBB
I am almost distract to find none of my Letters

[c 24 June 1798]   2 p 8vo   BM(Bar)
to CBFB
But I thank my dearest Charlotte for her

2<6> June [1798]   4 p fol   NYPL(B)
from SBP
At length I have received a letter to *Myself* my

also   copy   6 p LB   Arm

28–[29] June   6 p 4to   BM(Bar)
from Maria (Allen) Rishton
I shoud have written to you some time ago

June   3 p 4to   BM(Bar)
from Maria (Allen) Rishton
I have hardly a moment to scribble

1 July   copy   4 p LB   Osb
to Lady Keith
Your kind idea of ornamenting my little cottage

5 July   3 p 4to   BM(Bar)
from Maria (Allen) Rishton
the storm is broke over my head at last

6 July   4 p to   NYPL(B)
to SBP
I seize with avidity the hope that a Letter may

[10 July 1798]   2 p 4to   BM(Bar)
from Maria (Allen) Rishton
I bow to the Rod, & love the Hand that is

⟨20⟩ July [1798]   4 p fol   NYPL(B)
from SBP to FBA & M d'A
In the midst of the most harrassing uncertainty

also   copy (dated 30 July)   5 p LB   Arm

1 Aug   4 p 4to   NYPL(B)
to EBB
My dearest Esther, I earnestly hope, has not

14 Aug   4 p 4to   NYPL(B)
to CBFB
I have deferred writing, my dearest Charlotte,

[28 Aug 1798]   4 p 4to   NYPL(B)
to SBP
If I could find words — but the language does

29 Aug   2 p 4to   NYPL(B)
to Molesworth Phillips
Dear Major — Send us off your Wife &

[Aug–Sept 1798]   22 p 4to
to SBP   NYPL(B)
accomplishments. This, certainly must make

[2 Sept 1798]   1 p 4to   BM(Bar)
from Maria (Allen) Rishton
I dont know what to say — or write but to you

[3 Sept 1798]   4 p fol   BM(Bar)
from Maria (Allen) Rishton
I cannot help saying it was a cruel

5 Sept [1798]   4 p 4to   BM(Bar)
from Maria (Allen) Rishton
I am afraid my last letter was almost

8–11 [Sept 1798]   4 p 4to
from SBP   NYPL(B)
My beloved Fanny must have received two

also   copy   5 p LB   Arm

10 Sept   4 p 4to   NYPL(B)
to GMAPWaddington
Your very interesting pacquet, my dear

20 Sept   6 p 4to   NYPL(B)
to SBP
I can only grieve now thus uselessly — &

[post Sept 1798]   4 p scrap
from SBP   NYPL(B)
a few lines for yourself alone my dearest —

[3 Oct 1798]   4 p 4to   NYPL(B)
to EBB
I meant to have written a few lines to my dear

9 Oct   4 p fol   NYPL(B)
from SBP
The same day on which I had sent an answer

also   copy   8 p LB   Arm

9 Oct [1798]   4 p 4to   BM(Bar)
from Maria (Allen) Rishton
I will leave all Congratulations on the Glorious

[19 Oct 1798]   4 p 4to   BM(Bar)
from Maria (Allen) Rishton
I suppose your Father will write you word that

23 Oct   3 p fol   BM(Bar)
from Maria (Allen) Rishton
I am truly glad I was at home this Morning

30 Oct [1798]   4 p 4to   BM(Bar)
from Maria (Allen) Rishton
Once more at your request I will enter upon the

8 Nov   2 copies   1 p 8vo   BM(Bar)
from   ?
We are all invalids here & with the ever

22 Nov   4 p 4to   NYPL(B)
to EBB & Marianne (Burney) Bourdois
    (with PS from M d'A to EBB)
I cannot wonder, my dearest Esther, you were

[28 Nov 1798]   1 p 8vo   NYPL(B)
from Lady Rothes
Your Note prevented mine I had written to you

30 Nov–5 Dec   4 p fol   NYPL(B)
from SBP
Oh my dearest Fanny. — I have been for some

also   copy   9 p LB   Arm

Nov   6 p 4to   BM(Bar)
from Maria (Allen) Rishton
Your Father mentioned to me your having

13–15 Dec   8 p 4to   NYPL(B)
to SBP
My dearest dearest Susan — that I could but

[18 Dec 1798]   4 p 4to   BM(Bar)
to CB
Whether you call your Letter sprightly or not,

28 Dec   4 p 4to   BM(Bar)
to CBFB
You know what a vile unpunctual

[Dec 1798]   10 p 4to   NYPL(B)
to SBP
And now, my beloved Susan, I will sketch —

1798, continued

[1798–99]   2 p 4to   NYPL(B)
from JB
I have written in answer to M^r. d'Arblay

[post 1798]   1 p fol   NYPL(B)
from Amelia (Locke) Angerstein
I return the *truly* gratifying letters my precious

1799

4 Jan [1799]   2 p 4to   NYPL(B)
to CB
The sweet kindness of this invitation, my

5–11 Jan   4 p fol   NYPL(B)
from SBP
My dearest Fanny's, my M^{rs}. Locke's precious

also   copy   9 p LB   Arm

18 pmk Feb   4 p 4to   NYPL(B)
with M d'A to EBB
What! — a *Letter* to thank for too? — & how

[18 Feb] pmk 1799   3 p 8vo
from Maria (Allen) Rishton BM(Bar)
I hope a good < > and better weather

1 Mar   3 p 4to   NYPL(B)
from Ralph Broome & CBFB
Tho it were true, as Husbands oft complain /

[8] Mar [1799]   2 p 4to   NYPL(B)
to CB
It would have made me blush to have received

12 Mar   12 p 4to   NYPL(B)
to SBP
The first Pen I take after a Lingering & most

13 Mar   4 p 4to   Osb
to Rosette (Rose) Burney
I have received such true pleasure from your

14 Mar   4 p 4to   NYPL(B)
to CB
What a terrible time we have passed since we

20 Mar   copy   2 p LB   Osb
to Lady Keith
I thought myself quite unfortunate in being a

21 Mar   4 p 4to   NYPL(B)
to CBFB & Ralph Broome
If Chance has not kindly stood my friend in

23 Mar   4 p 4to   NYPL(B)
to GMAPWaddington
Your last Letter, so interesting, so open, so

24 Mar   4 p 4to   NYPL(B)
with M d'A to EBB
You have entirely misunderstood me, my dear

[Mar 1799]   4 p fragment.
from SBP   NYPL(B)
rapacious! — Poor Charlotte! — Can she be

1 Apr   4 p 4to   NYPL(B)
to EBB
I quite regret that your Letter did not come to

3 Apr [1799]   1 p 4to   Hyde
to CB Jr
I have just received your Monday's Letter, my

[pre 4 Apr 1799]   2 p 4to   BM(Bar)
from Hester (Mulso) Chapone
If you have heard of the most recent of my

also   copy   3 p 4to   NYPL(B)

4 Apr   copy   2 p 4to   Osb
to Hester (Mulso) Chapone
It was from your own affecting account, my

also   copy   3 p 4to   NYPL(B)

14 Apr   5 p 4to   NYPL(B)
to SBP
I send one hasty fresh sheet — / one Copy of

20 Apr   3 p 4to   NYPL(B)
to GMAPWaddington
It is *HERE* I must hope to see you — in my

20 AP 1799 pmk   1 p scrap
from CBFB   NYPL(B)
the exe[cution] of your Commissions is always

20 Apr   copy   2 p 4to   NYPL(B)
from SHB (included in AL FBA to SBP
     8 May 1799)
Before you can have taken any step in the

21 Apr   copy   1 p 4to   NYPL(B)
to SHB (included in AL FBA to SBP
     8 May 1799)
With the greatest amazement I have

22 Apr   4 p 4to   NYPL(B)
to CBFB
You are very good, my dearest Charlotte, & Mr.

23 Apr   copy   1 p 4to   NYPL(B)
from SHB (included in AL FBA to SBP
     8 May 1799)
The Letters, my dearest sister, concerning

[pre 25 Apr 1799]   copy   1 p 4to
to CB   NYPL(B)
I heard with great happiness of your good

25 Apr   4 p 4to   NYPL(B)
to EBB
My dearest Esther, I have had a long Letter

25 [Apr 1799]   7 p 4to   BM(Bar)
from Maria (Allen) Rishton
I have heard such constant accounts

28 Apr   4 p 4to   NYPL(B)
from SBP
It is a sad thing to have no Mr. Windham, &

also   copy (dated 29 Apr)   7 p LB   Arm
It is a bad thing to have no Mr. Windham, &

2 May   copy   3 p 4to   NYPL(B)
to Frederica Locke
Poor Mr Seward! — I am indeed exceedingly

8 May   4 p 4to   NYPL(B)
to SBP (with PS by M d'A)
Your dear Letter, my most dear Susan, has

12 May   2 p 4to   NYPL(B)
from JB
I am greatly concerned that any

also   copy (in AL FBA to SBP 29 June 1799)
                               NYPL(B)

[c 13 May 1799] draft   1 p 4to
to JB   NYPL(B)
I thank you most sincerely for your Letter,

also   copy (in ALS FBA to SBP 29 June 1799)
                               NYPL(B)

13 May   copy   5 p 4to   Osb
to Frederica Locke
I write before due time to tell my dearest

[26 May 1799]   4 p 4to   NYPL(B)
to SBP
I have just heard that our dearest Mrs. Locke

30 May   4 p 4to   NYPL(B)
to EBB
I am extremely pleased with my Cloak, my

4–[8] June   4 p 4to   NYPL(B)
from SBP
I am uneasy lest you shd. be so my own dear

also   copy   7 p LB   Arm

17 June   4 p 4to   NYPL(B)
to EBB
I can hardly tell you, my dearest Esther, how

29 June   6 p 4to   NYPL(B)
to SBP
We have now all round heard from my darling

18 July   4 p 4to   NYPL(B)
from SBP
What treasures I have to thank you for my

also   copy   6 p LB   Arm

22 July   4 p 4to   NYPL(B)
to CBFB
My dearest Charlottenberg — you are a most

25 July   4 p 4to   NYPL(B)
to CB
Fore George, a more excellent song than

also   copy   5 p 4to   Osb

28 July–1 Aug   4 p 4to   NYPL(B)
to SBP
I have just received your dear Letter of the

10 Aug   4 p 4to   Osb
to Rosette (Rose) Burney
If you measure my concern for your happiness

14 Aug   4 p 4to   NYPL(B)
to SBP
I know that my most beloved Susan — my

28 Aug mutilated   4 p 4to   NYPL(B)
to SBP
The news with which this pacquet will turn,

14 Sept [1799]   4 p 4to   NYPL(B)
to EBB   & BM(Bar)
[2 p NYPL(B)] In the expectation of a visit

[2 p BM(Bar] This letter was begun upon

19 Sept   4 p 4to   NYPL(B)
to SBP
Yes, my sweetest Susan, I *am* comforted — the

25 Sept   4 scraps   NYPL(B)
to CB
What a Crowning to your Honours, my dearest

28 Sept   4 p 4to   NYPL(B)
to EBB
I can hardly settle with myself, my dearest

1799, continued

1 Oct   4 p 4to   NYPL(B)
to CB
What a sumptuous feast have you given me,

4 Oct [1799]   4 p fragment NYPL(B)
from SBP
do you not know that *langue*? — "toujours

12 Oct   4 p 4to   NYPL(B)
to SBP & Molesworth Phillips
My dear — darling Susan must not wonder at

15 Oct   4 p 4to   NYPL(B)
to CB
on Saturday, my dearest sir, I had a Letter

15–18 Oct   4 p 4to   NYPL(B)
to EBB
You have seen but too clearly, my dearest

18 Oct   4 p 4to   NYPL(B)
to CB
Nothing but my full conviction that all our

20 Oct   2 p 4to   NYPL(B)
from SBP to M d'A & FBA
My dearest, dearest Fanny — my kind &

also   copy   2 p LB   Arm

26 Oct [1799]   2 p 4to   NYPL(B)
to CB
God be praised, my dearest Father, I have just

27 Oct [1799]   4 p 4to   NYPL(B)
to EBB
I have had my answer most astonishingly soon,

[pre 19 Nov 1799]   4 p 4to   BM(Bar)
to SBP
My Heart is too full for expression, my best —

19 Nov   4 p 4to   NYPL(B)
to EBB
'Tis my turn now to have the dear commission

28 Nov   4 p 4to   BM(Bar)
to CB
At length, my dearest Father, in thanking you

28 Nov   4 p 4to   NYPL(B)
to EBB
I had just, my dear Hetty, received a Letter

[Nov or Dec? 1799]   ½ p 4to
                         BM(Bar)
from Hester (Mulso) Chapone
I was much in pain lest you & your servants &

4 Dec   4 p fol   NYPL(B)
from SBP
I owe you my Fanny I know not how many

also   copy   3 p LB   Arm

10 Dec   4 p 4to   NYPL(B)
to SBP
O my Susan — my Heart's dear Sister! — with

14 Dec   3 p 4to   Osb
to CB Jr (with PS from M d'A)
I read your Letter with Tears of pleasure, my

27 Dec   copy   2 p 4to   Osb
to Ralph Broome
I am much flattered by the entire concurrence

30 Dec [1799]   1 p 4to   NYPL(B)
from SBP
My own Fanny — My other beloved sister

31 Dec   4 p 4to   BPL
to CB Jr
Whatever all your crosses & disappointments,

1800

1 Jan [1800]   4 p 4to   Osb
to Rosette (Rose) Burney
In a few lines I have just had from my dear

7 Jan [1800]   4 p 4to   NYPL(B)
to CB
Excess of anxiety & alarming suspense have

7 Jan [1800]   4 p 4to   BM(Bar)
from Maria (Allen) Rishton
The difficulty of knowing where to begin

9 Jan   1 p 4to   NYPL(B)
to CB
My Mate will say all say — so I can only offer

9 [Jan 1800]   1 p 4to   NYPL(B)
to CB
O my dearest Father — the dreadful account

[post 9] Jan   copy   3 p 4to
to Frederica Locke   NYPL(B)
"As a Guardian Angel!" — yes my dearest

[12 Jan 1800]   3 p 8vo   NYPL(B)
to EBB
I begin now to long to see you my dearest

13 Jan [1800]   copy   4 p 4to
to Frederica Locke   NYPL(B)
Yes my dearest Friend I do indeed look up to

[17–20 Jan 1800]   1 p 8vo
from Maria (Allen) Rishton   BM(Bar)
When you can prevail on yourself

20 Jan   1 p 4to   BM(Bar)
from Hester (Mulso) Chapone
I should be a most ungrateful creature

[Jan 1800]   4 p 8vo   Osb
with M d'A to CB Jr
O my Charles — how can I write or see — or

[1?] Feb [1800]   2 p 4to
to M d'A   NYPL(B)
Je suis bien fachée que vous ne vous portez pas

[1 Feb 1800]   2 p 4to   NYPL(B)
from M d'A
Je t'ai mandé hier, ma chere amie, que Charles

3 FE 1800 pmk   2 p 4to   Osb
to CB Jr
Nothing could be better than your Letter, my

[7] Feb   copy   2 p 4to   NYPL(B)
to Frederica Locke
Here we are my beloved Friend — we came

[c 11 Feb 1800]   4 p 8vo
to EBB   NYPL(B)
My Kindest Esther will I know be glad to hear

[10–]11 Feb   copy   2 p 4to
to CB   NYPL(B)
I hasten to tell you, dearest Sir, Mr. H[arris]

11 Feb   copy   1 p 4to   NYPL(B)
to JB
Shall a blow like this strike us & shall we not

also   copy   1 p 4to   Osb

26 Feb [1800]   1 p 8vo   BM(Bar)
from Hester (Mulso) Chapone
I am extremely obliged to you my dear

[27 Feb 1800]   3 p 8vo   BM(Bar)
from Amelia (Locke) Angerstein
I will not try to express to my beloved Mrs

[pre 4 Mar 1800]   2 p 4to   NYPL(B)
to GMAPWaddington
I know not how to write to you — yet think it

4 Mar   4 p 4to   NYPL(B)
to CB
I feel very anxious, Dearest Sir, to know if your

4 Mar   4 p 8vo   Osb
with M d'A to CB Jr
We were very sorry, my dear Charles, to leave

11 Mar   4 p 4to   NYPL(B)
to EBB
If you knew not the cruel state of my Mind, my

22 Mar   4 p 4to   NYPL(B)
to CBFB
It seems very long since I have had any

22 Mar   2 p 4to   NYPL(B)
to CB
Day after Day I have meant to write to my

26 Mar   4 p 4to   NYPL(B)
to EBB
Your kind — tender Letter, was very balsamic

7 Apr   1 p 8vo   Osb
to CB Jr
Wednesday I arrive at Chelsea, & carry my Boy

27 Apr   4 p 4to   NYPL(B)
to CB
I was quite rejoiced in the good account I

⟨9⟩ MY 1800 pmk   2 p 4to   Hyde
to Fanny (Phillips) Raper
What a dear girl you are, my Fanny — what a

13 JU 1800 pmk   3 p 4to   NYPL(B)
to EBB
M. d'Arblay charges me, my dearest Esther, to

18 June   3 p 4to   BM(Bar)
from David Ritchie
I have the honour to inform you that a literary

[post 18 June 1800]   draft   3p 4to
to David Ritchie   BM(Bar)
I am much obliged to the good opinion & kind

20 June   3 p 8vo   Hilles
to Rosette (Rose) Burney
Alas, my dear Rosette, from me have you been

[post 20 June 1800]   draft   1 p 8vo
from Rosette (Rose) Burney   Hilles
To ask favors my Dear Madam merely to have

[25] June [1800]   4 p 4to   NYPL(B)
from Norbury Phillips
a thousand thanks to you, my Dearest Aunt for

1800, continued

[June 1800]   2 p fol   NYPL(B)
to EBB
A friend of M. d'A's — son of a physician, of

also   copy   3 p LB   Osb

4 July   pmk 1800   4 p 4to   NYPL(B)
to EBB
I hardly know how to write to you, my dearest

17 July   4 p 8vo   NYPL(B)
to M d'A
I am going to answer to-morrow Morning's

18 July   4 p 8vo   NYPL(B)
to M d'A
Votre cher Lettre ne m'a pas fait beaucoup de

21 July [1800]   4 p 4to   BM(Bar)
from Maria (Allen) Rishton
It has not been from want of time, or

22 July   4 p 4to   BM(Bar)
from Marianne (Burney) Bourdois
I am so sure of dearest Aunt d'Arblay's kind

[26 July 1800]   4 p 4to   NYPL(B)
to EBB
I fear lest this beautiful season should be lost

28 July   4 p 4to   NYPL(B)
to EBB
Monday will perfectly do for us, my dearest

31 July   4 p 4to   NYPL(B)
to CB
We shall delight to see you, my most dear

[July 1800]   4 p 4to   NYPL(B)
to EBB
With so very important an interest to discuss,

2 Aug   7 p 4to   BM(Bar)
from Antoine Bourdois
À la Garde de Dieu, et du cocher

9–12 Sept   3 p 4to   BM(Bar)
from Marianne (Burney) Bourdois
I should be the most *ungrateful of my sex* did

13 Sept   4 p 4to   NYPL(B)
to CB
With what solid & heartfelt satisfaction do I

13–[14] Sept   4 p 4to   NYPL(B)
to EBB
To wish Joy — to write congratulations to my

21 Sept   4 p 4to   NYPL(B)
to EBB
It is impossible for me not to give ease to your

[3 Oct 1800]   4 p 4to   NYPL(B)
to GMAPWaddington
Have you been hurt by my long silence, my

14 Oct   1 p 4to   NYPL(B)
from M d'A
Mon depart est decidé, ma chere amie: mais

[pre 30 Oct 1800]   4 p 4to   NYPL(B)
to EBB
When I received your first Letter, my dearest

17 Nov   4 p 4to   NYPL(B)
to CB
I think it very long not to hear at least *of* you,

18 Nov   4 p 4to   Comyn
to CB Jr
M. d'Arblay has just left Westhumble — to set

27 NO 1800 pmk   3 p 4to   NYPL(B)
to CB Jr
Would to God I *could* send my kind Charles as

11 DE 1800 pmk   1 p 4to   NYPL(B)
to CB Jr
I have just received the glad — glad tydings

16 Dec   2 p 4to   NYPL(B)
to CB
He is returned — my dearest Father —

16 Dec   4 p 8vo   McG
to CB Jr
I know the postage will be *cheap* that shall tell

16 Dec   4 p 4to   NYPL(B)
to EBB
Think of my joy — my surprise — my gratitude

16 Dec   2 p 4to   NYPL(B)
from Antoine Bourdois
Whether or not I shall be the first to tell my

17 Dec   4 p 8vo   NYPL(B)
from Frederica Locke
Yes, my beloved Friend, from the bottom of

1801

[16 Jan 1801]   1 p 4to mutilated
to M d'A   NYPL(B)
How tormenting that this ancle attack should

18 Feb   4 p 4to   NYPL(B)
to GMAPWaddington
Will you not be tempted to cast away my

23 Feb   4 p fragment   NYPL(B)
to M d'A
How kind to write me so much — when so

4 MR 1801 pmk   2 p scrap   McG
to CPB
I write to my dear Charles, in the confidence of

17 Mar   4 p 4to   NYPL(B)
to EBB
You may indeed believe me, my dearest Esther,

18 MAR 1801 pmk   2 p 4to   PML
to JB
I am quite gratified, my dear James, to find

29 Mar   3 p 4to   PML
with M d'A to JB (and FBA to SHB)
Your sister rejoices at your not being ordered

4 Apr   4 p 4to   NYPL(B)
to GMAPWaddington
Well may you, at last, my dear Marianne, join

[25 Apr 1801]   1 p 8vo   NYPL(B)
to CB Jr
I have been all this week in hopes of seeing

27 Apr   pmk 1801   2 p 8vo   Osb
to CB Jr and Rosette (Rose) Burney
Everything turns out so unluckily for our

20 May   4 p 4to   NYPL(B)
to CB
We have been so much occupied since our

23 MY 180⟨1⟩ pmk   4 p 4to
to CBFB   NYPL(B)
May I not congratulate my dearest Charlotte

[5 June 1801]   3 p 4to   BM(Bar)
to M d'A
Pleasure is seated in London — Joy, Mirth,

12 June   4 p 4to   BM(Bar)
to CBFB
It is a truly great blessing to me, my dearest

6 July   3 p 4to   NPG
to CFBt (one page written by FBA as
    from AA)
Joy to you, my dear Charlotte — joy to dear

13 Aug   4 p 4to   NYPL(B)
to EBB
The receipt arrived safe & sound — & will

⟨1⟩ Sept   4 p 4to   NYPL(B)
to CB
My dearest — kindest — cruellest Father! —

6 Sept   4 p 4to   Osb
to CB
Magnificent, my dearest Padre, quite

19 Sept   4 p 4to   NYPL(B)
to CBFB
It would have given Me so very much pleasure

[21 Sept 1801]   2 p 4to   NYPL(B)
to CB
The Tables are this minute arrived, my dearest

3 Oct   2 p 4to   NYPL(B)
to CB
God avert mischief from this Peace, my

[5 Oct 1801]   2 p 4to   NYPL(B)
to EBB
We shall have your kindest & warmest Wishes

12 OC 1801 pmk   3 p 4to   NYPL(B)
from M d'A
Un mot seulement, ma bonne amie, et cela pour

22 OC 1801 pmk   1 p 8vo   Osb
to CB Jr
Not at all knowing how to direct to M. d A at

[pre 26] Oct [1801]   2 p 4to
to M d'A   NYPL(B)
Mr. Locke came just now to tempt me to an

[26–27 Oct 1801]   1 p 4to NYPL(B)
from M d'A
J'arrive de Chelsea où ton pere qui m'a

27 Oct   4 p 4to   NYPL(B)
to EBB
I know how kindly you would partake in my

27 Oct   2 p 4to   NYPL(B)
from M d'A
M. Dumergue étant occupé, je t'écris de son

1801, continued

[27–28 Oct 1801]   2 p 4to   NYPL(B)
from M d'A
Je te remercie, mon amie, des *demi* bonnes

28 Oct   4 p 4to   BM(Bar)
to M d'A
The Trees for Mr. Angerstein & Mr. Thompson

28 [Oct 1801]   4 p 4to   NYPL(B)
from M d'A
Ne m'écris plus, ma bonne amie, parce que

29 Oct   4 p 4to   NYPL(B)
to CBFB
Your kind purpose, my ever kind Charlotte, of

30 Oct   4 p 4to   BM(Bar)
to M d'A
Enfin, I am beginning, I trust, a Letter to mon

30 Oct   2 p 4to   NYPL(B)
from M d'A
Quel excellent dejeuner je vais faire, ma bonne

2 Nov   4 p 4to   NYPL(B)
to CB
I was sure my dearest Father could not blame

2 Nov   4 p 4to   NYPL(B)
from M d'A
Je viens, ma chere bonne amie, de m'assurer

5 Nov   2 p 4 to   NYPL(B)
from M d'A
Assurement, ma bonne amie, si je vais ce

5 Nov   2 p 4to   NYPL(B)
from M d'A
Je t'écris, ma chere bonne amie, de Douvre où

7 Nov   3 p 4to   NYPL(B)
from M d'A
Je voudrais, ma bonne amie, pouvoir donner

11 Nov   4 p 4to   NYPL(B)
to CB
I did not purpose writing to my dearest Father

12 Nov   4 p 4to   NYPL(B)
to M d'A
Never shall I be able to tell you the Joy of this

12 Nov   1 p 4to   NYPL(B)
to CB
With what joy — my dearest Father, do I tell

12 [Nov 1801]   2 p 4to   Hyde
to CB Jr
Thank Heaven my Letter — destined as an

[12 Nov 1801]   4 p 4to   NYPL(B)
from M d'A
Il m'est impossible, ma chere Fanny, d'entrer

16 Nov   4 p 4to   NYPL(B)
from M d'A
J'ai eu aujourdhui un bien grand plaisir en

16 Nov   4 p 4to   NYPL(B)
from M d'A
Dernièrement il était question de Savoir au

[post 16 Nov 1801]   3 p 4to
                              NYPL(B)
from Antoine Bourdois to FBA & AA
Le G\ al\ . Alexandre D Arblay est venu ce matin

[21] Nov [1801]   3 p 4to   NYPL(B)
from M d'A & Louis, comte de Nar-
      bonne-Lara
Je me Sens tellement bien ce Soir que j'aurais

[26 Nov 1801]   4 p 4to   NYPL(B)
from M d'A
Quand j'ai t'écrit (le 20) Je devais partir le

29 Nov   4 p 4to   NYPL(B)
to M d'A
I sent you a few hurried lines

30 Nov   2 p 4to   NYPL(B)
from M d'A
Ecoute bien ma chere amie, et ne manque

4 Dec   4 p 4to   NYPL(B)
to M d'A
Ah, my dearest Friend, this indeed is a terrible

6 Dec   4 p 4to   NYPL(B)
from M d'A
Suivant toute apparence, ma chère amie, je

10 Dec [1801]   6 p 4to   NYPL(B)
from M d'A
Oh dear! dear! dearest Soul! What a wife!

[11 Dec 1801]   2 p 4to   NYPL(B)
to CB
Why, my dearest orkbonnerie Pappy — I really

11 Dec [1801]   2 p fol   NYPL(B)
from M d'A
Que de tresors mon adorable amie, la journée

15 Dec   4 p 4to   NYPL(B)
with AA to M d'A
The relief, the consolation of your frequent

[17 Dec 1801]   4 p 4to   NYPL(B)
to M d'A
I wrote instantly upon receiving

[post 25 Dec 1801]   2 p 4to
to CB   NYPL(B)
I have been quite enchanted at the Sight —

18 Dec   4 p 4to   NYPL(B)
from M d'A
Aujourdhui, ma chere amie, nous avons celebré

[29 Dec 1801]   2 p 4to   NYPL(B)
to M d'A
I hope & trust my most beloved Friend

19–21 Dec   4 p 4to   NYPL(B)
to EBB
Tears of pleasure, my dearest Esther — rare

[1801–02]   2 p 8vo   Osb
to Cassandra (Leigh) Cooke
Nothing short of a nearly continual expectation

1802

1–3 Jan [1802]   4 p 4to   NYPL(B)
from M d'A
Quand reverrai-je donc notre hermitage!

24 Jan   3 p 4to   NYPL(B)
from M d'A (PS to AA)
En core une lettre de moi, ma chere amie, car

5 Jan   4 p 4to   NYPL(B)
from M d'A to FBA & AA
Je me repens beaucoup d'avoir Hier trop

Jan [1802]   3 p 4to   NYPL(B)
with AA to M d'A
In the <fervant> hope you will be set out

also   copy   4 p 4to   NYPL(B)

[7 Jan 1802]   ½ p 4to   NYPL(B)
from M d'A
Je t'ai ecrit hier, ma chere amie, tout ce que je

[11 Feb 1802]   3 p 4to   NYPL(B)
to Margaret Planta
A most unexpected &, to me, severe event

10 Jan   4 p 4to   NYPL(B)
from M d'A
L'orage est detourné ma bonne amie. Je n'irai

15–19 Feb   4 p 4to   NYPL(B)
to M d'A
Ah my amico! — in what manner must I begin

[10 Jan 1802]   2 p 4to   NYPL(B)
from M d'A
Voici comment mon affaire a fini. Tu as

[17 Feb 1802]   4 p 8vo   NYPL(B)
to CB
M. d'Arblay is gone, my dearest Father — !

11 Jan   1 p 4to   NYPL(B)
from M d'A
Tu dois ma chere amie, recevoir par notre ami,

17 FE 1802 pmk   2 p 4to   BM(Bar)
from Frederica Locke
My more than Ever dear Mrs d'Arblay

12 Jan   4 p 4to   NYPL(B)
with AA to M d'A
A poor little moment only is allowed Me to say

[18 Feb 1802]   2 p 8vo   NYPL(B)
to CB
My poor little Boy is still too ill for removal, &

15 Jan [1802]   2 p 4to   NYPL(B)
to M d'A
I have just indulged my pen with a little of the

19 Feb   1 p 4to   NYPL(B)
from M d'A
Here I am, my dearest friend, after a long and

15 Jan   2 p 4to   NYPL(B)
to M d'A
This is my third Letter of this Morning — this

19 Feb   1 p 4to   NYPL(B)
from Harriet (Collins) de Boinville
Not many of those who are happy enough to be

22 Jan   2 p 4to   NYPL(B)
from M d'A
Je m'etais bien promis, ma chere amie de

19–22 Feb [1802]   2 p 4to   NYPL(B)
to M d'A
I sent off to my best Friend a diary, from the

1802, continued

26 [Feb or Mar]   4 p 4to   BM(Bar)
from Marquis de Lally-Tollendal?
Cela est vrai, ma chère Madame, j'ai reçu hier

2 Mar   2 p 4to   NYPL(B)
from M d'A
Je suis ici occupé du matin au soir, ma chere

2 Mar   4 p 4to   NYPL(B)
from M d'A
Lis, ma chere amie les copies que je t'envoye

[3 Mar 1802]   3 p 4to   NYPL(B)
to EBB
I had not intended answering your Letter, my

5 Mar   4 p 4to   NYPL(B)
to CB
I have purposed waiting for a 2^d. Letter from

7 Mar   4 p 4to   BM(Bar)
from Cassandra (Leigh) Cooke
Believe me I appreciate quite as I ought the

8 Mar   4 p 4to   NYPL(B)
from M d'A
Je t'écris par *Triplicata* ma position actuelle,

10 Mar   4 p 4to   NYPL(B)
from M d'A
Il me semble ma bonne amie qu'il y a un Siecle

14 Mar [1802]   4 p 4to   NYPL(B)
to M d'A
O my dearest Friend! — can the intelligence

17 Mar   4 p 4to   NYPL(B)
to CB
Another Letter has at length reached me, my

18 Mar   4 p 4to   NYPL(B)
to M d'A
O mon ami! never did I so wish for Wings as

22 Mar   4 p 4to   NYPL(B)
to CB
How is my life changed, my dearest Father,

22 Mar   4 p 4to   NYPL(B)
to EBB
I know well how my dearest Esther will feel

23 Mar   2 p 4to   NYPL(B)
to M d'A
Why cannot I fly to you instantly, my better

24 Mar   4 p 4to   Comyn
to CB Jr
A long & torturing suspense is at length — for

26–28 Mar   3 p 4to   PML
to JB
I know well with what satisfaction you will

28 Mar   4 p 4to   NYPL(B)
to M d'A
Amelia — the sweet lovely Amelia is safe — &

[post 28 Mar 1802]   2 p scrap
to M d'A   NYPL(B)
I have this moment received our certificate of

30 Mar   4 p 4to   NYPL(B)
to CB
Now, indeed my dearest Father, I am in an

4 Apr   2 p 4to   BM(Bar)
to M d'A with PS by AA
I have just received (N°. 12) my beloved

4 [Apr 1802]   1 p 8vo   PML
from Anne-Louise-Germaine (Necker)
    de Staël-Holstein
je voudrais vous temoigner mon empressement,

also   copy   1 p 4to   NYPL(B)

6 Apr   pmk 1802   2 p 4to   BM(Bar)
from Margaret Planta
I should have acknowledged the receipt of

11 Apr [1802]   2 p 8vo   Comyn
from Mary (Danby), Countess of Har-
    court
M^{rs}. Harcourt presents her Compt. to Madame

12 AP 1802 pmk   1 p 8vo   Hyde
to CB Jr
You will come I trust to embrace me on *Sunday*

14 Apr   1 p 4to   Osb
to CB Jr
The very night I saw you, I received from

[15] Apr [1802]   1 p 4to   BM(Bar)
to M d'A
J'arrive, mon ami! mon Cher — Cher ami!

15–19 Apr   4 p 4to   NYPL(B)
to CB
I seize, at length, upon the largest Paper I can

also   copy of this and following JLS to CB
    27 p 4to   NYPL(B)

15–19 Apr   20 p 4to   NYPL(B)
to CB
When I began my Journal, I meant to give you

15 Apr–4 May [1802] typescript copies
of excerpts   53 p   NPG
to CB
Thursday, April 15. Good little Molly

17 Apr   3 p 4to   PML
to CB
Here we are, my dear Father, — after such

20–21 Apr   4 p 4to   NYPL(B)
to CB
At length my dearest Padre, I come to our safe

20–21 Apr   copy   13 p 4to
to Frederica Locke   NYPL(B)
I go on with the day of our arrival (April 20)

also   typescript copy   10 p   NPG

also   imperfect copy (composite of extracts
from the above two letters, redated 1 Apr)
10 p 4to   NYPL(B)
continued confinement for 2 days, and 2 nights,

21 Apr   2 p 4to   BM(Bar)
to CB
An opportunity has just presented itself by

21 Apr   4 p 4to   NYPL(B)
to Margaret Planta
As I have just received a message that a

[22]–24 Apr   9 p 4to   NYPL(B)
to CB
For Madame cidevant PS^se. de Beauveau, &

22 Apr–5 May   composite copy   54 p
4to   NYPL(B)
Composite of extracts from letters of
this period
Almost immediately after my arrival in Paris

24–25 Apr   8 p 4to   NYPL(B)
to CB
In our way home, which was through the

[pre 27 Apr]   copy   12 p 4to
to Frederica Locke   NYPL(B)
As I think there is no one my beloved friends

27 Apr   copy   11 p 4to   NYPL(B)
to Margaret Planta
A week have I been here, my dear Miss Planta,

[Apr 1802]   copy extracts   NYPL(B)
to Frederica Locke (copied as foot-
notes on JL copy to Miss Planta,
27 Apr 1802)
M. de Beauveau has a serious countenance

[Apr–May 1802]   copy extract   1 p
NYPL(B)
to Frederica Locke (on p 7 of composite
copy JL to CB 15–19 Apr 1802)
As soon as the red trunk of poor Adrienne was

also   typescript copy   1 p   NPG

3–5 May   12 p 4to   NYPL(B)
to CB
May 3^d. I pass now to the Week following my

5 May   4 p 4to   NYPL(B)
to CB
I shall go on, my dearest Padre, with the grand

[5]–6 May   8 p 4to   NYPL(B)
to CB
what to say, She gently stammered "ma

6 May [1802]   3 p 4to   NYPL(B)
to CB (imperfect copy of parts of FBA
to CB [5]–6 May 1802 and 6 May
1802–5 Oct 1806)
May 6th. Mad. d'Henin having borrowed the

also   typescript copy extract   3 p   NPG

6 May [1802]–5 Oct 1806   4 p 4to
to CB   NYPL(B)
[Mme de] Poix & M^e. de Bouillon, with whom

also   copy extract   4 p 4to   NYPL(B)

also   typescript copy   4 p   NPG
Here, my dearest Father, ends all my old

10 May   copy extract?   1 p 4to
to Frederica Locke   NYPL(B)
How many are the Letters, my dearest —

24 May   4 p 4to   NYPL(B)
to EBB
I can never tell you, my dearest Esther, the

6 June [1802]   3 p 8vo   BM(Bar)
from Marianne (Burney) Bourdois
It is very kind of you my dearest Aunt,

10 June   2 p 4to   NYPL(B)
to CB
My beloved Father — a thousand thanks for

11 June   copy   4 p 4to   NYPL(B)
to Frederica Locke
I sent my most beloved friends a pacquet

25 June–17 July   4 p 4to   NYPL(B)
to CBFB
Ah my dearest Charlotte if you can forgive

1802, continued

16 July   3 p 4to   NYPL(B)
to CB
It is almost in despair, my dearest Sir, that I

17 July–20 Aug [1802]   copy   16 p
    4to   NYPL(B)
to Frederica Locke
I send off now, Nov. 1st a sheet written months

20 July [1802]   4 p 4to   NYPL(B)
to EBB
I shall give you, at least, the pleasure I have
also   partial copy   3 p 4to   NYPL(B)
With the nearest Relatives now

20 July   copy   6 p 4to   NYPL(B)
to Margaret Planta
I hope my last long letter arrived safely. I had
also   typescript copy   6 p   NPG

1 Aug   typescript copy excerpt   4 p
to Charlotte Cambridge   NPG
... I must now come to ourselves beginning

[pre 9 Aug 1802]   copy   17 p 4to
                NYPL(B)
to Queen Charlotte via Margaret Planta
The institution of Madame Campan is for a
also   typescript copy   17 p   NPG

31 AU 1802 pmk   4 p 4to   NYPL(B)
to GMAPWaddington
I know not by what Strange fatality it happens,

Aug–22 Nov   4 p 4to   NYPL(B)
to GMAPWaddington
Mr. Green has this moment left Me — & I

10 Oct [1802]   4 p 4to   BM(Bar)
from CBFB & CFBt
We had a good & quiet Journey, tho' not a

22 Nov   2 p 4to   NYPL(B)
to CB
It is so long since I have written to, or heard

Nov   typescript copy   6 p   NPG
to Charlotte Cambridge
What kindness is yours, my dear valuable

19 Dec   copy   9 p 4to   NYPL(B)
to Margaret Planta
Rarely, indeed my dear Miss Planta, I have
also   typescript extracts   4 p   NPG

28 Dec   copy   6 p 4to   NYPL(B)
to Frederica Locke
With what joy I have received your two last

[1802–1806]   2 p 8vo   NPG
from AA
When I shall have had fourteen superlatives

[1802–1806]   2 p 8vo   NYPL(B)
from M d'A and Louis, comte de Nar-
    bonne-Lara
Pardon mille et mille fois, ma vraie amie

21 June [1802–14]   2 p 8vo   Comyn
from Adrienne (de Noailles), comtesse
    de Tessé
Voici, Madame, ma petite lettre pour

[post 1802?]   2 p 8vo   BM(Bar)
from Diane-Adélaïde (de Damas d'An-
    tigny), comtesse de Simiane
tout etait <   > quand votre aimable petit

16 [post 1802?]   3 p 8vo   BM(Bar)
from ?
Je vous supplie d'avance de ne pas

1803

12 Jan   4 p 4to   NYPL(B)
from Maria (Allen) Rishton
I always feel too happy at seeing your signature

22 Jan   1 p 4to   Comyn
from Charles, 1st Earl Whitworth
Lord Whitworth presents his Compliments to

14 FEB 1803 pmk   4 p 4to   PML
with M d'A to JB
Je vous remercie Sincerement et de tout mon

7 Mar   3 p 8vo   NYPL(B)
to GMAPWaddington
No, no, a Letter — — no! I am too dreadfully

10 Mar   copy   14 p 4to   NYPL(B)
to Margaret Planta
It would be difficult to give you an idea of the
also   typescript copy   13 p   NPG

22 Mar   6 p 4to   NYPL(B)
to GMAPWaddington
Let me now more fully answer your last

also   typescript copy extract   4 p   NPG

23 Mar [1803]   4 p 4to   NYPL(B)
to CB
No, my dearest Padre, *bumptious!* — no! I

6 Apr–16 June   4 p 4to mutilated
to CBFB   NYPL(B)
I flagelate myself — *mentally!* — doubly &

[25 Apr 1803]   1 p 4to   HSP
to — (Hunter) de Cadignan
I am really sorry & quite sorry at my utter

30 Apr   copy   4 p 4to   NYPL(B)
to Frederica Locke
How to write I know not — at a period so

6 May [1803]   4 p 4to   NYPL(B)
to CB
If my dearest Father has the smallest idea of

14 May   2 p 4to   NYPL(B)
with M d'A to CB
The enclosed missed the opportunity for which

14 May   2 p 4to   NYPL(B)
with M d'A to EBB
ah my dearest Esther — my dear — dearest

12–16 June   4 p 4to   NYPL(B)
to EBB
How wretchedly all immediate hopes are

16 June   pmk 1803   2 p 4to   Osb
to CB Jr
What is become of you, my dearest Carluce?

8 July   draft?   1p 4to   NYPL(B)
to Ann (Astley) Agnew
How unkind must I have appeared to my dear

22 July   1 p 8vo   NYPL(B)
from [an official?] — — Mory
Etant ici le Commissionnaire

1804

11 Apr   2 p 4to   NYPL(B)
to CB
How impossible it is for me to say the sighing

[1 Oct 1804]   4 p 4to   NYPL(B)
to M d'A
The Letter of M. Hureau yesterday is truly

1 Oct [1804]   1 p 4to   NYPL(B)
from M d'A
Tout est fini, ma chere amie. Le malheureux

[3 Oct 1804]   4 p 4to   NYPL(B)
from M d'A
J'ai beau chercher, je ne vois dans ta lettre

[4 Oct 1804]   4 p 4to   NYPL(B)
to M d'A
Ah, Mon cher Ami! Quel terrible triste triste

[4 Oct 1804]   4 p 4to   NYPL(B)
from M d'A
Je suis allé trois fois à la poste inutilement. Je

[7 Oct 1804]   2 p 4to   NYPL(B)
from M d'A
Demain Lundy sur les onze heures il y a un

8 Oct [1804]   4 p 4to   NYPL(B)
to M d'A
Before I answer your too interesting too terrible

[9 Oct 1804]   4 p 4to   NYPL(B)
from M d'A
En verité, ma chere amie, il m'est impossible

[9–11 Oct 1804]   6 p 4to   NYPL(B)
from M d'A
Ah mon amie, quel triste voyage! Mon oncle

[13 Oct 1804]   2 p 4to   NYPL(B)
from M d'A
Ah mon amie! combien je souffre de ce que tu

[Oct 1804]   2 p 4to   NYPL(B)
to M d'A
Vous *en vouloir?* — no, mon ami, non, — God

[Oct 1804]   3 p 4to   NYPL(B)
to M d'A
Our uncle, my dearest Friend, occupies me

[Oct 1804]   2 p 4to   NYPL(B)
to M d'A
[tear] than 7 gentlemen! our poor Boy had

1805

[Jan 1805]   1 p scrap   NYPL(B)
from M d'A
Je te remercie ma tendre amie de la bonne

5 May   3 p 4to   NYPL(B)
to CB
Ah, my dearest — dearest Father, what a

29 May   4 p 4to   NYPL(B)
with M d'A to CB
Before I expected it, my promised opportunity

28 June   4 p 4to   NYPL(B)
to EBB
If my dearest Esther has received the letter I

2 July   2 p 4to   NYPL(B)
to GMAPWaddington
If my ever dear Marianne is within reach of

2–4 Aug   6 p 4to   BM(Bar)
from Marianne (Burney) Bourdois &
     Antoine Bourdois
My dearest Aunt will, I trust, with respect to

1 Nov   4 p 4to   BM(Bar)
from Marianne (Burney) Bourdois &
     Antoine Bourdois
I felt so persuaded that you were about this

7 NO 1805 pmk   1 p scrap   Osb
to CB
. . . My love to dear Fanny — & may Heaven

1806

20 Jan   4 p 4to   NYPL(B)
with M d'A to CB
At length, my most beloved Father, an

13 June   3 p 8vo   BM(Bar)
from Marianne (Burney) Bourdois
I *must* congratulate my ever dear Aunt upon

27 [June? 1806]   1 p 8vo   NYPL(B)
from Marquis de Lally-Tollendal
Si Mr et Madame d'Arblay veulent obliger

[Aug 1806]   1 p 4to   Osb
with M d'A to CB Jr
The amount of what our dear friend has left

13 Sept [1806]   4 p 8vo   BM(Bar)
from Marianne (Burney) Bourdois
I believe, my dearest Aunt, that unless you see

19 Sept [1806]   1 p 4to   BM(Bar)
from Marianne (Burney) Bourdois
In the total uncertainty whether, or not, I

[20 Sept 1806]   3 p 8vo   NYPL(B)
from Mrs Fermor
Your obliging note came to hand last night

[c Sept 1806]   2 p 4to   BM(Bar)
from Marianne (Burney) Bourdois
I have just had a visit from Mr. Bourdois

9 Oct   4 p 4to   PML
with M d'A to JB
'Tis so long, so very long since I have heard

10 Oct   copy   4 p 4to   NYPL(B)
to Frederica Locke
How was I touched at sight of your

15 Oct   4 p 4to   NYPL(B)
to CBFB
What a cruel length of time is it since I have

17 Oct   2 p 4to   McG
with Marianne (Burney) Bourdois to
     CB Jr
We languish for news from you, my dearest

22 Oct   12 p 4to   NYPL(B)
with M d'A to CB
And now, my dearly beloved Father, all my

29 Oct [1806]   3 p 8vo   BM(Bar)
from Marianne (Burney) Bourdois
The pill has operated at length, my dearest

11 Nov   4p 4to   NYPL(B)
to EBB
Though I have written so lately a Volume

11 Nov   4 p 4to   NYPL(B)
to GMAPWaddington
What a cruel length of time has passed

23 Nov [1806]   5 p 8vo & fol   BM(Bar)
from Marianne (Burney) Bourdois
The fates have decreed, my dearest Aunt,

25 Dec [1806]   4 p 12mo   BM(Bar)
from Marianne (Burney) Bourdois
I have heard of, and seen *nobody* since

29 Dec [1806]   4 p 8vo   BM(Bar)
from Marianne (Burney) Bourdois
I am vexed at being prevented from seeing you

[c 1806?]   2 p 12mo   NYPL(B)
from Mrs Fermor
You would have heard from us before this time

[1806–12]   2 p 8vo   NYPL(B)
from Harriet (Collins) de Boinville
Want of strength to put one foot before the

[1806–12]   1 p 8vo   NYPL(B)
from Marquis de Lafayette
J'ai été Retenu, chere Madame, par une affair

[1806–12]   1 p 8vo   NYPL(B)
from Marquis de Lafayette
I have just now a very good Opportunity to

1807

1 Jan   3 p 8vo   BM(Bar)
from Marianne (Burney) Bourdois
Oh! my dear Aunt, what a day of bitter

9 Jan [1807]   4 p 12mo   BM(Bar)
from Marianne (Burney) Bourdois
How are you today, my dearest Aunt? I hope

12 Jan [1807]   4 p 12mo   BM(Bar)
from Marianne (Burney) Bourdois
I dined yesterday, my dearest Aunt, with the

[post 12 Jan 1807]   2 p 12mo
BM(Bar)
from Marianne (Burney) Bourdois to
FBA & M d'A [included in AL from
E Potts to Marianne Bourdois post
12 Jan 1807]
My dear Aunt & Mr. d'Arblay expressed so

21 Jan [1807]   6 p 8vo & 4to   BM(Bar)
from Marianne (Burney) Bourdois
Lest by differing my account untill To morrow,

28 Jan   4 p 12mo   BM(Bar)
from Marianne (Burney) Bourdois
Since I saw you my dearest Aunt I have not

[post 28 Jan 1807]   3 p 4to   BM(Bar)
from Marianne (Burney) Bourdois
My dearest Aunt I have this moment received

[post 28 Jan 1807]   4 p 8vo   BM(Bar)
from Marianne (Burney) Bourdois
I have nothing new to tell my dearest Aunt

22 Apr   copy   1 p fol   NYPL(B)
to Frederica Locke
Tis but within an hour I have heard that there

29 Apr [1807]   4 p 4to   BM(Bar)
from Marianne (Burney) Bourdois
We have had the most delightful journey

3 May [1807]   4 p 8vo   BM(Bar)
from Marianne (Burney) Bourdois
I will not proceed, any further without

7 May   4 p 4to   BM(Bar)
from Marianne (Burney) Bourdois with
PS from Laborda ⟨Percer⟩
I purposed writing to my dearest Aunt

14 May [1807]   3 p 4to   BM(Bar)
from Marianne (Burney) Bourdois
I have only time to say, my ever dear Aunt,

18 May [1807]   4 p 4to   BM(Bar)
from Marianne (Burney) Bourdois
Nous sommes ici ma chere Tante depuis

13 June [1807]   4 p 4to   BM(Bar)
from Marianne (Burney) Bourdois
I trust, my dearest Aunt, that you received my

14 June [1807]   2 p 4to   BM(Bar)
from Marianne (Burney) Bourdois
I have just recollected my dearest Aunt that

16 Sept   2 p 4to   NYPL(B)
with M d'A to CB
I have just received a kind offer to send a few

[post 1807]   1 p 4to   NYPL(B)
to Susan Adams
Had the smallest idea crossed my Mind, upon

1808

24 Jan [1808]   3 p 8vo   NYPL(B)
from Frances (Sayer) de Pougens
I am quite impatient to hear My dear Madam,

Sept [1808]   2 p 4to   NYPL(B)
to CB (with PS by M d'A)
After being so long robbed of all means of

2⟨1⟩ Oct   4 p 4to   NYPL(B)
to M d'A
Je n'entends rien de cette poste, rien du tout,

23–24 Oct   4 p 4to   NYPL(B)
with AA to M d'A
J'avois grand peur que ma petite Lettre la

24–25 Oct   4 p 4to   NYPL(B)
from M d'A
Que je suis honteux, ma bonne amie et

1809

19 Feb   1 p 4to   BM(Bar)
from David Baillie Warden
Having heard, more than a year ago, that you

18 May   4 p 4to   BM(Bar)
from CBFB
Tho' I have the pen in my hand I can hardly

[1809]   1 p 4to   PML
from Louis, comte de Narbonne-Lara
j'allois ecrire à la plus heureuse et a la plus

1810

[28 Mar 1810]   2 p 4to   NYPL(B)
to CB
Various considerations have induced us to

1 May [1810]   4 p 4to   NYPL(B)
to CB
A happy May Day to my dearest Father! sweet

5 July   1 p 4to   MdHS
to David Baillie Warden
Madame d'Arblay is extremely ashamed to

16 Sept   4 p 4to   NYPL(B)
with M d'A to CB
Can I tell you my dearest Father! — Ah no, —

16 Sept   copy   2 p 4to   NYPL(B)
to Frederica Locke
Should this reach you my ever dearest Friend,

1811

[14 Apr 1811]   4 p 4to   NYPL(B)
with M d'A to CB
Many — or rather, countless as are the times

19 [May 1811]   2 p 8vo   BM(Bar)
from Adrienne (de Noailles), comtesse
      de Tessé
ma miserable santé me poursuit sans Relache,

[30 Sept 1811]   12 p 4to   NYPL(B)
to EBB (with PS by M d'A)
Separated as I have now so long — long been
also   partial copy   8 p fol   NYPL(B)
My hope of escaping the evil being now at an

[30 Sept? 1811]   1 p 8vo   NYPL(B)
from Dominique-Jean, baron Larrey
il etoit convenu entre nous tous que vous ne

6 Oct   1 p 8vo   BM(Bar)
from Adrienne (de Noailles), comtesse
      de Tessé
M^de de Tessé manque de forces pour supporter

20 Nov   2 p 4to   NYPL(B)
from Dominique-Jean, baron Larrey
Lorsque par l'interet que votre situation

9 Dec   2 p 4to   NYPL(B)
to CB
May I not judge my dearest Father by myself

17 Dec   1 p 8vo   NYPL(B)
from Jean-Baptiste-Gabriel Bazille
Je vais vaincre toutes difficultez à vous faire

1812

29 May   4 p 4to   NYPL(B)
to CB
A friend of Maria's has just informed me that a
also   copy   3 p 4to   NYPL(B)

[pre July 1812]   18 p 8vo   NYPL(B)
Journal
The intense desire of Bonaparte to conquer not
also   copy   10 p 4to   NYPL(B)

6 July   2 p 4to   NYPL(B)
to M d'A
Can vexation go beyond what I feel & have felt
also   copy   2 p 4to   NYPL(B)

7 July [1812]   2 p 4to   NYPL(B)
to M d'A
I had hoped to have seen the sight the next

8 July   2 p 4to   NYPL(B)
to M d'A
I had a desire, which kindness like your own

[8 July 1812]   2 p scrap   NYPL(B)
from M d'A
Brave et excellente amie dis moi donc que tu

10 July   4 p 4to   NYPL(B)
to M d'A
Ah, mon Ami, que j'avois du chagrin hier —

11 July   2 p 4to   NYPL(B)
to M d'A
O with what pleasure — what sighs of pleasure

12 July   1 p fragment   NYPL(B)
to M d'A
Mon bien — et s'il est possible tout les jours

13 July   2 p 4to   NYPL(B)
to M d'A
Alas — no Letter to day! I feel as disappointed

[13 July 1812]   2 p 8vo   NYPL(B)
from M d'A
Faudra t'il encore aujourdhui attendre en vain
also   copy   4 p 4to   NYPL(B)

[14 July 1812]   2 p 4to   NYPL(B)
from M d'A
Grace à Dieu, elle est partie la boëtte que j'ai

15 July   2 p 4to   NYPL(B)
with AA to M d'A
Oui, cher, cher Papa, vous l'aurez, cette satis-

[17 July 1812]   2 p 4to   NYPL(B)
from M d'A
Ma chere chere amie! je hazarde aujourdhui

[17–18 July 1812]   2 p 4to   NYPL(B)
from M d'A (PS to AA)
En cherchant la lettre p^r Alex que j'ai eu assez

19 [July 1812]   2 p 4to   NYPL(B)
from M d'A
On a bien raison de dire, ma chère amie, qu'à

23–24 July   2 p 4to   NYPL(B)
from M d'A
Voici, ma chere et toujours plus chere Fanny

27 July [1812?]   2 p 4to   NYPL(B)
to M d'A
Your samedi's Letter I have just read —
also   copy   2 p 4to   NYPL(B)

28 [July 1812]   2 p 4to   NYPL(B)
from M d'A
Amie de mon coeur, toi qui dois si bien savoir
also   copy   2 p 4to   NYPL(B)

[31 July 1812]   4 p 4to   NYPL(B)
from M d'A
Chere, excellente, incomparable amie quelle

1 Aug   2 p 4to   NYPL(B)
from M d'A
Dieu te conserve ta philosophie et ta tendre

2 Aug   4 p 4to   NYPL(B)
with AA to M d'A
Adieu, then, mon ami — the Word with which

2 Aug [1812]   4 p 4to   NYPL(B)
from M d'A
Je ne desire rien tant que de voir revenir cette

3 Aug [1812]   4 p 4to   NYPL(B)
from M d'A
Oh mon amie, du courage du courage! nous en

1812, continued

[4] Aug [1812]   2 p 4to   NYPL(B)
to M d'A
This morning I thought all *useless* parting at

5 Aug   2 p 4to   NYPL(B)
with AA to M d'A
Oh — I am sick — sick — sick! I have

[5 Aug 1812]   2 p 4to   NYPL(B)
from M d' A
Ah ma fanni! que Paris me parait changé

also   copy misdated 6 July   6 p 4to
                                   NYPL(B)

[5 Aug 1812]   3 p 8vo   NYPL(B)
from M d'A
J'espere ma chere amie que tu trouveras tout

6 Aug   4 p 4to   NYPL(B)
from M d'A
No unmixed *joy* far from thee my fanny! Joy

8 Aug   2 p 4to   NYPL(B)
to M d'A
The tumult of emotions caused by this

9 Aug   4 p 4to   NYPL(B)
to M d'A
Why — why — I am ready every moment to

[post 9? Aug 1812]   2 p 4to
to M d'A   NYPL(B)
He immediately enquired if I had not a little

12 Aug   2 p 4to   NYPL(B)
to M d'A
I am entered into the most hospitable house in

12–22 Aug [1812]   4 p 4to
to M d'A   NYPL(B)
Another opportunity already offers for writing

13 Aug   4 p 4to   NYPL(B)
with AA to M d'A
Encore! encore! — here, here Still! /

15 Aug   1 p 8vo   NYPL(B)
to CBFB
In a flutter of joy such as my tender Charlotte

also   copy   1 p 4to   NYPL(B)

[15 Aug 1812]   1 p 8vo   PML
to JB
Who will be more sincerely rejoiced — except

17 Aug   1 p 8vo   NYPL(B)
to CB
Here I am, in dear — dear old England, my

also   copy   1 p 4to   NYPL(B)

[18 Aug 1812]   4 p 12mo   NYPL(B)
from Lady Lucy (Fitzgerald) Foley
indeed my Dearest Mrs D'Arblay I speak

19 pmk [Aug 1812]   1 p 8vo
to GMAPWaddington   NYPL(B)
No hand but my own shall tell my ever dear

20 Aug   3 p 8vo   BM(Bar)
from Amelia (Locke) Angerstein
My ever beloved Mrs d'Arblay Though

25 Aug   2 p 4to   BM(Bar)
from Cassandra (Leigh) Cooke
Mrs. Broome must forgive me, but not

26 Aug   3 p 4to   BM(Bar)
from Emilia & Frances Waddington
I must write one line dear Madam to express

27 Aug   2 p 8vo   BM(Bar)
from Maria (Allen) Rishton
Welcome — a thousand times welcome, my

30 Aug [1812]   2 p fragment
to M d'A   NYPL(B)
every moment is filled up with interviews,

31 Aug [1812]   1 p 4to   Osb
to CB Jr
This moment — calling to see my dearest

31 Aug–Sept   2 p 4to   NYPL(B)
to M d'A
it is through my dear Sister Burney I am to

[Aug 1812]   2 p 8vo   NYPL(B)
from Lady Lucy (Fitzgerald) Foley
how have you slept? and how do you feel this

2 Sept [1812]   1 p 4to   NYPL(B)
from Lady Lucy (Fitzgerald) Foley
return to this Climate, being so near the River;

[3 Sept 1812]   2 p ½ 4to   NYPL(B)
from M d'A
Ma santé, ma chere Bonne amie est excellente;

[10 Sept 1812]   3 p 8vo   NYPL(B)
to CB
Huzza! / My dearest Father, / Huzza! / What

[18 Sept 1812]   4 p 4to   NYPL(B)
to CB
The World is pretty bad, already, — as we of

30 Sept   2 p 8vo   NYPL(B)
from Charlotte Beckedorff
La Reine etant a Whitehall, pour voir La

[Sept–Oct 1812]   2 p 8vo   NYPL(B)
to CBFB
to say Nay would be to have no heart — / I

13 Oct [1812]   2 p 8vo   NYPL(B)
with SHB to CB Jr
I am torn to pieces by the *embarras* not of

25 Oct [1812]   1 p 8vo   BM(Bar)
from Sophia (Thrale) Hoare
Lady Keith who I have seen very lately in

[c 31 Oct]   4 p 8vo   NYPL(B)
to GMAPWaddington
I have felt nothing more of that little touch,

2–4 Nov   4 p 4to   NYPL(B)
to CB
"Why, Fanny, you are Here, & There, & every

also   copy   4 p 4to   NYPL(B)

3 Nov   4 p 4to   BM(Bar)
from Marianne (Burney) Bourdois
Your kind, & very delightful letter, my dearest

[post 4 Nov 1812]   4 p 8vo
to CB   NYPL(B)
Your kind Letter written with such exquisite

[post 4 Nov 1812]   4 p 8vo
to CB Jr   NYPL(B)
I must write to you — for when we are

5 Nov   4 p 8vo   NYPL(B)
to CB
Yesterday I saw Lady Crewe, & I write to give

[10 Nov 1812]   2 p 4to   NYPL(B)
from M d'A
Quel bonheur inattendu ma chere Fanny! Une

14 NO 1812 pmk   4 p 8vo   NYPL(B)
to CBFB
If I wrote to you as often as I think of you, my

[17?] Nov   1 p 4to   NYPL(B)
to CB
My dearest Padre will, I am sure, be happy to

18 NO 1812 pmk   2 p 4to   NYPL(B)
to GMAPWaddington
Alexandre will, I hope, answer the very pretty

26 Nov [1812]   4 p 4to   BM(Bar)
from CBFB
Here I am, to be ready for Marianne, with

[Nov–Dec 1812]   1 p fragment
to [CPB]   Comyn
N B. Would it be possible that Alexander could

4 Dec   4 p 8vo   NYPL(B)
to CB
I am this moment setting off for Norbury Park,

10 pmk [Dec 1812]   4 p 4to
with AA to M d'A   NYPL(B)
Alex having undertaken to finish Clement, I

10 Dec   4 p 4to   NYPL(B)
to CB
Two Letters from my dearest Padre! — what

16 DE 1812 pmk   3 p 8vo   NYPL(B)
to CBFB & CFBt
My two dearest Charlottes with what delight

31 Dec   4 p 8vo   Osb
to CB Jr
How truly I am sorry for you, my dearest

[31 Dec 1812–Feb 1813]   2 p 4to
from M d'A   NYPL(B)
Ah! mon amie que j'eprouve en ce moment

[1812]   1 p 4to   NYPL(B)
to M d'A
While no Folios procurable to Mortal hands

[1812]   3 p 12mo   BM(Bar)
from Sophia (Thrale) Hoare
I shall be so delighted to see you again my dear

[1812–14]   2 p 4to   Osb
to CB Jr
Thanks for your ever kind zeal, my dearest

[1812–14]   1 p 8vo   BM(Bar)
from GMAPWaddington
I hope that we may fetch you dearest Mrs

[1812–15]   2 p scrap   McG
to [GMAPWaddington?]
so long awaited & eventful termination.

[post 1812?]   2 p scrap   PML
to JB
If you have not already made Sarah act, let

1812, continued

[post 1812]   2 p 8vo   NYPL(B)
from Marie de Maisonneuve
dans un peu de tristesse — Avez-vous vu a

[post 1812]   1 p 8vo   NYPL(B)
from [Princess ——]
I long to improve my acquaintance with Your

1813

13 Jan   4 p 8vo   NYPL(B)
to CB
How is my dearest Father? I long to hear —

21 JA 1813 pmk   4 p 8vo   Osb
to CB Jr
This spirited effect of your promised

22 Jan   1 p 4to   Osb
to William Lowndes
Madame d'Arblay returns Mr. Lowndes thanks

[25–26 Jan 1813]   4 p 8vo   Comyn
to CB Jr
The hope you held out to me of coming hither,

[26 Jan 1813]   3 p 4to   NYPL(B)
to CB
I am now going to write a very private Letter

[30 Jan 1813]   4 p 8vo   BM(Bar)
to CB
My dearest Padre would allow of but one

8 FE 1813 pmk   4 p 8vo   NYPL(B)
to CB
Your dear & kind invitation, my dearest Padre,

11 Feb   2 drafts   4 p 12mo
to Queen Charlotte   NYPL(B)
The Astonishment, the delight the gratitude

[11–23 Feb 1813?]   2 p 4to   Osb
to CB Jr
Lady K. desires me to return Lord Hood's

12 Feb   2 p 8vo   NYPL(B)
from Charlotte Beckedorff
Mrs Beckedorff presents her Compliments to

19 Feb   2 p 4to   Osb
from Dorothea (Scrivenor) Fisher
The Bishop of Salisbury & I had both of us

22 FE 1813 pmk   4 p 8vo   NYPL(B)
to CB
What can my most beloved — my kindest

[post 23 Feb 1813]   1 p 8vo   Osb
to CPB
If all the parents of all the bantlings who have

[26 Feb 1813]   draft   3 p 8vo
to Queen Charlotte   NYPL(B)
With all my long experience of your Majesty's

[Feb 1813]   2 p 8vo   Osb
to CB Jr
I forgot to mention, my dearest Charles, that

3 Mar   2 p 4to   NYPL(B)
from Charlotte Beckedorff
My Constant attendance upon Her Majesty,

[5 Mar 1813]   draft   2 p 4to
to Queen Charlotte   NYPL(B)
The truly feeling heart of your Majesty will

5 Mar   2 p 8vo   Comyn
from Frederica Locke
my dearly loved Friend I have not lost a

[c 6 Mar 1813]   3 p 8vo   Comyn
to CB Jr
Houra to your Worship! I shall have the

10 MR 1813 pmk   3 p 8vo   Osb
to CB Jr
I think, in sober reason, my dear Charles, *not*

16 Mar [1813]   4 p 8vo   NYPL(B)
to CB
How will my Kindest Father rejoice for me!

[16 Mar 1813]   draft   1 p 4to
to Queen Charlotte   NYPL(B)
Most humbly — yet with that chering

18 Mar   4 p 4to   NYPL(B)
to GMAPWaddington
My own hand alone must thank my kindest

19 Mar   3 p 4to   NYPL(B)
from Charlotte Beckedorff
Au moment que je recue Votre derniere pour

22 MR 1813 pmk   4 p 8vo   Osb
to CB Jr
Since we make use — than which nothing can

30 Mar   4 p 4to   NYPL(B)
to CB
I long for some news of my most dear Padre, &

2 Apr 2 p 4to Osb
to CB Jr
As to your Franking your Letters, my dear

[post 2 Apr 1813] 1 p 8vo Osb
to CB Jr
You can no where better enjoy a day or two of

4 Apr 4 p 8vo NYPL(B)
from Charlotte Beckedorff
Je n ai pas manquée de presenter Votre lettre

4 Apr [1813] 3 p 8vo Osb
from Mary (Danby), Countess of Harcourt
You was so very good & so kind as to say that

7 Apr [1813] 4 p 8vo Osb
from Mary (Danby), Countess of Harcourt
I am just come from Chelsea where I hoped to

[12 Apr 1813] 2 p ½ 4to NYPL(B)
from M d'A
Un mot seulement, ma chere Fanny, et c'est

29 Apr [1813] 2 p 4to BM(Bar)
from Jérôme-Marie Eon, comte de Cély
I can't help Myself without thanking you for

1 MY 1813 pmk 2 p 8vo McG
to CB Jr
A parcel is come for you, which

3 MA 1813 pmk 3 p 8vo NYPL(B)
to GMAPWaddington
Ah my dearest Mary! — kind, cruel —

11 May 4 p 4to NYPL(B)
to CB
Will my beloved Father be startled to receive

14 MY 1813 pmk mutilated 3 p 8vo
to CB NYPL(B)
his most welcome & truly *aimable Lettre*, &

15 May 3 p 4to NYPL(B)
to GMAPWaddington
How is this, my dearest Mary? — are you

17 MY 1813 pmk 2 p 12mo PML
from Maria Edgeworth
Mr. & Mrs. & Miss Edgeworth were flattered

23 May [1813] 6 p 8vo NYPL(B)
to CB
Oh how teized I am, my dearest Padre, by this

31 May 4 p 4to NYPL(B)
to M d'A
This very day, only our kind Made. Solvyns

3 JU 1813 pmk 1 p 8vo Osb
to CB Jr
I cannot answer for one moment of *Thursday*.

13 June 2 p 4to NYPL(B)
to GMAPWaddington
I need not — I am sure, tell my dearest Mary

[14 June 1813] 1 p fragment
to GMAPWaddington NYPL(B)
O yes —— I was sure you would understand

[post 13 June] 1 p 4to NYPL(B)
to GMAPWaddington
Thursday is a very late day indeed, my dearest

[post 13 June] 2 p fragment
to GMAPWaddington NYPL(B)
How my hopes are disappointed! you looked

[post 13 June] 1 p fragment
to GMAPWaddington NYPL(B)
You are singularly right in your belief — we

[post 13 June] 1 p fragment
to GMAPWaddington NYPL(B)
O that I had but time of my own — sweet

[post 13 June 1813] 3 p 12mo
to GMAPWaddington NYPL(B)
And why, dearest Mary, settle 3 days

[pre 29 June] 2 p 8vo NYPL(B)
to GMAPWaddington
Your zeal — Your kindness — can never

29 JU 1813 pmk 1 p 4to Osb
to GMAPWaddington
What a melancholy letter! I return it with real

2 JY 1813 pmk 4 p 4to Osb
to CB Jr
I was immensely disappointed, upon opening

[2 July] 1 p 8vo NYPL(B)
to GMAPWaddington
'Tis well you gave me no commission, dearest

6 July [1813] 2 p 4to PML
from Anne Letitia (Aiken) Barbauld
I hope you will not think me too officious

[10 July 1813] 4 p 8vo NYPL(B)
to CB
If the offering I prepare for you should not

1813, continued

12 JY 1813 pmk   2 p 8vo   NYPL(B)
to CB Jr
What is to be done? / We must settle

[14 July 1813]   4 p 4to   NYPL(B)
to CB Jr
I am more grieved at this cruel & unexpected

[14 July 1813]   draft   2 p 4to
                                NYPL(B)
for CB Jr to Henry Colburn (included
    in AL FBA to CB Jr [14 July 1813])
Dr. Charles Burney presents his compliments

15 July   3 p 4to   Osb
with Martin Charles Burney to CB Jr
I am longing to hear how you go on — I need

16–17 Aug   3 p 4to   NYPL(B)
to CPB
Alexander has not been, I trust, more a truant

21 Aug   4 p 4to   NYPL(B)
to CB Jr
What a most unnatural silence would this have

2⟨0⟩ Aug   4 p 4to   NYPL(B)
to GMAPWaddington
I cannot yet reconcile myself to your flight, my

24 Aug [1813]   4 p 8vo   NYPL(B)
to CB
Your Seal, my dearest Padre, waits but for an

27 Aug   1 p 4to   NYPL(B)
to MF
Have I received, by every opportunity, so

[Aug 1813?]   ½p 4to   NYPL(B)
to Frances (Waddington) Bunsen
I am quite grieved at this melancholy account

3 Sept [1813]   mutilated   3 scraps
to CB   NYPL(B)
Nothing was ever more opportune, my dearest

4 Sept [1813]   3 p 8vo   Osb
from Mary (Danby), Countess of Har-
    court
Now my dear M^rs d'Arblay here we are,

[5 or 12 Sept 1813]   3 p 8vo   PML
to JB
I concur with you both in opinion & feeling,

[pre 8 Sept 1813]   4 p 4to   NYPL(B)
to GMAPWaddington
Your Letter, dearest Mary, has followed me

8 Sept [1813]   4 p 4to   NWUL
to CB Jr
How often — since your attack, my dearest

[post 8] Sept [1813]   4 p 8vo
to CB   NYPL(B)
I have time but for a word to my dearest Padre,

23 Sept [1813]   3 p 8vo   NYPL(B)
with CBFB to CB Jr
I have received this with a joy that almost

30 Sept   2 p 4to   NYPL(B)
from Charlotte Beckedorff
Je Viens de recevoir les Ordres de la Reine de

12 Oct   4 p 4to   NYPL(B)
to CB
My most dear Padre will, I am sure,

14 Oct   2 p 4to   BPL
to CB Jr
As speedily as may be in your power, let me

[post 14 Oct 1813]   3 p 8vo   Osb
to CB Jr
Thanks by the Million, my dearest Charles, for

28 Oct   2 p 4to   NYPL(B)
from M d'A
Sois sans inquietude sur ma santé ma chere

[30 Oct 1813]   4 p 8vo   NYPL(B)
to CB
I have a joy so great, my dearest Padre, that I

4 Nov [1813]   3 p 4to   BM(Bar)
from Frederica Locke
I will not tell my beloved Friend how I

23 Nov   2 p 4to   NYPL(B)
from Charlotte Beckedorff
Je viens de reçevoir des Ordres de la Reine, de

2 Dec [1813]   4 p 4to   BM(Bar)
from Mary (Danby), Countess of Har-
    court
I have indeed been long in hopes & expectation

6 Dec pmk 1813 4 p 8vo NYPL(B)
to CB Jr
This is the very first moment I am able to write

[post 6 Dec 1813]   2 p 4to
to CB Jr   NYPL(B)
Nothing can be more untimely for me, my

13 DE 1813 pmk   1 p 8vo   Harv(H)
to Martin Charles Burney
All the Courtiers I have left at Windsor are

16 Dec   copy   2 p 4to   NYPL(B)
to Frederica Locke
Ah, my dearest Friend — how is my poor

24 DE pmk [1813]   1 p 8vo   PML
to JB
Alexander is not yet arrived, & I am in hourly

24 Dec   4 p 4to   NYPL(B)
to GMAPWaddington
You think, perhaps, my dearest Mary, that not

also   partial copy misdated 1815   2 p 4to
                              NYPL(B)
My Heart has been almost torn asunder, of late,

30 Dec   4 p 8vo   PML
to Sarah (Payne) Burney
I am quite anxious for news of my dear Brother.

Dec   copy   5 p 4to   NYPL(B)
from M d'A
Quelle perte ma chère Fanny! — et il faut

[Dec 1813]   4 p 4to   NYPL(B)
from Marie de Maisonneuve
je n'ai ou pu jus'qu'ici incomparable bien chere

[1813–17]   1 p 8vo   NYPL(B)
from Princess [Elizabeth?]
oh how delightful! but *do* come to dinner; You

1814

[3–4 Jan]   4 p 4to   NYPL(B)
to CBFB & CFBt
My most dear Charlottes — kind, beloved, &

5 JA 1814 pmk   4 p 8vo   Osb
to CB Jr
Let me begin with the only little word I have

[post 5 Jan 1814]   4 p 8vo   Osb
to CB Jr
Alas — My dearest Charles — alas! — What

13 Jan   4 p 4to mutilated   NYPL(B)
to M d'A
M'est il permis encore de m'addresser à mon

[Jan? 1814]   2 p 8vo   NYPL(B)
from M d'A
Les papiers publiés, ma chère amie t'ont appris

2 Feb   draft   2 p 4to   NYPL(B)
to Longman & Co
Madame d'Arblay acquaints Messrs. Longman

5 Feb   1 p 8vo   Comyn
to William Lowndes
Madame d'Arblay is much obliged to Mr.

6 Feb   draft   2 p 4to   NYPL(B)
to Longman & Co
Madame d'Arblay is overwhelmed with

10 Feb   2 p 8vo   NYPL(B)
from M d'A
Dans ce moment terrible d'une crise si

15 FE 1814 pmk   4 p 8vo   Osb
to CB Jr
The hope, according to his own intimation, of

16 FE pmk [1814]   4 p 4to
to CBFB & CFBt   NYPL(B)
Alas my dearest Charlottes — what an

23 FE 1814 pmk   4 p 8vo   Osb
to CB Jr
Dr. Davy certainly judged right, my dear

Feb   3 p 8vo   NYPL(B)
from Lady Crewe
Altho' Sr I. MacKn attacked Mr Burke on the

2 Mar   3 p 8vo   BM(Bar)
from Lady Banks
Lady Banks's best Complts to Made d'Arblay

2 pmk [misdated 3] Mar   3 p 8vo
to GMAPWaddington   NYPL(B)
Your Letter fills me with horrour, my dearest

7 Mar   pmk 1814   4 p 4to   NYPL(B)
from Harriet (Collins) de Boinville
Can it be that such feelings as you describe in

19 Mar   copy   3 p 4to   NYPL(B)
to Frederica Locke
I hasten to impart to my kind & most

21 Mar   1 p 8vo   PML
to JB
It disagrees with me to refuse you any thing;

1814, continued

22 Mar–2 Apr   4 p 4to   NYPL(B)
to CBFB
What an Age since I have written — at least

[post 22 Mar 1814]   1 p 8vo   PML
to JB
It is impossible for me to come to you, my dear

25 Mar [1814]   1 p 12mo   Osb
to CPB
I feel sure that my dear Charles will grant an

⟨28⟩ pmk [Mar?] pmk 1814   4 p 8vo
to CB Jr   Osb
Your Letter, my dearest Charles, arrived just

29 Mar   4 p 4to   BM(Bar)
from AA
In triumph do I resume my pen!

31 MR 1814 pmk   1 p 8vo   PML
to JB
with "perfect cordiality," my always dear

31 Mar [1814]   3 p 12mo   BM(Bar)
from Sophia (Thrale) Hoare
Believe me my Dear Madme D'Arblay I would

[pre 2 Apr 1814]   1 p 8vo   PML
to [JB?]
to be strongly printed for 3 times in All the

6 Apr   3 p 4to   NYPL(B)
from Charlotte Beckedorff and Sophie
    Beckedorff
Si Vous m'acceptez de la plus grande

6 Apr   4 p 8vo   Osb
to CB Jr
O what News, my dear Charles! — I scarcely

7 AV 1814 pmk   2 p fragment
to M d'A   NYPL(B)
garde sa chambre encore [obliteration] je ne

7 Apr [1814]   4 p 4to   NYPL(B)
from M d'A
Quel bonheur inattendu, mon adorable amie!

8 Apr   4 p 4to   NYPL(B)
from M d'A
Quel bonheur inattendu ma chere Fanny; une

11 Apr   4 p 4to   NYPL(B)
to CBFB
I know that our Brother James has given my

14 Apr   2 p 8vo   NYPL(B)
to M d'A
Ah mon ami! — mon meilleur et tous les jours

14 Apr   amanuensis   3 p 8vo
                           NYPL(B)
from Mary (Danby), Countess of Har-
    court
I cannot my Dear Madme. Dablay [sic] refrain

15–17 Apr   2 p 4to   NYPL(B)
with Frederica Locke to M d'A
Quelle consolation pour moi! — oh mon ami!

17 Apr   6 p 4to   NYPL(B)
from M d'A
Je t'écris, ma chere Fanny, chez Madame

[post 19 Apr 1814]   4 p 8vo   Osb
to CB Jr
Your going to the Drawing room fills me with

20 Apr   4 p 8vo   NYPL(B)
to M d'A
I hasten, my beloved Friend — to unsay all I

[21 Apr 1814]   4 p 8vo   Osb
from Lady Crewe
The dss. d'angouleme receives company

22 Apr   4 p 4to   NYPL(B)
to M d'A
The joy & the sadness that mix in all the

22–27 Apr   4 p 4to   NYPL(B)
with AA to M d'A
Maman vient de recevoir hier une lettre daté

[22 Apr 1814]   51 p 8vo   NYPL(B)
Journal [written down in 1825]
When, — walking one morning in Hyde Park

25 Apr   copy   6 p 4to   NYPL(B)
from Marquis de Lally-Tollendal
Oui, chère Madame, je vous écris de ce Paris

26 Apr [1814]   4 p 8vo   NYPL(B)
from Etiennette, princesse d'Hénin
chere madame ne parlons plus de nos

[pre 28 Apr 1814]   4 p 8vo   NYPL(B)
to GMAPWaddington
Alas my dear fervent but too precipitate

29 Apr   8 p 4to   NYPL(B)
to M d'A
The Sweet Amine has just sent me word that

[30 Apr 1814]   4 p 8vo   NYPL(B)
to CBFB
My ever kindest Charlotte will be amongst the

30 Apr   copy   1 p 4to   NYPL(B)
to Frederica Locke
My own dearest Friend must be the first — as

Apr   1 p 4to   PML
from Charles-Emanuel-Sigismond, duc
    de Luxembourg
j'ai l'honneur d'envoyer avec empresement à

6 May   2 p 4to   PRO
from Henriette (Guignot de Soulignac)
    de Maurville
L'aimable acceuil, et Votre tendre interet pour

16 May   draft   1 p 6.3 x 3.7   BM(Bar)
to Frederica Locke
Your last arrived just as M. d'A was Setting off

[c 20–21 May 1814]   3 p 4to   PML
to EBB
We are extremely sorry that James declines

[24 May 1814]   1 p 4to   BM(Bar)
from Amelia (Locke) Angerstein
of my feedings whilst writing it almost

24 May   copy   2 p 4to   BM(Bar)
to Frederica Locke
Ah Heaven — to Me is this Letter? & from

26 May [1814]   2 p 4to   NYPL(B)
from M d'A
Copie du billet de Mr de la Châtre / "Je vous

26 May [1814]   3 p 8vo   BM(Bar)
from Frederica Locke
I will not lose a moment in assuring my ever

27 [May 1814]   1 p 4to   NYPL(B)
from M d'A
Je suis arrivé en six heures, sans être malade

28 MY 1814 pmk   3 p 8vo   PML
to Martin Charles Burney
As no means we can devize or propose will

28 May [1814]   4 p 4to   BM(Bar)
from Amelia (Locke) Angerstein
I received my dearest M^rs d'Arblay's kind

[29? May 1814]   1 p 4to   BM(Bar)
from Amelia (Locke) Angerstein
angelic father, let it not

30 May   4 p 4to   NYPL(B)
to M d'A
What a kindness — what a delicious kindness

30 May   pmk 1814   3 p 8vo   BM(Bar)
from Frederica Locke
A thousand thanks my dearly loved Friend for

31 May [1814]   4 p 8vo   BM(Bar)
from Amelia (Locke) Angerstein
Alas why will my dearest M^rs d'Arblay

[May 1814]   1 p 8vo   PML
to Martin Charles Burney
My dear Martin will, I feel sure, pardon my

[May 1814]   4 p 4to   NYPL(B)
from M d'A
Avant mon depart de Paris, j'ai vu Mad^e la

[May–June 1814]   2 p 8vo   BM(Bar)
from Louisa (Hervey), Countess of
    Liverpool
I rec'd your letter just as I was

[1 June 1814]   4 p 8vo   BM(Bar)
to CBFB
So busy — so occupied, as well as so sad have

1 June   1 p 8vo   Soth67
to [Charlotte] Beckedorff
[first line not available]

3 June   pmk 1814   4 p 4to   NYPL(B)
to GMAPWaddington
My kind Mary will not have been angry, I am
also   partial copy   2 p 4to   NYPL(B)
at the instant / I am wholly ignorant of where

7 JU 1814 pmk   1 p 8vo   PML
to JB
I would gladly have adopted provisionally, the

[7 June 1814]   2 p 8vo   BM(Bar)
from Frederica Locke
My dearly loved Friend, I was preparing to

[pre 8 June 1814]   1 p 12mo
from Sophia Beckedorff   NYPL(B)
The Emperor is coming to the Queen's house

9 June   4 p 4to   NYPL(B)
to M d'A
Not a line yet from Paris! — how does the

[13 June 1814]   3 p 8vo   NYPL(B)
from AA
i can write but to [sic] or three words my dear

1814, continued

15 June   4 p 8vo   NYPL(B)
to GMAPWaddington
I am very glad my dearest Mary spared

16 June   3 p 8vo   Osb
to CB Jr
Sally has just communicated the unwelcome

[18 June 1814]   4 p 4to   NYPL(B)
to M d'A
Ah mon ami! You are really then well? really

[18 June 1814]   4 p fol   NYPL(B)
from M d'A
Je dois commencer, mon adorable amie, par te

20 June   3 p 8vo   Osb
from Mary (Danby), Countess of Harcourt
I wish I could give you any comfort about our

21 June [1814]   4 p 4to   BM(Bar)
from Maria (Allen) Rishton
Your letter was truly gratifying

23 June [1814]   6 p 8vo & 4to
from Frederica Locke   BM(Bar)
My dearly loved Friend I have this momᵗ recᵈ

24 June   2 p 4to   NYPL(B)
to M d'A
This Day concludes the 4ᵗʰ. Week since my

29 June   2 p 4to   NYPL(B)
to M d'A
One word only can I now write — in the

3 July   4 p 4to   NYPL(B)
from M d'A
Quoi mon adorable amie, ma chere et bien

6 July   4 p 8vo   Osb
to CB Jr
Certainly, my dear Charles, I shall be very

[c 11–17 July]   2 p 12mo   NYPL(B)
to GMAPWaddington
To-morrow, my sweet Friend — & after

[11 July–28 Aug]   1 p fragment
to GMAPWaddington   NYPL(B)
Be still better, my sweet Mary, on *Friday* —

[11 July–28 Aug]   1 p 4to   NYPL(B)
to GMAPWaddington
I have time but to thank my dear Friend &

13 July   6 p 4to mutilated
to M d'A   NYPL(B)
Yesterday I received my 2ᵈ. *Letter* from Paris!

14 July   4 p 8vo   Osb
to CB Jr
I need not say with what trepidation I read

15 JY 1814 pmk   4 p 8vo   NYPL(B)
to CBFB
How cruelly is this vexing, my dearest

17 July   4 p 4to   NYPL(B)
from M d'A
Chere et adorable amie, je m'empresse de te

19 July   3 p 8vo   BM(Bar)
from Frederica Locke
My most dear Friend, yesterday I had the

20 July   3 p 4to   BM(Bar)
from Cecilia (Ogilvie) Locke
I should sooner have acknowledged

23–29 July   2 p fol   NYPL(B)
from M d'A
une calamité! oh ma Fanny quelle terrible

2⟨4⟩–25 July [1814]   4 p 4to mutilated
to M d'A   NYPL(B)
"Approve what you have done? Oh yes, mon

July   copy   3 p 4to   NYPL(B)
to Frederica Locke
After a most painful suspence I have been at

5 Aug   1 p 4to   PRO
to Charles Raper
I enclose you the Letter of Madᵉ. la Comtesse

[9–]24 Aug   copy   3 p 4to
to Frederica Locke   NYPL(B)
The friends of M:d'A. in Paris are now

[10 Aug 1814]   2 p 4to   NYPL(B)
to M d'A
Ah, Mon ami! with what mixt sensations do I

15 Aug   2 p 4to   NYPL(B)
to M d'A
Enfin je respire, mon bien bon ami! Je viens de

19 Aug   4 p 4to   NYPL(B)
from M d'A
Depuis deux jours, ma chere amie, j'ai

26 Aug   2 p 4to   NYPL(B)
from M d'A
Depuis quelques jours, ma chere Fanny, je

27 Aug [1814]   4 p 4to   NYPL(B)
from M d'A
En arrivant en voiture à 8ʰ à l'hotel des

27 AU 1814 pmk   4 p 8vo   NYPL(B)
to CPB
The direction of M. d'Arblay for a visit, my

30 Aug   6 p 4to   NYPL(B)
from M d'A
Il n'y a que deux jours, ma bonne Fanny, que

[pre 4 Sept]   2 p fragment NYPL(B)
to GMAPWaddington
I was preparing to come to you my dearest

4 Sept   2 p 4to   NYPL(B)
to M d'A
I will not lose a day ere I thank you for the

5 Sept [1814]   2 p 4to   NYPL(B)
from M d'A
Je viens de passer près de 3 heures la tête dans

6 Sept   4 p 4to   NYPL(B)
to CB Jr
I gladly followed your counsel, my dear Carlos,

19 Sept   6 p 8vo & 4to   NYPL(B) &
to CB Jr   Osb
[NYPL(B) 8vo] I write now a formal address
[Osb 4to] My poor Alex frightens me to death!

19 [Sept 1814]   4 p 4to   NYPL(B)
from M d'A
chez le portier de l'hotel de la Marine où sont

[Sept 1814]   2 p 4to   NYPL(B)
to M d'A
I am grieved about the de Beau[veau]'s. Lʸ

4 Oct   4 p 4to   Osb
to CB Jr
O Charles — you have written me a dagger! —

7 [Oct 1814]   2 p 4to   NYPL(B)
from M d'A
Quoi bien reellement, ma chere amie tu as été

8 Oct   1 p 4to   BM(Bar)
from Emilie, marquise de Tracy
C'est de grand coeur madame que

13–18 Oct   4 p 4to   NYPL(B)
to GMAPWaddington
Eh bien, mes chères amies? are you becoming
also   partial copy   2 p 4to   NYPL(B)
I beseech you not to let your too ardent

14 Oct   4 p 4to   NYPL(B)
to CB Jr
The *result* I expected, my dear Charles, is just

[post 18 Oct 1814]   4 p 4to   NYPL(B)
from [Frances (Waddington) Bunsen?]
I am deeply alarmed, however gratified, by the

25 OC 1814 pmk   4 p 8vo   Osb
to CB Jr
Certainly, my dear Carlos, we will have written

25 Oct   3 p 4to   NYPL(B)
from Charlotte Beckedorff
Vous devez m'accuser de la plus grande

2⟨8⟩ OC 1814 pmk   2 p 4to   Osb
to CB Jr
If you write to me again upon a scrap that can

28 OC 1814 pmk   2 p 8vo   Hyde
to JB
I thank you cordially for your hospitable

28 [Oct 1814]   4 p 4to   NYPL(B)
from M d'A
O Ma pauvre amie que je suis faché de

1 Nov   8 p 4to   NYPL(B)
from AA
I suppose you have quitted *Richmond*

[1 Nov 1814]   2 p 8vo   NYPL(B)
from Princess Elizabeth
I trouble you with this note to enclose
also   copy dated 6 Nov   2 p 4to   BM(Bar)

8 Nov   1 p 8vo   NYPL(B)
to CBFB
Accept, my dearest Charlotte, & use — from

9 NO 1814 pmk   2 p 8vo   Osb
to CB Jr
A furious cold has decided M. d'Arblay not to

1 Dec   3 p fol   BM(Bar)
from Ann (Astley) Agnew
I have been anxiously waiting for

[pre 15 Dec 1814]   copy   9 p LB
to Princess Elizabeth   BM(Bar)
The high honour conferred upon me by the so

15 Dec [1814]   copy   3 p LB
to Princess Elizabeth   BM(Bar)
With equal humility, but with much lessened

28 Dec   3 p 4to   NYPL(B)
from Princess Elizabeth
This morning I received Your very delightful
also   copy   4 p 4to   BM(Bar)

1815

3 Jan–10 Feb   4 p 4to   NYPL(B)
with M d'A to AA
Reçois mon cher Alex, mes bien tendres

11 Jan–8 Feb   4 p 4to   NYPL(B)
to EBB
Ah my dearest Esther! What pain — suffering

30 Jan   copy   8 p LB   BM(Bar)
to Princess Elizabeth
Nobody can conceive the joy of my mind, &

[Jan–Feb 1815]   4 p 4to   PML
with M d'A to JB
"From whence will you write to me?" said my

11 Feb [1815]   3 p 4to   NYPL(B)
from M d' A
Que tu es aimable et bonne, mon excellente

[11 Feb–July 1815]   345 p 8vo
                                    NYPL(B)
Journal [written down in 1824]
I have no remembrance how where, whence,

[c 20 Feb 1815]   36 p 8vo   NYPL(B)
Journal [written down in 1825]
Having fulfilled — at length! — my long

20 Feb   copy   2 p 8vo   NYPL(B)
to the Duchesse d'Angoulême (included
        in Journal [20 Feb 1815])
Penetrée des bontes dont le Roi a daigné

22 FE 1815 pmk   3 p 4to   NYPL(B)
with M d'A to CBFB
How exquisitely kind was my ever kindest

22 FE 1815 pmk   4 p 4to   Osb
with M d'A to CB Jr
In the middle of all your fine library, my dear

22 FEV 1815 pmk   1 p 8vo   Comyn
from the Duchesse d'Angoulême
Madame Duchesse d'Angoulême charge la

10 [Mar?]   3 p 8vo   NYPL(B)
to M d'A
How am I rejoiced to open the shortest — I

13 Mar [1815]   3 p 4to   NYPL(B)
from Princess Elizabeth
Nobody has received somebodys letters, which

17 Mar [1815]   1 p 8vo   NYPL(B)
from M d'A
Nous avons de meilleures nouvelles! je ne puis

[18 Mar 1815]   2 p 8vo   NYPL(B)
from M d'A
Les nouvelles ne sont pas rassurante[s] —

[19 Mar 1815]   1 p 4to   NYPL(B)
from M d'A
Ma chère amie, tout est perdu! je ne puis entrer

[20 Mar 1815]   1 p 8vo   NYPL(B)
from M d'A
Le Moment est venu, mon amie, où d'un

23–26 Mar   2 p 4to   NYPL(B)
to AA
Ah Alexander! — will not even this calamitous

23–31 Mar   4 p 4to   BM(Bar)
to Princess Elizabeth
What dreadful & afflicting scenes &

26 Mar   1 p 8vo   NYPL(B)
to M d'A
This Moment I receive the blessed tidings that

27 Mar [1815]   4 p 4to   NYPL(B)
to CBFB
Ah my dearest Charlotte — I would not write

27 Mar   2 p 4to   PML
to JB
Give the enclosed — my dear Brother — to

27–29 Mar   4 p 4to   NYPL(B)
to AA
I know not whether my poor Alex has

29 Mar [1815]   4 p 4to   NYPL(B)
to M d'A
Oh mon ami! Mon ami! — Je viens de lire

30 Mar   4 p 4to   NYPL(B)
to M d'A
The happiest — at this moment — in defiance

[31 Mar 1815]   4 p 4to   NYPL(B)
from M d'A
J'ai tant de choses à te dire, ma chere et bien

31 Mar [1815]   2 p 4to   NYPL(B)
from M d'A
Je suis arrivé ici assez bien, et je suis convaincu

[Mar–June 1815]   1 p scrap
from M d'A   NYPL(B)
Nous nous trouvons Du Repaire Mr de

1 Apr   3 p 4to   NYPL(B)
from M d'A
Dieu soit loué, nous ne sommes qu'à 10 lieues

6 Apr   2 p 4to   PML
to JB
Oh my dear Brother I have just seen in an

7 Apr   2 p 4to   NYPL(B)
to CB Jr
Though not a word has reached me from my

8 Apr   2 p 4to   NYPL(B)
to EBB
Ah, my dearest Esther, when am I to write you

15 AP 1815 pmk   2 p 4to   NYPL(B)
to CFBt
An opportunity offering for England by which

20 Apr–16 May   4 p 4to   NYPL(B)
to CBFB
What balm was poured into my aching heart

[22 Apr 1815]   1 p 8vo   NYPL(B)
from M d'A
Nous nous sommes trompés, ma chere Fanny,

[23 Apr 1815]   2 p 4to   NYPL(B)
from M d'A
Hier, ma chere et bien chere Fanny, je serais je

26 Apr   4 p 4to   NYPL(B)
to AA
At length, my long expecting Eyes meet again

[Apr-May 1815]   2 p 4to
to M d'A   NYPL(B)
Mon ami — mon amico — mon ALL! I have

13–18 May   4 p 4to   NYPL(B)
to M d'A
Oh blessed be the coming anniversary of This

[16 May 1815]   1 p 4to   NYPL(B)
from M d'A
Mon amie, ma tendre amie ne peut savoir à

19–20 May   copy   5 p 4to
to Frederica Locke   NYPL(B)
Balsamic indeed have been your letters —

25 May   2 p 4to   NYPL(B)
from M d'A
Ne point recevoir de tes nouvelles quand je

25 May   3 p 4to   NYPL(B)
from M d'A
Pardon, mille et mille fois, ma tendre amie, de

28 May   4 p 4to   NYPL(B)
to M d'A
Oh for Wings to answer in person the 2 side

29–30 May   4 p 4to   NYPL(B)
to M d'A
I cannot & will not refuse myself the happiness

29 May   draft   6 p 4to   NYPL(B)
to Princess Elizabeth
Ah, that some good Genius wd. arise — or

29 May–4 June   4 p 4to   NYPL(B)
to M d'A
I am so much struck with THE DECLARATION

31 May   4 p 4to   NYPL(B)
from M d'A
Je t'écris ma chere bonne amie de chez la

2 June [1815?]   4 p 4to   NYPL(B)
from Princess Elizabeth
June 2d Somebody's letters have reached

3–4 June   4 p 4to   NYPL(B)
from M d'A
Helas! ma bien chere amie! mes desirs ni mes

3–5 June   8 p 4to   NYPL(B)
from Princess Elizabeth
A letter is begun & will be continued at the

5 June   4 p 4to   NYPL(B)
to M d'A
I have so much to say, I must take my largest

5 June   4 p 4to   NYPL(B)
from M d'A
[obliteration] plus j'y réfléchis, plus je me

[8]–11 June [1815]   4 p 4to
to M d'A   NYPL(B)
I will prepare a letter against my next invitation

9 June   2 p 4to   NYPL(B)
from M d'A
Point de lettre de toi ma chere, chere, et

[10–20 June 1815]   draft   4 p 4to
to Princess Elizabeth   NYPL(B)
The waters of Lethe? No, no, no! thank

11–12 June   4 p 4to   NYPL(B)
to AA (with M d'A to AA 13 May 1815
     on p 3)
Why I have no answer to the Letter I sent the

1815, continued

11–13 June   4 p 4to   NYPL(B)
to M d'A
The softly soothing idea which these, frequent

12 [June 1815]   4 p 4to   NYPL(B)
from M d'A
Je ne sais, ma bonne amie ce que je t'ai ecrit

12–23 June   4 p 4to   NYPL(B)
to AA
Your full, satisfactory, & interesting Letter, or,

13 June [1815]   1 p 4to   NYPL(B)
from M d'A
Mille et mille paisibles jours de bonheur à ma

14–16 June [1815]   4 p 4to
to M d'A   NYPL(B)
Every day I will keep to my purpose of saying

15–19 June   4 p 4to   NYPL(B)
to M d'A
Oh my beloved Ami — what dreadful times are

19 June   4 p 4to   NYPL(B)
from M d'A
Pardon ma bonne amie, mais je ne veux pas

19–21 June [1815]   4 p 4to
to M d'A   NYPL(B)
Monday, June 19th. The sitting up all Night,

22–23 June   4 p 4to   NYPL(B)
to M d'A
How more than ever precious is now the sight

23–24 June   4 p fol   NYPL(B)
from M d'A
Ou es tu à present, ma bonne bonne amie?

24 June   4 p 4to   NYPL(B)
to M d'A
With what inexpressible joy have I just

25–26 June   copy   5 p 4to
to Frederica Locke   NYPL(B)
Tis a solace indeed, — at a period of

26–28 June   4 p 4to   NYPL(B)
to M d'A
Why have I not a Balloon to be the first to tell

28 June   2 p 4to   NYPL(B)
from M d'A
J'ai eu et j'ai encore en ce moment un mal de

29–30 June   4 p 4to   NYPL(B)
to M d'A
O Cette chère Treves! — Treves encore June

30 June [1815]   4 p 4to   NYPL(B)
from M d'A
Nous avons ici tant d'alertes, les unes sur les

[June? 1815]   2 p 8vo   BM(Bar)
from Amédée, duc de Duras
Chere Madame d'Arblay il y a de Bonnes

1 July [1815]   2 p 4to   NYPL(B)
to M d'A
Ah mon ami — qu'êtes vous donc devenu et

1–3 July   4 p 4to   NYPL(B)
to EBB
I have long meant to write to my ever dear

2 July   4 p 4to   NYPL(B)
from M d'A
Je recois ma bonne amie ta seconde lettre

3 July   4 p 4to   NYPL(B)
to CBFB
For the Universe would I not add to the

3–4 July   4 p 4to   NYPL(B)
to M d'A
How truly am I thankful — though not to you,

3 July [1815]   4 p 4to   NYPL(B)
to GMAPWaddington
How is it that my ever dear Mary can thus on

3–12 July [1815]   4 p 4to   NYPL(B)
to AA
Another Letter from my dear Alex, though

4 July [1815]   2 p 4to   NYPL(B)
to M d'A
Mon ami! mon cher Cher ami! what joy! what

4–6 July [1815]   3 p 4to   NYPL(B)
from M d'A
Mon dieu, ma chere chere amie, que je serai

6 July [1815]   4 p 4to   NYPL(B)
to M d'A
Que de bonheur, mon bien aimé ami, que de

[6–8 July 1815]   2 p 4to   NYPL(B)
from M d'A
Que j'aime la phrase suivante, ma chere amie,

10 July   4 p 4to   McG
with CPB to CB Jr
Congratulations can never, I ween, be out of

10 July   4 p 4to   NYPL(B)
from M d'A
Si j'avais été prés de toi, ma bonne amie, je

10–11 July   4 p 4to   NYPL(B)
to M d'A
Croyez vous, donc, mon bien aimé ami! croyez

10–12 July   4 p 4to   PML
to JB
Little as I am habituated to the liberality of

11 July [1815]   1 p 4to   NYPL(B)
from M d'A
Mr. de Premorel vient, ma chere Fanny, de me

13 July [1815]   4 p 4to   NYPL(B)
to M d'A
Instantly & without one moment of hesitation,

15 July [1815]   1 p 4to   NYPL(B)
from M d'A
Chere et adorable Fanny! Si je ne dois pas

17–19 July   4 p 4to   NYPL(B)
to M d'A
An Opportunity offering to send my beloved

19 July [1815]   1 p 4to   NYPL(B)
from M d'A
Je n'ai que le tems mon adorable amie de te

[19 July–1 Oct 1815]   174 p 8vo
                              NYPL(B)
Journal [written down Sept 1824–19
     July 1825]
It had been a favorable desire of the best

22 [July]   1 p 4to   NYPL(B)
from M d'A
Au nom du Ciel, ma chere Fanny, arive, arive!

27 July   4 p fol   Osb
from AA
I came yesterday here, on a visit to dear Aunt

9–20 Aug   4 p 4to   NYPL(B)
to AA
I have waited, and not, I thank God! in vain,

20 [Aug] [misdated Apr] copy 3 p LB
to Lady Keith   BM(Bar)
In the midst of the almost continual evils or

28 Aug–30 Sept   4 p 4to   NYPL(B)
to AA
My dear Alex's Letter, written in concert with

[post Aug 1815]   1 p 8vo   NYPL(B)
to M d'A
Vous m'avez demandé, Mon ami, avec tant

26 Sept [1815]   4 p 4to   NYPL(B)
from ?
je reçois avec reconnaissance ma chere madame

27 Sept–3 Oct   4 p 4to   NYPL(B)
to CFBt
My first dear Charlotte will, I know, pardon

18 Oct   copy   2 p 4to   NYPL(B)
to Frederica Locke & Amelia (Locke)
     Angerstein
Last night, my ever dear Friends, we arrived

18 Oct   3 p 4to   NYPL(B)
from Mme de la Grange
Mon mari m'a informée que vous étiez

19 Oct   1 p 8vo   PML
to JB
We are just arrived, my dear Brother fatigued

20 Oct   3 p 8vo   NYPL(B)
to CBFB
My dearest Charlotte will I am sure bless the

23 Oct–29 Nov   4 p 4to   NYPL(B)
to CBFB
My kind Charlotte will sooner make peace with

23 OC 1815 pmk   3 p 8vo   Osb
to CB Jr
I am just come from visiting our poor Esther,

31 Oct   3 p 4to   NYPL(B)
from Marie de Maisonneuve
que vous êtes aimable et que tous vos amis

1 Nov   3 p 4to   NYPL(B)
from AA
I have just seen M. Chapman, who

12 Nov   2 p 4to   NYPL(B)
from AA
I received your letter this morning dear

12 Nov   2 p 4to   BM(Bar)
from Marianne (Burney) Bourdois
The enclosed half sheet, addressed to dear M.

22 pmk Nov 1815   4 p 4to   Osb
to CB Jr
I should at least, my dear Charles, have

1815, continued

22 Nov   4 p 4to   NYPL(B)
from Marie de Maisonneuve
Ma bien chere très-chere amie, il y a eu

22–29 Nov   4 p 4to   PML
to JB
I take the opportunity of enclosing to my dear
also   copy dated 30 Nov   2 p LB BM(Bar)
From Alexander I have not heard this fortnight

[Nov 1815]   copy   6 p LB   BM(Bar)
to Princess Elizabeth
Was it a mistake? an airy delusion of self

1 Dec   2 p 4to   NYPL(B)
to AA
Why — why — oh Alexander! this cruel

9 Dec [1815]   4 p 4to   NYPL(B)
from Princess Elizabeth
This morning brought me your kind letter
also   copy   4 p 4to   BM(Bar)

16 DE 1815 pmk   1 p 4to   NYPL(B)
to AA
Why do I not hear from you? I have written

19–26 Dec   4 p 4to   NYPL(B)
to GMAPWaddington
If my ever kind Mary knew in what restless

21 Dec   4 p 4to   NYPL(B)
with M d'A to AA
Je suis, mon cher Alex, tout à fait de l'avis de

21 Dec   copy   6 p LB   BM(Bar)
to Princess Elizabeth
What a mixture was there of grief in the

[post 21 Dec 1815]   copy   6 p LB
to Lady Keith   BM(Bar)
If I trust, — as How can I do otherwise? to

[1815?]   1 p 4to   NYPL(B)
from William Dimond
Your residence in Bath was not < >

[post 1815] copy extract 1 p fragment
from Princess Elizabeth   NYPL(B)
A novel said to be by the Author of Waverley

[1815–18]   1 p 8vo   NYPL(B)
from Charlotte (Jerningham), Lady
     Bedingfeld
Mrs Holroyd has kindly guessed my thoughts

[1815–18]   2 p 12mo   NYPL(B)
from Annet Bevan
Will you & Genl d'Arblay give us the pleasure

[1815–18]   1 p 8vo   BM(Bar)
from Harriet Bowdler
I have thought myself very unfortunate

[1815–18]   1 p 8vo   NYPL(B)
from Sarah Martha Holroyd
How does dear Madame d'Arblay & her Gentle-

[1815–18]   ½ p fol   BM(Bar)
from Sarah Martha Holroyd
I know the enclosed will give my dear M

[1815–18]   1 p 8vo   NYPL(B)
from Sarah Martha Holroyd
Pray dear friend do send me <   >

[1815–18]   2 p 8vo   NYPL(B)
from Sarah Martha Holroyd
I was delighted to see you

[1815–18]   1 p 8vo   NYPL(B)
from Sarah Martha Holroyd
Lord Hardwick & his sweet daughter Lady

[1815–18]   1 p 8vo   NYPL(B)
from Sarah Martha Holroyd
If ye are not engaged next *friday* evening my

[1815–18]   ⅓ p 4to   BM(Bar)
from GMAPWaddington
[signature only] ever yours / G M W

1816

11 Jan   4 p 4to   Osb
with AA to CB Jr
The time being now nearly come when
also   copy   n d   1 p   LB   BM(Bar)
The account of Mr. Porson's Trusteeship is

[pre 13 Jan 1816]   copy   1 p LB
to Frances (Phillips) Raper   BM(Bar)
I should sooner have availed myself of my

13 Jan   4 p 8vo   HEH
to Frances (Phillips) Raper
I gladly accept my dearest Fanny's offered

19 JA 1816 pmk   4 p 8vo   PML
to JB
A kind *Fanny Frank* going just now from my

6 Feb   3 p 4to   NYPL(B)
from Marie de Maisonneuve
il n'a été en mon pouvoir Ma bien chere

8 Feb   2 p 4to   NYPL(B)
from JB
I have been in constant longing to write to you

14–16 Feb [1816]   4 p 4to   NYPL(B)
with M d'A to AA
O Alexander! — no Letter! / Wednesday 15th

[pre 15 Feb]   4 p 8vo   NYPL(B)
to GMAPWaddington
If I were not under the dominion of certain

[c 15 Feb]   4 p 8vo   NYPL(B)
to GMAPWaddington
We *Never* dine out, my dearest Mary, but

[c 15 Feb]   1 p fragment   NYPL(B)
to GMAPWaddington
Since you will not decide, let it be *here*

15 Feb   copy   2 p 4to   NYPL(B)
with M d'A? to Frederica Locke
Incredible — to myself, incredible is the time

26 Feb   4 p 4to   NYPL(B)
to AA
Under the benign hope of the promised

26 Feb   copy   1 p 4to   NYPL(B)
with M d'A? to Frederica Locke
I thank you truly for the good tidings of sweet

[27? Feb]   1 p fragment   NYPL(B)
to GMAPWaddington
M d'A has been writing to the last minute &

[27? Feb]   1 p 12mo   NYPL(B)
to GMAPWaddington
Unfortunately I am muffled with a new cold &

[Feb–Mar]   1 p 4to   NYPL(B)
to GMAPWaddington
I am charmed with your suffrage, dearest Mary

[Feb–Mar]   1 p 4to   NYPL(B)
to GMAPWaddington
How I grieve at the account given by Miss M.

[Feb–Mar]   1 p 12mo   NYPL(B)
to GMAPWaddington
We have visits to make this morning *per force*

[Feb–Mar]   1 p 4to   NYPL(B)
to GMAPWaddington
Better, certainly, though much still oppressed

[Feb–Mar]   1 p 12mo   NYPL(B)
to GMAPWaddington
We will both *meet* you at Mrs. Maltbys, — for

[Feb–Mar]   1 p fragment   NYPL(B)
to GMAPWaddington
Your Mercury neither waited for an answer

[Feb–Mar]   1 p 12mo   NYPL(B)
to GMAPWaddington
I expect a Letter by the post that may demand

[Feb–Mar]   2 p fragment   NYPL(B)
to GMAPWaddington
I am now — alas — confined myself — &

[Feb–Mar]   4 p 8vo   NYPL(B)
to GMAPWaddington
How grieved I am — & how shocked will be

[c 1 Mar]   2 p fragment   NYPL(B)
to GMAPWaddington
I am quite lowered, dearest Mary, quite let

[c 1–7 Mar]   2 p fragment   NYPL(B)
to GMAPWaddington
You shock & surprise me dearest Mary! so soon

1 Mar   copy   4 p LB   BM(Bar)
to Lady Keith
How sweet is your account of your little

18 Mar   4 p 4to   NYPL(B)
from Marie de Maisonneuve
C'est ici Ma Bien chere amie, que j'ai reçu

29 MR 1816 pmk   4 p 4to   NYPL(B)
with M d'A to AA
Je te remercie, mon ami, pour ta bonne et

[Mar]   2 p fragment   NYPL(B)
to GMAPWaddington
I am glad your note came, though not much

5 AP 1816 pmk   4 p 4to & 2 scraps
to AA   NYPL(B)
I write to *MY* day, to give example with

8 AP 1816 pmk   4 p 4to   Osb
to CB Jr
Does my dearest Carlos think I do not feel

12 Apr   4 p 4to mutilated   NYPL(B)
to AA
While I always keep to MY day, let me hope

14 Apr   3 p 4to   BM(Bar)
from AA
And is this all that I am to hear about P — s?

20 AP 1816 pmk   2 p 4to mutilated
to AA   NYPL(B)
upon so light a subject her feelings would be

1816, continued

25 Apr   copy   4 p LB   BM(Bar)
to Lady Keith
Every thing I gather of your little treasure

2[6] Apr   pmk 1816   4 p 4to
to AA   NYPL(B)
I know well that long long ago you had settled

30 AP 1816 pmk   4 p 4to   NYPL(B)
to AA
I embrace you, my Alex, — I kiss you

2 May   4 p 4to   BM(Bar)
from AA
Thanks for the letter I just received, Dearest

4–5 May   4 p 4to   NYPL(B)
to AA
We are terribly anxious, my dearest Alexander,

5 May   4 p 4to   BPL
to CB Jr
We are quite disturbed, my dear Carlos, by a

also   copy   2 p LB   BM(Bar)

7–14 May   4 p 4to   Comyn
to CB Jr
O my dear Charles, how pleased shall I be —

7 May   3 p 4to   NYPL(B)
from JB
I saw Sarah to day at Chelsea, and learnt

10 May   4 p 4to   PML
to JB
Impatient, my dear Brother? — why M. d'A.

10 May   copy   2 p LB   BM(Bar)
to Frederica Locke
I should like mightily to have one life lent me

14 May   4 p 4to   NYPL(B)
to AA
How is it possible, at a period so anxious, you

15–24 May   4 p 4to   NYPL(B)
to CBFB
As nearly the same post that brought me my

16 May   4 p 4to   NYPL(B)
to CFBt
I will not make a single apology for not having

20 May   4 p 4to   NYPL(B)
from Marie de Maisonneuve
Si je ne Connoissois toute votre indulgence

22–24 May   4 p 4to   PML
to JB
We received your noble Book, my dearest

26 May   4 p 8vo   BM(Bar)
to GMAPWaddington
How is sweet Emily? / How is my lovely

31 May   4 p 4to   NYPL(B)
to AA
Joy to my dear — et, il faut bien que je

May   1 p 8vo   NYPL(B)
from Frances Bowdler
My yesterday has made me rich in pleasing

5 June   1 p 4to   NYPL(B)
to AA
Are you ill, my dear Alex? / If so beg your

5 JU 1816 pmk   4 p 4to   Osb
to CB Jr
Huzza! & Huzza! & Huzza! even for my poor

7 June   4 p 4to   NYPL(B)
to AA
I will always keep steady to my Friday, in the

[7 June 1816]   1 p 4to   Comyn
from Sarah Martha Holroyd
You were scarce out of the room my dear

12 JU 1816 pmk   2 p 4to   NYPL(B)
to AA
Certainly you were right not to disappoint me

27 June   draft   1 p 4to   BM(Bar)
to William Wilberforce
Had not Miss Maltby allured me yesterday

June   copy   5 p LB   BM(Bar)
to Princess Elizabeth
The rumour of the great & I trust most happy

⟨9⟩ July   4 p 8vo   NYPL(B)
to GMAPWaddington
The never-ending expectations with which we

9 July   4 p 4to   NYPL(B)
from Marie de Maisonneuve
Ma bien chere amie, il y a deux mois

22 July   copy   1 p LB   BM(Bar)
to Charlotte Beckedorff
Again, dear Madam, I entreat you

23 July   copy   1 p LB   BM(Bar)
to Princess Mary
The sweetness with which, almost from

26 JY 1816 pmk   4 p 4to   Osb
to CB Jr
Your Letter, my dearest Carlos, proved a

6–14 Aug [1816]   4 p 4to   NYPL(B)
to M d'A
Mon Ami, mon cher mon meilleur Ami! Dieu

7 Aug [1816]   3 p 4to   NYPL(B)
from M d'A
Un mot, mais helas, *un mot* seulement, à

11 [Aug 1816]   1 p 4to   NYPL(B)
from M d'A
J'ai quitté Douvres à Midy ½ et suis arrivé ici

16 Aug   2 p 4to   NYPL(B)
from M d'A
Arrivé ici mercredy matin 14 à 4ʰ ¼, J'ai

17–19 Aug   4 p 4to mutilated
                            NYPL(B)
to GMAPWaddington   & BM(Bar)
[NYPL 1⅓ leaves] I have been in a state of
[BM(Bar) ⅔ leaf] *that* endured, change of

24 Aug   draft   2 p 4to   NYPL(B)
to Princess Mary
Can it be reprehensible to do what to leave

26 Aug   2 p 4to   NYPL(B)
from M d' A
Pas encore un seul mot de toi, ma chere amie!

27–31 Aug   4 p 4to   NYPL(B)
to CBFB
How truly, truly do felicitate my most dear

1 Sept   4 p 8vo   Osb
to CPB
I have just read your sermon — I hear you

3 Sept   4 p 4to   NYPL(B)
from M d'A
Ma jambe qui m'a non pas inquieté, mais un

4 Sept   4 p 4to   NYPL(B)
from Marie de Maisonneuve
J'ai eu bien du guignon Ma bien chere

7 Sept   incomplete copy   5 p 4to
to Frederica Locke   NYPL(B)
If my ever dearest Friend knew how I lament

9 Sept   4 p 4to   NYPL(B)
to EBB
I should not, my ever dear Esther, at this

9 Sept   4 p 4to   NYPL(B)
from M d'A
Mon amie, ma chere et unique amie, si tu

18 Sept   4 p 4to   NYPL(B)
to M d'A
Comment! vous voulez plus souvent de mes

20 Sept   4 p 4to   NYPL(B)
from M d'A
Fanny, Ingrate Fanny, comme tu traites *ton*

also   copy   3 p 4to   NYPL(B)

21 Sept   3 p 4to   NYPL(B)
from JB
I am glad I have an excuse for writing to you

22 Sept   4 p 4to   NYPL(B)
to M d'A
Mon Ami! mon bien aimé ami! quelle Lettre

24–[27] Sept   4 p 4to   NYPL(B)
from M d'A
Malgré la meilleure tournure que

28 Sept   4 p 4to   NYPL(B)
to M d'A
Au Nom du Roi / Charles Philippe de France,

30 Sept   4 p 4to   PML
to JB
Had I a friend *in office* always at hand, as

1 Oct   2 p 4to   BM(Bar)
from M d'A
O mon amie! ma chère et bien aimée amie!

4 Oct   2 p 4to   NYPL(B)
to M d'A
Voilà ma quatrième Lettre depuis que Votre

8 [Oct]   4 p 4to   NYPL(B)
from M d'A
Quel *bonheur!* me suis-je recrié en ouvrant

12 Oct   4 p 4to   NYPL(B)
from M d'A
J'ai, ma chere amie, une bonne nouvelle à te

14 OC 1816 pmk   2 p 4to   NYPL(B)
to M d'A
I will not hurry or press you. Do not leave any

19 Oct   2 p 4to   NYPL(B)
from — (Bazille) Meignen
Miss. / If you please good health. en voila

1816, continued

20 Oct   2 p 4to   NYPL(B)
to M d'A
With a trembling heart I write, for fearful is

25 Oct   4 p 4to   NYPL(B)
to EBB
How's This? A second Letter from my dearest

28 Oct   4 p 4to   NYPL(B)
to M d'A
Certainement, et très certainement, mon bien

28–31 Oct   4 p 4to   NYPL(B)
to CBFB & CFBt
O lovely, charming Letters! / I'm in love with

29 Oct–2 Nov   4 p 4to   NYPL(B)
to M d'A
Here comes the Letter for which I have so

[post 31 Oct 1816]   2 p 4to
to CB Jr   NYPL(B)
Though I have not the conscience *an* like your

4 Nov   3 p 4to   NYPL(B)
from Marie de Maisonneuve
je ne vous ai point écrit dans le mois

[6 Nov 1816]   4 p 4to   NYPL(B)
to CB Jr
The place you describe, my dear Carlos,

7 Nov   copy   5 p LB   BM(Bar)
to Lady Keith
I have something to communicate, curious,

10 Nov   copy   4 p 4to   NYPL(B)
to Frederica Locke
Have the cheeks of my dearest Friend

21 Nov   4 p 4to   NYPL(B)
to M d'A
God be praised, mon cher ami — God be

30 Nov   copy   1 p LB   BM(Bar)
to Martin Davy
If ever Epistolography may hope for a place

30 NO 1816 pmk   3 p 4to   Osb
to CB Jr
Yes, certainly, my dear Carlos, I eccho [sic]

6 Dec   copy   6 p LB   BM(Bar)
from Lady Keith
Your account of the strange interview

23 Dec   2 p 4to   Osb
to CB Jr
My dear Carlucci's Letters are truly kind in

26 Dec   8 p 4to   NYPL(B)
from Princess Elizabeth
There is no truth so great as that

[Dec 1816]   copy   5 p LB
to Princess [Mary?]   BM(Bar)
The thoughts of the so very important events

[1816]   2 p 8vo   NYPL(B)
from Adrienne (de Chavagnac), vicom-
     tesse de la Bretonniere
je n'aurais pas osé Madame, vous ennuyer de

[1816?]   draft   2 p fragment
to Queen Charlotte   NYPL(B)
Presumption, I hope can never be allied with

[1816]   1 p 8vo   NYPL(B)
to [William Dimond]
I am truly sensible of your flattering

[1816?]   2 p scrap   NYPL(B)
from GMAPWaddington to FBA &
     M d'A
England, though I deeply lament the

[1816–18]   1 p 8vo   Osb
to [Sarah Martha Holroyd?]
I should surely require no promise beyond

[pre 1817]   4 p 8vo   NYPL(B)
to CFBt & CBFB
As a suppliant I now come before you — but

1817

7 Jan [1817]   copy   7 p LB
to Princess Elizabeth   BM(Bar)
What a delicious letter should I compose were

20 Jan   4 p 4to   Comyn
with AA to CB Jr
Suffer me to take this opportunity

22 Jan   4 p 4to   NYPL(B)
from Princess Elizabeth
You will excuse my delaying answering your

[post 22 Jan 1817]   2 p LB
to SHB   BM(Bar)
What a sure sign is it — though not, perhaps

5 Feb   copy   3 p LB   BM(Bar)
to Princess Elizabeth
I was just preparing to send off my

6 ⟨Feb⟩   4 p 8vo   NYPL(B)
from Princes Augusta
I ⟨really⟩ am ⟨   ed⟩ when I think how

9 Feb   copy   8 p LB   BM(Bar)
to Lady Keith
—— —— Of her son (Mr. d. F) I often

9 Feb   3 p 4to   NYPL(B)
from Henriette (Guignot de Soulignac)
    de Maurville
depuis bien du tems, je cherche Madame et

15 Feb   4 p 4to   NYPL(B)
from Marie de Maisonneuve
je me reproche tous les jours Ma bien chere

16 Feb   4 p 4to   NYPL(B)
from AA
To morrow evening, according to custom, my

21 Feb   4 p 4to   NYPL(B)
to AA
Well, now you have found out the very way

21 Feb   copy   4 p 4to   NYPL(B)
from Marquis de Lally-Tollendal
Chère Madame, voici encore une offrande que

22–23 Feb   4 p 4to   NYPL(B)
to EBB
At length, my dearest Etty, comes the

23 Feb   4 p 8vo   NYPL(B)
to CB Jr
For Me, my dear Carlucci, & for my Partner

5 Mar   1 p 4to   NYPL(B)
to AA
I *write* the Day BEFORE the important Day

7 Mar   4 p 4to   NYPL(B)
from AA
Hourray! Hourray! Hourray! / Hour-r-r-r-ray!
also   copy   3 p LB   BM(Bar)

8 Mar   copy   4 p LB   BM(Bar)
to Lady Keith
—— —— —— I see your insuperable

10 Mar   copy   2 p LB   BM(Bar)
to George Owen Cambridge
As I never lose sight of your goodness to my

11 Mar   4 p 4to   NYPL(B)
to CB Jr
At the moment I re-opened your re-opened

14 Mar   2 p 4to   NYPL(B)
with M d'A to AA
Hourra! Hourra! vive Hourra! Vive Alex! vive

14 [Mar]   copy   5 p LB   BM(Bar)
to Princess Elizabeth
The security in which, I trust, we are ALL

[post 14 Mar]   2 p 4to   NYPL(B)
with M d'A to AA
Comme ta maman n'a pas reçu des lettres

15 Mar   4 p 4to   NYPL(B)
from George Owen Cambridge
I hope & trust that by having delay'd for a day

16 Mar   3 p 4to   NYPL(B)
to CB Jr
Your Letter came too late for business on

25 Mar   4 p 4to   NYPL(B)
to CB Jr
Most certainly, my dear Carlos, I am ready to

27 Mar [1817]   2 p 12mo   BM(Bar)
from Frances Bowdler
I have been here on a visit to Lady Louisa

[11] Apr   4 p 4to   NYPL(B)
to CB Jr
Your Letter, my dear Carlos, has given me the

23 Apr   4 p 4to   NYPL(B)
from AA
I deferred writing till I had had an

25 Apr   4 p 4to   NYPL(B)
to AA
Why what a Rogue you are! — 4 Days in

25 AP pmk [1817]   3 p 4to   Osb
to CB Jr
I would have answered you, my dearest

28 Apr   1 p 4to   Osb
to CB Jr
Alas, my dear Charles — while preparing for

28 AP 1817 pmk   4 p 4to   NYPL(B)
to EBB
Ah my dearest Esther — I know how I shall

28 Apr   2 p 4to   PML
to JB
I know well how sincerely you will grieve for

1817, continued

2 May   4 p 4to   NYPL(B)
to AA
The afflicting event I thought myself destined

2 May   copy   7 p LB   BM(Bar)
to Lady Keith
I will not let a post pass without assuring my

3–6 May   4 p 4to   NYPL(B)
to CB Jr
Thanks, my dear Carlos, for your exactitude.

9 May [1817]   4 p 4to   NYPL(B)
from Marie de Maisonneuve
C'est bien cette lettre si desirée qui

10 May   copy   4 p LB   BM(Bar)
to Lady Keith
If I had not so kind, so stable, so trusting a

16 May   3 p 4to   NYPL(B)
with M d'A to AA
Tes raisonnemens, mon cher Alex, me

17 May   4 p 4to   NYPL(B)
to CBFB
How touched & how grateful am I for the

23 May   2 p 4to   NYPL(B)
to AA
Encore rien! — / O Alexander! — / We must

30 May   3 p 4to   NYPL(B)
to AA
Eh bien? — / And where is my promised long

May   draft   2 p 4to   BM(Bar)
to Maria (Allen) Rishton
Long as it is since I have either written to or

May   2 p 8vo   NYPL(B)
from Sarah Martha Holroyd
On tuesday eveng next I am to have the *two*

2 June   4 p 4to   NYPL(B)
to CBFB
How truly may I return the words of my very

3 June   4 p 4to   NYPL(B)
to CB Jr
On my word, my dear Rector, with all due

4 June   2 p 4to   NYPL(B)
from AA
De moanishe due for the last term

6 June   4 p 4to   BM(Bar)
with M d'A to AA
If ever there was a *Tormentor* in the World

12 June [1817]   2 p 8vo   BM(Bar)
from Lady Charlotte Fitzgerald
Might I ask you & General D Arblay to a very

12 June   2 p 4to   NYPL(B)
to M d'A
O mon ami! mon ami! on how inauspicious

13 June   4 p 4to   NYPL(B)
from M d'A
Bon jour bonne oeuvre, est un vieux dicton

14–18 June [1817]   4 p 4to
to M d'A   NYPL(B)
O yes, yes, my dearest Ami, you divined right

[15 June 1817]   ½ p 4to   NYPL(B)
from M d'A
J'arrive de chez l'ambassadeur avec qui

16 [June 1817]   2 p 4to   NYPL(B)
from M d'A
La mer, ma chere Fanny, est entre nous;

18–25 June   4 p 4to mutilated
to M d'A   NYPL(B)
My last Great Epistle finished with Alex's

[c 20 June 1817]   1 p 12mo
to Frances (Kemble) Twiss NYPL(B)
General d'Arblay is on his way to Paris: not

20–[24] June   2 p 4to   NYPL(B)
with AA to M d'A
O mon cher pere, quelle peine je vous ai faite!

20–24 June   4 p 4to   NYPL(B)
from M d'A
Me voici, ma chere amie, etabli chez M^r le

21–28 June   4 p 4to   NYPL(B)
to M d'A
Sat^y. June 21st. Alex & I spent the Evening in

23 June   draft   1 p 4to   NYPL(B)
to Henry Hoare (with AL draft to Princess Elizabeth [Oct 1817])
I beg the favour that you will forward to me

[25–27 June 1817]   4 p 4to
from M d'A   NYPL(B)
Je ne te quittais hier que p^r aller diner au

28 June   4 p 8vo   BM(Bar)
from Amelia (Locke) Angerstein
Lest some unwelcome obtruder

28 Jun [–2 July]   4 p 4to   NYPL(B)
from M d'A
Un peu tard. Non il ne sera pas dit que je me

29 June–4 July [1817]   4 p 4to
to M d'A   NYPL(B)
I must begin with replying to N°. 6, though
also   copy extracts   2 scraps   NYPL(B)
This very day of our arrival

June [1817?]   draft   10 p 4to
to Princess Elizabeth   NYPL(B)
I presume not to make a merit to your R.H.

[3–9 July 1817]   4 p 4to   NYPL(B)
from M d'A
La seule lettre que j'ai de toi est commencée

5–9 July [1817]   4 p 4to   NYPL(B)
to M d'A
I must now give you some account of this
also   copy extract   1 p scrap   NYPL(B)

10 July   3 p 4to   BM(Bar)
from M d'A
Est il possible, ma chere amie, que depuis un

10–17 July [1817]   4 p 4to
to M d'A   NYPL(B)
July 10th. How I languish to hear some of my

14 July   4 p 4to   NYPL(B)
to EBB
If my dearest Esther thinks I have been long

16[–23] July   4 p fol   NYPL(B)
from M d'A
Quelle chose vraiment inconcevable! J'ai

18 July–1 Aug   4 p 4to   NYPL(B)
to M d'A
I feel the most extreme anxiety for news that

23 July   4 p 4to   NYPL(B)
to CBFB
The kind though melancholy offering of my

29 July   3 p 4to   BM(Bar)
My dear Madame d'Arblay Comment faites

30 July   4 p 4to   NYPL(B)
from EBB
I am afraid My Dearest Fanny will have

2–7 Aug   4 p 4to   NYPL(B)
to M d'A
Having now resided here a month, I ought to

[3–7 Aug 1817]   4 p 4to   NYPL(B)
from M d'A   & BM(Bar)
[NYPL] Encore une lettre de toi (N° 8) et
[BM(Bar)] et toujours effectives, quoique

8–15 Aug   4 p 4to   NYPL(B)
to M d'A
You bid me write, my dear — dear Friend —

9 Aug   draft   4 p 4to   NYPL(B)
to Princess Elizabeth
Will yr. R. H. be surprised — I hope not! —

9 Aug [1817]   4 p 4to   BM(Bar)
from M d'A
Avant hier < > ce fils de Massiquet me

16–23 Aug [1817]   4 p 4to   NYPL(B)
to M d'A
My N°. 12 Letter is just gone — yet I must

19–21 [Aug 1817]   4 p 4to   BM(Bar)
from M d'A
Le diner chez <Ampere> n'a pas été aussi

21 Aug   5 p 4to   NYPL(B)
from Sarah Martha Holroyd
You will be surprised, dear Me. d'Arblay.

22 Aug   4 p 4to   BM(Bar)
to GMAPWaddington
I have often — almost *continually* — nay,

25 Aug–2 Sept [1817]   4 p 4to
to M d'A   NYPL(B)
With what regret — almost alarm, do I now

25 Aug [1817]   2 p 4to   BM(Bar)
from M d'A
Comme le *mieux* dont je te parlais hier non

[27–29 Aug. 1817]   4 p 4to
from M d'A   NYPL(B)
Mercredi matin. Ma lettre de ce jour vient de

28 Aug–3 Sept   4 p 4to   Comyn
to CB Jr
I saw your hand, my dearest Carlos, quite

30 Aug   copy   2 p 8vo   BM(Bar)
to Longman & Co
Madame d'Arblay begs leave to observe to

1817, continued

3 Sept   2 p 4to   BM(Bar)
from M d'A
Je me suis trompé hier ma chere Fanny, en

3–12 Sept [1817]   4 p 4to mutilated
to M d'A   NYPL(B)
With This, let me fly this subject! I am so

also   copy extract   1 p scrap   NYPL(B)
I have not mentioned a letter I have received

9 Sept   4 p 4to   NYPL(B)
from M d'A
[obliteration] telle que je viens enfin de

9 Sept   1 p 4to   BM(Bar)
from Dr Thomas Bowdler
Permit me my Dear Madam to express the

11 Sept   2 p 4to   Osb
to CB Jr
Imagine my surprise, my dearest Carlos, at

12 Sept [1817]   4 p 4to   NYPL(B)
to M d'A
Friday Sept. 12th. I have so much to say to my

[15 Sept 1817]   2 p 4to   BM(Bar)
from M d'A
J'ai été 2 ou 3 jours sans t'ecrire, ma bonne

[15 Sept 1817]   4 p 4to   BM(Bar)
from M d'A
Je t'ai dit ma chere amie que je ne te

15 Sept   4 p 4to   NYPL(B)
from Marie de Maisonneuve
qu'il y a long-tems Ma bien chere amie

[19 Sept 1817]   4 p 4to   NYPL(B)
from M d'A
Je ne puis resister d'un coté au plaisir

22 Sept [1817]   4 p 4to   NYPL(B)
to M d'A
The quantity I have had to write of discussion

27 Sept   4 p 4to   BM(Bar)
from M d'A
N'es tu pas un peu surprise, ma chere amie,

3 Oct   3 p 4to   BM(Bar)
from M d'A
Je suis tant et si serieusement occupé des

8 Oct   1 p 4to   NYPL(B)
from M d'A
All safe, from dear England once more;

8–9 Oct   7 p 4to   NYPL(B)
from Princess Elizabeth
You must indeed think me very remiss in

[17 Oct 1817] draft   4 p 4to
to Princess Elizabeth   NYPL(B)
This moment only I have recd. the high honour

also   copy   3 p LB   BM(Bar)
This moment only (Oct 17th) from

24 Oct   4 p 4to   NYPL(B)
from AA
Once more on this *classical ground* (as they

28 Oct   8 p 4to   NYPL(B)
from AA
My mamkin! my mamkin, my faithless

2 Nov   4 p 4to   NYPL(B)
with M d'A to AA
Why my Boy! my Man! my Alex! — if you are

2 Nov   4 p 4to   NYPL(B)
from AA
Why have I no letter to day? — O mammy!

7 Nov   4 p 4to   NYPL(B)
with M d'A to AA
Bath, hier dans les transports d'une joie bien

9 Nov   4 p 4to   NYPL(B)
to AA
Why, my dear Alex, Wrangler or NOT

9–15 Nov   4 p 4to   NYPL(B)
to GMAPWaddington
Can I still hope, my dearest Mary, for that

14 Nov 1817–4 Jan 1818   4 p 4to
to CBFB   NYPL(B)
What a good & kind Charlotte is my invaluable

16 Nov   4 p 4to   NYPL(B)
to AA
I had watched for the post, — in defiance of

17 Nov [1817]   5 p 8vo   BM(Bar)
from Etiennette, princesse d'Hénin
Chere madame j'ai differé depuis longtems

22 Nov   3 p 4to   NYPL(B)
from Princess Elizabeth
You ought to have had a letter before now to

28 NO 1817 pmk   2 p 8vo   Osb
from Frances Bowdler
I heartily rejoice that you could say *thank*

[Nov 1817]   copy   3 p LB
to AA   BM(Bar)
I was carried in a sedan last week to the Q —

[Nov 1817]   2 p 8vo   BM(Bar)
from Lady Charlotte Fitzgerald
Ten Thousand Thanks

5 Dec [1817]   4 p 8vo   NYPL(B)
from AA
I am going into the schools on *Tuesday*

20 Dec   1 p 4to   NYPL(B)
from JB to M d'A & FBA
My dear General, (on 2ᵈ thought I judged it

21 Dec   4 p 4to   NYPL(B)
from JB
I made a very inexcusable mistake about our

21 Dec   4 p 4to   NYPL(B)
from AA
Jacob has got the Law Tancred Scholarship

[pre 25 Dec 1817]   2 p 4to   Osb
to CPB
Oh my dear Charles what a dreadful alarm is

25 Dec   4 p 4to   PML
to JB
A merry Christmas / To my dear Brother &

25 Dec   4 p 4to   NYPL(B)
from AA
Thanks for your last, dearest Madre;

26 Dec 1817–14 Jan 1818   copy   1 p
      LB   BM(Bar)
to Lady Keith
I had begun this with intention to end the old

27 [Dec 1817]   copy   4 p LB
to Princess Elizabeth   BM(Bar)
"One line" / What sweetness is this! & how

28 Dec   4 p 4to   NYPL(B)
from AA
A happy year to my dearest excellent parents!

[29 misdated 30] Dec   3 p 4to
to AA   NYPL(B)
Alas my dearest Alexander how sudden a blow

31 Dec   2 p 4to   NYPL(B)
from AA
Fruitless indeed would have been the thought

[1817]   copy   2 p LB   BM(Bar)
to Mary (Danby), Countess of Harcourt
I rejoice with all my heart that the ever

[1817]   1 p scrap   NYPL(B)
from M d'A
positive bien, reellement dicté par mon coeur

[post 1817?]   copy   1 p fragment
                           NYPL(B)
from [Princess Elizabeth to FBA]
I almost went distracted when I was seventeen

1818

1 Jan   3 p 4to   NYPL(B)
from Princess Elizabeth
Alas! My dear Madame dArblay how can I

7 Jan   1 p 8vo   NYPL(B)
from Sarah Martha Holroyd
I have respected your affliction as what I hold

7 Jan [1818]   3 p 4to   NYPL(B)
from Princess Mary
My very dear kind Madame d'Arblay your

19 Jan–3 Mar [misdated 1817]   4 p 4to
to CBFB   NYPL(B)
Let us renew & keep to our former practice,

[24 Jan 1818]   1 p 4to   NYPL(B)
from AA
All is over! — / I shall be with you on

25 Jan   3 p 8vo   NYPL(B)
from Princess Elizabeth
You ought to have heard from me sooner & I

25 Jan   1 p 4to   NYPL(B)
from Princess Elizabeth
at it: thank Heaven people are beginning of

[25 Jan 1818]   2 p 8vo   NYPL(B)
from Frederica Locke & Amelia (Locke)
      Angerstein
and now I must try to < > how my heart

27 JA 1818 pmk   2 p 4to   NYPL(B)
from Frederica Locke
our precious Amine has taken my letter sheet

29 Jan [1818]   3 p 8vo   Comyn
from Harriet Bowdler
I cannot tell you how much

1818, continued

29 Jan   copy   1 p LB   NYPL(B)
from Frances (Phillips) Raper
We have just received read [sic] the name of

31 Jan   copy   2 p LB   NYPL(B)
from GMAPWaddington
One line of congratulation warm from my

[1 Feb 1818]   4 p 4to   NYPL(B)
to Frederica Locke
The *Bath Drops* keep perfectly well, & are

5 Feb   copy   1 p LB   NYPL(B)
from Sarah Baker
To felicitate dearest M^e D'ay is a call upon

5 Feb   copy   1 p LB   NYPL(B)
from George Owen Cambridge
An indisposition which for some days

6 Feb   3 p 4to   BM(Bar)
from Charlotte Beckedorff
vous êtes bien bonne de m'écrire

[9 Feb 1818]   1 p 8vo   NYPL(B)
from AA
I am actually scholar of X^t College

also   copy   1 p LB   NYPL(B)

10 Feb   copy   3 p LB   BM(Bar)
to Princess Elizabeth
A report has just reached the obscurity of my

12–13 Feb   copy   3 p LB   BM(Bar)
to George Owen Cambridge
The true & well understood sympathy with

13 Feb   copy   3 p LB   BM(Bar)
to Princess Elizabeth
I have wept over Y.R.H. letter with gratitude,

20 Feb [1818]   3 p 8vo   BM(Bar)
from Frances Bowdler
I have not annoyed you with billets of

20 Feb   4 p 4to   NYPL(B)
from Marie de Maisonneuve
cela a été un moment de bonheur

[25] Feb   4 p 4to   NYPL(B)
from AA
I had written several letters at

25 Feb   ½ p 4to   NYPL(B)
from HLTP
A Thousand Thanks Dear Madam — & a

26 Feb   copy   3 p LB   BM(Bar)
to CPB
Your letters, my dear Charles, have caused me

26 Feb   1 p 4to   NYPL(B)
from HLTP
I had company in the Room when Lady

26 Feb [1818] partly a copy   3 p 4to
to HLTP   NYPL(B)
There is no situation in which a kind

also copy (in HLTP to FBA 26 Feb 1818)
NYPL(B)

[Feb 1818]   1 p 8vo   NYPL(B)
from HLTP
I heard Yesterday from some of your Family

1 Mar   3 p 4to   NYPL(B)
to AA
Your Letter is melancholy to me, my dear

4 Mar   3 p 4to   BM(Bar)
from Anne (Leigh) Frodsham
I have long'd indeed my dear M^rs. D'Arblay

also   partial copy   1 p LB   NYPL(B)
The B^sp of London (D^r. March) is as good

5 Mar   1 p 8vo   NYPL(B)
from AA
I am to be to morrow elected or

7 Mar   2 p 4to?   BM(Bar)
from Richard Twining
Whilst my good Friend, Dr Hughes, was at

9 Mar   copy, extracts   1 p LB
to Lady Keith   BM(Bar)
How infinitely amiable of the p^ess. Eliza to

9 Mar   copy, extract   4 p LB
to Lady Keith   BM(Bar)
I have just received a letter — read one rather,

10 Mar   4 p 8vo   NYPL(B)
from AA
I have only just time

13 Mar   copy   4 p LB   BM(Bar)
to Princess Elizabeth
Is my remembrance faithful? Did I not see a

14 Mar   4 p 4to   NYPL(B)
to CBFB
I will not wait for the leisure of sending one of

14 Mar   4 p 4to   Osb
to CPB
Niggard as I am now become of all Letters not

also   copy extract   1 p LB   BM(Bar)
I much approve the plan of consulting

[14? Mar 1818]   1 p 8vo   NYPL(B)
from AA
I received your letter yesterday which I could

14 Mar   2 p 8vo   BM(Bar)
from Cassandra (Leigh) Cooke
How good to spare any particle of your most

15 Mar [1818 misdated 1817]   copy
     2 p LB   NYPL(B)
from George Owen Cambridge
Few things could have afforded us more

16 Mar   copy   1 p LB   NYPL(B)
from EBB
We always loved dear Alexander, & have

17 Mar   3 p 4to   NYPL(B)
from Princess Elizabeth
Never can I thank you enough for your great

19 Mar   2 p 4to mutilated   NYPL(B)
to GMAPWaddington   & BM(Bar)
[NYPL 2 pieces] Eagerly I seize a *pleasant*
[BM(Bar)] I hope you had a Letter from me

23 Mar   copy   4 p LB   BM(Bar)
to Princess Elizabeth
How sweetly smiling is this view of expected

27 Mar   4 p 4to   NYPL(B)
from AA
I have been prevented from writing — on the

28–29 Mar [1818]   4 p 4to
to CBFB   NYPL(B)
Yesterday, my dearest Charlotte, Miss

31 Mar   copy   1 p LB   BM(Bar)
to Richard Twining
Grievous, indeed, to me most heavily so, is my

Mar   draft   1 p 4to   BM(Bar)
to Maria (Allen) Rishton
The late fatal event in our family, I had

[Mar 1818]   3 p 8vo   BM(Bar)
from Sarah Baker
I take this small measure of paper

3 Apr   4 p 4to   NYPL(B)
from AA
Mr. Jackson and Mr. Isaacson are not yet

5 Apr   2 p 4to   NYPL(B)
to CBFB
The Epitaph, my dearest Charlotte, *can* be all

7 Apr   copy   3 p 4to   BM(Bar)
to Charlotte Beckedorff
At the feet of Her Mty I entreat you to lay

7 Apr   copy   1 p LB   BM(Bar)
to Princess Elizabeth
Happy be This Day to the Ral. Bde. of Great

[10] Apr   3 p 4to   NYPL(B)
from AA
I had begun some stanzas for dear papa which

17 Apr   4 p 4to   NYPL(B)
from Marie de Maisonneuve
quels Romans! quelle histoire plus intéressante

22 AP 1818 pmk   3 p 4to   NYPL(B)
to AA
Oh my Alex — my poor Alex — I fear you

[22 Apr 1818]   4 p 12mo   BM(Bar)
from Amelia (Locke) Angerstein
My very dear Mrs d'Arblay The hope

22 Apr [1818]   2 p 4to   BM(Bar)
from Frederica Locke
Here I am, my dearly loved Friend with my

25 Apr   4 p 8vo   NYPL(B)
with Sophia Burney to EBB
Oh my dear Hetty I think him a little better

27 Apr   3 p 4to   BM(Bar)
from Frederica Locke
I cannot return to my Vale without telling my

[Apr 1818]   ½ p 4to   BM(Bar)
from EBB
How kind my poor dear Fanny it is of you to

[Apr 1818]   1 p 4to   BM(Bar)
from EBB
Grieved to the soul by the accounts of

[1–3 May]   1 p 4to   NYPL(B)
to CBFB & CFBt
Yes — come to me — my tender Charlotte —

1818, continued

6 May   2 p 4to   NYPL(B)
from SHB
How shall I, my most dear Sister, find courage

7 May   3 p 4to   NYPL(B)
from CBFB
Oh my dearest Sister, that it were in my

16 May   2 p 4to   NYPL(B)
from JB
I say nothing of consolation. I hope time will

17 May   4 p 4to   NYPL(B)
from CBFB
Ah my dearest Sister, what grief it is to me not

19 May   3 p 4to   NYPL(B)
from — (Bazille) Meignen
Permettez moi de vous exprimer toute la part

20 MY 1818 pmk   4 p 4to   NYPL(B)
to CBFB
I make Alex write again, for both our sakes,

[c 20] May   3 p 4to   NYPL(B)
from Marie de Maisonneuve
que vous me rendez bien justice Ma bonne

20 May   incomplete?   1 p 4to
from William Wilberforce   Osb
Excuse this most hurried scrawl, interposed

also   copy   2 p 4to   NYPL(B)
It is perhaps well for you, as well as for me,

23 May   4 p 4to   BM(Bar)
from Sarah Baker
My dearest Mrs D'Arblay, my revered *Friend,*

24 May [1818]   3 p 8vo   NYPL(B)
from Etiennette, princesse d'Hénin
je ne sais comment <approcher> d'une

30 May   1 p 4to   NYPL(B)
from Marquis de Lafayette
Les gazettes venaient de nous annoncer notre

[May 1818]   2 p fol   NYPL(B)
from Sarah Martha Holroyd
I would not intrude upon you my dear friend

[post May 1818]   4 p 4to   NYPL(B)
from Princess Elizabeth
Long have I intended you a letter my dear

2 June   2 p 8vo   NYPL(B)
from Marquis de Lally-Tollendal
chere, trop chere Madame, quelles expressions

23 JU 1818 pmk   1 p 4to   NYPL(B)
to CBFB
Oh my Charlotte — my dear — dear

28 JU 1818 pmk   4 p 4to   NYPL(B)
to CBFB
Your prompt answer is just what I ought to

7 July   4 p 4to mutilated   NYPL(B)
to CBFB   & BM(Bar)
[NYPL(B) 6 pieces] 'Tis sad we cannot yet
[BM(Bar) fragment] With regard to

8 July   2 p 4to   NYPL(B)
from John Kaye
I was in the point of answering your Letter

14 JY 1818 pmk   2 p 4to   PML
to JB
I have made Alex promise my dear — alas my

21 July   2 p 4to   NYPL(B)
from JB
I am glad to find you so far settled in your

28 July   4 p 4to   NYPL(B)
from Marie de Maisonneuve
que j'avais besoin Ma bien chere

29 July [1818]   4 p 8vo   BM(Bar)
from Frederica Locke & Amelia (Locke)
     Angerstein
I longed to speed my heart felt thanks to

17 Aug [1818]   5 p 4to   NYPL(B)
from Princess Mary
The constant kindness I have experienced

20 Aug   4 p 4to   BM(Bar)
from Charlotte Beckedorff
Si je ne comptois pas sur Votre indulgente

25 Aug [1818]   4 p 4to   NYPL(B)
from Harriet Maltby
Your kind, and dateless letter my dear

30 Aug [1818?]   3 p 4to   NYPL(B)
from Henriette (Guignot de Soulignac)
     de Maurville
il me serait difficile Madame et chere amie

3 Sept [1818]   2 p 8vo   Comyn
from Frances Bowdler
My very dear Friend my heart thanked you,

7 Sept   2 p 4to   NYPL(B)
from John Kaye
My absence from Cambridge must be my

27 Sept   1 p 4to   NYPL(B)
to AA
I need not tell you, my dearest Bachelor —

[c 27 Sept 1818]   2 p 4to   NYPL(B)
to EBB
My dearest Esther will be much more sorry

27 Sept   1 p 4to   PML
to JB
On *Tuesday night* your truly Brotherly

2–7 Oct   4 p 4to   NYPL(B)
to EBB
I know how anxious my kind Hetty will be to

6 Oct   2 p 8vo   NYPL(B)
to AA
I will not let you wait the slow arrival of the

6 Oct   4 p 4to mutilated   NYPL(B)
to CBFB
Long indeed I have found it to be without any

11 Oct   4 p 4to   BM(Bar)
from EBB
Your Letter My Dearest Fanny was indeed

13 Oct   1 p 4to   NYPL(B)
to HLTP
From my general seclusion during this late

13 OC 1818 pmk   2 p 8vo
                            NYPL(B)
from Cécile (de Riquet de Caraman),
     marquise de Sommery
La pauvre francoise m'a dit, Madame

17 Oct   4 p 4to   NYPL(B)
to AA
Your Letter, my dear Deacon, required too

18 Oct   2 p 4to   NYPL(B)
from Cassandra (Leigh) Cooke
By a recent Letter from our ever kind M^rs

18 Oct [1818]   3 p 4to   NYPL(B)
from Sarah Martha Holroyd
I was very glad my dear friend to hear that

19 Oct [1818]   4 p 4to   Comyn
from Frances Bowdler
My dear, very dear Friend I found your most

20 Oct   4 p 4to   NYPL(B)
from Marie de Maisonneuve
Votre silence, Ma bien chere

[20 Oct 1818]   3 p 4to   NYPL(B)
from HLTP
It was very gratifying Dear Madam to find

22 Oct   4 p 4to   NYPL(B)
to AA
O fie, Mr. Deacon, fie! / *Wasting Time* Still?

24 Oct   copy   2 p 4to   NYPL(B)
to William Tudor
Ma^de d'Arblay presents her best Comp^ts. to

26 Oct   1 p 4to   NYPL(B)
from William Tudor
M^r. Tudor presents his respectful Compliments

27 Oct   1 p 4to   NYPL(B)
from William Tudor
Since writing the inclosed Letter, M^r. Tudor

28 Oct   3 p 4to   NYPL(B)
from Sarah Martha Holroyd
How my ever dear friend can I express as I

[10 Nov 1818]   4 p 8vo   BM(Bar)
from Frances Bowdler
An opportunity offers of sending a packet to

14 NO 1818 pmk   1 p 8vo   NYPL(B)
to AA
unreflecting Alex! / Does then no "still small

15–16 Nov   4 p 4to   NYPL(B)
to CBFB
Your tender & cordial invitation, my Charlotte,

16 Nov   4 p 4to   NYPL(B)
from Marie de Maisonneuve
Ma lettre d'octobre vous aura donné l'idée

25 Nov [1818?]   2 p 4to   NYPL(B)
from Etiennette, princesse d'Hénin
chere madame je m'unis du fond du coeur à

[c 26 Nov]–4 Dec   4 p 4to   NYPL(B)
to EBB
Your Letter touches me to take my pen the

[post Nov 1818]   4 p 4to   NYPL(B)
from Princess Elizabeth
Yesterday evening I received your very kind

1818, continued

4 Dec   2 p 4to   NYPL(B)
to EBB
I now enclose this to send by our valued &

10 DE 1818 pmk   2 p 4to   NYPL(B)
from Lady Keith
The weather here is delightful — Our park

11 Dec [1818]   7 p 4to   NYPL(B)
from Princess Mary
I can not let so kind

29 DE pmk [1818?]   2 p 4to
to AA   NYPL(B)
If you wish me to come either *to* you, or *for*

29 Dec [1818]   3 p 8vo   NYPL(B)
from Frances (Phillips) Raper
I went this morning to see Aunt Sarah who

[1818]   2 p 8vo   BM(Bar)
from Catherine (de Boullongne), vicom-
     tesse de Laval
Permettez moi tres chere Madame d'Arblay

[1818–19]   draft, notes   1 p scrap
to Princess Mary   NYPL(B)
Worldly Charge for Pss. Augusta like King

[post 1818?]   1 p 8vo   NYPL(B)
from Princess Augusta
I know you are an early Person like myself —

[post 1818?]   1 p 8vo   NYPL(B)
from Princess Augusta
If you are well enough to come to me this

[post 1818]   2 p 8vo   NYPL(B)
from Marie de Maisonneuve
dans un peu de tristesse — Avez-vous vu a

4 Mar [post 1818?]   8 p 8vo
from Princess Mary   NYPL(B)
Your kind note has given me much *pleasure*

21 July [post 1818]   4 p 8vo
from Princess Mary   NYPL(B)
Many thanks for your amiable & kind letter by

2 Aug [post 1818]   2 p 8vo   NYPL(B)
from Princess Mary
I am vexed to <   > at leaving Town

28 ⟨Dec⟩ [post 1818]   4 p 4to
from Princess Mary   NYPL(B)
Your kind offer and kind letter my dearest

[post 1818]   4 p 12mo   NYPL(B)
from Princess Mary
I am no longer 15 <passed> 25

[post 1818]   4 p 8vo   NYPL(B)
from Princess Mary
How kind of you to enquire after us —

[post 1818]   4 p 8vo   NYPL(B)
from Princess Mary
How kind of you to have thought of me &

[post 1818?]   1 p fragment   NYPL(B)
from Princess Elizabeth
Send me bound simply Evelina, Cecilia &

[post 1818]   1 p 4to   NYPL(B)
from Florimond de Latour-Maubourg
Alexandre S'en sauvé, Madame, sans vouloir

[post 1818]   3 p 8vo   NPG
from Princess Mary
Dear kind Darblay I grieve to find the cold

1819

1 Jan [1819]   7 p 8vo   NYPL(B)
from Princess Mary
Your kind obliging letter

1 Feb   4 p 4to   NYPL(B)
to EBB
Could I have devized anything to say of a

2 Feb   5 p 4to   NYPL(B)
from Marie de Maisonneuve
que de choses j'aurois a vous dire

4 Feb   3 p 4to   NYPL(B)
from Marquis de Lally-Tollendal
chere Madame je ne veux pas laisser partir

[9 Feb 1818]   1 p 8vo   NYPL(B)
from AA
I am actually scholar of Xt College
also   copy   1 p LB   NYPL(B)

10 Feb   4 p 4to   NYPL(B)
to AA
I was never more surprised! — How? — a

11 Feb   4 p 4to   NYPL(B)
to AA
My own Alex — This last letter is very dear

14 Feb [1819?]   1 p 4to   BM(Bar)
from Cassandra (Leigh) Cooke
When my Daughter called in Bolton St —

18 Feb   4 p 4to   NYPL(B)
to AA
What a blessing is this, my dear Alex! a Letter

22 Feb   2 p 4to   NYPL(B)
from Marie de Maisonneuve
quelle touchante lettre Ma bien chere

[c 27 Feb 1819]   draft   23 p MB
                              NYPL(B)
to Princess Mary & Princess Elizabeth
Little able as I still feel to do what I wish

2 Mar [1819]   3 p 4to   NYPL(B)
from Princess Mary
I have many thanks to return you for the kind

4 Mar   draft   18 p MB   NYPL(B)
to Princess Mary
The new marks of y^r. R.H. constant sweetness

5 Mar   3 p 4to   NYPL(B)
to AA
Oh my dear Alex what an Event! — what an

[c 5 Mar 1819]   draft   9 p MB
to Princess Mary   NYPL(B)
The most distant hope of having any thing to

6 Mar   draft   6 p MB   NYPL(B)
to Princess Mary
One line I cannot resist of most grateful thanks

8 Mar   4 p 4to   NYPL(B)
to CBFB
My Charlotte — my dearest kindest Charlotte

13 Mar   4 p 4to   NYPL(B)
to EBB
Now then — at last — & most wonderfully — I

21 Mar [1819]   3 p 8vo   BM(Bar)
from Cassandra (Leigh) Cooke
A thousand thanks my dear Madam for the

22 Mar   1 p 4to   NYPL(B)
to AA
I regret not having sent this ANSWER to your

24 Mar [1819]   3 p 8vo   NYPL(B)
from Princess Mary
Could you come to me Saturday morning at

24 Mar   draft   1 p MB   NYPL(B)
to Princess Mary
at the earliest Hour since yr. R.H. deigns to

27 Mar   2 p 4to   NYPL(B)
to AA
I do certainly think that of all persons existing

27 [Mar? 1819]   4 p 12mo   BM(Bar)
from Amelia (Locke) Angerstein
What a pleasure to me to receive in my

[Mar 1819]   4 p 8vo   BM(Bar)
from Frederica Locke
A thousand thanks, my dearly loved Friend

2 AP 1819 pmk   2 p 8vo   NYPL(B)
to AA
In the hope this will meet you before your

9 Apr [1819]   2 p 8vo   NYPL(B)
from Marie de Maisonneuve
mille et mille remerciments Ma bien chere

[10 Apr 1819]   1 p 12mo   NYPL(B)
from Marie de Maisonneuve
Je recois votre réponse en rentrant

14 Apr   4 p 4to   NYPL(B)
from Sarah Martha Holroyd
I was so much obliged to you my dear friend

16 Apr   4 p 4to   BM(Bar)
from Cassandra (Leigh) Cooke
I never, believe me, received any Letter

[18 Apr 1819]   1 p 8vo   NYPL(B)
from Marie de Maisonneuve
Ma bien chere amie, Victor vouloit profiter

19 Apr   3 p 8vo   NYPL(B)
to CFBt
To-morrow, I hope & trust, my two dearest

21 Apr   9 p 4to   NYPL(B)
from Princess Elizabeth
You have waited three posts for an answer

24 Apr   2 p 4o   BM(Bar)
from Cécile (de Riquet de Caraman),
     marquise de Sommery
Vous m'avés procuré une bien Consolante

26 Apr draft 1 p 4to   BM(Bar)
to Cécile (de Riquet de Caraman),
     marquise de Sommery
It is a solemn gratification to me that through

[post 27 Apr 1819]   1 p 4to
to George Edmund Hay   BM(Bar)
Your letter has extremely touched me, but the

1819, continued

29 Apr   2 p 4to   NYPL(B)
to EBB
If you are well enough — / Willing I am sure

18 May   4 p 4to   NYPL(B)
to EBB
You did attend, my dearest Esther, since such

22 May   pmk 1819   4 p 4to
from EBB   BM(Bar)
I have been doubly vexed, my Dearest Fanny

[May 1819]   1 p 8vo   NYPL(B)
from Marie de Maisonneuve
je me suis flatté jusqu'à ce moment

20 June   4 p 4to   NYPL(B)
to EBB
Your little Note, my kind Esther, was my first,

21 June [1819]   1 p 8vo   NYPL(B)
from Princess Mary
In the first place Augusta wishes to see you at

[25 June 1819]   3 p 8vo   BM(Bar)
from Frederica Locke
at my return, my beloved Friend, I found

[June 1819]   2 p 8vo   PML
from Marie de Maisonneuve
bien bien chere amie, j'ai été reçue de votre

3 July [1819]   2 p 8vo   NYPL(B)
from Princess Mary
Indeed you do me but justice to believe I

5 July   6 p 4to   NYPL(B)
from Sarah Martha Holroyd
If I could be content not to hear from ye or

12 [July 1819]   3 p 8vo   NYPL(B)
from Marie de Maisonneuve
Ma bien bien chere amie, Vous serez bien

17 July [1819]   1 p 8vo   NYPL(B)
from Princess Mary
I only returned last Night late

19 July   4 p 4to   BM(Bar)
from EBB
Your most kind Letter, my Dear, dated

[20 July 1819]   1 p 8vo   NYPL(B)
from Marie de Maisonneuve
pendant que Made Victor cause avec

24 July   9 p 4to   NYPL(B)
from Princess Elizabeth
My letters from You, tho', as you say, *long*

3 Aug [1819]   4 p 4to   Comyn
from Frances Bowdler
My dear Friend it has been very

4 Aug [1819]   2 p 8vo   NYPL(B)
from Princess Mary
In opening My parcel from <Elaine>, with

5 Aug [1819]   4 p 8vo   NYPL(B)
to CBFB
Every day — & all day long, for at least a

8 Aug   2 p 4to   NYPL(B)
from Princess Augusta
You must forgive me as *Dutchess Mary* says

9 Aug [1819]   4 p 4to   NYPL(B)
from Princess Mary
Woman, alass, [sic] we all know, after the fall

11 Aug [1819]   3 p 4to   NYPL(B)
from Princess Mary
What can I say to your sweet *friendly* I may

12 Aug   draft   7 p 4to   NYPL(B)
to Princess Augusta
A sweeter SURPRIZE, a more soothing

[14 Aug 1819]   4 p 8vo   BM(Bar)
from Frederica Locke
I hasten to say, my beloved Friend that our

[post 18 Aug 1819]   4 p 8vo
to [CFBt]   NYPL(B) & McG
Not alone my Consent but my greatest

[1 p 8vo at McG] methods of cure, to prevent

23 AU 1819 pmk   3 p 12mo   PML
to JB
Though I have never, myself, been uneasy

30 Aug–4 Sept   4 p 4to   NYPL(B)
to EBB
As Alex is now planning a visit to Bath, I will

1 Sept   4 p 8vo   NYPL(B)
to CBFB
A little line only to my dearest Charlotte to

8 Sept   4 p 8vo   BM(Bar)
from Frederica Locke
I cannot tell you, my beloved Friend, how

14 Sept [1819]   2 p 4to   NYPL(B)
from Marie de Maisonneuve
je ne veux pas m'éloigner encore plus de vous

26–27 Sept   4 p 4to   NYPL(B)
to EBB
What can I say to my poor Esther — but

30 Sept [1819?]   4 p 8vo   NYPL(B)
to CBFB
Unwilling — & ungayly we left you, my ever

Sept   copy   2 p 4to   NYPL(B)
to Frederica Locke
How very your own kindest Self was this so

3 Oct   6 p 4to   NYPL(B)
from Princess Elizabeth
Yes, dear Madame d'Arblay, a volume from

4 Oct   4 p 4to   NYPL(B)
to EBB
I receive your Letter with great thankfulness,

15 Oct [1819]   4 p 4to   NYPL(B)
to CBFB
'Twas a kind surprise to see your hand so

18 Oct [1819]   5 p 8vo   NYPL(B)
from Princess Mary
It is ages & ages since I have troubled you

[Oct 1819]   3 p 8vo   BM(Bar)
from Petronille (Van Ryssel) de Latour-
      Maubourg
Je suis bien fachée ma chère Madame d'Arblay

4 Nov   2 p 8vo   NYPL(B)
from Marie de Maisonneuve
je n'ai reçu que ce matin Votre bonne lettre

12–17 Nov   4 p 4to   NYPL(B)
to GMAPWaddington
Your very touching Letter my dear — ever

13 Nov [1819]   4 p 8vo   BM(Bar)
from Frances Bowdler
Your interesting letter has been much too long

17 Nov 1819–20 Mar 1820   147 p Note-
      book   NYPL(B)
FBA Journal
My soul visits ever more my Departed angel

2 Dec   2 p 8vo   Osb
from Marie de Maisonneuve
Ma bien chère amie, n'est ce pas qu'<il>

3 Dec   copy   3 p 4to   NYPL(B)
to Frederica Locke
Never was good news more seasonable nor

8 Dec   9 p 4to   NYPL(B)
from Princess Elizabeth
I return You many thanks for Your very

14–15 Dec   4 p 4to   NYPL(B)
from Marie de Maisonneuve
je n'ai pas encore eu de vos nouvelles

1819   copy excerpt   2 p 4to
to Frederica Locke   NYPL(B)
—— My invaluable Madame de Maisonneuve

[1819]   1 p 12mo   NYPL(B)
from Princess Mary
I quite long to see you, it appears ages &

[1819]   1 p fragment   NYPL(B)
to GMAPWaddington
I am quite distressed but so engaged for my

5 May [post 1819]   1 p 8vo
      BM(Bar)
from Marquis de Lally-Tollendal
Chere madame, Je suis au desespoir j'avais

27 Mar [post 1819]   4 p 8vo
from Princess Mary   NYPL(B)
Charmed at the sight of your hand writing

[1819–22]   1 p 12mo   BM(Bar)
from Elizabeth, Lady Templetown
Only one line to say can you come to me

[1819–22]   2 p 8vo   BM(Bar)
from Elizabeth, Lady Templetown
I am quite vexed dearest Me d'Arblay

[1819–22]   3 p 12mo   BM(Bar)
from Elizabeth, Lady Templetown
I am forbid to write to you my dear & valued

[1819–22]   3 p 12mo   BM(Bar)
from Elizabeth, Lady Templetown
I will now put you quite at ease my dear

[1819–22]   3 p 12mo   BM(Bar)
from Elizabeth, Lady Templetown
I find my dear Me. D'arblay that it would

[9 Mar 1819–22]   3 p 12mo BM(Bar)
from Elizabeth, Lady Templetown
It is not indifferent to me the getting a line

[1819–22]   3 p 12mo   BM(Bar)
from Elizabeth, Lady Templetown
You cannot conceive how I am disappointed

1819, *continued*

[1819–22]   2 p 12mo   BM(Bar)
from Elizabeth, Lady Templetown
Tell me dearest Mᵉ d'Arblay if I may hope to

[1819–23]   3 p 8vo   NYPL(B)
from Princess Mary
Pray thank dear Lady Templetown for her

[1819–23]   1 p 12mo   NYPL(B)
from Princess Sophia
Mary promised me to ask You & send to know

[1819–28]   1 p 8vo   NYPL(B)
from Princess Augusta
I must beg you to make my Excuses to Lady

[1819–28]   1 p 8vo   NYPL(B)
from Princess Augusta
Will you have the kindness to dine with *us*

[1819–28]   1 p 4to   BM(Bar)
from   ?
On after having written the inclos'd, the

[1819–28]   1 p 8vo   NYPL(B)
from Princess Mary
Sophia desires me to ask you if you will come

29 May [1819–28]   1 p 8vo
from Princess Mary   NYPL(B)
<Inchanted> to see you dearest d'Arblay &

[1819–28]   4 p 4to   NYPL(B)
from Princess Mary
Your friendly offer & kind letter deserves my

2 Feb [1819–28]   3 p 8vo
from Princess Sophia   NYPL(B)
Yesterday Evening brought me your kindest

1 July [1819–28]   3 p 12mo
from Princess Sophia   NYPL(B)
I am indeed *more* than pleased in the kindness

16 Aug [1819–28]   2 p 12mo
from Princess Sophia   NYPL(B)
Dear & kind Friend! The coast being clear of

<20> Aug [1819–28]   1 p 12mo
from Princess Sophia   NYPL(B)
Dear & kindest of Friends I hope it is the *Sun*

25 Oct [1819–28]   2 p 8vo
from Princess Sophia   NYPL(B)
My dear kind Friend I feel asured no one has

[1819–28]   2 p 12mo   NYPL(B)
from Princess Sophia
I am vexed beyond measure dearest kindest

22 [1819–28]   1 p 12mo   NYPL(B)
from Princess Sophia
Tuesday is the day my dear friend so I hope

<5> [1819–28]   1 p 12mo   NYPL(B)
from Princess Sophia
My dearest Soul! Let me know how you are, &

[1819–28]   1 p 12 mo   NYPL(B)
from Princess Sophia
<Let> me know how you are *dearest kindest*

22 [1819–28]   2 p 12mo   NYPL(B)
from Princess Sophia
May I say *Thursday* Evening dearest dear

[1819–28]   3 p 12mo   NYPL(B)
from Princess Sophia
My dearest kind Friend! Illness *alone* has made

near Easter [1819–28]   1 p 8vo   Osb
[to Princess Sophia]
O yes! sweet Princess, Yes! Good Friday

[1819–28]   2 p 12mo   NYPL(B)
from Princess Sophia
I am in a state of distraction dearest dear Mʳˢ.

[1819–28]   2 p 12mo   NYPL(B)
from Princess Sophia
Dear & kind Friend — My sister being still in

12 [1819–28]   3 p 12mo   NYPL(B)
from Princess Sophia
My dearest kind friend! You will say is this

1820

21–22 Jan copy 2 p 4to NYPL(B)
to Frederica Locke
— And while this alarm for Alex's health has

25 Jan   draft   2 p 4to   Osb
to William Wilberforce
Nearly on the commencement of the dread
also   copy   2p 4to   NYPL(B)

10 Feb   copy   2 p 4to   NYPL(B)
from William Wilberforce
Tho' a complaint in my Eyes allows me to

17 Feb   copy   3 p 4to   NYPL(B)
to Frederica Locke
No one, my dearest Friend, can live — and

17 Feb   3 p 4to   NYPL(B)
from Marie de Maisonneuve
J'ai été bien touchée et bien intéressée

23 Feb   8 p 4to   NYPL(B)
from Princess Elizabeth
Tho Your letter arrived dear Madame d'Arblay

[14 Apr 1820]   1 p 8vo   NYPL(B)
from Princess Mary
Will you come to me *tomorrow* at *three o'clock*

17 Apr   7 p 4to   NYPL(B)
from Princess Elizabeth
Our letters have crossed my dear Madame

[18 Apr 1820]   receipt   1 p cut fol
from Thomas King   NYPL(B)
Received April 18th. 1820 — of Madame

24 Apr   1 p 8vo   Osb
to Thomas Payne
Madame d'Arblay troubles Mr. Payne with a

28 Apr   2 p 4to   NYPL(B)
from John Kaye
I must, I fear, have appeared very negligent

30 Apr [1820]   3 p 8vo   NYPL(B)
from George Owen Cambridge
It would not be doing justice to my own

[Apr 1820]   3 p 8vo   NYPL(B)
from Sarah Baker
You *must* indulge my impetuous wishes

3 May   5 p 4to   NYPL(B)
from Princess Elizabeth
Happy as Your letters always make me, my

10–12 May   4 p 4to   NYPL(B)
to EBB
How kind — how very kind, my dear Hetty,

7 June   copy   1 p 4to   NYPL(B)
to Frederica Locke
All London now is wild about the newly

19 June   7 p 4to   NYPL(B)
from Princess Elizabeth
A very bad evening (which often is a <trial>

[June 1820]   2 p 8vo   BM(Bar)
from Frederica Locke
I hasten to confirm, my beloved Friend,

3 JY 1820 pmk   6 p 4to   NYPL(B)
to GMAPWaddington
I had not answered your preceding Letter, my

3 AU pmk [1820]   4 p 4to   NYPL(B)
to EBB
True Comfort — I may add, with Truth, also,

15 Aug   copy   4 p 4to   NYPL(B)
to Frederica Locke
How long it seems — "Seems, Madam! nay

22 Aug   9 p 4to   NYPL(B)
from Princess Elizabeth
To prove to You the pleasure Your letters ever

Aug   3 p 8vo   BM(Bar)
from SHB
My poor Alex came in Dearest Sister miserably

3 Sept [1820]   3 p 8vo   BM(Bar)
from Lady Keith
Will be glad to hear we are alive here & I can

<20>–25 Oct   4 p 4to   NYPL(B)
to EBB
My Letter-Conscience, my dearest Hetty,

23 Oct [1820 or 1826]   1 p 8vo
from Princess Mary   NYPL(B)
Will you come & see me to day

1 Nov [1820]   1 p 12mo   BM(Bar)
from Elizabeth, Lady Templetown
I cannot help sending you a little of the

[6 Nov 1820]   2 p 8vo   NYPL(B)
to CFBt
I trouble you I hope & trust for NOTHING,

[7–12 Nov]   3 p 8vo   NYPL(B)
to CBFB
How sorry I am to have made known my

28 Nov   16 p 4to   BM(Bar)
to EBB
How kind is my *dear Etty* to so liberally

2 DE 1820 pmk   draft   2 p 4to
                                 NYPL(B)
to Marquis de Lally-Tollendal
O M. de Lally! dear, excellent, benevolent &

2 Dec [1820]   4 p 8vo   BM(Bar)
from Frances Bowdler
What do you think I have done, (or rather am

1820, continued

4 Dec   9 p 4to   NYPL(B)
from Princess Elizabeth
After having finished a long letter to dear

4 Dec [1820]   4 p 4to   NYPL(B)
from Lady Keith
All you say of Alexander is very just my own

7 Dec   4 p 4to   BM(Bar)
from SHB
I take a sheet of letter, not of note paper,

15 Dec   4 p 4to   NYPL(B)
to HLTP
Now, at last Dear Madam with a real pen I

1821

10 Jan [1821]   2 p 8vo   NYPL(B)
from Marie de Maisonneuve
bien chere amie seulement encore un petit

18 Jan   4 p 4to   NYPL(B)
from HLTP
Dear Madame D'Arblay was very considerate

25 Jan [1821]   4 p 4to   NYPL(B)
from Lady Keith
However great the disappointment my Dear

[27 Jan 1821]   4 p 4to   PML
to JB
My dear Brother will think I have been very

6 Feb   4 p 4to   NYPL(B)
to HLTP
You would be re-paid, Dear Madam, if I still

6 ⟨Feb⟩   1 p 12mo   NYPL(B)
from Princess Augusta
Will you kindly come to me tomorrow

6 Feb   7 p 4to   NYPL(B)
from Marie de Maisonneuve
j'aurois voulu commencer l'année par

10–12 Feb   4 p 4to   NYPL(B)
to EBB
Great pain has — I am sure — been spared

[16 Feb]   4 p 8vo   NYPL(B)
to CBFB
I well know how my dearest Charlotte &

25 Feb   4 p 4to   BM(Bar)
from EBB
Oh my Dear Fanny we are sisters in affliction

28 Feb-1 Mar   4 p 4to   BM(Bar)
from EBB
Thanks a thousand times my kind hearted

4 Mar   8 p 4to   NYPL(B)
from Princess Elizabeth
It was out of my power to write by this days

15 Mar   4 p 4to   NYPL(B)
from HLTP
I feel quite happy in being able to reply to

2 Apr   3 p 8vo   Osb
to CPB
The sight of my hand — At last! — will lead

4 Apr   3 p 4to   BM(Bar)
from EBB
To *you* my Dearest Fanny deeply grieved &

7 Apr   4 p 8vo   NYPL(B)
to CBFB
I was just going to execute the melancholy

14 Apr   ?   AECB31
to Sarah (Burney) Payne
Accept my warmest and kindest wishes in

24 pmk [Apr 1821]   4 p 4to   NYPL(B)
to CBFB
I ought to have written to my dearest

28 AP 1821 pmk   3 p 4to   BM(Bar)
from SHB
I was very much in hopes that I should still

[Apr 1821]   3 p 8vo   BM(Bar)
from Frederica Locke
My own beloved Friend will want to hear that

2 MY 1821 pmk   4 p 4to   NYPL(B)
to CBFB
My Charlotte — my dearest Charlotte how I

[post 2 May 1821]   2 p 8vo   BM(Bar)
from Sophia (Thrale) Hoare
Many Thanks to you my dearest Mad^me

12 May   4 p 4to   NYPL(B)
from Princess Elizabeth
The post is gone, & I am still in Your debt my

26 May [1821]   4 p 8vo   BM(Bar)
from Frances Bowdler
Well but now, my ever dear Friend,

12 June   2 p 8vo   NYPL(B)
from Harriot Wilson
The sympathetic Interest wch. you so kindly

24 June   1 p 8vo   NYPL(B)
from Princess Augusta
If you are willing to come to me may I hope

27 June [1821]   3 p 8vo   BM(Bar)
from Lady Keith
What can I say my dear Friend but that I most

19 July   1 p 8vo   NYPL(B)
from Charles Wesley
M^r. Charles Wesley's best Comp^{ts} to Mad^{me}

21 July 2 drafts   2 p 8vo   NYPL(B)
to Charles Wesley
Made. d'Arblay regrets her inability to aid the

30 July   4 p 8vo   NYPL(B)
to CBFB
I am so sorry for this melancholy termination

1–5 Aug   8 p 8vo   NYPL(B)
from Marie de Maisonneuve
enfin me voila, < > Ma bien chere

7 Aug   1 p 8vo   NYPL(B)
to Edward Foss
Madame d'Arblay would be ungrateful not to

10 Aug   4 p 8vo   Osb
to CPB
I am sure I need not tell you, my dear Charles,

[12] Aug   1 p 4to   NYPL(B)
from JB
On Friday (is not that the day on which I

14 Aug   1 p 4to   NYPL(B)
from Sarah (Payne) Burney
We have just received from the Admiralty

[c 14 Aug 1821]   3 p 4to   PML
to JB & Sarah (Payne) Burney
My dear Admiral! — / My noble Admiral! /

[post 14 Aug 1821]   2 p 8vo   PML
to JB
If your present run of Uniform expenses would

17 Aug   2 p 4to   NYPL(B)
from JB
I was tolerably diligent for me. I received

20 Aug   4 p 4to   NYPL(B)
to AA
I must set aside alike Disappointment at your

21 Aug   4 p 4to   NYPL(B)
to CFBt
This is truly my Charlotte — my Charlotte

26 Aug   4 p 8vo   Osb
to CPB
My wish, my dear Charles, is *yours*, now I see

28 Aug   5 p 8vo & 4to   PML
to JB
What is your opinion, my dear Brother, of all

31 Aug [1821]   4 p 4to   NYPL(B)
from EBB
How sincerely do I thank you My Dearest

3 Sept   4 p 4to   NYPL(B)
to AA
You have forgotten to give me any address,

3 Sept   8 p 4to   NYPL(B)
to EBB
If I read with peculiar satisfaction, which

4 Sept [1821]   4 p 8vo   PML
to JB
If This is not provokuss, I know not what is!

6 Sept   4 p 8vo   NYPL(B)
from Marie de Maisonneuve
Ma bien chere très-chere amie, un petit mot

12 SP 1821 pmk   1 p 4to   Osb
to CPB
Alex — to my great regret, is alone — his

17 Sept   4 p 4to   NYPL(B)
to CBFB
At length, my best & dearest Charlotte, I think

21 SP 1821 pmk   3 p 4to   NYPL(B)
from Edward Jacob
I regret that being at present resident in the

22 Sept   10 p 4to   NYPL(B)
from Princess Elizabeth
You must indeed think me lost my dear

25 Sept   3 p 8vo   Osb
to CPB
I am very sorry I missed seeing you this

1821, continued

10 Oct   2 p 4to   Osb
from Gasparo Pacchierotti
That *Pen* — which after so glorious & so long

21 Oct   8 p 4to   NYPL(B)
to EBB
Your *Mind*, my dearest Esther, was always

also   copy   10 p 4to   NYPL(B)

2⟨4⟩ Oct   4 p 8vo   NYPL(B)
to CFBt
I am so pleased at your return, my dearest

19 NO 1821 pmk   3 p 4to   PML
to Sarah (Payne) Burney & Sarah
(Burney) Payne
Oh what a stroke! — my Brother — my dear

20 Nov   2 p 4to   NYPL(B)
from EBB
I cannot my Dearest Fanny describe to you

21 Nov   7 p 4to   NYPL(B)
from Frances (Phillips) Raper
Although I have little hope of being able to

[22 Nov 1821]   2 p 4to   NYPL(B)
from Sarah (Payne) Burney
My heart is penetrated with the warmest

23 Nov   4 p 4to   NYPL(B)
to EBB
I cannot — My dear — & alas more than ever

[25 Nov-18 Dec 1821]   4 p 4to
to AA   NYPL(B)
You know, then, my poor Alex, the fatal blow

26 NO 1821 pmk   4 p 8vo   PML
to Sarah (Payne) Burney
I will be with you certainly my dear Mrs

27 Nov-1 Dec [1821]   4 p 4to
from CBFB   BM(Bar)
Alas my dearest sister, little did we think we

29 Nov   3 p 4to   NYPL(B)
from Marie de Maisonneuve
avec quelle anxiété, nous attendons

10 Dec [1821]   3 p 8vo   BM(Bar)
from Elizabeth, Lady Templetown
Do not imagine my dear Madam that I have

11 Dec   4 p 4to   NYPL(B)
to CBFB
Ah, take care of yourself, my dearest

12–14 Dec   6 p 4to   NYPL(B)
to EBB
Your Letter has found me still here, my

25 Dec   ?   AECB31
to Sarah (Payne) Burney
. . . Are you surprised I say Mrs. Admiral

1821   2 p 4to   NYPL(B)
to Frederica Locke
How is my beloved Friend? and how *doing*?

[1821?]   5 p 8vo & 4to   BM(Bar)
from Amelia (Locke) Angerstein
I will not again my beloved M^rs d'Arblay

[1821]   4 p 8vo   NYPL(B)
from Sarah Baker
I cannot resist the opportunity of sending a

[post 1821]   7 p 8vo   BM(Bar)
from Lady Keith
I had always gladly imagined that here I was

[1821–23]   2 p 8vo mutilated
to Frederica Locke   NYPL(B)
of my Alex — Sympathy [cut] Alex is wild to

[1821–23]   4 p 8vo   NYPL(B)
to Frederica Locke
Will This billet also meet a Shake hand on the

1822

2 Jan   7 p 4to   NYPL(B)
from Princess Elizabeth
May be You think that I am dead my dear

22 Jan   4 p 8vo   NYPL(B)
from Marie de Maisonneuve
Votre si chere lettre finie le 15

23 Jan   3 p 8vo   NYPL(B)
from Harriot Wilson
I take the Liberty of forwarding you my

25 Jan   4 p 4to   NYPL(B)
to EBB
Would you not have been a little astonished,

27 Jan [1822]   6 p 8vo & 4to
to CBFB   NYPL(B)
How vexed I am, my dearest Charlotte, thus,

29 Jan-13 Mar   12 p 4to   NYPL(B)
to EBB
I so delight in your plan, my dearest Esther

4 Feb   4 p 4to   NYPL(B)
to AA
So the Letter from *Mr. Tit* — which I

14 Feb   4 p 8vo   Osb
to CPB
Not very gaily I have to request you will be so

14 Feb   3 p 4to   Osb
from William Wilberforce
For so I may be allowed to address a Lady to
also   copy   3 p 4to   NYPL(B)

15 Feb   3 p 4to   NYPL(B)
from Marie de Maisonneuve
c'est ici Ma bien chere amie, que j'ai reçu

2 Mar   1 p 12mo   NYPL(B)
from GMAPWaddington
All that I could bear to do, has been to remove

3 Mar   8 p 4to   NYPL(B)
from Princess Elizabeth
This evening I was favoured with Your letter

8 Mar   2 p 4to   NYPL(B)
from Harriot Wilson
I beg to assure you I have this Inst received

9 Mar   3 p 4to   NYPL(B)
from Marie de Maisonneuve
depuis mon retour de Lys il y a plus de 15

18 Mar   2 p 4to   NYPL(B)
from Marie de Maisonneuve
qu'il m'est triste, Ma bien chere amie, de ne

25 Mar   3 p 8vo   NYPL(B)
to AA
Still no *Alex*! / And no Letter! — / What upon

[post 25?] Mar   4 p 4to   NYPL(B)
to CFBt
No Alex — I avail myself therefore of your

28 Mar [1822]   1 p 4to   NYPL(B)
from Marie de Maisonneuve
Ma bien chere amie, Alex a été au Lys

17 Apr   2 p 8vo   NYPL(B)
from Marie de Maisonneuve
Nous attendions avec la plus vive impatience

[27 Apr *or* 4 May]   4 p 4to   NYPL(B)
to CFBt
The kind attention of the excellent

7 May   4 p 4to   NYPL(B)
to EBB
O Yes — my dear*est* Esther, the very idea of

17 May   2 p 4to   NYPL(B)
from Marie de Maisonneuve
j'apprends, Ma bien chere amie, que M^r

6 June   4 p 4to   NYPL(B)
from Marie de Maisonneuve
une occasion se présente Ma bien chere

25 JU 1822 pmk   3 p 4to   NYPL(B)
to CFBt
To resist so kind a proposal of dear Mrs.

4 JY 1822 pmk   4 p 8vo   NYPL(B)
to CFBt
Very vexed am I to miss you, my sweet

1 Aug   8 p 4to   NYPL(B)
from Princess Elizabeth
I will begin directly my dear Madame d'Arblay

15 Aug   1 p 8vo   BYU
to Anne (Phipps), Lady Murray
I have long been internally persuaded that to

21 Aug   4 p 8vo   NYPL(B)
to CBFB
I am very uneasy now for News of my dearest

21 Aug [1822]   1 p 12mo   NYPL(B)
from Princess Sophia
Is Mrs Locke at Eliot Vale & w^d You like

28 Aug   4 p 4to   NYPL(B)
from Marie de Maisonneuve
J'avois donc bien raison! Ma bien chere

4 Sept   1 p 4to   NYPL(B)
from Miss? H Haley
When I had the honour of speaking to you this

7 Sept   4 p 4to   NYPL(B)
to EBB
Long I thought your silence, my dearest

1822, *continued*

22 Sept   3 p 8vo   BM(Bar)
from Elizabeth, Lady Templetown
Whenever you are endeavouring to forego

24 Sept   3 p 4to   NYPL(B)
from Marie-Alexandre Lenoir
Qu'ai-je fait pour meriter la nouvelle preuve

10 Oct   4 p 4to   NYPL(B)
to AA
Why my Alex! — why how is *This here*? Why

11–14 Oct   11 p 4to   NYPL(B)
from Princess Elizabeth
You shall have a beginning but when You will

12 Oct   4 p 4to   NYPL(B)
from Marie de Maisonneuve
Votre Gros et si intéressant Paquet

14–17 Oct   4 p 4to   NYPL(B)
to EBB
Has my dear Hetty thought me lost? — Lost,

18 Oct   8 p 4to   NYPL(B)
from Princess Elizabeth
Tho You are in my debt dear Madame

30 Oct   3 p 4to   NYPL(B)
from Marie de Maisonneuve
C'est encore Mr Cardon de Sandran qui veut

9 Nov [1822]   4 p 8vo   BM(Bar)
from Amelia (Locke) Angerstein
I cannot bear to delay a single day,

10 Nov   1 p 8vo   NYPL(B)
from John Julius Angerstein
Many thanks for your kind communication, I

29 Nov [1822]   3 p 12mo   BM(Bar)
from Elizabeth, Lady Templetown
At length I have the power my truly dear Me

11–24 Dec   4 p 4to   NYPL(B)
to EBB
I have so much to say to my dear Esther, that

24 Dec   4 p 8vo   NYPL(B)
from Frederica Locke
Mr. Vansittart & Mr John Angerstein came

24 Dec [1822]   4 p 12mo   BM(Bar)
from Elizabeth, Lady Templetown
There is a great deal (indeed *every line*) of

26 Dec   3 p 12mo   NYPL(B)
from Frederica Locke
My dearly loved Friend my Son George called

28 Dec   4 p 4to   BM(Bar)
to Frederica Locke
Indeed, my dearest Friend, this is too much

30 Dec   4 p 4to   NYPL(B)
to CFBt
I am glad of this resistless Spur not to let the

[Dec 1822?]   2 p 12mo   BM(Bar)
from Amelia (Locke) Angerstein
I cannot refuse myself the pleasure of telling

[1822–23]   3 p 8vo   BM(Bar)
from Sophia (Thrale) Hoare
I promised to give you the Earliest Intelligence

[Sept 1822-Sept 1823]   4 p 8vo
to Frederica Locke   NYPL(B)
In waiting & waiting for opportunity — by

[Sept 1822-Sept 1823]   4 p 8vo
to Frederica Locke   NYPL(B)
I have obeyed the injunctions of the sweetest

[1822–23?]   2 p 4to   NYPL(B)
from Harriot Wilson
I have this inst. been favoured by your kind

21 May [1822–32]   4 p 12mo
from Princess Sophia   NYPL(B)
How can I find words adequate to my feelings

[1822–32]   4 p 12mo   NYPL(B)
from Princess Sophia
My dearest Mrs d'Arblay! The sight of your

25 Nov [post 1822]   3 p 12mo
from Princess Sophia   NYPL(B)
Dearest kind Friend! delicacy alone has kept

[post 1822?]   2 p 12mo   NYPL(B)
from Princess Sophia
Do not I pray you *call this* a bad *omen* but the

[post 1822?]   1 p 12mo   NYPL(B)
from Princess Sophia
Are you afraid of coming out this Evening?

⟨8⟩ Apr [post 1822?]   4 p 12mo
from Princess Sophia   NYPL(B)
I am quite distressed My dear and beloved

30 Dec [post 1822?]   4 p 12mo
from Princess Sophia   NYPL(B)
Dearest dear & kindest of Friends How can I

10 Feb [post 1822?]   2 p 12mo
from Princess Sophia   NYPL(B)
Your welcome note has indeed cheered me!

19 Mar [post 1822]   3 p 8vo
from Princess Sophia   NYPL(B)
My joy is inexpressible! at having at length

28 Nov [pre 1823]   2 p 4to   NYPL(B)
from Elizabeth, Lady Templetown
It is with grief of heart dearest Mrs. d'Arblay

1823

5 Jan   4 p 8vo   Osb
to CPB
I could answer for Alex no sooner, as only last

19–27 Jan   4 p 4to   NYPL(B)
to EBB
Our good & dear Edward will have accounted

29–30 Jan   4 p 4to   NYPL(B)
to CBFB
I hope you are now safe landed in your

30 Jan   3 p 8vo   NYPL(B)
from Marie de Maisonneuve
Ma bien chere amie, votre dernière lettre

2 Feb [1823]   1 p 8vo   NYPL(B)
from Princess Mary
I came to town yesterday & long to see you if

17 Feb [1823]   1 p fragment
from Princess Sophia   NYPL(B)
My dear Mme. D'Arblay? Are *you agreeable?*

18 Feb   1 p 8vo   NYPL(B)
from Princess Mary
Will you come to me Thursday evening at

19 Feb [1823]   4 p 4to   BM(Bar)
from Lady Keith
I have just received your kind Letter begun

29 Feb-10 Mar   12 p 4to   NYPL(B)
to EBB
I must needs hope I shall never live to hear of
also   copy   10 p 4to & scrap   NYPL(B)

29 Mar [1823]   4 p 12mo   BM(Bar)
from Elizabeth, Lady Templetown
I cannot go on another day without an anxious

[post Mar 1823]   ½ p fol   NYPL(B)
from Marie de Maisonneuve
Ce Paquet était tout prêt mais non parti

3 Apr [1823]   4 p 4to   BM(Bar)
from Lady Keith
We have been too well accustomed to each

[post 3 Apr 1823]   4 p 4to   NYPL(B)
to CFBt
Poor — excellent Mrs. C. Cambridge! to

9 Apr [1823?]   1 p 8vo   NYPL(B)
from Princess Mary
I am to be all alone to Morrow eveng if you

12 Apr [1823]   5 p 8vo & 4to   BM(Bar)
from Elizabeth, Lady Templetown
I am anxious to take up my trembling Pen

[post 12 Apr 1823]   4 p 8vo   BM(Bar)
from Elizabeth, Lady Templetown
You will think I am never *satisfied*

[post 12 Apr 1823]   4 p 12mo
                              BM(Bar)
from Elizabeth, Lady Templetown
Your very *charming* note dearest M d'Arblay

⟨22 AP 1823⟩ pmk   1 p 4to   NYPL(B)
to CFBt
staying till Monday, we shall arrive at Night,

1 May   5 p 8vo   NYPL(B)
from Marie de Maisonneuve
Votre lettre Ecrite en 9obre Mars et avril

6 MY 1823 pmk   4 p 4to   NYPL(B)
to EBB
Heartily as I thank you, my kind Esther, for

10 May [1823]   3 p 8vo   BM(Bar)
from Elizabeth, Lady Templetown
It is not my dearest Me. d'Arblay to get you

13 May   2 p 4to   BM(Bar)
from EBB
Your generosity nay yr liberality in regard

25–26 May   5 p 4to   NYPL(B)
from Princess Elizabeth
Well my dear Madame d'Arblay Your

21 June   4 p 4to   NYPL(B)
to EBB
What a regale, my dearest Esther! I am *at*

1823, continued

2–3 July [1823] 4 p 4to NYPL(B)
to CBFB
I begin my Letter with those emphatic — &

[25 July 1823] 1 p 12mo BM(Bar)
from GMAPWaddington
Tell me how you are my dearest Mme. d'Arblay

26 July 8 p 8vo NYPL(B)
from Marie de Maisonneuve
enfin Ma bien chere amie, me voila a vous

26 July [1823] 4 p 8vo NYPL(B)
from Henriette (Guignot de Soulignac)
  de Maurville
une bonne occasion se presente Madame

26 July 4 p 8vo BM(Bar)
from William Wilberforce
I am conscious that it may seem an

7 Aug [1823] 4 p 4to NYPL(B)
from Sarah (Burney) Payne
The first moment of leisure since my arrival

7 Aug [1823] 1 p 12mo BM(Bar)
from GMAPWaddington
My dearest Madame d'Arblay — Harriet

8 Aug copy 3 p 4to NYPL(B)
to Frederica Locke
I have spent two evenings, since I wrote last,

22 Aug 2 p 4to NYPL(B)
to EBB
Most fortunately — & by a chance that never

25 AU 1823 pmk 4 p 4to NYPL(B)
to CBFB
I may compare myself now to my poor Alex,

[pre Sept 1823] 4 p 8vo NYPL(B)
to Frederica Locke
I will not wait to the end of the Week to write

[pre Sept 1823] 1 p 12mo BM(Bar)
from Elizabeth, Lady Templetown
My brains are so confused & so be-

[pre Sept 1823?] 3 p 12mo BM(Bar)
from Elizabeth, Lady Templetown
What a day has this been! & what

18 [Sept or Dec 1823?] 3 p 8vo
        NYPL(B)
from Henriette (Guignot de Soulignac)
  de Maurville
nous avons eu Madame de grandes et vives

19 Sept 3 p fol BM(Bar)
from Lady Keith
As I have an Opportunity of writing from

2⟨0⟩ S⟨ ⟩ pmk [1823] 4 p 8vo
to CBFB   NYPL(B)
A thousand thanks for this *Volunteer* Bulletin,

22 Sept 1 p 4to NYPL(B)
from Marie de Maisonneuve
il faut Ma bien chere amie que je ferme

29 Sept–16 Oct 4 p 4to NYPL(B)
to EBB
But not a Goose Act is it to write to my

29–30 Sept 4 p 8vo NYPL(B)
to Frederica Locke
I feel very sure that not to me is left the

29 Sept 4 p 8vo NYPL(B)
from Arthur Percy Upton
My sister Sophia has desired me to acquaint

[post Sept 1823] 4 p 8vo BM(Bar)
from Sophia Upton
I am too much impressed with your kindness

[1 Oct 1823] 2 p 4to NYPL(B)
to CBFB
I thought — I flattered myself, my dearest

3 Oct 3 p 8vo NYPL(B)
from Marie de Maisonneuve
Ma bien chere Amie, ceci n'est point une

Oct copy 2 p 4to NYPL(B)
to Frederica Locke
I have received a very kind letter from Miss

22 Nov 8 p 8vo NYPL(B)
from Marie de Maisonneuve
je ne sais Ma bien chere amie, quelle réflexion

9 DE 1823 pmk 4 p 4to NYPL(B)
to CFBt
A model of Epistolary kindness is my dearest

[c 16]-23 Dec 4 p 4to NYPL(B)
to EBB
How I wish, my dearest Hetty, You had half

21 Dec [1823] 4 p 4to BM(Bar)
from Lady Keith
As I have an opportunity of sending to

[Dec 1823] 4 p 8vo NYPL(B)
to Frederica Locke
I would not, my dearest Friend, execute your

[Dec 1823]   2 p 8vo   NYPL(B)
to GMAPWaddington
My warm & truly affectionate good wishes &

[1823]   4 p 8vo   NYPL(B)
from Amelia (Locke) Angerstein
It is from this dear roof, under which I am

18 Dec [1823–24]   4 p 8vo   NYPL(B)
from Amelia (Locke) Angerstein
It is at the side of the son whom the Almighty

1824

6 Jan   4 p 4to   NYPL(B)
to AA
Come to *ME*, my dearest Alex! come to *ME* I

9 Jan   2 p 4to   NYPL(B)
to AA
In the midst of the wretchedness I

12 JA 1824 pmk   4 p 4to   NYPL(B)
to AA
You gave me great comfort, my Alex, by

14 Jan [1824]   4 p 4to   NYPL(B)
to AA
What an interesting Letter is this of Tuesday!

19 Jan   2 p 8vo   NYPL(B)
to JCBTM
Will my dear Julia oblige me with a few lines

27–29 Jan   8 p 4to   NYPL(B)
to EBB
How sorry will be my dearest Esther to hear

31 Jan–2 Feb [1824]   4 p 4to
with Edward Jacob to AA   NYPL(B)
After some delay Mr Lockhart wrote to me

5 Feb [1824]   2 p 12mo   NYPL(B)
from Princess Sophia
I am *to blame* I fully admit for my long

11 Feb   4 p 4to   NYPL(B)
with John Croft to AA
The first instalment of the Disworth <fine>

[c 23 Feb 1824]   4 p 4to   BM(Bar)
to JCBTM & CFBt
I thank you for your letter, & I address this

1 Mar   4 p 4to   BM(Bar)
from Frances (Sayer) de Pougens
Your charming spirits your delightful vivacity

9 Mar   4 p 4to   BM(Bar)
from Lady Keith
I have just received your kind Letter my dear

[31 Mar 1824]   4 p 8vo   BM(Bar)
from George Owen Cambridge
So I find my Dear Madame that the secret is

[Mar 1824]   4 p 8vo   NYPL(B)
to CFBt
The How do do of a moment is always better

[Mar 1824]   4 p 4to   NYPL(B)
to CFBt
My dearest Charlotta will enclose the enclosed

[post Mar 1824]   7 p 8vo   NYPL(B)
to CFBt
Not to write a word to my dear & generous

12 Apr   1 p 8vo   NPG
from Princess Augusta
Will you kindly come to me tomorrow

18 Apr   11 p 8vo   NYPL(B)
from Marie de Maisonneuve
Que vous êtes bonne et aimable Ma bien chere

21 Apr   2 p 8vo   NYPL(B)
from Henriette (Guignot de Soulignac)
     de Maurville
Le general Stapfort qui devait partir

[pre 23 Apr 1824]   4 p 4to   NYPL(B)
to CFBt
I know not when I have read a Letter that has

23–25 Apr   4 p 4to   McG
to EBB
Does my dearest Esther think me lost

27 Apr–1 May   8 p 4to   NYPL(B)
from Princess Elizabeth
Your very interesting letter I received too late

24 May   2 p 4to   BM(Bar)
from AA
I solemnly request you to be so kind as to make

1–5 June   4 p 4to   NYPL(B)
to CFBt
My pleasure is so very great at the unexpected

1824, continued

10–[16] June   4 p 4to   NYPL(B)
to EBB
Little Grace (Epistolary) as I know you allow

12 June   3 p 4to   BM(Bar)
from George Owen Cambridge
I had hoped to find a leisure half hour

17 June   pmk 1824   4 p 4to
to AA   NYPL(B)
As this Letter, in all human probability, will

17 June   2 p 8vo   NYPL(B)
from Marie de Maisonneuve
Ma bien chere amie, Votre bonne lettre la

25 June   2 p 8vo   NYPL(B)
from Marie de Maisonneuve
Ma bien chere amie, Votre cher Alex nous

1–8 July   4 p 4to   NYPL(B)
to EBB
Can I *know* there is something I could

5 July   4 p 4to mutilated   NYPL(B)
to CBFB
I was truly eager for news of you, my ever

11 July   3 p 4to   BM(Bar)
from Lady Keith
I have luckily an Opportunity of writing

12 July   2 p 4to   NYPL(B)
to CFBt
My sweetly dear Charlotta must not be worried

[16? July 1824]   2 p 8vo   NYPL(B)
to GMAPWaddington
There still you do me justice, my still — & I

19 July   3 p 4to   BM(Bar)
from GMAPWaddington
I do indeed rejoice at Alexander's appointment

1 Aug   1 p 8vo   Hyde
to Caroline Anna Moore
Madame d'Arblay presents her best

18 Aug   4 p 4to   NYPL(B)
from Marie de Maisonneuve
j'ai reçu bien maintenant Ma bien chere amie

[pre 31 Aug]   2 p 8vo   NYPL(B)
to CFBt
This old Note must needs go, my dearest

31 Aug   3 p 8vo   PML
to Sarah (Payne) Burney
Will you kindly relieve me, my dear & kind

Aug–2 Sept   4 p 4to   NYPL(B)
to CFBt
I am quite *consternated* — in the phrase of

1–7 Sept   4 p 4to mutilated   NYPL(B)
to EBB
To begin with what is nearest & dearest to me

12 Sept [1824]   4 p 8vo   BM(Bar)
from Frances Bowdler
Your really precious letter reached me

24 Sept   8 p 4to   NYPL(B)
from Princess Elizabeth
How to thank You my dear Madame d'Arblay

28 Sept [1824]   2 p 8vo   NYPL(B)
from Sarah (Payne) Burney
Your letter of enquiry was brought to me

4 Oct   4 p 4to   NYPL(B)
to CBFB
How long it is since I have seen the hand, —

8 Oct   2 p 12mo   NYPL(B)
from Princess Sophia
Mousey Mousey Mousey! Methinks I will try

11 Oct   copy excerpt   1 p 4to
to Frederica Locke   NYPL(B)
— Yesterday brought a letter of great grief to

14 Oct   4 p 4to   NYPL(B)
to CFBt
The circular *project* — never ending, because

15 Oct   1 p 4to   NYPL(B)
from Princess Sophia
My dear & kind Friend! If Sunday after

28 Oct [1824?]   1 p 12mo   NPG
from Princess Sophia
My dear kind Friend! Are you free tomorrow

12–17 Nov   3 p 4to   NYPL(B)
from Marie de Maisonneuve
Ma bien chere amie qu'il y a long tems que

17 Nov [1824]   1 p 12mo   Osb
from Princess Augusta
Mary and I are at my House in the stable yard

[post 17 Nov 1824]   1 p 12mo   Osb
from Princess Augusta
Will you indulge your two old friends at St

22 Nov   4 p 4to   NYPL(B)
to EBB
How very long it is since I have heard from

Nov   copy   6 p 4to   NYPL(B)
to Frederica Locke
I have missed my Bulletin to my beloved

3 Dec   1 p 12mo   NYPL(B)
from Princess Sophia
Dearest kind Friend! Silence has partly arisen

9 Dec [1824]   4 p 8vo   NYPL(B)
from Henriette (Guignot de Soulignac)
     de Maurville
Le general Stapfort part pour Londres

17 Dec [1824?]   1 p fragment
from Princess Sophia   NYPL(B)
Could you come to me Tomorrow Eving [sic]

18 Dec   3 p 8vo   Osb
from Princess Augusta
I came home today with Dear Mary who

1824   copy extract?   1 p 4to
to   ?   NYPL(B)
— I have, of late, been frequently led to see

[1824?]   4 p 8vo   NYPL(B) & McG
to CFBt
[1st leaf NYPL(B)] Not alone my Consent
[2nd leaf McG] Methods of cure, to prevent

[1824?]   4 p 4to   NYPL(B)
from Marie de Maisonneuve
Voici une occasion qui suppléera a ma

[1824]   2 p 12mo   NYPL(B)
from Princess Sophia
So this <dress> Shoe has found a foot to fit

[post 1824]   4 p 8vo   NYPL(B)
from AA
Your nice letter was a most agreeable welcome

[1824]   1 p 12mo   NYPL(B)
from Princess Sophia
Not having a line from You My kind & dear

[post 1824]   draft   4 p 8vo   Osb
to Longman & Rees
Memorandum for enquiry / What numbers

22   [post 1824]   2 p 12mo   Leeds
to Caroline Anna Moore
I received your appointment, my dear Mrs.

3 July [1824–28?]   2 p 8vo   NYPL(B)
from Charlotte (Jerningham), Lady
     Bedingfeld
If you wish to prove my Zeal, in yr Service

[1824–28]   3 p 4to   BM(Bar)
from Charlotte Fitzgerald, Baroness Ros
I was much disappointed not to have the

18 Aug [1824–29]   2 p 8vo   NYPL(B)
from Henriette (Guignot de Soulignac)
     de Maurville
j'avais cachette la lettre cy jointe

11 Apr [1824–29]   4 p 4to   NYPL(B)
from Henriette (Guignot de Soulignac)
     de Maurville
Votre aimable lettre Madame et chere amie

1825

10 Jan   3 p 4to   NYPL(B)
from Princess Augusta
I am sorry that it was out of my power to

11 Jan   1 p 8vo   BM(Bar)
from Henry Merrick Hoare
I was much obliged by your very kind note

18 Jan   2 p 4to   NYPL(B)
to CBFB
If already I was languishing for a baloon [sic]

23 Jan [1825]   4 p 8vo   BM(Bar)
from Frederica Locke
Indeed my beloved Friend it is very long

25 Jan   1 p 4to   NYPL(B)
from Princess Augusta
I should very much like to know if your Cold

6 Feb [1825]   2 p 8vo   NYPL(B)
from Marie de Maisonneuve
je trouve Made Victor faisent un paquet pour

25 Feb   1 p 4to   NYPL(B)
from Princess Augusta
I thank your <   > to cough <   >, that

[Feb 1825]   6 p 4to   NYPL(B)
to EBB
Never my dear Esther never was a Franked

1825, continued

[Mar 1825]   2 p 12mo   NYPL(B)
from Princess Sophia
Joy joy joy! Huzzah Huzzah Huzzah! what

6 AP 1825 pmk   4 p 4to   NYPL(B)
to CFBt
I am quite disheartened, my dearest Charlotte

7 Apr   4 p 4to   NYPL(B)
to CFBt
I am delighted to put an end to at least the

11 Apr   4 p 4to   NYPL(B)
to CFBt
The enclosed unreasonable demand & most

⟨1⟩ 2 MY 1825 pmk   4 p 4to
to CFBt   NYPL(B)
You will surely be as glad as I shall be, my

26 May   4 p 4to   NYPL(B)
from Marquis de Lally-Tollendal, Hen-
     riette de Maurville, and Elisabeth
     (de Lally-Tollendal) d'Aux
chère Madame, je puis encore me rappeler

4 JU 1825 pmk   4 p 4to   NYPL(B)
to CFBt
I earnestly recommend that at the very next

7 JU 1825 pmk   4 p 4to   NYPL(B)
to EBB
I should be in no speed to help my dear Esther

13 JU 1825 pmk   4 p 4to   NYPL(B)
to CFBt
Do not be utterly disgusted, my dearest

16–17 June   pmk 1825   7 p 4to
to CFBt   NYPL(B)
Now, then, the Mystery is unveiled, —

17 JU 1825 pmk   2 p scrap   NYPL(B)
to CBFB
My Eyes are now so injured by long ill usage,

24 June   4 p 4to   NYPL(B)
to CBFB
My own dear Charlottes' kind & quick reply

[c 24 June]   4 p 4to   NYPL(B)
to CFBt
With what a grace does my dear Charlotta

13 July   4 p 4to   NYPL(B)
from Marie de Maisonneuve
C'est le 2 de ce mois, que j'ai reçu

12 Aug   4 p 4to   NYPL(B)
to EBB
This MOMENT I have read your last Letter

18–20 Aug   4 p 8vo & 2 p 4to   NYPL(B)
to CFBt
To resist such kind pleading from a Pleader so

23 Aug   4 p 8vo   NYPL(B)
to CFBt
Another Commission, my dearest Charlotte —

23 Aug   8 p 4to   NYPL(B)
from Princess Elizabeth
It is too long that I have made you wait for an

[post 23 Aug]   draft   3 p 4to
to Princess Elizabeth   NYPL(B)
I never feel so ashamed as when Your R. H.

24 Aug [1825?]   4 p 12mo   NYPL(B)
from Princess Sophia
I opened your dear note in *fear* & *trembling*

11 Sept [1825]   4 p 8vo   NYPL(B)
from Harriet Bowdler
I cannot find in my heart to be sorry for the

23 Sept [1825?]   4 p 4to   BM(Bar)
from Sarah (Burney) Payne
Thank you for your kind answer to my

26 Sept [1825]   2 p 4to   NYPL(B)
from Frances Bowdler
My ever loved & valued Friend all

29 Sept   3 p 8vo   NYPL(B)
from Marie de Maisonneuve
j'aurais répondu tout de suite par un bien

13 Oct [1825]   3 p 8vo   NYPL(B)
from Amelia (Locke) Angerstein
On this day when I knew the dearest of all

⟨20⟩ Oct   4 p 4to   NYPL(B)
to EBB
Little as I am in the custom — as you too

23 Oct   4 p 8vo   NYPL(B)
from Marie de Maisonneuve
la lettre que je vous Ecrivis bien

10 Nov   4 p 8vo   NYPL(B)
from Marie de Maisonneuve
Voici Ma bien chere amie, la note et la lettre

28 Nov–9 Dec [1825]   4 p 4to
                         BM(Bar)
from CBFB to FBA & CFBt & MF
this will have your dear home on the direction,

30 Nov   4 p 4to   NYPL(B)
from Marquis de Lally-Tollendal
Mon coeur a eu peine à suffir à tous les

30 Dec 1825-5 Jan 1826   4 p 4to
to EBB   NYPL(B)
I am very happy, my dearest Esther, to find I

1826

14 JA 1826 pmk   4 p 8vo   NYPL(B)
to CFBt
Your beloved Mother's Letter has given me

9 May   4 p 4to   NYPL(B)
from Marie de Maisonneuve
Ce n'est que le 5 Mai, Ma bien chere

18 Jan   3 p 8vo   NYPL(B)
from Marie de Maisonneuve
Ma bien chere amie, C'est le 22 8bre que j'ai

19 May   3 p 4to   NYPL(B)
from Marquis de Lally-Tollendal
Vu Colonel Luc Allen, fils du Comte Allen

5 Feb   4 p 8vo & 1 p 4to   NYPL(B)
from Marie de Maisonneuve
je viens d'avoir la surprise de voir entrer dans

21 May   3 p 8vo   NYPL(B)
from Marie de Maisonneuve
Ma bien chere amie, ne recevant pas de

12 ⟨Feb⟩ [1826?]   4 p 12mo
from Princess Sophia   NYPL(B)
Alas! Alas! Alas! double, treble, quadrupled

⟨2⟩ 2 MY pmk [1826]   4 p 8vo
to CFBt   NYPL(B)
I long to know how my ⟨   ⟩ Charlotte is

17 Feb   3 p 8vo   NYPL(B)
from Marie de Maisonneuve
Le départ très-précipité de Mr le Cte

31 M[Y] pmk [1826]   1 p 4to
to CFBt   NYPL(B)
If you have written too lately, my dearest

2 Mar   2 p 8vo   NYPL(B)
from Marie de Maisonneuve
J'ai reçu avec une lettre très-aimable de votre

18 June   1 p 12mo   Hyde
to Caroline Anna Moore
I should be so much concerned to miss the

4 Mar   4 p 4to   BM(Bar)
from CBFB to FBA, CFBt & MF
My beloved Trio — I give my address in the

25 June–5 July   4 p 4to   NYPL(B)
to EBB
What an Age since I have written to my

30 Mar   10 p 4to   NYPL(B)
from Princess Elizabeth
I wish I could convey to You the extreme

7 Sept   pmk 1826   4 p 4to   NYPL(B)
from Sarah (Burney) Payne
As I have your kind permission to send you

5 Apr   4 p 8vo   NYPL(B)
from Marie de Maisonneuve
Ma bien chere amie, ceci n'est qu'un a

9 Sept [1826]   4 p 4to   BM(Bar)
from CBFB
"While all that passes inter nos, — / May be

12 Apr [1826]   4 p 4to   BM(Bar)
from CBFB
This agreeable Mrs. Bernard is *about* to send

8 Oct   10 p 4to   NYPL(B)
from Princess Elizabeth
You will think me dead my dear Madame

[c 12 Apr]   4 p 4to   NYPL(B)
to CFBt
What an abominable ill treatment — —

9 Oct–4 Nov   4 p 8vo   NYPL(B)
from Marie de Maisonneuve
enfin, Ma bien chere Amie, me voila

17 Apr   4 p 8vo   NYPL(B)
to CBFB
Not a long Letter on Long Paper, such as I

19 Oct [1826?]   3 p 12mo   NYPL(B)
from Princess Sophia
Your welcome note did not reach me until

[Apr-Oct 1826]   4 p 4to   NYPL(B)
to CBFB & CFBt
My sweet Charlotte — You are certainly one

20 Oct   4 p 8vo   Osb
to CPB
If I had as strong a passion for Exordiums

1826, continued

–25 Oct   4 p 4to   NYPL(B)
to EBB
Charlotte — our dear valuable Charlotte —

27 Oct   4 p 8vo   NYPL(B)
from Marie de Maisonneuve
c'est le 12 que j'ai reçu votre si bonne

[Oct-Nov 1826]   4 p 4to   NYPL(B)
from Marie de Maisonneuve
Rue d'anjou ou je restois jusqu'au Soir

5 Dec   4 p 8vo   NYPL(B)
from Marie de Maisonneuve
je suis sure que ma bien chere amie desire

–8 Dec   4 p 4to   NYPL(B)
to EBB
Dear & excellent Edward! — Can it be possible

17 Dec   2 p 8vo   NYPL(B)
from Marie de Maisonneuve
il y aura beaucoup de monde

[1826?]   2 p 4to   NYPL(B)
from Princess Mary
a sad draw back to her <memory>

1827

29 Jan   3 p 8vo   NYPL(B)
from Princess Sophia
How can I find words to convey to my dear &

22 Feb   4 p 4to   NYPL(B)
from Princess Elizabeth
Your kind letter arrived last night my dear

2 Apr   8 p 8vo   NYPL(B)
from Marie de Maisonneuve
je suis en possession de ce Paquet fini le

11 Apr   1 p 4to   Osb
from Henry Hoare, Bankers
[printed] Agreeably to your request We

12 May   4 p 4to   NYPL(B)
from Marie de Maisonneuve
Je n'ai pas reçu un seul mot depuis ce que

18–22 May [1827]   4 p 4to   NYPL(B)
to EBB
My very dear Hetty is truly kind to write me

26 June   3 p 4to   Comyn
to CPB
I return you my cordial thanks for

7 July   4 p 8vo   NYPL(B)
from Marie de Maisonneuve
c'est le jour même du Départ de ce cher Alex

13 JY 1827 pmk   1 p fragment
to EBB   NYPL(B)
Let me beg you therefore to arrange your own

27 July [1827?]   2 p 12mo   NYPL(B)
from Princess Sophia
My dearest kind friend! Here I am again with

[Aug 1827]   1 p 4to   NYPL(B)
to EBB
YES — I am Unable to say — / NO — I am

17–22 Sept [1827]   4 p 4to   NYPL(B)
from Sarah (Burney) Payne
I have received so few letters, owing I believe

24 NO 1827 pmk   2 p 8vo   Osb
to CPB
Mrs. Sheriff Domville has this moment left me,

26 Nov   copy   2 p 4to   NYPL(B)
to Frederica Locke
How I bless this Frank! — / Is that blessing

1 DE 1827 pmk   1 p 4to   Osb
to CPB
I hasten to enclose you some of the new cards

5 Dec   2 p 8vo   NYPL(B)
from Marie de Maisonneuve
Ma bien chere amie, depuis 5 mois je n'ai pas

31 DE 1827 pmk   4 p 8vo   BM(Bar)
to CBFB & CFBt
The unwelcome — grievous news has just

1828

[7 Feb 1828]   4 p 4to   NYPL(B)
to EBB
I wish my dearest Esther could have seen my

15 Feb   8 p 4to   NYPL(B)
from Princess Elizabeth
At last I have received your letter wh is

16 FE 1828 pmk 4 p 4to NYPL(B)
to EBB
I am so thankful to have a Letter from you,

21 Feb   4 p 4to   NYPL(B)
from Marie de Maisonneuve
Ma bien chere amie, je ne sais ce que vous

13–19 Mar   4 p 4to   NYPL(B)
to CBFB
What a Charlotte is my dearest Charlotte! how

31 Mar   pmk 1828   4 p 8vo   BM(Bar)
to CBFB
I take Note paper to make an immediate

[11 June 1828]   3 p 4to   NYPL(B)
to EBB
How thankful I am for a *Frank* opportunity of

17 June   1 p 4to   Osb
to CPB
Great Pen-labour for our *never ending still*

23 June   10 p 8vo   NYPL(B)
from Marie de Maisonneuve
je ne puis Ma bien chere amie eu croire mes

15 Sept   3 p 8vo   NYPL(B)
from Marie de Maisonneuve
depuis le 16. 9bre date de ma derniere lettre

16 SE 1828 pmk   4 p 4to   NYPL(B)
to CBFB
With what double desire to join you, my ever

21 Sept   2 p 4to   NYPL(B)
from AA
As I was this morning my person adorning, lo!

28 Sept   2 p 4to   NYPL(B)
from Marie de Maisonneuve
Votre si chère lettre attendue avec tant

9 Oct–15 Nov   4 p 4to   NYPL(B)
from Marie de Maisonneuve
nous avons reçu bien exactement, Ma bien

[10 Oct]   4 p 4to   NYPL(B)
to CBFB & CFBt
If this poor Letter give *you* half as much pain

17 Oct   2 p 8vo   NYPL(B)
from Marie de Maisonneuve
nous sommes venus passer 6 jours a Paris

21 ⟨Oct⟩   4 p 4to   NYPL(B)
from Princess Augusta
I have many and grateful thanks to return

25 Oct   4 p 4to   NYPL(B)
to CBFB & CFBt
My dear Charlottes Twain — if *twain* be a

29 Oct [1828]   1 p 4to   NYPL(B)
from Princess Mary
⟨anxious⟩ — I ⟨   ⟩ to make an excuse

30 Oct   copy   2 p 4to   NYPL(B)
to Frederica Locke
It is quite a comfort to me to be apprized of a

⟨8⟩ Nov [1828]   4 p 8vo   NYPL(B)
from Clement Robert Francis
The Tancred to which we wish to obtain a

[post 1828]   2 p 4to   BM(Bar)
from John Julius William Angerstein
Stay in London, which deterred me from

[post 1828]   1 p 8vo   NYPL(B)
from Princess Augusta
I am truly sorry My Dear Madam d'Arblay

[post 1828]   1 p 4to   NYPL(B)
from Princess Mary
much to expect to see my ⟨Pss⟩ Mary's

⟨5⟩ Aug [1828–32]   1 p 8vo
from Princess Sophia   NYPL(B)
I am in despair, although I trust only till

[1828–32]   4 p 12mo   NYPL(B)
from Princess Sophia
Alas! Alas! Alas! Indeed My dear and kindest

26 Apr [1828–36]   2 p 8vo   NYPL(B)
from Princess Sophia
My dearest kind friend. Dare I venture to hope

[1828–37]   2 p 8vo   NYPL(B)
from Princess Sophia
I must thank you for your *dear, welcome kind*

1828, continued

4 Jan [1828–37]   1 p 12mo   NYPL(B)
from Princess Sophia
Tomorrow if you please dearest kind Friend

3 Jan [1828–37]   3 p 12mo   NYPL(B)
from Princess Sophia
You may indeed have reason to say (*sub Rosa*)

25 Jan [1828–37]   2 p 12mo
from Princess Sophia   NYPL(B)
I do not forgo *the delight* — I had anticipated

26 Jan [1828–37]   1 p 12 mo
from Princess Sophia   NYPL(B)
I am again compelled my dearest Friend to ask

2 Feb [1828–37]   2 p 12mo
from Princess Sophia   NYPL(B)
I cannot avail myself or *allow* myself

25 Feb [1828–37]   2 p 8vo   NYPL(B)
from Princess Sophia
Alas! Alas! I sigh from day to day & no note!

25 May [1828–37]   2 p 12mo
from Princess Sophia   NYPL(B)
My dearest kind Friend! I am really quite in a

14 June [1828–37]   2 p 12mo
from Princess Sophia   NYPL(B)
I am so vexed at being obliged to ask you to

23 June [1828–37]   2 p 12mo
from Princess Sophia   NYPL(B)
Thank God dearest dear! The *Sun Shines* &

3 Aug [1828–37]   1 p 12mo
from Princess Sophia   NYPL(B)
My dear dear Friend! I am *miserable* about you

22 Aug [1828–37]   1 p 12mo
from Princess Sophia   NYPL(B)
Are you as well as I wish you to be?

3 Sept [1828–37]   3 p 4to   NYPL(B)
from Princess Sophia
My dearest kind Friend! the first moment I am

11 Oct [1828–37]   1 p 12mo
from Princess Sophia   NYPL(B)
My dearest kindest Friend! How are you? May

4 Nov [1828–37]   2 p 8vo   NYPL(B)
from Princess Sophia
It is now about a fortnight since I saw you My

[1828–37]   2 p 8vo   NYPL(B)
from Princess Sophia
Pray let me know how you are & if I may

[1828–37]   2 p 12mo   NYPL(B)
from Princess Sophia
My dearest kind Friend I must *request* to

[1828–37]   1 p 12mo   NYPL(B)
from Princess Sophia
My dearest kind Friend. The weather has been

[1828–37]   1 p 12mo   NYPL(B)
from Princess Sophia
I must malgré <   > ask you to come

[1828–37]   3 p 12mo   NYPL(B)
from Princess Sophia
I cannot express my vexation when the carriage

5 Feb [1828–37]   3 p 12mo
from Princess Sophia   NYPL(B)
My dearest kind Friend! What can I say? it is

[1828–37]   2 p 12mo   NYPL(B)
from Princess Sophia
I look to Tomorrow (WEDNESDAY EVENING)

[1828–37]   3 p 12mo   NYPL(B)
from Princess Sophia
I must bien contre moi ask you to postpone till

[1828–37]   2 p 12mo   NYPL(B)
from Princess Sophia
Dearest kind Friend! Should you still be

[1828–37]   1 p 12mo   NYPL(B)
from Princess Sophia
My dearest dear kind Friend! After such a

[1828–37]   2 p 12mo   NYPL(B)
from Princess Sophia
My dearest kind Friend! *Instead* of delaying

[1828–37]   2 p 12mo   NYPL(B)
from Princess Sophia
I am distressed to the greatest degree my

[1828–37]   1 p 8vo   NYPL(B)
from Princess Sophia
Your kindest of notes *dearest* kind Mrs

[1828–37]   2 p 12mo   NYPL(B)
from Princess Sophia
One line dearest kind Friend to say that I am

[1828–37] 2 p 12mo NYPL(B)
from Princess Sophia
How vexed I am you continue so poorly My

[1828–37] 1 p 12mo NYPL(B)
from Princess Sophia
After all my dearest Friend I am obliged to put

[1828–37] 2 p 12mo NYPL(B)
from Princess Sophia
I will not bother you with a long letter my

[1828–37] 2 p 8vo NYPL(B)
from Princess Sophia
My dear kind Friend You are indeed a *kind*

27 [1828–37] 2 p 12mo NYPL(B)
from Princess Sophia
My dearest kindest friend! May I hope this

6 Mar [1828–37] 3 p 8vo NYPL(B)
from Princess Sophia
Your first kind note My dearest and kindest

1829

3 Jan 2 p 8vo NYPL(B)
from Marie de Maisonneuve
voici Ma bien bien chere amie, une lettre que

21 June [1829] 3 p 4to BM(Bar)
from CBFB
Sunday June 21st — longest day and not half

10 Jan 6 p 4to NYPL(B)
from Princess Elizabeth
There is so little from <home> worth relating

23 June 3 p 4to BM(Bar)
from Adolph, baron Billing
Si j'ai éprouvé une contrariété réelle, qui se

[13 Feb 1829] 1 p 8vo NYPL(B)
to JCBTM & HHBt
I am under the deepest uneasiness for some

26 June 2 p 4to NYPL(B)
from Marie de Maisonneuve
Je vous ai mandé dernierement, Ma bien chere

14 FE 1829 pmk 3 p 4to NYPL(B)
to CBFB
You are right / right /right / my dearest

2 July 2 p 8vo NYPL(B)
from Marie de Maisonneuve
Voici Ma bien chere amie l'extrait de deux

14 Feb 3 p 8vo NYPL(B)
from Marie de Maisonneuve
il m'arrive point de vos lettres, Ma bien chere

11 July 2 p 4to NYPL(B)
from Marie de Maisonneuve
je vous ai mandé hier pour le <   > de

[pre 17 Feb 1829] 2 p 4to NYPL(B)
from CBFB
Ah my dearest sister you will easily conceive

3 Sept 2 p 4to NYPL(B)
from Marie de Maisonneuve
je vous ai écrit le 25. 9bre Ma bien chere

19 FE 1829 pmk 4 p 4to NYPL(B)
to CBFB
How do I grieve for you my dearest dearest

4 Sept [1829] 7 p 8vo NYPL(B)
from Marie de Maisonneuve
j'ai eu bien du regret Ma bien chere

4 MR 1829 pmk 4 p 8vo NYPL(B)
to CBFB
How is my dearest loved Charlotte? — &

28 Sept 1 p 4to NYPL(B)
from AA
Safe landed here after a beautiful passage of

25 Apr 3 p 4to NYPL(B)
from Marie de Maisonneuve
que je suis contents Ma bien chere

4 Oct 3 p 8vo NYPL(B)
from Marie de Maisonneuve
c'est avec un coeur plein de joie, Ma bien chere

6 June 3 p 8vo NYPL(B)
from Marie de Maisonneuve
c'est au Lys Ma bien chere amie que j'ai reçu

6 OC 1829 pmk 4 p 4to BM(Bar)
to CBFB (with PS from EBB)
With a thousand Things to say to my dearly

17 June 2 p 8vo NYPL(B)
from Marie de Maisonneuve
Ma bien chere amie, je m'empresse de vous

6 Oct 3 p 4to NYPL(B)
from AA
I hope you have quite cured your cold,

1829, continued

9 ⟨Nov⟩ [1829?]   1 p 12mo
from Princess Sophia   NYPL(B)
My dearest dear kind friend — Will you come

10 Nov   3 p 4to   NYPL(B)
from Marie de Maisonneuve
bien chere amie, nous avons enfin, votre

25 Nov   2 p 4to   NYPL(B)
from Marie de Maisonneuve
quelle bonne et charmante Causerie que la

10 Dec   4 p 8vo   NYPL(B)
from Marie de Maisonneuve
Ma bien chere amie je me flatte que vous

11 DE 1829 pmk   2 p 4to   NYPL(B)
to CBFB
My own Charlotte — ever dear & patient —

1830

22 Jan–4 Feb   6 p 8vo   NYPL(B)
from Marie de Maisonneuve
J'ai reçu le 13 de ce mois votre si bonne si

10 Feb [1830?]   4 p 8vo   NYPL(B)
from Princess Mary
I was delighted to see your dear kind

17 Feb   2 p 4to   NYPL(B)
from Marie de Maisonneuve
je ne sais Ma bien chere amie, Si Made de

10 Apr   4 p 4to   NYPL(B)
from Marie de Maisonneuve
Ma bien chere si bonne si aimée amie

21 Apr–14 May   4 p 4to   NYPL(B)
to CFBt
How kind — how beautifully kind is my

24 Apr   3 p 4to   Osb
to John Jebb
I am penetrated with the most lively pleasure,

3 May   4 p 4to   NYPL(B)
from Marie de Maisonneuve
Depuis votre lettre du 12 avril

28 May   3 p 4to   NYPL(B)
from Marie de Maisonneuve
j'ai terminé au Mr Flandin

4 July [1830]   4 p 12mo   NYPL(B)
from Princess Sophia
I am anxious My dearest Dear kind friend to

28 Aug   3 p 8vo   NYPL(B)
from Princess Elizabeth
I trust I need not say how grieved I am that

28 Aug [1830]   2 p 8vo   NYPL(B)
from Marie de Maisonneuve
j'ésperois chaque jour avoir de vos nouvelles

29 Aug [1830]   3 p 12mo   NYPL(B)
from Princess Sophia
My dearest kind Friend! I hope now to be

14 Oct [1830]   1 p 12mo   NYPL(B)
from Princess Sophia
My dearest dear! I am D'ably sick! How are

[13] Nov   2 p 12mo   NYPL(B)
from Princess Sophia
Dearest kind Friend! To begin with an old &

21 Dec [1830]   1 p 12mo   NYPL(B)
from Princess Sophia
⟨In fear of any⟩ mistakes I write this — Did

25 Dec [1830]   2 p 12mo   NYPL(B)
from Princess Sophia
Dearest kind Friend! I was in an agony about

15 July [1830–36]   2 p 12mo
from Princess Sophia   NYPL(B)
I fear my dear Soul it must be Tuesday alas!

1831

22 Jan   3 p 8vo   NYPL(B)
to Caroline Anna Moore
What kind balm from my

29 Jan–11 Feb   4 p 4to   NYPL(B)
from Marie de Maisonneuve
C'est le matin Ma bien chere amie que votre

14 Mar [1831]   1 p 8vo   NYPL(B)
from Princess Mary
can you come to me to Morrow evening

19 Mar   3 p 8vo   NYPL(B)
from Marie de Maisonneuve
Depuis ma derniere lettre du 11 février

[23 May 1831 or 1836]   2 p 12mo
from Princess Sophia   NYPL(B)
Well! My dear Soul! Dare I name tomorrow

29 May [1831?]   1 p 8vo   NYPL(B)
from Princess Mary
I shall be delighted to see you Monday next at

30 May   2 p 8vo   NYPL(B)
from Princess Elizabeth
I need not say how happy it will make me to

31 May [1831?]   3 p 8vo   NYPL(B)
from Princess Mary
Your kind [note] was received with great

7 July   4 p 4to   NYPL(B)
from Marie de Maisonneuve
Ma bien chere amie, je ne vous ai pas écrit

[31] July [1831?]   1 p 4to   NYPL(B)
to [CBFB & CFBt]
My own beloved Best and Est, / To make the

8 Aug   4 p 4to   NYPL(B)
from SHB
I have been silent so long, that it were vain

25 Aug [1831]   4 p 12mo   NYPL(B)
from Princess Sophia
My dearest kind Friend! I was distressed

3 Oct   3 p 8vo   Good65
to Anna (Wilbraham) Grosvenor
. . . I had received a letter from the dear

9 Oct   4 p 4to   NYPL(B)
from Marie de Maisonneuve
je ne puis me persuader, Ma bien chere

19 Dec   1 p 4to   BM(Bar)
from William Watts
Being anxiously engaged in collecting the

[pre 1832] verses   2 p 4to   Osb
to EBB
My Sister dear / Your case is clear / And

21 Nov [pre 1832]   2 p 8vo   NYPL(B)
from Sarah (Payne) Burney
Incessant Spasms have prevented my seeing

1832

25 Jan [1832?]   5 p 8vo   NYPL(B)
from Princess Mary
As writing disagrees with me & I am

20 Mar   4 p 4to   NYPL(B)
from Marie de Maisonneuve
Ma bien chere toujours plus chere amie, je ne

30 Mar   4 p 4to   NYPL(B)
from SHB
Oh my poor Sister! How little dare I think of

12 AP 1832 pmk   1 p 8vo   Osb
to CPB
I take so kindly your offer to act for me, & to

29 AP 1832 pmk   1 p 4to   NYPL(B)
from AA
I take advantage of a gentleman just going up

8 JU 1832 pmk   1 p 8vo   NYPL(B)
from AA
Here I am / For the Bp's persuaded me to stay

13 June   3 p 8vo   Osb
from Sir James Prior
Give me leave to intrude upon you by asking a

20 June   2 p 4to   NYPL(B)
to Anna (Wilbraham) Grosvenor
Pardon me, dear, kind Mrs. Grosvenor, — I

14 July [1832]   1 p 8vo   NYPL(B)
from Princess Sophia
I confess I was becoming VERY VERY uneasy —

27 July   1 p 8vo   Osb
to CPB
THIS INSTANT Friday 2 o'clock, 27th. July

3 AU 1832 pmk   1 p 8vo   Osb
to CPB
Lest any kind idea of being able to serve me

8 Sept   2 p 4to   NYPL(B)
from AA
Here I am, sick and safe — / There is no

1832, continued

23 Sept   1 p 4to   NYPL(B)
from AA
I am just landed here safe

[Oct 1832]   copy   4 p 4to   NYPL(B)
to Rebecca (Burney) Sandford
How severe to me is the necessity of

11 Nov   8 p 4to   NYPL(B)
from Princess Elizabeth
Long Long have I wished to write to You dear

27 Nov   2 p 8vo   BM(Bar)
from Edward Chaplin
To be number'd among the friends

30 Nov   3 p 8vo   BM(Bar)
from William Harness
A thousand & one thanks for the kind

1 Dec   1 p 8vo   Comyn
from Thomas Faulkner
Mr Faulkner author of the History of Chelsea

6 Dec [1832]   4 p 8vo   NYPL(B)
from Princess Elizabeth
having an opportunity of sending a letter to

12 Dec   copy   3 p 4to   NYPL(B)
from John Jebb
This moment I have finished your most

21 Dec   1 p 8vo   NYPL(B)
from Thomas Faulkner
The Author of the History of Chelsea presents

27 Dec   1 p 12mo   Comyn
to Thomas Faulkner
Madame d'Arblay makes with pleasure an

[1832]   3 p 8vo   Osb
to John Jebb
I am so much mortified not to appear more

[1832]   1 p 8vo   BM(Bar)
from Edward Moxon
Mr. Moxon will be glad to know whether

[1832–36]   2 p 8vo   NYPL(B)
to CFBt
How I thank my dearest Charlotta for her very

1833

18 Jan   4 p 4to   Osb
from Johann Christian Hüttner
In an advertisement prefixed to your

22 Jan–12 Feb   4 p 4to   NYPL(B)
from Marie de Maisonneuve
C'est le 24 Décembre que j'ai reçu votre chere

23 Jan   1 p 8vo   Harv(H)
to [John] Nichols
Madame d'Arblay keeps no copies of the

9 FE 1833 pmk   1 p 8vo   NYPL(B)
to AA
In the earnest *hope* you will be upon your

19 Feb [1833]   4 p 4to   NYPL(B)
with CBFB & Cornelia (Mierop) Cambridge to CFBt
Oh my dearest — What can I say — Oh, that

22 Feb   4 p 4to   NYPL(B)
from AA
"Boy dood boy, mamma — boy edey dood boy,

24 Feb [1833]   4 p 8vo   NYPL(B)
from Amelia (Locke) Angerstein
One line of tender remembrance my beloved

14 Mar   4 p 8vo   NYPL(B)
to CPB
Will you do me the favour to take a little to

18 Mar [1833]   draft   4 p 4to
to Stephen Allen   NYPL(B)
At length, my dear Mr. Allen, my poor

18 AP 1833 pmk   2 p 4to   Osb
to CPB
As I know my dear Carlos — like his Father &

22 MY 1833 pmk   1 p 4to   Osb
to CPB
There is no time, I think, to be lost in

[15–] June [1833]   4 p 12mo
from Princess Sophia   NYPL(B)
Oh! What a happiness was the contents of your

26 June   7 p 8vo   NYPL(B)
from Marie de Maisonneuve
votre silence m'inquiete bien Ma chere

26 July–1 Aug   4 p 4to   NYPL(B)
to CBFB
Thanks, thanks, for so quick a sight of your

14 AU 1833 pmk   3 p 4to mutilated
with AA to CFBt & CBFB   NYPL(B)
My dear C [cut] / I am to preach [cut]

29 AU 1833 pmk   3 p 4to   NYPL(B)
to CBFB
Sweetly welcome to me was your Letter, My

6 Sept   6 p 4to   NYPL(B)
from Princess Elizabeth
Forget You! impossible my dear d'Arblay it is

25 Sept   4 p 8vo   BM(Bar)
from Charles Forster
Illness could alone have withheld the Bishop's

3 Nov   4 p 4to   NYPL(B)
to CFBt
I am quite vexed, my sweet Charlotte, not to

16 NO 1833 pmk   2 p 4to   NYPL(B)
to CBFB
My own sweet Charlotte — though I am unable

23 NO 1833 pmk   4 p 8vo   NYPL(B)
to CBFB
Not to lose a post by waiting till I can write

23 Nov   4 p 8vo   NYPL(B)
from Marie de Maisonneuve
Ma bien chere amie je voudrois me persuader

[Nov 1833]   2 p 8vo   NYPL(B)
to CBFB
God bless you, my sweetest — dearest —

2 Dec [1833]   4 p 4to   BM(Bar)
from CBFB & CFBt
This is Sunday — & therefore I begin my

[7 Dec 1833]   3 p 8vo   NYPL(B)
to CPB
I like the thought of the proposition, my dear

[13] Dec   4 p 4to   NYPL(B)
to CBFB
Wise in her Kindness is my dearest Charlotte

[1833]   draft   4 p 4to   NYPL(B)
to Stephen Allen
I am extremely sorry, my dear Mr. Allen, to

[1833?]   2 p 4to   NYPL(B)
from AA
I have been with Mr Verbeke all yesterday &

1834

1 JA 1834 pmk   4 p 8vo   NYPL(B)
to CBFB
Heaven bless my beloved Charlotte with a year

4 Jan   1 p 8vo   BM(Bar)
from Charles Forster
Your letter affected me more than I can express

5 Jan [1834]   4 p 4to   BM(Bar)
from CBFB
— dear Charlotte & I sent you off a Letter my

12 Jan–3 Feb   4 p 4to   NYPL(B)
to CBFB
This once for a marvel — I find the power to

12–20 Jan [1834]   4 p 4to BM(Bar)
from CBFB
One line if no more — I will indulge myself

21 Jan   4 p 12mo   NYPL(B)
from Princess Sophia
Prudence *alone* My dearest & kindest Friend

26 Jan–2 Feb [1834]   4 p 4to
from CBFB   BM(Bar)
I think this is very good Ink my dearest sister

[9]–13 Feb [1834]   4 p 4to BM(Bar)
from CBFB
Sun day — is one day — on which I love to

[23]–26 Feb [1834]   2 p 4to
from CBFB   BM(Bar)
I wish I cd see him to charge him to sport his

5–9 Mar [1834]   4 p 4to   BM(Bar)
from CBFB
Your dear sweet Letter arrived this morning my

17 Mar [1834]   4 p 4to   BM(Bar)
from CBFB
Your dear letter of yesterday arrived this

18 Mar   8 p 4to   BM(Bar)
from Ann (Astley) Agnew
Your last kind Letter gave me both Pleasure

1834, continued

23–24 Mar [1834]   4 p 4to   BM(Bar)
from CBFB
My dear dear affectionate tender darling

2⟨9⟩ Mar   4 p 8vo   NYPL(B)
to CBFB
Most thankfully I accept the sweet kindness of

30–[31] Mar [1834]   4 p 4to
from CBFB   BM(Bar)
Sunday being my day of rest, one of the

4–[7] Apr [1834]   4 p 4to   BM(Bar)
from CBFB
I now begin my Sundays Letter to my darling

13–15 Apr [1834]   3 p 4to   BM(Bar)
from CBFB
Here is Sunday come again — & poor dear Ju

[24–25 Apr 1834]   4 p 4to   BM(Bar)
from CBFB & CFBt
I *did* begin a bit of a Letter to you my very

[25] Apr–2 May [1834]   4 p 4to
from CBFB   BM(Bar)
this *ought* to have been begun my dearly loved

Apr–10 May [1834]   4 p 8vo
to CBFB   NYPL(B)
Rejoicing to my very soul is this improved

11–[16] May [1834]   4 p 4to
from CBFB   BM(Bar)
This Sunday I now make sure of to prevent

21–24 May [1834]   4 p 4to   BM(Bar)
from CBFB
I now begin our Bulletins my dearest sister for

23 MY 1834 pmk   2 p 4to   Osb
to CPB
I am truly concerned, my dear Carlos, not to

31 MY 1834 pmk   4 p 8vo   NYPL(B)
to CBFB
I never felt quite so little guilty in my

[c May 1834]   1 p 8vo   Osb
to CPB
It is impossible to me not to take pen to

12 JU 1834 pmk   4 p 8vo   NYPL(B)
to CBFB
With a warm & hoping heart I now write to

25 June   4 p 4to   NYPL(B)
from Marie de Maisonneuve
enfin Ma bien chere amie, me voila la plume

15 July   4 p 8vo   NYPL(B)
to CBFB
I had thought I should write no more to my

⟨1⟩ AU 1834 pmk   4 p 8vo   NYPL(B)
to CBFB
Ah my Charlotte! My dear dear Charlotte! what

21 Aug   3 p 12mo   NYPL(B)
to Frances (Phillips) Raper
Take, my dear Fanny, my most cordial

9 Sept   4 p 4to   BM(Bar)
from Ann (Astley) Agnew
I fear you will think me very neglectful in not

14 Sept   4 p 4to   NYPL(B)
from AA
After four days very pleasantly passed at

19 Sept   4 p 4to   NYPL(B)
from AA and Sarah (Burney) Payne
I shall endeavour to reach town

20 OC 1834 pmk   3 p 4to   NYPL(B)
to AA
a great & partial — but not blind friend of

23 Oct   1 p 4to   NYPL(B)
to AA
I am quite unused to this sort of transaction,

23 Oct   4 p 4to   NYPL(B)
from AA
As my prolonged stay has quite emptied

23 Oct   3 p 8vo   Osb
to CPB
Alex is still absent on his annual recruiting

[18 Nov 1834]   2 p 4to   NYPL(B)
from AA
This is just one month before my birthday alas

23–[24] Nov [1834]   4 p 4to
from CBFB & CFBt   BM(Bar)
My dearest sweetest of sisters — knowing that

1–18 Dec [1834]   4 p 8vo   NYPL(B)
to CBFB
When I got the great GREAT comfort of my

also   copy   3 p 4to   NYPL(B)

3 DE 1834 pmk   2 p 8vo   BM(Bar)
to CBFB
My ever dearest dearest Charlotte I Seize This

[c 1834]   3 p 12mo   NYPL(B)
from Sarah (Burney) Payne
If you are disengaged tonight, may we ask for

1835

13 Jan   3 p 4to   BM(Bar)
from Ann (Astley) Agnew
As a Friend is going to Town

15 Jan [1835]   4 p 4to   BM(Bar)
·from CBFB & CFBt
I must write to thank you for your sweet

16 Jan   4 p 4to   NYPL(B)
from Marie de Maisonneuve
enfin Ma bien chere amie toujours présente à

19 JA 1835 pmk   2 p 4to   NYPL(B)
to CFBt
My dear, my excellent Second — but second

26 JA 1835 pmk   4 p 8vo   NYPL(B)
to CBFB
Again must I take this short material for my

5 FE 1835 pmk   4 p 8vo   NYPL(B)
to CBFB
This is my small paper <twin> for my

6 Feb pmk 1835   4 p 4to   BM(Bar)
from CBFB & CFBt
This post brought me your dear sweet letter my

9 & 26 Feb   4 p 4to   Osb
to Mrs Temple
It is not without reluctance, & even pain, that I

21 pmk [Feb 1835]   4 p 8vo
to CBFB   NYPL(B)
Our Charotte, my own dearest Charlotte, will

17 Mar   2 p 8vo   NYPL(B)
from Zélie-Isaure-Elizabeth Larrey
Permit me to thank you for the great pleasure

30 Mar   4 p 4to   NYPL(B)
from SHB
Some ladies I am acquainted with

[1 May 1835]   1 p 4to   NYPL(B)
to AA
Take my tenderest — & delighted Benediction,

14 MY 1835 pmk   3 p 8vo   BM(Bar)
to CBFB
Alas — I greatly fear our kindest Charlotte

14 May [1835]   4 p 4to   BM(Bar)
from CBFB
So much I have been engross'd since my arrival,

[19? May 1835]   4 p 8vo   BM(Bar)
from CBFB
according to custom our last epistles met on

[May 1835]   2 p 4to   NYPL(B)
to AA
Where could be my Heart — my dearest Alex

1< > JU 1835 pmk   4 p 8vo
to CBFB   BM(Bar)
My sweet Charlotte what kindness is yours to

16 June [1835]   3 p 4to   BM(Bar)
from CBFB
a Letter began — to be finished in odd

30 June [1835]   4 p 4to   BM(Bar)
from CBFB
Barrett has just called with the kind offer of

8–10 July   4 p 8vo   NYPL(B)
to CBFB
NOT OFFS & ONS, my sweet Charlotte —

13 July   1 p 8vo   NYPL(B)
from CPB
Ten thousand thanks for your prompt & most

16 July [1835]   3 p 8vo   BM(Bar)
from CBFB
I am involved in occupations, finding places for

1 Aug   5 p 4to   NYPL(B)
from Marie de Maisonneuve
je ne puis croire ce que je vois de la date de

4 Aug [1835]   3 p 4to   NYPL(B)
from CBFB
You will easily conceive my dearly loved Sister

31 Aug   4 p 4to   NYPL(B)
from SHB
I hear from various quarters such very

21 pmk SE 1835   4 p 8vo   BM(Bar)
to CBFB
What a happy coincidence there seems, my

1835, continued

23 Sept [1835]   4 p 4to   BM(Bar)
from CBFB
It is impossible to say how rejoiced I am my

12 Oct   4 p 8vo   BM(Bar)
to CBFB
Your sweet acceptance of my hoped for

12 Oct   2 p 4to   BM(Bar)
from Richard Bentley
It has for some time been my wish to include

16 Oct   1 p 8vo   Osb
to Richard Bentley
Madame d'Arblay has been prevented from

23 OC 1835 pmk   3 p 8vo   BM(Bar)
to CBFB
Will it not be better to write any thing than

4 Nov   2 p 8vo   Harv(H)
to Richard Bentley
I am much concerned that the obstinacy of a

[post 25 Nov 1835]   draft   1 p 8vo &
    scrap   NYPL(B)
to [James?] Prior
I have only just now, — through my retired

27 Nov   1 p 8vo   NYPL(B)
from William Raper
I have the pleasure to inform you that M^r.

2 Dec [1835]   4 p 4to   NYPL(B)
from CBFB
Whenever friends are going from Brighton to

8 Dec   4 p 4to   NYPL(B)
from SHB
I cannot allow dear Edward to leave Bath

[14 Dec 1835]   4 p 8vo   NYPL(B)
to CBFB
The delicious accounts I have received — from

[pre 18 Dec]   2 p ½ fol   NYPL(B)
to AA
I am Sick! Sick! Sick! / Sick at heart! — /

[1835]   4 p 8vo   NYPL(B)
from AA
I remember the error as our trouble &

[1835?]   4 p 4to   NYPL(B)
from AA
O I am very unhappy / I know not what to say

[1835]   2 p 4to   NYPL(B)
from AA
I got y^r letter to day at 12 —

[c 1835]   1 p scrap   NYPL(B)
from CBFB
. . . being of use notwithstanding his poor Eyes

1836

24 Jan   4 p 4to   NYPL(B)
from SHB
I can let slip no private opportunity

24 Jan   4 p 8vo   NYPL(B)
from Marie de Maisonneuve
Ma bien chere amie, toujours plus aimée et plus

30 JA 1836 pmk   1 p 4to   NYPL(B)
from Mary Ann Smith
Were I constantly with him, to rouse him into

17 Feb   3 p 8vo   NYPL(B)
from Charles Forster
If you have not forgotten one, who would be

[c 20 Mar]   draft?   4 p 8vo
to Charles Forster   NYPL(B)
It is not Mr. Forster — the kind, & to me, long

25 Mar   4 p 8vo   NYPL(B)
from Marie de Maisonneuve
il y a deux Mois Ma bien chere amie, que je

28 Mar [1836]   2 p 12mo NYPL(B)
from Princess Sophia
Great was my joy on opening your dear *little*

1 Apr [1836]   2 p 4to   NYPL(B)
to AA
What is all this conduct, Alex? & What does it

3 May   4 p 8vo   Osb
to CPB
I wanted immediately to <write> my true

4 [pmk] May   pmk 1836   1 p 4to
to AA   NYPL(B)
My dear Mrs. Angerstein has just empowered

12 MY 1836 pmk   1 p 8vo   Osb
to CPB
Pray let the Captain know I have always

14 MY 1836 pmk   4 p 4to   NYPL(B)
to AA
I should delight in your passing so long a visit

17 May   2 p 8vo   NYPL(B)
to AA
Mr. Verger <Raper> has called upon me

29 June   1 p 4to   NYPL(B)
to AA
Mes Yeurx! [sic] / My prescription! / A note

11–16 July [1836]   4 p 4to   BM(Bar)
from CBFB & CFBt
I now begin what we talked of, a *journal*

14 JY 1836 pmk   2 p 4to   NYPL(B)
to CBFB
Could it be believed — I hope not! — that I

26 Aug   2 p 8vo   Cal(B)
to Alfred Turner
Now, indeed, I *must* write to beg your pardon,

30 Aug   1 p 4to   NYPL(B)
to Ann (Astley) Agnew
On my Mind's list, my dear Mrs. Agnew, how

Sept–21 Oct   4 p 4to   NYPL(B)
to CBFB & CFBt
My dearest sweetest Charlotte my loved my

also   copy   3 p 4to   NYPL(B)

7 Oct   4 p 8vo   NYPL(B)
from Marie de Maisonneuve
Ma bien chere amie, toujours plus aimée

21–25 Nov   pmk 1836   4 p 4to
to CBFB   BM(Bar)
Your sweet Letter my own dearest Charlotte

6 Dec [1836?]   1 p 4to   NYPL(B)
to [Sarah (Burney) Payne]
Some people would begin with saying I ought

1837

21 Jan   4 p 8vo   NYPL(B)
from Frances (Phillips) Raper
I wish I might see you [sic] grief as it will be,

[post Jan 1837]   2 p 8vo   NYPL(B)
to [CPB]
Your urgency to me to write to you is now for

[pre 11 Feb 1837]   4 p 4to   BM(Bar)
from CBFB
Friday — post does not go out Tomorrow, & no

11 Feb [1837]   3 p 8vo   BM(Bar)
from CBFB
I seize the opportunity of a line to my dearest

12 Feb [1837]   4 p 8vo   BM(Bar)
from CBFB
My sweetest, kindest most loved sister after I

17 FE 1837 pmk   4 p 8vo   NYPL(B)
to CBFB
Having something to communicate now in

also   copy   2 p 4to   NYPL(B)

[Feb? 1837]   4 p 4to   BM(Bar)
from CBFB
Your dear touching Heart felt Letter my most

6 pmk [Mar 1837]   4 p 8vo
to CBFB   NYPL(B)
My dear dear dearest Charlotte I write to you

16 MR 1837 pmk   3 p 8vo   Osb
to CPB
Woefully I have been disappointed by not

24 Mar   pmk 1837   3 p 4to
from SHB   NYPL(B)
How are you, my poor dear Sister? —

1 <Apr>   pmk 1837   4 p 8vo
to CBFB   BM(Bar)
Oh my Charlotte my dearest Charlotte —

3 Apr   1 p 8vo   Camb(F)
to Alfred Turner
I have just received a Letter from Dr. P.

3–4 Apr [1837]   4 p 4to   BM(Bar)
from CBFB
My poor pen *used* to be rather a merry pen —

10 [Apr 1837]   4 p 8vo   NYPL(B)
to CBFB
Ah my tenderest Charlotte my tenderest dearest

also   copy   3 p 4to   NYPL(B)

1837, continued

9 May [1837]   4 p 4to   BM(Bar)
from CBFB
Barrett is going to town & I take the

21 May   1 p 8vo   NYPL(B)
from GMAPWaddington
Within the last twenty four hours, I have first

22 May [1837]   3 p 8vo   NYPL(B)
from Amelia (Locke) Angerstein
My most precious Friend When you asked me

23 MY 1837 pmk 1 p 4to NYPL(B)
from Lady Llanover
I hope when you can see me you will send for

28–30 May [1837]   3 p 8vo   BM(Bar)
from CBFB
Debarred meeting as we so long unhappily

4 June [1837]   4 p 8vo   BM(Bar)
from CBFB
My dearest darling sister the softest comfort I

7 June [1837]   1 p 4to   BM(Bar)
from CBFB
It strikes me *now* my dearly loved sister, that,

12 JU 1837 pmk   4 p 8vo   NYPL(B)
to CBFB
Now then my dearest dearest Charlotte let me

also   copy   (misdated July)   3 p 4to
                                        NYPL(B)

⟨13⟩ JU 1837 pmk   2 p 8vo   NYPL(B)
to CBFB
From my own hand let my Charlotte first hear

13 June   1 p 4to   NYPL(B)
from SHB
My poor dear — VERY dear Sister! — I

15 JU 1837 pmk   1 p 8vo   Cal(B)
to Alfred Turner
Alas I am not ready! nor know I when I shall

15 June [1837]   3 p 8vo   BM(Bar)
from CBFB
Your sweet Letter my most tenderly loved

12 July [1837]   4 p 8vo   BM(Bar)
from CBFB
Well do I know how glad you will be, my own

20 JY 1837 pmk   2 p 8vo   BM(Bar)
to CBFB
Thanks — Thanks — my kindest dearest for

21 JY 1837 pmk   4 p 8vo   Osb
to CPB
I have found Mr. Hutton & I had him 20 times

22 AU 1837 pmk   4 p 4to   NYPL(B)
to CFBt
Now, then, my sweet Charlotte, that at length

1–2 Sept   4 p 8vo   NYPL(B)
to CBFB
How long my own beloved Charlotte, has my

also   copy (misdated Aug)   3 p 4to
                                   NYPL(B)

2 Oct   pmk 1837   4 p 8vo   BM(Bar)
to CBFB
Ah my dearest Charlotte, how have I been

9–11 Oct   pmk 1837   4 p 8vo
to CBFB   BM(Bar)
The deep & true interest with which we have

[c 25 Oct]   3 p 8vo   NYPL(B)
to CBFB
My dearest sister — I think I see land! — I

30 OC 1837 pmk   1 p 8vo   BM(Bar)
to CBFB
I have just sent to take my place for Thursday

13 Dec [1837]   2 p 4to   NYPL(B)
to CBFB & CFBt
And now, my dear Charlottes both I must

27 DE 1837 pmk   4 p 8vo   BM(Bar)
to CBFB
Why how is this, my dearest dears? Could I

[Dec 1837]   2 p 4to   NYPL(B)
to CBFB
My "errand of Love," as my dear Mrs.

[1837]   3 p 8vo   BM(Bar)
from CBFB
Thursday — we had hopes that this post would

[1837–38]   2 p 8vo   NYPL(B)
to CFBt
Ah, my Charlotte — how must I thank you for

also   copy   2 p 4to   BM(Bar)

[1837–38]   3 p 12mo   NYPL(B)
from Princess Sophia
What can I say? I have feared to write yet my

[1837–39]   3 p 8vo   NYPL(B)
from Princess Sophia
My dearest kind Friend! it w^d be difficult

1838

10 JA 1838 pmk   3 p 8vo   BM(Bar)
to CBFB
poor Minette has been so suffering in her Teeth

31 Jan [1838]   4 p 4to   BM(Bar)
from CBFB
It is high time my dear Sister to thank you for

[c Jan 1838]   2 p 8vo   BM(Bar)
to CBFB
[torn] me all night for only *intending* to let *our*

14 Feb   4 p 4to   NYPL(B)
from Marie de Maisonneuve
quelle precieuse marque de votre si chere

3 MR 1838 pmk   1 p 8vo   Osb
to CPB
I have thought of little else since I saw you —

6 pmk [Mar 1838]   4 p 8vo   NYPL(B)
to CBFB
What an age since I have written to my dearly

20 Mar   1 p 4to   Cal(B)
to Alfred Turner
Why do I not hear from, or see you? I

8 Apr [1838]   3 p 8vo   BM(Bar)
from CBFB
Muster Slater gives notage that he is to be off

[20 Apr 1838]   4 p 8vo   NYPL(B)
to CBFB
My dear darling Charlotte, though I am so
also   copy   3 p 4to   NYPL(B)

20 Apr   4 p 4to   NYPL(B)
from Marie de Maisonneuve
Ma bien chere toujours plus chere amie, nous

26 Apr [1838]   3 p 8vo   BM(Bar)
from CBFB
Pondering — pondering — pondering —

15 May [1838]   3 p 8vo   BM(Bar)
from CBFB
Barrett is going to town, & I cannot endure to

1 [July 1838]   1 p 8vo   Hyde
to CBFB
Is not this precarious weather my dearest

[15] July [1838]   3 p 4to   BM(Bar)
from CBFB
A thousand thanks my sweet dear darling for

[post 15 July 1838]   4 p 8vo
to CBFB   BM(Bar)
Ah my sweetest Charlotte — be not sorry as

4–7 Aug   4 p 4to   NYPL(B)
from Marie de Maisonneuve
Ma bien chere toujours plus chere amie,

29 [Aug misdated Sept]   1 p 8vo
to CPB   McG
I write in so much haste that I have time only

[pre 12 Sept 1838]   1 p 8vo   NYPL(B)
to CFBt
Now my dearest Charlotta shall have a Letter

[post 12 Sept]   2 p 8vo   NYPL(B)
to CFBt
<Oh> my Charlotte — if it be so — for I

23 Oct   4 p 4to   NYPL(B)
from Marie de Maisonneuve
Ma bien chere si precieuse amie, je vous

25 Dec   2 p 8vo   NYPL(B)
from C W Howard
Though a perfect stranger I have taken the

28 Dec   4 p 8vo   NYPL(B)
from Harriot Wilson
Your having authorized me, to apply at Xmas

10 Nov [1838–39]   copy   2 p 4to
to CFBt   NYPL(B)
Ah my Charlott*a*, you touch me now! when you

1839

8 JA 1839 pmk   3 p 8vo   NYPL(B)
to CFBt
I am *bodily* better certainly but worn — worn

21 [F]E 1839 pmk   2 p 8vo   Scot
to SHB
My dearest Sarah Harriet the affair is at length

1839, continued

28 FE 1839 pmk   3 p 8vo   NYPL(B)
from SHB
Before I thank you, my poor dear Sister,

2 MR 1839 pmk   1 p 8vo   Cal(B)
to Alfred Turner
Madame dd'Arblay [sic] begs the favour of Mr.

5 Mar   copy   3 p 4to   NYPL(B)
to CFBt
Ah my dearest! — how changed, changed I

1 MY 1839 pmk   3 p 8vo   NYPL(B)
to CFBt
So charmed I am that I *must* write my

30 July–21 Aug   4 p 8vo   NYPL(B)
to CFBt
I will not ask what my dearest Charlotta has

19 Aug [1839]   4 p 4to   NYPL(B)
from Sarah (Burney) Payne
I have waited to write until we should be

24 Aug   4 p 4to   NYPL(B)
from Maria (Burney) Bourdois
You were kind enough to throw out a gentle

1840

No letters extant.

ALEXANDRE JEAN BAPTISTE PIOCHARD D'ARBLAY   1754–1818

(M d'A)

See also letters to and from FBA, CB and CB Jr, and from SBP. M d'A also wrote many letters jointly with FBA; these are listed with her correspondence.

Holograph works and documents of General d'Arblay are chiefly in the Berg Collection, but some items are located in the following collections: Barrett, John Comyn, National Portrait Gallery, Osborn, Yale University Library.

1789

1 Sept   copy   1 p 4to   Vin
to — de Givry
Une affaire des plus pressantes m'appelle à

1791

[pre 26 Oct 1791]   1 p fol   Vin
to Jean-Baptiste Gouvion
Il resulte des decrets de l'Assemblée Nationale

[1791]   copy   3 p 4to   Vin
to the Military Committee of the National Assembly
Permettez qu'au nom de plusieurs Officiers

1792

4 Jan [1792]   2 p 8vo   NYPL(B)
from Louis, comte de Narbonne-Lara
je pars dans l'instant, Mon ami,

15 Feb 1792]   2 p 8vo   NYPL(B)
from Marquis de Lafayette
je reçois votre lettre, mon cher d'Arblay,

2 May   3 p 8vo   NYPL(B)
from Marie-Pierre Millin de Grandmaison
au moment ou j'ai recu Votre derniere epitre

15 June   copy?   1 p 4to   NYPL(B)
from Charles-François Dupérier Du-
   mouriez
Je reçois, Monsieur, la lettre que vous m'avez

[22 June 1792]   1 p 8vo   NYPL(B)
from Louis, comte de Narbonne-Lara
vous apprendrez bientot tous les details

24 June   3 p fol   NYPL(B)
from Marquis de Lafayette
J'ai reçu mon cher D'arblay, une lettre de vous

11 July   4 p 4to   AN
to Marquis de Lafayette
Je crois vous avoir mandé il y a quelques jours

23 July   2 p fol   AN
from le Directoire de Longwy
Nous avons l'honneur de vous faire passer

23 July   1 p 4to   AN
from Marquis de Lafayette
L'assemblée Nationale n'a rien encore décidé

24 July   3 p 4to   AN
to — Sionville
Je crois devoir avertir Monsieur Sionville

29 July   2 p fol   AN
to Marquis de Lafayette
Soyez tranquille, Je pourrais vous fournir

[July 1792]   1 p 4to   AN
from ?
La Personne que vien savez [sic] est revenue

29 Sept   copy   1 p 4to   NYPL(B)
to Louis, comte de Foucault de Lardimalie
J'ai l'honneur de vous adresser

2 Oct [1792]   3 p 4to   NYPL(B)
from Jean-Gabriel Peltier
oui, Monsieur, J'insére dans le supplement
also   copy   2 p 4to   NYPL(B)

2 Oct   copy   1 p 4to   NYPL(B)
to Jean Gabriel Peltier
Il m'est impossible, Mr. de fermer l'ocil
also   copy   2 p 8vo   NYPL(B)

10 Oct   copy   2 p 4to   NYPL(B)
from Louis, comte de Foucault de
   Lardimalie
J'arrivais de Verdun, Mr., lorsque j'appris

20 Oct   1 p 4to   NYPL(B)
from Louis, comte de Narbonne-Lara
Tu es malade, Mon pauvre ami,

[1792]   1 p 8vo   NYPL(B)
from Louis, comte de Narbonne-Lara
j'aimerois autant que nous ne fussions pas

[1792–94]   1 p 8to   NYPL(B)
from Louis, comte de Narbonne-Lara
je vais toujours demain a Londres, Mon ami

[1792–94]   1 p 4to   NYPL(B)
from Louis, comte de Narbonne-Lara
je repars pour aller trouver nos amis

[1792–94]   1 p 4to   NYPL(B)
from Louis, comte de Narbonne-Lara
voila un paquet pour Mr Darblai

[1792–94]   2 p 4to   NYPL(B)
from Louis, comte de Narbonne-Lara
vous scavez de ja que la Martinique est

[1792–95]   1 p 8vo   NYPL(B)
from Marquis de Lally-Tollendal
Mon cher D'Arblay, je m'arrache à un

[1792–98]   1 p 12mo   NYPL(B)
from Louis, comte de Narbonne-Lara
jaurois bien voulu; Mon ami, vous embrasser

[1792–98]   1 p 8vo   NYPL(B)
from Louis, comte de Narbonne-Lara
avant hier Mon ami le capitaine a amené

[1792–98]   1 p 8vo   NYPL(B)
from Louis, comte de Narbonne-Lara
jesperois vous porter moi même Mon ami tous

[1792–1802]   2 p 4to   NYPL(B)
from Marquis de Lally-Tollendal
Mon cher d'Arblay, c'est tout le plus si j'ai

26 [1792–1802]   1 p 8vo   NYPL(B)
from Marquis de Lally-Tollendal
je m'apperçois dans l'instant mon cher

1793

28 Mar   1 p 4to   NYPL(B)
from William Locke
Capt Phillips has just called upon me to desire

19 June   2 p 8vo   NYPL(B)
from Anne-Louise-Germaine (Necker)
    de Staël-Holstein
mon cher d'arblay vous avez pitié de madresser,

[June? 1793]   copy   3 p 4to
                              NYPL(B)
to Charles-François Dupérier Dumour-
    iez
Permets à un ancien ami qui ne t'a pas perdu

[27 July 1793]   1 p 8vo   NYPL(B)
to JB
C'est demain, mon cher Capitaine, que

[28 July 1793]   1 p 12mo   NYPL(B)
to JB
Je desirerais infiniment que le Capitaine

5 Aug   1 p 4to   BM(Bar)
from Philippe de Noailles, prince de
    Poix
Votre Lettre du 1er de ce mois ne m'est pas

also   copy   1 p 4to   BM(Bar)

9 Aug   4 p 4to   NYPL(B)
from Marquis de Lally-Tollendal
Je m'étais plaint de vous, mon cher D'Arblay,

24 Sept   2 p 4to   NYPL(B)
from Jean-Baptiste de Boinville
Mon cher ami, ton billet en date du 2 du mois

8 Dec   1 p 4to   BM(Bar)
from Philippe de Noailles, prince de
    Poix
Pardon mille fois Mon Cher d'Arblay de ne pas

9 [Dec 1793]   3 p 4to   NYPL(B)
from Marquis de Lally-Tollendal
Mettez moi, mon cher ami, aux pieds de

[1793–94]   1 p 8vo   NYPL(B)
from Louis, comte de Narbonne-Lara
je ne vais pas vous voir, Mon ami, attendu que

3 Sept [1793–96]   2 p 8vo   NYPL(B)
from Louis Romeuf
Je ne puis, mon cher d'arblay, quitter

[1793–98]   1 p 4to   NYPL(B)
from Louis, comte de Narbonne-Lara
je vous ai attendu avec impatience, Mon ami

[1793–1802]   2 p 4to   NYPL(B)
from Marquis de Lally-Tollendal
Autant qu'un autre, Mes amis

1794

18 Jan   2 p 4to   PML
from Arnail-François, marquis de Jau-
    court
J'espere mon cher D'arblay que M. de

12 Feb   3 p 8vo   NYPL(B)
from Marie-Louise, marquise de Ron-
    cherolles
j'ai vu avec le plus grand plaisir, Monsieur,

17 Feb   2 p 4to   NYPL(B)
from Marquis de Lally-Tollendal
J'ai recours à vous, mon cher D'Arblay

[Feb 1794]   1 p 4to   NYPL(B)
from Louis, comte de Narbonne-Lara
je comptois vous voir ce matin Mon ami,

[Feb 1794]   2 p 8vo   NYPL(B)
from Louis, comte de Narbonne-Lara
Si vous n'aviez pas, Mon ami, une autrement

[Feb 1794]   1 p 8vo   NYPL(B)
to SBP (with AL Narbonne-Lara to M
    d'A [Feb 1794])
Je ne sais pas votre Secret à tous

1 Mar   2 p 4to   NYPL(B)
from Bon-Albert Briois de Beaumetz
Adieu done, Mon cher D'Arblai, mon cher

2 Mar   copy   2 p 4to   NYPL(B)
from Charles-Maurice de Talleyrand-
    Perigord to FBA & M d'A
adieu mon cher d'Arblay; je quitte votre pays

15 Mar   2 p 4to   Osb
to *The Times*
Je crois acquerir des droits à votre

[Mar 1794]   ¾ p 4to   NYPL(B)
from Louis, comte de Narbonne-Lara
je suis arrivé hier au soir,

6 May   2 p 4to   NYPL(B)
to L M Barral, évêque de of Troyes
Vous avez reçu probablement, Monsieur, par

9 May [1794]   2 p scrap   NPG
from Charles Maurice de Talleyrand-
      Périgord
Le 14 Mars j'etois encore à falmouth et le 28

7 July   4 p 4to   NYPL(B)
from Louis, comte de Narbonne-Lara
C'est a votre tour a être ennuye de moi

16 July [1794]   3 p 4to   NYPL(B)
from Angélique, comtesse de Montrand
Vous mavez oubliée Monsieur et may

21 July   3 p 4to   NYPL(B)
from Angélique, comtesse de Montrand
Comme je Connais les tourmens de l'incertitude

[28 July 1794]   2 p 4to   NYPL(B)
from Angélique, comtesse de Montrand
Eh! bien Monsieur, Cette reponse

31 July   2 p 4to   NYPL(B)
from Angélique, comtesse de Montrand
Le detail de la maison que vous avez

5 Aug   2 p 4to   NYPL(B)
from Denise-Victoire, marquise de
      Germigney
j'ai recu Votre lettre du 18 juin, monsieur

7 Aug [1794]   5 p 4to   NYPL(B)
from Angélique, comtesse de Montrand
Nous nous sommes écrit en même temps

21 Aug   3 p 4to   NYPL(B)
from Louis, comte de Narbonne-Lara
je ne m'accomode pas du tout, Mon ami, de

22 AU 1794 pmk   3 p 4to   NYPL(B)
from Angélique, comtesse de Montrand
J'ay attendu que je fusse enfin passée

[Aug-Sept 1794]   draft   1 p 4to
                              NYPL(B)
to Denise-Victoire, marquise de
      Germigney
Oui, Madame: ma conscience est mon juge

23 Sept   4 p 4to   NYPL(B)
from Louis, comte de Narbonne-Lara
j'ai eu deux lettres de vous, Mon ami,

6 Nov   3 p 4to   NYPL(B)
from Louis, comte de Narbonne-Lara
j'ai heureusement appris a la fois, Mon ami,

15 [Nov? 1794]   2 p 4to   NYPL(B)
from Louis, comte de Narbonne-Lara
vous ne vous <lassez> pas, Mon ami, de me

18 Dec   2 p 4to   PML
with SBP to JB & PS by FBA
In a very few years, my dear James, Martin

27 Dec   4 p fol   NYPL(B)
from Marquis de Lally-Tollendal
Quoi qu'il y ait, mon cher D'Arblay

31 Dec   2 p 4to   NYPL(B)
from Antoine-Marie-René Terrier de
      Monciel
Je suis bien faché, mon cher Darblay, davoir

[1794]   1 p 4to   NYPL(B)
from William Locke
Nothing can be more natural than Mme.

6 Nov   3 p 4to   NYPL(B)
from Jean-Baptiste Le Chevalier
Comment voulez vous, Mon ami, que j'ecrive

[1794?]   2 p 4to   NYPL(B)
from Jean-Baptiste Le Chevalier
je sors de chez le Ministre

1795

28 Feb   2 p 4to   NYPL(B)
from Marquis de Lally-Tollendal
Dites moi, je vous en prie, mon Cher D'Arblay

[23 Mar 1795]   2 p 4to   PML
to JB (with PS by FBA)
your sister, my dear James, would be very
[PS by FBA] I am dying to see these

1795, continued

10 or 12 Apr   4 p 4to   NYPL(B)
from Louis, comte de Narbonne-Lara
depuis trois mois, Mon ami, je n'ai fait

10 Aug   4 p 4to   NYPL(B)
from ?
Oui Monsieur j'avois su que vous aviez eu la

10 Sept   3 p 4to   NYPL(B)
from Marie Charlotte (Bontemps), mar-
    quise de Jaucourt
j'ai esperé Monsieur que vous trouveriez

18 Sept   3 p 4to   NYPL(B)
from Angélique, comtesse de Montrand
Je voulais vous ecrire

11 Oct   6 p 4to   NYPL(B)
from Angélique, comtesse de Montrand
Je suis libre et tranquille, Monsieur,

17 OC 1795 pmk   4 p 4to   NYPL(B)
from Angélique, comtesse de Montrand
je n'entens point parler de vous monsieur

14 Dec   4 p 4to   NYPL(B)
from Charles Sicard
je vous remercie bien Sincerement Mon cher

[1795]   3 p 4to   NYPL(B)
from William & Frederica Locke
I have received your kind note my dear

[1795–1802]   3 p 4to   NYPL(B)
from Marie Charlotte (Bontemps), mar-
    quise de Jaucourt
enfin, il faut renoncer a tous ces projecs

[1795–1802]   3 p 8vo   NYPL(B)
from ?
Ah que je voudrais *consoler* et ranimer notre

1796

24 Jan   3 p 4to   NYPL(B)
from Louis, comte de Narbonne-Lara
Ce sort aura beau faire

28 Feb   4 p 4to   NYPL(B)
from Angélique, comtesse de Montrand
Eh! bien monsieur, ma souscription ne va pas

4 Mar   1 p 4to   NYPL(B)
from L M Barral, évêque de Troyes
j'ai l'honneur de vous renvoyer, Monsieur,

[16 Mar 1796]   4 p 4to   NYPL(B)
from Angélique, comtesse de Montrand
je ne sais par ou Commencer ma Lettre

6 AP pmk [1796]   4 p 4to   NYPL(B)
from Angélique, comtesse de Montrand
bonjour Monsieur, je vous écris

19–20 [Apr 1796]   3 p fol   NYPL(B)
from Angélique, comtesse de Montrand
J'ay bien peur Monsieur, qu'une lettre que j'ai

27 MA 1796 pmk   4 p 4to   NYPL(B)
from Angélique, comtesse de Montrand
Enfin monsieur ma robbe c'est a dire Celle de

22 July   2 p 4to   Comyn
from William Clarke
I received your obliging Letter of the 13th.

5 Sept   2 p 4to   NYPL(B)
from Angélique, comtesse de Montrand
Je doute, Monsieur, et je me plais même a

29 Nov   5 p 4to   NYPL(B)
from Angélique, comtesse de Montrand
J'avais donc bien raison, Monsieur, d'être si

12 Dec   3 p 4to   NYPL(B)
from Angélique, comtesse de Montrand
Je voulais vous ecrire, Monsieur, pour

[1796]   2 p 4to   NYPL(B)
from Etiennette, princesse d'Hénin
c'est avec le coeur tout rempli de notre chere

[1796?]   2 p 4to   NYPL(B)
from Etiennette, princesse d'Hénin
J'ai été sensiblement touchée de votre

[1796?]   4 p 4to   NYPL(B)
from Angélique, comtesse de Montrand
Je voulais avoir le plaisir bien plutot

1797

30 Jan [1797]   2 p 4to   NYPL(B)
from Etiennette, princesse d'Hénin
Vous sentez bien monsieur que vous m'avez

5 Feb   3 p 4to   NYPL(B)
from Marquis de Lally-Tollendal
Coment [sic], monsieur vous avez la bonté de

[17 Feb 1797]   4 p fol   NYPL(B)
from Angélique, comtesse de Montrand
Votre lettre m'a fait tant de plaisir

23 Mar   3 p 4to   NYPL(B)
from Angélique, comtesse de Montrand
Je suis payée, Monsieur et Madame,

30 Mar   pmk 1797   8 p 4to
                              NYPL(B)
from Angélique, comtesse de Montrand
Voicy ma petite histoire

16 AP 1797 pmk   4 p 4to   NYPL(B)
from Angélique, comtesse de Montrand
Je suis une ingratte

9 May   4 p 4to   NYPL(B)
from Angélique, comtesse de Montrand
Mais que pensez vous de moy Monsieur

12 May   2 p 4to   NYPL(B)
from Charles Sicard
il y a un Siecle, Mon cher Darblay, que je

26 May   4 p 4to   NYPL(B)
from Charles Sicard
il y a quatre jours, Mon cher Darblay, que

22 [July 1797]   4 p 4to   NYPL(B)
from Angélique, comtesse de Montrand
Eh! mon dieu non, Monsieur, je ne doutais pas

24 July [1797]   4 p 4to   NYPL(B)
from Angélique, comtesse de Montrand
Eh! bien Monsieur, je ne reçois point de vos

28 [July 1797]   4 p 4to   NYPL(B)
from Angélique, comtesse de Montrand
Non, Monsieur, je ne seray pas partie Lundy

8 Aug–1 Sept   4 p 4to   NYPL(B)
from Jean-Baptiste-Gabriel Bazille
il est donc vray, Mon cher Alexandre, que tu

12 Aug   2 p 4to   NYPL(B)
from Charles Sicard
je suis extremement touché, Monsieur

16 Nov–17 Dec   4 p fol   NYPL(B)
to SBP
La date de cette lettre est déjà une reponse

[Nov? 1797]   copy   1 p fol
                              NYPL(B)
from Marquis de Lafayette (included in
    AL M d'A to SBP 16 Nov–17 Dec
    1797)
Je savais bien d'avance que votre interest nous

[post 16 Dec 1797]   3 p fol
to SBP   NYPL(B)
Quelle lettre que la vôtre ma chere amie!

[1797?]   2 p 4to   NYPL(B)
from Angélique, comtesse de Montrand
Je prens une petite feuille si fine

[post 1797]   1 p 8vo   PML
from Claire (de Kersaint), duchesse de
    Duras
Je vous remercie mille fois Monsieur de la

1798

[18 Mar 1798]   1 p 4to   NYPL(B)
to SBP
Eh bien oui c'est encore moi

28 Aug   2 p 4to   NYPL(B)
from Louis, comte de Narbonne-Lara
surement, Mon D'Arblay, j'ai bien besoin

13 Nov   2 p 4to   NYPL(B)
from William Lane
Driven by an unfortunate accident

25 Nov   draft   1 p 4to   NYPL(B)
to William Lane
Je n'etais pas sans inquietude

15 ⟨Jan⟩ [post 1798?]   1 p 12mo
from Marquis de Lafayette   NYPL(B)
J'ai reçu, mon cher d'arblay, une tres aimable

1799

1 Feb   3 p 4to   NYPL(B)
from Louis, comte de Narbonne-Lara
vous voyez, Mon ami, par la datte de ma lettre
also   copy   3 p 4to   NYPL(B)

[Feb-Mar?]   copy   1 p 4to
from Pierre Victor Malouet   NYPL(B)
Nous pouvons nous considerer

1799, continued

[Feb-Mar?]   copy   1 p 4to
to SBP   NYPL(B)
J'ai ecrit à M. Mallouet pour

26 Mar   pmk 1799   3 p 4to
from Pierre Victor Malouet   NYPL(B)
je me peux Monsieur vous donner aucun

23 Aug   3 p 4to   BM(Bar)
from Marquis de Lally-Tollendal
Jai reçu hier, mon cher D'arblay, votre lettre

18 Oct   3 p 4to   PML
from Frederic-Seraphin, marquis de
    Latour du Pin
je n'ai point oublié, Monsieur, que vous m'avez

1800

25 Feb   3 p 8vo   NYPL(B)
from Marquis de Lally-Tollendal
Mon cher D'Arblay, tout est très simple

[pre Apr 1800] draft   ½ p 4to
to Louis-Alexandre Berthier   NYPL(B)
Ni l'eclat de tes exploits guerriers, ni

9 JY pmk [1800]   1 p 8vo   PML
from Marquis de Lafayette
Si vous avez reçu la Lettre que je vous Ecrivis,

9 Dec   2 p 4to   NYPL(B)
from ?
Je reçois ta Lettre dans l'instant, Mon cher ami

1801

15 Sept   4 p 8vo   NYPL(B)
from Marquis de Lally-Tollendal
Mon cher Bon ami, Je vous recommande

[2–8 Oct 1801]   copy   1 p 4to
to Louis-Alexandre Berthier   NYPL(B)
Il y a 10 mois que sur la nouvelle

26 Dec [1801]   1 p 8vo   NYPL(B)
from Marquis de Lafayette
Je ne sais ou vous etcs, mon cher d'arblay,

[1801?]   draft   1 p 4to   NYPL(B)
to Louis-Alexandre Berthier & Louis,
    comte de Narbonne-Lara
J'ose reclamer de votre justice

[1801]   copy   1 p 4to   NYPL(B)
to Charles Maurice de Talleyrand-Péri-
    gord
Je viens mettre à l'epreuve

[1801]   copy   1 p 4to   NYPL(B)
to Adrien du Bosc, comte Dutaillis
Je vous prie, mon cher Gᵃˡ, de mettre

14 June [pre 1802?]   1 p 4to   NYPL(B)
from Sir William Burrell
Sir William <Burrell> presents his

1802

2 Jan   copy   1 p 8vo   NYPL(B)
to Louis-Alexandre Berthier
Mʳ Bar. ne reçoit qu'a l'instant

[2 Jan 1802]   1 p 4to   NYPL(B)
to William Locke
Mon respectable ami, lisez ce lettre

10 Jan   1 p 4to   Vin
to Louis-Alexandre Berthier
Jaloux de repondre à la bienveillance du
also   copy   2 p fol   NYPL(B)

12 Jan   2 p 4to   NYPL(B)
from William Locke
I have barely time for a single line my dear

[17 Jan 1802]   2 p 8vo   PML
from Marquis de Lafayette
J'esperais le plaisir de Vous voir ici, mon cher

27 Jan   1 p fol   NYPL(B)
from Louis-Alexandre Berthier
Je vous préviens, Citoyen, que d'après
also   copy   1 p 8vo   NYPL(B)
also   28 Jan   draft   2 p fol   Vin

10 Feb   copy   1 p 4to   NYPL(B)
to Louis-Alexandre Berthier
Le Citoyen Gan qui avait bien voulu

14 Feb   2 p 8vo   PML
from Arnail-François, marquis de Jau-
    court
Adieu, Mon cher D'arblay, bon voyage, et en

20 Feb   1 p fol   NYPL(B)
from Louis-Alexandre Berthier
J'ai reçu, Citoyen, votre lettre datée

also   25 Feb   copy   ½ p 4to   NYPL(B)

25 Feb   copy   ½ p 4to   NYPL(B)
from Adrien du Bosc, comte Dutaillis
Je vous fais passer, mon cher Darblay, la lettre

[Feb 1802]   copy   1 p 4to
to Louis-Alexandre Berthier   NYPL(B)
J'apprens avec une extrême douleur,

[Feb 1802]   copy   2 p 4to
to Napoleon Bonaparte   NYPL(B)
La generosité et la grandeur etant inseparable

1 Mar   copy   1 p 4to   NYPL(B)
from Adrien du Bosc, comte Dutaillis
J'ai mon ami à vous remettre

3 Mar   copy   3 p 4to   NYPL(B)
to Marquis de Lafayette
Tel est, mon G^{al}., le resultat de ma lettre au

28 June   3 p 4to   NYPL(B)
from William Locke
I write by this post, mon cher ami, to Messrs

11 Dec   2 p 4to   NYPL(B)
from William Locke
I did not immediately answer you kind letter,

[1802]   1 p 12mo   NYPL(B)
from Marie Charlotte (Bontemps), mar-
    quise de Jaucourt
Nous avons eprouvé le plus grand plaisir

[1802]   1 p 8vo   PML
from Marquis de Lafayette
lorsque le < > a voulu <enver > un

9 Oct [post 1802]   1 p 12mo
from Marquis de Lafayette   NYPL(B)
je me felicite de tout mon coeur avec vous, mon

1 Dec post 1802]   1 p 4to
from Marquis de Lafayette   NYPL(B)
Vous savez surement, mon cher d'arblay, que

[1802–05]   1 p 12mo   NYPL(B)
from Adrienne (de Noailles), comtesse
    de Tessé
Me de Tessé ne concevoit pas que Monsieur

[1802–06]   3 p 4to   PML
with Antoine Bourdois to JB
Vite un mot, mon cher James, pour vous dire

[1802–14]   2 p 4to   NYPL(B)
from   ?
La complaisance que vous avez eu en

1803

5 Feb   2 p 4to   NYPL(B)
from William Locke
I did not sell your Omnium My d^r d Arblay

5 Mar   1 p fol   Vin
to Napoleon Bonaparte
Daignez accueillir avec indulgence la prière

5 Mar   4 p 4to   PML
to JB (with PS by FBA)
J'ai recu, mon cher James; votre second envoi

27 Mar   2 p 4to   NYPL(B)
from William Locke
My dear d Arblay The hope which I have

9 Apr   1 p 4to   Vin
to   ?
Je vous dois et vous fais les remerciemens les

22 May   2 p 4to   NYPL(B)
from William Locke
I have no courage My dear d'Arblay to enter

27 Dec   2 p 4to   NYPL(B)
to [Gilles] Ragon
Non seulement, mon cher ami, j'accepte

[1803]   draft   1 p 8vo   NYPL(B)
to Gabriel, comte d'Hédouville
J'ignore, mon cher General, quelle est

[1803?]   1 p 4to   NYPL(B)
from Pierre-Marie, marquis de Grave
J'ai bien du regret, mon cher camarade, de la

1803–13]   1 p 4to   NYPL(B)
from — Barbier Neuville
Tachez, mon Cher Bon Monsieur D'arblay,

1804

3 Mar [1804?]   1 p 4to   NYPL(B)
from Marquis de Lafayette
Voici, mon cher d'arblay, une recommendation

12 Sept   1 p 12mo   NYPL(B)
from Victor de Latour Maubourg
Votre bon coeur et votre amitié pour moi

21 Sept [1804]   2 p 8vo   NYPL(B)
from César, comte de Latour-Maubourg
je n'avois que trop prévu mon cher D'Arblay

24 Oct [1804]   2 p 4to   Comyn
to AA
Mon cher petit Alex. Je souffre au delà de tout

[Oct 1804?]   2 p 4to   NYPL(B)
to AA
Soigne bien ta Santé, mon cher petit Alex,

[Oct 1804?]   1 p 4to   NYPL(B)
to AA
je n'ai pas voulu t'éveiller mon cher petit bon

7 Nov   1 p 8vo   NYPL(B)
from Mathieu, comte Dumas
Voici, mon cher D'arblai, l'apostille que

[c 1804–05]   1 p 8vo   NYPL(B)
from Catherine (de Boullogne), vicom-
    tesse de Laval
mattieu et *gerrando* — désire que vous

1805

[10 Mar 1805]   draft   1 p 4to
    NYPL(B)
to Mathieu, duc de Montmorency
Vous savez, mon cher Montmorency, le

14 Mar   2 p 4to   NYPL(B)
from Joseph, baron de Gerando
Son Excellence Le Ministre de l'Interièur

14 Mar [1805]   1 p 8vo   NYPL(B)
from Mathieu, duc de Montmorency
je ne saurois aller vous dire, mon cher darblay

2 Apr   1 p 8vo   NYPL(B)
from [Jean-Nicolas Desmeunier?]
Je ne peux decemment vous feliciter, Monsieur

3 Apr   3 p 4to   NYPL(B)
from J G Lacuée, comte de Cessac
personne n'a pu apprendre avec plus de plaisir

7 Apr   1 p 4to   NYPL(B)
from Marquis de Lafayette
Oui sans doute, mon cher d'Arblai, c'est avec

13 Apr   1 p 4to   NYPL(B)
from Charles Dulauloy, comte de Ran-
    don
C'est ici dans tes anciennes galaries

19 May   1 p 4to   NYPL(B)
from — Montmarin
Dès que j'ai entendu prononçer votre nom

May   1 p 4to   NYPL(B)
from Gilles Ragon
j'ai vu avec Grand plaisir Monsieur

24 Oct 1805?]   1 p 4to   NYPL(B)
from Marquis de Lafayette
je recois, mon cher d'arblay, une lettre de

1806

19 Nov   2 p 4to   NYPL(B)
from César, comte de Latour-Maubourg
On dit qu'on ne repond pas aux Sollicitations

19 Nov   1 p 4to   NYPL(B)
from François, duc de Liancourt
Vous avez bien raison mon cher darblay,

[1806?]   2 p 8vo   BM(Bar)
from Marquis de Lally-Tollendal
Mon cher ami, je serois si heureux & si fier de

1807

3 Aug   2 p 4to   PML
from César, comte de Latour-Maubourg
M^de de Maubourg a eu de <l'espriz> comme

17 Dec   1 p 4to   NYPL(B)
from Jean-Jacques-Basilicn, comte de
    Gassendi
C'est au contraire moi qui t'importune

1808

[30 Apr 1808]   1 p 8vo   NYPL(B)
from Louis, comte de Narbonne-Lara
je ne sais pas comment vous servir, Mon ami,

[c 1808]   1 p 8vo   NYPL(B)
from — Meneret
Je ferai bien volontiers ce qui peut être

[1808–09]   copy   1 p 4to
                              NYPL(B)
to Jean-Pierre, comte de Montalivet
Non moins penetré de respect pour la place

1809

27 Jan   1 p fol   NYPL(B)
from Felix Pontonnier
J'ai l'honneur de vous adresser la figure

9 Apr   3 p 8vo   NYPL(B)
from Marquis de Lally-Tollendal
Je vous avais écrit une longue lettre

3 Sept   3 p 8vo   NYPL(B)
from Florimonde de Latour Maubourg
je n'ai point oublié Monsieur votre aimable

12 Sept   4 p 4to   NYPL(B)
from Victor de Latour Maubourg to
     M d'A & AA
Ta lettre du 4

26 ⟨Nov⟩   2 p 8vo   NYPL(B)
from E Paisy
⟨   ⟩ a vos ordres, Monsieur, j'ai

1810

4 Mar   1 p 8vo   NYPL(B)
from Jean-Pierre, comte de Montalivet
[printed] Le Ministre de l'Interieur et Madame

11 June [1810?]   1 p 8vo   NYPL(B)
from Denise-Victoire, marquise de
     Germigney
Ma fille est partie pour la franche-comté

21 July [1810?]   1 p 4to   NYPL(B)
from Denise-Victoire, marquise de
     Germigney
Comme il vous ⟨   ⟩ bien d'obliger

20 Sept [1810]   1 p 8vo   NYPL(B)
from Adrienne (de Noailles), comtesse
     de Tessé
notre chère malade savoit bien

16 Nov   1 p 4to   NYPL(B)
from César, comte de Latour-Maubourg
Je suis arrivé depuis huit jours

[1810]   1 p 8vo   NYPL(B)
from Marquis de Lally-Tollendal
je vous renvoye, mon cher D'arblai, ce

[1810]   1 p 8vo   NYPL(B)
from Louis, comte de Narbonne-Lara
chez le Ministre de la police

[1810]   1 p 8vo   NYPL(B)
from Adrienne (de Noailles), comtesse
     de Tessé
je ne puis defferer de Repondre cette foi

[1810–11]   ½ p 4to   NYPL(B)
from Louis, comte de Narbonne-Lara
je suis bien faché, Mon ami,

[1810–11]   1 p 8vo   NYPL(B)
from Louis, comte de Narbonne-Lara
je ne peux pas vous dire, Mon ami

[1810–15]   1 p 8vo   NYPL(B)
from [Louise-Joséphine de Montesqui-
     ou, comtesse de] Fézensac
ce n'est en vérité pas ma faute si je n'ai pas eu

1811

8 June [1811]   2 p 8vo   NYPL(B)
from Adrienne (de Noailles), comtesse
    de Tessé
quelle singuliere aventure! Monsieur

June   1 p 8vo   BM(Bar)
from Jean-Jacques-Basilien, comte de
    Gassendi
Je n'ai osé aller chez toi, mon cher d'Arblay

28 Aug   1 p 8vo   NYPL(B)
from Nicolas Seguier, marquis de Saint-
    Brisson
je n'ai pas oublié monsieur l'offre que vous

[pre Oct   1811]   1 p 12mo
                              NYPL(B)
to baron de Larrey & Antoine Dubois
Monsieur le Baron Larrey a rendu l'esperance

21 Oct [1811]   1 p 4to   BM(Bar)
from Anne (de Beauveau), princesse de
    Poix
Mad. d'Arblay a reçu tant de temoignages de

[1811?]   draft 1 p ½ fol NYPL(B)
to Jean-Pierre, comte de Montalivet
Permettez que sans detour je dis a Monsieur de

[1811]   1 p 8vo   NYPL(B)
from Louis, comte de Narbonne-Lara
je ne vais pas vous voir, Mon ami, parceque je

[c 1811]   1 p 8vo   Osb
from Marquis de Lafayette
j'ai passé par paris en Revenan d'Aulnay

1812

[June 1812]   1 p 8vo   NYPL(B)
from Marquis de Lally-Tollendal
Cher bon ami je suis chez des < > jusqu'au

9 July 181⟨2⟩   1 p 8vo   NYPL(B)
from Denise-Victoire, marquise de
    Germigney
avez vous des nouvelles des êtres qui

16 Sept   1 p 4to   NYPL(B)
from Jean-Jacques-Basilien, comte de
    Gassendi
Je te renvoye, Mon cher D'Arblay, le manuscrit

10 Oct   3 p 8vo   NYPL(B)
from Nathalie, princess de Beauveau
vous avez été bien bon Monsieur

[1812?]   2 p 8vo   NYPL(B)
from — Noguer
J'ai été touché jusqu'aux larmes

1813

18 Jan   3 p 4to   NYPL(B)
from L M Barral, évêque de Troyes
il n'est pas possible mon cher Darbelai, [sic]

28 Feb [1813?]   1 p 8vo   NYPL(B)
from Denise-Victoire, marquise de
    Germigney
Si vous pouviez obtenir de M. de Gassendi

8 Mar [1813?]   1 p 8vo   NYPL(B)
from Denise-Victoire, marquise de
    Germigney
N'écrivez pas cher ami aux personnes qui

9 Mar   3 p 8vo   PML
from Marquis de Lally-Tollendal
Cher bon ami je n'ai qu'un moment et je

26 May   4 p 8vo   NYPL(B)
to Mme Brou
L'objet de votre voyage me donne l'espoir

22 June [1813]   2 p 8vo   NYPL(B)
from Adrienne (de Noailles), comtesse
    de Tessé
ce coup a ebranlé toutes mes fibres

11 Oct   1 p 4to   NYPL(B)
from baron d'Astrel
Mr le directeur général aura l'honneur de

[Nov-Dec 1813]   1 p 8vo   PML
from Arnail-François, marquis de Jau-
    court
J<envoye> Savoir de vos nouvelles mon cher

2 Dec [1813]   1 p 8vo   NYPL(B)
from Marquis de Lafayette
Lorsque je vous ecrivais, mon cher d'arblay,

3 Dec [1813]   1 p 8vo   NYPL(B)
from Denise-Victoire, marquise de
     Germigney
Je ne peux resister au besoin de vous dire

[1813?]   1 p 8vo   NYPL(B)
from Denise-Victoire, marquise de
     Germigney
Je ne peux vous dire avec quel regret j'ai

[1813?]   1 p 8vo   NYPL(B)
from Marquis de Lafayette
j'ai appris avec grand plaisir, mon cher d'arblai,

[1813–15]   1 p 12mo   NYPL(B)
from Catherine (de Boullogne), vicom-
     tesse de Laval
Moi qui connois si bien votre

1814

[2 Jan 1814]   1 p 8vo   NYPL(B)
from Marquis de Lally-Tollendal
Voilà donc une Lettre reçu de cet ange

30 Mar   2 p 4to   NYPL(B)
from — Fauchat
Messieurs, j'ai l'honneur de vous transmettre

5 May   draft   2 p 4to   NYPL(B)
to William Locke Jr
Je vous renvoie, mon cher William, de ce que

19 May   copy   1 p 8vo   NYPL(B)
to William Locke Jr
La conference concerning Camilla Lodge

25 [May 1814]   copy   1 p 4to
                                  NYPL(B)
from Claude-Louis, duc de la Châtre
     (in ALS M d'A to FBA 26 May
     [1814])
Je vous prie mon cher d'A. de bien soigner

28 May   1 p fol   Vin
with Marquis de Lafayette to Laurent,
     marquis de Govion-Saint-Cyr
Nommé Marechal de camp dans l'intervalle du

[May 1814]   2 p 4to   PML
to JB
I beseech you not to give a hasty refusal to

[May 1814]   draft   2 p 4to
to William Locke Jr   NYPL(B)
Difficulties, very unexpected

[May 1814]   1 p 4to   BM(Bar)
from William Locke Jr
En consultant Mr Murray

5 June   1 p 8vo   NYPL(B)
from Amédee de Durfort, duc de Duras
Le Roi a permis que vous lui

9 June   1 p fol   Vin
to Louis XVIII
D'aprés l'assurance que je devais être porté sur

[9 June 1814]   1 p fol   NYPL(B)
from Marquis de Lafayette
Voici, mon cher d'arblay, mon attestation, si

28 June [1814]   3 p 8vo   NYPL(B)
from [César, comte de] Choiseul-Praslin
Je mempresse Monsieur de vous prevenir

29 June   2 p 4to   NYPL(B)
from Duc de Luxembourg
Je <vous Voulais> bien monsieur le chevalier,

11 July   4 p 4to   NYPL(B)
from — de Gault de Malaville
Quelque hâte que j'aie voulu mettre

19 July   1 p fol   NYPL(B)
from Duc de Luxembourg
Monsieur le Chevalier, j'ai l'honneur de vous

[July–Aug 1814]   1 p fol   NYPL(B)
from Duc de Montesquiou-Fézensac
J'apprends avec plaisir, Monsieur, que S.

8 Aug   1 p 4to   NYPL(B)
from Duc de Luxembourg
J'ai mille Graces à vous rendre Monsieur le

9 Aug   draft?   2 p 4to   NYPL(B)
to Duc de Luxembourg
Mr. le duc de Luxembourg, si aimable si bon

1814, continued

7 NO 1814 pmk   2 p 4to   NPG
to Mr Hudson
Comment puis je reconnaitre j'aurais

3 Dec   2 p 4to   NYPL(B)
from — d'Albini
Je reçois a l'instant, très honnoré et cher

[1814]   4 p 4to   NYPL(B)
to Duc de Luxembourg
(Pour vous seul) / Pardon Pardon / Lorsque

[1814]   copy?   2 p 8vo   NYPL(B)
to Duc de Luxembourg
Sous un Tyran et lorsque les Français

[1814]   1 p 4to   NYPL(B)
from Duc de Luxembourg
D'après toutes les Reflexions

[1814–15]   2 p 8vo   NYPL(B)
from Maria-Teresa (Poniantowski),
        comtesse de Tyszkiewicz
M. de Cyzkiewiz a été désolée de ne pouvoir

[1814–18]   1 p 4to   BM(Bar)
to AA
Ne sois pas trop malheureux mon cher et bien

1815

[7]–12 Jan   1 p fol   Vin
from Laurent, marquis de Gouvion-
        Saint-Cyr
Monsieur Jai reçu la demande que vous avez

27 Mar [1815]   2 p 4to   NYPL(B)
to Henriette (Guignot de Soulignac)
        de Maurville
arrivé ici, et sur le point de partir

2⟨8⟩ Mar   1 p 4to   NYPL(B)
to [Louise (Ferraro-Fieschi)] Duchesse
        d'Ursel
Dans l'inquietude la plus vive

1 Apr [1815]   1 p 8vo   NYPL(B)
from Duc de Luxembourg
Le Duc de Luxembourg regrettera beaucoup

16 Apr   4 p 4to   NYPL(B)
from Duc de Luxembourg
J'ai fait remettre en arrivant ici

4 June   copy   1 p 4to   NYPL(B)
from General Kleist de Hollendof (in
        ALS M d'A to FBA 5 June 1815)
J'ose vous prier, Monsieur le General

1 July   1 p 4to   Vin
to [Duc de Feltre?]
La Gendarmerie m'a encore ammené deux

6 July   3 p 4to   Vin
to [Duc de Feltre?]
J'ai eu l'honneur de rendre à Votre Excellence

3 Aug   2 p 4to   NYPL(B)
from Elizabeth-Charlotte, marquise
        d'Ambly
C'est une vielle connaissance, a vous mon

5 Aug [1815]   4 p 4to   BM(Bar)
from Etiennette, princesse d'Hénin
je vous envoie mes chers amis une lettre de

20 Aug   2 p 4to   NYPL(B)
to ?
On me flatte, mon cher commandant, de

20 Aug   3 p 4to?   Vin
to [Duc de Feltre?]
Officier superieur des Gardes du Corps, et

31 Aug   copy   1 p fol   NYPL(B)
from Laurent, marquis de Gouvion-
        Saint-Cyr
Général, la mission que Sa Majesté a bien voulu

[Aug 1815]   copy   2 p fol
to Duc de Luxembourg   NYPL(B)
Monʳ Durand de Premorel, chef d'une famille

[Aug 1815]   2 p 4to   NYPL(B)
from Marie de Maisonneuve
après avoir pris la part la plus sensible à

1 Sept   1 p fol   NYPL(B)
from Duc de Luxembourg
J'ai reçu, mon cher d'Arblay, votre lettre

3 Sept   1 p 4to   Vin
to Richard, comte D'Arcy
J'ai l'honneur de vous prier de vouloir bien

7 Sept 3 p 4to NYPL(B)
from — Durand de Prémorel
j'ai porté avant hier vos lettres à Madame

11 Sept 2 p fol Vin
to [Duc de Feltre?]
Vous le savez, loin de Solliciter la mission

also copy 3 p fol NYPL(B)

25 Sept 2 p 4to NYPL(B)
from Victor de Latour-Maubourg
Mon cher Darblay la remise de

11 Oct 1 p 4to NYPL(B)
from — (Host) Leclerc
Je me suis présentée chez vous samedy

[Oct 1815] 1 p 8vo NYPL(B)
from Louise-Joséphine, comtesse de
Montesquiou Fézensac
je vais remettre à l'instant

[1815] 3 p 4to Vin
to [Duc de Feltre?]
Les progrés inconcevables des Alliés ne me

[1815] 1 p scrap NYPL(B)
from ⟨Kiamensky⟩
Partant a deux heures du matin, j'ai l'honneur

[1815–1816] 1 p 4to Vin
to ?
Vous avez eu la bonté de me promettre, il y a

1816

15 Jan 4 p 4to NYPL(B)
from Victor de Latour Maubourg
Mon cher et bien cher Darblay

27 Mar 3 p 4to NYPL(B)
from — Carle
Je profite de l'occasion d'un voyageur

29 Apr 2 p fol Vin
from Duc de Feltre
Monsieur le Comte, Vous avez réclamé le

12 May 3 p 4to NYPL(B)
from J-B Theuillier de Beaufort
Votre lettre du 1er avril vient, Mon tres cher

27 Sept 3 p 4to NYPL(B)
from Marie-Pierre de Grandmaison
Si je savois que vous vinssiez me voir

27 Sept draft 1 p 4to NYPL(B)
to Marie-Pierre de Grandmaison
Il m'est impossible ma chere et bien aimée

28 Sept 1 p 4to NYPL(B)
from ⟨Kaurz⟩
J'ai l'honneur de vous adresser l'autorization,

[Sept 1816] 1 p 4to Vin
to Vicomte ?
J'ose me flatter que vous voudrez bien

Sept 2 p fol Vin
to Duc de Feltre
L'article X de l'Instruction du 4 Septembre

28 [Sept–Oct 1816] 1 p 4to
NYPL(B)
from Marie-Pierre de Grandmaison
Votre reponse cher frere, me confirme ce que

6 Nov 2 p fol Vin
to [Duc de Feltre?]
Parti de Bath aussitot que mes Plaies à peine

6 Nov 1 p fol Vin
to [Duc de Feltre?]
J'ai l'honneur d'adresser à Votre Excellence

9 Nov 1 p 8vo? Vin
to ?
Vous avez eu la bonté de me dire lorsque j'ai

29 Nov 1 p 8vo BM(Bar)
from Adrienne (de Chavagnac), vicom-
tesse de LaBretonnière
Je compte assez sur l'amabilité de Monsieur

[1816] 1 p 8vo NYPL(B)
from Catherine (de Boullogne), vicom-
tesse de Laval
vous nêtes pas si indigne que moi

[1816] 4 p 8vo NYPL(B)
from Marie de Maisonneuve
Rue d'anjou ou je restois jusqu'au Soir

[1816] 2 p 4to NYPL(B)
from Felicité, comtesse de Choiseul
Sans trop s'etendre sur ma position

[1816] 1 p 4to Wms
from Marquis de Lafayette
je ne vous ai point ⟨averti⟩, mon cher

[1816?] 2 fragments NYPL(B)
to AA
Je te remercie, pour ma part, mon cher

1817

29 Jan   pmk 1817   3 p 4to   NYPL(B)
from Lady Lucy (Fitzgerald) Foley
pour le moins tout les jours je me demande le

6 June   translation   2 p 4to
to AA   [postscript only]   BM(Bar)
I ought now to be seeing to our affairs in Paris

15 Aug   2 p 8vo   NYPL(B)
from Victor de Latour Maubourg
Mon cher Darblay, nous te croyions parti

8 Sept   2 p 4to   NYPL(B)
from Marc-Etienne, prince de Beauveau
Voici le moment mon Cher ami ou vous desiriez

[Sept 1817]   draft   4 p fol
                              NYPL(B)
to Catherine (de Boullogne), vicom-
      tesse de Laval
Rien, sans doute, de plus étrange

[Sept 1817]   draft   4 p fol
to Duc de Luxembourg   NYPL(B)
À mon depart de Gand, pour

also   copy   8 p 4to   NYPL(B)

28 Oct   1 p scrap   NYPL(B)
from   ?
Monsieur Tarnier, à qui vous avez écrit à

24 Dec   1 p scrap   BM(Bar)
from Henry Hoare
nous sommes toujours, avec une vrai

1818

12 Jan   3 p 4to   NYPL(B)
from Victor de Latour Maubourg
J'ai reçu ta lettre du 8 X^{bre}

15 Mar   1 p 4to   NYPL(B)
from Victor de Latour-Maubourg
Mon cher D'arblay, j'avois prié mon parent

[1817]   1 p 8vo   NYPL(B)
from Etiennette, princesse d'Hénin to
      [M d'A]
Vous ne me dites pas, cher ami, si cette lettre

ALEXANDER CHARLES LOUIS D'ARBLAY 1794–1837

(AA)

*See also letters from and to FBA, CFBt, CB Jr and CPB, and letters from
M d'A, JB, Frances Raper.*

*Holograph works of Alexander d'Arblay are located in the Barrett, Berg
and British Museum collections.*

1801

[1801–02]   2 p 4to   BM(Bar)
to M d'A
Papa, I hope Uncle Bazile is well

1802

⟨15⟩   [1802]   1 p 4to   NYPL(B)
to M d'A
dear Papa Cousin Maria has one day given me

1803

26 Jan   typescript copy   3 p   NPG
to Amelia (Locke) Angerstein
My Dear Amene I thank ye very much for

[2 Nov 1803?]   3 p 4to   NYPL(B)
from Précourt Bazille
Mon bon cousin, que votre amitié

1804

[Oct 1804?]   4 p 4to   NYPL(B)
to M d'A
Je vais t'ecrire une bien longue lettre,

1812

[pre 20 July 1812]   1 p 4to   Comyn
to M d'A (with ALS M d'A to CB Jr 20
    July 1812)
We cannot wait any longer for the letter for it

1814

7 July   3 p 4to   NYPL(B)
to M d' A
I am here with Mamma reading for

13 July   3 p 8vo   NYPL(B)
to M d'A
Miss Planta part demain (Jeudi)

[15–17] Oct   1 p 4to   NYPL(B)
to M d'A
Cher cher adorable pere!

[1814–18]   2 p 4to   BM(Bar)
to M d'A
Si j'ai differé jusqu'à present

1815

4 July [1815]   4 p 4to   BM(Bar)
from Frederica Locke
My dear Alexr. if you have not already rec'd

13 Sept [1815]   4 p 4to   NYPL(B)
from Sophia Burney
Pourquoi n'avez vous pas repondu a la lettre

23 Oct   3 p 8vo   BM(Bar)
from GMAPWaddington
How have you rejoiced my heart by writing

17 May [post 1815]   1 p 8vo   PML
from Marquis de Lally-Tollendal
Mon cher alexandre, comment <imaginer>

[post 1815]   1 p 8vo   PML
from Petronille-Jacoba (Van Ryssel) de
    Latour-Maubourg
Voici, mon cher Alexandre, un billet pour la

1816

[1816–18]   4 p 4to   Osb
from [Hugh James Rose]
I have only been prevented by an ocean of

1817

7 Mar   4 p 4to   NYPL(B)
to M d'A
Malgré que j'aie déjà écrit à Maman

13 May   3 p 4to   NYPL(B)
to M d'A
Quand passerons nous donc ce jour-ci

1817, *continued*

4 Nov   3 p 4to   NYPL(B)
to M d'A
Edward Jacob, Esqr. / 17. Everell Street,

30 Dec   1 p 4to   NYPL(B)
to M d'A
L'an prochain, ou comme l'on dit à Joigny,

1818

19 May   3 p 4to   NYPL(B)
from Marie-Alexandre Lenoir
Il n'est donc plus en ce monde de misères le

20 MY 1818 pmk   4 p 4to   BM(Bar)
to Frederica Locke & Amelia (Locke)
     Angerstein
If I have not written sooner in answer to your

22 May [1818]   1 p 8vo   BM(Bar)
from Catherine (de Boullogne), vicom-
     tesse de Laval
je suis digne <en effet> monsieur de sentir et

30 May   1 p 4to   NPG
from Marquis de Lafayette
J'ai lu votre touchante lettre à Victor

30 May [1818?]   2 p 4to   NYPL(B)
from Cécile (de Riquet de Caraman),
     marquise de Sommery
Je suis chargée, Monsieur, de la part de

31 May   2 p 4to   NYPL(B)
from Victor de Latour Maubourg
Mon cher Alexandre, j'ai été pour vous

1 June   3 p 4to   NYPL(B)
from Nathalie (de Mortemart), prin-
     cesse de Beauveau
je ne puis vous exprimer Monsieur, combien

5 June   1 p 4to   NYPL(B)
from Florimond de Latour Maubourg
J'étais à la Campagne, Mon cher Alexandre,

<16> Sept   2 drafts   1 p 4to
                              NYPL(B)
to George Hay (on verso of ALS CB Jr
     to FBA 18 Nov 1816)
My mother commissions me to beg upon

19 Sept   2 p 8vo   NYPL(B)
from William Tudor
I have to acknowledge the receipt of your

[post 1818]   draft   2 p 4to
to George Hay   BM(Bar)
We shall be very much obliged to you if you

1819

27 Apr   1 p 4to   BM(Bar)
from George Hay
I have as you say received numberless orders

1 June   1 p 4to   BM(Bar)
from John Brenan
I have had the honour of receiving your letter

1 June   1 p 4to   BM(Bar)
from George Hay
I have just time to say I received your letter

26 July [1819]   1 p 4to   NYPL(B)
from Étiennette, princesse d'Hénin
j'espere mon cher alexandre que vous n'avez

26 Aug   1 p 8vo   NYPL(B)
from Victor de Latour Maubourg
L'Ambassadeur de France & Mme: la Mise de

6 Dec   pmk 1819   4 p 8vo
                              BM(Bar)
from Maria (Burney) Bourdois
Madame de Beaurepaire has just called,

[post 1819]   3 p 4to   NYPL(B)
from Henry Raper
A *Fallacy.* / Calculus of *Differences.* / To

1820

11 Apr   1 p 4to   NYPL(B)
from Thomas King
[accounts] agreeable to your desire have

1 May   2 p 4to   NYPL(B)
from Thomas King
[copy of inscription for memorial tablet for
    M d'A]
[letter p 3] Agreeable to your desire I have

19 May   2 p 4to   NYPL(B)
from Thomas King
I have the satisfaction of informing you the

1821

5 Mar   1 p 4to   BM
to Charles Babbage
Captain Burney has just been writing a theory

14 Apr   ?   AECB31
to Sarah (Burney) Payne
Having been disappointed in my hope and

[1821–24]   2 p 4to   PML
from Sir John Herschel
Understanding you were to return from

1822

29 Mar   1 p 8vo   PML
from Marquis de Lally-Tollendal
Mon cher Alexander voila le petit paquet que

[1822?]   1 p 8vo   NYPL(B)
from Petronille-Jacoba (Van Rysell) de
    Latour-Maubourg
Mon cher Alexandre, vous seriez bien aimable

1829

12 JU 1829 pmk   1 p 4to   BM
to Charles Babbage
I only hesitated from imagining

18 June   2 p 4to   BM
to Charles Babbage
Believing, as I do, that the return of Mr

1830

8 Sept   draft   4 p 4to   NYPL(B)
to Richard Allen Burney
Hudibras has said long ago that / He that's

13 [Dec 1830]   1 p 8vo   BM(Bar)
from Edward A Chaplin
Mr. & Mrs. Edward A Chaplin request the

1831

18 Jan   4 p 4to   BM(Bar)
to MF
I thank you very sincerely for your kind note,

20 Jan   4 p 4to   NYPL(B)
to MF
This may truly be called *your Psalm*

1832

19 Mar   2 drafts mutilated   2 scraps
to the Foundling Hospital   NYPL(B)
Mr d'Arblay presents his compliments to the

19 July   1 p 8vo   NYPL(B)
from Charles Babbage
Will you have the kindness <   > the

1832, continued

29 July   3 p 4to   BM
to Charles Babbage
I don't know the exact french word for

[1832]   3 p 8vo   NYPL(B)
from Clarissa Marion (   ) Bolton
The General's return to Leamington induces

[c 1832]   2 p 4to   NYPL(B)
to Clarissa Marion (   ) Bolton
its CONSEQUENCES — if he exchange an iron

1833

13 Mar   1 p 8vo   PML
from Robert Southey
I am very much obliged to you for the Memoirs

also   copy   2 p 4to   NYPL(B)

1835

13 May   1 p 4to   NYPL(B)
from John Graham
I have this day desired Messrs < > to

17 Aug   1 p 8vo   NYPL(B)
from John Meyer & Sons
We respectfully beg to inform you that in

21 SP 1835 pmk   3 p 4to   NYPL(B)
from Clarissa Marion (   ) Bolton
My friend how did you get to town — more

[post 21 Sept 1835]   1st draft   2 p 4to
                                   NYPL(B)
to Clarissa Marion (   ) Bolton
Seven long days have I passed in painful

[post 21 Sept 1835]   2nd draft   3 p 4to
                                   NYPL(B)
to Clarissa Marion (   ) Bolton
Is your health improving and is your mind

1836

3 Feb   2 p 4to   NYPL(B)
from C T P Metcalf
With reference to your letter of the 22nd. April

12 Oct [1836]   1 p 8vo   NYPL(B)
from George Owen Cambridge
If you are now in London I shall be obliged

III

(CB Jr)

See also letters from FBA, CB, and CPB.

Holograph works, documents and other original material of Charles Burney, DD are chiefly located in the Osborn Collection, with some items in the following: Bodleian; British Museum; University of Chicago; Folger; Records Office, Gloucestershire; Fitzwilliam Museum; Hyde; John Comyn; John Rylands; Lambeth Palace Library; National Portrait Gallery; Trinity College, Cambridge; Yale (Historical Mss).

1767

[1767–71] 3 p fol Osb
to FB
I hope you are well and all friends in and out

1768

13 Dec 1 p 4to Osb
to FB
I Am very much surprised at never Hearing

1769

11 Oct 5 p 4to Osb
to FB
I was very much pleased at your kind answer.

1774

3 May 3 p 4to Osb
to FB
Whilst you are *flirting* ab^t. town, / In linnen

12 June 3 p 4to Osb
to FB
I came here, My dear Sister, on Monday last,

1778

[1778–79] 2 p 4to Osb
to [FB]
I have read Evelina, & like it *vastly much* — I

[1778–81] 5 p 4to Osb
from Gilbert Gerard
Spare your reproaches my dear Burney for

1779

18 Mar [1779] 4 p 4to Osb
from SEB
of talking or being silent according to the

31 Mar ⟨1779⟩ 3 p 4to Osb
from Robert Burnside
You may think it very well that I do not date

1779, continued

14 Apr   1 p 8vo   Osb
from J[ames?] Beattie
I wished to have waited upon you, to thank

24 May   draft   7 p 4to   Osb
to the *Aberdeen Journal*
Poetical compositions of merit are, in the

2⟨4⟩ May   3 p 4to   Osb
from James Dunbar
I had the pleasure of your's; And considering

31 May   6 p 4to   Osb
from Robert Burnside
I have been considering for some time past

30 Aug   3 p 4to   Osb
from Percival Stockdale
I am happy, from this place, to pay my

14 Sept   4 p 4to   Osb
from Robert Burnside
I did not think when I began my last Letter

25 Sept   3 p 4to   Osb
from Percival Stockdale
I should *now* be ashamed to look at the Date

[23 Oct 1779]   1 p 4to   Osb
from Percival Stockdale
I cannot return you good Paper, but I can

Dec   copy   2 p 4to   Osb
to Abercrombie Gordon
It has often been remarked, that no state of

1780

31 Jan   4 p 4to   Osb
from Percival Stockdale
I have your kind Letter of Dec. 19th. 1779: on

4 Mar [1780]   4 p 4to   Osb
from Edward Francesco Burney
The Difficulties of writeing [*sic*] to you are

17 Mar   1 p 4to   Osb
from Percival Stockdale
I shall not at present trouble you with a prolix

18 Mar   3 p 4to   Osb
from Gilbert Gerard
The charge of Laziness you have too justly

20 Apr   4 p 4to   Osb
from Robert Burnside
You begin to think by this time perhaps that

23 Apr   3 p 4to   Osb
from Alexander Gerard
I received your kind & agreeable letter some

29 Apr   4 p 4to   Osb
from James Gray
I am eager to seize the only alleviation for a

5 May   3 p 4to   Osb
from Gilbert Gerard
Just the same old man I find you are —

24 May   6 p 4to   Osb
from James Gray
You cannot conceive, My dear Burney, how

13 June   4 p 4to   Osb
from Percival Stockdale
I have just read two Letters from you which

28 June–6 Aug   18 p 4to & 31 p fol   Osb
to CAB, FB, & SEB
The late Sir A. Grant died last year, near 90.

30 June   4 p 4to   Osb
from Robert Burnside
Your laziness is great — most astonishing! But

25 July   3 p 4to   Osb
from Gilbert Gerard
I once thought you had taken a journey to the

11 Aug   3 p 4to   Osb
from Gilbert Gerard
You must excuse my not writing to you so often

25 Aug   4 p 4to   UAb
to [William Rose]
The kindness, my dear Sir, with which you

3 Sept   copy extract   2 p 4to   Osb
to Abercrombie Gordon
I can no longer keep silence — or refrain from

3 Sept   4 p 4to   UAb
to William Rose
I am very sorry that the Moor fowl were

9 Sept   3 p 4to   UAb
to William Rose
I hope my dear Sir, that your supposition

11 Sept   4 p fol   Osb
from Abercrombie Gordon
Don't you perceive how my pen *blushes* as it

14 Sept   3 p 4to   Osb
from Gilbert Gerard
You are still upbraiding me my Dear Burney

15 Sept   2 p 4to   Osb
from Thomas Gordon
The letter you favoured me with, directed to

15 Sept   8 p fol   Osb
from James Gray
I wish, my dear Burney, I could make Aber's

2 Nov   4 p 4to   Osb
from Percival Stockdale
You most friendly and affectionate Letter of

[1780]   4 p fol   Osb
to FB
[tear] can my heart [tear] <dear>est Fanny

[1780?]   2 p 4to   Osb
to FB
But let me change the subject — & talk of

[1780–82]   2 p 4to   Osb
to FB
In respect to me she has behaved like an angel

[1780–86]   1 p 4to   Osb
from Thomas Tyrwhitt
M[r] Tyrwhitt presents his Compl[ts] to M[r] C. B.

1781

17 Jan   3 p 4to   Osb
from Lord Findlater
If you were unacquainted with my Heart or

21 Jan   copy extract   1 p 4to   Osb
to Abercrombie Gordon
—— —— I have been but two weeks in Ab[dn]

29 Jan   7 p 4to   Osb
from AMR
Your letter of the 21 I received last week —

2 Feb   3 p 4to   Osb
from Robert Burnside
I don't know what you ever wrote me a Letter

6 Feb   3 p 4to   Osb
from E L Baines
I return you my kind thanks for y[r] Letter.

11 Feb   3 p 4to   Osb
from Lord Findlater
It's now three Weeks, My Dearest Burney,

24 Feb   2 p 4to   Osb
from Charles Cordiner
I was favoured with yours & made enquiries

6 Mar   4 p 4to   Osb
from Robert Burnside
It is impossible for me to comply with your

10 Mar   5 p 4to   Osb
from AMR
I thank you my good Friend for your last

16 Mar   4 p 4to   Osb
from Lord Findlater
My Dear Burney, I have been so shamefully

29 Mar   4 p 4to   Osb
from E L Baines
I acknowledge myself guilty of too long a

[11 Apr 1781]   ⅓ p 4to   Osb
from William Ogilvie
M[r]. Ogilvies compliments — begs Mr. Burney

13 Apr   2 p 4to   Osb
from Lord Findlater
I would have answered your Letter of March

20 Apr   2 p fol   Osb
to SEB
Your letter, my dear Susan, is just arrived. I

26 Apr   3 p 4to   Osb
from Gilbert Gerard
After the *hard labour* of the Winter Session I

2 May   2 p 4to   Osb
from Abercrombie Gordon
I congratulate you on your acquisition of

21 MY pmk [1781]   2 p fol   Osb
to FB, SEB, & CAB
Tell Ned, I am afraid, that I shall myself be

4 June   3 p fol   Osb
from Percival Stockdale
I am extremely obliged to you for your Letter

1781, continued

29 June   8 p 4to   Osb
to CAB, SEB, & FB
When I last wrote — my dearest Sisters —

18 July   3 p 4to   Osb
from Charles Cordiner
I am favoured with your agreeable letter and

29 July   3 p 4to   Osb
from Robert Burnside
I am glad to hear of your safe arrival. Your

4 Aug   3 p 4to   Osb
from E L Baines
I am just returned from Ipswich after being

25 Aug   3 p 4to   Osb
from [James Gray]
When a man, whose mind possesses that

27 Aug   3 p 4to   Osb
from Robert Burnside
You will not, I am sure, <impute> the length

Aug   3 p 4to   Osb
to Lord Findlater
Though we are now so far separated, I flatter

5 Sept   2 p 4to   Osb
from E L Baines
I have been much engaged lately making

Nov   2 p fol   Osb
to FB
Susan tells me that a frank is going off — so I

[1781?]   1 p 4to   Oxf(AS)
from Samuel Parr
Our Enquiry (for it is not in dispute

31 Mar [post 1781]   amanuensis?
2 p 4to   Comyn
from Brownlow North
I thank you for your obliging Letter

1782

5 Mar   3 p 4to   Osb
from Richard Payne Knight
Not having lately turnd [sic] my attention to

15 Aug [1782?]   2 p 4to   Comyn
from John Hoole
Many thanks for your kind favour

[1782]   2 p 8vo   Osb
to FB
Read this last / Gordon goes I believe — so

[post 1782?]   copy?   3 p 4to
from Samuel Parr   Oxf(AS)
Philosophus loquitor / Milton —

1783

7 Jan 178<3> [or 5?]   1 p 4to   Osb
from Joseph Warton
Dr Warton's best compts to Mr Burney; is

9 Jan   4 p 4to   Osb
to FB
Your letter to our sweet Rosette was received,

24 June   1 p 4to   Comyn
from SBP to CB Jr & Rosette (Rose)
   Burney
Though not with you my dear Brother & dear

[post June 1783]   4 p 4to   Osb
to FB
I hope, my dearest Fanny, that the storm

7 Oct   2 p 4to   Osb
from James Gray
I have been prevented from writing to You

[1783–85]   1 p 4to   Osb
from George Colman
I have just recd. the inclosed. I hoped to have

[1783–85]   ⅔ p 4to   Osb
from George Colman
Just come & sorry to find I have lost you —

3 Aug [1783–86]   2 p 4to   Osb
from George Colman
Permit me, my dear Sir, to thank you again &

[1783–86]   1 p 4to   Osb
from Dr F[rancis?] Riollay
I am very sorry my dear Sir for this

[1783–87]   1 p 4to   Osb
from Richard Owen Cambridge
I was very much vext that my New Servant

[post 1783]   1 p 8vo   Osb
from Philippe de Loutherbourg [to CB
    Jr?]
I am extreemly sorry to be prevented by my

1784

26 [Jan]   1 p 4to   Osb
from Alexander Chalmers
I have just sent yᵉ Theatrical MSS to Bostock

17 Feb   1 p 4to   Osb
from Alexander Chalmers
I know not how. I might have received your

8 June   4 p 4to   Comyn
from Thomas Macknight
After so long neglecting my Duty in

3 July   3 p 4to   Oxf(AS)
with Jane (Morsingale) Parr to Rosette
    (Rose) Burney
If you have the least grain of compassion

24 Sept   2 p 4to   Osb
from William Rose
Yesternight I was favoured with yours, and

28 Sept   8 p 4to   Osb
from Thomas Gray
I have just dispatched the last page of the

30 Dec   1 p 4to   Osb
from George Colman
I have (as my friend Mʳ O Bryan says in his

28 JU pmk [1784–85]   2 p 4to
from Samuel Parr   Oxf(AS)
I wish you well in your new undertaking

7 OCT pmk [1784–85]   1 p 4to
from Samuel Parr   Oxf(AS)
Come & dine with us, on Friday, I meet

[1784–85]   1 p 4to   Oxf(AS)
from Samuel Parr
Come & dine with us

1785

11 Feb   3 p fol   Osb
from G I Huntingford
Your letter found me literally and truly

26 July   4 p 4to   Osb
to FB
Oui, Oui, Madamoiselle —— Je promettois

26 July   1 p 4to   Osb
from Louis-George de Brequigny
Vir calendiossime / cum ego anglicae linguae

25 Aug   1 p 4to   Osb
from William Rose
A few hours ago, I was favoured with yours,

[20 Oct 1785]   3 p 4to   Oxf(AS)
from Samuel Parr
Last night I returned from a second long

[1785?]   1 p 4to   Osb
from Paul Henry Maty
This being the last week of the <review>

[Oct 1785-July 1786]   2 p 4to   Osb
from James Gray
Dʳ. Parr's visit was most critically opportune

1786

3 Feb   2 p 4to   Osb
from Francis Woollaston
By a letter received from Cambridge this day,

4 Feb   1 p 4to   Oxf(AS)
from Samuel Parr
I am now at <Whits> — but

21 Feb   4 p 4to   Oxf(Bod)
with FB to CBF
I have caught Fanny not in the fact but just

[pre 7 Mar 1786]   ⅔ p 4to   Osb
from Samuel Parr
On Tuesday you'll <see> <Porson> &

1786, continued

19 Mar　　2 p 4to　　　　　　　Osb
from Mary Berry
I called at Dr Rose's this Morning hoping to

3 Apr　　1 p 4to　　　　　　　Pforz
from Bennet Langton
I desire leave to mention to You that D^r. Parr

7 July　　1 p 4to　　　　　　　Osb
from Joshua Iremonger
I am exceedingly concerned for the death of

[July 1786]　　2 p 4to　　　　　Osb
from James Gray
I heard of your late loss accidentally, and for

22 Sept　　3 p 4to　　　　　　Osb
from Richard Porson
I received yours of last week, which, to say

22 Oct [1786–91]　3 p 4to　　Folger
from Ralph Griffiths
Most friendly, gay and liberal Carlos, My very

[1786–91]　　1 p 4to　　　　Oxf(AS)
from Samuel Parr
I am sorry I cannot

[1786–91]　　2 p 4to　　　　Oxf(AS)
from Samuel Parr
Last week I heard at or <saw> from

[1786–91]　　1 p 4to　　　　Oxf(AS)
from Samuel Parr
Windham's in Bath — / I thank you for the

[1786–91]　　1 p 4to　　　　Oxf(AS)
from Samuel Parr
Anglicanus will do — first upon the authority

[1786–91]　　1 p 4to　　　　Oxf(AS)
from Samuel Parr
I will, if not [tear] come

OC pmk [1786–91]　1 p 4to　Oxf(AS)
from Samuel Parr
When you tell me I <　　> say they are

[1786–91]　　1 p 4to　　　　　Osb
from Samuel Rose
Agreeably to your wish I yesterday called at

21 Mar [1786–91]　　1 p 4to　　Ham
from William Windham
If an absence from this time till the 7th of

1787

12 Jan　　3 p 4to　　　　　　　Win
to G I Huntingford
Your three kind letters, my dear friend, are

13 Jan　　3 p 4to　　　　　　　Osb
from James Fordyce
[verses] Virtuous Indignation . . . [ALS] The

22 Jan　　2 p 4to　　　　　　　Hyde
to James Fordyce
Were my Lyre, dear Sir, like yours, strung by

28 Jan　　3 p 4to　　　　　Oxf(AS)
from Samuel Parr
It is not from motives of disrespect

[Jan 1787?]　copy　2 p 4to　Osb
from Samuel Berdmore (included in
　AL CB Jr to FB 4 Feb 1787)
Your young man is received; &, I doubt not,

4 Feb　　4 p 4to　　　　　　　Osb
to FB
Your kind and most pleasant note, my dearest

8 Mar　　1 p 4to　　　　　　Hyde
to Isaac Reed
D^r. Rotheram has just sent me the inclosed

9 Mar　　3 p fol　　　　　　　Osb
from James Fordyce
'Tis natural for us to recall the image of those,

11 Mar [1787?] 1 p 4to　　　　Osb
from H Maty
My Sister is too Ill to take up her pen

22 Apr　　3 p 4to　　　　　　　Win
to G I Huntingford
You too well know how constantly and fully

28 Apr　　2 p 4to　　　　　　　Osb
from Thomas Twining
I will not let slip the opportunity of thanking

16 May　　2 p 4to　　　　　　　Osb
from Sabrina Bicknell
Accept my dear M^r & Mrs Burney my ardent

4 JU 1787 pmk　　4 p 4to　　Oxf(AS)
from Samuel Parr
After <　　> you, as I do sincerely

3 [July 1787]　　1 p 4to　　　Osb
from William Windham
Your letter is a very unexpected <pleasure>,

20 AU 1787 pmk   2 p 4to   Oxf(AS)
from Samuel Parr
[10 lines of Greek] Dᵣ Sir — You yes, I think

21 AU 1787 pmk   1 p 4to   Oxf(AS)
from Samuel Parr
[12 lines of Greek] let us go on

[Aug 1787]   3 p 4to   Comyn
from George Colman
On my return from Richmond yesterday

6 pmk   Sept   3 p 4to   Oxf(AS)
from Samuel Parr
After thanking for your kind & comfortable

[1787–90]   1 p fol   Osb
from John Ash
On reading over the Manuscript I find, *Entre*

7 OC? pmk [1787–91] 1 p 4to Hilles
from James Boswell
I should have been very happy to wait

[1787–91]   1 p 4to   Comyn
from James Bruce
Mᵣ Bruce returns Compˢ to Mᵣ Burney and is

[1787–91]   2 p 4to   Osb
from James Gray
I apprehend that you have misunderstood

[1787–91]   1 p 4to   Osb
from Ralph Griffiths
It is *Appendix-month,* my Dear Carlo! — It

[1787–91]   1 p 4to   Osb
from [Sir Thomas?] Lawrence
P.S. Pray write me <aᵗ.> your convenience

[1787–91]   1 p 4to   Osb
from William Thomas Lewis
I have not Tickets for *Three* at home but

[1787–91]   1 p 4to   Osb
from William Seward
Mᵣˢ Boscawen means us all as you see by

[1787–91]   1 p 4to   Osb
from William Seward
I am obliged to you for recommending me the

16 Feb [1787–93]   1 p 4to   Osb
from William Beloe
In the page of Plutarch to which you refer me,

1788

15 Jan   1 p 4to   Oxf(Bod)
to Isaac Reed
Some particular engagements of Mᵣ. Walter

23 Jan   1 p 4to   Osb
from Richard Penneck
Tho' I wish your School may be as full as it

23 Jan   1 p 4to   Osb
from Percival Stockdale
I have been in Town for ten weeks; I wish

22 FE 1788 pmk   amanuensis 2 p 4to
from Samuel Parr   Oxf(AS)
I applaud your diligence and sagacity,

28 Feb   2 p 4to   Comyn
from Clement Francis and CBF
This is to give you notice, and a short account

14 Mar   1 p 4to   Osb
from Louisa (Maty) Jortin
As Mᵣˢ Maty will not be in town till Easter

31 MR 1788 pmk   1 p 4to   Hyde
to FB
Murphy has extorted a promise from me to

23 Apr   1 p 4to   Osb
to [Thomas Cadell]
My answer, dear Sir, will be short. — I accept

27 Apr   1 p 4to   Osb
to FB
I had but little talk with Mr. W. — He seemed

20 Aug   1 p 4to   Osb
from George Colman
<L'ingo> amico suo meritissimo Burneo

23 Aug   1 p 4to   Osb
to Isaac Reed
It is proposed to hold the *extra Athenian* Club,

2 Oct   1 p 4to   Osb
from Joseph Goodall
The only Requisites to be admitted on the

4 Oct [1788]   1 p 4to   Osb
to FBA
The Papers deceived me — & so I lost a most

2 Nov   3 p 4to   Osb
from Thomas Burgess
During a few weeks residence at Leyden this

1788, continued

5 Nov   1 p 4to   Osb
from John Lempriere
I beg you will honor me with acceptance of

9 Nov   4 p 4to   Osb
from Thomas Burgess
I had great pleasure in the perusal of your

20 NO 1788 pmk   3 p 4to   Oxf(AS)
from Samuel Parr
I should be wanting in respect to you, if I did

26 Nov   1 p 4to   PML
to James Duff, 2nd Earl Fife
I send my dear Lord Fife a few lines

15 Dec   3 p 4to   Osb
from John Young
To your kind & obliging Letter received thro

18 Dec [1788]   1 p 4to   Osb
from Bennet Langton
Mr. Langton presents his Compliments to Mr.

1788 pmk   amanuensis   2 p 4to
from Samuel Parr   Oxf(AS)
And I am confirmed in my opinion of the

[1788–91]   2 p 4to   Osb
to FB
I have not yet taken any step abt. Berdmore,

[1788–91]   2 p 4to   Osb
from Thomas Macknight
I hope you are well & have received my

11 May [post 1788]   1 p 8vo   Osb
from Robert Nares
Permit me to congratulate you very cordially

1789

1 Feb   1 p 4to   Comyn
from Thomas Warton
I left Town last Friday, and this Morning

18 Mar [1789]   1 p ⅔ 4to   Osb
from Ralph Griffiths
Thou didst say something to me, on Saturday,

6 Apr   1 p 4to   Comyn
from Thomas Warton
I am much obliged to you for your very just

13 AP 1789 pmk   1 p 4to   Oxf(AS)
from Samuel Parr
I am getting off —

15 Apr   4 p 4to   Osb
from James Dunbar
When I parted with you in London, The

11 July   1 p 4to   Oxf(AS)
from Samuel Parr
I <wrote> to Mr Adder, desiring him to

2 Aug   3 p 4to   Osb
from George Henry Glasse to [CB Jr]
It is impossible for me to express the

4 Aug   2 p 4to   Osb
from James Dunbar
I am just on the wing for W. Britain — &

16 Sept   3 p 4to   Osb
from George Henry Glasse
I have just received the honour of your letter.

28 Sept   copy   6 p 4to   Osb
to Thomas Twining
My father yesterday shewed me part of a letter

29 Sept   3 p 4to   Win
to G I Huntingford
Will you, my dear Sir, pardon my suffering

7 Oct   1 p 4to   Osb
from George Henry Glasse
I inadvertently carried off <Salmarius> with

21 Oct   4 p fol   Osb
from Thomas Twining
I am extremely obliged to you for your letter,

[9 Nov 1789]   3 p 4to   Oxf(AS)
from Samuel Parr
I was prevented from answering your friendly

also   typescript   2 p   Lewis

19 Nov   1 p 4to   Osb
from John Barlow Seale
Dr. Seale's Comps. to Mr. Burney — He has

22–29 Nov   3 p 4to   Osb
from Thomas Burgess and Richard
    Porson
My respect for Mr. Twining, & the interest,
I shall do the needful. The double *I have seen*

23 NO 1789 pmk   3 p 4to   Oxf(AS)
from Samuel Parr
nothing, Dr Sir, nothing can be more clear —

23 Nov [1789]   3 p 4to   Oxf(AS)
from Samuel Parr
a Word, like a stitch, in time, saves nine

22 Dec   2 p 4to   Osb
from Bennet Langton
In reply to your obliging Letter wherein you

30 Dec   2 p 4to   Osb
from Ralph Griffiths
On being informed, this morning, at breakfast,

30 Dec [1789]   2 p 4to   Osb
from SBP
I can never think a visit from you *inconvenient,*

30 Apr [1789–91]   1 p 8vo   Osb
from William Windham
W Windham presents his compliments to M[r]

1790

6 Jan   4 p 4to   Osb
to Samuel Parr
From D[r]. Farmer, I have not yet heard. I have

[c 15 Jan 1790?]   3 p 8vo   Osb
from Sir William Scott
Many Reasons would induce me to oblige you

23 Jan   2 p 4to   Oxf(AS)
from Samuel Parr
Your former letter answered

27 Jan   2 p 4to   Osb
from G I Huntingford
Grata superveniet quae non sperabitur hora

23 FE pmk [1790]   3 p 4to   Oxf(AS)
from Samuel Parr
I am satisfied as to the fact

28 MA 1790 pmk   2 p 4to & scrap   Osb
from J Morley
<   > <   > Fife, & with the aid thereof

13 Apr   3 p 4to   Osb
from G I Huntingford
The proper mode of conducting the business

18 Apr   2 p 4to   Osb
from G I Huntingford
As I am disappointed in my lodgings at

22 AP 1790 pmk   2 p 4to   Oxf(AS)
from Samuel Parr
According to our Plan he not only would have

25 Apr   4 p 4to   Osb
from Joseph Warton
I shall with the greatest readiness & pleasure

28 Apr   2 p 4to   Osb
from John Douglas
I had an Opportunity of bearing my

30 Apr   1 p 4to   Osb
from M J Routh
It gives me pleasure that I have it in my power

30 Apr   1 p 4to   Osb
from Joseph Warton
I have punctually delivered your letters &

[3 May 1790]   3 p 4to   Oxf(AS)
from Samuel Parr
Last night very late I came home from

8 MA 1790 pmk   1 p 4to   Oxf(AS)
from Samuel Parr
<   > — never mind connections

8 May   3 p 4to   Osb
from John Young
I send this Letter by your young Friend &

10 MA 1790 pmk   1 p 4to   Oxf(AS)
from Samuel Parr
Having received yours at Birmingham

[13 May 1790]   1 p 4to   Oxf(AS)
from Samuel Parr
Yesterday I received, read, signed

16 May [1790?]   2 p 4to   Osb
from Henry Kett
I am desired by M[r]. Warton to inform you

20 May   1 p 4to   Comyn
from John Hey
You do me great Honour in sending your

23 May   3 p 4to   Osb
from Thomas Twining
I have just discovered that D[r]. Hey is to be in

24 May   1 p 4to   Osb
from Sir George Baker
Sir G. Baker hopes that this note from M[r].

1790, continued

25 May   2 p 4to   Osb
from Thomas Winstanly
Mr. Burgess not being here, I have just now

27 May   2 p 4to   Osb
from Thomas Twining
I thank you for your last. I will certainly tell

3 JU 1790 pmk   1 p 4to   Oxf(AS)
from Samuel Parr
Why < > <Evil>! I am sorry for the

8 JU 1790 pmk   1 p 4to   Oxf(AS)
from Samuel Parr
The < > I wished to hear from you

12 June   1 p 8vo   Osb
to FB
Expect me on Wednesday Evening, at the

14 JU 1790 pmk   1 p 4to   Osb
from Richard Porson
Run immediately to Egerton's & tell him that

15 June   1 p 4to   Osb
from James Hutton
To day the inclosed Letter has been put into

18 JU 1790 pmk   1 p 4to   Osb
from Richard Porson
Convey this with all possible speed, and do

5 July   2 p 4to   Osb
from Thomas Twining
Quis finis standi? quo me dicet usque teneri?

7 July   1 p 4to   Osb
from Sir James Gray
When you invite gentlemen to watering

[pre 13 July 1790]   draft   1 p 4to   Osb
to ?
I was honoured with your letter this morning.

13 JY 1790 pmk   1 p 4to   Oxf(AS)
from Samuel Parr
My amazement < > I cannot describe

14 July   3 p 4to   Osb
from John Hey
Dr. Hey desires that Mr. Burney would accept

16 July   pmk 1790   3 p 4to   Osb
from SBP
My Captain is in town, & seeing your hand I

20 July   2 p 4to   Osb
from William Seward
Je prends la liberté de vous introduire par

25 July   1 p 4to   Comyn
from Joseph Warton
I am beyond expression hurt & surprised at the

26 July   3 p 4to   Osb
from Bennet Langton
I was very sorry to find, by the last Letter that

6 Aug   3 p 4to   Osb
from Thomas Twining
I reproach myself for my silence. I ought, long

7 Sept   1 p 4to   Osb
from John Ash
I shall have a fine Haunch of Venison

10 Sept   amanuensis   2 p 4to
from Samuel Parr   Oxf(AS)
I was very happy to hear from you & rejoyce

27 Sept   1 p 4to   Osb
from Joseph Warton
As I observe in one of your letters to my

23 Oct [1790?]   2 p 4to   Osb
from Henry Kett
I take the first opportunity to acknowledge

29 Oct   pmk 1790   2 p 4to   Osb
from SBP
We, i.e. James, Mrs. B: & myself, hope you

11 Nov   1 p 4to   Osb
from Samuel Berdmore
Prest, as I am, with business, & that not always

22 Nov   1 p 4to   Osb
from Joseph Warton
I am desired by Mr *Cross* at Oxford to say he

28 Nov   2 p 4to   Osb
from Thomas Twining
Ay — Critics will *nibble*, as you say; & it is

1 Dec   copy   4 p 4to   Osb
to Thomas Twining
I assent to almost all your remarks, which

9 Dec   1 p 4to   Osb
from Charles Cross
I have return'd the Proofs with the Revises for

[1790?]   draft?   4 p 4to   Osb
from Thomas Twining
[p 2] In giving my remark upon

[pre 1791]   1 p 8vo   Osb
from C W Berd
Yr. last note is all Hebrew — I have no person

[pre 1791]   1 p 4to   Osb
from James Gray
Mr. Nicol having engaged himself to dine with

[pre 1791]   1 p 12mo   Oxf(AS)
from Samuel Parr
I was anxious to see & hear from you

[pre 1791?]   2 p 4to   Osb
from Richard Sharp [to CB Jr?]
I sent down to Mitchener's, My Dear Sir,

1791

9 Jan   3 p 4to   Osb
to FB
Many thanks to my dear Fanny, for her letter,

12 Feb   2 p fol   Osb
from Bennet Langton to [CB Jr?]
I send you inclosed the two Letters of

23 FE 1791 pmk   3 p 4to   Oxf(AS)
from Samuel Parr
Our conversation, . . . amounted to this

10 Apr [1791]   1 p 8vo   Osb
from Anna (Dillingham) Ord
Mrs. Ord desires to return Dr. Charles Burney

18 Apr   1 p 4to   Oxf(AS)
from Samuel Parr
it should seem, that you were rather puzzled

4 May   1 p 4to   Osb
from M J Routh
Congratulations from such men as Mr Burney

24 May   ½p 4to   Comyn
from John Moore
The Archbishop of Canterbury presents his

28 May   1 p 4to   PRO
to William Pitt the younger
I take the liberty of soliciting the honour of

10 June   pmk 1791   amanuensis
from Samuel Parr   3 p 4to   Oxf(AS)
I beguiled the passing hours of Sunday

11 June [1791]   2 p 4to   Osb
from Henry Kett
I am sorry my short stay in Town will deprive

11 July   3 p fol   Oxf(AS)
from Samuel Parr (with PS by M J
   Routh)
Dr Charles — I write this in the <presidence>

25 Aug   2 p 4to   Osb
from Thomas Burgess
The day before yesterday I received a letter

5 Sept   1 p 4to   Comyn
from William Windham
I did not think to inquire of you before my

7 Sept   2 p 4to   Osb
from Thomas Burgess
When I had the pleasure of seeing you last,

11 Oct   4 p 4to   Scot
from John Young
A Thousand thanks for your exact Punctuality

31 Oct   4 p 4to   Osb
from William Ogilvie
I beg leave to introduce to you Mr Thomas

23 Nov   3 p 4to   Osb
from John Young
Your quondam's Trunk having stray'd for

5 Mar [post 1791]   1 p 4to   Osb
from William Beloe [to CB Jr?]
I am too experienced to pay money for Sons

[post 1791]   2 p 8vo   Osb
from Richard Twining Sr?
When I put my letter into the post, I received

[1791–94]   1 p 4to   Osb
from William Seward
At the recommendation of the great little Dr

21 Aug [1791–95]   1 p 4to   Osb
from Ralph Griffiths
Thou art quite a fugitive, my Dear Carlo! —

[1791–95]   3 p 4to   Cal(B)
from William Seward
We shall meet at Bath I hope about Xmas.

[post 1791]   1 p 4to   Osb
from Alexander Chalmers
You have now an opportunity of doing a good

1792

2 Jan   1 p 4to   Oxf(Bod)
from James Boswell
I am appointed by my friend Mr Dilly

18 Jan   1 p 4to   Osb
from Thomas Burgess
The Photius arrived safe. My delay in writing

22 Jan pmk 1792 1 p 4to Oxf(AS)
from Samuel Parr
This day write fully to our friend Mʳ.

16 Feb   2 p 4to   Osb
from Osborne Wight
Tho' my short acquaintance with You at

21 Feb   1 p 4to   Oxf(AS)
from Samuel Parr
This will be delivered to you by my friend Mr

[Feb 1792]   1 p scrap   Osb
to [John?] Aiken
As I am obliged to attend the funeral of my

5 Mar   1 p 4to   Hilles
from Richard Farmer
After a Confinement of 3 Weeks

7 Mar   2 p 4to   Osb
from John Young
This Day a proposal was made in Senate to

24 MR 1792 pmk   amanuensis   2 p 4to
from Samuel Parr   Osb
Many thanks to you for your short note

4 Apr   2 p 4to   Osb
from [James Fordyce]
I have just read in the Diary a very pleasing

1 May   3 p 4to   Osb
from John Young
Mʳ Millar My Colleague, who is just setting

22 May   1 p 4to   Osb
from James Boswell
I called on Mʳ. Pott (Lieutenant good master

7 June   3 p 4to   Osb
from G I Huntingford
In confidence I acknowledge to You, what of

[pre 11 June 1792]   1 p 4to   Yale (Bo)
from James Boswell
At your desire I wrote down at Windham's

11 June   3 p 4to   Osb
from William Ogilvie
I have taken the liberty of causing Mr. Waller

12 June   2 p 4to   Oxf(AS)
from Samuel Parr
I am sending out my circular letters

17 June   4 p 4to   Osb
from Joseph Goodall
Mʳ Raine had promised to call on me, at Eton,

18 JU ⟨1792⟩ pmk 3 p 4to Oxf(AS)
from Samuel Parr
⟨Quintum⟩, I say to my correspondents,

25 June [1792]   2 p 4to   Osb
from William Robert, Viscount Feilding
I have to thank you for the very polite note

6 July   1 p 4to   Osb
from Joseph Goodall
The Provost has desired me to say that he will,

11 July   1 p 4to   Osb
from Joseph Warton
I beg you will do me the justice to believe that

12 July   3 p 4to   Osb
to FB
Your News, as far as it was Jacobian, — I will

⟨3⟩ Aug   3 p 4to   Osb
from John Young
A Thousand thanks for the Trouble you have

6 Aug   4 p 4to   BM
to Arthur Young
A friend of mine has desired me to present

13 Aug   1 p 4to   Comyn
from Arthur Young
Four days past I recᵈ. the honour

30 Aug   1 p 4to   Osb
from G I Huntingford
A generous friend of mine, to whom I

1 Sept   3 p 4to   BM
to Arthur Young
Accept my best thanks, for the time

3 Sept   3 p 4to   Comyn
from Thomas Twining
My tardiness will, at least, serve to prove,

14 Sept   1 p 4to   Osb
from Frederick North, 5th Earl of Guilford
Our respectable Friend Mr Langton made me

15 Sept   2 p 4to   Oxf(AS)
from Samuel Parr
A cold I caught last Monday, has confined

24 Sept   2 p 4to   Osb
from M — Riollay
I was prevented the pleasure of answering

25 SE 1792 pmk   2 p 4to   Osb
from Samuel Berdmore
I was flatterd [sic], when I last saw you in

29 Sept   1 p 4to   Osb
from Thomas Burgess
My time has been so divided by a variety of

11 Oct   2 p 4to   Osb
from Matthew Raine
Banks dined with me to day & wishes much to

18 Oct   2 p 4to   Osb
from Joseph Goodall
Waiting for the Provosts Arrival at Eton,

19 Oct   1 p 4to   Osb
from Shute Barrington
The Bishop of Durham presents his comps. to

22 Oct   2 p 4to   Osb
to FB
I cannot suffer a post to go out, without

24 Oct   1 p 4to   Osb
from Thomas Burgess
I have inclosed a draft for fifty pounds payable

29 Oct   2 p 4to   Osb
from Thomas Burgess
I hope that you received safe my last letter

19 Nov [1792]   2 p 4to   Osb
from Henry Kett
I really must crave a double portion of your

20 Dec   1 p 4to   Osb
from G I Huntingford
On the first day of tolerable convenience I

27 July [1792–95]   3 p 4to   FLP
from Bennet Langton
I am afraid there is some apology due in

1793

2 Jan   2 p 4to   Osb
to [John?] Aikin
I have desired Payne, at the Mews Gate,

[Jan? 1793]   1 p 4to   Osb
from Richard Graves
She flatters herself therefore <that> <Dr>

22 FE 1793 pmk   1 p 4to   Oxf(AS)
from Samuel Parr
I called in the <   > coach at Fair Lawn

14 Mar   2 p 12mo   Osb
from John Philip Kemble
Whenever you, or Mrs Burney with any

5 May   3 p 4to   Osb
from John Young
I must have expressed myself very carelessly

13 June   2 p 8vo   Osb
to FB
Pray desire the <Seer> to transcribe, as I

31 July   1 p 4to   Comyn
to FBA
With a hand debilitated by illness, but with

20 Aug   1 p 8vo   Osb
to Robert Lawless of Payne & Cadell
Dr. Charles Burney informs Mr Lawless, that

20 Sept [1793]   1 p 8vo   Comyn
from Louis, comte de Narbonne-Lara
Will Dr Charles Burney be so Kind as to

[1793–94]   1 p 4to   Comyn
from Louis, comte de Narbonne-Lara
I beg Dr Charles Burney to be excused for not

[1793–94]   1 p 4to   Comyn
from Louis, comte de Narbonne-Lara
I am so much accustomed to the kindness of

1794

12 Jan   4 p 4to   Osb
from M d'A
Many thousand thanks, my dear Charles, for

18 May   3 p 4to   Osb
from SBP
Your goodnature & kindness of heart

12 Mar   1 p 8vo   Osb
to Payne & Cadell
Dr Charles Burney begs Mr Cadell would find

14 July   2 p 4to   BM
to William Windham
The Gazette, which announces your having

30 Mar   2 p 4to   Osb
from William Windham
It is very true, that at the time you mentioned

31 Oct   1 p 4to   Osb
from Joseph Goodall
I am sorry to say that not a Document remains

1 May   3 p 4to   Osb
from John Young
Notwithstanding your Advertisement

27 Dec   2 p 4to   NYPL(B)
to M d'A
I had set my heart so very seriously and

7 [May 1794]   3 p 4to   Osb
from Alexander Chalmers
After having read, in Sundry papers, an

30 DE 1794 pmk   3 p 4to   Oxf(AS)
from Samuel Parr
having our < > to send to the post next

1795

17 Jan   amanuensis   3 p 4to
from Samuel Parr   Oxf(AS)
I do very heartily thank you & my godson

19 Mar   1 p 4to   Osb
from SBP
I have my dearest Charles been long wishing

24 Jan   verses   2 p 4to   Osb
from William Parsons
In fields of blood, & feats of arms / I own I see

1 Apr   pmk 1795   3 p 8vo   Osb
from SBP
Tho' I have just finished a letter to my dear

2 FE 1795 pmk   4 p 4to   NYPL(B)
to M d'A & FBA
To the Queen's House I went, when I'd

24 Apr   pmk 179⟨5⟩   2 p 4to   Osb
from Ralph Griffiths
Thy pleasant Letter, Dear Carlo, found me

3 Feb   2 p 4to   Osb
from William Keate
I am much obliged to you for the conveyance

4 June [1795]   1 p 4to   Osb
from Ralph Griffiths
R.G.'s loving Comps. to C.B. — R.G. has

11 Feb   6 p 4to   Osb
from William Keate
I am highly flattered by your approbation of

9 JU 1795 pmk   3 p 4to   Oxf(AS)
from Samuel Parr
As your ears have by this time

13 Mar   pmk 17⟨95⟩   3 p 4to   Osb
from Ralph Griffiths
I hear, — with sincere pleasure hear, — such

30 June   1 p 4to   NYPL(B)
from Cadell & Davies
Cadell junr. & Davies present their Respects

16 Mar [1795]   4 p fol   NYPL(B)
to M d'A & FBA
In those dark ages, when a Druid's hand

12 July [1795]   2 p 4to   NYPL(B)
to FBA & M d'A
I recd. your letters yesterday

28 MR 1795 pmk   3 p 8vo   Osb
from SBP
I did not my dear Charles receive your letter

[post July 1795]   2 p 4to   Osb
to M d'A & FBA
Our Letters meet & our wits jump. — I

11 Nov [1795]   amanuensis   1 p 4to
from Samuel Parr   Oxf(AS)
I return you very many thanks for

1795 pmk   1 p 4to   Oxf(AS)
from Samuel Parr
I <   > <   > <   > that you

17 Nov   2 p 4to   Comyn
from William Mason
(For one of the oldest Friends of your worthy

[post 1795]   1 p 8vo   Osb
from John Armstrong
I shall be at your house tomorrow morning

19 Dec   1 p 4to   Osb
from Ralph Griffiths
Thy kind promises will, I hope, & trust, be

9 Dec [1795–99?]   2 p 4to   Osb
from Ralph Griffiths
Can you give me any intelligence concerning

19 Dec [1795]   3 p 8vo   Osb
from SBP
I think it an age since I have seen anything of

[1795–1813]   card   Osb
to Shute Barrington
With Dr. Charles Burney's respects to the

[1795?]   1 p 4to   Oxf(AS)
from John Nichols to [CB Jr?]
I trouble you with one more proof of Dr

1796

31 Jan – 1 Feb   2 p 4to   Osb
from SBP
Here I am just returned from Norbury Park &

17 July   3 p 4to   Osb
to FBA & M d'A
I last night finished Camilla; and now write to

12 Feb [1796]   3 p 8vo   Osb
from SHB
I cannot deny myself the pleasure, even at the

20 July   pmk 1796   4 p 4to
                              NYPL(B)
with Rosette (Rose) Burney to CB
I lose no time in begging You to send me Wolf's

8 May [1796?]   1 p 4to   Osb
from Joseph Warton
Many thanks to you for the List of Books

[Nov 1796]   2 p fragment   Osb
from SBP
I bespoke a scrap of my poor Norbury's blotted

[18 May 1796]   ½ p 4to   Comyn
from Richard Porson
The accounts that Perry received

14 Sept [1796–1812]   1 p 8vo   Osb
from John Nichols to [CB Jr?]
My Friend the Revd *Auley Macauley*, Vicar of

[19 May 1796]   ½ p 4to   Osb
from Richard Porson
Parry has written from Bristol. He says that

1797

15 Apr   4 p 4to   Osb
from Richard L Edgeworth
I have hoped from day to day for a private

28 Nov   2 p 4to   Osb
from Sir William Herschel
It seems to be an established custom with me

28 June   pmk ⟨1797⟩   1 p 4to   Osb
from Samuel Parr
Accept my most hearty thanks for your most

1798

7 Apr   4 p 4to   Osb
from John Young
I have been roused from a most unwarrantable

[9 May 1798]   1 p 4to   Comyn
from John Young
By a Letter from Mrs Young just received, I

1798, continued

18 May   2 p 4to   Osb
from John Young
Your σηματα were *not* λυγρα. They have

2 June   1 p 4to   Osb
from John Young
My *Guts* are so deranged to Day & yesterday

[13 June]   1 p 4to   Osb
from John Young
I *was* at home at ½ past 6 — &, what is more,

15 June   1 p 4to   Osb
from John Young
I wrote you this morning to your *"Academy"*

30 June   1 p 4to   Osb
from Thomas Kidd
Please to accept this pamphlet as a testimony

2 July   pmk 1798   1 p 4to   Osb
from John Young
I am here. Ergo I will be soon *there.* Come

9 July   3 p 4to   Osb
from John Young
I wrote you a hurried line from Newcastle

21 July   3 p 4to   Osb
from Molesworth Phillips & SBP
I never doubted your kindness nor your wish to

28 July   1 p 4to   Folger
to George Steevens
Your lovely valuable present met me, just as I

28 July   2 p 4to   Osb
from William Vincent
Having been sometime at work upon the most

13 Aug   pmk 1798   4 p 4to   Osb
from J[ames?] Young
Mr Young having been from home since

18 Aug   3 p 4to   Comyn
from Edmond Malone
In settling the chronology of Dryden's disputes

22 Aug   3 p 4to   Hyde
to [Edmond Malone?]
I recollected the passage in Aristotle, as soon

25 Aug   1 p 4to   Osb
from John Young
My Dearest Graduate, Here I am — & there I

27 Aug   1 p 4to   Osb
from John Young
This will be *handed* you by Your Young Ward.

[28 Aug 1798]   1 p 4to   Osb
from John Young
I have your Note. glad the Cargo wth Bill of

30 Aug   1 p 4to   Osb
from John Young
I am baffled beyond description. My Business

[5] Sept [1798]   1 p 8vo   Osb
from John Young
I am still Baffled. I am to make another attempt

6 Sept   1 p 4to   Folger
from Edmond Malone
In your remarks on Boswell, there is a word

8 SP 1798 pmk   1 p 8vo   Scot
from John Young
I *will* set out by Eleven or Sooner — if there

[13 Sept 1798]   1 p 8vo   Osb
from John Young
I am in chambers here, without having made

[Sept 1798]   1 p 4to   Osb
from John Young
I have, as usual, been run down. "With what?"

7 Oct   2 p 4to   Osb
from John Young
I am this Moment returned to Alma Mater. I

22 Oct   1 p 4to   Osb
from M J Routh
I should be very much obliged to you for a

1 Nov   4 p 4to   Osb
from John Young
I have to acknowledge on My own part & that

2 Nov   pmk 1798   4 p 4to   Osb
from Molesworth Phillips & SBP
Your extreme kindness my dearest Charles

4 Nov [1798?]   2 p 4to   Osb
from John Young
It was really very kind in you to write so very

13 Nov [1798?]   2 p 4to   Osb
from John Young
Well — Here *is* "a sweet word" for the good

30 Nov   1 p 8vo   Osb
to Cadell & Davies
Dr. Charles Burney begs Messrs. Cadell &

2 Dec   2 p 4to   Osb
from John Young
James has mentioned to me an invitation he has

[1798]   1 p 4to   BM
to Lady Collier
Dr. Charles Burney presents his respects to

[1798]   1 p 8vo   Comyn
from John Philip Kemble
Ah, my dear Burney, I am most miserable

[pre 1799]   1 p 4to   Comyn
from William Seward
You are now & then applyd to for a

1799

8 Jan   pmk ⟨1799⟩   4 p 4to   Osb
from Ralph Griffiths
It shall have a *title*. Suppose we call it "*Notices*

10 Jan [1799?]   1 p fol   Osb
from G E Griffiths
I learnt yesterday that you have been at

13 Jan   2 p 4to   Osb
from John Young
You are Many Letters in my Debt. Scraps of

15 Jan   1 p fol   Osb
from G E Griffiths
I send you some more of Hecuba; & in this

17 Jan   4 p 4to   Osb
with CPB to Rosette (Rose) Burney &
      Sabrina Bicknell
[CPB] I shall now tell you how we have spent

2⟨0⟩ Jan   3 p 4to   Osb
from John Young
I have this Moment received Your Letter of the

23 Jan   1 p 4to   Osb
from Josiah Thomas
The mountain cannot come to Mahomet, &

25 Jan   1 p 4to   Osb
from George Dance
It gives me pain to tell you that before I

[1 Feb]   3 p 4to   Osb
from John Young
To a letter of yours — containing sundry

6 Feb   pmk 1799   1 p fol   Osb
from G E Griffiths
The Compositors are waiting for the Page of

10 Feb   pmk 1799   1 p 4to   Osb
from G E Griffiths
The printers are standing still for p. 70 of the

14 Feb [1799]   2 p 4to   Osb
from G E Griffiths
I send you now proofs of the whole remainder

18 Feb   4 p 4to   Osb
from John Young
I hope by this Time *the Needful* has moved

4 Mar   pmk 1799   3 p 4to   Osb
from G E Griffiths
I was obliged to stop, in the Rev. for Feb.,

12 Mar   2 p 4to   NYPL(B)
to FBA & M d'A
A Chance frank offers itself; — so let me know

13 Mar [1799?]   1 p 4to   Osb
from John Young
Here Cometh a little Morsel of Sweet Words

20 Mar   1 p 4to   Osb
from [Joseph?] White
Dr. White's best Respects to Dr. Burney. The

24 Mar   1 p 4to   Osb
from John Young
More "Sweet words"! — The same sweet

29 Mar   2 p 4to   Osb
from Joseph ⟨Passlay⟩
The Liberty I am now taking in writing to you

10 Apr   3 p 4to   Osb
from John Young
What Meaneth the good Clerk Burney that he

15 Apr   1 p 8vo   NYPL(B)
to Edward Foss
Pray let my friend Mr. Hagen have the opera

21 Apr [1799]   2 p 4to   Osb
from John Young
This will be delivered to you by Mr Chas

1799, continued

6 May   1 p 4to   Osb
from Charles Butler
When I appointed, next Wednesday, for You

7 [May misdated March]   pmk 1799
        3 p 4to   Osb
from G E Griffiths
If you are in the dark, I am only in the twilight

8 May   1 p 4to   Osb
from Richard L Edgeworth
I am very sorry to have missed you —

17 May   3 p 4to   Osb
from John Young
I have seen your "*third* of Exchange," &

3 June   1 p 4to   Osb
from G E Griffiths
The hurry, confusion, & anxiety of the last

13 June   4 p 4to   Osb
from John Young
A Letter begun on the 22ᵈ of May & finished

1 July   4 p 4to   Osb
from John Young
Your Letter of the 25ᵗʰ ult came to me here

4 July   pmk 1799   1 p fol   Osb
from G E Griffiths
I send you herewith a proof of the first eight

5 Aug   1 p 4to   Osb
from G E Griffiths
I now forward to you, in two packets, the

5 Aug   4 p 4to   Osb
from John Young
And so, Good Academician, My Cadet is off —

21 Aug   1 p 4to   Osb
from Richard Heber
I write from the George Inn, York amidst the

21 Aug   2 p 4to   Folger
from Edmond Malone
Many thanks, Dear Sir, for the trouble you

26 Aug   3 p 4to   Osb
from Thomas Twining
You will, probably, be surprised, when I tell

9 Sept   pmk 1799   4 p 4to   Scot
from John Young
A thousand thanks for your attention to my

23 Sept   4 p fol   Osb
from Thomas Twining
[Notes; Letter p 3] I have read your Critique

24 Sept   1 p fol   Osb
from John Philip Kemble
I couldn't get the Card till this Morning. —

27 SP 1799 pmk   3 p fol   Osb
from Thomas Twining
p. 432. o. 787. Is it so clear, that any

4 Oct   3 p 4to   Scot
from John Young
I wrote you about a Month ago, on some

16 Oct   4 p 4to   NYPL(B)
to Thomas Twining
Many thanks for your very kind & learned

17 Oct   3 p 4to   Osb
from William Vincent
Will you allow me to tease you once more

23 Oct   3 p 4to   Osb
from William Vincent
In order to recall your memory (which upon

30 Oct   4 p 4to   NYPL(B)
to FBA
Huzza! Huzza! Huzza Mʳ. H. admires the table

5 Nov   2 p 4to   Osb
from Thomas Burgess
Your letter of Aug 24ᵗʰ. I received, & intended

8 Nov   4 p 4to   NYPL(B)
to M d'A
Your News about our dearest Susan rejoiced

8 Nov   4 p 4to   Scot
from John Young
I have a Letter from the Marchioness of

23 Nov   3 p 4to   Osb
from Josiah Thomas
I have just met the Dean of Waterford who

23 Nov   1 p 4to   Scot
from John Young
I thank you for your prompt Reply to my

26 Nov   2 p 4to   Osb
from William Vincent
I promised you before I printed to submit to

28 Nov   2 p 4to   Osb
from M J Routh
The Thirty <   > or Scholarships, of

2 Dec   1 p 4to   Osb
from John Stuart, 1st Marquis of Bute
My Good Friend Professor Young having

2 Dec   4 p 4to   BM
to Thomas Twining
I have never been able, till this day

[3 Dec 1799]   3 p 4to   Scot
from John Young
We have this Moment a line from James, in

11 Dec   3 p 4to   Osb
from Thomas Twining
Your *MS* shall go by the Colchester Coach

14 [12? Dec 1799]   2 p fol   NYPL(B)
from SBP
I return you an answer *by return of post* as you

17 Dec   pmk 1799   1 p 4to   Osb
from John Young
I have only ¼ of an Hour to desire you &

27 Dec   3 p 4to   Osb
to FBA
Though times are hard, & though postage is

27 Dec [1799]   2 p 4to   BM(Bar)
to CB
Poor Susan has been driven into Holyhead: —

[c 1799]   2 p 4to   Osb
from Bennet Langton
As it happens that I have been induced to come

1800

1 Jan   4 p 4to   BM(Bar)
to CB
A most happy year to my dear Father! —

2 Jan   3 p 4to   BM(Bar)
with Molesworth Phillips to FBA &
      M d'A
I at length write under the same roof with our

6 Jan   3 p 4to   BM(Bar)
to CB
I want alas! that consolation, which I would

8 Jan   4 p 4to   NYPL(B)
to FBA & M d'A
I have been afraid to write to my dear

8 Jan   3 p 4to   BM(Bar)
to CB
I must write again to my poor dear Father,

9 Jan   4 p 4to   NYPL(B)
from EBB
Oh my Dearest Charles — What a task has

10 Jan [1800]   3 p 4to   BM(Bar)
to CB
I am thus far on my road towards Greenwich

20 Jan   1 p 4to   Scot
from John Young
You will not doubt that I sympathise with you

21 JA 1800 pmk   1 p 8vo   Osb
from M d'A
Without your help I shall never get the better

22 Jan   2 p 4to   Osb
from John Young
[tear] <Pr>ofession of my Regrets. I heard

1 Feb   3 p 4to   BPL
to Edmond Malone
Some time ago, I mentioned to Mr. Twining

2 Feb   2 p 4to   Scot
to James Sykes
By a letter, which I recieved lately from

3 Feb   draft   1 p 4to   Scot
from James Sykes (on p 4 ALS CB Jr to
      J Sykes 2 Feb 1800)
I have recd yr Letter, and whatever Ct.

5 Feb   1 p 8vo   PML
to Cadell & Davies
Dr. Charles Burney requests the favour being

6 Feb   1 p 8vo   PML
from Cadell & Davies
After so repeatedly charging us with wilfully

6 Feb   1 p 4to   Folger
from Edmond Malone
I am much obliged to you and Mr Twining, for

7 Feb   1 p 4to   Osb
to Cadell & Davies
Dr. Charles Burney is obliged to Messrs. Cadell

10 Feb   pmk 1800   1 p 4to
from Samuel Parr   Oxf(AS)
I remember that when you accepted

1800, continued

11 Feb   3 p 4to   Osb
from John Young
Holla ὦ οὗτος — ! Have you, or have you not

28 FE ⟨1800⟩ pmk   3 p 4to
from Samuel Parr   Oxf(AS)
I am exceedingly sorry that I was

11 MR 1800 pmk   1 p 4to   Osb
from John Philip Kemble
If I had a vote to give, you know how entirely

12 MR 1800 pmk   4 p fol   Win
to G I Huntingford
I have scribbled hastily on the opposite half

[15 Mar 1800]   1 p 4to   Osb
 from John Young
I write a few lines on the last page of a Letter

16 Mar   4 p 4to   Win
to G I Huntingford
First, for ⟨   ⟩ ⟨disyllabics⟩, your

20 Mar   2 p 4to   Win
to G I Huntingford
Again, my dear friend. — Compare your verse,

1 APR 1800 pmk   4 p 4to   Osb
from John Young
I am anxious to learn how my young Friend

25 Apr   1 p 4to   Comyn
from Samuel Hoole
I beg to return you my thanks for the favour

30 Apr   1 p 4to   Folger
from Edmond Malone
I hope you received by the Greenwich Coach

11 May   1 p 4to   RSA
to Charles Taylor
Dʳ. Charles Burney presents his compᵗˢ. to

11 July [1800]   3 p 4to   Osb
from John Young
"The Lads" outsailed your Letter. They were

17 July   2 p 4to   Osb
from John Young
Agreeably to your desire I *have* issued my

1 Sept   1 p fol   Osb
from G E Griffiths
The inclosed is just come to hand from Mʳ.

29 Oct   2 p 4to   Osb
from John Young
Having but little Room left me in the Frank I

31 OC 1800 pmk   1 p 4to   Oxf(AS)
from Samuel Parr
Huzza [the rest illegible]

⟨7⟩ Nov   1 p 8vo   NYPL(B)
to CPB
Let us hear, when you receive

20 Nov   2 p 4to   Yale(Be)
to [William] Davies
I was going to write, in order to request you to

30 Nov   4 p 4to   Scot
from John Young
Your little extract from Dʳ Huttons Letter was

10 DE 1800 pmk   3 p 8vo   Osb
from EBB
I acknowledge that it is a species of cruelty to

[1800?]   1 p 8vo   NYPL(B)
to CPB
I can only say, stay according to Lord

[c 1800]   ½ p 4to   Osb
from John Young
I have borrowed a Scrap of John's Letter to

[c 1800–1810]   2 p 8vo   Osb
from Priscilla Kemble
I am myself going to the Play to morrow

1801

8 Jan   2 p 8vo   Cal(SB)
to Samuel Lysons
I have been confined by a strain, ever since I

9 Jan   4 p 4to   Osb
from John Young
Your Protegé arrived by the Mail at

18 Jan   2 p 4to   Comyn
to Edward Foss
I send you a New Year's Gift. — It goes to you

19 Jan   3 p 4to   Osb
from John Young
Every new Line you write letteth me nearer

2 Feb   2 p 4to   Osb
from John Young
Your Enclosures came safe to hand this Day.

19 Feb   1 p 4to   Osb
from Mary Berry
A copy of Belmour lays by me destined for you

5 Mar   2 p 4to   BM
to CBFB
It was not in my power yesterday

7 MR 1801 pmk   3 p 4to   Osb
from John Young
I have been, rather impatiently, expecting some

7 Mar   1 p 4to   Osb
from Thomas Burgess
I have sent you below the title for my [li]ttle

11 Mar   2 p 4to   Osb
from John Young
Now, My Good Dear Doctor we are sore

16 Mar   2 p 4to   Osb
from Sir George Pretyman Tomline
I happened to be in Suffolk last week, or I

20 Mar   2 p 4to   Osb
from John Young
We yet on the Tenter Hook. No Letter from

22 Mar 1801 pmk   2 p 4to   Osb
from John Young
I have no Letter from Carruthers — but one

24 Mar [1801]   4 p 4to   Osb
from John Young
A thousand kind thanks for a thousand kind

[Mar 1801]   1 p 4to   Scot
from John Young
<   > Day. Even these pressing Demands

11 Apr [1801 misdated 1800] 1 p 4to
from John Young   Scot
I have just heard shortly from James. He has

12 Apr   3 p 4to   Osb
from John Young
This London Post! It comes so late as only to

22 Apr   4 p 4to   Osb
from John Young
I have to acknowledge your kind Letter

23 Apr   1 p 4to   Osb
from John Kaye
I yesterday received the Books, the selection

1 May   3 p 4to   Osb
from John Young
I write this Short Line to introduce to you Mr

9 May   2 p 4to   Osb
from John Young
In Times of sheer Distress the children of

30 MY 1801 pmk   1 p 4to   Comyn
from John Hoole
Mrs Hoole & I are now in town

[pre 8 Aug 1801]   4 p 4to   Osb
from John Young
I have received your Letter & your Bill. Thanks

8 Aug   1 p 4to   Osb
from Henry John Todd
I trust you will pardon the liberty I take in

22 Nov   3 p 4to   Osb
from John Young
Now for an Advertisement describing a "Stolen

13 Dec   4 p 4to   Osb
from John Young
The Parcel did come to hand safe & I am at this

[c 1801]   2 p 4to   Folger
from Edmond Malone
Many thanks, Dear Sir, for your <Classick>

1802

19 Jan   4 p 8vo   Osb
to FBA
What with rheumatics & griefs, and vexations,

29 Jan   4 p 4to   Osb
from John Young
No doubt you expected to receive Letters from

[Jan 1802]   1 p scrap   Osb
from [John Young]
Memorandum. Being a request that the Good

3 Feb   2 p 4to   NYPL(B)
with FBA to CBFB
Many thanks for your Shawl, which I shall find

1802, continued

6 Feb   1 p 8vo   PML
to William Davies
Pray, send me the Copies of the new Camilla.

19 Feb   1 p 4to   Osb
from Henry Fuseli
the paragraph which I saw in the Herald is

22 Feb   2 p 4to   Osb
from John Young
I send you, in Course, the <Monies>; for so I

26 Mar pmk 180<2>   3 p 4to   Osb
from John Young
If that my Dog Rayner did not cut

11 Apr   pmk 1802   1 p 4to
from Samuel Parr   Oxf(AS)
I hope you will not condemn me

25 Apr   2 p 4to   Osb
from G I Huntingford
I will tell you fairly I did hope my friend

26 Apr   3 p 4to   Osb
from John Young
I have been hunting after a Mathematician for

5 May   1 p 4to   Osb
from John Philip Kemble
I have the Pleasure to tell you that your Name

12 May   3 p 4to   Osb
from John Young
Here are we tied to the spot by our total

18 MY 1802 pmk   1 p 4to   Osb
from John Young
Your Letters, Lines, Notices, and others came

20 May   4 p 4to   Osb
from Jean-François Boissonade
J'ai reçu per mr Crooke la note des MSS. de la

22 May   1 p 4to   Osb
from Thomas King
When your very liberal and polite note came

[22 May 1802]   1 p 4to   Osb
from [Rosette (Rose) Burney]
I opened the Letter hoping I coud [sic] return

[26 May 1802]   1 p 8vo   Osb
from John Young
It hath so happened that we have detained the

[May–June 1802]   1 p 8vo   Osb
from John Young
Positively, at what Hour on Sunday will you

[May–June 1802]   1 p 12mo   Osb
from John Young
Instead of taking me up here, take me up at

[May–June 1802]   1 p 4to   Osb
from John Young
I return the borrowed Goods. My Dear Friend

<1 JU> 1802 pmk   1 p 4to   Osb
from John Young
We have got Mr Coutt's Box for the Opera

21 June   3 p 4to   Osb
from Sir Joseph Banks
I have seen Boissonnade this Morning, and

24 JU 1802 pmk   1 p 4to   Osb
from John Young
Imprimus let me beg you to take the charge

24 JU <1802> pmk   1 p 4to   Osb
from John Young
Call from time to time at N° 47 — & pick

18 Aug   4 p fol   Osb
from John Young
I write you on the long. Whether I shall be

6 Sept [1802]   3 p 4to   Osb
from Jean-François Boissonade
J'ai eu l'honneur de vous écrire il y a six

8 Oct [1802]   1 p 4to   Osb
from Jean-François Boissonade
Perdonnez moi de vous importuner encore. —

13 Oct   2 p 4to   BN
to Jean-François Boissonade
I am quite concerned, my dear Sir, that a letter

21 Oct   4 p 4to   Osb
from Jean-François Boissonade
J'ai reçu ce matin de Mr. Perregrin la somme

22 Nov   draft   1 p 4to   HSP
from Benjamin West
It becomes my duty in the Station I have the

23 Nov   2 p 4to   Comyn
from M d'A (PS by FBA)
In spite of my certainly *improved in Worse*

26 Nov   1 p 4to   Osb
from Jean-François Boissonade
M. Darblay m'a remis il y a une quinzaine de

9 Dec   2 p 4to   Osb
from Thomas Dampier
I am much obliged to you for the little Tract

11 Dec   2 p 4to   Osb
from G I Huntingford
You have written many things well; but none

21 Dec   3 p 4to   Osb
from Peter Paul Dobrée
An ardent desire of improvement in classical

25 Dec   3 p 4to   Osb
from John Young
Before all other matters let me request you to

29 Dec   1 p 4to   Osb
from Sir George Beaumont
I am sorry to see by the date of your obliging

30 Aug [1802–11]   1 p 8vo   Osb
from Nevil Maskelyne [to CB Jr?]
I shall be very happy to receive the Bishop of

[post 1802?]   1 p 4to   Osb
from Jean-François Boissonade
J'ai l'honneur de vous offrir un exemplaire de

4 May [post 1802]   1 p 4to   Osb
from Francis North, 4th Earl of Guilford
Will you and Charles meet

15 June [post 1802]   3 p 8vo   Osb
from John Young
The little Specimen Work is now out of the

[1802–08]   1 p 8vo   Osb
from Thomas Dampier
I am so very unwell that I have informed his

[1802–12]   2 p 4to   Osb
from Francis North, 4th Earl of Guilford
The Prince of Wales dines with the Saint to

[1802–17]   2 p 4to   Osb
from Francis North, 4th Earl of Guilford
I expect the Prince of Wales here on Friday

[pre 1803]   1 p 8vo   Osb
from [Ralph Griffiths]
Hoping, & trusting, Dear Carlo, that thou art,

[pre 1803]   2 p 4to   Osb
from [Ralph Griffiths]
(But first let me mend my pen.) I am very

1803

26 Feb   1 p 8vo   Osb
to Alexander Chalmers
I have gotten some *Tatlers* not *printed* in the

1 Mar   pmk 1803   1 p 4to   Oxf(AS)
from Samuel Parr
[illegible]

2 Mar   4 p 4to   Osb
from John Young
I thank you Cordially — *most* Cordially &

5 MR 1803 pmk   2 p 4to   Oxf(AS)
from Samuel Parr
I am engaged till Tuesday — on

6 Mar   1 p 4to   All
from Benjamin West
I am sorry you should not have been present at

17 MR 1803 pmk   amanuensis   3 p 4to
from Samuel Parr   Oxf(AS)
I think the passage intelligible

22 Mar   1 p 8vo   Osb
from Joseph Nollekens
In persuance to your request, I have had twelve

25 Mar   1 p 4to   Osb
from Sir Joseph Banks
I cannot entertain a doubt of the Thankfullness

25 Mar   1 p 4to   Osb
from Thomas Twining
You could not gratify & oblige me more than

29 Mar   1 p 4to   Osb
from George Owen Cambridge
As it is likely that several questions may arise

3 Apr   3 p 4to   Osb
from George Owen Cambridge
I am vexd [sic] that a mistake of Cadells in the

23 Apr   1 p 4to   Osb
from George, 2nd Earl Spencer
I received your obliging Letter here this

1803, continued

2⟨6⟩ Apr   1 p 4to   BM
from J W Bacon
The favor of your Company is requested

4 May   1 p 4to   BM
from J W Bacon
I see in my Notices and Summons

9 MAY 1803 pmk   2 p 4to   Comyn
from Thomas Twining
All safe & sound! — No fracture,

13 May   1 p 4to   BM
from J W Bacon
I beg leave to remind you of your engagement

22 June   2 p 4to   Comyn
from Elizabeth Inchbald to [CB Jr]
I trust you will pardon the Liberty I take

24 June   4 p 4to   Osb
from John Young
Now — That you *do* owe me *three* Answers,

25 June [1803]   2 p 4to   Comyn
from Elizabeth Inchbald to [CB Jr]
I cannot resist the pleasure of returning you

13 July   3 p 4to   Osb
from G I Huntingford
This Week I am at home to every body, & No

8 Aug   3 p 4to   Comyn
from George Owen Cambridge
You have I hope before this received a copy

22 AU 1803 pmk   2 p 8vo   Osb
from Sir Thomas Lawrence
I shall be glad to have the pleasure of a visit

4 Sept   3 p 4to   Osb
from John Young
Yes! York! Here have I been, bag & Baggage,

20 Oct   2 p 4to   Osb
from George, 2nd Earl Spencer
By this Evening's Mail Coach I shall send to

6 Nov   2 p 4to   Osb
from John Young
This Letter will be delivered to you by Master

6 Nov   4 p 4to   Osb
from John Young
I have, this Moment, finished a Letter to you

9 Nov   4 p 8vo   Osb
from Shute Barrington
I shall with pleasure see both you & your

9 NOV 1803 pmk   4 p fol   Osb
from [Lady Crewe]
I take a large sheet because I *literally* mean to

10 Nov   3 p 4to   Osb
from G I Huntingford
"That strain I heard was of a higher mood"

25 Nov   1 p 4to   Osb
from George, 2nd Earl Spencer
I am very sorry that an Engagement in the

28 Dec   2 p 4to   Osb
from Shute Barrington
I enclose a draft on Mess.rs Drummond for five

23 Feb [post 1803]   1 p 8vo   Osb
from Thomas Gaisford
I inclose a rude & unpolished and I may add a

[pre 1804?]   1 p 4to   Osb
from [Reginald] Heber
Owing to a delay, which has taken place in

1804

4 Jan   receipt   1 p fragment   Osb
from Joseph Nollekens
Received of D.r Charles Burney the sum of

7 Jan   2 p 4to   Osb
from Thomas Burgess
I hardly know how to apologize to you for my

16 Jan   pmk 1804   amanuensis
      1 p fol   Oxf(AS)
from Samuel Parr
Yesterday I received your letter together

20 Jan   2 p 8vo   Osb
from John Reeves
I am puzzled with this affair of Harris

30 Jan   1 p 8vo   Osb
from William Siddons
A few friends of your acquaintance chiefly —

11 Feb   4 p 4to   Osb
from John Young
By Prescription, I have acquired a claim on you

19 Feb   3 p 4to   Osb
from G I Huntingford
Your partiality for me is shewn in a manner of

27 Feb   2 p 4to   Osb
from G I Huntingford
Particular occasions require suitable Letters.

8 Mar   1 p 4to   Osb
from Martin Davy
I have been requested by Profʳ Porson to

10 Mar   2 p 4to   Osb
from Shute Barrington
As your name appears among the contributors

13 Mar   1 p 4to   Osb
from John Kaye
Accept my sincere thanks for your kind

20 Mar   1 p 4to   Osb
from Henry Fuseli
I thank you for your friendly condescension.

24 Mar   4 p 4to   Osb
from John Young
Les Voila. They are not to be Eyed as

25 Mar   4 p 4to   Osb
from John Young
As a great Minister (and eke a small) has not

[31 Mar? 1804]   4 p 4to   Osb
from John Young
I have no Answer from you to my two Letters.

11 Apr   4 p fol   Osb
from John Young
Dear Friend. Χαριν — χαριτας — χαιρειν! —

17 AP 1804 pmk   2 p 4to   Osb
from John Young
I ruin you with Postages. This I write to

27 Apr   3 p 4to   Osb
from John Young
Not being able to convince either Mother or

29 Apr   1 p 4to   Osb
from Richard Heber
Having luckily had an opportunity of

[29 Apr 1804]   3 p 4to   Osb
from John Young
John has just been telling us of your Friendship

2 May   pmk 1804   1 p 4to   Osb
from Reginald Heber
I have been to make enquiry respecting the

7 May   pmk 180⟨4⟩   1 p 4to   Osb
from Henry Kett
On opening a Box which I have had for some

[27 May 1804]   1 p 8vo   Osb
from John Young
Rayner goes by the 5 o'Clock coach. "Why

1 June   pmk 1804   1 p 4to   Oxf(AS)
from Samuel Parr
⟨Bartlam⟩ left me this morning

6 June   3 p 4to   Osb
from John Young
I am just *come* from the Opera. You see what

10 June [1804?]   1 p fol   Oxf(AS)
from Samuel Parr
I send you back the inclosed with my blessing

13 June   2 p 4to   Comyn
from Robert Nares
I send you the result of my Enquiries

16 June   amanuensis   3 p 4to
from Samuel Parr   Oxf(AS)
Bartlam came to me yesterday, &

4 JY 1804 pmk   4 p 4to   Osb
from John Young
By some unaccountable carelessness or

5 July [1804?]   3 p 4to   Osb
from Thomas Maurice
I hope you have not imputed that delay in

5 July   1 p 4to   Osb
from George, 2nd Earl Spencer
Having understood that you are desirous of

20 July   4 p 4to   Osb
from John Young
So you are determined to fob me off

21 July   1 p 8vo   Comyn
from Joseph Nollekens
Mʳ Nollekens presents his Compᵗˢ. to Dʳ.

16 Aug   1 p 4to   Osb
from William Sharp
Mʳ: Sharp has the pleasure to inform Dʳ:

1804, continued

8 Sept [1804]   4 p 4to   Osb
from John Young
First Receive my Congratulations. Your 43

26 Sept [1804]   3 p 4to   Osb
from John Young
I ordered John Yesterday to inform you that I

28 Sept   1 p 4to   Osb
from Henry Fuseli
Absence must plead my excuse for not

28 Sept   3 p 4to   Osb
from John Kaye
I am sorry that I cannot at present avail myself

29 SP 1804 pmk   2 p 4to   Osb
from Martin Davy
I assure you I have been extremely unwell for

3 OC 1804 pmk   1 p 8vo   Osb
from Horace Twiss
I have called at the hospital, & found Mr Jones

9 Oct   1 p 4to   Osb
from G I Huntingford
I enclose the Copy of a Letter which has

12 Oct   3 p 4to   Win
to G I Huntingford
My incessant occupations had prevented my

17–18 Oct   4 p 4to   Osb
to CPB
This letter, my dear Charles, will be delivered

22 Oct   4 p 4to   Osb
to CPB
Your letter was most acceptable to us all,

22 Oct   3 p 4to   Win
to G I Huntingford
How good and thoughtful are you, my kind

28 Oct [1804]   4 p 4to   Osb
from John Young
What is the Reason why "Carol-a-Grenovic"

1 NO 1804 pmk   4 p 4to   NYPL(B)
to CPB
Only a few lines — & those in haste

6 Nov   4 p 4to   NYPL(B)
to CPB
Your letter has made me more sorry

8 NO 1804 pmk   4 p 4to   Osb
from Mrs Crewe
I really feel ashamed to scribble so often

19 Nov   4 p 4to   Osb
to CPB
I should have written, last Week

22 Nov   2 p 4to   Osb
from Peter Paul Dobrée
I have thus long denied myself the pleasure of

27 Nov   3 p 4to   Osb
from G I Huntingford
I write under some degree of uneasiness, lest

5 Dec   3 p 4to   Osb
to CPB
I have only time to say, bring up all the Books,

6 Dec   pmk 1804   2 p 4to   Oxf(AS)
from Samuel Parr
I send <   > to you —

12 DE 1804 pmk   1 p 4to   Osb
from Sir George Beaumont
I cannot express to you how much I am obliged

12 Dec [1804]   1 p 4to   Oxf(AS)
from Samuel Parr
I thank you for your Critical Letter

20 Dec   1 p 4to   Oxf(AS)
from Samuel Parr
Charles Burney, LLD, Charles Parr Burney,

24 Dec   pmk 1804   1 p 4to   Oxf(AS)
from Samuel Parr
do you or Charles come to see me

26 Dec [1804]   3 p 4to   Osb
from JB
I am very sincerely grieved for the death of

[1804?]   2 p 8vo   Osb
from Sir Thomas Lawrence
A very pleasant and clever Woman and I think

1805

8 Jan   pmk 1805   1 p 4to   Oxf(AS)
from Samuel Parr
I am very anxious to see you

14 Jan   1 p 8vo   Osb
from Thomas Kidd
Permit me to return you my unfeigned thanks

18 Jan   3 p 4to   Osb
from Jean-François Boissonade
Permettez moi de vous présenter MM. *Antoine*

18 Jan   1 p 8vo   Osb
to John Robinson
Your letter followed me to the North —

2 FE 1805 pmk   3 p 4to   Osb
from Peter Paul Dobrée
Yesterday morning I told Mr Lunn your

5–6 Feb   5 p 4to   Osb
to CPB
I travelled sullenly to Salt Hill, after we parted.

12 Feb   4 p 4to   Osb
to CPB
An Appendix to the Monthly Reviews was left

12 Feb   3 p 4to   Osb
from John Young
My Dear Charles would communicate to you

17 Feb   4 p 4to   Osb
with Rosette (Rose) Burney to CPB
Your omission of the Number of the House, or

1 Mar   4 p 4to   Osb
to CPB
In a few days you may expect a parcel; but I

5 Mar   4 p 8vo   Osb
to CPB
Edward Foss *wisely* came to D L. & got an act

5 Mar   3 p 4to   Osb
from John Kaye
Nothing would be more gratifying to me than

⟨8 MR 1805⟩ pmk   2 p 4to   Osb
from Richard Payne Knight
I can find nothing nearer to τα νεα than

18 Mar   4 p 4to   Osb
to CPB
I have been sadly hurried — or I would not

20 MR 1805 pmk   1 p 4to   Osb
from Richard Payne Knight
Many thanks, my Dear Sir, for your Line,

20 MR 1805 pmk   1 p 4to   Osb
from Richard Payne Knight
Having been interrupted while writing to you

21 MR 1805 pmk   2 p 4to   Osb
from Richard Payne Knight
Surely οιδα & ειδεναι in the Line you quote, are

25 Mar   4 p 4to   Osb
to CPB
I must be brief — but I will not wait, till I

26 Mar   4 p 4to   Osb
from John Young
I ought to have made long ere now a Return

27 Mar   2 p 4to   Osb
to CPB
The Warden is very kind; as the inclosed will

29 Mar   3 p 4to   Osb
from Peter Paul Dobrée
Soon after you had done me the favour of

4 Apr   2 p 4to   Osb
to CPB
I have only time to say, that your Mother

4 Apr   1 p 8vo   Yale(Be)
to [Robert Harding?] Evans
Mr. Evans is requested to send to Dr. C Burney

8 APR 1805 pmk   amanuensis   1 p 4to
from Samuel Parr   Oxf(AS)
My godson and I separated last Wednesday

18 Apr   3 p 4to   Osb
from John Young
Where, My Dear Friend, are you Wandering?

6 May   3 p 4to   Osb
from John Kaye
During the Easter Vacation I was away from

13 May   4 p 4to   Osb
to CPB
Your second letter, my dear Boy, was a

15–17 May   3 p 4to   Osb
to CPB
I have been much pressed by various

1805, continued

[pre 17 May 1805?]   3 p 4to   Osb
from Peter Paul Dobrée
My dearest Sir, for so I must call you after

17 May   2 p 4to   Osb
from Peter Paul Dobrée
The copy of the Bentleian catalogue has

26 May   3 p 4to   Osb
from John Kaye
I was not in College when your Letter arrived;

30 May   4 p 4to   Osb
to CPB
Much longer than I wished, my dear Boy, have

31 May   4 p 4to   Osb
from John Young
Confessing myself rather Heathenish in not

2 June   2 p 4to   Osb
to CPB
I hope that your excursion will prove pleasure.

5 June   2 p 4to   Osb
from John Kaye
I have completed the Extract, which you

7 June   2 p 4to   Osb
from Peter Paul Dobrée
I am much concerned to hear that your cough

15 June   3 p 4to   Osb
from Peter Paul Dobrée
I have just looked at the MS Harpoeratis; & the

16 June   4 p 4to   Osb
to CPB
My dear Boy's letter is dated the 9th but I

17 June   1 p 4to   Osb
from John Kaye
I have sent by Ainslie the part of Photius

18 June   2 p 8vo   Osb
to CPB
As I find that my supposition about

[21 June 1805]   3 p 8vo   NYPL(B)
to CPB
This is merely as a <make-weight>

28 JU 1805 pmk   1 p 4to   Osb
from William Robert Spencer
Why did you fail us yesterday at Rogers's?

30 June   2 p 4to   Osb
from John Kaye
I intend myself the pleasure of being with you

5 July   1 p 4to   Oxf(Bod)
from Thomas Gaisford
I arrived here to-day, and on my arrival

5 July   2 p 4to   Comyn
from William Windham
I must write in haste, but I may go, I think,

7 July   1 p 4to   Osb
from Henry Fuseli
You have so often answered my questions

13 July   1 p 4to   Osb
from Richard Payne Knight
Thank[s], my kind Friend, for this additional

[23 July 1805]   3 p 4to   Osb
from Peter Paul Dobrée
As I was book-hunting in Trin Lib. this

28 July   1 p 8vo   Osb
from T J Mathias
Mr. Sneyd was extremely sorry he was

[July 1805?]   3 p 4to   Osb
from Peter Paul Dobrée
I forgot, I do not know how, the *Appendix ad*

[July 1805]   1 p 4to   BM
to [William Windham]
Allow me to assure you, & that without a

[July 1805?]   1 p 8vo   Comyn
from William Wilberforce
Will you & Mr Burney do me the favour to

23 Sept [1805]   1 p 8vo   Folger
from Edmond Malone
Euripides somewhere says, that "*no lie ever*

22 Oct   ½ p 4to   Osb
from John Inigo Richards
The inclosed Pamphlet not having been

25 Oct   2 p 4to   Osb
from John Kaye
I received your Letter by Ainslie on Monday

31 Oct   4 p 4to   Osb
from Thomas Gaisford
I have in compliance to your request inclosed

3 Nov   4 p 4to   Osb
to CPB
I now begin my correspondence with you, at

5 Nov   3 p 4to   Osb
to CPB
The inclosed, my dear Boy, is for your private

6 Nov   1 p 4to   Osb
from G I Huntingford
A very diligent & ingenuous Young Man has

8 Nov   3 p 4to   Osb
from John Kaye
I have finished the Transcript from the Index

9 Nov   3 p 4to   Osb
from John Young
Yes Yes. The Doctor Charles Burney is a very

⟨15⟩ Nov   2 p 4to   Osb
from John Kaye
I herewith send my Copy from the Index of

20 Nov   4 p 8vo & 1 p fol
to CPB   Comyn & Osb
I must be very brief — First, however
[fol in Osb] PS. I am glad that you return

21 Nov   1 p 4to   Osb
from Thomas Daniell
All the Academicians as well as some of the

22 Nov   1 p 4to   Comyn
from William Thomas Fitzgerald
Though I have not seen you for an Age, I

22 NO 1805 pmk   1 p 4to   Oxf(AS)
from Samuel Parr
pray take care of your eyes — when

26 Nov   2 p 4to   Osb
to CPB
I would not trouble the Warden, I think; but

[Nov 1805]   3 p 8vo   Osb
from Sir George Pretyman Tomline
I thank you for your Letter & am much obliged

2 Dec   3 p 4to   Osb
to CPB
I must send five lines. — You are assuredly

6 Dec   1 p 4to   Osb
to CPB
I am sorry to warn you, that you will find your

6 Dec   3 p 4to   Osb
from G I Huntingford
You will greatly oblige me, if you will look at

13 DEC 1805 pmk   3 p 4to   Osb
from John Young
A many thanks, My Dearest Friend for your

20 Dec   4 p 4to   Osb
from G I Huntingford
I have enclosed a draft, from which I beg you

23 Dec   1 p 4to   Osb
from William Vincent
I have been nursing a Cough & hoarseness

[post 1805]   3 p 4to   Osb
from Thomas Sheridan to [CB Jr?]
May I ask a favor of you? I have some thought

[1805–11?]   1 p 4to   Osb
from Thomas Sheridan
If you should by good fortune be disengaged

1806

6 Jan   1 p 4to   Osb
from Samuel, 1st Viscount Hood
Lord Hood presents his Compliments to

8 Jan   3 p 4to   Comyn
from EBB
Tho I do not think a mere note

9 Jan   pmk 1806   1 p 4to   Oxf(AS)
from Samuel Parr
John . . . of the Temple or ⟨Hervey⟩

23 Jan   1 p 4to   Osb
from Charles Butler
I lament much, that so much time has elapsed

23 Jan   2 p 4to   Osb
from John Kaye
I had promised myself the pleasure of paying

28 Jan   3 p 4to   Osb
to CPB
Keep aloof from Ch. Ch. — for some time to

1806, continued

30 Jan   3 p 4to   Osb
from John Young
You owe me a Letter, My Dear Friend; & I

2 Feb   1 p 8vo   Osb
to ?
I have got a share in an Hogshead of

2 Feb   4 p 8vo   Osb
to CPB
I have been & still am much pressed with

16 Feb   2 p 4to   Osb
to CPB
Did I not tell you, my dear Boy, that I had

17 Feb   2 p 4to   Osb
from John Kaye
I promised to inform you of the Result of my

18 Feb   4 p 4to   Osb
from John Young
In a letter to Charles, about a week ago, I

24 Feb   3 p 4to   Osb
to CPB
I am so excessively pressed by business of

28 Feb   4 p 4to   Osb
from John Young
I received your Letter of No Date, Yesterday.

1 Mar   4 p 4to   Osb
from EBB
I thank you for your kind note, & am glad to

4 Mar   4 p 8vo   Osb
to CPB
The inclosed for friend Gaisford. — His

6 Mar   pmk 1806   2 p 4to   Osb
from G E Griffiths
Many thanks, my dear Sir, for your inclosure

12 Mar   2 p 4to   Osb
from John Kaye
I delivered your Letter and the Memorial,

14 Mar   4 p 4to   Osb
with Rosette (Rose) Burney to CPB
You are right as to the Rivickzi Binding

16 Mar   3 p 4to   Osb
from John Young
I am delighted, my Dear friend, with the

17 Mar   pmk 1806   1 p 4to   Osb
from William Parsons
I have proposed you at the R.I. Club & have

⟨20⟩ MR 1806 pmk   2 p 4to   Osb
from William Parsons
THANKS, my dear Aristarchus! I kiss the rod

22 Mar   1 p 4to   Comyn
to CPB
Your Mother & I dine with the Bishop of

[23 Mar 1806]   1 p 4to   Comyn
to CPB
As I was in town on Saturday, I called for the

23 Mar   4 p 4to   Osb
from Henry Petty-FitzMaurice, Marquis
     of Lansdowne
Having fully considered the subject of your

24 MR 1806 pmk   3 p 4to   Osb
from William Parsons
Ware! Ware! my Dear Burney! for without

8 Apr   pmk 1806   1 p 4to   Osb
from Henry Kett
It is very extraordinary how you could

13 Apr [c 1806?]   1 p 4to   Oxf(AS)
from Samuel Parr
Come to me — I shall

16 Apr [1806]   4 p 4to   Osb
with Rosette (Rose) Burney to CPB
Your father my Dear Charles has so much

19 Apr   1 p 8vo   Osb
from Thomas Dampier
I dined yesterday at Lambeth, & the Abp

28 Apr   2 p 8vo   Osb
from Thomas Kidd
Lunn informs me that you have sent for

2 May   1 p 8vo   Osb
from Thomas Gaisford
I enclose to you the fragments of Bernards

3 May   2 p 4to   Comyn
from William Hayley
You have surprised me, Sir, politely,

5 May   pmk ⟨1806⟩   1 p fol   Osb
from John Young
Holla! Mark our Maypole! A very seemly pole

10 May   1 p 8vo   Osb
from Joseph Nollekens
After I had the pleasure of seeing you on my

12 May   4 p 4to   Osb
to CPB
I have so much involved in business of my

14 May   1 p 4to   RSA
to Charles Taylor
D^r. Charles Burney is much obliged to M^r.

19 MY 1806 pmk   2 p 8vo   Osb
from Samuel Rogers
Happy indeed should I be to assist in sweeping

21 May   9 p 4to   Osb
from Thomas Kidd
I have anxiously waited for an opportunity of

26 May [1806]   1 p 4to   Osb
from Henry John Todd
I have not been able to see the bishop of

1 June   2 p 8vo   NYPL(B)
to CPB
Time only for one line — to my dear Charles

4 JU 1806 pmk   3 p 4to   Osb
from William Parsons
My rage against Loughborough was kindled

6 June   2 p 4to   Osb
from G E Griffiths
In M^r. Knight's book on Taste, I see that he

⟨9⟩ June   2 p 4to   NYPL(B)
to CPB
Your letter of Monday made us rather uneasy

14 June   2 p 4to   Osb
from John Kaye
I am desired by Lord Henry Petty to

15 June   3 p 4to   Osb
from John Young
1st Charles writeth sundries bearing upon

24 June   1 p 4to   Osb
from Sir William Weller Pepys
I was not favor'd with your very obliging

4 July   pmk 180⟨6⟩   1 p 4to   Osb
from G E Griffiths
You spoke of Payne's & Rennell's Greek Odes

9 July   4 p 4to   Osb
from John Young
Odd as it may seem, the *Veto* of your

11 July   2 p 8vo   Osb
from William Bentinck, 3rd Duke of
      Portland
The Duke of Portland presents his Compts to

23 July   1 p 4to   Osb
from G I Huntingford
Your kind letter did not reach me till Sunday

28 July [1806?]   3 p 8vo   Osb
from John Young
I had sent one or two scraps of Messages to

2 Aug   1 p 4to   Osb
from Charles Manners-Sutton
Miss Carlyle by a Letter of this Day's Post

[13 Aug]   2 p 8vo   Osb
to CPB
I am sorry to hear such an account of your

16 Aug   3 p 4to   Wy
to CPB
My heart sunk, my dear Boy, at the sight of

17 Aug   1 p 4to   Osb
to CPB
Inclosed you have two ones — £1.00 & £1.00

[20 Aug 1806]   2 p 8vo   Osb
to CPB
Your Mo[ther], my dearest Boy, is better; but

25 Aug   2 p 8vo   NYPL(B)
to CPB
My wish is, my dear Charles, that you

27 Aug   3 p 8vo   Osb
to CPB
I am glad, that your introduction is over.

28 Aug   3 p 4to   Osb
to William Parsons
Your friendship, my dear friend, for Charles

30 Aug   2 p 8vo   Osb
to CPB
Commands from Royal Personages must be

2 Sept   2 p 4to   Osb
from Marianne (Burney) Bourdois
At this cruel moment, my best of Uncles, I am

1806, continued

2 SP 1806 pmk   3 p 4to   Osb
from William Parsons
Two of the greatest amusements of writing

4 Sept   1 p 8vo   Osb
to G A Hatch
D^r. Charles Burney begs to thank M^r. Hatch

5 SP 1806 pmk   3 p 4to   Osb
from [William Parsons]
Nothing amuses me more than this kind of

14 Sept   1 p 4to   Oxf(AS)
from Samuel Parr
Accept my best thanks for your

17 Sept [1806?]   3 p 4to   Osb
from John Young
I have not much to say. Yet I cannot think of

⟨3⟩0 SP ⟨1806⟩ pmk   3 p 4to   Osb
from William Parsons
Your criticisms are most of them perfectly

7 Oct   3 p 8vo   Osb
from John Young
Doc/thor Ch/harle/s Bhurney! &c &c &c [sic]

12 Oct [1806]   1 p 4to   Osb
from Martin Davy
D^r. Parr & I are very anxious that you sh^d.

13 OC 1806 pmk   1 p 4to   Osb
from William Vincent
Ὑπόφοξον occurs in the Periplus p. 10. but is

15 Oct   3 p 8vo   Osb
to CPB
Lay out — & let the Basilian Homily march to

15 Oct   1 p fol   Osb
from John Young
Pray despatch these — Mrs Lindsey's, if you

15 Oct   1 p fol   Osb
from John Young
Here they are — the pretties! of various papers

27 Oct   2 p 4to   Osb
from William Parsons
I am truly sorry that I could not keep Charles's

28 Oct [1806]   2 p fol & scrap   Osb
from John Young
Holla! / Look at the Enclosed Letter. It is

29 OC 1806 pmk   1 p 4to   Camb(F)
from Samuel Parr
During this Michaelmas turmoil

3 Nov   3 p 8vo   Comyn
to CPB
I am glad, that L^d. ⟨Glenbervie⟩ & M^r

7 Nov   3 p 4to   Osb
from Sir George Beaumont
We are in town for a few days & I have just

8 Nov   3 p 8vo   Osb
to CPB
I send for Kaye's patent Cover, the Catalogue

12 Nov   2 p 4to   Osb
from John Young
This Letter will be handed to you by D^r

1⟨3⟩ NOV 1806 pmk   4 p 4to   Osb
from John Young
Did you or did you not — you Dr Charles

14 Nov   2 p 4to   Osb
from Sir George Beaumont
You have not yet informed me when, where,

18 Nov   4 p 4to   Osb
to CPB
Your Parcel and its various contents came by

22 Nov   1 p 8vo   Comyn
to CPB
I will not detain their letters, —

25 Nov   3 p 4to   Osb
from John Young
Oyes! Oyes! Oyes! A Letter, as long as *ten* of

25 NO 1806 pmk   1 p fol   Osb
from John Young
Done! My Dear Burney! Thank you for the

2 Dec   5 p 8vo   Osb
to CPB
I have been — & am still full of various

14 Dec   4 p 4to   Osb
from John Young
Dhoc/thor Cha/arles / Bhur/hurney How

[post 1806]   ½ p 4to   Comyn
from John, 1st Baron Crewe
If I do not learn that it will

23 Apr [1806–09]   2 p 4to   Osb
from Henry Petty-FitzMaurice, Marquis
   of Lansdowne
Not being myself concerned in directing the

[post 1806?]   2 p 4to   Osb
from Henry John Todd
As very unexpected business has prevented

[pre 1807?]   2 p 4to   Osb
from Frederic North, 5th Earl of Guilford [to CB Jr?]
One of my Turkish Friends has promised to

1807

1 Jan   4 p 4to   Osb
to CPB
As far as I can just now recollect, my dear

4 Jan   2 p 4to   Osb
to CPB
Your letter, and its *Boat-Cloke* of wrappers

6 Jan   3 p 4to   Osb
to CPB
Take my Valckenaer's Theocritus — the Edit

10 Jan   1 p 4to   Bath
to J W Bacon
I have just received a summons to attend a

11 Jan   3 p 8vo   Osb
to CPB
All arrived safely — but there are no News

13 Jan   4 p 4to   Osb
to CPB
When John Young arrives, do you and M^rs

15 Jan   3 p 4to   Osb
from G I Huntingford
Your kind donation to M^rs. Williams I have

16 Jan [1807]   1 p 4to   Osb
from Henry Kett
I request the favour of your Company at

17 Jan   1 p 4to   Osb
from John Young
Holla! There it is. Thank you. The object is

18 Jan   4 p 4to   Osb
to CPB
I am but poorly with a cold & so shall probably

24 Jan   1 p 4to   Osb
to CPB
I shall hope to get to Oxford, on Monday: —

24 Jan   1 p 4to   Osb
from HLTP
Doctor Charles Burney's Letter is a very

2 Feb   amanuensis   1 p 4to
from Samuel Parr   Oxf(AS)
a Friend of mine is collecting autographs

2 Feb   3 p 4to   Osb
from John Young
I knew little of You for Weeks. I hope you

23 Feb   4 p 4to   NYPL(B)
to CPB
I write on a matter, my dear Charles,

26 Feb   2 p 4to   Osb
to CPB
Five lines I must send — and scarcely more

3 MR 1807 pmk   2 p 4to   Oxf(AS)
from Samuel Parr
Nothing can be more agreeable to my wishes

3 Mar   4 p fol   Osb
from John Young
First of all why do you keep Coughing on so

10 Mar   3 p 4to   Osb
to CPB
Whenever the Warden says, "March," my

16 Mar   1 p 4to   Osb
from John Young
Le Voici: le sieur Hugon — qui parle pour soi

21 Mar   4 p 4to   Osb
from John Young
A Letter of Mine, which you would receive

3 Apr   2 p 4to   Osb
from Shute Barrington
Accept my earliest thanks for your information

21 Apr   4 p 4to   Osb
to CPB
My first letter must be in part a warning Bell.

21 Apr   2 p 4to   Osb
to Richard Clark
I hope that you will pardon the liberty, which

1807, continued

24 Apr   1 p 4to   Osb
from Sir John Soane
I am favored with your Letter & shall on all

28 Apr   3 p 8vo   Osb
from Sir John Sinclair
Sir John Sinclair presents his compliments to

[29 Apr 1807]   4 p 8vo   Osb
to CPB
I send you the Livy — Vol. 1 & 2, as you may

[2 May 1807]   3 p 8vo   Osb
to CPB
I can only say, that my Father's better — & I

⟨9⟩ MY 1807 pmk   2 p 4to   Osb
from Peter Paul Dobrée
M. Raper's copy of Kuster's Aristophanes was

⟨10⟩ May   2 p 8vo   NYPL(B)
to CPB
Our friend the Enderbys have

12 May   4 p 4to   Osb
to CPB
A short letter is preferable to none. —

13 May   1 p 4to   NYPL(B)
to CPB
Edward's auction catalogue has just arrived.

14 May   2 p 4to   NYPL(B)
to CPB
The Book has been kindly sent

25 May   4 p 4to   NYPL(B)
to CPB
First — the *Catalogues* lodges

1 June   3 p 8vo   NYPL(B)
to CPB
Mr Sampson is going to the Exhibition

6 June [1807?]   3 p 4to   Osb
from C J Blomfield
I have taken the liberty of addressing you

8 June   4 p 4to   NYPL(B)
to CPB
We are soon to meet; — and

11 June   4 p 4to   NYPL(B)
to CPB from CB Jr & Edward Foss
When you apply to our good friend

11 June   3 p 8vo   Osb
from Thomas Gaisford
Inclosed are the papers with which you

[14 June? 1807]   4 p 4to   Osb
from John Young
Memorandum / To call at Murray Bookseller's,

22 June   3 p 8vo   Comyn
from T J Mathias
Though I fear that you have a greater

22 June   2 p 8vo   Osb
from T J Mathias
This morning I had done myself the pleasure

[22 June 1807]   4 p 8vo   Osb
from Frances (Phillips) Raper
To plague you again so soon is too bad my

22 June   1 p 4to   Osb
from William Vincent
Tho I am perfectly lippous I must take up

23 June   1 p 4to   Comyn
from George Canning
I accept with many acknowledgements

25 June   3 p 4to   Osb
from T J Mathias
I wrote you a letter yesterday to return my

26 JU 1807 pmk   2 p 4to   Osb
from Frances (Phillips) Raper
I cannot tell you my dearest Uncle how much

27 June   1 p 4to   Osb
from G I Huntingford
In my official capacity, as Warden of

27 June   2 p 8vo   Osb
from T J Mathias
Many thanks for your kind letter. I am obliged

27 June   pmk 1807   3 p 4to   Osb
from John Young
Did I not Date my Letter from *Edinr*? &/or

29 June   2 p 4to   Osb
from Peter Elmsley
I am very much obliged to you for your

[29 June 1807?   1 p 4to   Osb
from T J Mathias
I was out of town yesterday, — and on my

29 June   pmk 1807   2 p 4to   Osb
from Frances (Phillips) Raper
Once more receive my thanks my dearest

1 JY 1807 pmk   2 p 4to   Comyn
from Martin Davy
As I find from your last letter

8 JY 1807 pmk   2 p 4to   NYPL(B)
to CPB
Many thanks, my Charles, for your letter

11 July   1 p 8vo   Osb
to A Gray
D^r. Charles Burney will be obliged to M^r. A

14 July   amanuensis   1 p 4to
from Samuel Parr   Oxf(AS)
You forgot in your last to

20 July   3 p 4to   Osb
from John Young
We arrived here upon the 18th — and were

22–[23] July   3 p 4to   NYPL(B)
to CPB
One line, I must write to my dear Charles from

[22 Aug 1807]   3 p 4to   NYPL(B)
to CPB
This is for your private eye. —

22 Aug   2 p 4to   Osb
from George, 2nd Earl Spencer
I received your Letter of the 15th. on a little

24 Aug [1807?]   2 p 4to   NYPL(B)
to CPB
Your mode of proceeding has been perfectly

25 Aug   4 p 4to   Osb
from G I Huntingford
Your eminence as a Scholar, and the very

26 Aug   3 p 4to   Scot
from John Young
Here are we still — still breathing — but

[Aug 1807]   3 p 4to   BM
to William Windham
You were, many years ago, kind enough

12 SP 1807 pmk   1 p 4to   Osb
from John Hoppner
I return you many thanks for the favour of your

18 Sept   4 p 4to   Scot
from John Young
Liz has a Letter from James by this fleet. It is

24 Sept 18⟨07⟩   1 p 8vo   Osb
from Sir William Scott
I shall be glad to see you on Saturday

28 Sept   1 p 4to   Osb
from Henry Addington, 1st Viscount
   Sidmouth
Lord Sidmouth presents his Compliments to

5 Oct   1 p 8vo   HEH
to Thomas Frognall Dibdin
D^r. Charles Burney begs to thank M^r. Dibdin

9 Oct   1 p 4to   Osb
from G I Huntingford
On my return to this place, I found a letter

9 Oct   2 p 4to   Osb
from Sir William Scott
I ⟨found⟩ your Letter here last night on my

10 Oct   1 p 8vo   Osb
from Sir William Scott
Your Letter came to me after mine had gone to

12 Oct   1 p 4to   Osb
from Thomas Dampier
As Mr Mathew is not a licenced Curate within

12 Oct   1 p 4to   Osb
from Sir William Scott
I most heartily congratulate you — and the

26 Oct   3 p 4to   Osb
from John Young
I overflow! My Joy runneth over! So doth that

27 Oct   2 p 4to   Oxf(AS)
from Samuel Parr
I came from Oxford yesterday

27 Oct   pmk 1807   3 p 4to   Comyn
from Walter Savage Landor
In this bad weather my mind is haunted

[Oct–Nov 1807]   draft   6 p 4to   BM
from [Samuel Butler]
Encouraged by the high respect I feel for you

4 NOV 1807 pmk   3 p 4to   Scot
from John Young
Well — & so I have done the very thing I

1807, continued

[c 5 Nov 1807]   4 p 4to   Osb
from S[amuel] Butler
After a long and painful deliberation I venture

[9 Nov 1807]   4 p 4to   BM
to Samuel Butler
I am much obliged to you for your letters. Dr

[13 Nov 1807]   draft   4 p fol   BM
from [Samuel Butler]
I lose no time in offering you

14 Nov   3 p 4to   Osb
to CPB
I give you joy, my dearest Charles, with all my

[16 Nov 1807]   4 p 4to   Osb
to CPB
I would advise you by all means to wait on the

18 Nov   3 p 4to   Osb
to CPB
If you feel *mending*, stay and enjoy quietly the

20 Nov   2 p 4to   Osb
from John Kaye
Allow me to congratulate you upon an event,

20 Nov [1807]   4 p 4to   Scot
from John Young
I have (Novr 20th) a Corner in a frank which

22 Nov   2 p 4to   Osb
from Roger Wilbraham
Two days since I dined with your highly

26 Nov   4 p 4to   Osb
to CPB
My eyes will not suffer me to write — and

1 Dec   4 p 4to   Osb
to CPB
My eyes are still weak, my dearest Boy — but

5 Dec   1 p 4to   Comyn
to CPB
Happy shall I be to see you —

17 Dec   2 p 4to   Osb
to Charles Manners-Sutton
I went yesterday to Finsbury Square; and in

31 Dec   2 p 4to   Scot
from John Young
I have undertaken what I may not be able to

5 Aug [1807–12]   3 p 4to   Osb
from Henry John Todd to [CB Jr]
Twice within some weeks past did I intend

29 July [1807–12]   1 p 8vo   Scot
from John Young
They are Just going off. Why should I write a

27 June [1807–14]   1 p 8vo   PML
from Caroline, Princess of Wales
The Princess of Wales requests Dr. Burney to

7 Apr [post 1807]   1 p 4to   Osb
from Thomas Maurice
My answer to your obliging invitation for

[pre 1808]   1 p 4to   Osb
from James Gray
I understand from Porson that you wish

1808

2 Jan   1 p 4to   Osb
from Scrope Berdmore
I have found your very obliging Letter on my

4 Jan   4 p 4to   Comyn
to CPB
I am sorry, that you had so regulated

5 Jan   4 p 4to   Osb
from John Young
This is most shameful. Shall a Bat have Eyes?

11 Jan   4 p 4to   Osb
to CPB
As Mr. Aiken thinks proper to leave me thus

14 Jan   8 p 4to   Comyn
to CPB
Your letter, my dearest Charles, has filled my

14 Jan [1808?]   3 p 8vo   Oxf(AS)
from Samuel Parr
I am too feeble to < > say much

15 Jan   4 p 4to   Comyn
to CPB
After a disturbed night, during much of which

15 Jan   pmk 1808   3 p 4to   Osb
from John Young
I bewail your Eyes. Do they bleed — ie Leech

17 Jan   4 p 4to   Osb
to CPB
Into what a situation have you plunged

18 Jan   3 p 4to   Comyn
to CPB
Amid hurry & confusion of calls & other

19 Jan   4 p 4to   Osb
to CPB
When I used the word dishonourably, I knew

25 Jan   3 p 4to   Osb
to CPB
I sorrow at your delayed journey — & hoped

25 Jan   pmk 1808   1 p 4to
from Samuel Parr   Oxf(AS)
I <   > <   > will you mark me at

29 Jan   3 p 4to   Osb
to CPB
Tomorrow I cannot write, — as there is no

29 Jan   pmk 1808   4 p 4to
from Samuel Parr   Oxf(AS)
Take care of your eyes — I

31 Jan   receipt   1 p fragment   Osb
from Henry Fuseli
I Print from Milton viz Silence — — — 1. 1.0

31 Jan pmk 1808 1 p 4to Oxf(AS)
from Samuel Parr
I received to day as I was going to

1 Feb   1 p 4to   Osb
to CPB
I could not write, as I hoped on Saturday — &

1 Feb   pmk 1808   3 p 8vo   Osb
from SHB
I know not to whom the exclamation of, "Oh

7 Feb   4 p 4to   Osb
from Thomas Gaisford
I have examined the different copies of the

10 Feb   3 p 4to   Osb
to CPB
My time is crowdedly engaged — & I am very

11 Feb pmk 1808 1 p 4to Oxf(AS)
from Samuel Parr
pray send me back the matter

11 Feb pmk 1808 1 p 4to Oxf(AS)
from Samuel Parr
This, Dr Sir, is the second Letter

12 Feb   3 p 4to   Osb
to CPB
Merely to fill this envelope to Dr. Parr's letter,

13 Feb   3 p 4to   Comyn
from James Currey
Inclosed I send a transcript of the 20th

24 FE 1808 pmk   2 p 4to   Oxf(AS)
from Samuel Parr
I have <   > <   > to Dr Davy on

24 Feb pmk 1808 3 p 4to Oxf(AS)
from Samuel Parr
I rec'd your letter with your solicitation

26 Feb   2 p 4to   Osb
to CPB
I want the 1st & 2d Editions <Pearson> on the

29 Feb   2 p 4to   Osb
from Shute Barrington
All your hopes & mine from the evidence

7 Mar   3 p 4to   Osb
to CPB
My eyes are again rather better — that is

7 Mar   2 p 8vo   Osb
from John Philip Kemble
Your recommendation of Dr. Bancroft would

14 Mar   4 p 4to   Osb
to CPB
My eyes have now been five days without any

15–21 Mar   4 p 4to   Osb
to CPB
It was my intention to have answered the

21 Mar   3 p 4to   Osb
from John Kaye
You have always taken so kind an interest in

23 Mar   2 p 4to   Osb
to CPB
Hurried and driven almost beyond my bearing,

24 Mar [1808]   4 p 4to   Osb
from Thomas Gaisford
Your business is at length performed, & I hope

1808, continued

29 Mar   3 p 4to   Osb
from John Kaye
I am very sorry to find that the state of your

29 Mar [1808]   4 p 4to   Osb
from John Young
Sit down immediately & rectify a word in your

[Mar 1808?]   3 p 4to   Osb
to CPB
My eyes have again failed me — so I must be

13 Apr   1 p 4to   Osb
from John Kaye
I am so completely confined at present, that it

19   pmk APR 1808   3 p 4to   Osb
from John Young
A thousand thanks, with as many supplemental

25 Apr   pmk 1808   1 p 4to   Oxf(AS)
from Samuel Parr
pray call on Dr Maltby, & employ him

27 Apr   1 p 4to   Osb
from Henry John Todd
The book which is in the printed Library, the

28 Apr   1 p 4to   Osb
from John Blagden-Hale
I should have received particular satisfaction

7 May   2 p fol   Osb
from John Young
I am charged by the Marchioness of Bute to

18 May   3 p 4to   Osb
from John Kaye
Both our Master and Dr Davy were in town

3 June   3 p 4to   Osb
from John Kaye
The Books arrived yesterday; our Master

4 June   2 p 8vo   Comyn
to CPB
I send the Mags & <Arist.> Polit.

6 June   1 p 8vo   Osb
from T J Mathias
I have a pleasure in offering to your acceptance

7 June   3 p 4to   Osb
to CPB
Secure your Lodgings for the year. — If the

8 June   3 p 4to   Osb
from John Young
I have again lost sight of you μη γενοιτο that

13 June   2 p 4to   Osb
from M J Routh
I have just received an answer to my

15 June   copy extract   1 p 4to   Osb
to Abercrombie Gordon
"pray come and pass next Sunday with me — I

16 June   4 p 4to   Osb
to CPB
First, Lord Breadalbane has requested me to

19 June   4 p 4to   Osb
from John Kaye
The Advertisement was inserted in the

20 June   3 p 4to   Osb
from John Young
Did I not write? did I not interrogate? Have I

22 June   4 p 4to   Comyn
to CPB
I must be concise, though my head & heart are

22 June   2 p 4to   Osb
from William Lort Mansel
Till this morning I have not been able to say

23 June   1 p 4to   Osb
from John Kaye
I write these few lines to say that the Petition

23 June [1808?]   1 p 4to   Osb
from Henry John Todd
I beg to return you my best thanks for your

26 June   3 p 4to   Osb
from John Kaye
Both your Letters reached me this Morning; in

29 June   1 p fol   Osb
from G I Huntingford
"Respexit tamen, et longo post tempore venit,"

30 June   2 p 4to   WHM
from Sir Joseph Banks
it gives me Sincere Pleasure To Learn from

1 July   1 p 4to   Osb
from John Kaye
With this Letter you will receive a Cambridge

7 July   3 p 8vo   Osb
to CB
Only five lines, my dearest Sir, — I am

7 July   3 p 4to   NYPL(B)
to CPB
On July 8, I hope to dine at Cambridge

[12 July 1808]   2 p 4to   Osb
from John Young
Your Hysteroptericks have thrown us

1 Aug   amanuensis   4 p 4to
to CPB   NYPL(B)
To save my eyes, which are better, M^r. Kerr

6–8 Aug   3 p 4to   Osb
to CPB
Here I am, my dear Charles — very contrary

9 Aug   4 p 4to   Osb
to CPB
An hasty scratch off, is all that I can give. —

10 Aug [1808]   3 p 4to   Osb
from John Young
Take me up Ernulphus's Curse, or any other

17 Aug   pmk 1808   1 p 4to   Osb
from Richard Payne Knight
D^r. Davies shall be very welcome to a Copy

17 Aug [1808]   1 p 4to   Scot
from John Young
Holla! / Go immediately to Laeschman —

25 Aug [1808]   4 p 4to   Osb
to CPB
Your Mother is again *domesticating* in her

28 Aug   2 p 4to   Osb
to CPB
I have not had one vacant moment, my dear

3 Sept   4 p 4to   Osb
to CPB
Your wish to hear at Bristol compels me to be

4 Sept   2 p 8vo   Osb
from Thomas Dampier
I accept most thankfully your <Luctus> &

7 Sept   3 p 8vo   Osb
to CPB
I can only tell you, that we shall receive you

10 Sept   1 p 4to   Osb
to CPB
I write from Richmond whither I am come to

[10 Sept 1808]   2 p 4to   BM
from [Samuel Butler]
On the other side you will find a note

13 Sept   3 p 4to   BM
to Samuel Butler
Schutz is of all Editors the most presumptuous

20 Sept   4 p 4to   Scot
from John Young
First I give you all due congratulations on the

[23 Sept 1808]   1 p 4to   Osb
from James Perry
I entreat you to come up in the morning and

24 Sept   3 p 4to   Scot
from John Young
A Gentleman, lately arrived from India, Mr

25 Sept   1 p 4to   Osb
from James Perry
I lament to tell you that he is considerably

26 SP 1808 pmk   1 p 4to   Osb
from James Perry
Our dear friend departed after a long & most

28 Sept   3 p 4to   Osb
from William Lort Mansel
Truly do I lament when *You* ask what *I* cannot

29 Sept   3 p 8vo   Osb
from William Lort Mansel
Why am I to start any thing which may imply

29 Sept   1 p 4to   Osb
from Matthew Raine
All stands as before and you must stand. So

30 Sept   2 p 4to   Scot
from John Young
<Soft> you a While! Is it even so? Then God

30 Sept   1 p 4to   Osb
from Samuel Butler
I think it probable that you will offer for the

also   1 Oct draft   1 p 4to   Oxf(AS)

3 Oct   1 p 8vo   Osb
from William Lort Mansel
Being obliged to run out of College for a little

1808, continued

6 Oct   1 p 4to   Oxf(AS)
from Samuel Butler
From the information which reached me last

6 Oct   3 p 4to   Osb
from John Young
Impatience & Anxiety give rise to this Letter.

9 Oct [1808]   3 p 4to   Osb
from John Young
I am quite impatient to learn tidings of your

12 Oct   1 p 8vo   Osb
from John Philip Kemble
A thousand thanks, my dear Burney, for your

12 Oct   3 p 4to   Scot
from John Young
Holla, again! / A quondam Pupil of mine, and

[17 Oct 1808]   1 p fol   Osb
from John Young
What may this mean? / That thou poor Ghost

19 Oct   pmk 1808   2 p 4to   Osb
from Peter Paul Dobrée
If I can write in a warm room, I will attack the

19 Oct   1 p 4to   Comyn
from Joseph Nollekens
I received the favour of yours of the 15th.

24 Oct   2 p 8vo   Osb
from Sir George Pretyman Tomline
I have read the Proof Sheet of the Articles

30 Oct   3 p 4to   Osb
from John Young
Now My Dear Friend, the M. of Bute Suspects

1 NO 1808 pmk   2 p 4to   Osb
from Peter Paul Dobrée
By a note which I have just received from

4 Nov   4 p 4to   Osb
to CPB
I have abridged my morning short ride to

4 Nov   3 p 4to   Osb
from Edward Maltby
I will with great pleasure submit to your

5 Nov   pmk ⟨1808⟩   3 p 4to   Osb
from Samuel Parr
It may excuse you to censure, if you like

7 Nov   4 p 4to   Osb
to CPB
Some expectations, which Mr Warburton has

10 Nov   4 p 4to   Osb
to CPB
Your open and ingenuous letter, though it cost

21 NO 1808 pmk   3 p 8vo   Osb
from Peter Paul Dobrée
On Friday, unless I hear from you before, I

21 Nov   pmk 1808   2 p 4to   Osb
from Richard Payne Knight
I send you a proof Copy of my Prologomena

24 Nov   pmk 1808   1 p 4to   Osb
from Richard Payne Knight
I am apprehensive that in sending your Copy

26 Nov   pmk 1808   3 p 4to   Osb
from Richard Payne Knight
Do not be alarmed, my Dear Burney, nor

26 Nov   2 p 8vo   Osb
from Anthony Noll ⟨   ⟩
When I called at your house on Friday I did

28 Nov   4 p 4to   Osb
to CPB
I have been so much hurried and worried,

5 Dec   4 p 4to   Osb
with Rosette (Rose) Burney to CPB
By all means, accept Lady Crewe's dear

5 Dec   pmk 1808   2 p 4to   Osb
from Richard Payne Knight
I mean to be in Town the first Week in January

9 Dec   2 p 8vo   Osb
from Roger Wilbraham
I was far from insensible to your kind Civility

15 Dec   1 p 4to   Osb
from John Kaye
I have seen Mr Currey, who informs me that

16 Dec   5 p 4to   Osb
from G I Huntingford
So long as I have existence in this World, &

19 Dec   2 p 4to   Osb
from William Vincent
I am well at present, & nothing

26 Dec   4 p 4to   Osb
to CPB
I can wait for the arrival of a third letter from

28 Dec   2 p 4to   Scot
from John Young
Here I am, & Kaye at my Elbow. How long I

[1808]   3 p 4to   Osb
from Thomas Gaisford [to CB Jr?]
Articles of Edw. VI in the Collection by

[post 1808?]   1 p 8vo   Oxf(AS)
from Samuel Parr
I have written to Mr. <Dewes>

7 Feb [post 1808?]   1 p 4to   Osb
from William Beloe to [CB Jr?]
We feel ourselves highly gratified by your

[1808–1812?]   1 p 4to   Oxf(AS)
from Samuel Parr
<   > <   > <   > to day by post

[1808–1812?]   1 p 4to   Oxf(AS)
from Samuel Parr
I <   > <   > <   > set my own

4 Mar [1808–12]   3 p 4to   Osb
from John Young
If the late Kinnairds Banking House has not

1809

5 Jan   4 p 4to   Osb
to CPB
My second expedition to Cambridge proved

5 Jan   2 p 4to   McG
to John Nicholls
I have sent my Secretary, Mr. Kerr

5 Jan   amanuensis   3 p 4to
to Cadell & Davies   Oxf(Bod)
I am just returned from a second trip to

17 Jan   4 p 4to   Osb
to CPB
We left Greenwich on Monday Evening —

23 Jan   3 p 4to   Osb
to CPB
We shall be at Oxford on Thursday — or if not

5 Feb   3 p 4to   Osb
from Hugh Rose
I had the pleasure of addressing a few lines to

6 Feb   3 p 4to   Osb
to CPB
I write hurried to Death — — Your Mother's

8 Feb   1 p 4to   Scot
from John Young
On the Other Leaf you have that which will

16 Feb   4 p 8vo   Osb
to CPB
Only 3 lines — as I am hurried sadly. This is

18 Feb   2 p 4to   Osb
from G I Huntingford
By the post of this day I forwarded to Sir John

26 Feb   1 p 4to   Osb
from Thomas Gaisford
I enclose the cancels according to your desire

26 Feb   2 p 4to   Osb
from James Perry
On my return from Merton I found your

5 Mar   1 p 8vo   Osb
to CPB
Inquire of Cooke, or at the Clarendon press,

[7 Mar 1809]   1 p 4to   Osb
from James Perry (on p 3 Printed Notice
          re Porson Fund same date)
I have sent all the letters, and hope you will

14 Mar   3 p 4to   Osb
to CPB
If you feel perfectly clear on the subject of

15 Mar   2 p 8vo   Osb
to CPB
This will be brought by our friend, Mr Smith

18 Mar   1 p 4to   Osb
from John Young
I am uneasy about my India parcel and you

18 MR <1809> pmk   4 p 4to   Osb
from Sir George Beaumont
I am very sorry I have been prevented from

24 Mar   1 p 4to   Osb
to [John?] Pridden
Dr. Charles Burney presents his compts. to

4 Apr   1 p 4to   Osb
from Peter Paul Dobrée
The book, from which the inclosed extract was

1809, continued

7 Apr   4 p 4to   Osb
from John Young
Me Voici, qui enrage! I *am*, indeed, My Dear

16 Apr   2 p 4to   Osb
from John Kaye
I did not receive your Letter until this morning.

30 Apr   2 p 4to   Osb
from John Kaye
You are acquainted, I believe, with M^r

30 Apr   4 p 4to   Osb
from John Young
I received both your Letters — first your

6 May   2 p 4to   Osb
to CPB
Your letter, my dear Charles, affords the only

8 May   2 p 4to   Osb
to CPB
I never *doubted* in the slightest degree, your

14 May [1809]   3 p 4to   Osb
from John Young
Your Second "Circular," My Dear friend, is a

c 16 May   1 p 4to   Osb
from John Young
Take Care the enclosed is put into the proper

17 May   4 p 4to   Osb
to CPB
I sent your Johnson yesterday <per> coach

21 May   3 p 8vo   Osb
to CPB
The Book which serves to protect the

25 May   2 p 4to   Osb
with Rosette (Rose) Burney to CPB
I have only time, my dear Boy, to say that I

30 May   2 p 4to   Osb
to CPB
All my views have been disappointed.

2 June   2 p 4to   Osb
from John Kaye
I congratulate you sincerely on Charles's

7 June   4 p 4to   Osb
to CPB
When an opportunity offers, pray thank Mr

8 June   1 p 4to   Osb
from G I Huntingford
In my way towards Winchester, at Ramsey I

16 June   4 p 4to   Osb
with Rosette (Rose) Burney to CPB
I congratulate you *heartily* on the success of the

19 JU 1809 pmk   2 p 4to   Osb
from Martin Davy
I have just heard (having been absent a few

20 June   3 p 4to   Osb
to CPB
I accept your <Minerval>, my dear Charles,

29 June   4 p 4to   Osb
to CPB
I wrote in haste, my dear Boy; — and, indeed,

30 June   1 p 8vo   Comyn
from Nevil Maskelyne
D^r. Maskelyne's compliments to D^r. Burney,

[June 1809?]   card   Osb
from Caroline, Princess of Wales (per
    Lady Charlotte Campbell)
Lady Ch^tte: Campbell is commanded by

5 July   2 p 4to   Osb
to CPB
I have been obliged to give up my Cambridge

11 July   2 p 4to   Osb
from John Kaye
I have received from Dr Davy the Prize Essay,

15 July   1 p 4to   Osb
from Shute Barrington
Accept my thanks for the real pleasure which I

[17 July 1809]   1 p 8vo   NPG
from William Wilberforce
Many thanks my dear Sir for your very obliging

18 July [1809]   3 p 4to   Osb
from Martin Davy
I deferred sending the enclosed ½ doz. copies,

21 July   2 p 4to   Osb
from Thomas Kidd
On Wednesday I received a Letter from Town

28 July   1 p 8vo   Osb
from Thomas Dampier
We shall be very happy to see you and Charles

26 Aug   1 p 4to   Liv(P)
to Patrick Kelly
The Curate of Deptford, with whom I placed

11 Sept   4 p 4to   Osb
with Rosette (Rose) Burney to CPB
Your mother is getting better faster than She

15 Sept   3 p 8vo   Osb
to CPB
My hurries, my dear Boy, press too hardly on

18 Sept   3 p 4to   Osb
to CPB
I have not been able to see Mr Crew, and so I

26 Sept   3 p 8vo   Osb
from John Young
I am here. I shall be here till the 6th <Prox>

28 Sept   2 p 4to   Osb
from Thomas Dampier
I am much obliged to you for the second Sheet

29 Sept   2 p 4to   Osb
with Rosette (Rose) Burney to CPB
This will, I know, wish you & your fellow

[Sept–Oct 1809?]   4 p 4to   Osb
to CPB
I do not wonder at the Warden's feeling

3 Oct   5 p 4to   Osb
to CPB
I cannot be longer silent, — though I have

8 Oct [1809?]   1 p 4to   Oxf(AS)
from Samuel Parr
Dr & learned Dr Burney — The <   > is

9 Oct [1809]   3 p 4to   Osb
to CPB
Old Martyr — for I begin where you end is

18 Oct   2 p 8vo   Osb
to CPB
This is merely to tell you, that our next *Anon*

23 OC 1809 pmk   3 p 4to   Osb
from Peter Paul Dobrée
I have not the least recollection of the pacquet

29 Oct   pmk 1809   2 p 4to   Oxf(AS)
from Samuel Parr
I thought <   > of a Wednesday last

31 Oct   1 p 4to   Oxf(AS)
from Samuel Parr
Yours come last night — I had

[Oct 1809?]   2 p 4to   Osb
to [CPB?]
dear friend Parr to tell you all his <thoughts>

4 Nov   1 p 8vo   Oxf(Bod)
to Edmond Malone
I return this Inscription, —

10 Nov   2 p 8vo   Osb
from Richard Twining Sr
I crave your pardon for the Liberty, which I

11 Nov   3 p 4to   Folger
from Edmond Malone
Mr Courtenay wishes to erect a stone to the

27 Nov   2 p 8vo   HSP
to Patrick Kelly
Frazer has, I hope, returned to you. — He will

3 Dec   3 p 4to   Osb
from Scrope Berdmore
I am now on a melancholy attendance upon a

[post 7 Dec 1809]   2 p 8vo   Osb
to CPB
You must get a positive & direct mandate from

9 Dec   2 p 4to   Osb
from John Kaye
In my Letter to Charles I promised to visit

13[–14] Dec   4 p 8vo   Osb
to CPB
I am woefully hurried. but must tell you we

14 Dec   3 p 8vo   Osb
to CPB
I am just come from the Antiq. Society, & you

16 Dec   4 p 8vo   Osb
to CPB
I am much hurried; but must write. — Your

16 Dec   2 p 4to   Osb
to CPB
The Poets sing, that sylphs & Fayes / Protected

16 Dec   4 p 4to   Win
to G I Huntingford
Many thanks for your excellent Charge

1809, continued

19 Dec   1 p 8vo   Pforz
from William Godwin
M^rs. Godwin would be happy to be favoured

23 Dec   2 p 8vo   PML
to William Davies
The Pearson should if possible, be published,

26 Dec   1 p 4to   Osb
from James Perry
Your Note enclosing the draft on Mr Barnes

29 Dec   2 p 4to   Comyn
from Benjamin West
No event would have given me more

1810

2 Jan   1 p 4to   Osb
from Joseph Goodall
Forgive my Delay in not having answered

4 Jan   7 p 4to   Osb
from G I Huntingford
A most welcome New Year's Gift was your

9 Jan   1 p 4to   Mich
from George Canning
I accept with many acknowledgements, the

10 Jan   1 p 8vo   Oxf(AS)
from Samuel Parr
[illegible]

24 Jan   1 p 4to   Pforz
from William Godwin
I am happy to inform you that I have been

29 Jan   1 p 8vo   Osb
to ?
I hope that Pearson stirs in the trade. —

29 Jan   2 p 8vo   Osb
to Sir Francis Freeling
I think it right to acquaint you, that the

2 Feb   4 p 4to   Osb
from Josiah Thomas
I return you many thanks for your most

3 Feb [1810]   1 p 8vo   Osb
from Thomas Dampier
I shall be very glad to see you to morrow, If

7 Feb [1810]   1 p 4to   Osb
from Samuel Rogers
Pray dine with me, if you can, on Saturday

7 Feb   4 p 4to   Cal(B)
from John Young
Is there, my dear Burney, a Wight, hight

18 Feb   pmk 1810   2 p 4to   Osb
from John Young
Hang your preaching — I fear it may have

25 Feb   2 p 4to   Osb
from John Young
I burst in & with impatience to hear something

27 Feb   1 p 4to   Osb
from George, 2nd Earl Spencer
I have the Honour to inform you that you

2 Mar   2 p 4to   Osb
from [Spencer] Percival
Mr. Percival presents his Compliments to D^r

3 Mar   4 p 4to   Osb
from Josiah Thomas
I have received with the utmost pleasure both

6 Mar [1810]   3 p 4to   Osb
from John Young
There is a certain *Mouseley*, Late Fellow of

9 Mar   1 p 4to   Osb
from Charles Manners-Sutton
I will take ye first opportunity that offers, to

9 Mar   pmk 1810   3 p 4to   Scot
from John Young
Again, My Dear Reductionist, I <spin> you;

16 Mar   2 p 8vo   Osb
from T J Mathias
A very pleasant note has just reached me, and

[Mar–Apr? 1810?]   2 p 4to   Osb
to CPB & Frances (Young) Burney
The sky looks clearer — & I shall, at last, see

2 Apr   3 p 4to   Oxf(AS)
from Samuel Parr
I am very glad that your ramble at

9 Apr   1 p 4to   Osb
from Thomas Gaisford
I have delivered the sheet of the articles to

13 Apr   3 p 4to   Osb
from G I Huntingford
In every great House of Business there is a

17 Apr [1810]   4 p 4to   Osb
to CPB
The delay of the Writing Desk was vexatious;

22 Apr   2 p 8vo   Osb
to CPB
Just come from assisting at the altar; — I

22 Apr   2 p 4to   Osb
to CPB
I have nothing to add to my scrap of

24 Apr   4 p 8vo   Osb
to CPB
I must be very short, as I have much to do —

11 May   2 p 8vo   Osb
to CPB
I am mending, but very slowly. — Call again

17 May   4 p 4to   Osb
to CPB
I ventured to town yesterday; and trust, that

20 May   3 p 4to   Osb
from John Young
It is most unlucky that this India Fleet should

21 May   amanuensis   3 p 4to   Osb
to CPB
Mr. Kerr writes because I am eating my

21 MY 1810 pmk   1 p 4to   Oxf(AS)
from Samuel Parr
Dear Dr. Burney — I have received a Bill

23 May   4 p 4to   Osb
to CPB
Your pacquet has arrived — & I have written,

24 May   4 p 4to   Osb
from G I Huntingford
In a letter to my Nephew I have this day

26 May   1 p 8vo   Osb
to CPB
Merely to say that I was appointed one of His

29 May   4 p 8vo   Osb
to CPB
I am going to dine in <Grote's> Buildings

29 May   1 p 8vo   Osb
from John Randolph
The Bishop of London presents his Compts to

31 May   3 p 8vo   Osb
to CPB
I saw *Spencer* yesterday; and told your tale

2 June   4 p 4to   Hyde
to CPB
My Court going intended for Monday is

2 June   4 p 4to   Osb
from John Young
It shall be done. Better thus — "It *is* done".

[4 June]   3 p 4to   Osb
from John Young
T'other Chaplain has got into Difficulties as to

5 June   2 p 4to   Osb
from Shute Barrington
My early thanks are due for a work which

5 June   2 p 4to   Osb
from Henry John Todd
Accept my best thanks for your very valuable

8 June   3 p 4to   Osb
to CPB
The objection raised by the V. Chr. is not to

11 June   3 p 4to   Osb
to C J Blomfield
I dare say, that you are right, for though I had

12 June   2 p 4to   Osb
to CPB
As matters stand, I think, that I had better

15 June   4 p 4to   Scot
from John Young
Holla!/Here! les Voici. There are two en un.

20 JU 18⟨10⟩ pmk   2 p 4to   Osb
to CPB
Your poor Mother has again relapsed; — & I

23 June   2 p 4to   Osb
to CPB
Pacquet and letter of yesterday & to day have

25 June   2 p 4to   Scot
from John Young
Thanks for your over Weight — rather *all*

29 June   3 p 4to   Osb
from Josiah Thomas
A letter from my boy announces that the holy

2 July   1 p 4to   Osb
to CPB
Your Mother & I called at the Youngs on

4 July   1 p 4to   Osb
to CPB
Vicisti, — I will be in Oxford, tomorrow. —

1810, continued

5 July   1 p 8vo   Osb
from George Isted
If you should perchance be disengaged

10 July   1 p 4to   Osb
from James Edwards
Having sold my house in Pall Mall I was

⟨11⟩ July   4 p 4to   Scot
from John Young
Go to *You*. The Bad Debt you speak of I have

13 July   1 p 8vo   Osb
from Elspet Gray
Permit me, Sir to add a few words in behalf

13 July   1 p 8vo   Osb
from William Ogilvie
From your well known humanity & liberality,

17 July   3 p 4to   Osb
to CPB
Your letter arrived, this Morning. So far, so

22 July   4 p 4to   Osb
to CPB
Your Lyme Regis has just reached me and I

22 July   1 p 4to   Osb
from John Courteney
Give me leave to enclose my ⟨anticipatory⟩

27 July   3 p 4to   Osb
to CPB
We arrived yesterday from South-End. Your

30 July   amanuensis   4 p 4to   Osb
to CPB
Your letter of the 24th., from Dawlish,

30 July   1 p 4to   Osb
from Thomas Dampier
Our Friends here will not allow us to quit

5 Aug   4 p 4to   Osb
to CPB
I am just returned from preaching in the

8 Aug   2 p 4to   Osb
to CPB
I have nothing to add, my dear Charles,

12 Aug   3 p 4to   Osb
from John Young
I am sorry My Dear Friend for the loss you

13 Aug   3 p 4to   Osb
from John Young
"This to your Heart" . . . Eh bien. It has

15 AU 1810 pmk   1 p 4to   Osb
from C J Blomfield
I take the liberty of troubling you with a

7 Sept   1 p 8vo   Osb
from William Sharp
I had the pleasure to receive your Letter last

2 Oct   1 p 4to   Folger
from Edmond Malone
A new edition (the 6th.) of Boswell's Life of

3 Oct   pmk 1810   3 p 4to   Osb
from John Young
Holla! — My Rascals tell me that "a great

4 Oct [1810]   amanuensis   2 p 8vo
from Caroline, Princess of Wales   Osb
With the deepest ⟨sense⟩ of gratitude to

11 Oct   2 p 4to   Folger
from Edmond Malone
In two places in Boswell's life of Johnson, the

12 Oct   4 p 4to   Osb
from John Young
I received your Letter in which you mention

27 Oct   4 p 4to   Win
to G I Huntingford
Many thanks, my dear Lord, for your

6 NO 1810 pmk   1 p 4to   Osb
from John Young
Not that it is a thing to be forced — but *if* it

26 Nov   3 p 4to   Osb
from Edward Copleston
On the same day on which I received your

26 Nov [1810?]   1 p 4to   Osb
from Lady Charlotte (North) Lindsay
Lady Charlotte Lindsay presents her Compts:

28 Nov   1 p 4to   Osb
from Josiah Boydell
Having left my house at Hampstead some

3 Dec   1 p 4to   Osb
from Lavinia (Bingham), Countess
     Spencer
I am encouraged by Lord Spencer to hope

25 Dec   2 p 4to   Osb
from John Kaye
I was in daily expectation of seeing you at

26 Dec   4 p 4to   Osb
to CPB
Many thanks for your Letter, — which I

26 Dec   amanuensis   6 p 4to   Osb
to [CPB]
Nº. 1 is a letter which I wrote in great haste

30 Dec   2 p 4to   Osb
from James Henry Monk
Your great kindness in offering me the use of

31 Dec   2 p 4to   NYPL(B)
to CPB & Frances (Young) Burney
The Crewian Packet arrived safely —

[post 1810]   1 p 8vo   Osb
to CPB
Ward comes on Wednesday & Edwards last

5 Mar [post 1810]   2 p 4to   Osb
from C J Blomfield to [CB Jr or CPB?]
I am about to take a liberty with you which

16 July [post 1810]   4 p 4to   Osb
from Henry W Hobhouse to [CB Jr? or
        CPB?]
In your Letters to my Father and my Cousin

1811

2 Jan   2 p 4to   Osb
to CPB
On Saturday, or early in next Week —

5 Jan   amanuensis   4 p 4to   Osb
to CPB & Frances (Young) Burney
I must be shorter than I could wish. The

7 Jan   1 p 4to   Osb
to CPB
If you think that the inclosed will do, send it

8 Jan   1 p 4to   Osb
to CPB
I am still out of sorts, — and tremble even at

9 Jan   2 p 4to   Osb
to CPB
Why my dear Boy do you talk of directing to

17 Jan   3 p 4to   Osb
to CPB
By a new pacquet Boat, I send you

19 Jan   2 p 8vo   Folger
from Edmond Malone
You were so good some time ago to furnish

28 Jan   3 p 4to   Osb
from Sir George Pretyman Tomline
I lament exceedingly that till this moment it

30 Jan   1 p 4to   Osb
from G I Huntingford
In the first place I will send you the wish of

8 Feb   2 p 4to   Comyn
from Matthew Raine
Whether it be that I did not come to

10 Feb   2 p 8vo   Osb
from Sir George Pretyman Tomline
Many thanks, My Dear Sir, for your Letter

17 Feb   1 p 8vo   Osb
from Sir George Pretyman Tomline
I am much disappointed & mortified by your

17 Feb   1 p 4to   Osb
from Sir George Pretyman Tomline
I did not receive your Book till Friday Noon

11 Mar   2 p 4to   Osb
from John Kaye
I have received a Letter from the Secretary

17 Mar   2 p 4to   Osb
from John Kaye
You will, I am sure, give me full credit when

2 AP pmk   1 p 4to   Oxf(AS)
from Samuel Parr
Excuse me for saying, now

11 AP 1811 pmk   2 p 8vo   Osb
to William F Rose
Charles & I are going tomorrow into Kent;

14 Apr   2 p 4to   Osb
from John Kaye
I was very sorry that your Royal Ducal

19 Apr   1 p 4to   Osb
from Patrick Wilson
Should you happen to be in want, at present,

29 May   2 p 4to   Osb
from Sir Thomas Lawrence
I shall be very happy in the honor of seeing

1811, continued

30 May　　pmk 1811　　2 p 4to　　Osb
from Richard Payne Knight
I have sketch'd out the following for an

18 June [1811]　　2 p 8vo　　　　Osb
from Thomas Dampier
I hope that, as the Wiltshire Living may be

22 June　pmk 1811　1 p 4to　　Osb
from Peter Elmsley
I have just seen the Edinburgh Review, and

[7 July 1811]　　3 p 12mo　　　Osb
from John Young
I returned Here from Dr Disneys last night

11 July　　1 p 8vo　　　　　　Osb
from John Young
Why are you silent? say something even

20 July　　amanuensis　3 p 8vo　Osb
to CPB
I have nothing to add to the intelligence of

27 July　　2 p 8vo　　　　　　Osb
from Thomas Dampier
I congratulate you in having got through all

9 Aug　　3 p 8vo　　　　　　Osb
to CPB
Yesterday Evening about six o'clock, the

20 Aug　　3 p 4to　　　　　　Osb
from John Young
Well! Jacta est alia. Aut Caesar aut

27 Aug　　3 p 4to　　　　　　Osb
from Thomas Dampier
I am glad to have it in my power to

1 Oct　　3 p 4to　　　　　　Oxf(AS)
from Samuel Parr
I thank you for returning the list of

8 OC　pmk 1811　　3 p 4to　　Osb
from Edward Cardwell
I greatly regret that I have not had it in my

8 Oct　　1 p 4to　　　　　　Osb
from Jonathan Raine
I am not yet by any means fit for inviting or

20 Oct　　2 p 4to　　　　　　Oxf(AS)
from Samuel Parr
You <thote> accurately

19 Dec　　1 p 4to　　　　　　Osb
from William Vincent
I am infinitely obliged to you for the

19 Dec　　1 p 4to　　　　　　Osb
from William Vincent
The Dean of Westr. feels himself highly

26 Dec　pmk 1811　　2 p 4to　　Osb
from Samuel Parr
The Print has not reached me

27 Dec　　4 p 4to　　　　　　Osb
from G I Huntingford
Alas! it is one, among other sorrows which

1812

15 Jan　　1 p 4to　　　　　　Osb
to CPB
Jones is off — but very civilly. — I sent the

21 Jan　　2 p 8vo　　　　　　Osb
to CPB
Dauncey has again brought his Son — but said

8 Mar　　4 p 8vo　　　　　　Osb
to CPB
Here we still are, my dear Brats — and

10 Apr [1812]　　2 p 4to　　Oxf(AS)
from Samuel Thomas Bloomfield
You must doubtless have been much surprised

24 Apr　　1 p 4to　　　　　　Osb
from J W Bacon
By suggestion of Mr. Knight, I take the liberty

30 AP 1812 pmk　　3 p 4to　　Oxf(AS)
from Samuel Parr
The <　　> <　　> disagreeable

4 May　　2 p 8vo　　　　　　Osb
from Caroline, Princess of Wales
The Princess of Wales wishes Both Grand

1<0> MY pmk　　1 p 8vo　　　Hyde
to Patrick Kelly
I will pay Cox's subscription

12 May　　3 p 4to　　　　　　Osb
from Thomas Maurice
Although an Indian Cycle has nearly elapsed

13 MY 1812 pmk　amanuensis　2 p 4to
from Samuel Parr　　　　　　Oxf(AS)
On Saturday I called and

16 May   1 p 4to   Oxf(AS)
to Thomas Maurice
Many thanks for your liberal present. — Be

15 June   1 p 4to   Osb
from Robert Nares [to CB Jr]
I cannot easily express how much I feel obliged

20 June   2 p 8vo   Osb
to G E Griffiths
I send you the remainder of my young friends

21 June   1 p 8vo   Osb
from B[asil] Montagu
Do not forget your kind promise of a copy of

22 June   2 p 4to   Osb
from Prince Hoare
I am entreated by the son of a late eminent

24 June   1 p 8vo   Osb
from George, 2nd Earl Spencer
As I perceive by the Card which you left with

29 June   2 p 4to   Osb
from Henry Addington, 1st Viscount
    Sidmouth
I have to acknowledge two letters, which I

1 July   1 p 8vo   Camb(F)
from John Philip Kemble
I return your Catalogue with a thousand thanks

20 July   4 p 4to   Comyn
from M d'A (on ALS AA to M d'A [pre
    20 July 1812])
Dearest charles, kindest of brothers & friends,

21 July   3 p 4to   Osb
from SHB
That French-headed, fluttering bustler, M^de

13   pmk AU 1812   3 p 8vo   Scot
from John Young
Well — here I am, My Dear Friend, again

[15 Aug 1812]   2 p 8vo   NYPL(B)
from AA
We are on the point of arriving at Deal from

[pre 26 Aug 1812]   2 p 4to   Osb
from Peter Paul Dobrée
I hardly know how to tell it, but I have been

7 Sept   4 p 4to   Osb
from Laurence Parsons, 2nd Earl of
    Rosse
I wish you would point out to Mr Woodfall or

25 Sept [1812]   2 p 4to   Osb
from Prince Hoare
I wrote to you on Saturday last, but recollecting

29 Sept   1 p 4to   Osb
to FBA
Dearest of the Fannies, — tho' others be

5 Oct   4 p 4to   Osb
from Samuel Butler
I congratulate, and as far as I am capable of

15 Oct   3 p 4to   Osb
from James Henry Monk
I thank you for your kind letter; but am really

2 Nov   3 p 8vo   Osb
from Joseph Planta
I duly received your favor of the 20th ult^e. and

11 Nov   1 p 4to   Osb
from John Kaye
I have procured a Tutor for <Parker>, M^r

15 Nov   2 p 4to   Osb
from Sir Benjamin Hobhouse
I cannot express the pleasure with which I

26 Nov   1 p 4to   Osb
from Henry Petty-FitzMaurice, Marquis
    of Lansdowne
Accept my best thanks for your obliging

29 Nov   2 p 4to   Osb
from George, 2nd Earl Spencer
I return you many thanks for the large Paper

2 Dec [1812]   3 p 4to   Osb
from G E Griffiths
I am so wretchedly ill with a debilitated

11 Dec   1 p 4to   Osb
from William Vincent
I want no inducement of a Royal Duke's

24 Dec   3 p 4to   Osb
from C J Blomfield
I am much indebted to you for your kind

26 Dec   1 p 8vo   Osb
to Patrick Kelly
I am off for Althorp on Monday — to spend

30 DE 1812 pmk   1 p 4to   Osb
from C J Blomfield
I am truly sorry that it was not in my power

1812, continued

[1812?]   4 p 4to   Osb
from Charles Greville to [CB Jr?]
Mr. Robson call'd upon me yesterday for the

[1812?]   2 p 8vo   Bord
from William Wilberforce
Many thanks my dear Sir, but my arrangements

[1812–13]   2 p 4to   BM
to [Samuel Butler]
Many thanks for your nice Book

[1812–17]   2 p 8vo   Osb
from Walker King
I cannot return you the compliment of saying

[1812–17]   3 p 8vo   Bord
from William Wilberforce
Will you & yr Son eat Mutton with me on

12 Mar [pre 1813]   2 p fol   Osb
from John Young
I am hurried as much as you was when you

[Sept pre 1813]   1 p 4to   Osb
from John Young
Unhappy Wight! — not *You* — but *I!* I

1 Nov [pre 1813]   amanuensis   1 p 8vo
from Caroline, Princess of Wales   Osb
The Princess of Wales presents her

[pre 1813]   1 p 4to   Oxf(AS)
from Samuel Parr
I <   > <   > to say, it was not

[pre 1813?]   2 p 4to   Osb
from Thomas Sheridan [to CB Jr?]
Mrs. Knight has requested me to request you

[pre 1813]   2 p 4to   Osb
from Thomas Sheridan
I write at the request of a particular Friend of

1813

12 Jan   1 p 8vo   NYPL(MS)
to [Patrick Kelly]
This is a most comfortable mansion; — & as

21 Jan   3 p 4to   Osb
from John Hewlett
I have collected something more than fifty

25 Jan   pmk 1813   2 p 8vo   Osb
from EBB
You may give me credit — when I say, that

26 Jan   2 p 4to   Osb
from John Hewlett
I like your proposed inscription for our friend

1 Feb   4 p 4to   Osb
from Samuel Butler
I inclose a £2 note being the subscription of

9 Feb   3 p 8vo   Osb
to CPB
If any *one*, or any *two* can come & dine, do so.

9 Feb   4 p 4to   Scot
from John Young
I begin again to lose sight of you. What are

8 Mar   3 p 4to   Osb
to C J Blomfield
The good news of the fate of Callimachus has

13 Mar   4 p 4to   Osb
from John Young
Mounseer Ellis has given us a World of

[1] Apr   1 p 8vo   Osb
from Peter Elmsley
I am sorry to have kept your Euripides so

22 Apr   1 p 4to   Osb
from C J Hunter [to CB Jr?]
Will you do me the favor of giving my Brother

4 May   1 p 4to   Comyn
from Francis Milman
I shall be at Home from one to two

10 May   2 p 4to   Pforz
from William Godwin
I have been enquiring in various quarters for

14 May   4 p 8vo   Pforz
from William Godwin
I beg leave to acknowledge the satisfaction I

19 May   2 p 4to   Pforz
from William Godwin
When I was at your house on Friday last, I

[20 May 1813]   1 p 8vo   Pforz
from William Godwin
Mr. Godwin has this moment received two

1 June   pmk 1813   1 p 8vo   Osb
from Richard Payne Knight
Pray come and partake of a dose of Greek,

10 June   pmk 1813   1 p 4to   Osb
from Prince Hoare
Have compassion once more on my ignorance,

11 JU 1813 pmk   1 p 8vo   Oxf(AS)
from Samuel Parr
I am to dine today with M^r

12 June   pmk 1813   1 p 8vo   Oxf(AS)
from Samuel Parr
To <   > <   > with poor pleasure

12 June   1 p 4to   Harv(H)
from William Godwin
I am extremely sorry I have not had an

26 June [1813]   1 p 4to   Osb
from R[ichard?] Heber
If you are at home, & in good heart, Boswell

30 June [1813?]   1 p 8vo   Osb
from Samuel Rogers to [CB Jr?]
If you have nothing better to do, pray dine

4 July   3 p 4to   Win
to G I Huntingford
A violent attack of rheumatism in my left arm

12 July   1 p 8vo   Mag 916(23)
to Mr Mason
[first line not available]

25 July   3 p 4to   Osb
from C W LeBas
M^r. <Dealtry>, having accepted the Living

3 Aug   2 p 4to   Osb
from C W LeBas
Accept my best thanks for your very gratifying

8 Aug   3 p 4to   Osb
from Thomas Sheridan
The state of my health, renders it advisable

9 Aug   3 p 4to   Osb
from C W LeBas
A thousand thanks for your prompt and

16 Aug [1813]   2 p 4to   Osb
to CPB
I sorrow at Your *plagues* which seem beyond

30 Aug   3 p 8vo   McG
to CPB
I cannot let my dear Party quit me without a

[31 Aug 1813]   2 p 8vo   Osb
from William Wilberforce
Perhaps I scarcely take ye best Method for

2 Sept [1813]   3 p 8vo   Osb
to CPB
Time is very short; for a day has been lost. —

5 Sept   4 p 4to   Osb
to CPB
The letter, my dear C.P.B. was for Alex. —

9 Sept   pmk 1813   4 p 8vo   Osb
to CPB
I am still here — and likely to be here; — for

10 Sept   1 p 4to   Osb
to CPB
This Gout is hostile; and I have no fleecy

11 Sept   2 p 4to   Osb
to CPB
PS. As to *Venison* — I should like to send

11 Sept   4 p 8vo   Osb
to FBA
Read directly. / If you can "elevate & surprise"

12 Sept [1813]   2 p 4to   Osb
to CPB
The dear, charming Pacquet arrived by Coach

19 Sept   3 p 4to   Osb
to CPB
What a glorious morning! — After a little

21 Sept   2 p 8vo   Osb
to CPB
As I take it for granted, that you are all dead,

23 Sept   4 p 4to   Osb
to CPB
At length *all* your letters — pears — apples,

27 Sept   2 p 4to   Osb
to CPB
The Venison did not arrive at York Place, till

[Sept 1813]   2 p 4to   Osb
to CPB
I must be at home all day — for the Gout has

1813, continued

3 Oct   4 p 8vo & 2 p fol   Osb
to CPB
My present plans are these: to leave Ramsgate

5 Oct   pmk 1813   2 p 4to   Osb
from Henry Kett
The kind expressions of my Friend Cleaver

21 Oct 18[13?]   3 p 8vo   Osb
to CPB & Frances (Young) Burney
When you can, send over Brightblossom to the

5 Nov   4 p 8vo   Osb
from Walker King
There is no end of the absurdities, and

26-30 Nov   4 p 8vo   Osb
to FBA
The Gout: — a foe, worse than Beau

1 Dec   1 p 4to   Osb
from William Vincent
I never failed to attend my brethren the

4 Dec   1 p 4to   Prin
to Edward Foss
I want an Act of Parliament for 1753 which

4 DE 1813 pmk   3 p fol   Oxf(AS)
from Samuel Parr
I applaud the measures & the <   > of the

8 Dec   1 p 4to   Comyn
from SHB
We are in a very poor way here, my dear

11 DE 1813 pmk   3 p 4to   Osb
to FBA
I am impowered by Lady Spencer to invite

13 Dec   pmk 1813   4 p 4to   Oxf(AS)
from Samuel Parr
I recognized your handwriting, &

18 Dec   2 p 8vo   Osb
to E H Barker
Dr. Charles Burney is much obliged to Mr. E.

29 Dec   3 p 8vo   Osb
from Thomas Greville
Your letter has followed me hither, as I had

12 Feb [post 1813]   1 p 8vo   Prin
to ?
Revd. Wm. Beloe lives in Kensington Square

[1813-14]   2 p 8vo   Osb
to FBA
I am just preparing to visit the Archbishop —

1814

26 Jan   4 p 8vo   Osb
from SHB
You remember, I hope, the good-natured

3 Feb   1 p 4to   Oxf(Bod)
from James Boswell Jr
Will you do me the favour to accept of a little

24 Feb   2 p 8vo   Yale(MS)
to [George Henry Law?]
Allow me to congratulate you on your

28 Feb   1 p 4to   Osb
from Charles Manners-Sutton
I, too, should have been confined as a Prisoner

13 Mar   2 p 8vo   Oxf(Bod)
to Robert Finch
Many thanks, my dear Finch, for your kind

16 Mar   1 p 8vo   Osb
to ?
I cannot let a Post go out without thanking you

[18 Mar 1814]   1 p 8vo   Oxf(Bod)
to Robert Finch
I have been so long detained

27 Mar   2 p 8vo   Oxf(Bod)
to Robert Finch
Some business has occurred, which

4 Apr   1 p 8vo   Oxf(Bod)
to Robert Finch
We shall be glad to see you; —

16 Apr   1 p 8vo   Oxf(Bod)
to Robert Finch
Accept my best thanks

18 Apr   1 p 4to   Osb
from Sir George Beaumont
I shall have a melancholy satisfaction in

19 Apr   1 p 8vo   Osb
from T J Mathias
I am much concerned that it will not be in my

4 May   2 p 4to   Osb
from Sir Joseph Banks
I thank you my dear Dr for your Friendly

14 May   1 p 4to   Osb
from Roger Wilbraham
When I was at Holkham last month I copied

27 May   4 p 4to   Osb
from G I Huntingford
The very first business, which I undertake on

31 May   1 p 4to   Osb
from Roger Wilbraham
Mr Coke having signified to me that Lord

4 June   2 p 4to   Oxf(Bod)
to Robert Finch
Thou hast rejoiced the cockles of my heart

6 JU 1814 pmk   1 p 4to   Yale(Bo)
from James Boswell
I find in the catalogue of Dr Burneys books

22 July   1 p 8vo   BM
to James White
If any Person should come to you commissioned

26 July   2 p 4to   Osb
to Edward Foss
If you had accepted my offer, when it was

31 July   1 p 8vo   Osb
from Sir David Wilkie
I have had the pleasure of presenting from you

3 Aug   3 p 4to   Osb
from John Young
I had from you no reactory Epistle to meet my

25 Aug   1 p 8vo   Osb
to Thomas Maurice
Many thanks for your literary *Scheda*.

29 Sept   4 p 4to   Osb
from Thomas Sheridan
I have received your Letter of the 18th: July

4 NO 1814 pmk   3 p 4to   Osb
to CPB
Now has not Sion Cottage a fine curat[e]

11 Nov   1 p 4to   Osb
from Douglas Kinnaird
I have look'd for the Bill you mention, & find

14 Nov   2 p 12mo   Ryl
to Frances Anne (Burney) Wood
Your Grandpapa sends you some more Prints.

27 Nov   4 p 8vo & 2 p 4to   Osb
from William Wilberforce
A Letter received this morng from one of Clem

4 Dec   3 p 8vo   Osb
to CPB
The horrours of packing up — Calls — &

9 Dec   2 p 12mo   NYPL(B)
to Edward Foss
I am this moment arrived from Cambridge

24 Dec [1814]   1 p 8vo   Osb
to CPB
Thanks for drafts <twain> — So, I must dine

27 Dec   2 p 4to   Osb
from G I Huntingford
When you next go to London, do me the

[1814]   3 p 8vo   Osb
from George Dyer
Tho' a sort of dead author, I do not come to

1815

1 Jan   4 p 8vo   Osb
to CPB
The Roads were so bad and heavy, that I slept

8 Jan   1 p 4to   Osb
to CPB
A power of the General Post induces me to

8 Jan   2 p 4to   McG
to CPB
This House is a most idle & delightful

8 Jan   3 p 4to   Osb
to Rosette (Rose) Burney
It did occur to me, Yesterday, that I might

10 Jan   4 p 8vo   Osb
to CPB
Thanks, dear Boy, for your pacquet. — the

14 Jan   4 p 4to   Osb
from John Young
Now, My Dear Sir, I know not whether I have

1815, continued

20 Jan   4 p 8vo   Osb
to Rosette (Rose) Burney
The Snow has been falling for some days, my

21 Jan   2 p fol   Osb
to CPB
Darlington, Joseph <Jekyl> Rye's Living, is,

1 Feb   2 p 4to   Osb
from Edward Copleston
By this time I presume you have reached home.

7 Feb   2 p 4to   Osb
from George, 2nd Earl Spencer
I am very much obliged to you for your kind

9 Feb [1815]   1 p 4to   Osb
from C J Blomfield
Will you have the goodness to inform me,

19 Feb   4 p 4to   Osb
from John Young
I am, like Old Lear, mustering possibilities of

21 Feb   2 p 8vo   Scot
from James Mackintosh
Mr. Elliott & myself are absolutely

22 Feb   pmk 1815   1 p 4to   Osb
from Henry Petty-FitzMaurice, Marquis
     of Lansdowne
Many thanks for your obliging note which I

24 Feb   1 p 4to   Osb
from George, 2nd Earl Spencer
Many thanks for the <Stackins> & Handel;

18 Mar   1 p 4to   V&A
to K Wyton
Not *from* Callimachus, my dear Friend; but

18 Mar   2 p 4to   Osb
from William Austin
I cannot miss the opportunity of writing to

27 Mar   1 p 4to   Osb
from JB
Among so much bad news as we have had of

5 Apr   3 p 4to   Osb
from Edward Maltby
The sight of your hand-writing, after such an

14 May   2 p 4to   Osb
from James Henry Monk
I am induced to trespass upon your goodness

22 May   1 p 4to   Osb
from George Henry Law
Lady Crewe called upon me yesterday

9 June   1 p 8vo   Osb
to Mr Richardson
Dr Burney begs Mr Richardson will purchase

15 June   1 p 8vo   BM
to [CPB]
I think at present; — but have not mentioned

28 June   receipt   1 p fragment Osb
from Joseph Nollekens
Received of Rev. Dr Burney the sum of

29 June   3 p 4to   Osb
from E H Barker
In a Memorandum, written by Mr Lunn on

9 July   4 p 4to   Osb
from Sir Benjamin Hobhouse
Next to that consolation which comes from

[post 1 Aug 1815]   2 p 8vo   Osb
from Sir H C Englefield
I fully intended to profit of your most kind

2 Aug   3 p 4to   Osb
from John Young
I am, every Day, pressed to write to you to

21 Aug   3 p 4to   RAA
to Sir Thomas Lawrence
At last, I have been able to get a sort of

3 Sept   1 p 4to   Osb
to Francis North, 4th Earl of Guilford
Do let me know when and where I shall send

23 Sept   3 p 4to   Osb
from John Young
We have scarcely yet been able καταπεψαι

5 Oct   4 p 4to   Osb
to FBA
My dearest of the Fanny tribe — / Though

21 Oct 1815 pmk   3 p 8vo   Osb
from George Dyer
The enclosed paper will explain its own

21 Oct   2 p 4to   Osb
from John Young
I thank you for your Letter — good Letter —

1 Nov   2 p 8vo   Osb
from Joseph Planta
I have too much confidence in your kindness,

19 Nov   2 p 4to   Osb
from John Kaye
I am sorry that you are obliged to postpone

25 Nov   4 p 4to   Osb
to FBA
Since you & my dear d Arblay left the Rectory

also   copy, extract   2 p 4to   BM(Bar)
On the 24th of October, a little before midnight

30 Nov   2 p 8vo   NYPL(MS)
to Patrick Kelly
If you wish for the service of Princes, you

4 Dec   1 p 8vo   Osb
from Thomas Phillips
I have the pleasure to tell you that I have

6 Dec   pmk 1815   3 p 4to   Osb
from John Young
I fear you are not, all of you, so well as you

15 Dec   1 p 8vo   Osb
from Joseph Nollekens
Nollekens presents his Respects to Dr Burney

[c 1815?]   amanuensis   1 p 4to   Osb
from EBB
I fear you will deem this letter too long by a

1816

[1 Jan 1816]   4 p 4to   Osb
to CPB
Joy, joy, joy, to my dear Charles! — May the

3 Jan   4 p 4to   Osb
to CPB
I shall get a frank, if I can; — but the Marquis

15 Jan   2 p 4to   Pforz
to FBA
Most grateful was your letter to me, and not

21 Jan   2 p 8vo   Osb
to Charles Matthews
The Bullock is arrived: and in rare good case;

also   copy   1 p 4to   Comyn

8 Feb   4 p 4to   Osb
from John Young
This Gout of yours vexes me. It comes too

13 Feb   1 p 4to   Osb
to Patrick Kelly
The Partner of my Nephew Mr. Martin Burney,

25 Feb   1 p 4to   Osb
from Count ⟨Zenobic⟩
Count Zenobic presents his compliments to

28 Feb   1 p 4to   Osb
from Charles Butler
The three Volumes arrived safe. I am much

3 Mar   3 p 4to   Osb
to CPB
Here I am, safely and snugly lodged, with Dr.

3 Mar   2 p 4to   Osb
to Rosette (Rose) Burney
Kerr's letter arrived this morning; and brought

4 Mar   2 p 4to   Osb
from William Lort Mansel
It is truly an act of *self-denial* in me, when,

9 MR 1816 pmk   2 p 4to   Osb
to CPB
By your opening the Bp of St. David's letter

15 Mar   1 p 8vo   Osb
from Edward Legge
I hope Mr. Gill has duly apprized you, as he

21 Mar   receipt   ½ p 4to   Osb
from W Whiffin
Recd. of the Revd. Charles Burney. D.D. Rector

12 Apr   1 p 8vo   Osb
from Sir George Pretyman Tomline
Many thanks for your Letter & kind offer.

3 May   1 p 4to   WHM
from Sir Joseph Banks
a difference of opinion has arisen Relative to

6 May   3 p 4to   Osb
to FBA
I dispatch two letters, — according to my dear

13   pmk [May 1816]   4 p 4to   Comyn
to FBA
Poor Dr. Kaye has lost his Father in law

1816, continued

20 May   copy   1 p 4to   Osb
to J Asperne
"Some particular circumstances have prevented

24 May   1 p 8vo   RS
to ?
The Hexameter about which you inquired, is

8 June   3 p 4to   Osb
from Peter Paul Dobrée
Kidd, as every one foresaw, is in Cambridge

4 July   1 p 8vo   Osb
from Sir George Pretyman Tomline
I have this morning returned the Box by the

6 July   pmk 1816   1 p 4to   Osb
from [Richard?] Heber
Since I agreed to dine with you it has occurred

9 JY 1816 pmk   2 p 8vo   Osb
from Peter Paul Dobrée
After several vain attempts to manage a

23 July   4 p 4to   Osb
to FBA
My dearest Fanny, while I can hold a pen, and

24 JY 1816 pmk   3 p 4to   Osb
from Peter Paul Dobrée
I found both your cards at my lodgings, but

27 July   1 p 4to   Osb
from Herbert Marsh
Though it is now nearly a fortnight since I was

20 Aug   2 p 8vo   Osb
from Sir George Pretyman Tomline
I sent the Box to the Deanery last Saturday,

23 Sept   4 p 4to   BM(Bar)
to FBA
What does all this mean, my <Lady> General

1 Oct   6 p 4to   Osb
from E H Barker
In a Letter, which I lately received from

[11 Oct 1816]   4 p 4to   NYPL(B)
to FBA
Beg Alex, my dearest Fanch, to draw

15 Oct   4 p 4to   Osb
from John Kaye
The words, to which the expression "sub

16 Oct   4 p 4to   Osb
from G I Huntingford
If the motto "Detur Dignion" *could* be my

4 Nov [1816]   2 p 8vo   Osb
from Thomas Maurice (on p 3 & 4 of
    printed notice)
Although you will be always entitled to every

5 Nov   1 p 4to   Oxf(AS)
to Thomas Maurice
Pray add my name to your List of subscribers

6 Nov   1 p 4to   Osb
from Henry Drury
Although I have not the honour of knowing

18 Nov   1 p 4to   NYPL(B)
to FBA
The inclosed has just arrived from Dr. Kaye

27 Nov   3 p 4to   Osb
from C J Blomfield
Your letter having been directed to me in

28 Nov   amanuensis   3 p 4to   Osb
from Richard Twining
As you happened to be at your Sister's when

[pre 1817]   2 p 4to   Osb
from Francis North, 4th Earl of Guilford
Richard is arrived here like a drowned rat, I

1817

5 Jan   2 p 4to   Oxf(AS)
from Samuel Parr
Dr & reverend Dr Burney — I read

10 Jan   2 p 4to   Osb
from Peter Paul Dobrée
Many thanks for the £20 which came to hand

10 Jan   2 p 4to   Osb
from George, 2nd Earl Spencer
No one can more sincerely lament the

[12] Jan [1817]   1 p 4to   Osb
to [William Howley]
May I beg leave to assure you that I should

20 Jan   copy   1 p LB   BM(Bar)
from AA
Suffer me to take this *opportunity* to express

23 Jan   1 p 4to   Glouc
to John Sayer
It will afford me great pleasure to receive

31 Jan [1817?]   1 p 4to   Osb
from R[ichard?] Heber
Will your engagements permit you to meet

18 Feb   1 p 4to   Osb
from John Ireland
Having caused an enquiry to be made by the

19 Feb   3 p 4to   Hilles
to FBA
I have, this moment, received a reply from the

20 Feb [1817 misdated 1815]   2 p 4to
from C J Blomfield   Osb
I ought to have written to you before on the

21 Feb   4 p 4to   Osb
to FBA
After my last triumphant Epistle, here

22 Feb   1 p 4to   Osb
from J H Gell
The Dean of Westminster having mentioned

14 Mar   copy   1 p 4to   Osb
to J Asperne
"Dr Burney begs to assure Mr Asperne that

21 Mar   1 p 8vo   Osb
from Sir George Pretyman Tomline
I thank you very much for your Letter & the

[22 Mar 1817]   2 p 4to   Osb
to FBA
So we are to appear, with the Lyre on the

[3 Apr 1817]   4 p 4to   Osb
to FBA
Brava! my dearest of the Fanny tribe! —

15 Apr   3 p 4to   BM
to Samuel Butler
Do not suppose *me* insensible of your great

18 Apr   1 p 8vo   Osb
to Thomas Maurice
I beg to inclose the Note, with thanks.

21 Apr   copy   1 p 4to   Osb
to J Asperne
"Dr Burney presents his compts. to Mr.

22 Apr   3 p 4to   Osb
from Peter Paul Dobrée
I got here on Saturday, but could not find the

2 May   1 p 4to   Osb
to J Asperne
Dr Burney presents his compliments to Mr.

10 May   1 p 8vo   Osb
from John Philip Kemble
I have great occasion to learn which of your

15 MY 1817 pmk   1 p 4to   Osb
to FBA
[. . .] its way — and so yours, also does, it

[20 May 1817]   1 p 4to   Harv(H)
from Eva Maria (Veigel) Garrick
Your kind letter I received at Hampton in May

29 May   2 p 8vo   Osb
to Sir John St Aubyn
My absence for a few days at < > where

29 May   1 p 8vo   Osb
from John Luxmoore
My Son is a Candidate for the Alfred and the

5 June   2 p 8vo   Osb
from Sir George Pretyman Tomline
A small Prebend in my Church of Lincoln is

12 June   4 p 4to   NYPL(B)
to FBA
I have again submitted the Inscription

27 June   pmk 1817   3 p 4to   Osb
from C J Blomfield
You must have thought me very dilatory in not

3 July   4 p 4to   Osb
to CPB
Well, my dear Brats and Bratikins, here am I,

5–6 July   4 p 4to   Osb
to CPB
My letter, written on the Road, I trust, reached

17 July   1 p 4to   Osb
from John Philip Kemble
Your friendly letter reached me only last night.

6 Aug   3 p 4to   Osb
from Josiah Thomas
How goeth on Canvass respecting Grays-Inn?

17 Aug   1 p 4to   Harv(H)
to Mr ⟨Miller⟩
Dr. Burney will be obliged to Mr. ⟨Miller⟩,

[20 Aug 1817]   4 p 4to   Osb
to FBA
Only one line & an half — I have a packet for

24 Aug   2 p 4to   Osb
to William Shield
Most heartily do I rejoice — and truly do I

1817, continued

4 Sept   2 p 8vo   Osb
from Sir George Pretyman Tomline
I really am very sorry that I omitted to send

13 Sept   1 p 4to   Osb
to John Gillies
Perry, Nicol, and Gordon dine with me on

18 Sept   4 p 4to   NYPL(B)
to FBA
Two letters! — that ought to imply two

23 Sept   2 p 4to   Osb
from Richard Twining
You are very good to have corrected me; and

8 Oct   1 p 4to   Osb
from William Scott
You cannot be ignorant of the Causes of my

10 Oct [1817]   8 p 8vo   Osb
to CPB
Your noble sheet full met me this morning, at

[10 Oct 1817?]   4 p 8vo   Osb
to CPB
The first hasty scrawl Mrs Bicknell forgot to

13 Oct   copy   2 p 4to   NYPL(B)
from Charles Manners-Sutton (in ALS
     CB Jr to FBA 21 Oct [1817])
If I did not feel, and to the degree, to which

[18] Oct [1817]   4 p 4to   Osb
to CPB
After a tedious Vestry, from which M^r. *Davey*

20 Oct   2 p 8vo   Osb
from George, 2nd Earl Spencer
When I had the pleasure of seeing you at the

21 Oct [1817]   2 p 4to   NYPL(B)
to FBA
I am just arrived from Tunbridge Wells —

29 Oct   1 p 12mo   NYPL(MS)
to [Thomas?] King
Dr Burney requests Mr King would purchase

26 Nov   2 p 4to   Osb
from G Woodfall [to CB Jr?]
As Hamlet settled our former business

7 Dec   3 p 4to   Osb
from John Young
Riddle me this. How am I comport [sic]

31 Jan   ?   ½ p 4to   Comyn
from William Heberden [to CB Jr or
     CPB]
Dr Heberden presents his comp^ts. & thinks

6 May   amanuensis   4 p 4to   Comyn
from Samuel Parr
When you left me I wrote to Mr Turnstall to

n d   1 p 4to   PML
to R Sharp [from CB Jr?]
Do not forget, my dear Sir, that we expect the

SARAH "ROSETTE" (ROSE) BURNEY 1759–1821

(Printed in *Catalogue:* Rosette (Rose) Burney)

See also letters to and from CB Jr and CPB, and letters from FBA, CBFB,
CB, EBB, Richard T Burney, SHB, SBP, Frances (Phillips) Raper.

29 May 1776   3 p 4to   Osb
from A Hirons
After gathering Gooseberrys making Pyes &c

⟨14⟩ June [1782?]   4 p 4to   Osb
from Clarissa [Morse?]
I now sit down to fulfill my promise to my

9 Oct 1783   3 p 4to   Osb
from Samuel Rose
I hope, My Dear Mrs Burney, that I have not

[1787–91]   1 p 4to   Comyn
from Samuel Rose
I am very sorry you should have

14 Oct 1792   3 p 4to   Osb
from M Riollay
I am very sorry that you should have suffer'd

8 NO 1797 pmk   1 p 8vo   Comyn
from Elizabeth Rose
I am happy my dear Sister, in again being able

[1797–1812]   1 p 4to   Osb
from [Sir Thomas] Lawrence
Mʳ. Lawrence with his Respects to Mʳˢ c.

23 Apr 1814   4 p 4to   Comyn
from Harriet Rose
I feel afraid, that you will deeply lament,

Charles Parr Burney, DD 1785–1864

(CPB)

See also letters from CB, CB Jr, FBA and CFBt.

A number of holograph works and original documents of Charles Parr Burney are in the Osborn Collection.

1797

18 [Apr 1797]   2 p 4to   Osb
to Rosette (Rose) Burney
We arrived at Bath on Monday night at eleven

1799

20 Jan [1799 misdated 1798]   3 p 4to   Osb
with CB Jr to Rosette (Rose) Burney
I shall now continue my journal; I dined last

15 Nov   2 p 8vo   Osb
to Rosette (Rose) Burney
I think you will be surprized to receive this

1800

2 Jan   2 p 4to   Osb
to Rosette (Rose) Burney
I should have written to you sooner but I have

9 Jan   1 p 4to   Osb
with CB Jr
to Rosette (Rose) Burney
I am truly sorry to be under the necessity of

15 Mar   1 p 4to   Osb
from James [Young]
I do return You my most hearty thanks for Your

3 MY 1800 pmk   1 p 4to   Oxf(Bod)
from R[ichard?] Heber
You know enough I daresay of Authorship

16 July   2 p 4to   Osb
to Rosette (Rose) Burney
You must excuse my not writing to you before,

1802

10 Jan   4 p 4to   Folger
to Rosette (Rose) Burney
You will be surprised, no doubt, to find us

13 July   4 p 4to   NYPL(B)
to Rosette (Rose) Burney
At last, my dear Mother we're safely arrived

1 Aug   4 p 4to   Osb
to Rosette (Rose) Burney
I received your letter, my dearest Mother, this

5 Aug   4 p 4to   NYPL(B)
to Rosette (Rose) Burney
Here am I up at six oclock to see the Youngs

19 Aug   4 p 4to   NYPL(B)
to Rosette (Rose) Burney
Well, *"after this, that & to'ther"* I arrived, my

23 Aug   4 p 4to   Osb
to Rosette (Rose) Burney
Many thanks, my dearest Mother, for your

11 Sept   4 p 4to   NYPL(B)
to Rosette (Rose) Burney
Many, many thanks, my dearest Mother

1803

9 Jan   1 p 4to   Osb
to Rosette (Rose) Burney
The Bishop of Gloucester kindly offers a *frank,*

18 June   1 p 4to   NYPL(B)
to Rosette (Rose) Burney
I acquaint you, with great satisfaction

20 Mar [pre 1804]   3 p 4to   Comyn
from Samuel Rose
As I daresay you are anxious for an answer

1804

24 Jan   4 p 4to   NYPL(B)
to Rosette (Rose) Burney
I have been waiting, my dear Mother

16 JY 1804 pmk   4 p 4to   NYPL(B)
to Rosette (Rose) Burney
Well, at last, I have a leisure minute

19 July   4 p 4to   Osb
to Rosette (Rose) Burney
I should have written yesterday, my dear

7 Aug   4 p 4to   Osb
to Rosette (Rose) Burney
I received on Sunday your nice long letter, for

[31 Aug] pmk 1804   1 p 8vo   Penn
from Edward Francesco Burney
Although I had almost determined not to go

[28 Sept] pmk 1804   3 p 8vo   Penn
from Edward Francesco Burney
I have plucked a feather out of the wing of

8 Nov   4 p 4to   NYPL(B)
to Rosette (Rose) Burney
The Box and all its valuable contents

1805

15 JA 1805 pmk   4 p 4to   Osb
from Josiah Thomas
I am directed to inform you of the complete

25 JA 1805 pmk   1 p 4to   Comyn
from Reginald Heber
I must thank you heartily for your kind letter

3 Feb   2 p 4to   Osb
to Rosette (Rose) Burney
Many, many thanks, my dear Mother, for your

13 Feb   1 p 12mo   Oxf(Bod)
to Robert Finch
I regret, that it is totally out of my power to

[c 16 Feb 1805]   1 p 4to   Oxf(Bod)
to Robert Finch
Dyson & I are having a *jolly* evening

28 July   4 p 4to   Oxf(Bod)
to Robert Finch
As I think your punctuality exemplary &

22 Sept   3 p 8vo   Oxf(Bod)
to Robert Finch
My most noble Finch / As I'm at a Pinch / For

25 Sept   3 p 8vo   Oxf(Bod)
to Robert Finch
Upon enquiry I am astonished at the distance

30 Sept   4 p 4to   Osb
from John Kaye
Many thanks for your Letters. It would have

22 Oct   4 p 4to   Oxf(Bod)
to Robert Finch
Many thanks for your Letter, though it was but

[15 Nov 1805]   1 p 12mo   Oxf(Bod)
to Robert Finch
The Fates are, at last, adverse, & I

[5 Dec 1805]   1 p 12mo   Oxf(Bod)
to Robert Finch
I shall regret much, if I miss you by being out

16 Dec   4 p 4to   Oxf(Bod)
to Robert Finch
I have not ceased from wishing to have my

1806

11 Jan   1 p 12mo   Oxf(Bod)
to Robert Finch
My Folks at home

15 JA 1806 pmk 3 p 12 mo Oxf(Bod)
to Robert Finch
I am grieved, that Thursday will not suit you:

16 Jan   3 p 12mo   Oxf(Bod)
to Robert Finch
You know not, my dear Finch, how mortified

23 Jan   1 p 12mo   Oxf(Bod)
to Robert Finch
My Friend Goodwyn has lost his mother

28 Feb   4 p 4to   NYPL(B)
to Rosette (Rose) Burney
As in my last letter to my Father,

21 Mar   3 p 4to   Osb
to Rosette (Rose) Burney
It is my intention to leave Merton early

2 Apr   4 p 4to   Oxf(Bod)
to Robert Finch
Since my return from Oxford I have been so

22 Apr   3 p 4to   Oxf(Bod)
to Robert Finch
I snatch a moment, my dear Finch, to thank

11 July   4 p 4to   Osb
to Rosette (Rose) Burney
Your kind letter is just arrived, & did it not tell

23 JY 1806 pmk   3 p 8vo   Oxf(Bod)
to Robert Finch
I am just returned from my *Touret*, & hear

28 JY 1806 pmk   3 p 8vo   Oxf(Bod)
to Robert Finch
I am quite ashamed of myself for not having

⟨8⟩ Aug   3 p 8vo   NYPL(B)
to Rosette (Rose) Burney
As I promised to write to you

29 Aug   3 p 4to   NYPL(B)
to CB Jr
Nothing ⟨sure⟩, my dearest Father, was ever

6 Oct   3 p 8vo   Oxf(Bod)
to Robert Finch
I have to thank you for a very nice journalizing

7 Oct   3 p 12mo   Oxf(Bod)
to Robert Finch
I am quite grieved to hear of your accident, —

12 Oct   pmk 1806   1 p 4to   Osb
from Martin Davy
Dr. Parr & I are very anxious that you shd.

14 Oct   4 p 4to   Oxf(Bod)
to Robert Finch
As you are still, I fear, an Invalid

20 Oct   2 p 12mo   Oxf(Bod)
to Robert Finch
Many, many thanks, dear Finch, for your letter

9 Nov   4 p 4to   NYPL(B)
to Rosette (Rose) Burney
My Father's kind little note arrived

[29 Nov 1806]   2 p 12mo   Oxf(Bod)
to Robert Finch
I am really quite ashamed of myself for

30 Nov   2 p 4to   Osb
to Rosette (Rose) Burney
As my Father tells me, that you feel very

[1806?]   4 p 8vo   NYPL(B)
to Rosette (Rose) Burney
I have, as Cowper says, just caught hold

1807

6 JA 1807 pmk   1 p 8vo   Oxf(Bod)
to Robert Finch
Pray join our party, ⟨ma chere Roberta⟩

20 JA 1807 pmk   1 p 8vo   Oxf(Bod)
to Robert Finch
I write in the utmost haste

8 Feb   3 p 8vo   Osb
to Rosette (Rose) Burney
You are quite kind, my dearest Mother, in

[15 May 1807]   1 p 12mo   Oxf(Bod)
to Robert Finch
I am sadly hurried, & over head & ears in

1807, continued

27 May   3 p 4to   Osb
from Josiah Thomas
Though my intercourse with the world has not

11 July   2 p 8vo   Oxf(Bod)
to Robert Finch
I am most unexpectedly called away to

14 July   4 p 4to   NYPL(B)
to Rosette (Rose) Burney
I take the earliest opportunity

5 Nov   4 p 4to   BM
from Samuel Parr
Dear namesake I not only confess but declare

1808

16 Jan   4 p 4to   Osb
to Rosette (Rose) Burney
Many thanks, my dear Mother, for your kind &

[June 1808]   4 p 4to   Osb
to Rosette (Rose) Burney
You know, my dearest Mother, how averse I

4 Oct   pmk 1808   4 p 4to   Osb
from Thomas Gaisford
Many thanks for your interesting but to me

17 OC 1808 pmk   1 p 8vo   Oxf(Bod)
to Robert Finch
I am not without my fears

17 Oct   3 p 4to   Osb
from Thomas Gaisford
I thank you for your extracts from the

21 OC 1808 pmk   1 p 8vo   Oxf(Bod)
to Robert Finch
I am sincerely sorry, my dear Finch

23 Oct   pmk 1808   3 p 4to   Osb
from Thomas Gaisford
The E. P. of Stobaeus is absolutely necessary to

24 OC 1808 pmk   1 p 8vo   Oxf(Bod)
to Robert Finch
I am rejoiced, my dear Finch, at your release

[1808–1816]   2 p 4to   Oxf(Bod)
to Robert Finch
Mind me, my dear Fellow, I insist

1809

4 Jan   4 p 4to   Osb
from Josiah Thomas
Your very short letter has given me the pleasure

17 Feb   4 p 4to   Osb
to Rosette (Rose) Burney
It is now very nearly a fortnight, since I heard

[29 May 1809]   1 p 4to   Oxf(Bod)
to Robert Finch
Many, many thanks, my dear Finch, for your

12 JUN 1809 pmk   2 p 4to   Osb
to Rosette (Rose) Burney
So sadly, my dearest Mother, have all my

14 July   1 p 4to   Osb
from [Sir Henry Charles?] Englefield
I return you many thanks for your kind

– 22 July   3 p 4to   Osb
from J Hirons
I am indebted to you, my dear Sir, for that

28 July   4 p 4to   Oxf(Bod)
to Robert Finch
Sad < > am I for not having replied to

31 July   4 p 4to   Osb
to Rosette (Rose) Burney
As our return, my dearest Mother, is deferred

9 Aug   2 p 4to   Osb
from Brownlow North
I fear I shall have appear'd very deficient

23 Aug   1 p 4to   Oxf(Bod)
to Robert Finch
If you give yourself *rectorial* airs,

29 Aug   3 p 4to   Osb
from Edward Nares
Our good friend Griffiths has been careful to

30 Aug   3 p 8vo   Oxf(Bod)
to Robert Finch
I positively am ashamed of having so long

14 Sept   4 p 4to   Oxf(Bod)
to Robert Finch
Your kind letter, my dear Finch, reached me

30 Sept   4 p 4to   Osb
to Rosette (Rose) Burney
Let me close, my dearest Mother, the series of

20 Oct   3 p 4to   NYPL(B)
to Rosette (Rose) Burney
I arrived here last night

3 Dec   amanuensis   5 p fol Oxf(AS)
from Samuel Parr
I take it for granted that you seriously mean to

23 DE 1809 pmk   1 p 8vo   Oxf(Bod)
to Robert Finch
Young is with me

28 Dec   1 p 8vo   Oxf(Bod)
to Robert Finch
Young & myself regret our privation sincerely

1810

14 Jan   4 p 4to   Oxf(Bod)
to Robert Finch
Your last letter to me is so pretty-spoken

6 Mar   3 p 4to   Comyn
from John Wilson
Tho' long since I have had any communication

29 Apr   2 p 8vo   Oxf(Bod)
to Robert Finch
You know too well from experience how

5 July   1 p 8vo   Osb
from George Isted
If you should perchance be disengaged

[post 1810]   1 p 4to   Osb
from Josiah Thomas
I am off *the Mail* this Evening. I have left your

1811

15 Jan [1811?]   1 p 4to   NYPL(B)
from John Crewe, 1st Baron Crewe
I received yours only a few days ago, &

26 Mar   3 p 8vo   Oxf(Bod)
to Robert Finch
Are we ever to meet again?

8 May   1 p 8vo   Oxf(Bod)
to Robert Finch
My Friend Everett of C.C.C. whom you must

31 May   1 p 8vo   Oxf(Bod)
to Robert Finch
Many thanks for your kind intentions to

13 Oct [1811?]   2 p 4to   Osb
from G E Griffiths
I cannot formally answer your formal but kind

[1811–22]   3 p 12mo   Osb
from John Cooke
I return your books — and request you will

1812

12 Jan [misdated 1811]   4 p fol   Osb
to Frances (Young) Burney
Why, — you naughty little Girl, — here is the

17 Jan   6 p 4to   Osb
to Frances (Young) Burney
Does my dear little Fanny think, that I have

10 Mar   2 p 8vo   Oxf(Bod)
to Robert Finch
It is with us no small mortification

24 Mar   3 p 8vo   Oxf(Bod)
to Robert Finch
Most heartily do I congratulate you

30 Mar   1 p 4to   Oxf(Bod)
to Robert Finch
I have been in hourly expectation of seeing

2 Apr   3 p 8vo   Oxf(Bod)
to Robert Finch
All turns out most provokingly

23 June   3 p 4to   Oxf(Bod)
to Robert Finch
Neither your Letter nor its kind contents have

24 June   1 p 8vo   Oxf(Bod)
to Robert Finch
I cannot be with you on Saturday

1812, continued

15 July   3 p 4to   Oxf(Bod)
to Robert Finch
This letter is positively wrenched from me

18 Sept   2 p 8vo   Oxf(Bod)
to Robert Finch
On Saturday I must be at the school.

24 Sept   2 p 8vo   Oxf(Bod)
to Robert Finch
I have written to Russell to appoint him

9 Oct   3 p 8vo   Oxf(Bod)
to Robert Finch
I very much regret your disappointment

10 Dec   1 p 8vo   Oxf(Bod)
to Robert Finch
Though I have no time to write you a letter

21 Dec   2 p 8vo   Oxf(Bod)
to Robert Finch
My Troops are all on the retreat

[post 1812]   3 p 4to   Osb
from Benjamin Travers [to CPB?]
I am sure you will be anxious to know the

1813

19 Jan   3 p 4to   NYPL(B)
to Rosette (Rose) Burney
My time here has been so fully

30 Jan   1 p 8vo   Oxf(Bod)
to Robert Finch
I much regret having missed you

18 Feb   2 p 4to   Oxf(Bod)
to Robert Finch
I enclose the promised *notuole*.

23 Feb   3 p 8vo   Oxf(Bod)
to Robert Finch
Plague take these *self-taught geniuses*

26 Feb   3 p 8vo   Oxf(Bod)
to Robert Finch
Cum prodicibus puellarum non habeo

8 Mar   1 p 8vo   Oxf(Bod)
to Robert Finch
By most untoward additions our *snuggery*

11 Mar   1 p 8vo   Oxf(Bod)
to Robert Finch
Your absence was really deplored yesterday

13 Mar   1 p 8vo   Oxf(Bod)
to Robert Finch
We shall be most happy to see

17 Mar   1 p 8vo   Oxf(Bod)
to Robert Finch
I write in desperate haste to say

26 Mar   1 p 8vo   Oxf(Bod)
to Robert Finch
Come to-morrow: — three we dine

26 Mar   2 p 8vo   Oxf(Bod)
to Robert Finch
Here goes! — it is, indeed, but a chance

30 Mar   1 p 8vo   Oxf(Bod)
to Robert Finch
Suit your own time about coming to-morrow,

1 Apr   1 p 8vo   Oxf(Bod)
to Robert Finch
But a moment to say

16 Aug   1 p 4to   Osb
to CB Jr (on p 4 ALS T Sheridan to CB
     Jr 8 Aug 1813)
I have opened this letter, but have thought it

[Oct 1813]   4 p 4to   NYPL(B)
to FBA
Alex leaves us by the Eleven o'clock

2 Dec   1 p 8vo   Oxf(Bod)
to Robert Finch
I do, indeed, long to see you, — pray then

3 Dec   1 p 8vo   Oxf(Bod)
to Robert Finch
Thou art quite *bonus puer* for coming

11 Dec   2 p 8vo   Oxf(Bod)
to Robert Finch
My preachment is deferred to my

14 Dec   1 p 8vo   Oxf(Bod)
to Robert Finch
I still am anxious to alter

30 Dec   4 p 8vo   Oxf(Bod)
to Robert Finch
Would that you could have come to our

31 Dec   1 p 8vo   Oxf(Bod)
to Robert Finch
My place is insured, but whether

22 Jan [post 1813]   2 p 4to   Osb
from E Weddell to [CPB?]
I think I cannot do better than transcribe the

1814

10 Feb   3 p 8vo   Oxf(Bod)
to Robert Finch
I am truly sorry, that we have not yet

17 Feb   1 p 4to   Oxf(Bod)
to Robert Finch
a *bonne Bouche* for the Dinner

17 Feb   1 p 8vo   Comyn
from Edward, Duke of Kent
I hereby authorize the Rev^d. D^r. Burney to

18 Feb   1 p 4to   Oxf(Bod)
to Robert Finch
The Rector will probably be in town

28 Feb   3 p 8vo   Oxf(Bod)
to Robert Finch
A Monsieur de <Meusm> / an half-pay

28 Feb   1 p 8vo   Oxf(Bod)
to Robert Finch
Hodgson will dine with me

4 Mar   3 p 8vo   Oxf(Bod)
to Robert Finch
You must go as *Magister Artium*

8 Mar   3 p 8vo   Oxf(Bod)
to Robert Finch
Thomas & his captain dine with me to-morrow

9 Mar   3 p 8vo   Oxf(Bod)
to Robert Finch
I am clearly against the delay. —

14 Mar   2 p 8vo   Oxf(Bod)
to Robert Finch
I delight, if but in the thought of

15 Mar   3 p 8vo   Oxf(Bod)
to Robert Finch
The best, — the heartiest thanks

21 Mar   3 p 8vo   Oxf(Bod)
to Robert Finch
I have again pestered Hodgson,

22 Mar   3 p 8vo   Oxf(Bod)
to Robert Finch
You & I shall be ruined in Postage

23 Mar   3 p 8vo   Oxf(Bod)
to Robert Finch
Here is a beauteous morning, —

25 Mar   1 p 8vo   Oxf(Bod)
to Robert Finch
Save your shoe Leather, —

29 Mar   2 p 4to   Oxf(Bod)
to Robert Finch
I am forced to be brief —

2 Apr   2 p 4to   Oxf(Bod)
to Robert Finch
Dearest of Literary Butchers, / I give you

4 Apr   1 p 4to   Oxf(Bod)
to Robert Finch
I have only time to say,

9 Apr   1 p 4to   Oxf(Bod)
to Robert Finch
You will greatly oblige me, if, while

13 Apr   1 p 8vo   Oxf(Bod)
to Robert Finch
I have only time to tell you

15 Apr   1 p 8vo   Oxf(Bod)
to Robert Finch
But a moment to say, that Henry Foss

18 Apr   4 p 4to   Oxf(Bod)
to Robert Finch
Your two last Letters are lying before me

19 Apr   2 p 8vo   Oxf(Bod)
to Robert Finch
I envy you, dear Finch, with all

19 Apr   1 p 8vo   Oxf(Bod)
to Robert Finch
We dine punctually on Thursday at three. —

19 Apr   1 p 8vo   Oxf(Bod)
to Robert Finch
As we meet on Thursday here, — you must

21 May   1 p 8vo   Osb
to James Lackington
Mr. C. P. Burney begs to thank Messrs.

4 June   4 p 4to   Oxf(Bod)
to Robert Finch
Your Letter, — had inclination alone been

1815

10 Jan   2 p 4to   Osb
from Edward Copleston
Nothing can be more grateful to one's

9 June   3 p 8vo   Osb
to Edward Foss Jr.
But a moment to say that my Fanny has just

1816

16 Mar   1 p 8vo   Osb
from Edward Legge
I hope Mr. Gele has duly apprized you, as he

2 Apr   2 p 4to   Osb
from Thomas Gaisford
You are exceedingly kind in offering your

7 Apr   1 p 4to   Osb
from Thomas Gaisford
Since I wrote to you I have received from an

4 June   4 p 4to   Oxf(Bod)
to Robert Finch
Do you recognize an once well-known hand

10 June   1 p 8vo   Osb
to Samuel Sotheby
Pray oblige me by purchasing for me in Dr.

12 June   1 p 4to   Glouc
to John Sayer
Years have passed since we met —

24 June   2 p 4to   Osb
from John Kaye
On many occasions, when an Author has sent

24 June   pmk 1816   4 p 8vo   Osb
from C[hristopher] Lipscomb
I feel much gratified at your kind recollection

26 June   3 p 4to   Osb
from John Bartlam
Your sermons arrived safe a few days ago. But

2 July   1 p 8vo   Osb
from William Van Mildert
Dr: Van Mildert presents his Compliments to

6 July   3 p 4to   Oxf(Bod)
to Robert Finch
I have only time to thank you most heartily

6 July [1816]   1 p 4to   Lewis
from William Beloe to [CPB]
As I go very seldom to Town I only received

6 July   2 p 4to   Osb
from John Bowles
Accept my warmest thanks for your valuable

7 July [1816?]   2 p 8vo   Osb
from Robert Nares
I felt a strong sense of obligation, when I

11 July   1 p 4to   Osb
from John Law
If I am gratified by the attention with which

18 July   4 p 4to   Oxf(Bod)
to Robert Finch
Thus far, my dear Friend, am I on my

19 July   2 p 4to   Osb
from Robert Finch
Here goes another epistle to my travelling

22 July   3 p 4to   Oxf(Bod)
to Robert Finch
Our Journey has been sadly impeded & we

28 July   1 p 4to   Oxf(Bod)
to Robert Finch
I arrived here on my way to Lausanne

31 July   4 p 4to   NYPL(B)
to Rosette (Rose) Burney
Though I shall in all probability

9 Sept   3 p 4to   Glouc
to John Sayer
Very many thanks for your kind remembrance

13 Sept   1 p 4to   Osb
from Ugo Foscolo
Le Sousigné aura l'honneur de presenter

16 Oct   3 p 4to   Osb
from Thomas Gaisford
After 5 months absence here I am once more.

29 Oct   2 p 8vo   Osb
from John Parsons
On my Return to this Place from

26 Nov   3 p 4to   Osb
from Gabriel Brequet
I received both your letters the 10th day in

1817

31 Jan   1 p 4to   Osb
from Rogers Ruding to [CPB?]
The state of my mind, at the time when Mr.

11 Feb   3 p 4to   Osb
from Gabriel Brequet
I just now received an answer of Mr. Berthoud

10 June   2 p 4to   Osb
from Gabriel Brequet
Je vous ecris la Présente par mon Secretaire

Aug 16   2 p 8vo   Osb
from Edward Legge
On my return from Whitney, I find your very

12 Dec   2 p 4to   Osb
from John Kaye
Blackburne's Rooms will be ready for him

31 Dec   1 p 4to   Osb
from G I Huntingford
Very afflicting indeed is your

31 Dec   3 p 8vo   Osb
from Edward Legge
I had heard, through a private channel, the

31 Dec   amanuensis   3 p 4to   Osb
from Brownlow North
It is with deep regret, that I receive this

[post 1817]   3 p 8vo   Osb
from J Bailey
Agreeably with your request (through Mr.

1818

1 Jan   2 p 4to   Osb
from William Howley
You judge very rightly of my feelings in

2 Jan   2 p 4to   Osb
from M J Routh
I was afflicted and surprised at seeing an

2 Jan   1 p 4to   Osb
from John Young
I write you a Line. More I cannot write —

5 Jan   3 p 4to   Osb
from J Asperne
As proprietor of the European Magazine, I

9 Jan   2 p 4to   Osb
from Thomas Burgess
It was with a truly heartfelt concern that I

9 Jan   3 p 8vo   Osb
from Sir George Pretyman Tomline
I thank you very much for your kind attention

13 Jan [1818?]   2 p 4to   Osb
from Anne Hayman to [CPB]
I have been much shock'd & concern'd by

18 Jan   2 p 8vo   Osb
from James Perry
I would before now have expressed to you my

22 Jan   4 p 4to   Oxf(AS)
from Edward Foss
I have received this morning a letter from Dr.

24 Jan   3 p 8vo   NYPL(MS)
to Patrick Kelly
Very many thanks for your kind exertions in

1818, continued

7 Feb   4 p 4to   NYPL(B)
to FBA
At last have I summoned resolution

16 Feb   1 p 4to   Osb
from Richard Payne Knight
I am happy to congratulate you on the

23 Feb   1 p 4to   Osb
from Charles Manners-Sutton
I am very sorry to hear from you, so bad an

25 Feb   2 p 4to   Osb
from JB
I send you a Memoir the Royal Society have

3 Mar   2 p 4to   Osb
from Martin Davy
Be assured that my silence under your heavy

4 Mar [1818]   2 p 8vo   Yale(Bo)
from James Boswell
I shall have great pleasure in dining with you

4 Mar   3 p 8vo   Osb
from Richard Payne Knight
The Reputation of Dr. Burney both as a Scholar

5 Mar   2 p 4to   Osb
from Richard Twining Sr
The Burney family & the Twining family

6 [Mar? 1818?]   2 p 8vo   Osb
from Richard Heber
I rejoice to learn by your two kind notes that

11 Mar   3 p 4to   Osb
from Edward Cardwell
Your welcome letter has found me employed

4 Apr   2 p 4to   Osb
from Nicholas Vansittart, Baron Bexley
I have the pleasure to acquaint you that the

8 Apr   2 p 4to   Harv(H)
from Henry Bankes
Mr. Bankes is extremely sorry that it has not

14 Apr   2 p 4to   Osb
from C J Blomfield
I write for the purpose of informing you that

15 Apr   1 p 8vo   RS
to Sir Joseph Banks
I have desired a Cast from the Bust of my

24 Apr   2 p 8vo   Osb
from Joseph Planta
It is sometime since, for cogent reasons, chiefly

5 May   2 p 8vo   Osb
from Nicholas Vansittart, Baron Bexley
The Resolution of the Committee of Supply

16 May   2 p 4to   Osb
from John Kaye
In consequence of my absence from

17 May   4 p 4to   NYPL(B)
to AA
You have not, I am sure, attributed my

1 June   3 p 4to   Osb
from John Kaye
Your Cousin made his appearance yesterday;

20 June   2 p 8vo   Osb
from E H Barker
In a parcel, which I received the other day

28 June   4 p 4to   Comyn
from AA
I have several times been on the point —

6 July   1 p 4to   Osb
from G I Huntingford
With what unsolicited attention & unabated

28 July   4 p 4to   Osb
to Rosette (Rose) Burney
Thus far are we on our journey towards Basle

3 Sept   2 p 4to   Osb
from Sir Henry Ellis
I have this Moment received a Note from the

9 SE 1818 pmk   2 p 4to   Osb
from John Parsons
NB *No* — in Memory of. — it is superfluous.

15 [Sept]   1 p 4to   Osb
from Frederick North, 5th Earl of Guil-
     ford
I arrived in Town last Night,

1 Oct   2 p 4to   Oxf(Bod)
to Henry Colburn
I beg you to do me the favour of informing

5 Oct   1 p 8vo   Osb
from Frederick North, 5th Earl of Guil-
     ford [to CPB?]
Many thanks for your very kind Note; and

19 Oct   3 p 4to   Osb
from John Young
I am more vexed than I can tell at the strange

22 Oct   2 p 4to   Osb
from L J Martin
Ayant appris que vous avez une collection de

[1818]   2 p 4to   Osb
from Richard Payne Knight
I am extremely sorry to hear that you have

[1818]   2 p 4to   Osb
from Richard Payne Knight
From the conversations which I have had with

23 Nov [1818–22]   1 p 4to   Osb
from John Nichols
My Son & myself are much obliged by your

3 July [post 1818?]   1 p 4to   Osb
from Richard Golding to [CPB?]
I hasten to acknowledge the receipt of your

1819

27 Feb   1 p 8vo   Osb
from Alexander Chalmers
In order to keep up my character with your

[post 6   AP 181⟨9⟩ pmk]   2 p 8vo
from George Dyer   Osb
Mrs. Burney is so kind as to convey this note,

4 May ⟨1819⟩   1 p 4to   Osb
from Edward, 3rd Baron Hawke
I am sorry you have had so much trouble in

7 May   2 p 4to   Osb
from John Kaye
I believe that your best plan will be to address

8 May   2 p 4to   Osb
from Alexander Chalmers
Accept my thanks for your elegant copy of the

21 May   4 p 4to   Osb
from William Lort Mansel
I must intreat of you not to conceive any

24 May   1 p 4to   Osb
from Sir Francis Chantrey
The sum which the late Dr. Burney agreed to

9 July   1 p 4to   Osb
from Sir Francis Chantrey
I am happy to inform you that the Monument

[post 9 July 1819]   1 p 4to   Osb
from Sir Francis Chantrey
I enclose a receipt conformable to your

10 Aug   4 p 8vo   Comyn
from William Wilberforce to [CPB?]
I do not Relish ye formality of dictating

14 Sept   3 p 4to   Osb
from John Kaye
On my return home yesterday I found your

17 Nov   3 p 8vo   Osb
to ?
I shall have the most sincere pleasure in taking

4 Dec [1819–20]   2 p 4to   Osb
from Henry John Todd to [CPB?]
Many thanks for both your letters. Your kind

1820

20 Jan   3 p 4to   Osb
from John Kaye
I was on the point of writing to you when I

11 Feb   3 p 8vo   Liv(P)
to ?
If you will kindly have the Copies of the

17 Feb   2 p 4to   Osb
from Hugh James Rose
I have been for the last year being about a

24 Feb   1 p 4to   Osb
from John Kaye
I have made enquiries respecting Blackburn,

10 Mar   pmk 1820   4 p 4to   Osb
from John Wilson
Will you confer a favour upon me?

22 July   pmk 1820   4 p 4to   Osb
from John Wilson
After the most savage contest ever known

1820, continued

24 July   1 p 8vo   Osb
from Sir George Pretyman Tomline
Many thanks for your kind wishes &

25 July   2 p 4to   Leeds
to John Wilson
The glorious tidings of your triumphant

5 Aug   pmk 1820   4 p 4to   Osb
from John Wilson
I answer your Letter, chiefly because it is

12 Aug   1 p 8vo   Osb
from Charles Butler
I had by no means forgotten my promise; —

19 Aug   3 p 8vo   Osb
to James Thomson
On Sunday, the twenty-seventh, I shall look

11 Sept   2 p 4to   Osb
from John Kaye
I confess my neglect, and the only excuse

28 Nov   3 p 4to   Osb
from John Kaye
I am at length enabled to return an answer

9 Dec   1 p 4to   Oxf(AS)
from John Bartlam to [CPB?]
The Dr reads no books & writes no Letters,

15 Dec   3 p 4to   Oxf(AS)
from Samuel Parr
You did well in communicating to me the

[1820]   2 p 4to   Osb
from Sir George Pretyman Tomline
The Carriage is coming to the door to convey

[1820–27]   3 p 8vo   Osb
from John Kaye
I arrived here yesterday for the purpose of

1821

18 Jan   3 p 4to   Oxf(AS)
from Samuel Parr
I hope to hear a better account of the Relatives

26 Jan   3 p 8vo   Comyn
from Edward Francesco Burney
As I mean to do myself the pleasure of waiting

5 Feb   3 p 4to   Osb
from John Kaye
I have delayed answering your Letter until I

11 ⟨Feb⟩   1 p 4to   Osb
from Richard Heber
⟨The opposition is vigorous, & must⟩

12 Feb   4 p 4to   Osb
from James Lindsay
The inclosed petition (or rather representation;

18 Feb   4 p 4to   Osb
from John Wilson
(Tell me that you, wife, & children are all

26 Feb   3 p 8vo   Osb
from G[eorge?] Pearson
The late circumstance of my family have

1 Mar   amanuensis   3 p 8vo   Osb
from William Wilberforce
I will certainly reserve my Vote for your poor

9 Apr   3 p 4to   Osb
from John Kaye
Will you be kind enough to say for me to

1 May   3 p 4to   Osb
from John Wilson
My friend and brother in Law, Mr F ⟨   ⟩

8 May   3 p 8vo   Osb
from Edward Francesco Burney
I am sorry that I have but a bad account to

8 May   4 p 4to   Osb
from EBB
I have two of your Lettters to answer. —

29 June   1 p 8vo   BM
to Sir Everard Home
As the proposed statue is the British Museum

12 July   3 p 4to   Osb
from Edward Cardwell
I have waited till today without replying to

15 Aug   1 p 4to   Osb
from Edward Cardwell
Herewith you have Heber's warrant for his

29 Aug   1 p 4to   Osb
from Richard Heber
Nobody is better entitled to my prompt &

6 Sept   2 p 8vo   Osb
from John Kaye
I can now speak with some degree of certainty

⟨8⟩ Sept   1 p 8vo   Osb
from J D Alexander
I will confine myself to one half of your

21 Sept   3 p 8vo   Osb
from John Kaye
An alteration has taken place in our

29 Sept   2 p 8vo   Osb
from Edward Francesco Burney [to
    CPB?]
When I wrote last I did not expect to have

9 Oct   2 p 4to   Osb
from Richard Allen Burney
Many thanks for your kindness in this and in

3 Nov   1 p 4to   Oxf(Bod)
to Andrew Spottiswoode
Dr. Burney presents his best Compliments to

7 Nov   1 p 4to   Comyn
from Thomas Campbell
Your kind invitation to dine with you last

10 Dec   3 p 4to   Comyn
from Sarah (Kemble) Siddons
Your very kind and gratifying letter

17 Dec   3 p 8vo   Osb
from Edward Francesco Burney
Many thanks are due to you for your note and

17 Dec   1 p 4to   Osb
from Thomas Campbell
I received your kind note last week. There

17 Dec   1 p 8vo   Osb
to James Lackington
Oblige me, if you please, by purchasing

1822

1 Feb   4 p 4to   Osb
from Richard Allen Burney
Your truly friendly letter, my dear Charles,

18 Mar   amanuensis   2 p 4to   Osb
from Samuel Parr
I send you a copy of a Letter which came to

19 Mar   3 p 8vo   Osb
to Edward Wedlake Brayley
Dr. Burney, at the request of Dr. Parr, begs to

20 Mar   3 p 4to   Osb
from Edward Wedlake Brayley
In reply to a Letter which I was yesterday

22 Mar   3 p 8vo   Osb
to Edward Wedlake Brayley
Dr. Burney presents his Compliments to Mr.

22 Mar   1 p 8vo   Oxf(AS)
from Samuel Parr
I have again heard from the intelligent person,

28 Mar   1 p 4to   Liv(P)
to John Wilks Jr
The Revd. Dr. Burney presents his

[7 Apr]   1 p 4to   Osb
from James Dallaway
Non deficit alter / Aureus! — There *should*

[pre 21 May 1822]   2 p 4to   Osb
from CBFB
Martin talks of writing to request you will

23 May   3 p 4to   Osb
from Samuel Butler
I am in want of an assistant after my

29 May   4 p 4to   Osb
from Samuel Butler
Time presses and I have not got the old rogue's

31 May   1 p 4to   Osb
from CBFB
In answer to your last kind note, my Hesitation

26 Sept.   1 p 8vo   Osb
to J H Burn
Dr. Burney begs Mr. Burn to send for him

29 Dec   pmk 1822   3 p 4to   Oxf(AS)
from Samuel Parr
Dr Richardson ⟨   ⟩⟨   ⟩

31 Dec   2 p 4to   Oxf(AS)
from Samuel Parr
I did like ⟨   ⟩⟨   ⟩ for one

[1822?]   2 p 4to   Osb
from Edward Wedlake Brayley
Agreeably to my promise I now inclose you

1822, continued

[1822–38]   2 p 4to   Osb
from William Daniel Conybeare
In the hurry of the two last days I have not

[post 1822]   1 p 4to   Osb
from Alexander Chalmers
You have now an opportunity of doing a good

1823

26 Jan   3 p 4to   Osb
from Laurence Parsons, 2nd Earl of
    Rosse
I have been much too long in acknowledging

30 Jan   3 p 8vo   Osb
from John Kaye
I send under two other Covers four Letters

31 Jan [1823]   1 p 4to   Osb
from Richard Heber
Will your engagements permit you to meet

12 Feb   2 p 8vo   Osb
to John Nichols
I shall feel greatly indebted to you for giving

16 Mar   2 p 8vo   Oxf(AS)
from Samuel Parr
I attended the funeral — <   > not

7 Apr   3 p 4to   Osb
from James T Law
I hope my Answer to your very kind Letter

18 Apr   3 p 8vo   Osb
from John Kaye
I am sorry to hear so unfavourable an account

28 Apr   3 p 4to   Osb
to George F Robson
About two years ago I had the pleasure of

7 May   3 p 8vo   Osb
from John Kaye
I have secured Mr Coddington, who says,

7 June   1 p 12mo   Pforz
to Thomas Cadell
Dr. Burney presents his compliments to Mr

25 June   2 p 4to   Oxf(Bod)
to Robert Finch
This letter will be delivered to you by those

30 Sept   2 p 8vo   Osb
from Arthur William Trollope
I should be very ungrateful if any wish of

25 Dec   4 p 8vo   Osb
from John Kaye
In the first place let me, in the old-fashioned

[1823–25?]   4 p 4to   Osb
from   ?
I have heard from Mrs Groombridge that you

19 June [post 1823?]   2 p 8vo   Osb
from Lewis Goblet to [CPB?]
being obliged to remain in Town owing to the

1824

16 Jan   3 p 8vo   Osb
from John Kaye
We shall be most happy to see you on

15 Feb   3 p 4to   Osb
from David Williams
You are too well acquainted with the various

16 FE 1824 pmk   2 p 4to   Osb
from Dawson Turner
<A   > mentioned to me a few days ago

17 Feb   3 p 8vo   Camb(T)
to Dawson Turner
Very many thanks for your kind Letter

24 Feb   3 p 4to   Osb
from G I Huntingford
Your kind letter and valuable Prints were duly

2⟨4⟩ Feb   4 p 8vo   Osb
from John Kaye
I delayed answering your Letter until I had

26 Mar   2 p 4to   Osb
from Christian Latrobe
I have had some of my Antigua jaspers &

27 Mar   1 p 8vo   NYPL(B)
from AA
I am just returned from Hartwell

29 May [1824]   3 p 8vo   Osb
from William Robert Spencer
You are quite right in your interpretation,

16 June   1 p 4to   Osb
from Henry Hervey Baber
I have the pleasure to acknowledge the

20 June   2 p 4to   Osb
from James T Law
I am just returned from the Visitation of my

23 June   3 p 8vo   Osb
from John Kaye
I think that you may with propriety add the

26 June   1 p 8vo   Osb
from Sir John Barrow
I have received a portrait, and a very good one

26 June   4 p 4to   Osb
from William Daniel Conybeare
The pressure of much melancholy business

28 June   1 p 8vo   Osb
from John Nichols
I am exceedingly obliged to you for our

10 July   1 p 4to   Osb
from James Tate
I feel myself much honored by your Letter of

14 July   2 p 8vo   Osb
from Henry Petty-FitzMaurice, Marquis
      of Lansdowne
Allow me to return you my sincere thanks for

19 July   1 p 4to   Osb
from Stephen Allen
Mr. Kidd has surprised me with your very kind

4 Aug   3 p 4to   Osb
from Edward Nares
I have reason to think from reports made to me

5 Aug   2 p 4to   Osb
from Samuel Butler
On my return home I have found your kind &

5 Aug   3 p 4to   Osb
from Christian Latrobe
Permit me to return my best thanks to YOU

20 Sept   4 p 8vo   Osb
from John Kaye
I must have expressed myself confusedly

27 Sept   4 p 4to   Osb
from William Gimingham
On my return home after some absence I

24 Oct [1824?]   3 p 8vo   Osb
from Peter Paul Dobrée
Many thanks for the print, which is as beautiful

26 Oct   3 p 8vo   Osb
from James Henry Monk
I am extremely sorry that your very kind &

29 Oct   2 p 8vo   Osb
to John Taylor
Accept, I beg, my best thanks for your kind &

3 Dec   3 p 8vo   BM
to Edward Griffith
I cannot alas! reach Harley St.

8 Dec   1 p 8vo   Osb
from Herbert Marsh
As you are not unacquainted with the situation

10 Dec   2 p 4to   Osb
from Frances Ann (Burney) Wood
I hope you will find me improved in my writing

18 Dec   4 p 8vo   Osb
from C J Blomfield
I accept with much pleasure the honourable

20 Dec   4 p 8vo   Osb
from John Kaye
You ask for a Bill of Health, and I am sorry

23 Dec   2 p 4to   Osb
from Alexander Chalmers
I am very happy that it is in my power to

[pre 1825]   2 p 4to   Oxf(AS)
from Samuel Parr [to CPB?]
I or <   > < ” > <   > to sleep, I

1825

21 Jan   3 p 4to   Osb
from R W White
I have received your letter within these five

25 Jan   4 p 4to   Osb
to Samuel Parr
Many, very many happy returns to you of

1825, continued

9 Mar   1 p 4to   Osb
from Edward Cardwell
The death of D^r. Elmsley has made a vacancy

6 Apr   4 p 8vo   Osb
from Richard Mant
Your letter has reached me at the moment of

4 May   3 p 8vo   Osb
to Thomas Joseph Pettigrew
I am extremely sorry to be compelled to return

20 May   2 p 4to   Osb
from Richard Mant
I hoped to have the pleasure of seeing you

24 May   2 p 4to   Osb
from E H Barker
Having been appointed by D^r. Parr's Executors,

6 June   3 p 4to   Osb
from G E Griffiths
When I was last at Greenwich, & conversing

14 June   3 p 4to   Osb
from E H Barker
I was this morning favoured with your

17 July   2 p 4to   Osb
from John Nichols
If Sympathy is anyway useful, you have it

9 Aug   2 p 8vo   Osb
from John Inglis
I cannot refrain from thanking you sincerely

12 Aug   3 p 8vo   Osb
to John Taylor
I have been absent from home for <seven>

23 Sept   1 p 4to   Osb
from Edward Nares
Our Poor Schoolmaster being still alive, and

9 Oct   3 p 4to   Osb
from Edward Nares
You have once more enabled me to gladden

30 Nov   1 p 8vo   Comyn
from John Gillies [to CPB?]
I hoped to have seen you this day

1826

3 Feb   2 p 4to   Osb
from M J Routh
The request I am about to make will perhaps

31 Mar   2 p 4to   Osb
from G I Huntingford
In consequence of your favour received this

2 May   2 p 8vo   Osb
to Thomas Joseph Pettigrew
I have thus long deferred any acknowledgments

22 May   2 p 8vo   Osb
to Thomas Joseph Pettigrew
I have again to thank you for your kind

23 May [1826]   4 p 8vo   Osb
from Henry John Todd
The moment I received your friendly letter

24 June   4 p 8vo   Osb
from John Kaye
Under the circumstances which you mention,

5 Sept   1 p 4to   Oxf(Bod)
to Robert Finch
These few lines will be delivered to you by

4 Nov   4 p 4to   Osb
from Robert Finch
I received your friendly <notule> but you

1 Dec   2 p 4to   Osb
from T Holt White
I have to apologize for not earlier acknowleging

5 Dec   4 p 8vo   Osb
from John Kaye
I was in town last week in order to take my

19 Dec   4 p 4to   Osb
from Henry Sass
At the request of a Mr. <Tinsley>, a young

23 Dec   4 p 4to   Osb
from Robert Finch
"You never write to a body!" Very true. Just

1827

9 Jan   3 p 4to   Osb
from Robert Finch
If the mighty "King John" were still in this

30 Jan   3 p 8vo   Osb
from John Kaye
So the poor Bishop of Oxford is gone: he will,

8 Feb   4 p 4to   Osb
from Robert Finch
Your pleasant Christmas box flung a reflective

15 Feb   3 p 8vo   Osb
from John Kaye
Report for once speaks truth. I came to

17 Feb   4 p 4to   Osb
from Robert Finch
Again I strike the chords of the responsive

28 Feb   pmk 1827   4 p 4to   Osb
from Hugh James Rose
Many thanks to you, my dear Dʳ Burney, for

1 Mar   4 p 8vo   Osb
from John Kaye
I came to town in order to go thro' the

10 Apr   2 p 4to   Osb
from Robert Finch
The ever kind and fraternal interest you have

1 June   3 p 8vo   Osb
from John Kaye
<Parkwood> should be admitted before the

11 June   3 p 8vo   Osb
from John Lonsdale
I am desired by the Dean of Canterbury to

30 June   1 p 8vo   Oxf(Bod)
to Robert Finch
A moment, & only a moment

10 July   2 p 8vo   Oxf(Bod)
to Robert Finch
Where are you, — where is your Lady?

23 July   1 p 8vo   Prin
to ?
I beg to thank you for your obliging Present,

15 Aug   1 p 8vo   Oxf(Bod)
to ?
Our Friend Finch & his Lady have fixed upon

16 Aug   2 p 8vo   Oxf(Bod)
to Robert Finch
On Saturday I shall be in readiness

30 Aug   3 p 4to   Osb
from Hugh Percy
Having arranged for the holding an Ordination

24 Sept   3 p 8vo   Oxf(Bod)
to Robert Finch
It has been really a mortification to me

26 Sept   1 p 4to   Osb
from James Tate
Your good nature will excuse this intrusion. I

28 Sept   3 p 8vo   Oxf(Bod)
to Robert Finch
One hurried line or two, — spite of

5 Oct   2 p 4to   HEH
to William Upcott
I have much pleasure in so far acceding to

11 Nov   1 p 4to   Osb
from Edward Copleston
It has often happened, to my great concern,

8 Dec   3 p 8vo   Osb
from John Kaye
All that I can say respecting your Friend

30 Dec   1 p 8vo   Osb
from James Tate
You will see that the letter which accompanies

[1827?]   2 p 4to   Osb
from Theodore E Hook
having accidentally discovered a memorandum

1828

2 Jan   1 p 4to   Osb
from W G Whitcombe
Believing that you are good enough to feel an

15 Jan   3 p 8vo   Oxf(Bod)
to Robert Finch
Your note, arriv'd from <Post> just in the

1828, continued

17 Jan   3 p 8vo   Oxf(Bod)
to Robert Finch
All is as cross, — as very cross, — as needs be

18 Jan   3 p 8vo   Oxf(Bod)
to Robert Finch
I send you a Ticket of admission for the

2 Feb   2 p 8vo   Osb
from John Lonsdale
Your most friendly congratulations demand &

8 Feb   1 p 8vo   Osb
to Sir Anthony Carlisle
Dr. Burney presents his Compliments to the

14 Feb   2 p 8vo   Osb
from [Robert Finch]
I am just renested after a flight to Oxenford,

15 Feb   2 p 8vo   Osb
from Robert Finch
Old Parr said "Vice versa, Sir, in common

18 Feb   3 p 4to   Osb
from T F Dibden
The illustrious Payne, the Elder (the

20 Feb   2 p 8vo   Oxf(Bod)
to Robert Finch
I have not written, because I had hoped

3 Mar   2 p 8vo   Oxf(Bod)
to Robert Finch
When we talked on Saturday of your

21 Mar   2 p 8vo   Oxf(Bod)
to Robert Finch
I will be with you to-morrow

6 May   1 p 8vo   Roch
to Robert Balmanno
Dr. Burney presents his Compliments to Mr.

10 May   1 p 8vo   Osb
from G I Huntingford
Your God-Father Dr. Parr used to say he could

24 May   1 p 12mo   Oxf(Bod)
to Robert Finch
Pray fail not to dine with me on Saturday

24 May [1828?]   4 p 4to   Osb
from J[ohn?] Penrose
It is very kind of you, and very much like

30 May   3 p 8vo   Osb
from John Kaye
My acquaintance with Mr Penrose is very

31 May [1828]   1 p 4to   Osb
from G I Huntingford
As Dr. Wooll & I cannot have the pleasure of

2 Aug   4 p 4to   Oxf(Bod)
to Robert Finch
Day after day, — nay week after week,

6 Aug   2 p 4to   Osb
from E H Barker
I beg your acceptance of my *opusculum* on

22 Aug   3 p 12mo   Oxf(Bod)
to Robert Finch
Come, when you please!

26 Aug   1 p 12mo   Oxf(Bod)
to Robert Finch
I will, if it is possible, see you

26 Nov   3 p 8vo   NYPL(B)
from Edward Kaye Burney
I am sure you must now be as anxiously

17 Dec   1 p 4to   NYPL(B)
to Joseph Skelton
I write to thank you for your letter, & to say

1829

18 Feb   2 p 8vo   Osb
from A V Copley Fielding
I hope that you will excuse my troubling you,

16 Mar   2 p 4to   Osb
from[William Stanley]Goddard
I fear that you have thought me inattentive;

25 Apr   3 p 8vo   Osb
from John Kaye
I thought that my best course was to put that

26 May   2 p 8vo   Osb
from Edward Blore
I had discovered the error in the Card you

3 June   2 p 4to   Osb
from CB IV
I could not let this opportunity pass, without

23 July   pmk 1829   1 p 4to   Osb
from Samuel Prout
Your young ladies must have put me down as

27 July   3 p 8vo   Osb
from J ⟨Bégny⟩ to [CPB?]
J'ai été si occupé toute la saison qu'il ne m'a

11 Aug   4 p 8vo   Osb
from John Kaye
I know the exact person for Dr Williams's Son.

6 Nov   1 p 4to   Osb
from James Henry Monk
You will remember your kind promise of

12 Nov   1 p 4to   Osb
from Thomas Scott
Sir, I have not the Honour of being known

13 Nov   5 p 4to   Oxf(Bod)
to Robert Finch
It is true, & "Pity 'tis, tis true," that

16 Dec   2 p 8vo   Osb
to Thomas Joseph Pettigrew
Accept, I beg, my best thanks for your most

1830

30 Jan   4 p 8vo   Osb
from John Kaye
The report which has reached you respecting

25 Feb   2 p 4to   Osb
from M J Routh
I began to be afraid, that it was not intended

9 Apr   3 p 8vo   Osb
from John Kaye
We are proceeding with our equipment, and

22 Apr   pmk 1830   2 p 4to   Osb
from Alexander Crombie
I should be truly happy to resume my seat at

19 MY 1830 pmk   1 p 4to   Osb
from George Fennel Robson
I have deferred acknowledging your kind

21 June   2 p 8vo   Osb
from Theodore E Hook
When I parted from Mr ⟨Croker⟩ Saturday

28 July   2 p 4to   Osb
from John Kaye
I congratulate you on your safe return from the

9 Aug   3 p 8vo   Osb
from John Kaye
I am afraid that young Hopeful will not reach

8 Sept   1 p 4to   Osb
from T F Dibden
As you value my high & good opinion, insert

15 SP 1830 pmk   1 p fol   Osb
from T F Dibden
Here comes the pamphlet — touching which

2 Oct   pmk 18⟨30⟩   1 p 4to   Osb
from T F Dibden
Me voici donc! This is the day of *parturition*

24 Nov   1 p 8vo   Osb
to Thomas Joseph Pettigrew
I am totally in the dark as to all the *Revolutions*

6 Dec [c 1830?]   4 p 8vo   Osb
from T F Dibden
Oblige me by granting the following request.

15 Dec   4 p 8vo   Osb
from John Kaye
I send a Note for Jack: our ⟨Brother⟩ will

24 Dec   3 p 4to   Osb
from Thomas Turton
I feel your kind remembrance of me very

⟨6 Aug⟩ [post 1830?]   2 p 8vo   Osb
from Frederick Christian Lewis Sr
Mr Keith Milnes has placed in my care a

1831

30 Mar [1831?]   1 p 8vo   Osb
from Molesworth Phillips
-men, by asking other questions why did not

7 Apr   2 p 4to   Osb
from E H Barker
I am glad to find that the *Greek Lexicon* finds

17 May   2 p 8vo   Osb
from AA
I had almost vowed a vow that I never would

5 June   1 p 4to   Osb
from William Scott, 1st Baron Stowell
I received your kind invite yesterday and shall

1831, continued

29 June   2 p 8vo   Osb
from Molesworth Phillips
It is with reluctancy I thus trespass (even for

24 Sept   3 p 8vo   Osb
to Thomas Joseph Pettigrew
Your Note ought long since to have been

27 Sept   4 p 8vo   Osb
from John Kaye
I perfectly remember Mr Armstrong: he was a

7 Oct   1 p 8vo   Osb
to Richard ⟨Best⟩
I shall be punctually at my Post on Tuesday

19 Oct   1 p 4to   Osb
from Alexander Chalmers
I hope to deliver your MSS. to-day in person

2 ⟨   ⟩183⟨1⟩   2 p 8vo   Osb
from Molesworth Phillips
I yesterday was favoured by your very obliging

1832

19 Jan   4 p 8vo   Osb
from John Kaye
If all is well Jack will make his appearance

16 Mar   1 p 4to   Osb
from Henry Cox
Dʳ Charles McDermott has handed me a letter

7 Apr   1 p 8vo   Osb
from Edward Francesco Burney
In the last letter I received from Mʳˢ. Bourdois

3 May   pmk 1832   1 p 4to   Osb
from T F Dibden
DB; which means either,/Dearly Beloved, or

11 May   2 p 8vo   Osb
from Richard Goodwin Keats
I have not and will not forget your application

4 June   1 p 4to   Osb
from [David?] Roberts
Mʳ Roberts presents his respectfull comptˢ. to

7 June   1 p 4to   draft   Osb
to Henry Cox
I beg to acknowledge with my best thanks

20 June   2 p 8vo   Scot
to [a publisher]
I trouble you with these few lines merely to

10 July   2 p 8vo   Scot
to [a publisher]
Your kind Note followed me on my Travels.

7 Sept   3 p 4to   Osb
from E H Locker
Your artist friend will find abundance of

15 Sept   1 p 8vo   Osb
from Edward Blore
On my return from a journey I have found

18 SP 1832 pmk   1 p 4to   Osb
from J D Harding
I cannot leave England without thanking you

20 SP 1832 pmk   2 p 8vo   Osb
from J D Harding
I have only a moment to say that I can now go

29 Oct   4 p 8vo   Osb
from John Kaye
Together with your Letter arrived one for ⟨

14 Nov   1 p 4to   Osb
from Richard Goodwin Keats
I regret and so will you that my Journey and

21 Nov   1 p fol   Osb
from Stephen Allen
Twice I have been gratified by an interview &

29 Nov   2 p 4to   Osb
from Stephen Allen
When I took the liberty, from my total

29 Nov   3 p 8vo   Osb
from John Kaye
I conclude that young ⟨   ⟩ is a Member

4 Dec   3 p 4to   Osb
from John Kaye
I shall be in town D.V. on Monday next.

12 Dec   4 p 4to   Osb
from [Dr Charles] McDermott
I received your very kind letter by the

21 Dec   1 p 4to   Osb
from Stephen Allen
Why need I trouble M. D'Arblay to write to me

29 Dec   1 p 8vo   Osb
to ?
Your Nephew is, I am happy in assuring you,

1833

24 Jan   1 p 4to   Osb
from Stephen Allen
Were I not ignorant of Madame D'Arblay's

28 Jan   3 p 4to   Osb
from Sir James Prior
A communication of Mr. Heber to Mr. Amyot

11 FE pmk   2 p 4to   Osb
from Alexander Chalmers
Had you shown the printed article, which I

12 Feb   1 p 4to   Osb
from Stephen Allen
It is in truth with no slight hesitation that I

21 Feb   6 p 4to   Osb
from George M Musgrave
The letter-press accompanying this

13 May   2 p 4to   Osb
from Solomon Alexander Hart
I purpose visiting some of the Cathedrals in

21 June   2 p 4to   Osb
from William Henry, 3rd Baron Lyttel-
    ton
I spoke to the Chancellor yesterday about you.

3 July   1 p 8vo   Osb
to Thomas Joseph Pettigrew
I beg to thank you for your kind Note & its

11 JY 1833 pmk   3 p 4to   Osb
from T W C Edwards
Dr George Matthews is no more — the Revᵈ.

30 July   4 p 4to   Osb
from Richard Twining Jr
I did not mean to be so long before I write to

22 Sept   2 p 4to   Osb
from Richard Twining Jr
When I sent my last packet I little thought it

2 Oct   4 p 8vo   Osb
from John Kaye
Tho' I could have wished it to be otherwise I

2 Oct   2 p 4to   NYPL(B)
to [Mr Norton]
Circumstances & considerations of various

3 Nov   2 p 4to   Comyn
from Martin Davy
Sʳ. Henry Halford has been here,

25 Nov   3 p 8vo   Osb
from John Kaye
Jack informed us that in the first instance he

10 Dec   2 p 8vo   Osb
from William Wyon
I have been reproaching myself many times

1834

14 Jan   4 p 8vo   Osb
from John Kaye
I doubt not that your time and thoughts are

17 Jan   2 p 4to   Osb
from J S Cotman [to CPB?]
As I cannot afford to lose a Friend. allow me

27 MR 1834 pmk   3 p 8vo   Osb
from R G Greville
I was rejoiced to see again your handwriting,

29 Apr   1 p 4to   Osb
from Sir Francis Chantrey
I have the pleasure to inform you that you are

3 May   1 p 8vo   Osb
to Thomas Joseph Pettigrew
With very many thanks for your kindness in

20 May   2 p 8vo   Osb
from John Kaye
I am sorry that I missed you when you called

26 May   1 p 4to   Osb
from H ⟨Klaprotky⟩
D'après une note que je viens de

6 June   3 p 4to   Osb
from Thomas Rickman
Thy very kind favor of 22ᵈ Ult. has reached

4 Sept   pmk 1834   1 p 4to   Osb
from T F Dibden
Behold! — I will make the most interesting

22 Dec   2 p 8vo   Osb
from Charles Richard Sumner
Herewith I send the correct list of the Surrey

1834, continued

[post 1834]   3 p 8vo   Osb
from Samuel Prout
There is but one other most kind friend to

⟨7 Jan⟩ [pre 1835]   1 p 8vo   Osb
from William Linley
I am sorry to say that a sudden and sharp

13 Jan [pre 1835]   3 p 8vo   Osb
from W[illiam] Linley
My conscience will not suffer me to let you

1835

2 Jan   2 p 4to   Osb
from T F Dibden
It is essential that I should write to You — not

2 Feb   3 p 4to   Osb
from Thomas Rickman
I am so fully convinced that thou must have

3 Feb   2 p 8vo   Osb
from Sir John Taylor Coleridge
I have longed to answer your very kind and

5 Mar   4 p 8vo & 4to   BM
to Stacey Grimaldi
Your kind note, for which

18 Mar   1 p 8vo & 4to cover   BM
to Stacey Grimaldi
The Petition for the ⟨Gravesend⟩ Railway

19 Mar   3 p 8vo & 4to   BM
to Stacey Grimaldi
I made a vain effort to find you

1 Apr   1 p 8vo & 4to cover   BM
to [Stacey Grimaldi]
You are once more, I suppose, fixed

4 Apr   2 p 8vo & 4to   BM
to Stacey Grimaldi
I am extremely sorry, that your

14 Apr   1 p 8vo & 4to cover   BM
to Stacey Grimaldi
A Committee is to meet here

15 Apr   3 p 8vo & 4to   BM
to Stacey Grimaldi
Let me first thank you

13 May   1 p 8vo   HSP
to Francis Boott
Dr. Burney presents his compliments to Mr.

6 June   1 p 8vo   Osb
to Thomas Joseph Pettigrew
Assuredly it is my full hope & intention to

18 Nov [post 1835]   2 p 8vo   Osb
from Alexander Baring, Baron Ashbur-
     ton
The application to me by your note received

1836

15 Feb   3 p 8vo   BM
to Stacey Grimaldi
I think it my duty to let you

10 Apr   2 p 8vo   Osb
with Frances (Young) Burney to Anne
     (Warner) Burney
Your Uncle & I have thought again & again,

2 May   2 p 8vo   Osb
to Thomas Joseph Pettigrew
Many thanks for your kindness in sending me

3 June   1 p 8vo   Osb
to Thomas Joseph Pettigrew
The Bp. of Llandaff has some months ago found

30 Aug   1 p 8vo   HEH
to [William Upcott]
Accept, I beg, my very best thanks for your

13 Oct [post 1836]   4 p 8vo   Osb
from Edward Maltby
I have received your acceptable present of the

11 Nov [post 1836]   4 p 8vo   Osb
from Edward Maltby
My letters are like Angels' visits, in that they

1837

23 Jan   3 p fol   Osb
from Thomas Rickman
I think when I was favoured with thy kind visit

18 Feb   2 p 8vo   Osb
to Thomas Joseph Pettigrew
Very many thanks for your kindness in thinking

6 June   1 p 8vo   Osb
to Thomas Joseph Pettigrew
I shall be at my Post, — as in duty bound, —

19 June   1 p 8vo   Osb
to Anne (Warner) Burney
My Birth-day Offering, — accidentally, but

12 Aug   1 p 4to   Osb
from V Lagrencé
J'ai beaucoup entendu parler de votre belle

26 Oct   1 p 4to   Osb
from M J Routh
My rule is, to admit as a Candidate for a Day's

[Aug pre 1838]   4 p 4to   Osb
from Alexander Crombie
I perceive, by the Professor's letter, that he

1838

3 Mar   3 p 8vo   Osb
to Thomas Joseph Pettigrew
Cordially let me thank you for your very kind

9 Mar   3 p 4to   Osb
from CBFB
My very dear Nephew, for very dear you are

11 Mar   3 p 4to   Osb
from S P Rigaud
You only did me justice in thinking that I

10 May   3 p 4to   Osb
from Samuel Prout
The question has no doubt been asked why has

25 May   1 p 8vo   draft   inc   Osb
to Lord ?
These few lines are merely to say, that Dinner

1 Nov   3 p 8vo   Osb
to Thomas Joseph Pettigrew
What is Club Law for the Class of *Non*

1 Dec   2 p 4to   NYPL(B)
to CFBt
You judged most rightly, & most kindly

1839

12 SP 1839 pmk   2 p 4to   Osb
from Henry Crabb Robinson
I have read over with attention and interest the

25 SP 1839 pmk   4 p fol   Osb
from Martin Charles Burney
Since writing my last letter to you Mr Turner

30 Sept   1 p fol   Osb
from Martin Charles Burney
Alfred Turner has written to me that he has had

8 Nov 183[9 misdated 8]   1 p fol   Osb
from Alfred Turner
We have this morning received from Mr

29 Nov   3 p fol   Osb
from Martin Charles Burney
I have received a long letter from Barrett, full

11 DE 1839 pmk   2 p 4to   Osb
from Samuel Prout
I expect to be in Town tomorrow evening, it

18 Dec   1 p 4to   Osb
from Henry Barrett
In order to cut short any further delay,

25 Dec   3 p 4to   Osb
from Martin Charles Burney
It has not been in my power to sit down

1839, continued

26 Dec   1 p 4to   draft   Osb
to Henry Barrett
You must, I fear, have thought me not only

27 Dec   3 p 4to   BM(Bar)
to CFBt
I think it only my duty as a Trustee in a matter,

28 Dec   2 p 8vo   Osb
from C J Blomfield
'We shall be happy to see you on the 10th. &

1840

1 Jan   draft   2 p 8vo   Osb
to Samuel Whitlock Gandy
In the account of myself & of my Cousins, Mr.

3 Jan   4 p 4to   Osb
from Henry Barrett to CPB & Martin
      Charles Burney
I must take it for granted that you have read

10 June   2 p 4to   Comyn
from Edward Francesco Burney
I went to the Atheneum on Friday the fifth

4 Oct [1840]   2 p 8vo   Osb
from Edward Maltby
No one of your friends could receive with more

8 Oct   3 p 8vo   Camb(T)
to Christopher Wordsworth
Accept, I beg, my best thanks for your kind &

9 Oct   4 p 4to   Osb
from Samuel Prout
If I tell you all the truth, you will scarcely

5 Nov   3 p 8vo   Osb
to A V Copley Fielding
One & all of us exclaimed on receipt of your

10 Nov   1 p 8vo   Osb
to Thomas Joseph Pettigrew
Unexpectedly, — & much to my annoyance, —

15 Dec   3 p 8vo   Osb
from Josiah Forshall
I am directed by the Trustees to request your

[post 1840]   3 p 12mo   Osb
from John Mitford
I venture once more to trouble you touching

18 July [post 1840]   2 p 8vo   Osb
from C G Lynn Fryer
I desire most sincerely to thank you for yr

[post 1840]   1 p 4to   Osb
from Henry Philpott
It is desirable that the plan, if submitted to the

1841

7 Jan   4 p 8vo   Ryl
to [Frances Paulet Wood]
Baby-bo's Birthday, & not a line from Grand-Pa

6 Aug   3 p 8vo   Osb
from John Mitford
I wish you would be kind enough to excuse this

10 Aug   1 p 8vo   Osb
to John Mitford
How much pleasure in promoting your kind

21 Aug   1 p 8vo   Osb
to John Mitford
Did you get my Answer to your Enquiry

21 Aug   2 p 8vo   Osb
from John Mitford
I have many thanks to give you for your kind,

23 Aug   3 p 8vo   Osb
to John Mitford
Your very friendly Note reached me this

27 Aug   1 p 8vo   Osb
to Thomas Joseph Pettigrew
You will oblige me, — if it be not already done

21 Sept   1 p 8vo   Osb
to John Mitford
I have been hoping to hear from you; — about

5 Oct   4 p 4to   Osb
from Henry John Rose
I beg to return you my best thanks for a copy

11 Oct   4 p 8vo   Osb
from Sir John Taylor Coleridge
Many thanks for your charge which has just

12 Oct   4 p 8vo   Osb
from John Lonsdale
On my return to this place last week, I found

20 Oct   3 p 4to   Osb
from John Lynes
Thank you again & again for your excellent

20 Oct   4 p 8vo   Osb
from John Mitford
I have to account to you for my long Silence,

16 Nov   4 p 8vo   Osb
to John Mitford
You have not, I am sure, done me the very great

1842

13 Jan   1 p 8vo   APS
to John Edward Gray
I am quite sorry, that you are too late in the

2 Apr   3 p 8vo   Osb
from W J Copeland
I seem quite unable to help writing to you,

23 May   3 p 8vo   Osb
from H E Manning
It was not until some time after the arrival of

21 Oct   4 p 8vo   Osb
to Thomas Joseph Pettigrew
It has caused me many a pang, before I

27 Oct   3 p 8vo   Osb
to Thomas Joseph Pettigrew
There is some satisfaction in knowing, that you

10 Nov   3 p 8vo   Osb
to Thomas Joseph Pettigrew
I thought of you, & of those, who gathered

5 Dec   4 p 8vo   Osb
to Anne Hayman
Your warm-hearted, affectionate Letter ought

1843

7 Feb   2 p 8vo   Osb
to Mrs Pond
You are, — may I be permitted plainly, —

22 Feb   4 p 8vo   Osb
from John Kaye
When you see Dr Walton, thank him in my

4 Mar   3 p 8vo   Osb
from H E Manning
I have to thank you for the two notes, & for

30 May   1 p 8vo   Osb
from Henry Philpott
I have received a begging letter from a person

1844

27 Apr   1 p 8vo   Osb
to William Thomas Brande
Should you be at the Athenium-Ballot on

5 Aug   4 p 4to   Osb
from Aubrey George Spencer
Your very kind and welcome letter of the

10 Aug   1 p 8vo   Osb
to Thomas Joseph Pettigrew
Will you trust me for a Guinea, until we meet

14 Aug   3 p 8vo   Osb
to Thomas Joseph Pettigrew
From this Bœotian neighborhood you must not,

17 Aug   4 p 8vo   Osb
to Thomas Joseph Pettigrew
I am very troublesome, and you have

30 Aug   3 p 8vo   Osb
to Thomas Joseph Pettigrew
Your friendly *Notuscle* followed me hither,

7 Sept   1 p 8vo   Osb
to Thomas Joseph Pettigrew
Your Letter, — friendly and cordial as its

10 Oct   4 p 8vo   Osb
from Christopher Wordsworth
Allow me to offer my very Sincere thanks for

2 Dec   2 p 8vo   Osb
from C J Blomfield
Mr Dalton has forwarded to me your kind letter

1845

5 Apr   3 p 8vo   Osb
from Thomas Turton
Pray accept my best thanks for your kind

4 June   1 p 8vo   Osb
from Christopher Wordsworth
I am extremely obliged by your very kind

1 Aug   1 p 8vo   Osb
from C J Blomfield
It is very forgetful of me — but I cannot

8 Aug   2 p 8vo   Osb
from C J Blomfield
It has just occurred to me that if you are not

8 Sept   4 p 4to   Osb
from George Shepherd [to CPB?]
It was very kind in the Knaresbro' Host and

1846

4 Jan   3 p 8vo   Osb
from George Murray
I hope you have by this time recovered from

26 Jan   2 p 8vo   Osb
from George Murray
I shall be happy to see you at Danbury on

13 Mar   1 p 8vo   Osb
from C J Blomfield
I have directed my Bankers to pay £200 to your

21 Apr   2 p 4to   Osb
from John Graham
The marble stone, with the inscription which

18 May   1 p 8vo   Vas
to ?
I write to acknowledge with my best thanks

[13 Aug 1846]   2 p 8vo   Osb
from George Murray
We arrived here Saturday evening from

19 Aug   4 p 12mo   Osb
from John Mitford
I have many thanks to return for your obliging

2 Nov   4 p 8vo   Osb
from John Mitford
I only got your obliging Letter this morning,

20 Nov   4 p 8vo   Osb
from John Kaye
I had heard of your lameness; but until I

4 Dec   1 p 4to   Osb
from H M Clark
Miss Burney has returned from Cambridge

1847

3 Feb   5 p 8vo   Osb
from John Kaye
Many thanks for Your congratulations. We

7 July   4 p 8vo   Osb
from Sir John Taylor Coleridge
I venture upon the strength of old friendship to

25 July   2 p 8vo   Osb
from Sir John Taylor Coleridge
I have not found time to thank you for your

1 Oct   4 p 4to   Osb
from Henry Philpott
I owe you great apology for having allowed so

1848

9 Jan   4 p 8vo   Osb
from Hugh Chambers Jones
Very glad was I to receive Your letter — and

28 Feb   4 p 8vo   Osb
to John Mitford
By this post I write to my kind Friend at

20 Mar   3 p 8vo   Osb
to John Mitford
I must, I fear, in the whirlwind of removal

21 Mar   3 p 8vo   Osb
from John Graham
I beg to thank you very sincerely for your kind

19 Sept   3 p 8vo   Osb
from William Daniel Conybeare
It is some years since we <have> met — but

4 Oct   3 p 8vo   Osb
from John Mitford
I must now commence the printing of the Gray

5 Oct   2 p 8vo   Lewis
to John Mitford
The Post of to-day brought me your interesting

1<0> Oct   1 p 8vo   Lewis
to John Mitford
The Inclosed has been forwarded to me hither

26 Dec   3 p 8vo   Osb
from William Daniel Conybeare
at this season especially which reminds one of

29 Dec   1 p 8vo   Osb
from H H Thomas
This letter went down to Torquay for me, but

30 Dec   1 p 8vo   Osb
to William Daniel Conybeare
I thank you heartily . . . hardly more . . . for

1849

27 Aug   3 p 8vo   Osb
from George Murray
We are involved in disagreeable mess with M^rs

7 Nov   2 p 8vo   Oxf(Bod)
to Henry Hart Milman
When I look back upon by-gone days, &

12 Nov [1849]   3 p 8vo   Osb
from Henry Hart Milman
I could receive the congratulations of few older

10 Nov [post 1849]   3 p 8vo   Comyn
from Henry Hart Milman [to CPB?]
Singularly enough mother's God-daughter

1850

11 Feb   photostat   3 p 8vo   Lewis
from John Mitford
I am bound in gratitude to write to you, and in

16 Feb   1 p 8vo   Osb
to Mrs Hudson
Your kindness is very great, — the temptation

18 Feb   3 p 12mo   Osb
to CB IV
The Quit Note from the new Rectory is to my

23 Apr   1 p 8vo   Osb
from C J Blomfield
I like your Address to the B^p. of Rochester, and

24 Aug   1 p 4to   Osb
from James Haliburton
I am no letter writer at any time — and

[23 Sept 1850]   2 p 8vo   Osb
from George Murray
I have sent a surplice to be Exchanged for my

<3> Oct   1 p 8vo   Osb
from C J <Thorne>
Your kind order came to hand this morning, &

4 Oct   draft   2 p 8vo   Osb
to W K Borton
Your silence was but too significant, — & the

23 Oct   4 p 8vo   NYPL(B)
to CFBt
We have been staying at Fulham,

27 Dec   1 p 8vo   Osb
from Henry Jarvis
As the Clerical Association Secretary to the

[c 1850]   3 p 8vo   Osb
from George Murray
I heartily wish that you could have given me

[pre 1851]   photostat 3 p 8vo   Lewis
from John Mitford
Your kindness in thinking of me in all your

1851

1 Jan   draft   1 p 8vo   Osb
to Henry Brown
Most heartily do I congratulate you & your

28 Apr   1 p 8vo   Osb
to Mr Harvey
I have some notion that there is already some

23 May   3 p 8vo   Lewis
to John Mitford
I am quite ashamed of making such tardy

15 Aug   1 p 8vo   Camb(T)
to William Whewell
I am quite ashamed of having inadvertently

1851   1 p 8vo   Osb
from John Mitford
As I must send this to the Mason,

1852

15 May   2 p 8vo   Osb
from John Mitford
You will be grieved to hear that Mr

14 Aug   2 p 8vo   Osb
from A V Copley Fielding
I have just returned to Worthing with my

25 Oct   4 p 8vo   Osb
from John Kaye
Mr <Sturman> is what he represents himself

16 Nov   mutilated   ½ 4to   Osb
from ?
We have received your favor of the 15th

[c 1852?]   3 p 12mo   Osb
from John Mitford
I should feel truly obliged if you would have

1853

24 Feb [1853]   3 p 8vo   Osb
from William Frederic John Kaye
You have already learnt from my sister, how

28 Feb   draft 2 p ½ 4to   Osb
to William Frederic John Kaye
By a most unfortunate accident your Letter of

2 Mar [1853]   3 p 8vo   Osb
from E D Mortlock
You will, I know, be desirous to know how all

24 June   3 p 8vo   Osb
from David Williams
The Election begins on Monday the 11th. & the

18 July   draft   1 p 8vo   Osb
to Thomas Hepworth
I was not on the late Commtee for the Selection

1854

1 May   4 p 8vo   Osb
from William Hale Hale
You will be glad to hear that all the

11 Dec   1 p 8vo   Osb
from John William Colenso
I beg to thank you most sincerely, on behalf

1855

17 Feb   4 p 8vo   Osb
from George Murray
There are some Institutions to vacant Livings

1857

10 Feb   2 p 8vo   Osb
from William Ayrton
I have delayed acknowledging your letter of

24 Mar   4 p 12mo   Osb
to CB IV
My chief purpose in writing to you is to have

1 Apr   4 p 8vo   Osb
to CB IV
I am better, — but stupid, — & little worth.

4 Apr   3 p 8vo   Osb
to CB IV
We do not, I fear, get on quite cleverly, on

23 May   2 p 8vo   Osb
to Henry Philpott
My absence from home on my Visitations alone

30 Oct   3 p 8vo   Osb
from William Gilson Humphry
I thank you much for your letter. It is indeed

20 Nov   4 p 12mo   NYPL(B)
to CB IV
We all grieve, that you cannot

27 Nov   3 p 8vo   Osb
from William Gilson Humphry
Upon receiving your letter forwarded to me by

1858

14 May   4 p 12mo   Osb
to CB IV
Here I am, dearest Charles, & have left the

22 June   4 p 8vo   Osb
to CB IV
Dearest Madre, who is pronounced by her

26 Aug   2 p 8vo   Osb
to CB IV
We are comforted this morning by another

24 Sept   4 p 8vo   Osb
to CB IV
I found with pleasure your Letter, awaiting my

16 Oct   1 p 12mo   Roch
to Charles Alfred L'Oste
Pardon my troubling you with your Paper of

21 Dec   1 p 8vo   Osb
from C J ⟨Ellicott⟩ to [CPB?]
Our friend Prof^r. Browne was kind enough to

[c 1858]   4 p 12mo   Osb
to CB IV
I return, with many thanks, the very gratifying

1859

18 Mar   2 p 8vo   Osb
to CB IV
Among the manifold & great mercies

1860

31 Mar   3 p 8vo   Osb
from C[harles] Forster
I feel that I should be wronging your long-tried

8 May   4 p 8vo   Osb
from Joseph Cotton Wigram
One scrap, my dear Archdeacon, to express the

20 July [1860]   3 p 4to   Osb
from Sarah (Burney) Payne
I want you very much to come to my help —

5 Sept   3 p 8vo   Osb
from Joseph Cotton Wigram
Your kind wish to have me with you at the

1860, continued

17 Sept   2 p 8vo   Ryl
to [Frances Paulet Wood]
Let me be the FIRST to draw a Cheque in

28 Sept   4 p 8vo   Osb
from John James
Truly do I thank You, as for bearing me in

3 Nov   4 p 8vo   Osb
from John James
Though my letter will not be posted till

1861

1 May   4 p 8vo   Osb
to CB IV
The Inclosed took me by surprize this Morning,

13 May   3 p 8vo   Osb
from Joseph Cotton Wigram
Archdeacon Grant, as you Know, is interested

7 July   1 p 8vo   Osb
from Charles Forster
I cannot refrain from writing a Sabbath Day's

20 July   3 p 8vo   Osb
from Joseph Cotton Wigram
You have probably been aware of your *brothers*

26 Nov   2 p 8vo   Osb
from W L Leitch
I am quite grieved that you should have been

1862

6 Feb   4 p 8vo   Osb
from William Hale Hale
Having failed to see you and heard nothing

29 Sept   1 p 8vo   Osb
to —— Colnaghi
Kindly excuse my troubling you to answer

9 Oct   3 p 8vo   Osb
from James Holland
It affords me much pleasure once again to see

undated

?   1 p 8vo   Osb
to   ?
My Master & my Host sends you very kind

FRANCES BENTLEY (YOUNG) BURNEY c 1792–1878

See also letters to CFBt and letters from CPB, EBB.

[Dec? 1826–27?]   1 p 4to   Osb
from Charles Wild
Your Note did not reach me until late on

19 May 1822   3 p 8vo   Osb
from George M Musgrave
I send you your Album, the perusal of whose

24 July 1822   3 p 4to   Osb
from Dr Benjamin Travers
I am much gratified by your favorable report

31 Mar   pmk [1825]   2 p 4to   Osb
from Paul Sandby Munn
I hasten to acknowledge with our best &

15 Apr 1825   3 p 4to   Osb
from Frances Anne (Burney) Wood
I received the parcel last night, and I am very

10 June 1825   1 p 4to   Osb
from CB IV
Our Midsummer Holidays will begin on

11 July 1825   4 p 4to   Osb
from CB IV & F E Hall
I must not praise myself but hope Miss Hall

[9 Nov] 1826   1 p 8vo   Osb
from J[ohn Bowyer] Nichols
Mr Nichols presents his kind Respects to Dr.

10 June 1828   1 p 4to   Osb
from CB IV
With no small pleasure do I take up my pen

4 May 1829   1 p 4to   Osb
from Filippo Pistrucci
E vero che io andava a Blackeath da Mrs

[1830–36]   2 p 4to   Osb
from Edward Kaye Burney
I have now a very good opportunity to have

[c 1832?]   1 p 8vo   Osb
from E H Locker
So — I find your gudeman has told you

4 Apr 1835   copy extract   2 p 8vo
to AA   BM(Bar)
. . . My friend MAS is very good & we often

2 ⟨Dec⟩ 1862   2 p 8vo   Osb
from Sir James Prior
Sir James Prior presents his compliments and

16 Mar [1864–78]   3 p 8vo   Liv(U)
to [Allen Page Moor]
I am much obliged to you for your kind note

18 Mar [1864–78]   3 p 8vo   Liv(U)
to [Allen Page Moor]
Pray accept my best thanks for the Autographs

14 July 1865   2 p 8vo   Osb
from Joseph Cotton Wigram
Your kind & liberal Contribution to the

18⟨71⟩   4 p 8vo   Osb
to ?
I beg to offer to you my Apologies for not

?   2 p 4to   Osb
from M L Randolph
I am desired by my Friend Mrs. ⟨Vigor⟩ to

IV

See also letters to and from FBA, letters to CB, CB Jr, CPB and CFBt, and letters from M d'A.

Holograph works, documents and other material of James Burney are located in the following collections: Berg; British Museum; Mitchell Library; Osborn; Pierpont Morgan; Public Record Office; Royal Society.

1772

18 Nov   1 p fol   PML
from James Cook
Whereas I have appointed the Second

1781

18 June   copy   3 p 4to   PML
to Molyneux, 1st Baron Shuldham
I take the liberty to lay before your Lordship

7 July   copy   1 p fol   PML
from Philip Stephens (included in JB
       to CB 16 July 1781)
My Lords Commissioners of the Admiralty

1782

24 June   2 p 4to   PML
from Samuel Johnson
The Bearer is the young Man whom I have

21 Aug   2 p 4to   PML
from Alexander Dalrymple
I send you some Plans of parts on the Coast of

2 July   2 p 4to   PML
from John Montagu, 4th Earl of Sand-
     wich
as I am informed that you are destined for the

13 Sept [1782]   1 p 4to   PML
from John Jervis, Viscount St Vincent
Dear Sir! you will oblige me very much by

1783

17 Apr   4 p fol   Osb
to Philip Stephens
My last Letter dated Dec^br. 17th. 1782 from

7 May   4 p 4to   PML
to [CB?]
I have now been 3 weeks in India and feel

1784

9 Aug   2 p 4to   PML
from John Montagu, 4th Earl of Sand-
     wich
I yesterday received a letter from Captain

1 Dec   3 p 4to   PML
from Sir Edward Hughes
Being to sail for England this morning

1786

4 May   2 p 4to   PML
from Samuel Gambier
I made an attempt to see you when you was

1791

26 July ? Mag20
from William Bligh
. . . Among the things which I wish to remark

5 Sept 3 p 4to NSW
to Sir Joseph Banks
The first proof came to me only this morning,

also copy 2 p fol BM(NH)

13 Oct copy 3 p fol BM(NH)
to Sir Joseph Banks
I hoped I should have been able to have gone

22 Oct 3 p 4to HSP
to Sir Joseph Banks
I am so much gratified by your approbation of

also copy 2 p fol BM(NH)

1795

9 Mar 1 p 4to PRO
to [Sir Evan Nepean]
I take the liberty, in consequence of the notice

1796

6 May 1 p 8vo PML
from Marquis de Lally-Tollendal
a sudden emergency compels me to go to

5 Nov 1 p 4to PRO
to [Sir Evan Nepean]
I beg the favour of you to lay this, my request

[post 1796?] 1 p 4to Comyn
to [SHB]
M^r. Payne has settled for us to go to

1797

15 June copy 4 p fol PML
to George, 2nd Earl Spencer
It is with considerable embarrassment that I

1798

22 July ? AECB31
from Molesworth Phillips
I feel myself infinitely obliged to you for your

[pre 2 Sept 1798] 1 p 4to BM(Bar)
to Maria (Allen) Rishton (on p 1 M
    Rishton to FBA [2 Sept 1798])
"Dear Mrs R. Be so kind to give the inclosed

1801

6 Jan 1 p 4to PRO
to [Sir Evan Nepean]
I beg leave to renew my application to the

[25 Jan 1801] 1 p 8vo BM
to Thomas Poole
I have not the pleasure of being acquainted

8 Oct 1 p 4to PML
from Thomas Coke, 1st Earl of Leicester
    of Holkham
Every good Citizen must rejoice in the blessings

1802

[post 1802?] draft 2 p 4to PML
to Adam Ivan Krusenstern
When I received your Letter which I did with

[post 1802?] 1 p 8vo Osb
to S[haron?] Turner
M^r. Murray has made a proposition which if

1803

14 Mar   1 p 4to   PRO
to Sir Evan Nepean
I beg the favour of you to acquaint the Lords

[27? July 1803]   4 p 4to   HEH
with Charles Lamb to John Rickman
We are at Cowes, the whole flock, Sheep and

[1803?]   1 p 8vo   PML
from Adam Ivan Krusenstern
According to your kind promise of the

1804

24 Jan   4 p 4to   HEH
with John Rickman to Robert Southey
My old friends the Friendly islanders I see

27 Mar   3 p 4to   HEH
to Robert Southey
Having learnt from our friend Rickman that

22 June   3 p fol   PRO
to William Marsden
I request the favour of you to lay the enclosed

1805

1 Aug   3 p 4to   HEH
to Robert Southey
I am in the hands of the Printer and his devils,

1–13 Sept   2 p 4to   HEH
from Adam Ivan Krusenstern
If I have not wrote you yet, it is I assure you

1806

29 Apr   2 p 4to   PRO
to [William Marsden]
I addressed a Letter to the Board of Admiralty,

30 May   1 p 4to   PRO
to [William Marsden]
It gives me concern to find that my

30 June   copy   1 p 4to   NYPL(B)
from John Jervis, Viscount St Vincent
          (included in ALS JB to FBA 21
          Dec 1817)
I do assure you that I have not received the

29 Dec   1 p 4to   PML
from John Jervis, Viscount St Vincent
Whenever I am referr^d to, I shall be ready to

1807

1 Jan   2 p 4to   PRO
to William Marsden
I beg you will do me the favour to acquaint

1808

15 July   4 p fol   LC
to William Wellesley-Pole, Earl of
     Mornington
Understanding that the Board of Admiralty

1809

4–9 Mar   3 p 4to   HEH
with John Rickman to Robert Southey
The Article of the Cid had not been disposed

1812

15 Jan   2 p 4to   Hyde
to — Allen
I am taking a liberty for which I know not how

1815

17 May   copy   1 p 4to   PML
to William Hazlitt
It would be strange, if not wrong, after years

1816

5 Oct   2 p 4to   NYPL(B)
to M d'A
I have just time to catch at an opportunity to

1817

July   1 p 4to   PML
from Jean-Pierre Abel-Rémusat
As it is your capital work I have acquired

24 Nov   copy   2 p fol   PML
to John Pond
So long as forty years ago I adopted

31 Dec   2 p 8vo   PML
from Thomas Coke, 1st Earl of Leicester
    of Holkham
I have to <return> you my best thanks for

[1817]   1 p 4to   PML
from Thomas Coke, 1st Earl of Leicester
    of Holkham
I would have you wait upon Ld St Vincent to

[1817]   ?   AECB31
with Sarah (Payne) Burney to Sarah
    (Burney) Payne
Your Mother has brought to town with her my

1818

27 Jan   3 p 4to   PML
from Adam Ivan Krusenstern
It is highly provoking that the letter you have

5 May   1 p 4to   NYPL(B)
to AA
I just learn from my Sister Burney that what

13 Aug   3 p 4to   PML
from Adam Ivan Krusenstern
Your letter of the 29 April reached me late in

29 Nov   3 p 4to   PML
from Adam Ivan Krusenstern
It is so long my dear Sir, since I wrote to you,

30 DE 1818 pmk   1 p 4to   PML
from Conrad Malte-Brun & J B Eyries
Nous avons l'honneur de vous addresser ci-

1819

27 July   2 p 4to   PML
from James Rennell
I fear you have long since set me down for a

20 Dec   4 p 4to   PML
from Adam Ivan Krusenstern
It is now upwards of a twelve month since I

1820

4 Aug   1 p 4to & fol   PML
from William IV (Duke of Clarence)
In answer to yours of 2ᵈ instant I can easily

5 Aug   ?   AECB31
to William IV (Duke of Clarence)
Whatsoever may be the fortune of my petition,

⟨18⟩ Aug   1 p 4to   NYPL(B)
to CBFB
Your letter for Esther has not come

29 [Aug]   2 p 4to   NYPL(B)
to CBFB
I thank you for the trouble you have taken

9 Nov   ½ p 4to   Osb
to ?
I have not been able to send you the paper

1821

23 AP 1821 pmk   ?   AECB31
with Sarah (Payne) Burney to John &
     Sarah (Burney) Payne
We received Sarah's letter after common post

[May 1821]   ?   AECB31
to John Payne
. . . They gave me and Mrs. B. ten days good

20 June   1 p 4to   PML
from William IV (Duke of Clarence)
In answer to yours I am <   > that I have

28 June   ?   AECB31
to John Payne
Your letters are not tiresome, but they are very

19 July   ?   AECB31
to John Payne
[no text available]

19 Nov   4 p 4to   PML
from Adam Ivan Krusenstern
The last letter I had the pleasure to receive

SARAH (PAYNE) BURNEY c 1758–1832

1 July 1781   2 p 4to   Essex
from Samuel Crisp to [Patricia Payne]
     & Sarah (Payne) Burney
Kate has got an Inflammation in her Eyes, &

10 July 1781   1 p 4to   Essex
from Samuel Crisp to [Patricia Payne]
     & Sarah (Payne) Burney
I have the Pleasure to inform You, that our

17 Sept 1782   1 p 4to   Essex
from Samuel Crisp
We last night reced the Pacquet mention'd in

31 Dec 1795   1 p 4to   PML
from Marquis de Lally-Tollendal
The Princess is very, very sorry she cannot

30 Aug [1814?]   1 p 4to   Comyn
to [EBB?]
It is with much reluctance that I write to say

[26 or 27 Apr 1821]   ?   AECB31
to Sarah (Burney) Payne
Aunt Sally [SHB] and I dined with the Lambs

17 Aug [1821]   ?   AECB31
to Sarah (Burney) Payne
. . . on this same day there has been exhibited

[c 24 Aug 1821]   ?   AECB31
to Sarah (Burney) Payne
. . . he [JB] talks of wintering at Lisbon or

Aug 1821   ?   AECB31
with Martin Burney to Sarah (Burney)
     Payne
They use me very badly for the Postman's last

1828   copy?   1 p 8vo   Buff
to Martin Charles Burney
I have packed up for tomorrow to go to

Sarah (Burney) Payne 1796 – post 1867

4 Sept 1813   2 p 4 to   BM(Bar)
to CBFB
Papa bids me say, Martin shall see after the

24 Aug [1818]   4 p fol   NYPL(B)
to MF with CBFB to MF & HHBt
Oweing to some queerality or other, *both* y^r.

17 Sept pmk 1823 4 p 4to NYPL(B)
to Sarah (Payne) Burney
My dearest Mamma — It was the very greatest

[July 1829?]   5 p 4to   NYPL(B)
to HHBt
Every moment I can spare from the darling

3 Aug [1831?]   4 p 4to   NYPL(B)
to Frances (Phillips) Raper
You cannot think with how much pleasure I

[post June 1833] 1 p 8vo NYPL(B)
from Lady Caroline Morrison
As Madame d'Arblay is so kind as to consent

22 Aug [1858]   3 p 8vo   Wms
to Henry Crabb Robinson
Returning to London from a country visit, I

28 Aug pmk 1860 4 p 8vo NYPL(B)
to Henry Hart Milman
I have not been unmindful of my engagement

10 Sept 1861   4 p 8vo   Wms
to Henry Crabb Robinson
I am too pleased to be your correspondent

20 Dec 1861   4 p 8vo   Wms
to Henry Crabb Robinson
Your letter was a great pleasure to me

V

SUSANNA ELIZABETH (BURNEY) PHILLIPS 1755–1800

(SEB, SBP)

*See also letters to and from FBA, CB and CB Jr and letters from M d'A,
CBFB, and Maria (Allen) Rishton.*

1777

[post 1777]   3 p 4to   BM(Bar)
from Louisa (Skrine), Lady Clarges
I thank you for your kind letter;

1778

7 Sept   4 p 4to   BM(Bar)
from Catherine (Southwell-Clifford)
    Coussmaker
That Evelina should be the production of the

[c 1778]   4 p 4to   BM(Bar)
from Catherine (Coussmaker) Lindsay
Good God! My Dearest Susy I hope Evelina

1779

29 Jan [1779]   4 p 4to   NYPL(B)
to CAB
I am every minute in hopes of the Baker's

1780

2 [May 1780]   3 p 4to   BM(Bar)
from Louisa (Skrine), Lady Clarges
You are very kind & *tender* my Dear Miss

[21 Sept 1780]   4 p 4to   BM(Bar)
to CAB
Your clever, goodhumour'd, comical Letter

29 [Sept or Dec 1780]   4 p 4to
                                  BM(Bar)
from Louisa (Skrine), Lady Clarges
I was eccessively [sic] sorry to miss seeing of

[1780]   1 p 4to   BM(Bar)
from Louisa (Skrine), Lady Clarges
Huzza huzza, I am so happy Pachierotti is

1782

9 May [1782]   1 p 4to   NYPL(B)
from James Hutton to SBP & Moles-
    worth Phillips
I <read> dear C. Philips Lr. just now & went

10 July [1782]   3 p 4to   NYPL(B)
to CAB
Your letter has been a day later in coming

23 July   6 p 4to   BM(Bar)
from Catherine (Coussmaker) Lindsay
'Tis an awkward thing I am going to do

24 July   6 p 4to & fol   NYPL(B)
from Lady Mary Hales
May I hope my dear Mrs. Phillips that you are

[post Oct 1782]   3 p 4to   BM(Bar)
from Louisa (Skrine), Lady Clarges
We shall set out in a few days

1783

24 July [1783] 2 p 4to Comyn
to Rosette (Rose) Burney
I have just received your letter my dear M^rs.

1 Dec 4 p 4to NYPL(B)
to CAB
I hope I have not trespassed too far on y^r.

1786

9–10 Jan 3 p 4to NYPL(B)
to CBF
If I expected immediate answers to my letters

4 Mar 4 p 4to NYPL(B)
to CBF
Your letter my dearest Charlotte found me

1787

[2 Feb 1787] copy 1 p 4to Osb
from Betty Parker (included in AJS
   SBP to FB 15 Jan 1787 to 17 Feb
   1787)
I hope you will not be angry at my giving you

6 Feb [1787] copy? 4 p 4to Osb
to Charlotte Cambridge
I will not apologize my d^r. Miss Cam: for
also copy 3 p LB Arm

[9? Feb. 1787] 4 p 4to Osb
from Charlotte Cambridge
What can I say my Dear Mrs Phillips that will
also copy 2? p LB Arm

1788

7–11 Sept [1788] 4 p 4to NYPL(B)
to CBF
Has my dear Charlotte thought herself very

1790

26 Apr [1790] 3 p 4to Comyn
to Rosette (Rose) Burney
If my Brother & you have not heard the

1791

16 June [1791] 4 p 4to NYPL(B)
to CBF
I have delayed day after day writing to you

1792

18 [Sept] 4 p 4to NYPL(B)
to CBF
I begin to be anxious for news of you my

3 Nov [1792?] 1 p 4to NYPL(B)
from Anne-Germaine (Necker) de Staël-
   Holstein
je me suis decidée à passer l'hyver en

1793

6 Mar 2 p 4to BM(Bar)
to M d'A
M. d'Arblay must not think the request he had

2 Apr copy 3 p 4to NYPL(B)
to Frederica Locke
I must however say something of Juniper

1794

[Jan 1794]   3 p 4to   NYPL(B)
from Louis, comte de Narbonne-Lara
vous avez bien voulu; avec votre bonté

also   copy   4 p 4to   NYPL(B)

20 Feb [1794]   1 p 4to   NYPL(B)
from Bon-Albert Briois de Beaumetz
je ne comprends pas, Moi même, Madame,

1 July   copy   1 p 4to   NYPL(B)
from Louis, comte de Narbonne-Lara
Je vous ecris d'Utrecht mon aimable soeur

22 Sept   ?   AECB31
to JB?
. . . I hope my dearest James your anxiety for

[23 Sept 1794]   4 p 4to   NYPL(B)
to M d'A
Il n'est pas necessaire de vous dire la peine

[post 28 Dec 1794]   1 p 4to   NYPL(B)
from Frederica Locke
Thank God my dearest Friend I can today

[30? Dec 1794]   1 p 4to   NYPL(B)
to M d'A
I rec^d. this letter last night my dear Brother

[1794]   1 p 4to   PML
from Charles Maurice de Talleyrand-
    Périgord
il faut qu'il y ait eu de l'impossibilité pour ce
also   copy   1 p 4to   NYPL(B)

1795

9 Feb   ?   AECB31
to JB
It seems an age to me since we have seen or

[Feb 1795?]   1 p 4 to   NYPL(B)
to William Locke
I am very sorry my Mitter [sic] Lock it will

13–14 Oct   4 p 4to   NYPL(B)
to Frederica Locke
I do not think I shall feel perfectly settled,

also   copy   4 p LB   Arm

[1 Nov 1795]   1 p 4to   NYPL(B)
from Etiennette, princesse d'Hénin
Ma chere Madame je suis heureuse de pouvoir

8 [Nov 1795]   1 p 8vo   NYPL(B)
from Etiennette, princesse d'Hénin
Les dentelles sont vendues 25 guinées

[Nov 1795]   1 p 4to   NYPL(B)
from Etiennette, princesse d'Hénin
voici ma chere Madame le jupon que

1796

9 JA 1796 pmk   3 p 4to   NYPL(B)
from Etiennette, princesse d'Hénin
j'ai reçu presque en meme tems

13 JA 1796 pmk   2 p 4to   NYPL(B)
from Etiennette, princesse d'Hénin
Ma chere Madame je suis tout a fait honteuse

2⟨9⟩ JA pmk [1796]   3 p 4to
    NYPL(B)
from Etiennette, princesse d'Hénin
Ma chere Madame il faut donc toujours avoir

[Jan 1796]   3 p 4to   NYPL(B)
from Etiennette, princesse d'Hénin
il y à une bonté d'un genre si particulier

[Feb-Mar 1796]   2 p 4to   NYPL(B)
from Etiennette, princesse d'Hénin
Ma chere Madame, seriez vous assez bonne

20–21 Apr [1796]   4 p 8vo   NYPL(B)
from Frederica Locke
my own M^rs. Phillips your dear lines arrived

3 July   3 p 8vo   NYPL(B)
to M d'A
Lest you should have left town before the
also   copy   2 p LB   Arm

[July 1796]   4 p 4to   NYPL(B)
from Etiennette, princesse d'Hénin
jai besoin de vous communiquer toute

2 Aug [1796]   3 p 4to   NYPL(B)
from Etiennette, princesse d'Hénin
Ma chere Madame votre bon coeur souffrira

[Aug 1796]   4 p 4to   NYPL(B)
from Etiennette, princesse d'Hénin
Ma chere Madame votre bonne et tendre

8 Oct   4 p 4to   NYPL(B)
to CBF
I am once more in James Street my dearest

23 Nov   4 p 4to   NYPL(B)
to Frederica Locke
I have already sealed a letter to my dearest
also   copy   6 p LB   Arm

5 Dec   4 p 4to   NYPL(B)
to CBF
I don't know whether Sally has told my dearest

1797

26–28 Oct   4 p 4to   NYPL(B)
to CBF
Tho' I so well know your indulgence my

1798

25 June [1798]   4 p 4to   NYPL(B)
to CBFB
If I were not sure that my dearest Charlotte

1799

31 Mar   4 p 4to   NYPL(B)
to CBFB
I shall a second time, & nearly as innocently

FRANCES (PHILLIPS) RAPER 1782–1860

*See also letters to and from FBA, CFBt, CB, CB Jr, and letters from SHB
and Sarah (Payne) Burney.*

[1800–07]   2 p 4to   Osb
to Rosette (Rose) Burney
The extreme hurry which Grand Papa is in,

9 Apr 1803   2 p 8vo   Osb
to Rosette (Rose) Burney
Grand papa has given me a very difficult task

[1805]   copy   1 p   Osb
from Emma Crewe (included in CB's
    Memoirs)
You cannot I think have more pleasure in

28 Dec [1806]   2 p 8vo   Osb
to Rosette (Rose) Burney
Many thanks for your very kind letter my dear

[6 May 1818]   4 p 4 to   NYPL(B)
to AA
It is not in the vain hope of offering consolation

15 Aug 1826   5 p 4to   NYPL(B)
to HHBt
I will give the first proof of my earnest desire

25 Aug 1826   4 p 4to   NYPL(B)
to HHBt
I am very much concerned to see by your little

11 Sept [1826]   4 p 4to   NYPL(B)
to HHBt
I have this evening received a most kind but

[1826]   4 p 4to   NYPL(B)
to HHBt
I began a long letter which I intend to dedicate

12 Jan   pmk 1831   4 p 4to   BM(Bar)
with Minette (Raper) Kingston to
    JCBTM
As usual your letter ought to have been

12 SE 1832 pmk   4 p 4to   NYPL(B)
to Minette (Raper) Kingston
I am in much sorrow for the loss of my poor

[1834–36]   8 p 8vo   BM(Bar)
to CBFB
How *very very* kind you are my dearest aunt

12 June 1841   4 p 4to   NYPL(B)
to Minette (Raper) Kingston
My own darling Minny what interesting

[post 1841]   2 p 8vo   NYPL(B)
to Minette (Raper) Kingston
My ever Darling Minny will think me cold and

VI

ESTHER (BURNEY) BURNEY 1749–1832
(EBB)

See also letters to and from FBA, CFBt, CB Jr, and CPB and letters from CBFB, and Sarah (Payne) Burney.

Holograph material and documents of this branch of the Burney family are located in the Berg and Barrett collections. Works (drawings etc) by her husband's brother Edward Francesco Burney are to be found in the National Portrait Gallery, Pierpont Morgan Library, and Royal Academy of Arts.

28 Feb 1786   verses   3 p 4to   Osb
from Clement Francis
Tho' I don't think it right, / For *one* Man to

[post 1793]   2 p 8vo   BM(Bar)
from Hester (Mulso) Chapone
You are very kind my dear Madam

[post 1793]   1 p 8vo   BM(Bar)
from Hester (Mulso) Chapone
M^{rs} & Miss Ord are to drink tea with me

3 Mar [1798]   ½ p fol   BM(Bar)
from Hester (Mulso) Chapone
I am made very happy Dear Madam

5 May [1805]   2 p 4to   NYPL(B)
from Marianne (Burney) Bourdois
  (with ALS EBB to Sophia Burney
  8 Dec 1805)
My dear Aunt having kindly offered to send a

8 Dec 1805   1 p 4to   NYPL(B)
to Sophia Burney (with ALS Marianne
  (Burney) Bourdois to EBB 5 May
  [1805])
I consider this Letter as a treasure — it is one

6 Sept 1806   4 p 4to   Osb
from Marianne (Burney) Bourdois
I have already dispatched by different convey-

4 Aug 1816   3 p 4to   BM(Bar)
from Eliza Hill
I feel exceedingly flattered, my dear M^{rs}.

30 Dec 1817   2 p 4to   Osb
to Rosette (Rose) Burney
Without knowing well what to say that has not

1 Mar 1824   4 p 4to   BM(Bar)
from Frances (Sayer) de Pougens
Your charming spirits, your delightful vivacity

10 May 1827   4 p 4to   Osb
to Frances (Young) Burney
I have been in bed these three days with

17 Oct 1828   4 p 4to   BM(Bar)
to CBFB
I am a sad Correspondent Dearest Charlotte

2⟨3⟩ Jan 1829   4 p 4to   NYPL(B)
to CBFB
"Your Letter is before me." — I will not finish

26 Feb 1829   4 p 4to   NYPL(B)
to CBFB
Dearest & truly loved Charlotte. How can I tell

25 Oct 1829   4 p 4to   NYPL(B)
to CBFB
Having a friendly conveyance in mine Eye I sit

CHARLES CRISP BURNEY 1774–1791

Nov 1785   3 p 4to   BM(Bar)
to Richard Allen Burney
I am now encouraged to write to you merely

VII

SARAH HARRIET BURNEY 1772–1844

(SHB)

*See also letters to and from FBA, CFBt, and CB Jr and letters from CB,
JB, and Maria (Allen) Rishton.*

1792

4 Dec   4 p 4to   BM(Bar)
to Mary Young
This will be the *first* letter

[mid-Sept 1792]   2 p 4to   Hilles
to [FB?]
I went away laughing at this good humoured

1793

28 June   4 p 4to   BM(Bar)
to Martha (Allen) Young
My history compared to yours, is such a blank

7 Oct   3 p 4to   BM(Bar)
to Martha (Allen) Young
To a letter so earnest, & pressing as yours

2 Aug   4 p 4to   BM(Bar)
to Mary Young
The date of this letter will surprise you

1794

19 Oct   2 p 4to   Osb
to [SBP]
Look at the edges of this paper — Do you see?

1796

Mar   1 p 4to   NYPL(B)
to CBF
Brava, Brava! Keep it up! I applaud your spirit,

12 Nov   2 p 4to   BM(Bar)
to Martha (Allen) Young
The books you mention were all carefully

10 [Oct 1796]   3 p 4to   BM(Bar)
to [Mary?] Young (with PS by Eliza-
    beth (Allen) Burney)
How in the world came it ever to enter your

12 Dec   2 p 4to   BM(Bar)
to Martha (Allen) Young
According to your directions, received

20 Oct   1 p 4to   BM(Bar)
to Martha (Allen) Young
As a duty, however melancholy and dreadful

29 Dec   2 p 4to   BM(Bar)
to Martha (Allen) Young
I received the favour of your last letter

28 Oct   3 4to   BM(Bar)
to Martha (Allen) Young
Although I flatter myself that by this time

1797

19 Mar [1797]   1 p 4to   BM(Bar)
to Martha (Allen) Young
I sent a note to M^r. Young requesting we might

1798

[2 Sept 1798] copy 1 p fol BM(Bar)
to Molly Waters (included in Maria
    (Allen) Rishton to FBA [3 Sept
    1798])
I beg that when your Master returns you will

22 Oct [1798] copy 1 p fol BM(Bar)
to Molly Waters (included in Maria
    (Allen) Rishton to FBA 23 Oct
    1798)
I am much concerned my dear Molly to hear

1807

[1807–11] 3 p 4to NYPL(B)
to Frances (Phillips) Raper
To my utter surprise, my dear Father

19 Apr [1807–14] 2 p 4to Osb
to ?
Your flattering letter has this moment come to

1808

3 Nov 1 p 4to Osb
to Johann Christian Hüttner
My father would have done himself the

[1808] 2 p 8vo BM(Bar)
to CBFB
My father read your note with the utmost

1809

16 JA 1809 pmk 3 p 8vo Osb
to Johann Christian Hüttner
I beg you will not attribute to negligence or

[pre Nov 1809] 1 p 8vo Osb
from R[ichard] Y[ates?] to [SHB?]
I have very great pleasure in < > the

28 Feb 2 p 4to Osb
to Johann Christian Hüttner
Your letter, with its very punctual enclosure,

14 Nov 3 p 8vo Osb
to Johann Christian Hüttner
My father was much gratified by the

28 May 3 p 8vo Osb
to Johann Christian Hüttner
I have little more to trouble you with than I

1810

[1 Aug 1810] 4 p 4to NYPL(B)
to Henry Barrett (with PS CBFB to
    CFBt)
If Moll's noise, for I am in Chenies Street,

1814

24 Jan 3 p 4to Oxf(Bod)
to Henry Colburn
I hope that considering the thickness of the

1815

4 Oct 3 p 8vo Osb
to Rosette (Rose) Burney
It is possible that you may receive the

1816

[post 1816]   1 p 4to   PML
to ?
You will be concerned to hear, that

1819

30 Mar   4 p 4to   NYPL(B)
to CBFB
No, no, my kindest of Sisters — nor no such a

1820

6 Jan   1 p 8vo   Osb
to Henry Colburn
I venture to inclose a fresh list of books

7 June   2 p 4to   NYPL(B)
to CBFB
When I saw you last, my dear Sister, and

1821

29 June   ?   Osb
to Henry Colburn
I am leading just now a very secluded life

1822

14 Mar [1822]   2 p 4to   NYPL(B)
to CBFB
Tell our sweet Charlotte, my dear sister,

2 June [1822?]   4 p 4to   NYPL(B)
to Anna (Wilbraham) Grosvenor
Our Mrs. Gregor leaves this place

17 Mar   2 p 4to   BM(Bar)
to CBFB
I might have saved you much plague, my dear

1829

22 Feb   2 p 4to   NYPL(B)
to CBFB
Oh my dearest Sister! I can find no words to

28 Nov [1829]   3 p 8vo   Oxf(Bod)
to Robert Finch
I know not how to thank you sufficiently

26 June   4 p 4to   NYPL(B)
to CBFB
I will venture to say, that I am not undeserving

11 Dec   3 p 4to   NYPL(B)
to Anna (Wilbraham) Grosvenor
Very bad weather — very atrocious smells

1830

[9 Jan 1830]   1 p 12mo   Oxf(Bod)
to Maria (Thomson) Finch
Miss Burney presents her best compliments to

5 June [1830 misdated 1826]   4 p 4to
to Henry Crabb Robinson   Wms
Business must take the lead — I therefore

19 Mar [1830]   3 p 4to   Wms
to Henry Crabb Robinson
It will be pleasant to you if I begin

19 July [1830]   4 p 4to   Wms
to Henry Crabb Robinson
to be what I have called you is a great

19 May   4 p 4to   Wms
to Henry Crabb Robinson
I begin with the due formality of which your

12 Aug   3 p 4to   Wms
to Henry Crabb Robinson
We are inexpressibly anxious to hear the

30 Aug [1830]   4 p 4to   Wms
to Henry Crabb Robinson
Mʳ. Richmond gave me yesterday afternoon

13 Nov   2 p 4to   NYPL(B)
to Anna (Wilbraham) Grosvenor
We have heard at length from Mʳˢ. Gregor

28 Nov   4 p 4to   Wms
to Henry Crabb Robinson
There was a passage in your letter that made

29 Nov   4 p 4to   NYPL(B)
to Anna (Wilbraham) Grosvenor
"If you *do* write;" — I wonder at your

1831

6–11 Feb [1831]   4 p 4to   Wms
to Henry Crabb Robinson
In these "spirit-stirring times," I thought a

28 Mar   3 p 4to   Wms
to Henry Crabb Robinson
Mais arrivez-donc! — I have been hoping to

1832

15 Jan   4 p 4to   NYPL(B)
to Anna (Wilbraham) Grosvenor
Buon giorno, la mia carissima Sposina. — Are

9 May   4 p 4to   NYPL(B)
to Anna (Wilbraham) Grosvenor
Oh my dearest Nannie, how you (I mean your

4 July   3 p 4to   Wms
with Guiseppe Niccolini to Henry Crabb
     Robinson
E veramente singulare che gli

16–30 Aug [1832]   4 p 4to   NYPL(B)
to Anna (Wilbraham) Grosvenor
My poor dear Anna, how truly concerned I was

1833

25 FE 1833 pmk   4 p 4to   NYPL(B)
to Emma Wilbraham
Ah, poor dear Sister Emma! — how sorry I am

14 Dec   4 p 4to   NYPL(B)
to Anna (Wilbraham) Grosvenor
I have just finished a long letter to my poor

1834

26 Mar   4 p 4to   NYPL(B)
to Anna (Wilbraham) Grosvenor
By way of being young and giddy, my dearest

12 June   2 p 4to   BM(Bar)
to CBFB
Never suspect *me* of being exacting on the

1835

23 Jan   pmk 1835   4 p 4to   NYPL(B)
to Anna (Wilbraham) Grosvenor
My dearest Anna (for Anna — *my* Anna —

18 Feb   4 p 4to   Wms
to Henry Crabb Robinson
How shall I thank you for the opportunity

28 May   pmk 1835   4 p 4to   NYPL(B)
to Anna (Wilbraham) Grosvenor
My dearest Anna will forgive me for not

1837

23 Feb   4 p 4to   NYPL(B)
to Anna (Wilbraham) Grosvenor
It was like yourself to write to me

1838

15–21 Jan   4 p 4to   NYPL(B)
to Anna (Wilbraham) Grosvenor
My dearest Mʳˢ. Grosvenor — or, *do* let me say

20 Apr   4 p 4to   Wms
to Henry Crabb Robinson
Shall I say, "*Dear* Mʳ. Robinson?" — No, I

1839

22 Mar   4 p 4to   NYPL(B)
to Anna (Wilbraham) Grosvenor
I take it most kindly, my dearest Anna

4 June   3 p 4to   NYPL(B)
to Anna (Wilbraham) Grosvenor
It grieves me to the heart to hear so alarming

3 Apr   3 p 4to   Wms
to Henry Crabb Robinson
I must say, my dear friend, tho' with thanks

1840

26 Feb   4 p 4to   Wms
to Henry Crabb Robinson
Your most kind & welcome letter

10 Aug [1840?]   3 p 8vo   NYPL(B)
to Anna (Wilbraham) Grosvenor
I am at Clifton an' please you,

8 June   3 p 8vo   NYPL(B)
to Anna (Wilbraham) Grosvenor
I have alas! quite given up all thoughts of a

29 Aug   3 p 8vo   Wms
to Henry Crabb Robinson
Many thanks, my kind friend, for the excellent

1842

9 Dec   5 p 8vo   Wms
to Henry Crabb Robinson
You really *are* a good boy, and deserve the

[Jan]–2 Feb [1842–44]   4 p 8vo
                                 NYPL(B)
to Anna (Wilbraham) Grosvenor
I have seldom, dear Annie, read a letter with

30 Jan – 6 Feb [1842–44]   4 p 8vo
                                 NYPL(B)
to Anna (Wilbraham) Grosvenor
My dearest Anna — for I cannot accustom

18 May [1842–44]   2 p 8vo   NYPL(B)
to Anna (Wilbraham) Grosvenor
Only think, dearest, of its being considered by

1843

4 Mar   4 p 8vo   Wms
to Henry Crabb Robinson
My dear friend — Let me plunge at once into

17 Sept   4 p 8vo   Wms
to Henry Crabb Robinson
I have been upon the tramp ever since the 8th

9 Mar   3 p 8vo   NYPL(B)
to Anna (Wilbraham) Grosvenor
I am desired, dearest Annie, to return Mr.

29 Sept–5 Oct   7 p 8vo   NYPL(B)
to Anna (Wilbraham) Grosvenor
When you think me graceless enough

VIII

10 Apr 1790   4 p 4to   Comyn
to [Rosette (Rose) Burney]
Allow me to acknowledge the receipt of your

IX

CHARLOTTE ANN (BURNEY) FRANCIS BROOME 1761–1838

(CAB, CBF, CBFB)

See also letters to and from FBA, CB, and CPB, and letters from Henry Barrett, EBB, JB, SHB, C R Francis, MF, JCBTM, Sarah (Burney) Payne, SBP, and Frances (Phillips) Raper.

1780

[1780–82]   ½ p 4to   BM(Bar)
from Samuel Crisp
I thank the lovely *Churrlotte* for her

1781

8 Feb   4 p 4to   BM(Bar)
to Samuel Crisp
Sir — "But musn't I say *dear* Sir?"

22 Oct   2 p 4to   NYPL(B)
from Samuel Crisp
I thank you kindly for your funny, lively letter

1782

[6 May 1782]   2 p 4to   NYPL(B)
from Samuel Crisp
I don't know by your letter whether you had

4 Aug   2 p 4to   NYPL(B)
from Samuel Crisp
You are an excellent live Creature — not

26 Oct   2 p 4to   Essex
with Samuel Crisp to Sarah (Payne)
     Burney
I am employ'd by your Friend Charlotte to

[1782]   1 p fragment   NYPL(B)
from Samuel Crisp
Yr Daddy is but just determined to go, &

1783

15 Aug [1783]   4 p 4to   Comyn
to Rosette (Rose) Burney
My Father desires his best love to you & my

25 Oct [1783]   4 p 4to   BM(Bar)
to SBP
I ought to have written as soon as I came

3 Dec [1783]   4 p 4to   NYPL(B)
to SBP
Many thanks, my dearest Susan, for your kind

[1783–86]   1 p 4to   Comyn
from Arnaud Berquin
M. Berquin a l'honneur de Saluer la gentille

1784

[15 Jan 1784]   4 p 4to   BM(Bar)
to SBP
I now sit down to thank you for *all favours*, &

[1784]   16 p 4to   BM(Bar)
to SBP
I am sorry you shd. think of apologizing

13 Apr [1784–86]   2 p 4to   Osb
to Christian Latrobe
desires his affectionate Compliments & is

1785

1785   3 p 4to   BM
to Arthur Young
presuming on your goodnature, & *making free*

1786

[pre Feb 1786]   1 p 4to   BM(Bar)
from Albinia (Mathias) Skerrett
Many thanks my d^r Mrs Burney for your

10 Feb   2 p 4to   BM(Bar)
from Albinia (Mathias) Skerrett &
     Marianne (Popple) Mathias
I am much obliged to you for your letter

20 Feb   3 p fol   Comyn
from Arthur Young
You know enough of me to be well assured

1788

5 Mar   4 p 4to   with draft 3 p fol   BM
to Arthur Young
I am much oblig'd to you for your

24 May [1786–92]   1 p 4to   NYPL)B)
from Ralph Griffiths to CBF & Clement
     Francis
My Governess commands me to present her

2 May [1788]   1 p 4to   NYPL(B)
from Ralph Griffiths
I am glad to hear that you, and good M^r.

[4 Aug 1788]   3 p 4to   NYPL(B)
from Benjamin Latrobe
Here I am, / Eleven miles from Aylsham /

8 Aug   2 p fol   NYPL(B)
from Christian Latrobe
I went to Chelsea a few Days ago to enquire

1789

10 Mar   4 p fol   NYPL(B)
from Benjamin Latrobe
Very well I thank you! and how does yourself

11 June   2 p 4to   Osb
to Rosette (Rose) Burney
I am much obliged to you for your kind Letter

7 Aug   3 p 4to   NYPL(B)
from Ralph Broome
I thank you for forwarding the Letter which

10 Sept   3 p fol   NYPL(B)
from Ralph Broome
Coming home this Morning I found your

6 Oct [1789]   3 p 4to   Osb
from James Hutton to CBF & Clement
     Francis
Here I received the kindest L^r of you both &

[1789–93]   4 p 4to   Osb
to Rosette (Rose) Burney
Welcome as the Face of a Friend almost

1790

26 Feb   3 p 4to   NYPL(B)
with Clement Francis to [Ralph?]
     Broome
I dined at Mr Hastings after the Trial on

1792

17 NO pmk [1792–97]   1 p 4to
from Ralph Broome   NYPL(B)
I have just time to say that I have received

1794

7 Jan   1 p 8vo   BM(Bar)
from Thomas James Mathias
I flatter myself you will do me

1 May [1794?]   2 p 8vo   BM(Bar)
from Sarah Wesley
I enclose the lines on Mrs D'Arblay's marriage

11 Dec   3 p 8vo   BM(Bar)
from Thomas James Mathias
As you are so kind as to allot

26 Dec [1794?]   2 p 8vo   BM(Bar)
from Thomas James Mathias
I have at last been lucky enough to find

2 Mar [1794–98]   1 p 8vo   BM(Bar)
from Thomas James Mathias
Many thanks for all your patience with Rowly

[1794–98]   2 p 8vo   BM(Bar)
from Thomas James Mathias
You have obliged me much

1795

30 Jan   3 p 4to   BM(Bar)
from Thomas James Mathias & Mari-
    anne (Popple) Mathias
As you are a very eloquent agent

27 Feb [1795]   1 p 4to   NYPL(B)
from Veronica Boswell
My Father and I will with pleasure wait on

1797

3 July [1797]   2 p 4to   Osb
from Frances Reynolds
I hope my Dear Madam you did not expect

4 NO 1797 pmk   1 p 4to   NYPL(B)
from Ralph Broome
⟨Your⟩ Letter has so affected me that I know

1801

⟨6⟩ JU 1801 pmk   3 p 4to   NYPL(B)
from Anne (Cox) Woodrooffe
Apologies for Negligence in writing are so

1807

9 May [1807]   3 p 8vo   BM(Bar)
from Sarah Wesley
Do not imagine I estimate the attachment

18 Dec [1807]   2 p 4to   NYPL(B)
from Sophia Burney
Your very kind letter my dearest Aunt would

1808

22 MR 1808 pmk   1 p 8vo   BM(Bar)
from Sh[aron] Turne[r]
I am extremely sorry that the ⟨pressure⟩ &

31 Mar   amanuensis   2 p 4to   Osb
from Christian Latrobe
I groped & groped, & hunted, as for little

[1808]   1 p 8vo   BM(Bar)
from Charles Wesley
Pray accept my best thanks for your kind

1809

6 Aug   1 p 8vo   Osb
from Thomas James Mathias
You will do me a great pleasure in accepting

4 Oct [1809]   4 p 4to   NYPL(B)
from Matthew Rolleston
I recollect Miss Francis once told me, she was

1810

3 Mar   3 p 4to   NYPL(B)
from Christian Latrobe
Your Letter finds me just setting out for

[1810]   1 p 8vo   BM(Bar)
from Thomas James Mathias
I was sorry not to see you

2 Nov pmk 1810   2 p 4to   BM
to Arthur Young
It is so long since we met that I fear I am

[1810–12]   1 p fol   Comyn
from Arthur Young
I have long been much concerned that your

6 Dec [1810]   1 p 8vo   Osb
from Thomas James Mathias
You are very good in thinking of me. I cannot

1811

15 July   3 p 8vo   BM(Bar)
from Thomas James Mathias
I cannot help expressing in writing

6 Nov   4 p fol   BM
to Arthur Young
Most sincerely do I thank you my dear friend

9 Aug   3 p 4to   BM
to Arthur Young
In answer to your kind Letter, & repetition

14 Dec   4 p fol   BM
to Arthur Young
I must first thank you for the pleasure your last

21 Oct [1811]   3 p 4to   NYPL(B)
from Arthur Young
You will persist in talking of pleasure

1812

17 Feb   2 p 4 to   BM
to Arthur Young
I hope you can send me word that you are

17 July   amanuensis   4 p 4to
from Arthur Young   NYPL(B)
I intended long ago to have done myself the

1813

14 July   1 p 8vo   BM(Bar)
from Thomas James Mathias
I am vexed that I was so unlucky

23 Jan [1813–14]   1 p 12mo   Osb
from William Weller Pepys
Sir W. W. Pepys will be very happy to wait on

1814

7 Jan   3 p 4to   BM(Bar)
from Thomas James Mathias
It is always a great pleasure

25 Aug [1814]   3 p 8vo   NYPL(B)
from William Wilberforce
I have heard today with no little concern of

1815

19 AP 1815 pmk   3 p 4to   BM
with CFBt to Arthur Young
Ever since I heard of the death of poor Mrs.

24 July   3 p 4to   BM
to Arthur Young
We are thinking with much pleasure of our

1815, continued

9 Sept   3 p fol   BM
to Arthur Young
Here is a sheet of folio paper that I could easily

20 Nov   3 p 4to   BM(Bar)
from Thomas James Mathias
I can assure you it always gives me great

1816

9 Jan   2 p 4to   NYPL(B)
from John Bickersteth
I felt much obliged by your letter, & if my

20 Jan   4 p 8vo   NYPL(B)
from William Wilberforce
I am almost ashamed to execute the Intention

1817

8 Dec   1 p 4to   NYPL(B)
from Sharon Turner
I have this morn^g Received the enclosed Bill

1818

21 July   3 p 4to   BM(Bar)
to Arthur Young
I don't exactly know what Marianne wrote to

24 Aug [1818]   4 p fol   NYPL(B)
to MF & HHBt (with Sarah (Burney)
    Payne to MF)
Oweing to some queerality or other, *both* y^r.

1819

14 Jan   1 p 4to   NYPL(B)
from Frys & Chapman
We have thy favor of the 13th Inst.

15 Jan   4 p 4to   BM(Bar)
to EBB
I have now to thank you for a kind &

1820

22 Mar   3 p 8vo   NYPL(B)
from Christian Latrobe
That my good brother in Yankee-Land may

3 Dec   1 p 8vo   NYPL(B)
from Thomas James Mathias
I am engaged, unfortunately for myself, on

1 Aug   2 p 4to   NYPL(B)
from R H Gaby
I remained in Town till Friday last much

1822

11 May   2 p 8 vo & 4to cover   BM(Bar)
from J[oseph?] Planta
The satisfaction I had in finding that I still

20 Oct [1822]   4 p 4to   NYPL(B)
to MF
That agreeable family of penns & paynters

1823

9 Sept [1823]   2 p 8vo   NYPL(B)
from Frances Bowdler
We never shall meet, unless we do so by

1826

18 Apr [1826]   1 p 8vo   NYPL(B)
from [César?] de Latour Maubourg
Comme la santé de Madame Broom est

7 Nov   pmk 1826   1 p 4to
from Esther Sleepe   NYPL(B)
This morning I have received your verry good

14 Aug   2 p 8vo   NYPL(B)
from Marie de Maisonneuve
Nous regrettons bien vivement, très-chere

1827

3 Nov   2 p 4to   NYPL(B)
from Alfred Turner
I have made the inquiry at <Jervin> Street

3 Jan [pre 1828]   1 p 8vo   NYPL(B)
from Charles Wesley
I take the liberty to hope you got no

[1827]   3 p 4to   NYPL(B)
from Alfred Turner
My father desires me to enclose the little

1828

30 May [1828]   2 p 12mo   NYPL(B)
from Charles Wesley
What a pleasure dear Madam do we anticipate

11 Dec   2 p 4to   NYPL(B)
from Charles Wesley
What can I say to express the thanks due to

1829

10 Mar   4 p 4to   NYPL(B)
from Charles Porter
I did not, till yesterday, know to what place I

10 Aug   2 p 4to   NYPL(B)
from John Shore, Baron Teignmouth
I can assure you with great truth, that I did

9 Apr   2 p 8vo   NYPL(B)
from John Kaye
The Bishop of Lincoln presents his respectful

[Aug 1829]   4 p 8vo   NYPL(B)
from Caroline Anderson
I was very sorry that I had not the pleasure

6 May [1829]   3 p 8vo   NYPL(B)
from George Archdall
On my return to Cambridge after an Absence

10 Nov   2 p 4to   Osb
from Robert Southey
I was absent from home when yours of Oct

16 June   1 p 4to   Osb
from Robert Southey
Your letter, which has followed me from

12 Nov [1829]   3 p 8vo   NYPL(B)
from John Abel Smith
I thank you for your letter & for your

[June 1829?]   2 p 4to   NYPL(B)
from H V Elliot to [CBFB?]
I received just as I was setting off to

13 Nov   2 p 4to   NYPL(B)
from Harvey James Sperling
I have received in safety the little packet you

18 July   pmk 1829   3 p 4to   NYPL(B)
from Cornelia (Mierop) Cambridge
I cannot easily express how much I feel your

20 Nov   2 p 4to   NYPL(B)
from John Abel Smith
Your letter was forwarded to me here where

20   pmk JY [1829]   1 p 4to   NYPL(B)
from Sarah Baker
I cannot lay my head quietly on the Pillow to

25 Nov   1 p 4to   NYPL(B)
from John Abel Smith
Accept Mrs J. Smiths & my own united

1829, continued

7 DE 1829 pmk   2 p 4to   NYPL(B)
from Edward R Tunno
On receiving your letter this morning I

8 Dec   1 p 4to   NYPL(B)
from John Abel Smith
I have received back the parcel addressed for

9 Dec   1 p 8vo   NYPL(B)
from John Shore, Baron Teignmouth
You have judged very rightly in supposing

15 Dec   1 p 4to   Osb
from Robert Southey
The box has this day Safely arrived. — The

18 Dec   amanuensis   2 p 4to
from William Wilberforce   NYPL(B)
I return you my sincere thanks for your

[1829?]   3 p 4to   NYPL(B)
from Ed[ward] R Tunno
Your very kind letter of the 11th Inst. followed

1830

1 Dec [1830?]   4 p 4to   NYPL(B)
to MF
on the other half of this sheet you will find

1832

[1823–38]   2 p 8vo   NYPL(B)
to Minette (Raper) Kingston
I have this morning received a letter from our

1833

c 10 Dec 1833   7 p 4to   BM(Bar)
from [Alfred?] Turner
I have looked over your settlement with Mr

1834

14 Apr   4 p 4to   NYPL(B)
from Sharon Turner & W[illiam?]
    Turner
Happening to be in London when your

13 Feb   3 p 4to   NYPL(B)
from William Turner
I take up my pen with more pleasure than I

CLEMENT ROBERT FRANCIS 1792–1829

See also letters to and from CFBt.

1810

23 JY 1810 pmk   3 p 4to   Ryl
to HLTP
The long intimacy I have enjoyed with dear

28 July   4 p 4to   NYPL(B)
from HLTP
My dear Young Friend's Letter gave me

9 AU 1810 pmk   4 p 4to   Ryl
to HLTP
Dear Mrs. Piozzi's kindness in answering so

28 Aug   4 p 4to   Ryl
to HLTP
Matter is scarce in the dog days in London and

26 Oct   4 p 4to   Ryl
to HLTP
Dear Mrs. Piozzi's letter gave me great pleasure

13 Nov   4 p 4to   NYPL(B)
from HLTP
I thank you for your nice Letter — and would

1811

8 Jan   4 p 4to   Ryl
to HLTP
Had not my mind been much plagued or at any

13 Feb   4 p 4to   Ryl
to HLTP
Your illustration of the 8th verse of the 4C. of

24 JA 1811 pmk   4 p 4to   Ryl
to HLTP
Many thanks Dear Madam for your kind letter

12 JU 1811 pmk   3 p 4to   Ryl
to HLTP
I don't know whether I should have teazed

20 July   4 p 4to   Ryl
to HLTP
The life of a Rambler desultory but very busy

5 Nov   4 p 4to   Ryl
to HLTP
Though not buoyed up by hope or big with

18 Dec   4 p 4to   Ryl
to HLTP
Dear Mrs. Piozzi's letter did come among the

1812

31 Jan   4 p 4to   Ryl
to HLTP
Dear Mrs. Piozzi's kind letter of 20. Decr. has

3 SE 1812 pmk   4 p 4to   Ryl
to HLTP
Dearest Mrs. Piozzi's kindness I too well know

1813

22 DE 1813 pmk   4 p 4to   Ryl
to HLTP
If silence were a symbol of fickleness in friend-

25 Dec [1813]   2 p 4to   NYPL(B)
to M d'A
I should have replied earlier to your letter, had

1814

17 Jan   3 p 4to   Osb
from HLTP
It was very kind in you to write so attentively

9 Mar   4 p 4to   NYPL(B)
from HLTP
You are all of you too kind, dear Mr. Francis;

1816

14 May [1816?]   4 p 4to   Ryl
to HLTP
Your kind remembrance of me in your last

19 June [1816]   2 p 4to   Ryl
to HLTP
I quite regretted that it was intirely [sic] out

July   3 p 4to   NYPL(B)
from HLTP
My dear Mr. Francis's very kind and Christian-

1817

19 Mar   3 p 4to   Ryl
to HLTP
I know not how it is but ye lassitude arising

[pre 1818]   4 p 4to   Ryl
to HLTP
Many thanks for your kind and prompt

1818

3 DE 181⟨8⟩ pmk   4 p 4to   Ryl
to HLTP
Driven from study by severe sickness, I have

1819

17 Apr   4 p 4to   Ryl   31 Dec   4 p 4to   Ryl
to HLTP   to HLTP
It is so long since any letter has reached me   It is so long since I have had the pleasure of

1820

29 Jan   2 p 4to   Ryl
to HLTP
The day is now past, and I trust without any

1822

20 Aug   3 p 4to   NYPL(B)
from Charles Shephard
Looking over the Chronicle I saw your name &

1826

9 Jan   4 p 4to   NYPL(B)
to CBFB
My dearest Mama, I was much disappointed in

MARIANNE FRANCIS 1790–1832

(MF)

See also letters to and from CFBt, and from AA, FBA, CBFB, and JCBTM.

1798

12 June [1798?]   2 p 4to   Myers
to Rosette (Rose) Burney
My dear Aunt will I hope excuse my having

1806

9 June [1806]   4 p 4to   Ryl   10 Dec [1806]   4 p 4to   Ryl
with CBFB & CFBt to HLTP   to HLTP
How can I ever thank you enough   "What? Another Letter from Marianne

1807

5 Jan [1807]   4 p 4to   Ryl   19 June   4 p 4to   Ryl
to HLTP   to HLTP
In the greatest of all great hurries, (for the   From the interest my dearest Mrs Piozzi has

12 Jan   4 p 4to   NYPL(B)   21 July [1807]   4 p 4to   Ryl
from Sarah Wesley   to HLTP
I waited so long before I left Town for your   How kind and how good, and how better than

30 Apr   3 p 4to   Ryl   27 June [1807]   4 p 4to   NYPL(B)
to HLTP   from Sarah Wesley
To write or not to write? That is the Question   The first Letter I have received from you since

4 Sept [1807]   4 p 4to   Ryl
to HLTP
Dearest Mrs Piozzi what an age since I have

[Nov 1807]   4 p 4to   Ryl
to HLTP
August, September, October have elapsed, and

6 Oct [1807]   4 p 4to   Ryl
to HLTP
If Dearest Mrs Piozzi is not quite weary of

3 Dec [1807]   4 p 4to   Ryl
to HLTP
Tidings of Corilla! dear Mrs Piozzi — Charlotte

20 Nov [1807]   4 p 4to   Ryl
to HLTP
Dearest Mrs Piozzi, so you have been ill that

17 Dec   4 p 4to   Ryl
to HLTP
As I am not, unfortunately for my dear Mrs

1808

1 Feb   4 p 4to   Ryl
to HLTP
Much have I wished ere now to thank my

4 July   pmk 1808   4 p 4to   Ryl
to HLTP
Whether this will ever reach dearest Mrs

13 Feb [1808]   4 p 8vo   NYPL(B)
from Sarah Wesley
You have left our Neighbourood [sic] — and

9 July   pmk 1808   4 p 4to   Ryl
to HLTP
Can you forgive me, dearest Mrs Piozzi, for

19 Feb   4 p 4to   Ryl
to HLTP
I have begun this Letter, my own dear Mrs

23 July   4 p 4to   Ryl
to HLTP
Here we are dearest Mrs Piozzi! — AT LAST,

12 MR 1808 pmk   4 p 4to   Ryl
to HLTP
Dearest Mrs Piozzi has done more towards

13 Aug   4 p 4to   Ryl
to HLTP
My dearest Mrs Piozzi will forgive an intruding

28 Mar   4 p 4to   Ryl
to HLTP
How good of dear Mrs Piozzi to caution me

24 Aug   4 p fol   Ryl
to HLTP
Don't be frightened, dearest Mrs Piozzi, at my

24 Apr   4 p 4to   Ryl
to HLTP
But that reading dearest Mrs Piozzi's last

30 Aug [1808?]   4 p 8vo   NYPL(B)
from Sarah Wesley
It was very sweet of you to write to me your

14 MY 1808 pmk   2 p 4to   NYPL(B)
from Charles T T——
You are the most malicious creature in the

14 Sept   4 p 4to   Ryl
to HLTP
My dearest Mrs Piozzi's last charming letter

16   pmk MY 1808   4 p 4to
from Charles T T——   NYPL(B)
You have honoured me with the name of

21 Sept   pmk 1808   4 p 4to   BM(Bar)
from Sarah Wesley
So if you had not found a settled residence

19 May   pmk 1808   4 p 4to   Ryl
to HLTP
Dearest Mrs Piozzi would have heard sooner

4 Oct   4 p 4to   Ryl
to HLTP
Give me joy — dearest Mrs Piozzi, or rather

10 June   4 p 4to   Ryl
to HLTP
Dearest Mrs Piozzi guessed right — I *was*

24 Oct   4 p 4to   Ryl
to HLTP
Wish me joy again! dearest Mrs Piozzi — last

⟨ ⟩ JU ⟨1808⟩ pmk   4 p 4to
from Charles T T——   NYPL(B)
I have attempted as you may perceive to send

31 Oct   4 p 4to   Ryl
to HLTP
Now I'm going to have a good long chat, with

1808, continued

4 Nov [1808]   5 p fol   NYPL(B)
to Henry Barrett
I must first thank your goodnature, dear

21 Nov   4 p 4to   Ryl
to HLTP
Here are Spencer's Verses, dearest Mrs Piozzi:

13 Dec   4 p 4to   Ryl
to HLTP
Dear, dear, Mrs Piozzi — What an inducement

28 Dec [1808?]   4 p 8vo   NYPL(B)
from Sarah Wesley
But yesterday dearest Marianne I sent a Letter

[1808?]   4 p 8vo   NYPL(B)
from Sarah Wesley
I received dearest Marianes sportful Epistle

1809

3 Jan   4 p 4to   Ryl
from HLTP
Dear Mrs Piozzi, and your *Classical* Pun! —

9 Jan   2 p 4to   NYPL(B)
from Sarah Wesley
Heaviness of Heart retarded my pen — I have

30 Jan   4 p 4to   Ryl
to HLTP
Ah sweetest Mrs Piozzi, how shamefully, how

15 Feb   4 p 4to   Ryl
to HLTP
Ah dearest Mrs Piozzi — I *am* delighted with

16 Mar   (pmk 15)   4 p 4to   Ryl
to HLTP
The pleasure of writing to you, dearest Mrs

1 Apr   1 p 4to   Ryl
to HLTP
Dear, dearest, Mrs Piozzi shall not be thanked

6 Apr   2 p 4to   Ryl
to HLTP
Forgive me, my adored Mrs Piozzi, my loved,

1 May   4 p 4to   Ryl
to HLTP
I *have* waited, my beloved Mrs Piozzi

29 May   4 p 4to   Ryl
to HLTP
Dearest Mrs Piozzi who feels for every body,

6 June   4 p 4to   Ryl
to HLTP
It was Mad de Sevigné who first taught me to

13 June [1809]   4 p 4to   Ryl
to HLTP
Here begins again, provoking *paper*

27 June   4 p 4to   Ryl
to HLTP
You have sent me a noble letter to be sure, my

10 July   4 p 4to   Ryl
to HLTP
It was very good *indeed,* my dearest Mrs

28 July   4 p 4to   Ryl
to HLTP
No, my beloved Mrs Piozzi — I have

25 Aug   4 p 4to   Ryl
to HLTP
I do indeed thank my beloved Mrs Piozzi for

19 Sept   4 p 4to   Ryl
to HLTP
My dearest Mrs Piozzi will never get a holiday

11 Oct   4 p 4to   Ryl
to HLTP
I don't know whether my sweet Mrs Piozzi

7 Nov   4 p 4to   Ryl
to HLTP
There we are, dearest Mrs Piozzi, one more

14 Nov   4 p 4to   Ryl
to HLTP
"Crawl through 7 *years* more existence"!

13 Dec   4 p 4to   Ryl
to HLTP
Well dearest Mrs Piozzi, you *are* gay to be

1810

10 Jan   pmk 1810 [misdated 1809]
to HLTP   4 p 4to   Ryl
Not all the knocking in the world shall drive

6 Feb   4 p 4to   Ryl
to HLTP
There shall be a letter, my ever dear Mʳˢ

26 Feb   4 p 4to   Ryl
to HLTP
My affronted *hand* is at length prevailed upon

9 Mar   4 p 4to   Ryl
to HLTP
My dearest Mʳˢ Piozzi cannot digest a letter I

28 Mar   4 p 4to   Ryl
to HLTP
My dearest Mʳˢ Piozzi wrote me a delightful

31 May   4 p 4to   Ryl
to HLTP
Quite broken-hearted at **losing you my own**

6 June   4 p 4to   Ryl
to HLTP
No letter from Brynbella yet — Dearest Mʳˢ

11 JU pmk [1810]   4 p **4to**   Ryl
to HLTP
My dearest Mʳˢ Piozzi's beautiful *Letter* was

13 June   4 p 4to   Ryl
to HLTP
My beloved Mʳˢ Piozzi will grieve at the fate

15 June   1 p 8vo   NYPL(B)
from Thomas James Mathias
I send the Volume which I promised, & which

25 June   4 p 4to   Ryl
to HLTP
You are *very* good my dearest Mʳˢ Piozzi to

29 June   4 p 4to   Ryl
to HLTP
Here am I, dearest Mʳˢ Piozzi, fanning myself

10 July   4 p 4to   Ryl
to HLTP
Will you be quite ashamed of your little

28 July   4 p 4to   Ryl
to HLTP
How good of you, my dearest Mʳˢ Piozzi, to

6 July   (pmk AU)   4 p 4to   Ryl
to HLTP
Your model is like the snail's shell, dearest Mʳˢ

10 Sept   4 p 4to   Ryl
to HLTP
How can *you* talk about "lacking matters"

4 Oct   4 p 4to   Ryl
to HLTP
My dearest Mʳˢ Piozzi's beautiful letter

12 Oct   2 p 8vo   Osb
from William Wilberforce
I cannot well tell you how much I was

17 Oct   4 p 4to   Ryl
to HLTP
My dearest Mʳˢ Piozzi, *think* of the dilatory

9 Nov   4 p 4to   Ryl
to HLTP
How *should* I like either your Health, Face, *or*

3 Dec   4 p 4to   Ryl
to HLTP
My dearest Mʳˢ Piozzi's letter made me very

12 Dec   pmk 1810   3 p 4to   NYPL(B)
from Sarah Wesley
I much want your opinion on a subject I am

19 Dec   4 p 4to   Ryl
to HLTP
of nothing & nobody but Nixon have I thought,

[c 1810?]   1 p 8vo   Osb
from William Wilberforce
Farewell my dearest Marⁿⁿᵉ. I am ever your

[c 1810–11]   1 p scrap   Harv(H)
from HLTP to [? MF]
Meantime your Brother's Description of my

[1810–14]   1 p 8vo   Osb
from Thomas James Mathias
You are a great [deal] too good to me, & I am

1811

15 Feb   4 p 4to   Ryl
to HLTP
Since I had the happiness of writing to you last,

21 Mar   4 p 4to   Ryl
to HLTP
My Dearest, Cruelest Mrs Piozzi, what *are* you

27 Mar   4 p 4to   Ryl
to HLTP
My dearest Mrs Piozzi will be surprised to see

4 AP pmk [1811?]   3 p 4to   NYPL(B)
from Sarah Wesley
We are as completely separated by

16 Apr   1 p 4to   Ryl
to HLTP
Clem & I *tore away*, after we had the happiness

[post 16 Apr 1811]   2 p 4to   Ryl
to HLTP
My dearest Mrs Piozzi will not refuse to

22 Apr   1 p 8vo   NYPL(B)
to HLTP
Mrs Piozzi brought her little God Daughter's

3 May   4 p 4to   NYPL(B)
to CBFB
You were so good as to *tell* me to write, so I

1⟨4⟩ May   4 p 4to   Ryl
to HLTP
My dearest Mrs Piozzi's sweet letter had an

27 May   4 p 4to   Ryl
to HLTP
No Letter comes from my dearest Mrs Piozzi,

16 June   1 p 8vo   NYPL(B)
from Thomas James Mathias
I have been out of town, or I should have

17 June   pmk 1811   4 p 4to   Ryl
to HLTP
My dearest Mrs Piozzi would have heard from

1 July   4 p 4to   Ryl
to HLTP
My dearest Mrs Piozzi's delightful letter

16 July   4 p 4to   Ryl
to HLTP
My dearest Mrs Piozzi must think me located

31 July   4 p 4to   Ryl
to HLTP
My dearest Mrs Piozzi will, I trust have

15 Aug   2 p 4to   NYPL(B)
to Ralph Broome Jr
Mama is gone into the country to cure her

22 Aug   4 p 4to   Ryl
to HLTP
I have been waiting long & anxiously, my

8 Sept   4 p 4to   Ryl
to HLTP
My dearest Mrs Piozzi will certainly think

12 Sept   pmk 1811   2 p 4to NYPL(B)
from Sarah Wesley
I seem to have lost you my dear Mariane, but

24 Sept   4 p 4to   Ryl
to HLTP
My dearest Mrs Piozzi knows the way to win

4 ⟨OC⟩ 1811 pmk   3 p 4to   BM
to Arthur Young
If you were not like Cassius "aweary of the

18 Oct   4 p 4to   Ryl
to HLTP
I should certainly not "scape *whipping*" if I

22 Oct   4 p 4to   BM
with CBFB to Arthur Young
Your sad, afflicting letter reached me this

5 Nov   4 p 4to   BM
to Arthur Young
Answer your arguments? / No — my dearest

6 Nov   4 p 4to   Ryl
to HLTP
My dearest Mrs Piozzi's very curious &

16 Nov   4 p 4to   BM
to Arthur Young
Scold indeed! / Pray what encouragement

[23]–30 Nov [1811]   4 p 4to   BM
to Arthur Young
What — angry in *right earnest,* my dearest

2–4 Dec   amanuensis   4 p 4to
from Arthur Young   NYPL(B)
I have long had a desire to write to you in a

3 Dec   3 p 4to   Ryl
to HLTP
My dearest Mrs Piozzi has been cruelly silent

4 Dec   2 p 4to   BM
to Arthur Young
I have just 3 minutes, my dearest Sir —

6 Dec   amanuensis   3 p 4to
from Arthur Young   NYPL(B)
I intended to have filled a sheet by answering

8 Dec   3 p 4to   Ryl
to HLTP
Here we are, my dearest Mrs Piozzi, safe

17 Dec   4 p 4to   BM
to Arthur Young
I have been waiting, my dear Sir, long &

20 Dec   4 p 4to   BM
to Arthur Young
Your letters this moment arrived my dearest

26 Dec   4 p 4to   Ryl
to HLTP
Am I ever to have the happiness of hearing

26 Dec   amanuensis   4 p 4to
from Arthur Young   NYPL(B)
Two letters from you are on the table are truly

28 Dec   3 p 4to   Ryl
to HLTP
I blush, my dearest Mrs Piozzi, to persecute

1812

2–4 Jan   4 p 4to   BM
to Arthur Young
Good news, my dear Sir, for you — / I have

6 Jan   3 p 4to   Ryl
to HLTP
I wrote two letters, one in the 26, the other on

11 Jan 181[2]   amanuensis   4 p 4to
from Arthur Young   NYPL(B)
When you give the reins to your fancy you

15 Jan   8 p 4to   Ryl
with Anna Maria (de Blaquiere), Viscountess Kirkwall to HLTP
With an unsteady hand, but with a Heart ever

19 Jan   4 p 4to   BM
to Arthur Young
Your kind letter, my dearest Sir, reached me

[24 Jan 1812]   2 p 4to   BM
to Arthur Young
Safe arrived in London my dearest Sir, at last

25 Jan   3 p 4to   Ryl
to HLTP
I did swear, like Lord de Blaquiere to write

17 Feb   4 p 4to   Ryl
to HLTP
May it be long, very long, my dearest M^rs

12 Mar   4 p 4to   Ryl
to HLTP
Silence to my dearest Mrs Piozzi's kind &

9 Apr   4 p 4to   Ryl
to HLTP
How kind and good you are, my dearest M^rs

5 May   4 p 4to   Ryl
to HLTP
My dearest Mrs Piozzi's letters are full of

8 May   1 p 8vo   Osb
from Thomas James Mathias
I flatter myself that you will do me the favour

11 May [1812]   1 p 8vo   NYPL(B)
from Thomas James Mathias
Many thanks for your kind & good-natured

19 May [1812]   4 p 4to   Ryl
to HLTP
Monday *has* past quietly over, notwithstanding

1 July [1812]   4 p 4to   Ryl
to HLTP
My dearest Mrs Piozzi's long silence is very

10 Aug   4 p 4to   Ryl
to HLTP
Though the *uncertainty* my dearest Mrs Piozzi

1 Sept   4 p 4to   Ryl
to HLTP
Who do you think, my dearest Mrs Piozzi, is

26 Sept   4 p 4to   Ryl
to HLTP
I have been wishing repeatedly to write to my

1812, continued

23 Oct   4 p 4to   Ryl
to HLTP
My dearest Mrs Piozzi will call me a lunatic

31 Oct   4 p 4to   Ryl
to HLTP
My dearest Mrs Piozzi's kind note by Lake,

28 Nov   4 p 4to   Ryl
to HLTP
My dearest Mrs Piozzi must have thought me

16 Dec   4 p 4to   Ryl
to HLTP
My dearest Mrs Piozzi is not a collector of

28 Dec   amanuensis   3 p 4to
from Arthur Young   NYPL(B)
As I have already explained to you, I send

[1812?]   amanuensis   3 p 4to
from Arthur Young   NYPL(B)
As here is a letter to send I cannot let it go

1813

15 Jan [1813 misdated 1812]   4 p 4to
to HLTP   Ryl
My dearest Mrs Piozzi will conclude by the

23 Jan   4 p 4to   BM
to Arthur Young
You were so good as to desire an account of

26 Jan   amanuensis   2 p 4to
from Arthur Young   NYPL(B)
I am very glad to hear such good accounts

3 Feb   4 p 4to   Ryl
to HLTP
I had hoped to have heard from my dearest

24 Feb   4 p 4to   Ryl
to HLTP
My dearest Mrs Piozzi has been silent very

15 Mar   4 p 4to   Ryl
to HLTP
My dearest Mrs Piozzi was very good to write

1⟨3⟩ Apr   4 p 4to   Ryl
to HLTP
My dearest Mrs Piozzi would sooner have

22 Apr   4 p 4to   Ryl
to HLTP
My dearest Mrs Piozzi's letter gave me equal

23 Apr   4 p 4to   BM
to Arthur Young
Many thanks, my dearest Sir, for your

8 May   3 p 4to   Ryl
to HLTP
Here is the passage from Quintilian, about my

17 May   4 p 4to   Ryl
to HLTP
I have no language, my dearest Mrs Piozzi

[3 June 1813]   5 p 4to   Ryl
to HLTP
I write from Mrs Wilberforce's, with whom I

5 June   4 p 4to   NYPL(B)
from HLTP
Think not dear Marianne that I should employ

24 June [1813]   3 p fol   BM
to Arthur Young
Many thanks for your kind letter, which

3 July   4 p 4to   Ryl
to HLTP
My dear Mrs Piozzi's letter would not have

23 Aug   4 p 4to   Ryl
to HLTP
would have heard before now, if I had not

4 Oct   4 p 4to   Ryl
to HLTP
My dear Mrs Piozzi's kind letter deserves a

3 Nov   3 p 4to   BM
to Arthur Young
A thousand thanks for your kindness in getting

9 Nov   4 p 4to   Ryl
to HLTP
My dear Mrs Piozzi sees a new direction every

10 Nov   amanuensis   3 p 4to
from Arthur Young   NYPL(B)
I am much obliged to you for so early an

25 Nov   pmk 1813   4 p 4to
from A Cotterill   NYPL(B)
My dear Miss Francis shall not have to

21 Dec   5 p 4to   Ryl
to HLTP
will laugh when she hears what has kept me

1814

[17 Jan]   pmk 1814   amanuensis
          1 p 4to   NYPL(B)
from Arthur Young
I could not at the Lock return a written answer

23 Jan   4 p 4to   BM
to Arthur Young
This so long time I have been able to write to

26 Jan   4 p 4to   Ryl
to HLTP
At last, my dear Mrs Piozzi, I have the

10 Feb   4 p 4to   BM
to Arthur Young
I have been longing to write to you before now

11 Feb   4 p 4to   Ryl
to HLTP
Here I am at last, with my Mother & little

14 Feb   amanuensis   3 p 4to
from Arthur Young   NYPL(B)
I should have written to you long ago, but had

22 [Feb 1814]   1 p fol   BM
to Arthur Young
Many thanks for your interesting letter, my

22 Feb   amanuensis   3 p 4to
from Arthur Young   NYPL(B)
A thousand thanks for your kind letter, and

4 Mar   4 p 4to   BM
to Arthur Young
I lost no time in hastening to inform you of

16 Mar   3 p 4to   BM
to Arthur Young
Our last letters crossed, I believe, upon the

17 Mar   amanuensis   4 p 4to
from Arthur Young   NYPL(B)
I am in a rage. And yet I ought to be in none

18 Mar   4 p 4to   Ryl
to HLTP
Many sincere thanks, my dear Mrs Piozzi, for

26 Mar   amanuensis   3 p 4to
from Arthur Young   NYPL(B)
I am much obliged to you for your kind letter

11 Apr [1814]   2 p 4to   BM
to Arthur Young
I enclose Mrs Strachays note with many

13 Apr   4 p 4to   Ryl
to HLTP
My dear Mrs Piozzi will be sorry to hear the

13 Apr [1814]   3 p 8vo   BM
to Arthur Young
Your constant kind interest in what concerns

14 Apr   amanuensis   2 p 4to
from Arthur Young   NYPL(B)
At the great age of your grand father his death

3 May [1814 misdated 1813]   4 p 4to
to Arthur Young   BM
I am sure you will be anxious to hear about

[5 May 1814]   amanuensis   4 p 4to
from Arthur Young   NYPL(B)
This morning I found your very obliging letter

2 June   4 p 4to   Ryl
to HLTP
My dear Mrs Piozzi would have heard from

14 June   4 p 4to   Ryl
to HLTP
It was with great pleasure that I learnt your

23 June   4 p 4to   BM
to Arthur Young
You did not tell me the day of your departure

2 July   4 p 4to   Ryl
to HLTP
My dear Mrs Piozzi will start at the sight of

3 July   4 p 4to   BM
to Arthur Young
I know not whether a letter I directed to you

4 July   amanuensis   3 p 4to
from Arthur Young   NYPL(B)
The letter for which I am much obliged to you

11 July   amanuensis   2 p 4to
from Arthur Young   NYPL(B)
I should have replied to your 2nd letter sooner

13 July   4 p 4to   Ryl
with CFBt to HLTP
I am but just returned to Richmond, & could

13 July   4 p 4to   BM
to Arthur Young
Many thanks, my dearest Sir, for your last kind

1814, continued

21 July   amanuensis   3 p 4to
from Arthur Young   NYPL(B)
I recᵈ my dear little girl's letter which gave

27 July   4 p 4to   BM
to Arthur Young
Here I am, for a few days only, staying with

2 Aug   amanuensis   3 p 4to
from Arthur Young   NYPL(B)
A thousand thanks for your kind letter from

4 Aug   2 p 4to   NYPL(B)
from William Wilberforce
Dinner actually being on the table

5 Aug   4 p 4to   BM
to Arthur Young
Many thanks for your kind letter. It is always

12 Aug   amanuensis   4 p 4to
from Arthur Young   NYPL(B)
I am dissatisfied with myself when I do not

15 Aug   4 p 4to   BM
to Arthur Young
Many thanks, my dearest Sir, for your kind

22 Aug   amanuensis   3 p 4to
from Arthur Young   NYPL(B)
Your last kind letter gave me the greatest

24 Aug   4 p 4to   NYPL(B)
from William Wilberforce
This is so near yᵉ time when yʳ mother was so

29 Aug   4 p 4to   BM
to Arthur Young
I cannot have the pleasure of writing a long

7 Sept   4 p 4to   BM
to Arthur Young
You will wonder, my dearest Sir, at the date of

23 Sept   4 p 4to   Ryl
to HLTP
I have been waiting, with more anxiety than

24 Sept   4 p 4to   BM
to Arthur Young
Have you had a letter from me, dated from

1 Oct   amanuensis   5 p 4to
from Arthur Young   NYPL(B)
Your two very kind letters are now before

4 Oct   4 p 4to   BM
to Arthur Young
Your kind & interesting letter reached me this

10 Oct   4 p 4to   BM
to Arthur Young
I have not heard from you, since I wrote last—

11 Oct   amanuensis   3 p 4to
from Arthur Young   NYPL(B)
You should understand the deceitfulness of

20 Oct   4 p 4to   BM
to Arthur Young
I am glad to hear so good an account of you

25 Oct   4 p 4to   BM
to Arthur Young
Your kind & welcome letters are always

26 Oct   amanuensis   3 p 4to
from Arthur Young   NYPL(B)
Having recᵈ a letter from Mʳ. Quayle of

27 Oct   4 p 4to   Ryl
to HLTP
I have been long wishing to answer my dear

1 Nov [1814]   4 p 4to   BM
to Arthur Young
Many thanks for your kind letters & enclosures

25 Nov   3 p 4to   BM
to Arthur Young
My mother desires me to write & say,

25 Nov   amanuensis   3 p 4to
from Arthur Young   NYPL(B)
Before I say anything of your letter, I must

1 Dec   4 p 4to   BM
to Arthur Young
I did not go to Cambridge as I fully intended

7 Dec   amanuensis   4 p 4to
from Arthur Young   NYPL(B)
My dear Marianne must certainly think that I

10 Dec   4 p 4to   BM
to Arthur Young
I must have seemed, I fear, strangely remiss

21 Dec   4 p 4to   Ryl
to HLTP
I have not written for some time, for indeed

21 Dec   3 p 4to   BM
to Arthur Young
Clem & I are both now with the Wilberforces.

22 Dec   amanuensis   3 p 4to
from Arthur Young   NYPL(B)
I am horribly angry with myself on reading

29 Dec   4 p 4to   BM
to Arthur Young
On my return from Barham Court I found

7 ⟨Dec⟩ [1814–17]   2 p 8vo
from William Wilberforce   NYPL(B)
For I dont like to lose old ⟨Habits⟩ with old

1815

12 Jan   4 p 4to   BM
to Arthur Young
The new year has been ushered into us, with

1 Feb   3 p fol   BM
to Arthur Young
I know you will rejoice to hear that poor little

4 Feb   4 p 4to   BM
to Arthur Young
Many thanks for your kind letter from

16 Feb   4 p 4to   BM
to Arthur Young
Many thanks for your last kind letter

25 Feb   4 p 4to   BM
to Arthur Young
I received your letter this very evening, &

25 Feb   amanuensis   4 p 4to
from Arthur Young   NYPL(B)
There have been two reasons for the silence

4 Mar   6 p 4to   Ryl
to HLTP
My dear Mrs Piozzi's last letter almost brought

10 Mar   4 p 8vo   BM
to Arthur Young
I was just sitting down to write to you

6 Apr   4 p 4to   BM
to Arthur Young
Many thanks for your letter, & friendly

8 Apr   4 p 4to   BM
to Arthur Young
I looked for you in vain at the ⟨Locke⟩

22 Apr   4 p 4to   Ryl
to HLTP
My dear Mrs Piozzi is so entirely in the living

[25 Apr 1815]   3 p 8vo   BM
to Arthur Young
I received your letter last night, & am very

4 May   3 p 4to   BM
to Arthur Young
I have been planning & contriving how to dine

17 May   6 p 4to   Ryl
to HLTP
The following is a curious story of a Russian

17 June   4 p 4to   BM
to Arthur Young
It grieves me to say that neither my mother or

27 June   4 p 4to   BM
to Arthur Young
I write, among other reasons, for the pleasure

6 July   4 p 4to   Ryl
to HLTP
It is very long since I last had the pleasure of

6 July   4 p 4to   BM
to Arthur Young
I was much disappointed at not having the

15 July   4 p 4to   BM
to Arthur Young
I was in hopes to have heard from you by this

20 July   3 p 4to   BM
to Arthur Young
Mr W goes tomorrow, D.V — on his

5 Aug   3 p 4to   BM
to Arthur Young
I have been longing to write, & to thank you

9 Aug [1815?]   4 p 8vo   NYPL(B)
from William Wilberforce
You must have supposed me to have lost my

17 Aug   4 p 4to   Ryl
to HLTP
My dear Mrs Piozzi will see by the date of this

Aug   4 p 4to   BM
to Arthur Young
I wrote you a few days ago, to say that Mama's

1815 continued

9 Sept   4 p 8vo   NYPL(B)
from William Wilberforce
I have been for some days thinking of writing

7 Oct   4 p 4to   Ryl
to HLTP
Ah my dear Mrs Piozzi, I have been in a world

9 Oct   4 p 4to   BM
to Arthur Young
Gardner was here today, & begs I will tell you

10 Oct   amanuensis   4 p 4to
from Arthur Young   NYPL(B)
I have this moment taken leave of your dear

13 Oct   4 p 4to   BM
to Arthur Young
Many sincere thanks, for your kind & welcome

16 Oct   amanuensis   4 p 4to
from Arthur Young   NYPL(B)
Can it be necessary for me to tell you that your

17 Oct   copy   3 p 8vo   BM(Bar)
from Arthur Young
You desire me to give you advice,

20 Oct   4 p 4to   BM
to Arthur Young
Many thanks for your kind present, of the hare

25 Oct   amanuensis   3 p 4to
from Arthur Young   NYPL(B)
My conscience reproaches me with not having

26 Oct   4 p 4to   BM
to Arthur Young
I wish I cd give you any positive intimation of

31 Oct   amanuensis   3 p 4to
from Arthur Young   NYPL(B)
As I suppose you are now in the habit of often

1 Nov   4 p 4to   BM
to Arthur Young
I have heard from dear Mr W. who is so good

4 Nov   amanuensis   3 p 4to
from Arthur Young   NYPL(B)
Your last letter gives me a very deep concern,

6 Nov   4 p 4to   BM
to Arthur Young
Your kind letter arrived to-day, accompanied

7 Nov [1815]   amanuensis   3 p 4to
from Arthur Young   NYPL(B)
Your telling me in the letter now recd. that the

10 Nov   4 p 4to   BM
to Arthur Young
Your kind letter, carried by Mr W. is just

11 Nov   6 p 4to   Ryl
to HLTP
Whether the richest people are the best, my

18 Nov   amanuensis   3 p 4to
from Arthur Young   NYPL(B)
I forgot the French Revolution before, and

20 Nov   4 p 4to   BM
to Arthur Young
We are safely arrived at Brighton, thank God.

3 Dec   4 p 4to   BM
to Arthur Young
I believe it is not my *turn* to write, but I am

5 Dec   amanuensis   3 p 4to
from Arthur Young   NYPL(B)
I have two very kind letters of yours to

10 Dec   4 p 4to   BM
to Arthur Young
Many thanks for yr kind letter, my dearest Sir.

18 Dec   4 p 4to   BM
to Arthur Young
It would do you good to see the delight Mr

20 Dec   amanuensis   4 p 4to
from Arthur Young   NYPL(B)
I am really ashamed to find by the date of your

26 Dec   4 p 4to   BM
to Arthur Young
Many thanks for your kind letter. I am now

26 Dec   4 p 12mo   NYPL(B)
from Sarah Wesley
The Time of Mr Wilberforce being so much

26 Dec   amanuensis   4 p 4to
from Arthur Young   NYPL(B)
What am I to say to the extreme kindness of

[1815?]   amanuensis   3 p 4to
from Arthur Young   NYPL(B)
Is it not very unreasonable [sic] in me to

1816

1 Jan [1816 misdated 1815]   4 p 4to
to Arthur Young   BM
I can write but a very few hurried lines, my

3 Jan   amanuensis   4 p 4to
from Arthur Young   NYPL(B)
Your letters are so pleasing to me, and I read

9 Jan   4 p 4to   BM
to Arthur Young
Many thanks for your kind letter, my dearest

11 Jan   amanuensis   4 p 4to
from Arthur Young   NYPL(B)
I was much concerned to find by your last

16 Jan   4 p 4to   Ryl
to HLTP
Many thanks, my dear Mrs Piozzi, for your

16 Jan   amanuensis   3 p 4to
from Arthur Young   NYPL(B)
I now begin what I presume will be my last

19 Feb   2 p 4to   NYPL(B)
from Sarah Wesley
Ah my dear Miss Francis! that I should have

1 Mar [1816]   4 p 8vo   NYPL(B)
from William Wilberforce
I am truly sorry that your warm & friendly

[11 Mar 1816]   6 p 4to   Ryl
to HLTP
One day when to Jove the black list was

17 Apr [1816]   4 p 8vo   NYPL(B)
from William Wilberforce
Having as I trusted so little more to do to

1 May   5 p 4to   Ryl
to HLTP
This is a glorious week. I wish you were in

8 May [1816]   2 p 8vo   NYPL(B)
from William Wilberforce
Be assured you always gratify me by applying

29 May   4 p 4to   BM
to Arthur Young
I have been often wishing to write to you

4 June   amanuensis   3 p 4to
from Arthur Young   NYPL(B)
I called the other day on Captain Burney, but

11 June   4 p 4to   BM
to Arthur Young
It was a great pleasure to us all to see you the

13 June [1816]   amanuensis   5 p 4to
from Arthur Young   NYPL(B)
I received your very kind letter, and I am sure

26 June   4 p 4to   Ryl
to HLTP
I envied Clem, my dear Mrs Piozzi, greatly,

6 July   4 p 4to   BM
to Arthur Young
You are very good to be angry with me for not

5 pmk   Aug   4 p 4to   Ryl
to HLTP
Here am I, once more, my dearest Mrs Piozzi

20 Sept   4 p 8vo   NYPL(B)
from William Wilberforce
I should be the most ungrateful Wretch alive

1 Oct   4 p 4to   Ryl
to HLTP
I had hoped, long before this, to have

4 Nov   amanuensis   3 p 4to
from Arthur Young   NYPL(B)
Your kind letter gave me much pleasure, for

28 Nov   4 p 4to   Ryl
to HLTP
Here we are, once more, my dear Mrs Piozzi,

28 Nov   4 p 4to   BM
with CBFB to Arthur Young
I wrote first to Charlotte, because I thought

4 DE 1816 pmk   inc   2 p 4to   Osb
from William Wilberforce
[ri]dings on Horseback had proved in ye

10 Dec   4 p 4to   BM
to Arthur Young
Many grateful thanks, my very dear Sir, for

14 Dec   amanuensis   3 p 4to
from Arthur Young   NYPL(B)
So all of you are arrived safely at Richmond,

21 Dec   4 p 4to   BM
to Arthur Young
Many thanks for your kind letter, my dearest

27 Dec   amanuensis   3 p 4to
from Arthur Young   NYPL(B)
I trust that your next letter will give an

28 Dec   4 p 4to   BM
to Arthur Young
My dearest Sir, though I wrote so lately, yet

20 Mar [pre 1817]   3 p 8vo   Osb
from William Wilberforce
How could you ask such a Question? Will you

1817

6 Jan   4 p 4to   BM(Bar)
to Arthur Young
Allow me, my dearest Sir, to Thank you

22 Jan   4 p 8vo   NYPL(B)
from William Wilberforce
My Eyes have of late been so indifferent as to

23 Jan   amanuensis   4 p 4to
from Arthur Young   NYPL(B)
Your account of Marianne Fairs has given us

28 Jan   4 p 4to   Ryl
to HLTP
I am sure, my dearest Mrs Piozzi, you will

[8] Feb   4 p 4to   BM(Bar)
to Arthur Young
I fear you will think that lately,

⟨10⟩ FE 1817   amanuensis   1 p 4to
from Arthur Young   NYPL(B)
Since the inclosed was written, I have received

19 Feb . amanuensis   3 p 4to
from Arthur Young   NYPL(B)
Your Brother Clem: called on me this morning

21 Feb   4 p 4to   BM(Bar)
to Arthur Young
Many thanks, my very dear Sir, for your

27 Feb   3 p 4to   BM(Bar)
to Arthur Young
I am happy to say that I expect

11 Mar   4 p 4to   Ryl
to HLTP
My letters to you, my dear Mrs Piozzi, instead

11 Mar   4 p 4to   BM(Bar)
to Arthur Young
Ever since we left you last, poor Dolph

15 Mar   amanuensis   3 p 4to
from Arthur Young   NYPL(B)
I cannot sufficiently thank you for your last

18 Mar [misdated] 1816   4 p 4to
to Arthur Young   BM(Bar)
You will be glad to hear, my dearest Sir, that

16 Apr   4 p 4to   BM(Bar)
to Arthur Young
As we missed Clem, & he was not

[19 Apr 1817]   3 p 8vo   BM(Bar)
to Arthur Young
Will you do me a great kindness?

23 Apr   3 p 4to   BM(Bar)
to Arthur Young
My journey is at length fixed. I go directly to

30 Apr   3 p 4to   BM(Bar)
to Arthur Young
I arrived at this melancholy abode

3 May   amanuensis   3 p 4to
from Arthur Young   NYPL(B)
Though you will soon quit Bath, &

6 May [1817]   4 p 4to   NYPL(B)
from William Wilberforce
Tho I am extremely prest for time I must try

12 May   4 p 4to   BM(Bar)
to Arthur Young
I have been wishing, & intending, for many

14 May   amanuensis   4 p 4to
from Arthur Young   NYPL(B)
Your reference to a passage in ⟨   ⟩

16 May   4 p 4to   Ryl
to HLTP
I think my dear Mrs Piozzi will be glad to hear

19 May   4 p 4to   BM(Bar)
to Arthur Young
You shall not say this time

26 May   amanuensis   3 p 4to
from Arthur Young   NYPL(B)
Yesterday I attempted to hear the famous D^r

27 May   3 p fol   BM(Bar)
to Arthur Young
Your kind & welcome letter reached

[May? 1817]   6 p 8vo & 4to   Ryl
to HLTP
Though I trust I shall have the happiness of

3 June   amanuensis   3 p 4to
from Arthur Young   NYPL(B)
Your Letter, my Dearest Friend, was very

5 June   4 p 4to   BM(Bar)
to Arthur Young
I hasten to tell you, my dearest Sir, what are

17 June   4 p 4to   BM(Bar)
to Arthur Young
Marianne <Fairs> is arrived safe. I saw her

19 June   4 p 4to   BM(Bar)
to Arthur Young
I am quite grieved, my dearest Sir, not to have

19 June   amanuensis   3 p 4to
from Arthur Young   NYPL(B)
You are become a sad correspondent — for I

25 June   pmk 1817   4 p 4to   BM(Bar)
to Arthur Young
Our last letters crossed upon the road,

3 July   4 p 4to   BM(Bar)
to Arthur Young
I lose no time in writing to you, my dearest

5 July   4 p 4to   Ryl
to HLTP
We wander about, my dear Mrs Piozzi, in

9 July   4 p 4to   BM(Bar)
to Arthur Young
I am quite grieved to find

14 July   amanuensis   3 p 4to
from Arthur Young   NYPL(B)
A thousand thanks for your very obliging

19 July   4 p 4to   BM(Bar)
to Arthur Young
Many thanks for your kind letters my dearest

25 July   amanuensis   3 p 4to
from Arthur Young   NYPL(B)
Without any power of dictating, I have

31 July   4 p 8vo   NYPL(B)
from William Wilberforce
Not, out of Ceremony; of that you would not

5 Aug   4 p 4to   BM(Bar)
to Arthur Young
You will have heard ot us from Charlotte,

13 Aug   amanuensis   4 p 4to
from Arthur Young   NYPL(B)
Your last letter had a commencement too

26 Aug   4 p 4to   Ryl
to HLTP
My dear Mrs Piozzi's remark on Lady Edwd

26 Aug   4 p 4to   BM(Bar)
to Arthur Young
There is a most marvellous person here, M^r

5 Sept   amanuensis   3 p 4to
from Arthur Young   NYPL(B)
All your letters are sure to be full of interesting

20 Sept   4 p 4to   BM(Bar)
to Arthur Young
I have seen a very curious sight to-day

27 Sept   4 p 8vo   NYPL(B)
from William Wilberforce
Indeed my dear Marianne I can plead Not

28 Sept   2 p 4to   NYPL(B)
from William Wilberforce
Never Apologize my dear Mar^{nne}. for opening

29 Sept   amanuensis   3 p 4to
from Arthur Young   NYPL(B)
It was with much pleasure that I rec^d. my dear

7 Oct   3 p 4to   BM(Bar)
to Arthur Young
It is twelve at night, my dearest Sir,

6 Nov   4 p 4to   Ryl
to HLTP
Here we are, once more, my dear Mrs Piozzi,

1817, continued

8 Nov   6 p 4to   NYPL(B)
from J I Hoare
I do not know that I should thus soon have

6 Dec   4 p 4to   BM(Bar)
to Arthur Young
You will be kindly wishing, perhaps,

10 Dec   amanuensis   4 p 4to
from Arthur Young   NYPL(B)
I cannot let the dear Charlotte go without

19 Dec   4 p 4to   BM(Bar)
to Arthur Young
I should sooner have acknowledged your kind

27 Dec   4 p 4to   Ryl
to HLTP
I had hoped to have written before we left

1818

1 Jan   4 p 4to   BM(Bar)
to Arthur Young
All hail, to you, my dear Sir, on this

24 Jan   3 p 4to   BM(Bar)
to Arthur Young
Many thanks, my dearest Sir, for your kind

12 Feb   3 p 4to   BM(Bar)
to Arthur Young
Here I am, once more, my dear Sir,

23 Feb   4 p 4to   Ryl
to HLTP
I am just returned from a visit to Mr & Mrs

24 Feb   amanuensis   3 p 4to
from Arthur Young   NYPL(B)
Your last of the 12th ought to have been

5 Mar [1818]   4 p 4to   Osb
from HLTP
My dear Marianne / will have Reason to be

5 Mar   amanuensis   3 p 4to
from Arthur Young   NYPL(B)
My dear friend is become a very pretty sort of

7 Mar   4 p 4to   BM(Bar)
to Arthur Young
It is so long since I wrote last

11 Mar   amanuensis   3 p 4to
from Arthur Young   NYPL(B)
I have so much business on my hands at

19 Mar   4 p 4to   BM(Bar)
to Arthur Young
What shall I say to you, my dearest Sir,

24 Mar   amanuensis   3 p 4to
from Arthur Young   NYPL(B)
Your last favour with your dear Mama's kind

2 Apr   4 p 4to   BM(Bar)
to Arthur Young
I hasten to answer the questions

11 Apr   amanuensis   4 p 4to
from Arthur Young   NYPL(B)
The first page of your last favor was very

22 Apr   4 p 4to   BM(Bar)
to Arthur Young
I have been intending for several days

25 Apr   4 p 4to   Ryl
to HLTP
I turn to Bath with melancholy thoughts, my

4 May   amanuensis   4 p 4to
from Arthur Young   NYPL(B)
I have continued so busy in reading and

6 May   4 p 4to   BM(Bar)
to Arthur Young
I lose no time in replying to your

14 May   amanuensis   3 p 4to
from Arthur Young   NYPL(B)
What! does my dearest friend talk of a poor

20 May   4 p 4to   BM(Bar)
to Arthur Young
Your letter was, as usual, very welcome to me

21 June   2 p 8vo   Osb
from John Sinclair
I have now the pleasure of sending you a copy

25 June   3 p 4to   BM(Bar)
to Arthur Young
Since I saw you last, I have been

26 June   4 p 4to   Ryl
to HLTP
My dear Mrs Piozzi's welcome letter should

6 July   4 p 4o   BM(Bar)
to Arthur Young
On my return home to Richmond, my

22 Oct   4 p 4to   NYPL(B)
from S Langton
It was with the deepest regret that I heard

14 July   amanuensis   3 p 4to
from Arthur Young   NYPL(B)
I have had your letter too long in my pocket

26 Oct   4 p 4to   NYPL(B)
from E Cardigan
It sounds rather paradoxical; but the kind

18 July   3 p 4to   BM(Bar)
to Arthur Young
Many thanks my dearest Sir for your letter

29 Oct   amanuensis   3 p 4to
from Arthur Young   NYPL(B)
The beginning of your last letter was a very

21 [July 1818]   amanuensis   1 p 4to
from Arthur Young   NYPL(B)
The messenger waits for this letter and

5 Nov   4 p 4to   BM(Bar)
to Arthur Young
Many thanks for your 2 kind letters

28 July   3 p 4to   BM(Bar)
to Arthur Young
Many thanks for your kind & welcome

16 Nov   amanuensis   3 p 4to
from Arthur Young   NYPL(B)
You deserve a very good dressing if I had the

10 Aug   5 p 4to   NYPL(B)
from Camilla Sinclair
Before I left Ham I used to promise myself

17 Nov 1817   pmk 1818   4 p 4to
to Arthur Young   BM(Bar)
I have been intending to write before

23 Sept   4 p 4to   Ryl
to HLTP
I have been very tardy, my dear Mrs Piozzi, in

27 Nov   amanuensis   4 p 4to
from Arthur Young   NYPL(B)
If I was not well assured of your friendship I

30 Sept   4 p 4to   Osb
from HLTP
My dear Marianne will accept my Answer to

4 Dec   4 p 4to   BM(Bar)
to Arthur Young
I have 2 kind & welcome Letters

1 Oct   4 p 4to   NYPL(B)
from William Wilberforce
I wonder whether our dear & valuable old

8 Dec   4 p 4to   Ryl
to HLTP
'Time flies, we know not how, away; but none

12 Oct   2 p 4to   BM(Bar)
to Arthur Young
We arrived safely at this place, Thank God,

17 Dec   amanuensis   4 p 4to
from Arthur Young   NYPL(B)
In answer to the introduction to your last

19 Oct   amanuensis   3 p 4to
from Arthur Young   NYPL(B)
I should have answered your portion of the

23 Dec   4 p 4to   BM(Bar)
to Arthur Young
You are very kind in desiring to have

21 Oct   4 p 4to   BM(Bar)
to Arthur Young
As I hope always, unless particularly

1819

4 Jan   amanuensis   3 p 4to
from Arthur Young   NYPL(B)
I find by your last favor that I gave you an

5 Feb   3 p 4to   BM(Bar)
to Arthur Young
I cannot let your last kind letter

14 Jan   4 p 4to   BM(Bar)
to Arthur Young
You will be pleased to hear that

13 Feb   pmk 1819   1 p 4to   Osb
from William Wilberforce
I have long earnestly wished to have you once

1819, continued

24 Feb   3 p 4to   BM(Bar)
to Arthur Young
I have been quite grieved, ever since I left you

26 Feb   4 p 4to   NYL(B)
from C J Hoare
Will you excuse the pen of a hasty writer in

11 Mar   3 p 4to   BM(Bar)
to Arthur Young
I have now been for a few days

22 Mar [1819]   3 p 4to   NYPL(B)
to HHBt
As my eyes feel rather better this morn^g than

23 Mar   4 p 4to   Ryl
to HLTP
My dear Mrs Piozzi's last kind letter has too

29 Mar   4 p fol   BM(Bar)
to Arthur Young
It is time to tell you something of my

25 Apr   3 p 4to   BM(Bar)
to Arthur Young
You will be grieved to hear that

28 Apr   3 p 4to   BM(Bar)
to Arthur Young
Not having been well enough

11 MY 1819 pmk   4 p 4to   BM(Bar)
to Arthur Young
I had a safe journey hither

1 June   4 p 4to   BM(Bar)
to Arthur Young
It was so hurried a visit

14 June   3 p 4to   BM(Bar)
to Arthur Young
I am quite vexed with myself

12 July   4 p 4to   BM(Bar)
to Arthur Young
I rejoice to find, by your letter,

14 Aug   4 p 4to   BM(Bar)
to Arthur Young
I give our present address, Mama having

29 Sept   4 p 4to   BM(Bar)
to Arthur Young
I feel quite like a most ungrateful

12 Oct   amanuensis   3 p 4to
from Arthur Young   NYPL(B)
I ought sooner to have acknowledged the

25 Oct   4 p 4to   BM(Bar)
to Arthur Young
It was with great pleasure that I

27 Oct   4 p 4to   Ryl
to HLTP
It is so very very long since I have had the

24 Nov   4 p 4to   BM(Bar)
to Arthur Young
Since I wrote last to you I have been on a

23 Dec   4 p 4to   BM(Bar)
to Arthur Young
I have often been wishing to write to you

[pre 1820]   amanuensis   3 p 4to
from Arthur Young   NYPL(B)
I send you the Missionary Registers, and Miss

1820

18 Jan   4 p 4to   BM(Bar)
to Arthur Young
Your last letter was particularly acceptable

23 Feb   4 p 4to   BM(Bar)
to Arthur Young
We are all truly rejoiced to hear

11 Mar   3 p 4to   BM(Bar)
to Arthur Young
I have been daily expecting to hear

4 Apr   3 p 4to   BM(Bar)
to Arthur Young
We have been rather occupied again

14 Apr   4 p 4to   Ryl
to HLTP
I should not have been thus tardy in replying

3 May   3 p 4to   NYPL(B)
from Mary Young
I am much gratified to find that you are kindly

14 Sept   4 p 4to   Ryl
to HLTP
Much more time has elapsed since the receipt

21 Sept [1820]   4 p 4to   Osb
from HLTP
I was glad to see Dear Marianne's kind letter

[post 1820]   2 p fragment   NYPL(B)
to HHBt
My darling Hett I am very glad to hear

[post 1820?]   2 p 4to   NYPL(B)
to JCBTM
I owe many thanks to you, my dearest Julia,

[post 1820?]   4 p 8vo   NYPL(B)
to HHBt
Since all <these> letters were finished, yr's

9 Apr [1820–28]   4 p 8vo   Ryl
from Sarah Wesley
Your mighty pretty Billet I have just received,

1823

22 July   4 p 8vo   NYPL(B)
from William Wilberforce
I cry you mercy — yet as was said by the

1824

18 Feb   3 p 4to   BM(Bar)
to JCBTM & HHBt
My dearest little Ju & Hett I suppose by this

23 Sept   3 p 8vo   NYPL(B)
to J Mendham
Having received an official Invitation to the

[22 Mar 1824]   4 p 4to   NYPL(B)
to CBFB
You liked this, my dearest Mama, so I employ

1825

29 MR 1825 pmk   4 p 4to   NYPL(B)
from Margaret Gandy
It pains my heart to hear Miss Francis talk of

1826

11 Aug   4 p 4to   NYPL(B)
to JCBTM & HHBt
Excuse my writg to you both together, havg

[1826?]   2 p 4to   NYPL(B)
to HHBt
I hope you recd a letter from me enclosg one

17 Sept   4 p 4to   NYPL(B)
to HHBt
Being very sick with a bilious & bowel attack,

[1826?]   3 p 8vo   NYPL(B)
to HHBt
I wrote you a long letter a week ago, when I

[1826?]   3 p 4to   NYPL(B)
to HHBt
I cant let them go without a line to you tho' so

1827

5 May   3 p 4to   BM(Bar)
from Charles Wesley
I am the voice of my sister, who cannot face

19 July   4 p 8vo   NYPL(B)
from William Wilberforce
I prefix private to my manuscript, not because

8 May   2 p fol   BM(Bar)
to CBFB
I rec'd yr kind letter of Ap. 11th

20 Dec   6 p 4to   NYPL(B)
to CBFB
Your most welcome letter, & dearest Char's, &

7–11 June   2 p 8vo   NYPL(B)
from Charles Wesley
I regret not being at home when you call'd;

[1827–30?]   4 p 4to   NYPL(B)
to CBFB
This is in answer to your kind & Char's

1827, continued

4 July [pre 1828]   2 p 8vo   Comyn
from Hannah More
Tho you were so considerate as to desire me

1828

21 Mar   4 p 4to   NYPL(B)
to JCBTM & HHBt
I think you did quite right in send^g me that

13 JU 1828 pmk   2 p 4to   BM(Bar)
to CBFB
Julia called on Tuesday for about 3 quarters

June   2 p 4to   BM(Bar)
from Charles Wesley
I have examined your airs, and have

22 Aug [1828]   4 p 4to   BM(Bar)
to CBFB
Yr kind letter was most welcome to me, who

15 Sept   4 p 4to   BM(Bar)
to CBFB
I lose no time in writing that this may go

3 Nov   1 p 4to   BM(Bar)
from Charles Wesley
I find you have not heard of the irreparable

18 Nov [1828]   4 p 4to   BM(Bar)
to CBFB
I am almost ashamed to write,

18 Nov [1828]   4 p 4to   BM(Bar
to JCBTM & HHBt
I consider myself the shabbiest of mortals

29 Nov – 1 Dec   4 p 4to   NYPL(B)
from William Crotch
I beg to return you many thanks for the very

[c1828]   1 p 4to   BM(Bar)
from Charles Wesley
Ye have had a most miraculous

1829

21 Feb   4 p 4to   NYPL(B)
from William Wilberforce
Poor Clement! or rather let me say poor

3 Mar   4 p 4to   NYPL(B)
from J I Hoare
Had I heard before the arrival of your letter

31 Mar   4 p fol   NYPL(B)
from Mary S Buchan
I cannot very well express the delightful

28 Apr   1 p 4to   NYPL(B)
from Charles Wesley
I much regret I hapend to be out when you

[6 May 1829]   4 p 4to   NYPL(B)
to CBFB
It is grievous to know that you are in town, &

27 May [1829?]   3 p 4to   NYPL(B)
from William Wilberforce
I cannot venture to express for fear of

28 May   4 p 4to   NYPL(B)
to CBFB
Yr kind letter arrived yesterday — & I shd

1830

7 Sept   4 p 4to   BM(Bar)
to CBFB
The Maid recommended by

14 Sept   4 p 4to   BM(Bar)
to CBFB
I am quite ashamed to <teaze> you so often

15 Nov   4 p 4to   NYPL(B)
from John Bickersteth
I thank you for your kind letter of Condolence

[1830–32]   2 p 8vo   NYPL(B)
from Ridley Haim Herschell
My dear Sister in a crucified & risen Saviour.

1831

24 JA 1831 pmk   1 p 4to   BM(Bar)
from William Wilberforce
I am told there is not perhaps one living

21 Feb   3 p 8vo   NYPL(B)
from William Wilberforce
By all means write to Simeon & tell him such

1 Aug   4 p 4to   NYPL(B)
to CBFB
I hope you have found a suitable lodging, &

12 Aug [1831]   4 p 4to   NYPL(B)
to CBFB
Yr most kind & welcome letter is just arrived,

[?23 Aug 1831]   4 p 8vo   NYPL(B)
from James E Gordon
I feel obliged by your kind note, and am sorry

24 Aug   4 p 4to   NYPL(B)
from Fanny Williams
A thousand thanks for the papers which

25 Aug [1831]   4 p 4to   NYPL(B)
to CBFB
You will be glad, I know, in yr kindness, to

26 Aug [1831]   4 p 4to   NYPL(B)
to CBFB
Yr letter (many thanks to you for it) is this

1 Sept   4 p 4to   NYPL(B)
to CBFB
I have *two* of yr kind dear welcome letters to

3 Sept   4 p 4to   NYPL(B)
to CBFB
Yr letter about M^r <Burrowes> is just

3 SE 1831 pmk   1 p 4to   NYPL(B)
from Julia Strachey
How very kind it was of the dear good

14 Sept [1831]   4 p 4to   NYPL(B)
to CBFB
Yr dear kind letter is this moment arrived: &

14 Sept   pmk 1831   4 p 4to   NYPL(B)
from Julia Strachey
Mr Strachey tells me of a packet from you

29 Sept   6 p 8vo & 4to   NYPL(B)
from Fanny Williams
I hope My very dear friend you will forgive

[c1831?]   4 p 8vo   NYPL(B)
from Fanny Williams
My dear Sister in Jesus and fellow-traveller to

[1831–32]   1 p 4to   NYPL(B)
from Margaret J Taylor
I feel quite ashamed at giving you the trouble

undated

?   3 p 8vo   NYPL(B)
to Henry Barrett
Hearing that you have offered Mr Talbot

?   4 p 8vo   NYPL(B)
from Mary S Elliot
Ever since I received your note my dear Miss

?   3 p 4to   NYPL(B)
from Charles Noel, 2nd Baron Barham
I send you a letter from M^r. Wilberforce and

?   2 p 4to   NYPL(B)
from Charles Noel, 2nd Baron Barham
I am quite <sorry> that I have detained this

?   1 p 4to   NYPL(B)
from [Margaret Gandy]
I feel quite at variance with myself, when I

?   1 p 4to   NYPL(B)
from Margaret Gandy
early and rest your weariness, in quiet with me

?   4 p 8vo   NYPL(B)
from Margaret Gandy
I thank you for your little note tho' I needed

?   4 p 8vo   NYPL(B)
from Margaret Gandy
How I looked out of the Window & grudged

?   4 p 8vo   NYPL(B)
from Margaret Gandy
M^r. Cotterill has read M^{rs}. Tighe's book

?   6 p 4to   NYPL(B)
from Margaret Gandy
I should be very glad to learn from yourself

?   1 p 12mo   NYPL(B)
from Mrs & Miss Roberts
M^{rs}. & Miss Roberts intended themselves the

CHARLOTTE (FRANCIS) BARRETT 1786–1870

(CFBt)

See also letters from FBA and CPB.

Holograph works, documents and other material relating to the Broome, Francis, and Barrett families are in the Berg and Barrett Collections except for a commonplace book with copies of poems by various members of the Burney family in the hand of CBFB, which is in the Houghton Library, Harvard.

1800

[8 Sept 1800]   1 p fol   NYPL(B)
from Clement Robert Francis
I long to see you I should like to act a play In

1801

31 Jan [1801]   2 p 4to   NYPL(B)
from Clement Robert Francis
I am so unhappy that I am gone away from

[1801?]   2 p 4to   NYPL(B)
from Clement Robert Francis
pray write me a letter in a Day or two and

1802

[8 June 1802]   2 p 8vo   NYPL(B)
from JB & SHB
I wish to write to your mother, but she has

[23] July   4 p 4to   NYPL(B)
from S Kingston
My dear Charlotte requests to hear of my safe

[post 17 Sept 1802]   2 p 4to   BM(Bar)
from Sarah Baker
My friend who loves you dearly wishes you to

23 Oct [1802]   4 p 4to   BM(Bar)
with CBFB to FBA
We arrived with reluctance last night in

1803

20 Mar   4 p 4to   NYPL(B)
from SHB
Why, the people think, at least those that I

2 Apr [1803]   4 p fol   NYPL(B)
from MF
I should not answer your kind letter so soon,

[12 May 1803]   4 p 4to   NYPL(B)
from SHB
Will you think this letter worth reading,

1804

4 Jan   4 p 4to   NYPL(B)
from SHB to CFBt & CBFB
Long looked for, come at last —

1 June [1804]   4 p 4to   NYPL(B)
from Sophia Burney
Your long silence is petrifying, & cuts me to the

17 Oct   4 p 4to   NYPL(B)
from Clement Robert Francis to CFBt,
    CBFB & MF
Thou the only comforter of the absent Clem I

26 Oct   4 p 4to   NYPL(B)
from SHB
Now I hope that this will not come popping

3 Nov [1804]   4 p fol   NYPL(B)
from SHB
Dear Me! You have been in Monmouthshire,

1805

29 June – 1 July   4 p 4to   NYPL(B)
from   ?
I have been debating a long time whether to

1806

5 Jan [1806]   4 p 4to   NYPL(B)
from Sophia Burney
I am extremely obliged to you for your

18 Jan [1806?]   4 p 4to   NYPL(B)
from Sophia Burney
Your silence is petrifying & Barbarous.

9 Mar [1806]   4 p 4to   NYPL(B)
from Sophia Burney
I received your entertaining Epistle of the

23 Apr [1806?]   4 p 4to   NYPL(B)
from Sophia Burney
Your Gallant Major Gardiner called here

[10 June 1806]   4 p 4to   NYPL(B)
from SHB
I have no objections in life to plucking my old

7 July   4 p 4to   NYPL(B)
from Sarah Wesley to CBFB, CFBt &
    MF
I have thought of my dear Mrs Broome every

18 Aug [1806]   4 p 4to   Ryl
with MF & CBFB to HLTP
I jumped about the room like "Miss Hett"

26 Aug   4 p 4to   NYPL(B)
from Sarah Wesley to CBFB & CFBt
Write a Letter to a dear Friend from Brighton!

Aug [1806]   4 p 4to   NYPL(B)
from Sophia Burney
I take the earliest opportunity of franking

27 [Sept 1806?]   4 p 4to   NYPL(B)
from Clement Robert Francis
My Dearest Charlotte now for an epistle to

16 Oct [1806]   4 p 4to   NYPL(B)
from Sarah Wesley to CBFB & CFBt
On the arrival of your prized Triumvirate (so

25 Oct   4 p 4to   BM(Bar)
from Frederic Thurston
Familarity, they say, breeds contempt or I

20 Nov [1806?]   4 p 4to   NYPL(B)
from SHB
I know you will not answer me

27 Dec [1806]   4 p 4to   NYPL(B)
from Sarah Wesley
You shall not again reproach me in the most

[1806?]   4 p 4to   NYPL(B)
from SHB
I will not venture to assert that this scrib,

[pre 1807]   4 p 4to   NYPL(B)
from Mary Eakin
I do not mean to trouble you with a

[1806 – June 1807]   2 p 4to
to FBA   NYPL(B)
Next to the delight of hearing *from* you I value

1807

22 Jan   4 p 4to   NYPL(B)
from Sarah Wesley to CBFB, CFBt &
    MF
Here I come my dear Mrs Broome like a well

8 Apr   3 p 4to   NYPL(B)
from Sarah Wesley
My dear Charlottes pretty letter requires

[6 May 1807]   3 p 4to   NYPL(B)
from SHB
With a great coarse sheet of vulgar paper

16 May [1807]   4 p 4to   BM(Bar)
from CBFB
My dearest Charlotte, your two last Letters I

1807, continued

22–[23] May [1807]   4 p 4to
from CBFB   BM(Bar)
I have been wanting to write to my dearest

May [1807]   4 p 4to   NYPL(B)
from SHB
My dearest Charlotte would not have been

[pre June 1807]   1 p 4to   BM(Bar)
from MF
The Girl waits & won't wait; & I can

3 June   2 p 4to   NYPL(B)
from Nathaniel G Woodrooffe
You would have had an earlier information of

4 June [1807]   3 p 4to   NYPL(B)
from Sophia Burney
I should not so soon trouble you with another

20 June   4 p 4to   NYPL(B)
from Clement Robert Francis
What a house we have got to our backs now.

26 June   4 p 4to   NYPL(B)
from SHB
Why truly I must be in high favour indeed!

26 June   4 p 4to   NYPL(B)
from Mary Cooke
Dear Charlotte since the single state / You've

5–9 July   4 p fol   BM(Bar)
from CBFB & Clement Robert Francis
I shall now begin a Letter to write by agrees

30 July [1807]   4 p 4to   NYPL(B)
from MF
Mercy 'pon me! If you knew what has befallen

2–11 Aug [1807]   4 p fol   NYPL(B)
from CBFB to CFBt & Henry Barrett
Friday last I forwarded a Sermon of three

12–24 Aug [1807]   4 p fol   NYPL(B)
from CBFB
Yesterday my dearly beloved Travellers I sent

25 Aug [1807]   3 p 8vo   NYPL(B)
from SHB
Charlotte, my love, and Henry / my Soul —

29 Nov [1807]   4 p 4to   NYPL(B)
from Sophia Burney
I have been many many weeks waiting for a

[18] Dec [1807]   2 p 4to   NYPL(B)
from Sophia Burney
Chide on, chide on — / Thy soft reproaches

14 Sept [1807–09]   4 p fol   BM(Bar)
from Cecilia Saunderson
This letter will probably reach you

1808

2 FE 1808 pmk   4 p 4to   NYPL(B)
from MF
Imprimis — read this to nobody but Barrett,

5 Mar   pmk 1808   4 p 4to   BM(Bar)
from MF
I should have annoyed you and Barrett with a

19 Mar [1808?]   4 p 4to   NYPL(B)
from MF
The <Lodging> commission gave Clem & me

20 JU 1808 pmk   4 p 4to   BM(Bar)
from MF
Mama thinks it, no doubt, highly dissolute

27 June [1808]   4 p 4to   BM(Bar)
from MF
I cannot let the parcel go, dearest Charlotte,

2 July [1808]   4 p 4to   NYPL(B)
from MF
Having not a great deal, Dearest Charlotte, to

9 July [1808]   4 p 4to   NYPL(B)
from MF
We were very unhappy at leaving you, &

12 July [1808]   4 p 4to   NYPL(B)
from MF
What the Deuce my dear Charlotte is after, I

20 Sept [1808]   4 p 4to   NYPL(B)
from MF
We are delighted my dearest Char, at the

24 Nov [1808]   3 p 4to   NYPL(B)
from Sarah Wesley
In weather which depresses every faculty of

[1808?]   2 p 4to   NYPL(B)
from MF
Your Budget arrived safe this ev^g. darling Char

[1808]   5 p 4to   BM(Bar)
from MF
This is to go to you by young Garratt,

[1808–18]   4 p 4to   NYPL(B)
from MF
It was a matter of the most severe regret to us

[1808–18]   4 p 4to   NYPL(B)
from MF
I am this moment come from Kens. G. & send

1809

[13 Feb 1809]   1 p 4to   NYPL(B)
from SHB
I have this moment received

11 Dec   4 p 4to   NYPL(B)
from MF
You have been most excessively kind darling

[28 Mar 1809]   3 p 4to   NYPL(B)
from SHB
Instead of me, who in my own proper person

12 Dec   3 p 8vo   NYPL(B)
from MF
Your note reached me this morning at one

23 Oct [1809]   4 p 4to   NYPL(B)
from Sarah Wesley
I returned but this morning, & to convince you

[29 Dec 1809]   6 p 4to   NYPL(B)
from SHB
Your well-packed, and well-stored basket

5 Dec   3 p 4to   NYPL(B)
from Sarah Wesley
I returned from <   > with the <   >

1810

6 JA 1810 pmk   3 p 4to   NYPL(B)
from SHB
I began a letter to you yesterday,

30 Mar   3 p fol   NYPL(B)
from Ralph Broome Jr
Thank you for your kind letter. You and I have

10 Jan   6 p 4to   BM(Bar)
from MF
I was very happy to hear from Mama that Julia

3 Apr   4 p 4to   NYPL(B)
from MF
Read this to yourself, Lovely, by all means —

25 Jan [1810]   4 p 4to   BM(Bar)
from MF
I am *quite* grieved & vexed & disappointed

5 Apr   3 p 8vo   NYPL(B)
from MF
Yesterday Morning Clem & I rose early dearest

29 Jan   4 p 4to   BM(Bar)
from MF
It was very good of you in the midst of your

23 Apr   4 p fol   NYPL(B)
from MF
Dont be frightened darling Char at the length

10 Feb   2 p 4to   NYPL(B)
from MF
I cannot let Mama's letter go, darling Char,

10 May   4 p 4to   BM(Bar)
from MF
Dear darling Charlotte you are very kind to

16 Feb   2 p 8vo   NYPL(B)
from Sarah (Payne) Burney
Receive my thanks for yours and M^r. Barretts

15 May   4 p 4to   BM(Bar)
from MF
Can I ever thank you enough darling Char for

16 Mar   4 p 4to   BM(Bar)
from MF
I can't let the Boys go, darling Char without

16 May   4 p 4to   NYPL(B)
from MF
We got home quite safe & happily darling Char,

18 Mar [1810]   4 p 4to   NYPL(B)
from Sarah Wesley
Your letters dearest Mrs Barrett afford me

18 May   4 p 4to   BM(Bar)
from MF
I am quite ashamed, darling Char, to pester

1810, continued

21 May   pmk 1810   4 p fol   BM(Bar)
from CBFB
My dearest Charlotte don't hinder & bother

12 JU 1810 pmk   1 p fol   NYPL(B)
from MF
I was some time debating, dearest Char,

19 June [1810]   4 p fol   NYPL(B)
to Henry Barrett
I should have written to you before, but I was

21 June   4 p 4to   NYPL(B)
from Henry Barrett
This will serve to acquaint you that I shall

[23 June 1810]   4 p 4to   NYPL(B)
from SHB
Were I so circumstanced as to be able

[1 Aug 1810]   4 p 4to   NYPL(B)
PS only from CBFB (in ALS SHB to
    Henry Barrett)
My dearest Charlotte I was much thunderstruck

15 Aug   3 p 4to   NYPL(B)
from SHB
The sweet Catalani! — I should break my heart

28 Sept   4 p 4to   NYPL(B)
from MF
You must have sent your last letter in a loaded

[1810?]   4 p 4to   NYPL(B)
from MF
Now Mama is gone dearest Charlotte, *you* are

[c 1810?]   3 p 4to   NYPL(B)
from Ralph Broome Jr
I thank you very much for the present and letter

1811

30 JA 1811 pmk   3 p 4to   NYPL(B)
from SHB
I write to say that I am grown so inveterately

18 Feb   4 p 4to   NYPL(B)
from MF
I am delighted to be at length able to write &

28 Feb [1811]   3 p 4to   NYPL(B)
from Samuel Wesley
Time always has encreased my friendships and

6 Mar [1811]   4 p 4to   NYPL(B)
from Samuel Wesley
Thanks dearest Mrs Barrett for the information

21 Mar   4 p 4to   NYPL(B)
from MF
I hope you wont be angry with me, dearest

9 Apr   3 p 8vo   BM(Bar)
from MF
Mirror of punctuality that you are my dearest

13 May   4 p 8vo   NYPL(B)
from MF
My dearest Charlotte must forgive this little

17 May [1811]   draft?   4 p 4to
to SHB   NYPL(B)
I ought to have written to you sooner, for *your*

17 May [1811?]   4 p 4to   NYPL(B)
from Sarah Wesley
I have been subpaened in a court of Law — I

1 June   4 p 4to   BM(Bar)
from CBFB
Sweet Ju has left a pinbefore & some of her

26 JU 1811   pmk   4p 4to   NYPL(B)
from SHB
No, darling Charlotte, I remember not a word

26 July   4 p 4to   NYPL(B)
from MF
Mama desires me to give you her kindest love

1 AU 1811 pmk   6 p 4to   NYPL(B)
from SHB
I shall put no date to this letter, dearest Char,

13 Aug [1811]   4 p 4to   NYPL(B)
from SHB
I reckoned, my dearest Charlotte, without my

16 Aug   4 p 4to   NYPL(B)
from MF
You will rejoice thoroughly my dearest Char,

12 Sept   4 p fol   NYPL(B)
from CBFB & MF to Ralph Broome Jr &
    CFBt
I am glad you have had the pleasure of seeing

29 Sept [1811]   3 p 4to   NYPL(B)
from Sarah Wesley
Thanks dear Mrs Barrett for your obliging

4 Oct   4 p fol   NYPL(B)
from CBFB & MF to Ralph Broome Jr &
    CFBt
I thank you for your French Letter — &

5 OC 1811 pmk   4 p 4to   NYPL(B)
from SHB
I have just finished off a noble long rigmarole to

[18 or 25] Oct [1811]   4 p 4to
from SHB   NYPL(B)
Behold Charlotte, my love, I send you

9 Dec   4 p 4to   NYPL(B)
from MF
So my dearest — Lady K came at last you

1812

20 Jan   4 p 4to   NYPL(B)
from SHB
How very droll, dearest Charlotte, that your

31 Jan   pmk 1812   4 p 4to
from MF   BM(Bar)
Many thanks my dearest for your kind letter

[Jan 1812]   3 p 8vo   BM
to Arthur Young
We have all to thank you for a very fine

19 Feb [1812]   4 p 4to   NYPL(B)
from SHB
Dearest Char — Last night, or rather, this

[1 Apr 1812]   3 p 4to   NYPL(B)
from SHB
I thank you, my dearest Charlotte, for the

15 AP pmk [1812?]   2 p 4to   NYPL(B)
from MF
I hear is surprising. He is now < >

3 Aug [1812?]   4 p 4to   NYPL(B)
from CBFB
Ever since I wrote to you last I have been

10 Aug   4 p 4to   BM(Bar)
from MF
Many thanks, my dearest, for your kind letter

14–17 Aug [1812]   3 p 4to   NYPL(B)
from SHB
Your letter to M^{de}. Gomer procured me a visit

26 [Aug 1812]   4 p 4to   BM(Bar)
to MF
You will be glad to hear that dear Aunt

7 Sept   3 p 4to   NYPL(B)
from SHB
I am an ungrateful wretch to have left

8 Oct   pmk 1812   4 p fol   BM(Bar)
to MF
You owe this attack to Tighe, who came

31 Oct   4 p 4to   BM(Bar)
from MF
I have been long intending to answer

1813

[26 Apr 1813]   3 p 4to   BM
to Arthur Young
Do not be angry with me if I tell you that we

24 May [1813]   4 p 4to   NYPL(B)
from MF
I begin my letter you see, in a true irish spirit

2 July   4 p 4to   BM(Bar)
from MF
Here I am my dearest Char, almost tired of

7 Nov [1813?]   3 p 4to   NYPL(B)
from Clement Robert Francis
Tho I may have little or nothing to say yet

10 Nov   4 p 4to   NYPL(B)
from SHB
I too am reading Mme. de Staal [sic]

[1813]   4 p 4to   NYPL(B)
from MF
Will you forgive me, & not think it

1814

[1 Jan 1814]   6 p 4to   BM(Bar)
to FBA
I write at my dear Mother's elbow

7 May [1814]   4 p 4to   NYPL(B)
to MF
I have plenty of things to tell you if I knew

9 July   1 p 4to   NYPL(B)
from HLTP
Our Marianne plays us very false — does she

14 July   1 p 4to   NPG
from HLTP
H: L: Piozzi will wait on dear Mrs. Barrett on

23 July   3 p 4to   NYPL(B)
from Richard Tighe
Your letter of 20th May reached my hands at

27 July [1814]   4 p 4to   NYPL(B)
to FBA
I must entreat you to pity our disappointment

10 Sept   pmk 1814   4 p 4to
from SHB   NYPL(B)
Oh, the bustles and fusses that I was in,

1815

28 Jan   4 p 4to   NYPL(B)
from SHB
I have scarcely been at home a day

5 Apr   4 p 4to   NYPL(B)
from SHB
If ever you do me the undeserved honour

21 Apr   4 p 4to   NYPL(B)
from MF
Many thanks for your letter, my dearest Char.

29 Apr [1815]   4 p 4to   NYPL(B)
from Clement Robert Francis to CBFB
    & CFBt
Your kindness in excusing my long silence not

20 June   4 p 4to   BM
to Arthur Young
Mama & Marianne are talking very happily

22 June [1815]   3 p 4to   BM
to Arthur Young
We thank you most gratefully for your very

[25 June 1815]   3 p 4to   BM
to Arthur Young
Nothing can be so kind as your letters &

[29 June 1815]   3 p 4to   BM
to Arthur Young
I am ashamed to trouble you with so many

30 June   4 p 4to   NYPL(B)
from Agathe, comtesse de Gomer
Je me serois empresée de vous ecrire

4 July [1815]   4 p 4to   BM
to Arthur Young
I hope this letter may find you safely arrived

8–10 July [1815]   4 p 4to   BM(Bar)
to FBA
You must imagine our thankfulness at hearing

10 July   4 p 4to   NYPL(B)
from MF
Before I forget it again, let me enclose, what

31 July [1815]   4 p 4to   BM
to Arthur Young
I rejoice to tell you that at last our house is let

4 Aug [1815]   3 p 4to   BM
to Arthur Young
I have only time to write shortly & save

2 Oct   4 p 4to   NYPL(B)
from Agathe, comtesse de Gomer
Il m'est impossible de vous exprimer combien

6 Oct   4 p 4to   BM(Bar)
from MF
I enclose a letter to dr Mr Young

11 Oct [1815]   4 p 4to   BM
to Arthur Young
We all arrived here safely though very

13 Oct   4 p 4to   NYPL(B)
from MF
You will rejoice, I know, to hear, that by the

19 Oct   4 p 4to   NYPL(B)
from MF
I fear that both you & Barrett will think I have

24 Oct [1815]   4 p 4to   BM
to Arthur Young
Your kind letter gave us great pleasure though

2 Nov   4 p 4to   NYPL(B)
from MF
Your kind & interesting letter arrived today.

8 Nov   4 p 4to   NYPL(B)
from MF
Many thanks, my dearest Char^e for your kind

13 Nov [1815]   4 p 4to   BM
to Arthur Young
I received your very kind letter at Harwich, &

18 Nov [1815]   5 p 4to   BM(Bar)
to FBA
Joy to us all, a thousand times over

25 Nov   amanuensis   3 p 4to
from Arthur Young   NYPL(B)
The cart gone to Bury with the trunks and

4 Dec [1815]   4 p 4to   BM
to Arthur Young
I am delighted to find that you are arrived in

20 DE 1815 pmk   5 p 4to   BM
to Arthur Young
The melancholy account of your bad health

22 Dec   2 p 4to   NYPL(B)
from JB
Evil communication has certainly disturbed my

[1815]   4 p 4to   inc   BM(Bar)
to FBA
me that Aunt Burney had some opportunity in

[1815?]   1 p 4to   NYPL(B)
from JB & Sarah (Payne) Burney
I received the Dividends this morning

1816

1 Mar   4 p 4to   NYPL(B)
from SHB
I do begin, my dearest, humbly to flatter myself

29 Mar [1816]   4 p 4to   BM
to Arthur Young
Mama and I fully hoped to have met you at the

24 Apr [1816]   4 p 4to   BM
to Arthur Young
I congratulate you on the return of fine weather

30 May [1816]   5 p 4to   BM
to Arthur Young
I thank you for your kind letter & for your very

[15 June 1816]   4 p 4to   NYPL(B)
to FBA
I am most grateful not only for the sweet &

[26 June 1816]   4 p 4to   BM
to Arthur Young
I venture to write today in the hope that this

4 Sept   4 p 4to   NYPL(B)
from SHB
How many sweet, and cordial, and amusing

[Nov 1816]   5 p 4to   BM(Bar)
to FBA
Joy to us all, a thousand times over

6 Dec [1816]   3 p 4to   BM
to Arthur Young
I know you will be kindly pleased to hear that

27 Dec   6 p 4to   BM(Bar)
to Arthur Young
Your kind letter gave me great pleasure

[1816]   2 p 4to   BM(Bar)
to FBA
The last accounts which my dear Mother gave

[1816]   4 p 8vo   NYPL(B)
from MF
You are very kind & good My dearest Charlotte

24 Apr [c 1816–17?]   4 p 4to
                            BM(Bar)
from Cecilia Saunderson
Really my dear Charlotte you are the best Girl

1817

16 JA 1817 pmk   4 p 4to   BM(Bar)
to Arthur Young
I begin to fear you will not give me another

10 Feb   pmk 1817   4 p 4to   BM(Bar)
to Arthur Young
As I conclude you are now arrived

22 Feb   pmk 1817   4 p fol   BM(Bar)
to Arthur Young
We were all grieved to hear so

8 Apr [1817]   6 p 4to   BM(Bar)
to Arthur Young
You may judge with what

16 Apr   pmk 1817   6 p 4to   BM(Bar)
to Arthur Young
I owe you double & treble thanks for a

10 May [1817]   4 p 4to   BM(Bar)
to Arthur Young
In all the melancholy hurry of our

26 May [1817]   4 p 4to   BM(Bar)
to Arthur Young
I must confess that your kind letter deserved

16 June [1817]   4 p 4to   BM(Bar)
to Arthur Young
I wish I had another sermon to send you

3 JY 1817 pmk   3 p 4to   BM(Bar)
to Arthur Young
Your kind letter dated Tuesday

29 July [1817]   4 p fol   NYPL(B)
from CBFB & MF
Your dear Letters my beloved Charlotte are

6 Aug   4 p 4to   NYPL(B)
from Agathe, comtesse de Gomer
j'esperois, ma chere Madame Barrett, en

11 Sept   4 p 4to   NYPL(B)
from Clement Robert Francis
I have long been intendᵍ. to write to you but

23 Oct [1817]   4 p 4to   NYPL(B)
from SHB
Ten millions of thanks for telling me

13 DE 1817 pmk   4 p 4to   BM(Bar)
to Arthur Young
I know you will be pleased to hear that we

16 Dec   4 p 4to   NYPL(B)
from SHB
Well, how do you do, my dearest Charlotte?

28 Dec   4 p 4to   BM(Bar)
to Arthur Young
I wish you, & all around you a merry Christmas

1818

12 Jan [1818]   4 p 4to   BM(Bar)
to Arthur Young
I am sure you will have been shocked

23 Jan [1818?]   4 p 4to   BM(Bar)
to HHBt
I was very glad to receive

24 Jan [1818]   6 p 4to   BM(Bar)
to Arthur Young
I hope, my dear Sir, that you are now

28 Jan [1818]   4 p 4to   BM(Bar)
to FBA
We all join in congratulating you & Genˡ.
also   copy   1 p LB   NYPL(B)

6–7 Mar [1818]   5 p 4to   BM(Bar)
to Arthur Young
Marianne tells me you are so good as to wish

18 Mar [1818]   5 p 4to   BM(Bar)
to Arthur Young
I take the opportunity of saving your pence

25 Mar [1818]   6 p 4to   BM(Bar)
to Arthur Young
I was really ashamed of myself

6 Apr   4 p 4to   BM(Bar)
to Arthur Young
I hasten to give you what little information

9 Apr   amanuensis   3 p 4to
from Arthur Young   NYPL(B)
Pray return a thousand thanks from me to Mʳ

[16 Apr 1818]   3 p 4to   BM(Bar)
to Arthur Young
I write in haste to say that Mama, Barrett & I

4 May   4 p 4to   NYPL(B)
from AA
All — all is over my dearest Charlotte! —

[4 May 1818]   2 p 4to   NYPL(B)
to FBA
How can we express how deeply we all feel for

6 May [1818]   3 p 4to   NYPL(B)
to AA
Alas! my dearest Alexander we can only grieve

9 May [1818]   4 p 4to   BM(Bar)
to Arthur Young
I conclude that Marianne has told you of poor

15 May [1818]   4 p 4to   NYPL(B)
to FBA
Our dear Alexander desires me to write to you

18 May [1818]   4 p 4to   BM(Bar)
to Arthur Young
I duly received your kind letter

[21 May]   pmk 1818   3 p 4to
to Arthur Young   BM(Bar)
We shall I hope have the pleasure

7 June   4 p 4to   NYPL(B)
from Agathe, comtesse de Gomer
Depuis le moment ou j'ai reçu votre derniere

11 June   4 p 4to   BM(Bar)
from MF
Many thanks for your kindness in writing twice

27 June   pmk 1818   4 p 4to
to Arthur Young   BM(Bar)
At last our day for departing is fixed

7 July   2 p 4to   NYPL(B)
from Cassandra (Leigh) Cooke
You will I am certain pardon this trespass upon

9 July   pmk 1818   4 p 4to
from CBFB   NYPL(B)
This post my dearest Charlotte brought me y^r.

13–16 July [1818]   4 p 4to   BM(Bar)
to Arthur Young
We have arrived thus far on our journey

23 July   amanuensis   4 p 4to
from Arthur Young   NYPL(B)
I cannot sufficiently thank you for the most

25 July   4 p 4to   NYPL(B)
from MF & HHBt to CFBt & JCBTM
I have been waiting several days in hopes of a

28 July   pmk 1818   4 p 4to   BM(Bar)
to Arthur Young
Here is another letter from Paris where Julia &

3 Aug   4 p 4to   BM(Bar)
to Arthur Young
We have been at Tours <four> days

12 Aug   4 p 4to   NYPL(B)
from Arthur Young & MF
Can it be necessary for me to tell you how much

17 Aug   4 p 4to   BM(Bar)
to Arthur Young
This is the last day of our stay at Lyons

19 Aug   4 p 4to   NYPL(B)
from MF
A letter from Mama yesterday, mentions, with

27 Aug [1818]   4 p 4to   NYPL(B)
to MF
Your kind letter to Tours was a great treat &

28–30 Aug [1818]   4 p 4to   BM(Bar)
to Arthur Young
We arrived at Sesto this evening

9–16 Sept [1818]   4 p 4to   BM(Bar)
to Arthur Young
We arrived at Geneva from Turin & Mont

25 Sept [1818]   4 p 4to   BM(Bar)
to Arthur Young & MF
This is the second day of our journey from

26–29 Sept   4 p 4to   NYPL(B)
from Arthur Young & MF
I employ Marianne's pen, in the 1st place, to

6 Oct   pmk 1818   4 p 4to   BM(Bar)
to Arthur Young & MF
I have just received your & dear Marianne's

8 Oct   4 p 4to   NYPL(B)
from MF
This is my 9th letter since your absence, & as it

12 Oct [1818]   2 p 4to   BM(Bar)
to Arthur Young
We are safely arrived at Brighton

1818, continued

10 Nov [1818]   4 p 4to   BM(Bar)
to Arthur Young
I have been silent longer than I wished, but

1–2 Dec   pmk 1818   4 p 4to
to Arthur Young   BM(Bar)
I have received your kind letter

23 Dec   pmk 1818   4 p 4to   BM(Bar)
to Arthur Young
I have a great part of my Journal ready

23–24 Dec   amanuensis   4 p 4to
from Arthur Young   NYPL(B)
It shall arrive in a very few days! Oh you are a

29 Dec [1818]   4 p 4to   BM(Bar)
to Arthur Young
I received your letter & am

1819

4 Jan   amanuensis & ALS   3 p 4to
NYPL(B)
from Arthur Young & Mary Young
I have read your Journal with the greatest

17 Jan [1819]   4 p 4to   BM(Bar)
to Arthur Young
Your kind letter was forwarded

5 Feb [1819]   4 p 4to   BM(Bar)
to Arthur Young
I have to thank you for a very fine hare

9 Feb [1819]   4 p 4to   BM(Bar)
to Arthur Young
We are truly concerned to hear of your cold

10 FE 1819 pmk   1 p fol   BM(Bar)
to Arthur Young
PS. I am sorry to trouble you my dear Sir with

[24 Feb 1819]   3 p 4to   BM(Bar)
to Arthur Young
How very kind you are in exerting yourself for

[11 Mar 1819]   1 p 4to   NYPL(B)
from Clement Robert Francis
I take great blame to myself for having been so

2 Apr [1819]   4 p 4to   BM(Bar)
to Arthur Young
I thank you very gratefully for your

[12 Apr 1819]   4 p 4to   BM(Bar)
to Arthur Young
I had not written to Mr Gandy

22 Apr [1819]   4 p 4to   BM(Bar)
to Arthur Young
I owe you a thousand thanks

10 May [1819]   4 p 4to   BM(Bar)
to Arthur Young
I was much vexed when last in Town

7 JU 1819 pmk   4 p 4to   BM(Bar)
to Arthur Young
I hope you like this fine weather

9 June [1819]   4 p 4to   BM(Bar)
to Arthur Young
I wrote to you a few days ago,

23 June   pmk 1819   4 p 4to   BM(Bar)
to Arthur Young
I hope this will find you somewhat

[June 1819]   2 p 4to   BM(Bar)
to FBA
Mrs. Parker begs leave to offer you

16 July   pmk 1819   4 p 4to   BM(Bar)
to Arthur Young
You will see by the date of this letter

23 Aug [1819]   4 p 4to   BM(Bar)
to Arthur Young
We have been returned from Brighton

6 Sept   pmk 1819   4 p 4to   BM(Bar)
to Arthur Young
Accept our best thanks for

5 Oct   pmk 1819   4 p 4to   BM(Bar)
to Arthur Young
You ask me in your kind letter of Septr 20th.

17 Oct   pmk 1819   4 p 4to   BM(Bar)
to Arthur Young
You will have seen in the news paper

11 Nov   pmk 1819   4 p 4to   BM(Bar)
to Arthur Young
I received your last kind letter for which I beg

[1819–26]   6 p 4to   BM(Bar)
to CBFB
These opportunities of Mrs. Mellish's set my

22 Nov   4 p 4to   BM(Bar)
to Arthur Young
I have not had the manners to thank you

[pre 1820]   3 p 8vo   BM(Bar)
to Arthur Young
I will not interrupt you by too early a visit

7 Dec   5 p 4to   BM(Bar)
to Arthur Young
Your kind & interesting letter

1820

25–26 Jan   4 p 4to   BM(Bar)
to Arthur Young
I reproach myself with having

22 Oct [1820]   3 p 4to   NYPL(B)
from P L Costantini
E meglio tardi che mai, è un proverbio per i

10 Feb   4 p 4to   BM(Bar)
to Arthur Young
You have doubtless been concerned

27 Oct [1820]   4 p 4to   NYPL(B)
from SHB
My dearest Char — for sundry reasons, too

21 Feb [1820]   6 p 4to   BM(Bar)
to Arthur Young
As you were expected in London according

1 NO 1820 pmk   4 p 4to   NYPL(B)
from SHB
No, my dearest, I do not by any means think

13 MR 1820 pmk   3 p 4to   BM(Bar)
to Arthur Young
I have only a few minutes to say

19 Dec [1820?]   4 p 8vo   BM(Bar)
to FBA
For a fortnight I have been trying

29 Mar [1820]   4 p fol   BM(Bar)
to Arthur Young
You will I hope excuse a rough sheet of foolscap

22 Dec   3 p 4to   NYPL(B)
from JB
I am very glad you have published your journal.

19 Apr   4 p 4to   NYPL(B)
from Mary Young
Pray accept my sincere thanks for your kind

[1820]   4 p 4to   NYPL(B)
to Sarah (Burney) Payne
Your kind note received last night has given me

11 Sept   3 p 4to   NYPL(B)
from Mary Young
I have the pleasure of sending you by the

[1820]   4 p 4to   NYPL(B)
from William and Barbara Wilberforce
I long to send you a few lines to express our

1821

27 Feb   4 p 4to   NYPL(B)
from SHB
My dearest — that part of your letter which

7 May [1821]   3 p 4to   NYPL(B)
from Frances (Phillips) Raper
Raper desired me to tell you and M^r. Barrett

21 Apr [1821]   4 p 4to   NYPL(B)
from Frances (Phillips) Raper
We were awakened from our long sleep of

May 1821   4 p 4to   NYPL(B)
from Clement Robert Francis
You will I am sure be glad to hear some account

7 May   4 p 4to   NYPL(B)
from Agathe, comtesse de Gomer
il y a si si longtems, ma chere Madame Barrett

16–22 June [1821]   4 p 4to   BM(Bar)
from CBFB & MF
I have just finished N°. 3 to dispatch

1821, continued

18 June [1821?]   draft   3 p 4to
to CBFB   BM(Bar)
I begin this letter during my travels though it

29 June [1821]   copy   2 p LB
to MF   BM(Bar)
all your letters arrived safely

29 June [1821]   copy   3 p LB
to Elizabeth Morton   BM(Bar)
We have now been here long enough

29 June [1821]   2 p LB   BM(Bar)
to Caroline Penn
We heard with great interest

1 July [1821]   summary   1 p LB
to Clement Robert Francis   BM(Bar)
Julius back — Dick Election — Flemings

4 July   4 p 4to   NYPL(B)
from MF to Henry Barrett, CFBt &
    HHBt
I sit down to give you an acct of all

[pre 9 July 1821] copy   2 p LB
to CBFB   BM(Bar)
Henry's Head / I have painted portraits

9 July [1821]   copy   2 p LB
to CBFB   BM(Bar)
Arthur & I were walking in the fields

26 July   4 p 4to   NYPL(B)
from MF to CFBt, JCBTM & Henry
    Barrett
I am obliged to write on business to Barrett, by

28 July [1821] copy   1 p LB
to CBFB   BM(Bar)
We are safely returned & found the little ones

28 July [1821] copy   3 p 4to
to Anne (Cox) Woodrooffe   BM(Bar)
We have now been self banished from England

31 July–[3 Aug 1821]   4 p 4to
to CBFB   BM(Bar)
When you receive this you may be sure

7 Aug [1821]   copy   3 p LB
to Frances (Phillips) Raper   BM(Bar)
I have been 3 months in Ghent & never received

5 Sept [1821] copy   3 p LB
to CBFB   BM(Bar)
I do not like to miss my weekly

7 Sept   4 p 4to   NYPL(B)
from SHB
I write, dearest Charlotte, for the interested

19 Sept [1821]   copy   4 p LB
to Clement Robert Francis   BM(Bar)
I was quite grieved to hear from dear Mama

[c 20 Sept 1821]   copy   4 p LB
to CBFB   BM(Bar)
Your two kind letters 12 & 13 arrived

20 Sept [1821]   copy   4 p LB
to MF   BM(Bar)
Your kind letter in Mr P's pacquet

28 Sept [1821]   copy   3 p LB
to FBA   BM(Bar)
Your most kind & charming letter claims & *has*

28 Sept [1821]   copy   1 p LB
to CBFB   BM(Bar)
I don't know why Alex is travelling in

29 Sept [1821]   copy   1 p LB
to [William?] Penn   BM(Bar)
The King is at Brussels

[Sept 1821]   draft   2 p LB   BM(Bar)
to [William?] Penn
It gave us much pleasure

5 Oct [1821]   copy   5 p LB
to SHB   BM(Bar)
Your kind & beautiful letter only arrived to day

5 Oct [1821]   copy   4 p LB
to Sarah (Burney) Payne   BM(Bar)
Your very kind & very pleasant letter was a

[20? Oct 1821]   copy   1 p LB
to FBA   BM(Bar)
Now I am *Penning* my last letter <carrier>

[post 1821]   10 p 8vo   BM(Bar)
from Sarah (Burney) Payne
When I begin to want a letter

[1821]   1 p 8vo   BM(Bar)
to Cornelia (Mierop) Cambridge
I have *divided* my case of Chinese Vermillion &

1822

8 Jan [1822]   4 p 4to   NYPL(B)
from JCBTM
I was very glad indeed to receive your last

10 Mar   3 p 4to   NYPL(B)
from SHB
My dearest, I write to you, *under the rose*

10 July [1822]   4 p 4to   NYPL(B)
from CBFB & MF
Yʳ. dear letters by Mʳ. ⟨Garrick⟩ are just

16 July   copy   2 p LB   BM(Bar)
to MF
Directions about Dick / Mrs Kingston

18 July   4 p 4to   NYPL(B)
from MF
This is my 1ˢᵗ to you, Mama wishing to write a

24 July [1822]   3 p 4to   NYPL(B)
from ⟨Laetitia⟩ Hawkins
You have a new neighbour in the house over

26 July [1822] copy 4 p LB BM(Bar)
to MF
Mrs Langtons death has shocked us

28 July [1822] copy 4 p LB BM(Bar)
to MF
I have teized you sadly

2 Aug [1822] copy 4 p LB BM(Bar)
to MF
You will receive this before you get a budget

26 Aug [1822] copy 4 p LB BM(Bar)
to MF
Your kind letter arrived yesterday & relieved

28 Aug [1822] copy 3 p LB BM(Bar)
to CBFB
Marianne writes me word that you &

4 Sept   4 p 4to   NYPL(B)
to FBA
This letter must contain no secrets of State as
also   copy   4 p LB   BM(Bar)

4 Sept [1822] copy 2 p LB BM(Bar)
to MF
Dicks going he can upon occasion

9 Sept [1822] copy 4 p LB BM(Bar)
to CBFB
A gentleman who is going to London

9 Sept [1822] copy 1 p LB BM(Bar)
to Elizabeth Morton
I have not forgotten that you desired

10 Sept [1822]   copy   1 p LB
to MF   BM(Bar)
Count de Salis says it is much believed in the

14 Sept [1822]   copy   5 p LB
to CBFB   BM(Bar)
Your most wellcome letter of Sepʳ 4

20 Sept [1822]   4 p 4to   NYPL(B)
with JCBTM to Clement Robert Francis
Though it is now so late for new expeditions,
also   partial copy   2 p LB   BM(Bar)
Prices at Boulogne / We have had the Beauty

22 Sept [1822]   copy   4 LB
to MF   BM(Bar)
Many thanks for your kind thought

22 Sept [1822]   copy   5 p LB
to Frances (Phillips) Raper   BM(Bar)
It is my turn to apologize for not immediately

29 Sept   4 p 4to   NYPL(B)
from MF
I think this letter will have some chance of

4 Oct [1822] copy 3 p LB BM(Bar)
to CBFB
Both your kind letters arrived

21 Oct [1822] copy 3 p LB BM(Bar)
to FBA
We are at last thus near you

21 Oct [1822] copy 1 p 4to BM(Bar)
to Richard Barrett
We arrived at home last Wedʸ night

23 Oct [1822] copy 4 p LB BM(Bar)
to CBFB
I hope I shall soon be indulged with a letter

28 OC 1822 pmk   2 p 4to   NYPL(B)
from B[arbara] Hofland
When Mʳ Holland came over the other day to

3 Nov   copy   3 p LB   BM(Bar)
to CBFB
As you predicted your kind letter for Marianne

12 Dec   4 p 4to   NYPL(B)
from Agathe, comtesse de Gomer
Il y a si long-temps que je n'ai eu le plaisir

1823

[1822–26]   2 p 4to   BM(Bar)
to CBFB
Marianne's Jelly / 1 Calves foot / I Lemon —

19 Jan   4 p 4to   NYPL(B)
from Agathe, comtesse de Gomer
Pourquoi faut-il, ma chere Madame Barrett

Jan   3 p 4to   NYPL(B)
from AA
As Le soir of Lamartine is one of your

1 AP 1823 pmk   3 p 4to   NYPL(B)
to FBA
With what joyful and thankful alacrity I obey

25 May pmk 1823 4 p fol BM(Bar)
from JCBTM to CFBt & HHBt
As Grandmama has given me this large sheet

13 June [1823]   3 p 4to   NYPL(B)
from SHB
I am quite disappointed, dearest, at

24 JU 1823 pmk   4 p 4to   BM(Bar)
from JCBTM & CBFB to CFBt & Henry
    Barrett Jr
Clem desires me to say

8 Aug   4 p 4to   NYPL(B)
from MF
Kind Mrs Cambridge sent, last night offerg to

15 Aug   4 p 4to   BM(Bar)
from MF
Barrett brought me, very kindly, yr most

31 Aug [1823] copy 3 p LB BM(Bar)
to MF
I have been every day hoping to hear

7 Sept [1823] copy 4 p LB BM(Bar)
to Caroline Holland
I should have written earlier to

16 Sept [1823]   copy   3 p LB
to CBFB   BM(Bar)
I am very thankful for your kind letter

20 Sept [1823]   copy   2 p LB
to Caroline Holland   BM(Bar)
You will but too easily

29 Sept – 2 Oct 4 p 4to BM(Bar)
from MF
I have 2 kind & most welcome letters

31 Oct   4 p 4to   BM(Bar)
from MF
Mrs Cambridge (whom I can never find at

10 Nov   4 p 4to   BM(Bar)
from MF
I hope you rec'd 2 or 3 pacquets by Mrs

19 Nov   4 p 4to   BM(Bar)
from MF to Henry Barrett & CFBt
I have drawn for some of the £110 from

29 Nov   4 p 4to   NYPL(B)
from MF
I know you will rejoice to hear, that I have the

2 Dec   11 p 8vo   NYPL(B)
from SHB
Why your <impurance> and your insurance!

4 Dec   4 p 4to   NYPL(B)
from MF
I am quite in *despair* about the Maids. *What* do

15 Dec [1823]   4 p 4to   BM(Bar)
to FBA
I should have written immediately

[1823?]   3 p 4to   BM(Bar)
to FBA
How deeply I grieved at the sad account

1824

26 Jan   4 p 4to   BM(Bar)
from MF
I am grieved indeed to hear of yr sad illness

13 FE 1824 pmk 2 p 4to NYPL(B)
from MF
him so, with my kind love. <This> is the only

<8> Mar pmk 1824 2 p 4to
from Richard Barrett   BM(Bar)
My dear Papa and Mama I hope you are well

12 Mar   2 p 4to   NYPL(B)
from MF
Yr kind letter wh, arrived yesterday, was most

9 Apr   8 p 4to   NYPL(B)
from Samuel Whitlock Gandy
I am at a loss to know which is most sluggish,

23 Apr pmk 1824 4 p 4to BM(Bar)
from Cornelia (Mierop) Cambridge
I lament that this fine rain today prevents my

10 May [1824]   1 p 4to   NYPL(B)
from Clement Robert Francis
I hope you will consult Wallace à la privato at

19 June [1824]   4 p 8vo   NYPL(B)
from SHB
My dear Charlotte was kind enough to say

29 June   4 p 4to   NYPL(B)
from MF & CBFB
I have been so upon the whirl ever since you

24 Aug   4 p 4to   BM(Bar)
from MF
Yr welcome letter reached me last Saturday

3 Sept [1824]   4 p 4to   BM(Bar)
from CBFB
I yesterday recd. yr most welcome letter

21 Oct [1824?]   4 p 4to   BM(Bar)
to MF
We are all wondering & grumbling at your

29 Dec   4 p 4to   NYPL(Bar)
from Samuel Whitlock Gandy
I am quite grieved at having allowed your very

[1824–25]   2 p 4to   BM(Bar)
from Elizabeth Jenyns
Having got an opportunity of getting a frank

1825

16 Jan [1825]   4 p 4to   NYPL(B)
to Henry Barrett, JCBTM & HHBt
I arrived here safely as you may guess and

19 [Jan 1825]   4 p 4to   NYPL(B)
to Henry Barrett & JCBTM
Your kind letter this morning gave us all great

23 Jan [1825]   6 p 4to   NYPL(B)
to Henry Barrett
If you were all so kindly pleased on the arrival

29 Jan [1825]   4 p 4to   NYPL(B)
from MF
The Maid Ann Larkin will, I hope, bring you

20 Mar [1825]   4 p fol   NYPL(B)
to Henry Barrett & JCBTM
I shall begin this letter to be filled by degrees,

24 Apr [1825]   4 p fol   BM(Bar)
to CBFB
The above is very carefully copied from Dr.

6 JY pmk [1825?]   4 p 4to   NYPL(B)
to HHBt
Unless any thing very unexpected should occur,

11 July   3 p 8vo   NYPL(B)
from SHB
I have fumbled over your puzzle,

27 AU 1825 pmk   4 p 4to   BM(Bar)
from JCBTM to CFBt, Richard Barrett
    & HHBt
We arrived here quite safely about six o'clock

29 Aug pmk 1825 4 p fol BM(Bar)
from JCBTM to CFBt, Richard Barrett
    & HHBt
Many thanks for your Letter which

16 Sept [1825]   4 p 4to   NYPL(B)
from Clement Robert Francis
I am sorry to make yr confession, as it may

17 SP 1825 pmk   4 p fol   BM(Bar)
from JCBTM & Elizabeth Jenyns to
    CFBt & HHBt
Many thanks for both your letters.

[24 Sept 1825]   4 p fol   BM(Bar)
from JCBTM & Elizabeth Jenyns
As if I don't write today

[10 Oct 1825]   4 p fol   NYPL(B)
from JCBTM & Elizabeth Jenyns
I have just received your letter & many thanks

[18 Oct 1825]   4 p 4to   BM(Bar)
from JCBTM & Elizabeth Jenyns to
    CFBt & HHBt
I have just received your letter

23 Oct   4 p 4to   NYPL(B)
from EBB
Your Letter with its pleasing communication

24 Oct   4 p fol   NYPL(B)
from MF, Henry Barrett & JCBTM to
    CFBt & HHBt
Bt generously offers me this side so I rejoice in

1825, continued

1 Nov   4 p 4to   NYPL(B)
from MF to CFBt & HHBt
As you are not com^g home directly, perhaps you

[4 Nov 1825]   4 p 4to   NYPL(B)
from JCBTM with MF to HHBt
No news I grieve to say from Grandmama

10 Nov [1825]   8 p 8vo   NYPL(B)
from SHB
My dearest Charlotte, notwithstanding your

15 Nov [1825?]   4 p 4to   NYPL(B)
from JCBTM & Minette (Raper) King-
    ston to CFBt & HHBt
The other day on coming down to breakfast and

6 Dec [1825]   4 p 4to   NYPL(B)
from Clement Robert Francis
As you and Marianne will I am sure be glad of

[c 1825]   4 p fol   NYPL(B)
from JCBTM
As D^r. Wollaston is going to London tomorrow,

27 Dec [1825–27]   4 p 4to   NYPL(B)
from JCBTM
I have been for some days expecting to hear

1826

10 Jan   4 p 4to   NYPL(B)
from EBB
Your Letter my Dearest Mrs. Barrett, gave me

9 Feb   4 p 4to   BM(Bar)
from Mary Harwood
I have often talked of writing to you

18 Apr [1826]   4 p 8vo   BM(Bar)
to SHB
You're not to suppose That wisdom like mine

20 Apr [1826]   4 p 4to   BM(Bar)
from CBFB
Y^r. 23^d. dear Letter — dated April 11th. I have

12 May [1826?]   4 p 4to   NYPL(B)
to FBA
You will guess how sorry I am to have such a

9 Aug   6 p 4to   NYPL(B)
from Samuel Whitlock Gandy
I thank you for your kind little quota of a letter

13 Aug   4 p 4to   BM(Bar)
from EBB
Your Letter My Dear & amiable Charlotte was

23 Aug   4 p 4to   NYPL(B)
from MF to CFBt & HHBt
I have 2 of yr welcome kind letters to thank

17 SE 1826 pmk   2 p 4to   BM(Bar)
from Elizabeth Jenyns
A thousand thanks for your kind

4 Oct [1826]   4 p 4to   NYPL(B)
from Clement Robert Francis
My Dearest Lot, as I know you at least would

8 Oct   4 p 4to   NYPL(B)
from MF to CFBt & JCBTM
A thousand thanks for yr most kind & welcome

26 Oct [1826]   3 p 4to   NYPL(B)
from Clement Robert Francis
I have written this day to Mama at Richmond,

27 Oct [1826]   4 p 4to   NYPL(B)
from Clement Robert Francis
I wrote owing to accident in such a hurry by

31 Oct   4 p 4to   NYPL(B)
from Richard W Jelf
I hope you will not have attributed my long

31 Oct – 1 Nov   4 p 4to   BM(Bar)
from CBFB & JCBTM
I have been wishing to write ever since I left

[Oct 1826]   4 p 4to   BM(Bar)
from Mary Harwood
How I should like to shake you by the hand

[Oct 1826]   2 p 4to   BM(Bar)
from Elizabeth Jenyns to CFBt & HHBt
Harriet sends her kind love, & is very much

3 Nov [1826]   4 p 4to   BM(Bar)
to CBFB
I put myself in a hurry to scribble

4–[5] Nov [1826?]   4 p 4to   BM(Bar)
from CBFB & JCBTM
I don't like any letter should go to you

8 Nov   pmk 1826   4 p 4to   BM(Bar)
from CBFB & JCBTM
Sweet Julia & myself had a grand treat

19 Nov [1826]   4 p 4to   NYPL(B)
from Clement Robert Francis
Received 2 journal letters from Oct 14 to 31.

23–24 Nov [1826]   4 p 4to   BM(Bar)
from JCBTM, MF & CBFB
You see I am at last here,

26 Nov   pmk 1826   3 p 4to   NYPL(B)
from Richard Barrett to Henry Barrett,
    CFBt, Henry Barrett Jr, & HHBt
The Holidays begin on Friday the 8th of

26 Nov   4 p 4to   NYPL(B)
from SHB
"Send you the letter that I owe you," quotha?

28 Nov [1826]   4 p 4to   NYPL(B)
from JCBTM
Many thanks for your two last letters, & to

[2 Dec 1826]   4 p 4to   NYPL(B)
from Sarah (Burney) Payne
I should much sooner have written to you, but

4 Dec [1826?]   4 p 4to   NYPL(B)
from Clement Robert Francis
My Dearest Lot, I now begin a club letter to

7 Dec   4 p 4to   NYPL(B)
from JCBTM, MF & CBFB
My last letter was written in such a desparate

[18 Dec 1826]   2 p 4to   NYPL(B)
from JCBTM, MF & CBFB
<so> I hope you are going on well — I hear

[1826]   2 p ½ fol   BM(Bar)
to CBFB
The two enclosed arrived last night

[1826]   4 p 4to   BM(Bar)
from Cornelia (Mierop) Cambridge
It has indeed been most unwelcome

[1826]   3 p 8vo   NYPL(B)
from MF
Hetty asked me in a letter to send her some

[1826?]   4 p 4to   NYPL(B)
from MF
Mr Gerard Noel has been lately on a visit to the

[1826?]   4 p 4to   NYPL(B)
from MF
This is to go by dear Mama or Julia, tho' I am

[1826]   4 p fol   BM(Bar)
from JCBTM
I think you will not find fault

[1826–27]   4 p 8vo   NYPL(B)
from JCBTM
I was very glad indeed to receive your last

11 Jan [1826–29] draft   4 p 4to
to Mary Harwood   NYPL(B)
Your kind & delightful letter & your injunction

1827

23 JA 1827 pmk   2 p 4to   NYPL(B)
to FBA
avert so horrible a visitation! — this is my

25 Jan [1827]   4 p 4to   NYPL(B)
from JCBTM
I know the Archdeacon is now writing to Papa

12 Feb   6 p 8vo   NYPL(B)
from SHB
My dearest Charlotte — Julia's well bred and

14 Feb   4 p 4to   NYPL(B)
from MF
I have now *two* most kind & valuable letters of

15 Feb [1827]   4 p 4to   NYPL(B)
from JCBTM
There is just now arrived a letter from Mrs.

15 Mar [1827]   4 p 4to   NYPL(B)
from Clement Robert Francis
As Mama's return is uncertain, I cannot let

11 Apr   4 p 4to   BM(Bar)
from MF
Yr kind & most welcome letter of Ap 2d

29 Apr   pmk 1827   4 p 4to   BM(Bar)
to MF
Many thanks my dearest Marianne for your

1827, continued

17 May [1827] 4 p 4to NYPL(B)
to FBA
I have long been wishing and waiting for an

22 June 4 p 4to BM(Bar)
from MF
I write almost in fear & trembl[g] darling Char,

20 July [1827] 4 p 4to BM(Bar)
from CBFB
I have been longing to write to you my dearest

11 Aug pmk 1827 4 p 4to NYPL(B)
from H[arriet?] Martin
I have not tried to read this over — so Excuse

30 Oct 4 p 4to BM(Bar)
from Mary Harwood
I have just received a very kind intimation

9 Dec [1827] 4 p 4to NYPL(B)
to FBA
Dicky arrived last night and we had been

10 Dec 1 p fragment NYPL(B)
to FBA
of for ever — I have had observed for

19 Nov [1827–28] 4 p 4to BM(Bar)
to SHB
I have long been wishing to write

1828

17 Feb 6 p 4to NYPL(B)
from SHB to CFBt & CBFB
Ye are, both Mother and Daughter, most

23 Feb 3 p 4to BM(Bar)
from Henry Barrett Jr to CFBt & Henry Barrett Sr
I received your last letter on Sunday the 17th

5 Mar [1828] 4 p 4to BM(Bar)
from M Roberts
I received your parcel safe,

14 Mar 5 p 4to NYPL(B)
from Mary Jelf
I feel quite confident that I shall be doing a

22 Mar 4 p 8vo NYPL(B)
from SHB
Dearest Charlotte, how kind of you to

9 [Apr misdated May 1828] 4 p 4to NYPL(B)
to FBA
Alas, my dearest Aunt, I delayed

12 Apr pmk 1828 4 p 4to BM(Bar)
from A[ugusta?] Brudenell
Dear M[rs] Barrett I am going . . for a very

13 Apr 4 p 4to BM(Bar)
from MF
What a noble pacquet you have sent me

25 Apr 4 p 4to NYPL(B)
from SHB
I have been in town about a month, with only

3 May 3 p 4to NYPL(B)
from Samuel Whitlock Gandy
Your friendly Sister sends me word that she

30 MY 1828 pmk 4 p fol BM(Bar)
from JCBTM & Cornelia (Mierop) Cambridge
We arrived here on Wednesday evening

2 June [1828] 3 p 4to NYPL(B)
from Clement Robert Francis
As to Easter & Whitsun Holidays, those times

9 June [1828] 4 p fol BM(Bar)
from JCBTM & Cornelia (Mierop) Cambridge
If I could have found an instant

17 [June] 4 p 8vo NYPL(B)
from SHB
You have not surprised me, dearest Charlotte,

16 July 4 p fol BM(Bar)
from MF
Here I am at last, an ungrateful wretch

28 July [1828] 4 p 4to BM(Bar)
from JCBTM
Your letter arrived on Saturday to my great

30 July [1828] 4 p 4to NYPL(B)
from CBFB & MF
Now that Clement has put to Sea, there is

15 Aug 4 p 4to BM(Bar)
from MF (with PS by JCBTM)
Thank you for your kind letter in dearest

1829

20 Sept   4 p 4to   BM(Bar)
from MF
Your welcome letter, my dear Char,

[22 Sept 1828]   4 p 4to   NYPL(B)
from Sarah (Burney) Payne
I received your letter this morning only, but am

4 Oct   4 p 4to   BM(Bar)
from MF to CBFB & CFBt
I hope you rec'd, & dear Char, a parcel each

9 Oct [1828]   4 p 8vo   NYPL(B)
to FBA
How are you my dearest Aunt? We are longing

25 Oct   2 p 4to   NYPL(B)
from Mary Jelf
The hope of a frank, from London induces me

7 Dec   4 p 4to   BM(Bar)
from MF to CFBt & CBFB
I have 2 kind letters of yr's to acknowledge

[Dec 1828]   2 p 4to   BM(Bar)
from MF to [FBA], CBFB & CFBt
kind letter: ask dr Mama to read her & my own

[1828?]   4 p 4to   NYPL(B)
from Sarah (Burney) Payne
Your kind letter has been a very great treat,

[1828]   4 p 4to   NYPL(B)
from Frances (Phillips) Raper
Pray forgive me my dearest Charlotte for not

16 Jan [1828–29]   4 p 8vo   NYPL(B)
to FBA
You will kindly rejoice with us at the

11 June [1828–29]   4 p fol   NYPL(B)
from MF
Here begins a vol I have long been wishing to

[1828–29]   2 p 4to   NYPL(B)
from MF to CBFB & CFBt
in the streets. But I must leave off to thank

[1828–29]   2 p 4to   NYPL(B)
from MF to CFBt & CBFB
Many thanks, my dearest Char, for yr most

[1828–29]   2 p 4to   NYPL(B)
from MF to CBFB & CFBt
I have told all my news to dearest Mama, so

20 Apr [post 1828]   5 p 4to   NYPL(B)
from Mary Jelf
I have <ever> been led to consider a Duke

4 Jan [pre 1829]   2p 4to   NYPL(B)
to MF
Mama has just brought me your kind letter, &

[pre 1829]   2 p fragment   NYPL(B)
from MF [to CFBt?]
be obliged to send my own also to

29 June [pre 1829]   4 p 8vo   BM(Bar)
from Cornelia (Mierop) Cambridge
I have deferred thanking you

28 JA 1829 pmk   4 p 4to   BM(Bar)
from JCBTM
Grandmama only sent us your letter

2 FE 1829 pmk   1 p 4to   NYPL(B)
from Clement Robert Francis
I cannot but send a line to say how deeply

5 Feb   amanuensis   1 p 4to   NYPL(B)
from Clement Robert Francis per John
    Okes
Your brother requests me to write to request

6 [Feb 1829]   4 p 8vo   NYPL(B)
to FBA
Though I have but little to tell you, I only

10 FE 1829 pmk   4 p 4to   BM(Bar)
from JCBTM & HHBt
I am glad that you are (as you must be by

[11 Feb 1829]   2 p 4to   BM(Bar)
from JCBTM
I could not let Grandmama go without

12 Feb   4 p 4to   NYPL(B)
from MF
Your very afflicting letter written Monday,

[pre 13 Feb 1829]   4 p 4to   NYPL(B)
to FBA
I grieved to send you such a note with so few

[pre 13 Feb 1829?]   1 p scrap
to FBA   NYPL(B)
Very bad, my dearest Aunt. Mr Vances

13 FE 1829 pmk   4 p 4to   BM(Bar)
from JCBTM (with copy LS from Har-
    riet Page)
There came this morning a letter from Harriet

17 Feb   4 p 4to   NYPL(B)
to Henry Barrett
All is over! this afternoon at 5 o clock my poor

1829, continued

18 FE 1829 pmk   4 p 4to   BM(Bar)
from JCBTM, HHBt & Henry Barrett
Your two last letters made us all very sorrowful

[c 19 Feb 1829]   2 p 4to   BM(Bar)
from JCBTM
Enclosed is Miss Morton's letter

[25 Feb 1829]   6 p 4to   BM(Bar)
from JCBTM
Your letter was brought to us last night

[Feb 1829]   3 p 8vo   NYPL(B)
from MF
Dear Mama wishes me to write for her to say,

20 Mar [1829]   4 p 4to   BM(Bar)
from M Roberts
I return you my most sincere thanks for your

24 MR 1829 pmk   1 p 4to   NYPL(B)
from SHB
Need I tell you how sensibly gratified

29 Mar [1829]   3 p 4to   NYPL(B)
to FBA
Marianne leaves us tomorrow and will take this

[Mar 1829]   5 p 4to   BM(Bar)
from JCBTM
I am just returned from my dinner

[Mar-Apr 1829]   4 p fol   NYPL(B)
to Henry Barrett & JCBTM (with
    HHBt to JCBTM)
Your nice parcel came safely and we were as

1 AP 1829 pmk   4 p 4to   NYPL(B)
to Henry Barrett
As you will be anxious to know what Dr Batty

[3 Apr 1829]   4 p fol   BM(Bar)
with HHBt to JCBTM
I promised to write as soon as we had

6–7 Apr   4 p 4to   NYPL(B)
from SHB
Your dear letter, my kind Charlotte, reached

11 Apr   4 p 4to   NYPL(B)
from MF
Tho' I address you because you were <so>

12 AP 1829 pmk   4 p 4to   BM(Bar)
to JCBTM
My last letters have given you such gloomy

22 AP 1829 pmk   4 p fol   BM(Bar)
from Frances Raper (with Minette
    Kingston to HHBt)
I am penetrated with shame and vexation

[Apr? 1829]   4 p fol & 2 p 4to
from JCBTM   BM(Bar)
Your letter this morning gave us great comfort

6 MY 1829 pmk   4 p 4to   BM(Bar)
from JCBTM
Your letter arrived this morning, and I have

7 MY 1829 pmk   4 p 4to   NYPL(B)
from MF
Your deeply afflicting letter, my dearest *darling*

[10 May 1829]   4 p fol   BM(Bar)
with HHBt to JCBTM
I sent a letter to you last night

27 MA[Y] 1829 pmk   4 p 4to   BM(Bar)
with HHBt to JCBTM & Henry Barrett
My dearest Julia would you send

26 June   3 p 4to   BM(Bar)
from George Vance
I am sorry to learn that Miss Barrett

26 June   3 p 4to   NYPL(B)
from Henry V Elliott
I will entreat your kind offices to prevail upon

7 July   pmk 1829   4 p 8vo   NYPL(B)
to FBA
We little expected to remain long enough at

27 Aug   4 p 4to   NYPL(B)
from MF
Ever since yr dr letter 9th Aug. arrived, I have

30 Aug   pmk 1829   4 p 4to   BM(Bar)
from CBFB & Richard Barrett
I first write to <you> to thank you for yr.

[10 Sept 1829]   2 p fol   NYPL(B)
from JCBTM & Henry Barrett
Your letter arrived this morning, and you shall

5 Dec   4 p 4to   BM(Bar)
from CBFB
My dearest Charlotte, I begin my letter on this

14 Dec   4 p 4to   NYPL(B)
from MF to CFBt & HHBt
My darling Char I recd yr last dear kind letter

18 DE 1829 pmk   4 p 4to   BM(Bar)
from Richard Barrett & Henry Barrett
   Jr to CFBt, HHBt & JCBTM
I should have written to you from Eton

[1829]   3 p 8vo   BM(Bar)
from HHBt
We were glad to hear this morning

[1829]   4 p 8vo   BM(Bar)
from HHBt
I wrote to you last night but as

1830

3 Jan   4 p 4to   BM(Bar)
from Henry Barrett & Richard Barrett
My dearest Charlotte — Your letter dated

28–30 Jan   4 p 4to   NYPL(B)
to FBA
I have very long restrained my wish of writing

16–17 Feb   4 p 4to   NYPL(B)
from CBFB & MF
The 8th of this month I sent you my No. 5 —

1 Apr   4 p 4to   NYPL(B)
from Frances Raper to CFBt & HHBt
   (with Minette Kingston to JCBTM)
It is very kind of you to wish for a few lines

23–30 Apr [1830]   4 p 4to   NYPL(B)
to Henry Barrett
We hoped for letters from you and lines from

26 May [1830]   4 p 4to   NYPL(B)
from MF
I shd not have been so slow in writg, but that

10 JU 1830 pmk   2 p 4to   BM(Bar)
from Frances (Phillips) Raper
My dearest Charlotte our hopes by Mr Barretts

11 June   4 p 4to   BM(Bar)
from Mary Elliott
My dear Friends at Pisa are so frequently

18 June [1830]   4 p 4to   NYPL(B)
to FBA
You can but faintly imagine the very great

24 June   4 p 4to   NYPL(B)
from MF & CBFB
I am sure you will be glad to hear that dearest

3–9 July   4 p 4to   NYPL(B)
from CBFB & MF
Oh, my dearest, what comfort yr. last letter has

5 JY 1830 pmk   4 p 4to   BM(Bar)
from Richard Barrett to CFBt, HHBt &
   JCBTM
I am much obliged to you for your last letter

15 July pmk 1830 4 p 4to NYPL(B)
from George Owen Cambridge
Many thanks, for your most kind &

23 pmk   Aug [1830]   4 p 4to
to Henry Barrett   NYPL(B)
I received yesterday your kind letter, of the

⟨2⟩ Oct   4 p 4to   NYPL(B)
from John A Methuen
I regret that I should have missed sending a

15 Oct   4 p 4to   NYPL(B)
from MF
Your kind but afflictg letter of 20 Sept, Pisa, is

19 Oct   2 p 4to   BM(Bar)
from SHB
The above has lain by me some days

8 Nov   3 p 4to   BM(Bar)
from C Delap
I am anxious to thank you for your welcome

4 Dec   4 p 4to   BM(Bar)
from John A Methuen
Mrs Methuen has been waiting day after day

15 Dec   4 p 4to   NYPL(B)
from MF
I wrote last, but do not stand upon etiquette if

[1830–32]   4 p 4to   BM(Bar)
from Frances (Phillips) Raper
Your truly kind letter was a most welcome feast

[1830–33?]   1 p 8vo   NYPL(B)
from A Bianchette
Sono veramente ⟨dispiacentissimo⟩, che

1831

18 Jan   4 p 4to   NYPL(B)
from MF
Yr dear kind interestg letter of Dec 24 is just

21 Jan   4 p 4to   NYPL(B)
from Mary Elliot
Had I been free to obey the impulse of my

31 Jan – 1 Feb   4 p 4to   NYPL(B)
from MF & CBFB
Dearest Mama says she will write to-morrow,

15 MR 1831 pmk   4 p 4to   NYPL(B)
from MF
I have 2 of yr valuable letters to acknowledge

22 MR 1831 pmk   4 p 4to   BM(Bar)
from Richard Barrett to CFBt, HHBt &
    JCBTM
I should have written to you before

12–14 Apr   4 p 4to   BM(Bar)
from CBFB & MF
I yesterday rec^d. y^r. dear Letter N°. 26,

14 Apr [1831]   4 p 4to   NYPL(B)
to Henry Barrett & Arthur Barrett
This morning brings your kind letter of March

28–30 Apr [1831]   4 p 4to   NYPL(B)
to Henry Barrett
I always like to begin about Hetty, particularly

6 May [1831]   4 p 4to   NYPL(B)
to Henry Barrett
Your Deed arrived safely on Monday — the

2 June   4 p 4to   BM(Bar)
from SHB
Many thanks, my dearest Charlotte, for the

8 June [1831]   4 p 4to   NYPL(B)
to Henry Barrett & Arthur Barrett
We are safely arrived & have a pretty lodging

2 Aug [1831]   4 p 4to   BM(Bar)
from C Delap
I have to thank you for your kind letter

7 Aug [1831]   4 p 4to   NYPL(B)
with HHBt to Henry Barrett
We received 3 days ago, your kind letter of

15 Aug   4 p 4to   NYPL(B)
from MF
This is an answer to a good scrap of yr's in a

1 Sept   4 p 4to   NYPL(B)
from SHB
Before I allow myself any of my usual gossip

9 Sept   4 p 4to   NYPL(B)
to CBFB
I was very glad to hear you were at Brighton

12 Sept   4 p 4to   NYPL(B)
from MF
I have just had a long & most interestg letter

21 Oct [1831]   4 p 4to   NYPL(B)
to CBFB
I had yesterday the pleasure of receiving your

4 Nov   4 p 4to   NYPL(B)
from CBFB & MF
I now have the pleasure to thank you for y^{rs}.

17 Dec   4 p 4to   NYPL(B)
from MF
I have a most interestg letter of yrs to

24 Dec   4 p 4to   NYPL(B)
from   ?
My dear M^{rs}. Barrett your kind letter was

22 May [pre 1832]   4 p 8vo   NYPL(B)
from MF
My darling Char since writg the enclosed

1832

19 Jan [1832]   4 p 4to   NYPL(B)
to CBFB
I begin another letter to be ready against

3 Feb   4 p 4to   BM(Bar)
from CBFB & MF
Be so good as to go to Mess^r. Torlonia

22 Feb   4 p 4to   NYPL(B)
from MF
I write by dearest Mama's desire, to mention

23 Feb [1832]   4 p 4to   NYPL(B)
to Henry Barrett
I begin this that it may be ready to send off

29 Feb   4 p 4to   NYPL(B)
from Matilda Aufrère
When a bad soldier is brought to a court

6–7 Apr [1832]   4 p 4to   BM(Bar)
to Henry Barrett
I have this moment received your kind letter

16–17 May [1832]   4 p 4to   BM(Bar)
with HHBt & JCBTM to Henry Barrett
You will be glad to hear we have passed

29 May – 11 June [1832]   4 p 4to
to Henry Barrett   BM(Bar)
Your kind letter of May 3ᵈ. was duly

26–28 June [1832]   4 p 4to   BM(Bar)
from CBFB
My dearest of dears, — I now thank you for

30 June – 6 July [1832]   4 p 4to
with JCBTM to Henry Barrett NYPL(B)
I wrote to you just before our leaving Pisa —

16 JY 1832 pmk   4 p 4to   NYPL(B)
from Richard Barrett to CFBt, JCBTM
    & HHBt
I am much obliged to you for your letters,

29 July   4 p 4to   NYPL(B)
from Henry Barrett, Richard Barrett &
    Arthur Barrett
Your letter of the last date July the 8ᵗʰ is come

31 July – 11 Aug   pmk 1832   4 p 4to
                              BM(Bar)
with HHBt & JCBTM to Richard Barrett
We have just received your beautiful letter

8 [Aug 1832]   4 p 4to   BM(Bar)
from JCBTM to CFBt & HHBt
Here I am quite safe & going to be very

13–20 Aug [1832]   4 p 4to   NYPL(B)
to Henry Barrett
Your letter of July 29 arrived this morning & I

14 AU 1832 pmk   4 p 4to   BM(Bar)
from JCBTM to CFBt & HHBt
This is our donkey party riding in the King's

16 Aug [1832]   4 p 4to   BM(Bar)
to JCBTM & Lady Caroline Morrison
Yesterday was what my Richmond cap maker

16–17 Aug [1832]   4 p 4to   BM(Bar)
from JCBTM to CFBt & HHBt
Your "gratissima" arrived the day before

22 Aug [1832]   4 p 4to   BM(Bar)
from JCBTM to CFBt & HHBt
Two nights ago Mʳ. & Mʳˢ. Dashwood

24 Aug [1832]   4 p 4to   NYPL(B)
to Henry Barrett
Now, I am very sorry to have troubled you

27 Aug   4 p 4to   NYPL(B)
from Henry Barrett, CBFB & Richard
    Barrett
I write as soon as I can to inform you that

30 Aug [1832]   4 p 4to   BM(Bar)
from JCBTM to CFBt & HHBt
Your gratissima of Augᵗ 19ᵗʰ &c arrived

30 Aug–3 Sept [1832]   4 p 4to
to JCBTM   BM(Bar)
I begin my answer immediately to yours of

10 Sept   4 p 4to   NYPL(B)
from Henry & Richard Barrett to CFBt,
    JCBTM & HHBt
I received yesterday your long expected letter

11 Sept [1832?]   4 p 4to   NYPL(B)
from JCBTM
Your beautiful packet arrived last night; a

14–[17] Sept [1832]   4 p 4to
to JCBTM   BM(Bar)
I had begun half a sheet yesterday

20 SE 1832 pmk   2 p 4to   BM(Bar)
with HHBt to JCBTM
Many thanks for your two letters

20–[22] Sept [1832]   4 p 4to
to JCBTM   BM(Bar)
Arrived yesterday at Lucca

22 Sept [1832]   4 p 4to   BM(Bar)
from JCBTM
I have waited a day longer

[30 Sept]–1 Oct [1832]   4 p 4to
to JCBTM   BM(Bar)
Yours of wise demurs about Sally & houses

6 Oct [1832]   4 p 4to   BM(Bar)
to JCBTM
We received your letter yesterday

8 Oct [1832]   3 p 4to   BM(Bar)
to JCBTM
This one letter I send to Torlonias,

1832, continued

19 Oct [1832]   4 p 4to   BM(Bar)
to JCBTM
Your letter from Rome came this morning

19 Oct [1832]   4 p 4to   BM(Bar)
from JCBTM
Houses are so scarce that I wish very much

24 Oct   4 p 4to   NYPL(B)
from [2 names illegible] & from Eliza
      Spence to HHBt
We should have liked vastly to have popped

26–[27] Oct [1832]   4 p 4to
to JCBTM   NYPL(B)
Many thanks my darling Julia for yours of

[post 19 Oct 1832]   4 p fol   BM(Bar)
with HHBt to JCBTM
Your kind letter to Hett is just come

16 NO 1832 pmk   4 p 4to   BM(Bar)
from JCBTM to CFBt & HHBt
I am arrived quite safely without any

23–26 Nov [1832]   4 p 4to   BM(Bar)
to Henry Barrett
By this time you have probably received my

28 Nov   6 p 4to   NYPL(B)
from ?
You will have received a note from me

15 Dec [1832]   4 p 4to   NYPL(B)
to Henry Barrett
Your letter of Novr. 25 is safely arrived with

[1832]   4 p 4to   NYPL(B)
from JCBTM to CFBt & HHBt
Is it not provoking? The Packet does not sail

1833

1 Feb [1833]   4 p 4to   NYPL(B)
to Henry Barrett
Alas my dearest Barrett what a sad sad letter

3 [Feb 1833]   3 p 8vo   NYPL(B)
from Mary Wilberforce
I find that my dear husband & myself were at

[3 Feb 1833]   2 p 8vo   NYPL(B)
from William Wilberforce Jr
When I called at your lodging the day before

4 Feb [1833]   2 p 8vo   NYPL(B)
from Isabella Galton
I beg to offer you my deepest sympathy

5 Feb   3 p 4to   NYPL(B)
from W Spence
You will believe what extreme grief it gave us

6 Feb [1833]   4 p 4to   NYPL(B)
to Henry Barrett
By then you will have received my last sad

11 Feb [1833?]   draft   3 p 4to
to Matilda Aufrère   NYPL(B)
Before I thank you for your most interesting

19 Feb   4 p 4to   NYPL(B)
from Henry Barrett
I have broken this morning the Seal of your

3 Mar   3 p 4to   NYPL(B)
from Matilda Aufrère
It would be very difficult for me, if not wholly

9 Mar   3 p 4to   NYPL(B)
from W Spence
I will not omit writing a line to express the

11 Mar   4 p 4to   BM(Bar)
to Henry Barrett
Yesterday we received your letter of Feby 19

5 Apr [1833]   4 p 4to   BM(Bar)
to Henry Barrett
This I hope will be my last letter

21 Apr [1833]   3 p 4to   NYPL(B)
to FBA
I am all concern my dearest Aunt, to think that

25 Apr   pmk 1833   4 p 4to   BM(Bar)
to Henry Barrett
We arrived at this place last night

3 May [1833]   4 p 4to   BM(Bar)
to Henry Barrett
We arrived here yesterday to remain till

13 May [1833]   4 p 4to   BM(Bar)
from CBFB
May 13th. — old May day — Monday, an

15 May [1833]   4 p 4to   BM(Bar)
from Elizabeth Jenyns
What a variety of thoughts crowd in upon me

18 May [1833]   4 p 4to   NYPL(B)
to Henry Barrett
Here we arrived last thursday and were very

28 June [1833]   draft   2 p 4to
to Maria Rousseau   NYPL(B)
Your kind letter claimed an earlier answer, my

28 June   3 p 4to   BM(Bar)
from Mary Paynter
Pray allow one of your old, & I trust

[June 1833?]   3 p 8vo   NYPL(B)
to FBA
Let me hope, my dearest Aunt, that you are

4 July   4 p 4to   BM(Bar)
from Matilda Aufrère
It is just like yourself my very dearest

18 JY 1833 pmk   3 p 4to   BM(Bar)
from JCBTM
We arrived safely and I found Miledi

24 [July] pmk 1833 4 p 4to BM(Bar)
from JCBTM
Many thanks for your letter — I will be sure

29 JY 1833 pmk   4 p 4to   BM(Bar)
from JCBTM
I had not time to get a letter ready

1 Aug   pmk 1833   4 p 4to   BM(Bar)
from JCBTM
Many thanks for your last letter —

[5 Aug 1833]   4 p 4to   BM(Bar)
from JCBTM
I am very sorry poor Dick has been so ill

6 Aug [1833]   4 p 4to   NYPL(B)
from JCBTM
I send this allo privato not for any secrets of

11 Aug pmk 1833 4 p 4to BM(Bar)
from JCBTM
Many thanks for your pacquet

18 Aug [1833]   draft   4 p 4to
to Frances Mackenzie   NYPL(B)
I flatter myself that you will be interested in

19 AU 1833 pmk   4 p 4to   BM(Bar)
from JCBTM
I should have written before but we

[1833?]   3 p 8vo   NYPL(B)
from George W Mylne
You asked me the evening I spent with you,

[1833]   3 p 8vo   NYPL(B)
from George W Mylne
I was not surprised that you did not see me

[1833–38]   6 p 4to   BM(Bar)
from Elizabeth Jenyns
The delight with which I read your letter my

1834

8 Jan   4 p 4to   BM(Bar)
from Matilda Aufrère
I was so perfectly aware of what

11 Feb [1834?]   draft?   3 p 4to
to Matilda Aufrère   NYPL(B)
Before I thank you for your most interesting

12 Feb [1834?]   3 p 4to   BM(Bar)
to FBA
We have been waiting for this opportunity

12 Feb [1834?]   4 p 4to   NYPL(B)
to FBA
Here comes my bulletin again My dearest

16 Apr   4 p 4to   BM(Bar)
from Matilda Aufrère
Are you tired hoping that the Post will bring

17 JU 1834 pmk   4 p 4to   NYPL(B)
from Arthur Barrett to CFBt & Henry
     Barrett
I hope Ju is improving rapidly. Mr <Haron>

28 JU 1834 pmk   4 p 4to   BM(Bar)
from JCBTM & Richard Barrett
Julia says that I forgot to bid you good bye

1 JY 1834 pmk   4 p 4to   BM(Bar)
from Henry Barrett & JCBTM
I arrived in London at twelve o'clock

3 JY 1834 pmk   3 p 4to   BM(Bar)
from Henry Barrett & JCBTM
This will still reach you,

20 July [1834]   4 p 4to   BM(Bar)
from Frances Mackenzie
I am really too ashamed of my abominable

25 July   4 p 4to   NYPL(B)
from Emma Jelf? & Cornelia (Mierop)
     Cambridge
You must well know what a sacrifice it is to my

[July 1834]   4 p 4to   BM(Bar)
from Henry Barrett
I have just now received your letter

1834, continued

26 Aug   4 p 4to   BM(Bar)
from Matilda Aufrère
I am more than usually obliged by your letter

9 Oct   4 p 4to   NYPL(B)
from Lady Caroline Morrison
Your kind letter from London arrived

22 Oct [1834]   4 p 4to   BM(Bar)
from JCBTM
Mr. Jenyns has offered to get me a Frank

26 Oct pmk 1834 4 p 4to BM(Bar)
from JCBTM
All your letters and parcels are at last

28 Nov [1834]   4 p 4to   BM(Bar)
from JCBTM
You will be surprised at my

10 Dec [1834]   4 p 4to   BM(Bar)
from JCBTM
A great many thanks for your letter

[25–31 Dec 1834?] 2 p 4to NYPL(B)
to FBA
Do not suppose, my dearest Aunt, that you are

27 Dec pmk 1834 4 p 4to BM(Bar)
from JCBTM & Cornelia (Mierop)
      Cambridge
I am ashamed not to have answered

29 Dec [1834]   4 p 4to   BM(Bar)
from [M Roberts?]
I cannot sufficiently thank you

[c 1834?]   draft   3 p 4to NYPL(B)
to Cornelia (Mierop) Cambridge
How I wish that my spirits and heart were

1835

2 Jan   4 p 4to   BM(Bar)
from Lady Caroline Morrison
A thousand thanks for your very kind letter

16 Jan   4 p 4to   BM(Bar)
from Matilda Aufrère
Had I the looking Glass in Le <Bete> et

29 Jan [1835]   4 p 4to   NYPL(B)
to FBA
How beautifully true, my dearest Aunt, was

12 Feb [1835]   4 p 4to   NYPL(B)
to FBA
How very thankful I ought to be, my dearest

11 Mar [1835]   4 p 4to   BM(Bar)
from JCBTM
We arrived quite safely on Monday,

10 Apr [1835]   4 p 4to   BM(Bar)
from JCBTM
Many thanks for your letter by Miss Newcome

21 Apr pmk 1835 4 p 4to BM(Bar)
from JCBTM
Many thanks for your note which I received

2 MY 1835 pmk   4 p 4to   BM(Bar)
from JCBTM
Many thanks for both your letters

22 June [1835]   4 p 4to   BM(Bar)
to FBA
My dearest Aunt will, I know,

[25 June 1835]   4 p 4to   BM(Bar)
from JCBTM & Minette (Raper)
      Kingston
We arrived here quite safely and very

29 June [1835]   4 p 4to   BM(Bar)
to FBA
Here comes my weekly bulletin dearest Aunt

[1835?]   2 p 4to   NYPL(B)
to FBA
was so kind hearted. Our friends the Jenyns

1836

[11] pmk MY 1836 4 p 4to BM(Bar)
from JCBTM
I am very sorry I could not write before

2 June [1836]   4 p 4to   BM(Bar)
to CBFB
I began the beginning yesterday

6 June [1836]   4 p 4to   BM(Bar)
to CBFB
We have had visitors ever since breakfast

8 June [1836]   4 p 4to   BM(Bar)
to CBFB
I am quite grieved at the great worry

9 June [1836]   4 p 4to   BM(Bar)
to FBA
Il n'est pas donné à tout le monde

14 JU 1836 pmk   4 p 4to   BM(Bar)
to CBFB
Your kind letter came this morning

30 June [1836]   4 p 4to   NYPL(B)
with CBFB to FBA
My dearly loved Sister, the tandem, touching

1 July   4 p 8vo   NYPL(B)
from Henrietta de Salis
It was with sincere pleasure I read Mr Barrett's

2 July   4 p 4to   NYPL(B)
from James Thomas
You have I'm sure many correspondents and

7 AU 1836 pmk   3 p 4to   NYPL(B)
from JCBTM
I was most delighted to receive your letter this

11 Aug [1836]   4 p 4to   BM(Bar)
to CBFB
We all arrived here safely last night

11 Aug   3 p 4to   NYPL(B)
from Lady Caroline Morrison
Having this morning heard of your Daughter's

[pre 17] AU 1836 pmk   4 p 4to
from JCBTM   NYPL(B)
The Pilot is going in a short time; so I take the

17–23 Aug [1836]   4 p fol   NYPL(B)
from JCBTM
I begin now, in hopes of meeting a ship, to tell

25 Aug [1836]   4 p 4to   NYPL(B)
from JCBTM
I take the opportunity while the gentlefolks are

29 Aug [1836]   4 p 4to   NYPL(B)
from JCBTM
The Captain has just told us that he expects to

6–21 Oct   4 p fol   NYPL(B)
from JCBTM & James Thomas
I finished off a long letter to you the other day,

24 Oct [1836]   4 p 4to   NYPL(B)
from JCBTM
As we have a quarter of an hour before going

14 Nov–24 Dec [1836]   4 p fol
from JCBTM   NYPL(B)
They say we may possibly meet a Ship in about

28 Dec [1836]   4 p fol   NYPL(B)
from JCBTM & James Thomas
I am afraid you will receive this letter at the

[1836–38?]   2 p 4to   NYPL(B)
to Minette (Raper) Kingston
My dear Mother sends you her kind love &

[1836–39]   4 p 8vo   NYPL(B)
from Minette (Raper) Kingston
I went to Fortenum's on Saturday & gave your

1837

⟨7 Jan⟩   4 p 4to   NYPL(B)
from JCBTM
I have just heard that there is a dispatch

11 Jan [1837]   4 p fol   NYPL(B)
from JCBTM
I go on with my journal against we shall hear

21 Jan [1837]   3 p 4to   BM(Bar)
to FBA
Oh, my dearest Aunt, how broken hearted we

21–23 Jan [1837]   4 p 4to   BM(Bar)
from Cornelia (Mierop) Cambridge
How very kind & good you are my dearest Mrs

31 Jan pmk 1837   4 p 4to NYPL(B)
from JCBTM
I have been most eagerly expecting the last

[Jan 1837]   4 p 8vo   NYPL(B)
to FBA
This small sheet shall be the limit of my

also   draft   4 p 8vo   NYPL(B)

9 Feb pmk 1837   4 p 4to NYPL(B)
from JCBTM
Here is an elegant specimen of instruction for

1 Mar pmk 1837   4 p 4to NYPL(B)
from JCBTM
We have had but short notice of this ship, so I

8 Mar pmk 1837   4 p 4to NYPL(B)
from JCBTM
Another ship arrived, & no letters! I hope I

23 Mar – 2 Apr [1837]   4 p 4to
from JCBTM   NYPL(B)
This morning I had a visit from two Hindoo

1837, continued

30 MR 1837 pmk   4 p 4to   BM(Bar)
from Elizabeth Jenyns
Your precious letter has long deserved

3 Apr   4 p 4to   BM(Bar)
from Matilda Aufrère
But for the vile Influenza your *Cat* letter

12 Apr   pmk 1837   4 p 4to   NYPL(B)
from JCBTM
This letter is to go by the overland dispatch

25 Apr – 9 May [1837]   4 p fol
from JCBTM   NYPL(B)
You may fancy my delight on Saturday after

16–19 May   pmk 1837   4 p fol
from JCBTM   NYPL(B)
Think of the beggar boys being so lazy that

23 May   4 p 4to   NYPL(B)
from James Thomas
You must I am sure be anxious to have

29 May   pmk 1837   4 p 4to
from JCBTM   NYPL(B)
I find the ship by which I sent my last letter

1–17 June   pmk 1837   4 p fol
                              NYPL(B)
from JCBTM & James Thomas
Here begins my journal again — not to be

21 June [1837]   4 p 8vo   NYPL(B)
to FBA
Your welcome letter came this morning very

1 July   4 p 4to   NYPL(B)
from JCBTM & James Thomas
In preference to giving you my own account I

6–12 July   pmk 1837   4 p fol
from JCBTM   NYPL(B)
Here begins again my journal which I hope

30 July [1837]   4 p 4to   BM(Bar)
from JCBTM
at last we have got through our packing

11–14 Aug [1837]   4 p fol   NYPL(B)
from JCBTM
Here we go on very comfortably, and are

29 Aug   pmk 1837   4 p fol   NYPL(B)
from JCBTM
A parcel from John has just brought your

13–25 Sept   pmk 1837   4 p 4to
from JCBTM   NYPL(B)
This morning's Post brought me your most

2 Oct [1837]   3 p 4to   NYPL(B)
to FBA
Here is one more Bulletin from *me*, and next

3–4 Oct   pmk 1837   4 p 4to
from JCBTM   NYPL(B)
If this should turn out a short letter, do not be

15–17 Oct   pmk 1837   4 p 4to
from JCBTM   NYPL(B)
Of late I have been stopped short in letter

31 Oct   pmk 1837   4 p 4to   NYPL(B)
from JCBTM
Jellicoes left us yesterday, & I am not at all

23 Nov   pmk 1837   4 p fol   NYPL(B)
from JCBTM
Enclosed is a bill for *£105.* which will you be

15 Dec   pmk 1837   4 p 4to   NYPL(B)
from JCBTM & James Thomas
The day before Yesterday, we returned from

19 Dec   4 p 4to   NYPL(B)
from Matilda Aufrère
No doubt there are a variety of ways of proving

21–28 Dec [1837]   4 p 4to   NYPL(B)
from JCBTM
I have just despatched a letter to you, & I owe

[post 1837]   4 p 8vo   NYPL(B)
from Richard Barrett
I received your letter dated 21ᵗ and as by that

1838

8 Sept   pmk 1840   3 p 8vo   BM(Bar)
to Col Henry Burney
Lest your great kindness should bring you to

6 Jan [1838]   2 p 4to   NYPL(B)
to FBA
Let me despatch a Bulletin to keep your

10 Jan [1838]   3 p fol   NYPL(B)
from JCBTM
This will be nothing but a Catalogue of the

15 Jan   pmk 1838   4 p 4to   NYPL(B)
from JCBTM
I have just despatched to you a box of rubbish

29 Jan   pmk 1838   4 p fol   NYPL(B)
from JCBTM
I think I always forgot to tell you that Diana's

9 Feb   pmk 1838   4 p 4to   NYPL(B)
from JCBTM
I have just despatched you a long

13–22 Feb   pmk 1838   4 p 4to
from JCBTM   NYPL(B)
I find that the overland Mail which brought us

8 Mar   pmk 1838   4 p 4to   NYPL(B)
from JCBTM
Yesterday while I was dressing, I heard an

12 Mar [1838]   4 p 8vo   NYPL(B)
to FBA
Your dear letters were a welcome comfort to

20 Mar – 3 Apr   pmk 1838   4 p 4to
from JCBTM   NYPL(B)
James & I have been making all possible

23–26 Apr   pmk 1838   4 p 4to
from JCBTM   NYPL(B)
there have been no ships for England all this

27 Apr   pmk 1838   4 p 4to   NYPL(B)
from JCBTM
This morning I despatched you a letter by

15 May [1838]   4 p 4to   NYPL(B)
to FBA
How are you now? Have you suffered from

4 June   4 p 4to   NYPL(B)
from Matilda Aufrère
As you — on 18th May, began by a "saying"

22 June – 9 July   pmk 1838   4 p 4to
from JCBTM   NYPL(B)
On looking over my drawing materials today, I

10–16 July   pmk 1838   4 p 4to
from JCBTM   NYPL(B)
At last there is another Steam[er] advertized,

[July – Aug 1838]   3 p 8vo   NYPL(B)
to FBA
Your kind and wise letter, my dearest Aunt,

10–24 Aug   pmk 1838   4 p 4to
                               NYPL(B)
from JCBTM & James Thomas
You must not think it my fault that I do not

10 SP 1838 pmk   4 p 4to   BM(Bar)
to Henry Barrett
I have just received your letter

13 Sept [1838?]   4 p 4to   NYPL(B)
from JCBTM
Here is another box of curiosities for you, &

18 Sept   4 p 8vo   NYPL(B)
from Charles Maitland
We were both not a little affected on hearing

18–26 Sept   pmk 1838   4 p 4to
from JCBTM   NYPL(B)
This is intended to go by the *Minerva*, and I

1–10 Oct   pmk 1838   4 p 4to
from JCBTM   NYPL(B)
Your letter No. 34 *did* come by ship I find after

18–20 Oct   pmk 1838   4 p 4to
                           NYPL(B)
from JCBTM & James Thomas
This will be a very short & stupid letter for I

29 Oct [1838]   4 p 4to   NYPL(B)
from Cornelia (Mierop) Cambridge
The Archdeacon & I are sure that it will afford

13 Nov   pmk 1838   4 p 4to   NYPL(B)
from JCBTM
I have another letter to you in hand which shall

15 Nov [1838]   draft?   4 p 4to
to Matilda Aufrère   NYPL(B)
I began a letter to you my dear Mrs Aufrère

11–20 Dec   4 p 4to   NYPL(B)
from JCBTM & James Thomas
I can only write a few lines because I have

[1838]   4 p 8vo   NYPL(B)
to FBA
what a sincere thanksgiving our hearts offered

1839

8 Jan   pmk 1839   4 p 4to   NYPL(B)
from JCBTM
There is only time for a short letter, as the

18–22 Jan   pmk 1839   4 p 4to
from JCBTM   NYPL(B)
The Steamers have been so irregular lately

28 Feb – 8 Mar   4 p 4to   NYPL(B)
from JCBTM
I have so much to tell you I hardly know where

30 Mar – 2 Apr   pmk 1839   4 p 4to
NYPL(B)
from JCBTM & James Thomas
Here we arrived this morning, & are enjoying

10–29 Apr [1839]   4 p 4to   NYPL(B)
from JCBTM
I am rich in beautiful letters from you just now,

17 Apr   4 p 4to   BM(Bar)
from SHB
You can say nothing, dear Charlotte, however

4 May [1839]   4 p 4to   BM(Bar)
to SHB
It is now 3 months since Dr. Kingston paid

24 May [1839]   3 p 4to   BM(Bar)
to FBA
An *opportunity* of writing you a line

25 May – 20 June [1839]   4 p 4to
from JCBTM   NYPL(B)
I have just received an < > letter from you

10–21 June   pmk 1839   4 p 4to
from JCBTM   NYPL(B)
The day before yesterday was Etta's birthday,

6 AU 1839 pmk   4 p fol   NYPL(B)
from JCBTM
As there is no Steamer till the 16th of Septr. 1

24–26 Sept   pmk 1839   4 p 4to
NYPL(B)
from JCBTM & James Thomas
Here is the Steamer going, & almost gone, & my

24 Oct–1 Nov [1839]   4 p fol
from JCBTM   NYPL(B)
Your long expected letter No. 57 by the last

[19–20 Nov 1839]   4 p 4to   BM(Bar)
to Henry Barrett
I received your kind letter & am glad

21 Nov   copy   3 p 8vo   NYPL(B)
from Thomas Babbington Macaulay
— Though I had not the honour of knowing

4 DE 1839 pmk   4 p 4to   BM(Bar)
to Henry Barrett
I have just received your second

7 Dec [1839]   4 p 4to   BM(Bar)
to Henry Barrett
Above is Dr. Holland's prescription

[12? Dec 1839]   2 p 4to   BM(Bar)
to Henry Barrett
This letter from Mr Turner

1840

[3 Jan 1840]   2 p 4to   Osb
to CPB
I hope the letter I now send is written in due

3 Jan   1 p 4to   Osb
to CPB & Martin Charles Burney
I request the Trustees of my Mothers Marriage

6 Jan   draft   1 p 4to   NYPL(B)
to Lydia Morton
If you have thought at all of such an unworthy

[6 Jan 1840]   4 p 4to   NYPL(B)
from Frances (Phillips) Raper
I cannot prepare you or say anything — but

[8 Jan 1840]   2 p 4to   BM(Bar)
to Henry Barrett
I write in great haste to tell you what will

9 JA 1840 pmk   2 p 4to   BM(Bar)
to Richard Barrett
Your kind Aunt in her Will

11 Jan [1840]   4 p 4to   NYPL(B)
to Henry Barrett
I am very sorry to hear your Cough is so bad

[Jan 1840]   4 p 8vo   BM(Bar)
to Henry Barrett
I write a line just to say that I went

[Jan 1840]   4 p 8vo   BM(Bar)
to Henry Barrett
I went this mornᵍ to Turner's Alfred

[6 Feb 1840]   4 p 4to   BM(Bar)
to Richard Barrett
Your very kind letter & parcel

29 Feb   4 p 4to   BM(Bar)
from Alfred Turner
I think that though the Dividends on the

9 Mar [1840]   2 p 8vo   NYPL(B)
from Princess Augusta per Lady Mary
   Pelham
Lady Mary Pelham presents her Compliments

30 Mar   4 p 8vo   NYPL(B)
from Frances (Waddington) Bunsen
I never had a greater, & seldom a more

2 Apr [1840]   draft   3 p 8vo
                             NYPL(B)
to [Amelia(Locke) Angerstein]
I was most truly concerned to hear of your

24 May   1 p 4to   NYPL(B)
from A N Beaven
It is with pleasure I fulfil my promise

13 July [1840]   3 p 4to   Wms
to Henry Crabb Robinson
You must have thought me a compound of

16 July [1840]   4 p 8vo   NYPL(B)
from Frances (Phillips) Raper
I dare not begin with apologies they can not

18 JY 1840 pmk   3 p 4to   BM(Bar)
from JCBTM & Minette (Raper) Kingston
Many thanks for your letter which is just come

[25 July 1840]   4 p 4to   BM(Bar)
from JCBTM
Many thanks for your yesterday's

[28 July 1840]   3 p 4to   BM(Bar)
from JCBTM
Many thanks for your nice letter of this

12 Nov   3 p 4to   BM(Bar)
from Alfred Turner
I thought that I had before given the

[post 1840]   draft 3 p 8vo NYPL(B)
to [Augusta (Waddington) Hall?]
You will be surprized at receiving this letter &

[post 1840?]   4p 4to   BM(Bar)
from Sarah (Burney) Payne
As I sent you my Revᵈ. C. Southey letter

[post 1840?]   12 p 8vo   BM(Bar)
from Sarah (Burney) Payne
now doubt but that there must be, a little

[post 1840?]   2 p 8vo   BM(Bar)
to JCBTM?
to furreiners, so sat promiscuous

[1840–47]   draft 2 p 4to NYPL(B)
to ?
I am sincerely concerned to hear of you. The

1841

1 May [1841]   4 p 4to   BM(Bar)
from JCBTM
We are all here, safe & well. Babies all come

[4 or 11 May 1841]   4 p 4to BM(Bar)
from JCBTM
Many thanks for your letter which is just come

[31 May] pmk 1841 3 p 4to BM(Bar)
from JCBTM
I have had my poor little Poolly very ill again

8–9 June   pmk 1841   4 p 4to
from JCBTM   BM(Bar)
Here is Dicky, quite safe & well,

22 JU 1841 pmk   3 p 4to   NYPL(B)
from JCBTM & Maria Thomas
At last, I hope I have time to write a letter to

6 Aug [1841]   3 p 4to   NYPL(B)
from JCBTM
Many thanks for both your letters from

7 pmk   Aug   3 p 8vo   BM(Bar)
from Henry Colburn
I have just received your favor of the 5ᵗʰ.

30 Oct [1841]   2 p 8vo   NYPL(B)
from Henry Crabb Robinson
Your letter gives me great pleasure and I will

1841, continued

2 Dec   4 p 8vo   BM(Bar)
from Mary Ann Smith
In the hurry of answering the letter

8 Dec [1841]   2 p 8vo   BM(Bar)
from Amelia (Locke) Angerstein
Seeing in the papers this morning that your

[Dec 1841]   draft   4 p 8vo   BM(Bar)
to [Amelia (Locke) Angerstein]
Let me hasten to send you my grateful thanks

27 Nov [post 1841]   4 p 4to   NYPL(B)
from Richard Barrett
Arthur's book is out; Deighton has sold fifty

1842

1 Feb   4 p 8vo   BM(Bar)
from SHB
No, my dearest, I did *not* "quake from top to

5 Feb   4 p 8vo   NYPL(B)
from R C Murryn
My dear and respected friend's affectionate

16 Feb [1842]   3 p 8vo   NYPL(B)
from Lady Keith
Lady Keith presents her Com^s. to M^{rs}. Barrett.

23 Mar   4 p 8vo   NYPL(B)
from Henry Colburn
I have the pleasure to send you <Slips> 249

1 May [1842]   4 p 8vo & 1 p 4to
from Marianne Skerrett   BM(Bar)
When you look at the bottom of this note

5 May   4 p 8vo   NYPL(B)
from <J> Jones
In returning the second Vol. of Madame

[pre 9 June 1842]   4 p 8vo   BM(Bar)
from JCBTM
I write in the depth of haste —

9 June   pmk 1842   4 p 4to   BM(Bar)
from JCBTM
For fear of hindrance

29 June [1842]   4 p 8vo   BM(Bar)
from Frances (Phillips) Raper
I seem ungrateful for a moment to delay my

29 July [1842]   4 p 8vo   Wms
to Henry Crabb Robinson
You will be surprised to receive a letter from

7 Aug   4 p 8vo   NYPL(B)
from Henry Crabbe Robinson
You will take for granted that

8 Sept   4 p 8vo   NYPL(B)
from Frances (Waddington) Bunsen
I have experienced your kind regard, & wish to

30 SE 1842 pmk   4 p 4to   BM(Bar)
from JCBTM
I have just received Mrs Hackley's letter

2 OC 1842 pmk   2 p 4to   NYPL(B)
from JCBTM
I was very thankful to get your little scrap, and

[6 Oct 1842]   4 p 4to   BM(Bar)
from JCBTM
Your letter to day was a great comfort to me,

12 Oct [1842]   4 p 8vo   BM(Bar)
from SHB
How little did I imagine, my dear Charlotte,

11 Nov   1 p 8vo   NYPL(B)
from Henry Colburn
As I cannot keep the types standing any longer

[c 1842?]   draft   2 p fol   NYPL(B)
to Henry Colburn
I am requested by 2 gentlemen

[1842]   3 p 4to   NYPL(B)
from Frances (Phillips) Raper
You too well know the difficulty of moulding

[1842]   4 p 8vo   BM(Bar)
from Frances (Phillips) Raper
Minette has not sent off my scraps

[1842–43]   4 p 8vo   BM(Bar)
from Lydia Morton
We have seen Mrs Bedford lately

21 Nov [1842–46]   2 p 8vo   BM(Bar)
from Mary Ann Smith
I received your kind note on my return home

[1842–47]   2 p 4to   NYPL(B)
from Minette (Raper) Kingston
I enclose one of the troublesome lists for your

23 Mar [post 1842] 2 p 8vo BM(Bar)
from Mary Gwatkin
Seeing in your appendices to Madam

[post 1842?]   2 p 8vo   NYPL(B)
from [Dr Henry?] Holland [to CFBt?]
I resist for a moment my impatience to begin

[post 1842]   4 p 8vo   BM(Bar)
to Dr Peter Nugent Kingston
I was much gratified by what you kindly

[3 June post 1842] 2 p 4to BM(Bar)
from Charles Maitland
I must add a few lines to counteract

[post 1842]   4 p 8vo   NYPL(B)
from JCBTM
I am still in bed, not much better — Charles

[post 1842]   4 p 8vo   NYPL(B)
from JCBTM
an enormous Pedestal which they call a

[post 1842]   4 p 8vo   NYPL(B)
from JCBTM
I do not know how to thank you enough for all

[post 1842]   8 p 8vo   NYPL(B)
from JCBTM
I am very sorry indeed to hear of your bilious

[post 1842]   8 p 8vo   NYPL(B)
from JCBTM
Many thanks for your nice letter yesterday —

[post 1842]   4 p 8vo   BM(Bar)
from   ?
It is with much pleasure

1843

4 Feb [1843]   6 p 8vo   BM(Bar)
from Frances (Phillips) Raper
I returned full of conflicting feelings my dearest

3 Mar   7 p 8vo   BM(Bar)
from Mary Harwood
Day by day for a long time past, my dear Mrs.

7 Mar [1843]   4 p 8vo   BM(Bar)
from Frances (Phillips) Raper
We are all deeply grieved my dear, dear

24 May [1843?]   6 p 4to   BM(Bar)
from JCBTM
We came back last night, & found

3 June [1843]   4 p 4to   BM(Bar)
from JCBTM
Many thanks for your letter this morning

23 JU 1843 pmk   4 p 4to   BM(Bar)
from JCBTM
I find we have not a Bank of England

[28 June 1843]   4 p 4to   BM(Bar)
from JCBTM
I am very glad to be able to write again

1 July [1843]   4 p 8vo   BM(Bar)
from Frances (Phillips) Raper
As usual I am a hateful wonder to myself

16 July [1843]   4 p 8vo   BM(Bar)
from SHB
Here am I dearest Charlotte, at Cheltenham

19 July   4 p 8vo   BM(Bar)
from Frances (Phillips) Raper
How delightful a prospect your kindness

5 Sept [1843]   4 p 4to   NYPL(B)
from JCBTM
Many thanks for your note of yesterday, but I

13 Oct   2 p 4to   BM(Bar)
from SHB
Do not be frightened, dearest Char: — I by no

19 Dec   4 p 12mo   NYPL(B)
from SHB
Thanks my most dear Charlottte for so very

[1843?]   4 p 4to   NYPL(B)
from JCBTM
I just scribble a line in a hurry while Charles is

[1843]   4 p 4to   NYPL(B)
from JCBTM
I am afraid I have been very bad lately about

1845

6 Jan [1845]   4 p 4to   NYPL(B)
from Richard Barrett
Enclosed is a letter from the Dover Railway,

2 Dec   4 p 8vo   NYPL(B)
from Frances (Phillips) Raper
You will I know be sorry for poor Caroline

12 Dec [1845]   4 p 4to   NYPL(B)
from Richard Barrett
I have received a paper from the Dover

15 Dec [1845]   6 p 8vo   NYPL(B)
from JCBTM
I have been rayther in hopes of a letter from

[1845?]   6 p 8vo   NYPL(B)
from JCBTM
Jemmy has just had a letter from Dick in which

1846

23 Jan   2 p 8vo   NYPL(B)
from Henry Colburn
Various causes have to my great regret,

27 JA 1846 pmk   7 p 4to   BM(Bar)
from JCBTM
What a shame it seems that I never answered

30 MR 1846 pmk   5 p 4to   BM(Bar)
from JCBTM
Many thanks for all your letters

21 Apr   pmk 1846   4 p 4to   BM(Bar)
from JCBTM
Your letter from Boulogne arrived this morning

3 MY 1846 pmk   4 p 4to   BM(Bar)
from JCBTM
I cannot think it is any harm

9 May [1846]   4 p 4to   BM(Bar)
from JCBTM
I begin a letter ready to send as

14–16 May   pmk 1846   4 p 4to
from JCBTM   BM(Bar)
Just after I had dispatched my last letter

26 May   pmk 1846   4 p 4to   BM(Bar)
from JCBTM
At last I have my time for once regularly to

6 June   pmk 1846   4 p 4to   BM(Bar)
from JCBTM
If you have any thing like *our* heat now

6 JY 1846 pmk   4 p 4to   BM(Bar)
from JCBTM
I am quite vexed to think of your having been

10 Oct [1846?]   2 p 4to   BM(Bar)
from JCBTM
I sent off a letter to you enclosing some

20 Oct [1846]   3 p 8vo   NYPL(B)
from Henry Colburn
Your note of Tuesday has given me some

23 Oct   pmk 1846   4 p 4to   BM(Bar)
from JCBTM
I have been putting off writing to you

21–23 Nov   pmk 1846   4 p 4to
from JCBTM   BM(Bar)
I begin a letter now to go on

14 Dec   pmk 1846   4 p 4to   BM(Bar)
from JCBTM
I am more glad every day that Dick

19 Dec [1846]   4 p 4to   BM(Bar)
from Minette (Raper) Kingston
How can I ever thank you Dearest Mrs Barrett

25–26 Dec   pmk 1846   4 p 4to
from JCBTM   BM(Bar)
A happy new year to you

[1846]   4 p 4to   NYPL(B)
from JCBTM
Thank you for telling me of Ackermanns old

[1846]   4 p 4to   NYPL(B)
from JCBTM
At last I can "take up my pen" — The party

[post 1846]   2 p 8vo   BM(Bar)
to [Minette (Raper) Kingston?]
Here is a query nearly as important which I

[post 1846]   4 p 8vo   NYPL(B)
from Arthur Barrett
Many thanks for your kindness in

1847

1 Jan   pmk 1847   4 p 4to   BM(Bar)
from JCBTM
A very happy new year to you

29 Jan [1847]   4 p 8vo   BM(Bar)
from Henrietta Ann Thomas
My dearest Grandmama Mama sends you her

3 Feb   4 p 4to   BM(Bar)
from Matilda Aufrère
You are indeed a dear Darling creature

5 Feb   pmk 1847   4 p 4to   BM(Bar)
from E[lizabeth] Morton to CFBt &
   Richard Barrett
Now, that the consideration of the Donors

29 Mar   4 p 8vo   BM(Bar)
from Charles Maitland
I have to thank you for remembering

6 Apr [1847]   4 p 4to   BM(Bar)
from Elizabeth Jenyns
I have put off answering your two

10 Apr   pmk 1847   4 p 4to   BM(Bar)
from JCBTM
This being my last chance, I write a line

13 Apr   pmk 1847   4 p 4to   BM(Bar)
from Elizabeth Jenyns
Mr Parsons has *Just* paid me the rent

6 May   pmk 1847   4 p 4to   NYPL(B)
from JCBTM
I have been quite what old Coleman used to

27 OC 1847 pmk   2 p 4to   BM(Bar)
from JCBTM
but his brother; He found that

5 Nov [1847]   4 p 4to   BM(Bar)
from JCBTM
I was very glad to get your note from

10 Nov   pmk 1847   4 p 4to   BM(Bar)
from JCBTM
Can you read my writing

2 Dec [1847]   2 p 4to   BM(Bar)
from JCBTM
Many thanks for your long letter of the 29th.

[pre 19 Dec 1847]   4 p 4to   BM(Bar)
from JCBTM
I know you will like even such a short scribble

19 DE 1847 pmk   5 p 4to   BM(Bar)
from JCBTM
I have not written for some days

23 DE 1847 pmk   4 p 4to   BM(Bar)
from JCBTM
I am very sorry indeed to hear

30 Dec   pmk 1847   3 p 4to   BM(Bar)
from JCBTM
I meant to write this evening Post,

[Dec 1847]   4 p 4to   BM(Bar)
from JCBTM
While "Médecin Maitland" (as Etta called

29 Aug [post 1847]   4 p 8vo   BM(Bar)
from Richard Barrett
Mary has given me for you £36.5.6

[post 1847]   1 p 8vo   NYPL(B)
from Adam Sedgwick
The warm sun tempted me out & the cold wind

[post 1847]   1 p 8vo   NYPL(B)
from Adam Sedgwick
I am grieved that I cannot have the pleasure

1848

5 Jan   pmk 1848   4 p 4to   BM(Bar)
from JCBTM
I am very sorry your cough is so bad

[9 Jan 1848]   4 p 4to   BM(Bar)
from JCBTM
I hope your cough is getting better, & that

14 Jan   pmk 1848   4 p 4to   BM(Bar)
from JCBTM
I have not written for some days because

[17]   pmk JA 1848   5 p 4to   BM(Bar)
from JCBTM
Many thanks for both your two last. I hope

1848, continued

[22 Jan? 1848]   8 p 8vo   BM(Bar)
from JCBTM
Doctor is gone to church, & I do not go in the

[25 Jan? 1848]   4 p 8vo   BM(Bar)
from JCBTM
We have just got the last Quarterly — Nº.

3 Feb [1848?]   2 p 4to   BM(Bar)
from Richard Barrett
Now won't I be a comfort &c!! I got to

3 Feb [1848]   4 p 4to   BM(Bar)
from JCBTM
Now that you are [on] the move again,

[17? Feb 1848]   4 p 4to   BM(Bar)
from JCBTM
I hope you have got into a tolerably

[22 Feb 1848]   4 p 8vo   BM(Bar)
from JCBTM
Here is your poor Judy in bed again

[25]   pmk FE 1848   5 p 8vo   BM(Bar)
from JCBTM
I know you will like a letter though ever so

28 Feb [1848]   4 p 4to   BM(Bar)
from JCBTM
I am better to night and down to tea

2 Mar [1848]   4 p 4to   BM(Bar)
from JCBTM
Mʳˢ. Montgomerie has plenty of letters now

3 Mar [1848]   3 p 4to   Wms
to Henry Crabb Robinson
It is so long since we met that perhaps

7 Mar   4 p 4to   Wms
to Henry Crabb Robinson
A thousand thanks for your delightful letter

8 Oct [1848]   6 p 8vo   BM(Bar)
from JCBTM
I was very glad to hear you were at Folkestone

22 Oct [1848]   4 p 8vo   BM(Bar)
from JCBTM
I meant to write you a long letter this evening,

[Oct? 1848]   4 p 8vo   BM(Bar)
from JCBTM
I am glad you have avoided the sea voyage

[1848]   4 p 8vo   BM(Bar)
from JCBTM
Many thanks, but do not make yourself

[1848]   4 p 8vo   BM(Bar)
from JCBTM
All the crossings of our letters

[1848]   4 p 8vo   BM(Bar)
from JCBTM
I am very sorry to hear you have been

[1848?]   8 p 8vo   BM(Bar)
from JCBTM
I made Poolly write you a line last night

[1848–53]   4 p 8vo   NYPL(B)
from JCBTM
Your nice letter was a most agreeable welcome

1849

[13 Jan 1849]   6 p 8vo   BM(Bar)
from JCBTM
Mrs. Chesterman's letter by Post

[18]–19 Jan [1849]   4 p 4to   BM(Bar)
from JCBTM
Many thanks for the sovereign which

[Jan 1849]   4 p 8vo   BM(Bar)
from JCBTM
about dolls than Jemmy is."

[Jan? 1849]   2 p 4to   BM(Bar)
from JCBTM
Yours just come to my great delight.

24 Mar [1849]   4 p 8vo   BM(Bar)
from JCBTM
I have just heard from Rob that

[30 Mar 1849]   4 p 4to   BM(Bar)
from JCBTM
Charles thinks, if you would not mind

3 May [1849]   4 p 8vo   BM(Bar)
from JCBTM
I have just had a letter from my dear friend

[Sept 1849]   8 p 8vo   BM(Bar)
from JCBTM
Caroline is come home very well and brisk,

1 Nov [1849]   6 p 8vo   BM(Bar)
from JCBTM
How surprized you must have been on Sunday

[1849]   4 p 8vo   BM(Bar)
from JCBTM
I have heaps of these half sheets

13 Nov [1849]   4 p 4to   BM(Bar)
from JCBTM
I wait for one more letter from you

[1849]   2 p 8vo   BM(Bar)
from JCBTM
German professor — the great opposer

24 NO 1849 pmk   8 p 4to   BM(Bar)
from JCBTM
At last I am able to "take up my pen"

[1849]   4 p 8vo   BM(Bar)
from JCBTM
I am very glad you have had such a pleasant

15 Dec   4 p 8vo   BM(Bar)
from Henrietta Ann Thomas
I am very much obliged to you for your nice

[1849]   4 p 8vo   BM(Bar)
from JCBTM
I have been but a shabby correspondent

[Dec? 1849]   4 p 4to   BM(Bar)
from JCBTM
It is such a singlerly [sic] long time

[1849]   4 p 4to   BM(Bar)
from JCBTM
I am very glad your cold is

[1849]   4 p 4to   BM(Bar)
from JCBTM
I am very much obliged to you

[1849]   4 p 4to   BM(Bar)
from JCBTM
Many thanks for your last — Glad you have

[1849]   3 p 8vo   BM(Bar)
from JCBTM
Many thanks for all your nice letters

[1849?]   8 p 8vo   BM(Bar)
from JCBTM
I found your nice letter on my arrival. Many

[1849]   4 p 4to   BM(Bar)
from JCBTM
Many thanks for your last nice letter

[post 1849?]   4 p 8vo   Osb
from Adam Sedgwick
What a shame it was that I <   > your

[1849]   6 p 4to   BM(Bar)
from JCBTM
Many thanks for your letter

1850

3 Jan [1850]   4 p 4to   BM(Bar)
from JCBTM
I have been in bed with a headache

13 FE 1850 pmk   4 p 4to   BM(Bar)
from JCBTM
Many thanks for your letter, & Dick's Diagrams

8 JA 1850 pmk   2 p 4to   BM(Bar)
from JCBTM
I send you another sheet of verses

[15 Feb 1850]   4 p 4to   BM(Bar)
from JCBTM
I am very sorry to hear of your bad cold

15 JA 1850 pmk   4 p 4to   BM(Bar)
from JCBTM
Our letters have been a crossing of each other

[Feb? 1850]   6 p 4to   BM(Bar)
from JCBTM
I think it was very perlite

22 JA 1850 pmk   4 p 4to   BM(Bar)
from JCBTM
I am very sorry for your poor young

29 Apr   4 p 4to   NYPL(B)
from Elizabeth Morton
Many thanks for your charming letter & dear

[27] JA 1850 pmk   3 p 4to   BM(Bar)
from JCBTM
As I do not know Mrs. Skin[ner]'s direction

26 Aug [c 1850?]   4 p 8vo   BM(Bar)
from Frances Bentley (Young) Burney
Any thing and every thing I can do I will do

1850, continued

[post 26 Aug c 1850?]   2 p 8vo
                                    BM(Bar)
from Frances Bentley (Young) Burney
Before I return home I hope to pay Susan a

23 OCT 1850 pmk   4 p 4to   NYPL(B)
from Sarah (Burney) Payne & Giacomo,
    Cardinal Piccolomini
avendo il piacere di aver qui Mrs Payne le

12 NO 1850 pmk   4 p 4to   NYPL(B)
from JCBTM
Many thanks for letting me see <Essington's>

21 pmk [Nov 1850]   4 p 4to   NYPL(B)
from JCBTM
Young 'uns take particular delight in sending

22 NO 1850 pmk   4 p 4to   NYPL(B)
from JCBTM
Your nice letter this morning was very

[Nov 1850]   4 p 4to   NYPL(B)
from JCBTM
Charles was in such a hurry for my letter this

[c 1850]   2 p fragment   NYPL(B)
from Giacomo, Cardinal Piccolomini
Essendo quà a fare una visita a Mrs Payne mi

1851

[7? May 1851]   4 p 8vo   BM(Bar)
from JCBTM
I hope you enjoyed the Crystal Palace

[10? May 1851]   4 p 8vo   BM(Bar)
from JCBTM
I hope this will find you not overtired with

[14? May 1851]   4 p 8vo   BM(Bar)
from JCBTM
I hope you have not really got that horrid

20 May [1851]   4 p 8vo   BM(Bar)
from JCBTM
Yours & Dick's just come.

[May or June 1851]   6 p 8vo BM(Bar)
from JCBTM
I am going home this afternoon

12 JY 1851 pmk   4 p 4to   BM(Bar)
from Sarah (Burney) Payne & John T
    Payne
Your letter, you know how welcome it was! —

5 Aug [1851]   4 p 4to   BM(Bar)
from Sarah (Burney) Payne
I am in a hurry to write a message sent me

5 Sept pmk 1851 4 p 4to NYPL(B)
from Sarah (Burney) Payne
In post haste I write to beg of you, and Dick,

12 Sept   4 p 4to   BM(Bar)
from Sarah (Burney) Payne & John T
    Payne
I had your letter yesterday, and was

3 Nov   pmk 1851   4 p 4to   BM(Bar)
from Sarah (Burney) Payne
This last kindest of letters, was received long

[1851]   4 p 8vo   BM(Bar)
from JCBTM
At last I can just write a line

1852

5 Jan   4 p 8vo   NYPL(B)
from Emily Burney
It is so very long since we have met, or had any

<18> Jan   4 p 4to   NYPl(B)
from Sarah (Burney) Payne
I have been so rusty fusty all this long while,

1 June [1852]   4 p 4to   NYPL(B)
from Sarah (Burney) Payne
I am so tired of telling of being lame, that it

18 Sept [1852]   4 p 8vo   NYPL(B)
from Sarah (Burney) Payne
Your letter came this morning, to enliven &

1853

5 Jan   4 p 8vo   Wms
to Henry Crabb Robinson
Here I am at the *Water Cure* establishment

2<3> Jan   4 p 8vo   Wms
to Henry Crabb Robinson
a thousand thanks my dear Mr Robinson for

26 Feb [1853]   4 p 4to   BM(Bar)
from Sarah (Burney) Payne
I ought to be ashamed of myself not to have

18 Oct [1853]   3 p 8vo   Wms
to Henry Crabb Robinson
One of these days you will receive a bit of a

[1853]   4 p 8vo   NYPL(B)
from JCBTM
How are you going on? I hope, tolerably well,

7 Jan [post 1853]   8 p 8vo   NYPL(B)
from JCBTM
Very clever of you to <invent> a dodge for

1 Feb [post 1853]   8 p 8vo   NYPL(B)
from JCBTM
Many thanks for Table of Wages — very

17 Feb [post 1853]   4 p 8vo   NYPL(B)
from JCBTM
"Poor dear Ju" is still in bed — I have been

21 Nov [post 1853]   4 p 8vo   NYPL(B)
from JCBTM
Mr. Bugden says that in consequence of your

25 Nov [post 1853]   4 p 8vo   NYPL(B)
from JCBTM
The Mead, we find, is in two separate pitchers,

1854

2 Jan   4 p 8vo   NYPL(B)
from Adam Sedgwick
You are resolved that I should *never* be out

15 Feb [1854]   3 p 8vo   Wms
to Henry Crabb Robinson
With many thanks for your kind letter

14 Apr [1854]   3 p 8vo   Wms
to Henry Crabb Robinson
I am in great hopes that the enclosed

20 Nov   1 p 8vo   NYPL(B)
from Adam Sedgwick
I have experienced from you so many acts of

1855

21 Mar [1855]   4 p 8vo   Wms
to Henry Crabb Robinson
A letter from my daughter has just told me of

28 Mar [1855]   3?p 8vo   Wms
to Henry Crabb Robinson
Though I have great delight in a Bird in the

11 July   3 p 8vo   NYPL(B)
from Samuel Sharpe
Your beautiful tracing arrived quite safe this

18 Dec   4 p 4to   BM(Bar)
from Sarah (Burney) Payne
Best of creeturs [sic] that you are! — to

1857

30 Apr   4 p 4to   BM(Bar)
from William Ford
In a separate cover I send you

1859

16 Sept [1859?]   3 p 8vo   NYPL(B)
from Sarah (Burney) Payne
Just a few more *lines* — to tell you an anecdote

14 Nov   8 p 4to   BM(Bar)
from Alexander Crummell
I was made very happy last month

1860

23 Jan [post 1860?]   4 p 8vo   NYPL(B)
from Minette (Raper) Kingston
How very kind it is of you to think of sending

1861

5 Sept   8 p 8vo   BM(Bar)
from J[ohn] C[ouch] Adams
You will I know be glad to hear

1863

13 Apr   3 p 8vo   BM(Bar)
from Richard Penn
I have been delaying to Thank you

3 May   4 p 8vo   BM(Bar)
from Symes & Sandilands
The Death of Mr Penn, on the 1st of last

10 May   2 p 8vo   BM(Bar)
from Symes & Sandilands
I learn that the work of the candle screen

24 May   1 p 8vo   BM(Bar)
from Symes & Sandilands
We send you the Particulars of the late Mrs

14 July   4 p 4to   BM(Bar)
from William Ford
I have received both your letters dated the

[pre 15 Aug 1863] 2 p 8vo   BM(Bar)
from Catherine Carroll
Messrs. Symes & Sandilands have sent me your

15 Aug   4 p 8vo   BM(Bar)
from Catherine Carroll
I have been daily hoping to have a letter from

21 Aug   3 p 8vo   BM(Bar)
from Catherine Carroll
I return you M^r. Ford's letter, with thanks

1 Sept   3 p 4to   BM(Bar)
from William Ford
Mr Benett only returned from his vacation

11 Sept   3 p 8vo   BM(Bar)
from Catherine Carroll
By a note just received from my nephew

1864

20 Feb   3 p 8vo?   Wms
to Henry Crabb Robinson
If you have not already heard of my affliction

15 Mar   4 p 8vo   BM(Bar)
from Catherine Carroll
I hasten to answer your letter, as I can in some

1865

10 June [1865]   10 p 8vo   NYPL(B)
from Sarah (Burney) Payne
Your welcome, spoiling, letter I saved to

17 June [1865]   4 p 8vo   NYPL(B)
from Sarah (Burney) Payne
Here is a letter from Minet, which as it is a

[June 1865?]   6 p 8vo   NYPL(B)
from Sarah (Burney) Payne
The only letter, almost, that I ever did not

23 July [1865]   4 p 8vo   NYPL(B)
from Charles Henry Barrett
we have all been very sorry to hear that you

[23 July 1865]   4 p 8vo   NYPL(B)
from Francis W Barrett
My dear Grandmama we have all been sorry

23 [July]   3 p 8vo   NYPL(B)
from J[ohn] P Barrett
I am very sorry to hear you are so ill, and I

[c 1865?]   4 p 8vo   NYPL(B)
from Arthur Barrett
We all hope and trust you have recovered from

[1865]   4 p 8vo   NYPL(B)
from Arthur Barrett
I hope you are now better than when we last

1866

23 June   2 p 8vo   NYPL(B)
from Samuel Sharpe
As you mention Psalm 68, I send you my

1867

21 Jan   4 p 8vo   BM(Bar)
from William Selwyn
I wish I c^d have answer'd

12 Oct   4 p 8vo   BM(Bar)
from [Adam] Sedgwick
I returned to Cambridge last Tuesday Even^g

9 Apr   4 p 8vo   BM(Bar)
from Emily Sharpe
I thank you for your very kind letter

1868

20 Apr   6 p 8vo   BM(Bar)
from William Selwyn
We are very anxious

[post 30 May 1868]   3 p 8vo
from Sarah (Burney) Payne BM(Bar)
to your *real and true* convenience! / You & I,

30 May [1868]   8 p 8vo   BM(Bar)
from Sarah (Burney) Payne
My dear dearest Cousin I am the worst of those

[? Sept 1868]   4 p 8vo   BM(Bar)
from Sarah (Burney) Payne
In our united *after-dinner sleepiness* at

1870

?   draft   4 p 4to   NYPL(B)
to Agathe, comtesse de Gomer
Vous croirez aisement à mon regret en me

22 Dec [?]   4 p 8vo   NYPL(B)
from [Minette (Raper) Kingston]
From my heart do I wish you & yours all the

?   4 p 12mo   NYPL(B)
from Mary Berthan
M^r. Guthrie's address in the city, is D. C.

?   4 p 4to   NYPL(B)
from Elizabeth Morton
Thank you for your two dear letters & many

26 Sept–1 Oct [?]   4 p 8vo & 1 p 4to
           NYPL(B)
from George Owen Cambridge
Nothing can afford me greater pleasure than

?   3 p 4to   NYPL(B)
from Ann (Cox) Woodrooffe
I send you your kind order and I shall have

5 Oct [?]   2 p 8vo   Osb
from Thomas Hood
With many thanks I beg leave to return to you

?   1 p 8vo   NYPL(B)
from ⟨A F Colerobe⟩
I am much obliged to you for all the kindness

HENRY BARRETT c 1756–1843

See also letters to and from CFBt and CPB, and letters from Richard Barrett, SHB, MF, and JCBTM.

26 Apr [1811]   1 p 4to   NYPL(B)
from HLTP
Dear M^r. Barrett's Letter was mislaid in our

1 June [1816]   4 p 4to   BM
to Arthur Young
I am very grateful for the kind concern

24 Dec [1812]   5 p 4to   BM
to Arthur Young
I have to congratulate you upon your perfect

12 July [1823]   8 p 4to   NYPL(B)
from Samuel Whitlock Gandy
I fear I must have appeared negligent in regard

3 Nov [1815]   4 p 4to & 2 p fol   BM
to Arthur Young
I feel a great pleasure in sending you an

4 May [1827]   4 p 4to   BM(Bar)
from George Owen Cambridge
Your explicit & confidential communication

[1828–29]   2 p 4to   BM(Bar)
to CBFB
As Mr Painter is going from hence to Richmond

21 Feb [1832]   4 p 4to   Wms
to Henry Crabb Robinson
I beg leave to make a little entrait for your

[1833?]   2 p 8vo   NYPL(B)
from Charles Maitland
The little acquaintance I had picked up with

19 June [1839]   2 p 4to   BM(Bar)
from Jacob Boys
Mrs Barrett's third share of the £4268:13.9

29 Nov [1839]   copy   2 p fol   Osb
to Martin Charles Burney (in ALS M C
    Burney to CPB 29 Nov 1839)
Mr Barrett has perused Mr. Kindersley's

18 Dec [1839]   copy   1 p 4to   Osb
to Martin Charles Burney (in ALS M C
    Burney to CPB 25 Dec 1839)
In order to cut short any further delay inde-

3 Feb [1843]   5 p 4to   NYPL(B)
to Dr Peter Nugent Kingston & Minette
    (Raper) Kingston
I stare at myself! what a poor vermiculated

Julia Charlotte (Barrett) Thomas Maitland 1808–1864

(JCBTM)

*See also letters to and from CFBt and from FBA, MF, and Frances
(Phillips) Raper.*

[1820?]   4 p 8vo   BM(Bar)
to CBFB
We were very glad to have your last letter

15 June 1824   3 p 4to   BM(Bar)
to Richard Barrett
Papa is going to send you a parcel

[1824–29] verses 4 p 4to BM(Bar)
from [Mary] Harwood to JCBTM &
    HHBt
Six hearts by fairest hands entwined / In one

[1825–26?]   4 p 4to   NYPL(B)
to HHBt
As I find Papa is writing to Mama, and we have

15 Apr [1827–28]   4 p 4to   BM(Bar)
with HHBt to MF
Your parcel arrived quite safely

11 July [pre 1829]   4 p 4to   BM(Bar)
to HHBt
I cannot remember whether I wrote last to you

[pre 1829]   4 p 8vo & 2 p 4to
to HHBt   BM(Bar)
There is another note writing to you

[pre 1829]   6 p fol   BM(Bar)
to HHBt
As you wished to hear more of Mrs. de la

[pre 1829]   9 p fol   BM(Bar)
to HHBt
Here is an account for you of Dr Glasspoole's

[pre 1829]   6 p fol   BM(Bar)
to HHBt
I am very glad to find that Papa thinks it best

8 AP 1829 pmk   2 p 4to   BM(Bar)
to HHBt
In the first place I have to inform you

25 AP 1829 pmk   4 p fol   BM(Bar)
to HHBt
Many thanks for your letter by Dick & also

[Apr 1829?]   10 p fol   BM(Bar)
to HHBt
Those who attended to what was said.

[Apr 1829?]   8 p fol   BM(Bar)
to HHBt
I am afraid you will be disappointed

[1830?]   3 p 4to   BM(Bar)
to MF
As we have an opportunity of

18 June [1830–32]   copy   4 p 4to
to J B Sober   BM(Bar)
I should not have left your kind letter

6 Sept pmk 1832 4 p 4to NYPL(B)
to Henry Barrett
As I am here established, a lady on my own

7 Sept [1832] 4 p 4to BM(Bar)
to HHBt
Time passes quickly with you at Lucca

26–27 Sept [1832] 4 p 4to BM(Bar)
to HHBt
I treat you with a sheet of good paper

22 Oct [1832] 4 p 4to NYPL(B)
to HHBt
(I beg to observe I am 24!) I have just rec^d.

[1832] 4 p 4to BM(Bar)
to HHBt
List of Houses as I see them

26 July [1836] 4 p 4to BM(Bar)
from Elizabeth Jenyns
Though I am so tired & sleepy this evening

19 Oct [1836] 4 p 4to NYPL(B)
to CBFB
Here are all our ship's company engaged in

[Oct 1836] 6 p 4to NYPL(B)
to Arthur Barrett
Herewith you will receive a full true &

1 Mar pmk 1837 4 p 4to NYPL(B)
to Richard Barrett
Mind you write me word the minute the

28 May pmk 1837 4 p 4to NYPL(B)
to Richard Barrett
What a sweet boy you were to write me that

5–16 June 1837 4 p 4to BM(Bar)
to CBFB (PS by James Thomas)
Ten thousand thanks for your most kind

27 Oct 1837 4 p fol NYPL(B)
to CBFB
I have been waiting a long time past to answer

1 Oct [1837–38] 2 p 4to NYPL(B)
to Minette (Raper) Kingston
My dearest Minny — I only take half a sheet

28 Mar [1838] 2 p 4to NYPL(B)
from James Thomas
My very dear Julia — I am quite anxious for

30 Apr [1838] 2 p 4to NYPL(B)
to Sophia (Finch) Fielding
I have long been very much ashamed of myself

19 June pmk 1838 4 p 4to NYPL(B)
to CBFB
Two or three days ago I had the great pleasure

8 Feb [1838–39] 2 p 4to NYPL(B)
to Minette (Raper) Kingston
Best of girls! will you add to your favours that

4 Apr 1839 4 p 4to NYPL(B)
to Richard Barrett
I am in your debt for several very nice letters

31 DE 1847 pmk 4 p 4to BM(Bar)
to Richard Barrett
I dare say you require letters when

[Dec 1847] 4 p 8vo BM(Bar)
to Richard Barrett
Many thanks for your nice letter & kind

[1848] 4 p 4to BM(Bar)
to Richard Barrett
Many thanks for all your letters; and the Draft

10 Nov [1849] 4 p 8vo BM(Bar)
to Richard Barrett
I want to know how your sermon went

[1849] 2 p 8vo BM(Bar)
to Richard Barrett
I should be well now if it were not for

1 June [1851?] 4 p 8vo BM(Bar)
to Richard Barrett
I am about well now, i. e. about

Henrietta Hester Barrett 1811–1833
(HHBt)

See also letters to and from CFBt and letters from MF, JCBTM, Sarah
(Burney) Payne, and Frances (Phillips) Raper.

6 Feb 1824 copy 3 p 4to BM(Bar)
from Louisa Henslow
We have just heard from <Harriet> my dear

3 July 1826 copy BM(Bar
from Elizabeth Jenyns
Thank you very much for your last little letter

23 Aug 1826   4 p 4to   NYPL(B)
from Gerard Noel
Your Aunt having told me that you have been

[1826?]   copy   BM(Bar)
from Elizabeth Jenyns
For fear of my frank being over weight

[1826–29?]   typescript copy   2 p
from Elizabeth Jenyns   BM(Bar)
Julia would not be contented with such

22 Aug 1827   copy   2 p 4to   BM(Bar)
from Louisa Henslow
As you have not written to me to tell me

15 Nov 1827   copy   BM(Bar)
from Elizabeth Jenyns
Many thanks for your highly interesting share

12 June [1827–29]   copy   BM(Bar)
from Elizabeth Jenyns
Your last "highly interesting" letter deserves

[1827–29]   copy   BM(Bar)
from Elizabeth Jenyns
I am quite glad of this opportunity

13 Feb 1828   verses   1 p 4to
from Elizabeth Jenyns   BM(Bar)
Hetty! whom I will love so well / As ever yet

5 May [1828]   copy   2 p 4to
from Louisa Henslow   BM(Bar)
I shall begin my dear Hetty

11 July 1828   copy   BM(Bar)
from Elizabeth Jenyns
I hardly know how much I may venture

[pre 1829]   4 p 8vo & 1 p 4to BM(Bar)
from Cornelia (Mierop) Cambridge
Your sweet little Letter my dear Hetty

[pre 1829]   4 p 8vo   BM(Bar)
from Sir James Gambier
You never saw me in your life

22 Feb [pre 1829]   3 p 8vo   BM(Bar)
from Minette Raper
I did not think that my letter to Julia

21 Mar [pre 1829]   3 p 4to   BM(Bar)
from Minette Raper
Many thanks for your letter which I received

15 July [pre 1829]   3 p 8vo   BM(Bar)
from Minette Raper
Thank you for your note and beautiful pictures

28 Dec [pre 1829]   3p 8vo   BM(Bar)
from Minette Raper
I am very sorry you have been sick

[pre 1830]   4 p 8vo   NYPL(B)
from Henry V Elliott
In begging your acceptance of a Pocket Bible

28 Jan 1833   4 p 4to   NYPL(B)
from R H Spence
It was with the greatest sorrow that we heard

RICHARD ARTHUR FRANCIS BARRETT 1812–1881

See also letters to and from CFBt and from JCBTM.

[1832]   2 p 4to   BM(Bar)
to Henry Barrett
Mama has made a fool of me

Sept 1838   4 p 4to   BM(Bar)
from Leonidas Clint
The generous interest you have taken on my

28 Feb 1842   3 p 4to   NYPL(B)
from Martin Charles Burney
I am very much obliged to your Mother and to

15 Sept 1851   4 p 8vo   NYPL(B)
to Caroline (Maitland) Wauchope
I am very sorry to hear that your Mama is still

1 Feb 1867   3 p 4to   BM(Bar)
from William Ford
Since I saw you yesterday I have looked into

20 Aug 1868   4 p 8vo   NYPL(B)
to Caroline (Maitland) Wauchope
I am very much obliged to you for the <cork>

24 Apr 1878   4 p 8vo   Osb
to [CB IV?]
I am very much obliged to you for kindly

Additions

Charles Burney, Mus Doc

p 15 1778 *insert after* 21 Nov [1778]
22 Nov   1 p 4to   Osb
from John Montagu (Admiral)
Doctor Burney . . . has been canvassing

p 30 1792 *insert after* 3 Mar
12 Apr   2 p 4to   Osb
with Elizabeth (Allen) Burney to FB
   & SBP
I know you both wish me so much better

p 42 1800 *insert after* 16 July
23 July   2 p 4to   Osb
from George Canning
You wrote to me last year on behalf of a

p 48 1805 *insert after* 24 Mar
6 May   2 p 4to   Osb
from Brownlow North
I know not how to express my confusion, &

p 50 1806 *insert after* 12 Oct
19 Oct   2 p 4to   Osb
to Edmond Malone
I have with great difficulty got 4 vol[s].

p 154 *insert after last entry*
NOTE: *Draft letters, in French, from*
   FBA to Madame de Tessé, Marie
   de Maisonneuve, and other French
   women, 1802–06, will be found in 4
   holograph notebooks (thèmes in
   French), NYPL(B).

Frances (Burney) d'Arblay

p 161 1812 *insert after* [18 Sept 1812]
23 Sept [1812]   3 p 8vo   NYPL(B)
with CBFB to CB Jr
I have received this with a joy that almost

p 164 1813 *insert after* 15 July
[c 16 July 1813]   4 p 8vo   NYPL(B)
to CFBt & CBFB
As a suppliant I now come before you

p 165 1814 *insert after* [Jan? 1814]
22 Jan [1814]   1 p 4to   Osb
to William Lowndes
Madame d'Arblay returns Mr. Lowndes thanks

Charles Burney, DD

p 247 1790 *insert after* 28 MA 1790 pmk
10 Apr   2 p 4to   Osb
from Bennet Langton
I write this line just to mention

p 257 1800 *insert after* 22 Jan
30 Jan   1 p 12mo   Car311(247)
from John Philip Kemble
Pray be so good as to drive

p 258 1800 *insert after* 12 MR 1800
[7 Apr 1800]   2 p 8vo   Osb
to William Sotheby
Pray, accept my best thanks for your kind

p 259 1801 *insert after* 30 MY
20 June   1 p 4to   NYPL(Mus)
to Samuel Lysons
Many thanks for the kindness of your

p 261 1803 *insert before* 26 Feb
21 Jan   2 p 4to   NYPL(Mus)
to [the President of the Royal Academy]
The honour, which has been conferred on

p 262 1804 *insert after* 11 Feb
18 Feb   1 p 4to   NYPL(Mus)
to George Henry Glasse
I have been in hopes of being

Charles Parr Burney, DD

p 305 1818 *insert after* 24 Jan
24 Jan   2 p 4to   Osb
to ?
I feel obliged by the very handsome expression

p 310 1822 *insert before* [1822–38]
[pre 1823?]   1 p 8vo   Osb
from Alexander Chalmers [to CPB?]
I proceed to answer your questions *seriatim.*

p 311 1824 *insert after* 29 Oct
18 Nov   3 p 4to   Nor
from J S Cotman
I have this day sent off

Charlotte (Francis) Burney

p 405 1840 *insert after* 12 Nov
[post 1840]   3 p 8vo   Osb
to Mrs Chapman
I send you a letter of D[r]. Burneys with

Revisions

Charles Burney, Mus Doc

p   4 1762 16 Sept
  for 4th Earl of Sandwich *read* (Admiral)

p 13 1776 19 July
  for 19 July [1776?] *read* 19 July 1774

p 15 1778 28 Dec
  for <Magellais> *read* Jean Magellan
  for <Magellais's> *read* Magellan's

p 33 1794 [5 Feb 1794]
  for [5 Feb 1794] *read* 5 Feb

p 43 1800 [post 1800] (3rd entry after 8 DE)
  for William Malings *read* Christopher
  T Maling
  for Miss Malings *read* Miss Maling

p 50 1806 [1806?] (2nd entry after 23 Dec)
  for Mr Lee *read* Stephen Lee

Elizabeth (Allen) Allen Burney

p 63 [Apr-Oct 1796]
  for M[ary?] Hales *read* Martha (Rigby)
  Hale

Frances (Burney) d'Arblay

p 83 1782 [July 1782], from CAB
  for PM(Bar) *read* BM(Bar)

p 109 1788 [13 Aug 1788]
  add NYPL(B)

p 140 1797 25 Sept, to CB: How very kind
  is this most dear —
  for 25 Sept *read* [29 Sept 1797] *and*
  place after next entry

p 143 1798 [28 Aug 1798]
  for [28 Aug 1798] *read* [28]–29 Aug
  [1798]
  for 4 p 4to *read* 6 p 4to

p 145 1799 28 July–1 Aug
  delete –1 Aug
  for 4 p 4to *read* 2 p 4to

p 151 1802 [17 Feb 1802]
  for 17 Feb *read* 16 Feb

p 156 1805 7 NO 1805 pmk
  this 1 p scrap *is part of the 1805 letter*
  to CB *dated* 5 May, *beginning*: Ah,
  my dearest — dearest Father, what a

p 160 1812 [post 9? Aug 1812]
  for He immediately enquired if I had
  not a little *read* This moment M.
  Dagneau has been to inform us
  1812 [3 Sept 1812]
  for [3 Sept 1812] *read* [Sept ? 1812]

p 161 1812 10 pmk [Dec 1812]
  for 10 pmk [Dec 1812] *read* –25 Sept
  and place after [18 Sept 1812]

  1812 [1812–14], to CB Jr, Thanks for
  your ever kind zeal,
  for [1812–14] *read* 1 Oct 1812 *and*
  place before 13 Oct [1812]

  1812 [1812–15]
  for [1812–15] *read* [post 7 Mar 1814]
  and for to [GMAPWaddington] *read*
  to [Harriet (Collins) de Boinville]
  and place in 1814 *after* 7 Mar

p 162 1812 [post 1812] (last entry)
  for [Princess ——] *read* [Princess
  Sophia?]

  1813 22 Jan, to William Lowndes, Madame d'Arblay returns Mr. Lowndes
  thanks
  delete entry

p 164 1813 [pre 8 Sept 1813]
  for [pre 8 Sept] *read* [post 21 Sept]
  and place before 23 Sept

  1813 [post 8] Sept [1813]
  for [post 8] *read* [post 17]

  1813 23 Sept [1813], with CBFB to
  CB Jr, I have received this with a
  joy that almost
  delete entry

p 166 1814 [pre 2 Apr 1814]
  for [JB?] *read* Longman, Rees etc

  1814 7 AV 1814 pmk
  this 2 p fragment *is part of the* **1814**
  letter to M d'A *dated* 13 Jan, *beginning:* M'est il permis encore de
  m'addresser à mon

p 168 1814 [18 June 1814], to M d'A
  for [18 June 1814] *read* [8–11 July
  1814] *and place after* 6 July

p 169 1814 [Sept 1814]
  this 2 p 4to *is part of the 1814 letter to*
  M d'A *dated* 15 Aug, *beginning:*
  Enfin je respire, mon bien bon ami!

p 170 1815 20 Feb
  for bontes *read* bontés

p 177 1816 19 Oct
  for —— (Bazille) Meignen *read* Marie-Euphémie-Claudine (Bazille) Meignen

p 178 1816 [pre 1817], to CFBt & CBFB, As a suppliant I now come before you
  delete entry

p 181 1817 29 July
  add from Frances Bowdler

p 186 1818 19 May
  for —— (Bazille) Meignen *read* Marie-Euphémie-Claudine (Bazille) Meignen

p 188 1819 [9 Feb 1818], from AA, I am actually scholar of X*t* College
  delete entry

p 192 1819 *near Easter* [1819–28]
  add draft

p 201 1824 1 Mar, from Frances (Sayer) de Pougens, Your charming spirits your delightful vivacity
  delete entry

p 209 1829 25 Apr
  for contents *read* contente

p 210 1830 24 Apr
  for 24 Apr 1830 *read* post 6 Nov 1832

Alexandre Jean Baptiste d'Arblay

p 223 1794 6 May
  2nd line, delete of

p 224 1796 [16 Mar 1796]
  for ou *read* où

p 227 1803 27 Dec
  for [Gilles] Ragon *read* C Ragon-Gillet

p 228 1805 13 Apr
  for galaries *read* galeries
  1805 May
  for Gilles Ragon *read* C Ragon-Gillet

p 229 1809 3 Sept
  for Florimonde *read* Florimond

p 230 1812 10 Oct
  for princess *read* princesse
  1813 11 Oct
  for d'Astrel *read* d'Hastrel

p 231 1814 28 May
  for Govion *read* Gouvion

Charles Burney DD

p 243 1784 28 Sept
  for Thomas Gray *read* James Gray

1786 3 Feb
  for Woollaston *read* Wollaston

p 245 1788 4 Oct [1788]
  for FBA *read* FB

p 248 1790 25 May
  for Winstanly *read* Winstanley

p 250 1792 [Feb 1792]
  for Aiken *read* Aikin

p 260 1802 21 Oct
  for Perregrin *read* Perregaux

p 286 1812 24 Apr
  for J W Bacon *read* John Bacon

p 293 1816 25 Feb
  for <Zenobic> *read* Zenobio

Charles Parr Burney, DD

p 309 1821 9 Oct
  for Richard Allen Burney *read* Richard Burney

p 314–318 passim *for* T F Dibden *read* T F Dibdin

p 316 1832 12 Dec
  for [Dr Charles] *read* W——

p 321 1843 30 May
  for Henry Philpott *read* Henry Phillpotts

p 326 1862 29 Sept
  for —— Colnaghi *read* Dominic Paul Colnaghi

Sarah (Burney) Payne

p 333 3 Aug [1831?]
  for [1831?] *read* [1853] *and place after next entry*

Susanna Elizabeth (Burney) Phillips

p 335 1792 3 Nov [1792?]
  for [1792?] *read* [1793] *and place in* 1793 *after* 2 Apr

Charlotte (Francis) Barrett

p 386 1821 29 June [1821] (3rd entry)
  for Caroline Penn *read* Hannah Penn

p 414 1863 10 May
  for Symes & Sandilands *read* John Coles Symes

p 415 1870
  for centered heading 1870 *read: undated*

In addition, a number of names, the spellings of which were originally derived from signatures or docketings, are silently corrected in the index.

APPENDIX

APPENDIX

Guide to the Order of the Barrett Collection, British Museum

THE BARRETT COLLECTION of Burney Papers (Egerton 3690–3708)
acquired by the British Museum in 1952 is analysed in a typescript catalogue and made available in the Students Room of the British Museum. A
summary, arranged alphabetically, is offered as follows [f = folio(s)]:

The Burney Family

CB *to*	CAB/CBFB	Eg 3700A	f 2–12b
	FB/FBA	Eg 3690	f 1–104
	SB/SBP	Eg 3700A	f 13–14b
	Misc	Eg 3700A	f 1, 15–18
To CB *from*	Misc	Eg 3700A	f 19–40b
CB Jr *to*	CB	Eg 3700A	f 22–31b
	FB/FBA	Eg 3698	f 78–81b
		Eg 3699B	f 6–6b (Letter Book)
CAB/CBFB *to*	CB	Eg 3700A	f 118–119b
	EBB	Eg 3700A	f 120–121b
	FB/FBA	Eg 3693	f 1–224b
	SB/SBP	Eg 3700A	f 123–134b
	CFBt	Eg 3700A	f 82–117b
	Misc	Eg 3700A	f 135–138b
To CAB/CBFB *from*	Misc	Eg 3700A	f 149–185b
Elizabeth (Allen) Burney (chiefly postscripts) *to*	CAB/CBFB	Eg 3700A	f 6–7b
	FB/FBA	Eg 3690	f 64–65, 77–79b
	Misc	Eg 3700A	f 230–231b
To Elizabeth (Allen) Burney *from*		Eg 3700A	f 239–240b (Mrs Thrale)
EBB *to*	CAB/CBFB	Eg 3700A	f 41–42b
	FB/FBA	Eg 3690	f 114–142b
	CFBt	Eg 3705	f 39–40b
To EBB *from*	Misc	Eg 3700A	f 45–52b
FB/FBA *to*	AA	Eg 3695	f 77–78b
		Eg 3699B	f 62b–63b
	M d'A	Eg 3693	f 229–239
		Eg 3696	f 82–83
	CB	Eg 3690	f 2–111b
	CB Jr	Eg 3699B	f 6b, 14b–15
	CAB/CBFB	Eg 3693	f 4–226b
		Eg 3700A	f 122b

FB/FBA *to, cont*	EBB	Eg 3690	f 122–135b
	JB	Eg 3699B	f 1
		Eg 3700A	f 122
	SHB	Eg 3699B	f 41b–42
	SB/SBP	Eg 3690	f 143–178
		Eg 3696	f 8–26, 170–183b
	CFBt & JCBTM	Eg 3695	f 80–82
	Misc	Eg 3694	f 8–135b (Samuel Crisp)
		Eg 3695	f 1–108 (incl Lowndes f 3–4, 8; and Mrs Thrale f 18–76b)
		Eg 3698	f 229, 248
		Eg 3699A	f 2–21 (Letter Book, incl Princess Elizabeth)
		Eg 3699B	f 1–77 (incl copies to Princess Elizabeth and Lady Keith)
		Eg 3701A	f 38–38b (Hay)
To FBA *from*	Misc	Eg 3694	f 2–136b (Samuel Crisp)
		Eg 3695	f 5–74b (Lowndes f 5–12; Mrs Thrale f 13–74b)
		Eg 3697	f 1–30b (Mrs Bourdois f 1–66; Locke 95–210b; Rishton 213–305b)
		Eg 3698	f 1–341
		Eg 3699A	f 1–15b (Princess Elizabeth)
		Eg 3699B	f 6–346 (incl Lady Keith f 188–206)
M d'A to	AA	Eg 3695	f 79
		Eg 3700A	f 186–188
	FBA	Eg 3693	f 227–256b
To **M d'A** *from*	Misc	Eg 3700A	f 189–206
AA to	FBA & M d'A	Eg 3701A	f 1–19
	Misc	Eg 3699B	f 35b
		Eg 3701A	f 21–31b
To **AA** *from*	Misc	Eg 3701A	f 32–47b
		Eg 3701F	f 9b
SHB *to*	CAB/CBFB	Eg 3700A	f 144–148
	FB/FBA	Eg 3698	f 82–91
	CFBt	Eg 3705	f 41–61b
	Misc	Eg 3700A	f 213–231b
SB/SBP *to*	CB	Eg 3700A	f 54–59b
	CAB/CBFB	Eg 3700A	f 60–61b
	FB/FBA	Eg 3691	f 1–175
		Eg 3692	f 1–196
		Eg 3700A	f 62
	M d'A	Eg 3700A	f 53
To **SB/SBP** *from*	Misc	Eg 3700A	f 64–79b

Miscellaneous Burneys

Charles Crisp Burney *to*		Eg 3700A	f 211–212b (Richard Allen Burney)
CPB *to*	CFBt	Eg 3708	f 123–124
JB *to*	FBA	Eg 3696	f 84

The Barrett-Francis-Broome Complex

CFBt *to*	CAB/CBFB	Eg 3702A	f 125–146b
		Eg 3706D	f 2b–58
	FB/FBA	Eg 3702A	f 4–67
		Eg 3706D	f 19–50b (Letter Book)
	Barretts: Henry, HHBt, RAFBt	Eg 3702A	f 68–217b
	& JCBTM	Eg 3706D	f 5
	CF	Eg 3706D	f 4, 15–16b, 44–45
	MF	Eg 3706D	f 3–54b
		Eg 3702A	f 162–182b
	Misc	Eg 3702A	f 1–185b
		Eg 3703A	f 1–153b (Arthur Young)
		Eg 3706D	f 1–58b
To **CFBt** *from*	Misc	Eg 3705	f 1–248b (incl Sarah Payne f 149–181b)
		Eg 3708	f 125–128b
HHBt *to* and *from*		Eg 3707	f 134–177
JCBTM *to*	CFBt	Eg 3704B	f 1–314b
	HHBt	Eg 3707	f 60–95b
	RAFBt	Eg 3707	f 96–108b
	CBFB	Eg 3707	f 109–115b
	Misc	Eg 3707	f 116–127b
To **JCBTM** *from*	Misc	Eg 3707	f 128–133b
RAFBt *to* and *from*		Eg 3707	f 178–203b
		Eg 3708	f 131–132b
MF *to*	CAB/CBFB & CFBt	Eg 3707	f 5–25
	CFBt	Eg 3704A	f 1–207b
	HHBt & JCBTM	Eg 3707	f 1–4b
	Misc	Eg 3703B	f 1–169b (Arthur Young)
To **MF** *from*	Misc	Eg 3707	f 38–59 (incl Wesleys, Wilberforce, etc)

INDEX OF CORRESPONDENTS

INDEX OF CORRESPONDENTS

Numbers at the ends of the entries refer to pages. Those in roman type, to the pages for letters written by, those in italic type, to those written to, a correspondent. Numbers in bold type supply the paging of sections devoted to the correspondence (arranged chronologically) of individual members of the Burney family.

There are cross references from maiden to married names, from earlier to later married names, and from the titles of the British nobility or the episcopacy to family names. Members of the British Royal Family are listed at the beginning of the H's (under H.M. or H.R.H.)

A number of names, the spellings of which were originally derived from signatures or docketings, are silently corrected in the index.

Abel-Remusat, Jean-Pierre (1788–1832), Oriental scholar, Collège de France 331

The Aberdeen Journal 240

Adam, Robert (1728–1792), architect *26*

Adams, John Couch (1819–1892), astronomer 413

Adams, Susan (1768-post 1816), servant to SBP *157*

Addington, Henry (1757–1844), 1st Viscount Sidmouth, politician 273 287

Agnew, Ann (Astley) (c 1748–1836) 121 169 213–15; *155 217*

Agujari, Lucrezia (1743–1783), singer 11 12

Aikin, Anna Letitia, *see* Barbauld, Anna Letitia (Aikin)

Aikin, John (1747–1822), MD *250–51*

Ailesbury, 1st Earl of, *see* Brudenell-Bruce, Thomas

Ailesbury, Earl of, 1st Marquess of, *see* Brudenell-Bruce, Charles

Ailesbury, Marchioness of, *see* Brudenell-Bruce, Henrietta Maria (Hill)

Albert d'Ailly, Marie-Joseph-Louis (1741–1793), duc de Chaulnes 33

Albini *or* Albizzi, — d' (fl 1799–1814), cousin of M d'A, adjoint au Maire de Joigny 232

Alcock, John (1715–1806), Mus Doc 7

Alexander, Josias Du Pré (c 1771–1839), MP 309

Alison, Dorothea Montagu (Gregory) (c 1755–1830) 81 116; *116*

Allen, —, at Rotterdam in 1812 *331*

Allen, Elizabeth (1761–?1826) *see* Bruce, Elizabeth (Allen) Meeke

Allen, Elizabeth (Allen) (1725–1796) *see* Burney, Elizabeth (Allen) Allen

Allen, Maria, *see* Rishton, Maria (Allen)

Allen, Martha, *see* Young, Martha (Allen)

Allen, the Rev Stephen (1755–1847) 311 316–17; *65 212–13*

Alsace-Hénin-Liétard, Adélaïde-Félicité-Etiennette d', *see* Hénin, princesse d'

Ambly, Elisabeth-Charlotte (Malus de Montarcy) (1775–1853), marquise d' 232

Amelot de Chaillou, Marie-Louise, *see* Pont-Saint-Pierre, Marie-Louise (Amelot de Chaillou) de

Anderson, the Hon Caroline Dorothea (Shore) (1802–1874) 351

Angerstein, Amelia (Locke) (1777–1848) 139–40 144 147 160 167 181 183 185–86 189 196 198 201 204 212 218 406; *173 235–36 405–06*

Angerstein, John Julius (1735–1823) 198

Angerstein, John Julius William (1801–1866) 207

Angoulême, Marie-Thérèse-Charlotte de France (1778–1851), duchesse d' 170; *170*

Anguish, Catherine, *see* Osborne, Catherine (Anguish)

Anonymous 11 59 141 143 154 173 192 221 224 226–27 234 310 324 375 396 398 407; *8 19 25 28 38 42 48–51 53 57 60 67 99 203 227 232–33 248 268 282 290 294 307 313 316 322 326–27 332 341–42 405 419*

Anon of Auxerre, post 1802 154

Anon, a lord in 1838 *319*

Anon, a publisher in 1832 *316*

Anon, a vicomte in [1816] *233*

Arblay, the Rev Alexander Charles Louis Piochard d' (1794–1837) [AA] **234–38**; 150–52 154 158–61 166–67 169 173–76 178–80 182–85 201 209 211–14 216 287 294 306 310 315 383 388; *150–51 159 170–76 179–80 182–85 187–89 195–98 201–02 212 214–17 228–29 232–34 306 327 331 337 383*

Arblay, Alexandre-Jean-Baptiste Piochard (1754–1818), comte d' [M d'A] **220–34**; 32 126–30 132–36 138–40 142–52 154–61 163–75 177 179–83 203 207 235 252 257 260 287; *32 126–32 133–34 136–38 140–41 143 146–52 155 157–61 163 165–73 177–78 180–83 234–36 252–53 255–57 287 331 335–36 353*

Arblay, Frances (Burney) d' (1752–1840) [FB/FBA] **64–220**; 13 24 32 223 227 243 259–60; *4 6 17–18 20–22 24–42 44 48–50 55 57–58 61–62 222 231–32 236 239–46 248–53 255–57 259 287 289–90 292–96 302 306 329–30 335 340–41 374–75 380–88 390–95 398–404 419; Journals 150 166 170 173 191*

DATE DUE

AG 5'65			